A New Star-Rating System & Other Exciting News from Frommer's!

In our continuing effort to publish the savviest, most up-to-date, and most appealing travel guides available, we've added some great new features.

Frommer's guides now include a new **star-rating system.** Every hotel, restaurant, and attraction is rated from 0 to 3 stars to help you set priorities and organize your time.

We've also added **seven brand-new features** that point you to the great deals, in-the-know advice, and unique experiences that separate travelers from tourists. Throughout the guide, look for:

Finds	Special finds—those places only insiders know about
Fun Fact	Fun facts—details that make travelers more informed and their trips more fun
Kids	Best bets for kids—advice for the whole family
Moments	Special moments—those experiences that memories are made of
Overrated	Places or experiences not worth your time or money
Tips	Insider tips—some great ways to save time and money
Value	Great values—where to get the best deals

Here's what the critics say about Frommer's:

"Here's everything you need to know about the various ports."
—*Boston Globe*

"Amazingly easy to use. Very portable, very complete."
—*Booklist*

"Detailed, accurate, and easy-to-read information for all price ranges."
—*Glamour Magazine*

"Hotel information is close to encyclopedic."
—*Des Moines Sunday Register*

"Frommer's Guides have a way of giving you a real feel for a place."
—*Knight Ridder Newspapers*

Frommer's®

Caribbean Ports of Call

4th Edition

by Heidi Sarna & Matt Hannafin

with Ken Lindley

Wiley Publishing, Inc.

Wiley Publishing, Inc.

909 Third Ave.
New York, NY 10022

ISBN 0-7645-6646-6
ISSN 1090-2617

Editor: Elizabeth Albertson
Production Editor: Tammy Ahrens
Cartographer: Elizabeth Puhl
Photo Editor: Richard Fox
Production by Wiley Indianapolis Composition Services

Front cover photo: USVI, St. Croix: Snorkeling near Buck Island
Back cover photo: Curaçao: View of Handelskade, Willemstad

For information on our other products and services or to obtain technical support, please contact our Customer Care Department within the U.S. at 800-762-2974, outside the U.S. at 317-572-3993 or fax 317-572-4002.

Wiley also publishes its books in a variety of electronic formats. Some content that appears in print may not be available in electronic formats.

Manufactured in the United States of America

5   4   3   2

Contents

List of Maps

About the Authors

Heidi Sarna has cruised on more than 75 ships of all shapes and sizes, from 100-passenger sailing ships to 3,000-passenger megas, and she loves them all (well, okay, some more than others). Aside from her ocean travel, she's done her share of exploring on land, too, from the rugged hinterlands of northern India and Brazil to the posh streets of Côte d'Azur and Singapore. She's never met a place she hasn't liked in some way. Heidi's a contributing editor to *Travel Holiday* magazine, and over the past 10 years her work has appeared in *Savoy, Bride's, New Choices, Diversion, Cigar Aficionado, Frommer's Budget Travel On-Line, Cruise Travel, AAA Westways, Porthole,* and *Travel Weekly* magazines. She has also written for major guidebooks, websites, and the *New York Times, Chicago Tribune, Washington Post, Boston Herald, Star Ledger,* and *Washington Times* newspapers. When she's not off cruising somewhere, you're bound to find her touring and inspecting the many ships that pass through New York City. She lives in the Big Apple with her husband, Arun.

Matt Hannafin is a freelance writer, editor, and musician based in New York City. A former senior editor/cruise editor at Frommer's and former senior online writer at *Expedia Travels* magazine, he currently brackets research trips and performance/teaching gigs with long, sleepless nights spent editing for various publishing houses and U.N. agencies. His articles have appeared in *Travel Holiday, Expedia Travels, Travel Weekly,* and *Porthole* magazines, the *Boston Herald,* and numerous travel guidebooks.

Ken Lindley believes every locale is interesting in some way but does keep a list of extremely dreadful destinations. He's lived in Asia, Europe, and around the United States, and although he's spent half his life in New York, call before dropping by—he may be someplace farther afield, like India, China, Peru, or Turkey. The author of *Frommer's Portable Aruba,* he's also contributed to *Out & About* travel newsletter and *Expedia Travels.* When he's not on travel assignment, he's on Wall Street, where he edits financial reports.

Acknowledgments

A select group of experienced travel journalists and experts contributed to this book.

Thanks to **Dr. Christina Colon,** respected academic, for her knowledge of sea life, fact checking, and role as Heidi's number-one cruise companion. Adventuress **Darlene Simidian** updated the Belize and U.S. Virgin Islands chapters. Thanks (and a rhetorical bottle of Paddy's whiskey) to **Jim and Cindy Tunstall,** authors of *Frommer's Walt Disney World® & Orlando* and *Walt Disney World® & Orlando For Dummies* and contributors to *Frommer's Florida,* for updating the Tampa section. Thanks to **Lesley Abravanel,** *Miami Herald* columnist and author of *Frommer's South Florida,* for her downtown, late-night take on what's cool in Miami. Thanks to **Mary Herczog,** author of *Frommer's New Orleans* and *Frommer's Las Vegas,* who advised us on the best of New Orleans—we still owe you that lox spread. Many thanks also to all the helpful public-relations staffs at the cruise lines, and to our editors at Frommer's, Liz Albertson and Naomi Kraus, for their conscientious work (and to Naomi also for writing the Orlando theme-parks section of chapter 5).

Last, but not least, Heidi thanks her dear husband, **Arun,** for his support, insight, and most important, his prodding around deadline time, when all she really wanted to do was watch TV.

An Invitation to the Reader

In researching this book, we discovered many wonderful places—hotels, restaurants, shops, and more. We're sure you'll find others. Please tell us about them, so we can share the information with your fellow travelers in upcoming editions. If you were disappointed with a recommendation, we'd love to know that, too. Please write to:

Frommer's Caribbean Ports of Call, 4th Edition
Wiley Publishing, Inc. • 909 Third Ave. • New York, NY 10022

An Additional Note

Please be advised that travel information is subject to change at any time—and this is especially true of prices. We therefore suggest that you write or call ahead for confirmation when making your travel plans. The authors, editors, and publisher cannot be held responsible for the experiences of readers while traveling. Your safety is important to us, however, so we encourage you to stay alert and be aware of your surroundings. Keep a close eye on cameras, purses, and wallets, all favorite targets of thieves and pickpockets.

New! Frommer's Star Ratings & Icons

Every hotel, restaurant, and attraction listing in this guide has been ranked for quality, value, service, amenities, and special features using a star-rating scale. In country, state, and regional guides, we also rate towns and regions to help you narrow down your choices and budget your time accordingly. Hotels and restaurants in the Very Expensive and Expensive categories are rated on a scale of one (highly recommended) to three stars (exceptional). Those in the Moderate and Inexpensive categories rate from zero (recommended) to two stars (very highly recommended). Attractions, towns, and regions are rated according to the following scale: zero stars (recommended), one star (highly recommended), two stars (very highly recommended), and three stars (must-see).

In addition to the rating system, we also use seven icons to highlight insider information, useful tips, special bargains, hidden gems, memorable experiences, kid-friendly venues, places to avoid, and other useful information:

| Finds | Fun Fact | Kids | Moments | Overrated | Tips | Value |

The following abbreviations are used for credit cards:

| AE | American Express | DISC | Discover | V | Visa |
| DC | Diners Club | MC | MasterCard | | |

FROMMERS.COM

Now that you have the guidebook to a great trip, visit our website at **www.frommers.com** for travel information on nearly 2,500 destinations. With features updated regularly, we give you instant access to the most current trip-planning information available. At Frommers.com, you'll also find the best prices on airfares, accommodations, and car rentals—and you can even book travel online through our travel booking partners. At Frommers.com, you'll also find the following:

- Online updates to our most popular guidebooks
- Vacation sweepstakes and contest giveaways
- Newsletter highlighting the hottest travel trends
- Online travel message boards with featured travel discussions

The Gulf of Mexico & the Caribbean

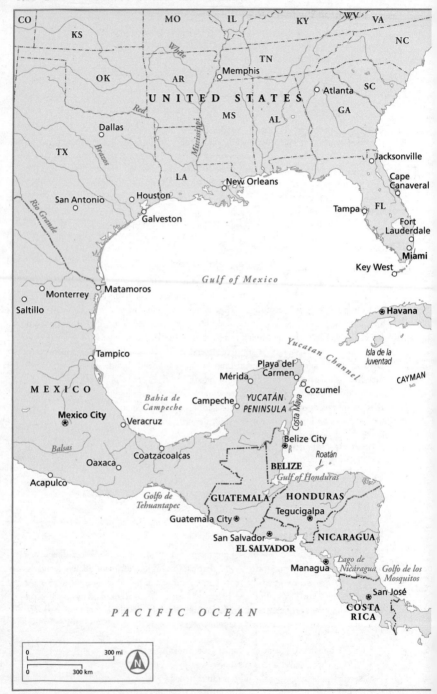

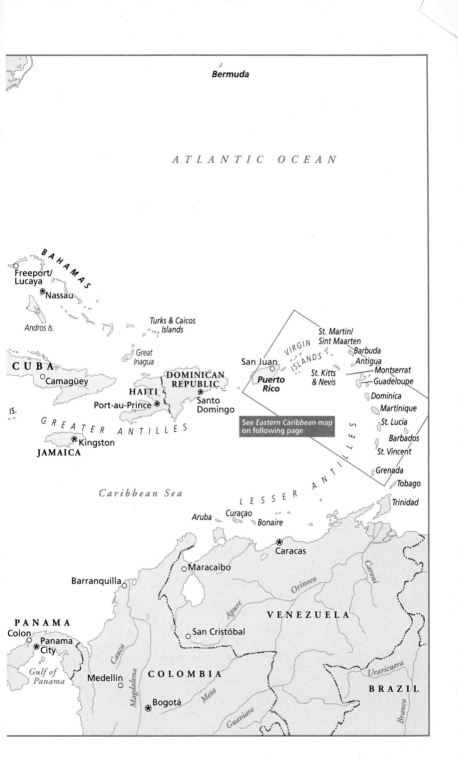

Bermuda

ATLANTIC OCEAN

BAHAMAS
Freeport/Lucaya
Nassau
Andros Is.
Turks & Caicos Islands
Great Inagua
CUBA
Camagüey
DOMINICAN REPUBLIC
HAITI
Port-au-Prince
Santo Domingo
San Juan
Puerto Rico
VIRGIN ISLANDS
St. Martin/Sint Maarten
Barbuda
Antigua
St. Kitts & Nevis
Montserrat
Guadeloupe
Dominica
Martinique
St. Lucia
Barbados
St. Vincent
Grenada
Tobago
Trinidad

See *Eastern Caribbean* map on following page

GREATER ANTILLES
Kingston
JAMAICA
IS.

LESSER ANTILLES

Caribbean Sea

Aruba
Curaçao
Bonaire
Caracas
Maracaibo
Barranquilla
Orinoco
Caroni
Apure
VENEZUELA
PANAMA
Colon
Panama City
San Cristóbal
Gulf of Panama
Cauca
Medellín
COLOMBIA
Magdalena
Bogotá
Meta
Guaviare
Uraricuera
BRAZIL
Branco

The Eastern Caribbean

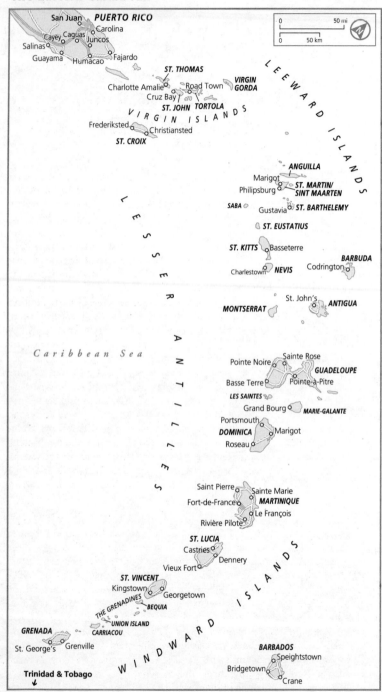

Introduction: Cruising to the Ports of Call

Here's the thing about cruises: They go places. What other kind of trip can you name where every morning you wake up in a different country, with the red carpet rolled out for you?

Of all the possible cruise destinations, the Caribbean remains a time-tested favorite, the classic picture-perfect island vacation destination. It's warm and sunny all year round, the major ports of embarkation are easily accessible and relatively cheap to reach by air (especially when compared with flying to Europe or Asia), and it's hassle-free because American, Canadian, and British citizens don't need visas to go there. Even as cruise lines set up more and more itineraries around the world, the Caribbean remains the most popular cruise destination. In fact, the area has never been more popular. The ports along Mexico's Yucatán Peninsula, and Central American ports like Belize and Honduras, are among the newest additions to the Caribbean cruise circuit, joining traditional eastern and western Caribbean routes, routes through the small islands of the southern Caribbean, and itineraries that make a full or partial crossing of the Panama Canal. It's an exciting time, with cruise lines like Princess, Holland America, Carnival, Royal Caribbean, Celebrity, Norwegian, and Star Clippers increasing their presence by adding new ships, and island nations building new and improved facilities in recognition of the economic potential of cruise ship arrivals. Shore excursions, too, are getting more interesting and more active, with biking, horseback riding, golfing, and river-tubing trips exposing cruisers to the natural splendors of the islands. So much for lounging on the Lido Deck . . . .

1 Choosing the Itinerary That's Best for You

If you count every rocky little outcropping and sandbar, there are hundreds of islands in the Caribbean, but of the 40 or 50 that make it onto the map, cruise ships regularly visit only about 25 of them. Most Caribbean cruises are 7 nights long and visit anywhere from three to six different ports, with the 2,000-passenger-plus megaships tending toward the lower number, spending the rest of their time on leisurely (and more profitable) days at sea. There are a handful of 3- and 4-night cruises out of Florida visiting the Bahamas or Mexico's Yucatán Peninsula; 4- and 5-night cruises out of Tampa, Miami, New Orleans, and Galveston, Texas, doing western Caribbean itineraries; and 10- to 14-night Caribbean cruises that transit the Panama Canal, typically sailing between Florida and Acapulco, visiting three to seven ports.

While they're all appealing in some way, the Caribbean islands are not all created equal. Some islands are better for shopping, others for beaches or scenic drives. Some are quite built up, while others are not developed at all. Some have

How Many Ports for You?

These days, many of the largest ships in the Carnival, Royal Caribbean, Princess, and Norwegian fleets are visiting only three ports during a typical weeklong cruise, and spending the rest of the days at sea. What's the story? Are ports too crowded? Are the ships too big to dock at other ports? Do cruise lines want to keep passengers on board to spend more money in the shops, bars, and casinos? Do passengers just *want* to stay on board? All of the above, if you ask us. A cruise including three ports may be just fine for you, if what you're looking for is pure, unadulterated relaxation—sitting by the pool with a good book and a steward to bring you fresh drinks. If you want to maximize the number of islands you visit, however, there are alternatives: Many mid-size and even large ships—like Celebrity's *Constellation,* Princess's *Sea Princess,* and NCL's *Norwegian Sky* and *Norwegian Majesty*—visit five ports on their 7-night southern Caribbean itineraries, and small-ship lines like Windstar, Star Clippers, Windjammer, Clipper, American Canadian Caribbean, and Seabourn really pack in the ports of call, visiting a different island nearly every single day and sometimes even making two stops, one in the morning and another after lunch. Contact the cruise lines to find out the number of port days and the number of sea days for each ship (contact information for various cruise lines is listed in chapter 2, "The Cruise Lines in Brief."

piers that can accommodate large ships, and others require that ships anchor up to a mile offshore and shuttle passengers back and forth in small, motorized launches called "tenders." Big ships tend to visit the more commercialized, developed islands, which host as many as 10 ships per day, while the small ships are able to access the less-developed, off-the-beaten-path islands. Typically, the big lines divide Caribbean itineraries into eastern, western, and southern routings, but smaller ship lines rarely adhere to such rigid labels.

MEGASHIP ITINERARIES

WESTERN CARIBBEAN   Most western Caribbean itineraries depart from Miami, Fort Lauderdale, or Tampa, Florida (a few depart from New Orleans and Galveston, Texas), and typically visit Grand Cayman, Jamaica, and Cozumel or one of the other ports on Mexico's Yucatán Peninsula. This is a popular itinerary for many lines, so you'll see throngs of other cruise passengers in each port—often three or four (or more) ships will be visiting at a time. Belize City and the Bay Islands of Honduras are also popping up more frequently on western Caribbean itineraries.

EASTERN CARIBBEAN   Eastern Caribbean itineraries also typically sail out of Florida, and may include visits to Puerto Rico, St. Thomas, St. Croix, St. Martin, and Nassau or Freeport, in the Bahamas—all very popular and busy ports of call, especially St. Thomas, Nassau, and Puerto Rico.

SOUTHERN CARIBBEAN   A southern itinerary is typically round-trip out of San Juan, Puerto Rico or sometimes out of Aruba. Southern routes, which often overlap with eastern Caribbean itineraries, may visit St. Thomas, St. Martin,

Barbados, St. Lucia, Martinique, Antigua, and maybe Dominica, Guadeloupe, Aruba, and Grenada or one of the other islands in the Grenadines.

SMALL-SHIP ITINERARIES

Most small ships cruise in the eastern and southern Caribbean, where distances between islands are shorter. Instead of Florida, they may sail out of Barbados, Grenada, St. Kitts, or San Juan, Puerto Rico, and visit more remote islands.

EASTERN CARIBBEAN   These itineraries may include visits to St. Barts, the British Virgin Islands, and the U.S. Virgin Islands (lush St. John as well as more touristy St. Thomas).

SOUTHERN CARIBBEAN   Southern Caribbean cruises may visit Guadeloupe, Dominica, Les Saintes, St. Kitts, Nevis, Martinique, St. Lucia, St. Vincent, Grenada, and Bequia, and maybe the truly unspoiled and remote Palm, Canouan, Mayreau, and Carriacou islands.

SHORTER ITINERARIES

Today, there are more 3-, 4-, and 5-night cruise itineraries than ever before (plus a small handful of 2-nighters), as cruise lines continually look for new ways to fill all of their big ships. Short and affordable, **2- and 3-night cruises** offer a more action-packed, nonstop party ambiance than longer 7-night Caribbean itineraries. It's obvious why: These are weekend cruises, departing Thursday or Friday afternoons, so people are ready to squeeze in as much fun, relaxation, drinking, gambling, dancing, and eating as possible during these weekends. Though you'll definitely find more 20- and 30-somethings on these shorties than on any other type of cruise, you'll still see a wide range of ages.

The ships that offer these minicruises tend to be the oldest in their fleets and are a bit beat-up compared to the newest megaships. We've also noticed that service is not as good on the weekend party cruises as compared to longer itineraries; the crews are overworked and probably a little bit fed up with the throngs of rowdies week after week. Then again, most passengers don't notice the difference; they're too busy having fun.

Because they typically depart on Sunday or Monday afternoon and sail through the workweek, **4- and 5-night cruises** represent the opposite end of the liveliness spectrum, tending to attract an older and less party-oriented crowd.

Aside from the fun factor, all of these shorter cruises are a great way for first-time cruisers to test the waters before committing to a full week. They're also a good idea if you're short on time or moola. The majority of the minicruises sail round-trip from Miami or Port Canaveral in southern Florida and visit the Bahamas and/or Key West and Cozumel. Others depart from Tampa, Galveston, and San Juan.

Many cruise lines offer weeklong **land-sea packages** that pair a cruise with a land vacation either before or after your cruise. For instance, Disney, Carnival, and Royal Caribbean will combine a 3- or 4-night cruise out of Port Canaveral with a 3- or 4-night visit to one of central Florida's theme parks, like Walt Disney World, Universal Studios, Sea World, or Busch Gardens.

MATCHING YOUR HABITS TO YOUR DESTINATION

Some ports are better for certain things than others. Here's a short rundown; see p. 73 for a comparison chart that rates shore excursions, activities, beaches, shopping, and dining for all the Caribbean ports. The island reviews in chapter 5, "The Ports of Call," provide detailed information.

PORTS FOR SHOPPERS

Eastern Caribbean: St. Croix, St. Martin, St. Thomas, Puerto Rico, Nassau. **Western Caribbean:** Grand Cayman, Cozumel. **Southern Caribbean:** Aruba, Barbados.

PORTS FOR BEACH LOVERS

Eastern Caribbean: Anguilla, British Virgin Islands, St. John, St. Martin. **Western Caribbean:** Grand Cayman, Jamaica. **Southern Caribbean:** Aruba, Grenada, Bequia.

PORTS FOR SCUBA DIVERS & SNORKELERS

Eastern Caribbean: St. Croix, St. John, St. Thomas, Dominica. **Western Caribbean:** Grand Cayman, Belize, Cozumel. **Southern Caribbean:** Bonaire, Curaçao.

PORTS FOR HISTORY & ARCHAEOLOGY BUFFS

Eastern Caribbean: Puerto Rico, Dominican Republic. **Western Caribbean:** Cozumel/Playa del Carmen/Calica. **Southern Caribbean:** Barbados, Curaçao.

PORTS FOR NATURE BUFFS

Eastern Caribbean: St. John, Puerto Rico. **Southern Caribbean:** Aruba, Dominica, St. Kitts, Grenada, Trinidad.

PORTS FOR FRANCOPHILES

Eastern Caribbean: Guadeloupe, Les Saintes, St. Martin, St. Barts, Martinique.

SHORE EXCURSIONS: THE WHAT, WHY & HOW

No matter what size ship you're on or what its itinerary is, you'll be able to choose from several shore tours (three or four tours in some ports, dozens in others) in any given port, from typical walking and bus tours to more active excursions like biking, hiking, snorkeling, scuba diving, horseback riding, golfing, kayaking, and river tubing. Prices range from about $25 to $200 per person, and most excursions are run by concessionaires on the islands rather than by the cruise lines themselves, though you'll book the excursions through the cruise lines, usually once you're aboard ship, with payments charged to your onboard account. A few lines, such as Royal Caribbean, Celebrity, and Princess, also allow you to pre-book excursions, as does the independent website www.port promotions.com. Some ports are best explored through these tours (which depart directly from the pier), and some ports are best seen on your own. In chapter 5, "The Ports of Call," we discuss shore excursions in more depth, providing information on the best excursions and noting where you can skip the excursions entirely and set out on your own.

2 When to Go

With temperatures in the balmy 80s almost year-round, dozens of ships stay in the Caribbean full-time, and a bunch more spend the winters there after summering in Alaska or Europe: The Caribbean is the only major cruise destination that never closes; it's the sea that never sleeps. The only trouble in paradise is **hurricane season,** which officially runs June 1 to November 30 but rarely causes cruisers any problems bigger than a few days of rain and a bit of rocking and rolling. We've taken many cruises in the Caribbean during this period and have only occasionally run into stormy weather; it's rare, but it's a risk you take. The chance of actually getting caught in the perfect storm is next to nil, as modern communications (and generally speedy vessels) allow captains to change course and pilot their ships out of danger as soon as they get word of a storm.

Defining seasons as "low" and "high" is hardly a science, since most lines seem to come up with their own unique pricing schemes, and some lines (like Carnival) have stopped bothering to divide rates by season at all. For those that do, it's generally accepted that **high season** in the Caribbean is mid-December through mid-April. During this time, weather will most likely be perfect, the islands and ships will be jampacked, and thus, the prices will be higher. The **holiday weeks** of Christmas, New Year's, Presidents' Day, and Easter are the absolute busiest and most expensive periods, especially on the family-oriented megaships—these are often the few times in the year when the cruise lines' brochure rates are not discounted.

Despite it being hurricane season, the **summer months** of June, July, and August are the next busiest times; in fact, many lines consider these months high season along with December through April, as families traditionally vacation during the summer and because many ships migrate to Alaska and Europe for the season, leaving fewer vessels in the Caribbean. Temperatures may be a bit hotter in summer, but the islands' colorful flowering trees are at their most lush, and the winds are mildest.

September, October, and early November are considered **low season** (often referred to as "value season") and are the times when you'll encounter the fewest crowds onshore and on board, and some of the lowest rates. Sometimes, there will be a lull during the first 2 weeks of January, just after the rush of the holidays, and sometimes in late April and May, so look for good prices then, as well.

The **Panama Canal cruise season** is roughly the same as the Caribbean's, generally between about November and April. A few lines, like Holland America, have ships doing Panama Canal cruises in September and October, too. Many ships do only two Panama Canal cruises annually, generally in April and September, when they are repositioning their ships between the summer season in Alaska and the fall/winter season in the Caribbean.

2

The Cruise Lines in Brief

People feel very strongly about ships. For centuries, mariners have bestowed their vessels with human attributes, and even though cruise passengers are typically only aboard for a week at a time, they really do bond with their ships. They find themselves in the gift shop, loading up on T-shirts with the ship's name emblazoned on the front. They get to port and the first question they ask other cruisers they meet is "Which ship are you sailing on?" and then engage in a friendly comparison, each walking away knowing in his heart that his ship is the best. We know people who have sailed the same ship a dozen times or more, and feel as warmly about the vessel as if it were their own summer cottage.

Following is a quick primer on the cruise lines operating in the Caribbean at press time. If you're an experienced cruiser you may already have a favorite, but if not, these will give you a little background to help you make your choice. The important thing is to find a cruise line and a ship that says "you." To make your selection easier (and to make sure you're not comparing apples and oranges), we've divided the cruise lines into four distinct categories based on the type of experiences they offer. If you want more info, with in-depth discussions of the different aspects of each line's onboard experience, detailed reviews of the different ships, and all scheduled Caribbean itineraries, pick up a copy of *Frommer's Caribbean Cruises & Ports of Call.*

1 The Mainstream Lines

These are the shopping malls of cruise ships—they're big, bustling, exciting affairs that attract a cross-section of mostly American guests. There's lots to eat, lots to buy on board, and lots of other people sharing the experience with you, though you can always hide out on your cabin balcony—these ships have hundreds of them—or stake out a quiet corner to commune with the sea and contemplate your vacation.

The term "mainstream" covers a lot of ground, and that's the point. These ships are generalists, attempting to offer a little something for almost everyone— all ages, backgrounds, and interests. You'll find people with lots of tattoos downing cans of beer, and you'll find genteel, sherry-sipping types with graduate degrees and subscriptions to *Smithsonian.* It's a mixed-bag kind of crowd if there ever was one.

Since the mainstream category is the most popular, it's the one that's seen the most growth, innovation, and investment in recent years, meaning the ships are, as a general rule, remarkably new—and also remarkably *big.* This is the category that houses the **megaships,** those hulking 1,200- to 3,200-passenger floating resorts that offer the widest variety of activities and entertainment on the ocean. Most of these lines (but particularly the "Big Four"—Carnival, Royal Caribbean, Princess, and Norwegian) have been pumping billions into building newer, bigger, and fancier ships, offering a wide variety of different cabins—inside (no windows), outside (with windows), suites, and cabins with private balconies and without. They offer both formal and several informal dining options, a wide array of entertainment (heavy on the Vegas-style stuff), Internet centers with e-mail access, and more activities than you can possibly squeeze into 1 day, from line-dancing lessons and bingo games, to informal lectures and art tours, plus the inevitable goofy pool games. Overall, the atmosphere is very social.

Within this category, the more elegant and refined of the lines are commonly referred to as **premium,** a notch up in the sophistication department from others that are described as **mass-market.** Quality-wise, for the most part, premium and mass-markets lines are all on equal footing and, overall, are more alike than they are different.

CARNIVAL CRUISE LINES

3655 NW 87th Ave., Miami, FL 33178-2428. ⓒ **888/CARNIVAL** or 305/599-2200. Fax 305/406-4740. www. carnival.com.

THE LINE IN A NUTSHELL The Wal-Mart of cruising, Carnival specializes in colorful, jumbo-size resort ships that deliver plenty of bang for the buck. If you like the flash of Vegas and the party-hearty attitude of New Orleans, you'll love Carnival's brand of flamboyant fun.

THE EXPERIENCE Nobody does it better in the party department. The line with the most recognized name in the biz serves up a very casual, down-to-earth, middle-American Caribbean vacation. While food and service are pretty average, there sure are a lot of choices to keep you satisfied, from round-the-clock entertainment to sushi bars. The line aims to please with unique features on various ships, from upscale supper clubs on the Spirit-class vessels to the smoke-free environment on *Paradise.*

The line's decor, like its clientele, has mellowed a bit since its riotous, exceedingly festive beginnings, but each ship is still an exciting collage of textures, shapes, and images. Where else but on these floating playlands would you find life-size mannequins of Hollywood stars like Marilyn Monroe and Humphrey Bogart, a San Francisco trolley car, or real oyster-shell wallpaper? The outrageousness of the decor is part of the fun: Carnival ships provide a fantasyland you can't get at home. Call it whatever you want, but don't call it dull.

PASSENGER PROFILE Carnival's passenger groups are a melting pot—couples, singles, and families; young, old, and lots in between—and span the whole range from Ralph Lauren shirts and Gucci glasses to Mötley Crüe T-shirts and tattoos. Carnival estimates about 30% of passengers are under age 35, another 40% are between 35 and 55, and 30% are over age 55. At least half of all passengers are first-time cruisers. While it's one of the best lines to choose if you're single, Carnival's ships certainly aren't overrun by singles—families and couples are definitely in the majority.

CELEBRITY CRUISES

1050 Caribbean Way, Miami, FL 33132. ⓒ **800/722-5941** or 305/539-6000. Fax 800/722-5329. www. celebrity-cruises.com.

THE LINE IN A NUTSHELL If you like elegance without stuffiness, fun without bad taste, and pampering without a high price, Celebrity is king.

THE EXPERIENCE With the most elegant big ships in the industry, Celebrity offers a refined cruise experience, yet one that is fun and active. Each of the line's ships is spacious, glamorous, and comfortable, mixing sleekly modern and vaguely art-deco styles and throwing in an astoundingly cutting-edge art collection to boot.

An exceedingly polite and professional staff contributes greatly to the sophisticated mood. Dining-wise, Celebrity shines, offering cuisine and dining service that's a cut above all the other mainstream lines; the dashing alternative restaurants on the Millennium-class ships are the best at sea.

Like all the big-ship lines, Celebrity offers lots for its passengers to do, but its focus on mellower pursuits and innovative programming sets it apart. Niceties such as roving a cappella groups lend a warm, personal touch, while expert-led seminars on personal investing, divorce-coping strategies, and handwriting analysis offer a little more cerebral meat than the usual facial demonstrations or Ping-Pong tournaments.

Celebrity gets the "best of" nod in a lot of categories: The AquaSpas on the line's megaships are the most attractive at sea, the art collections fleet-wide are the most compelling, the cigar bars are the plushest, and the onboard activities are among the most varied. Celebrity pampers suite guests with butler service, and treats all guests to in-cabin pizza delivery.

PASSENGER PROFILE   Celebrity tries to focus on middle- to upper-middle-income cruisers and even wealthy patrons, but these days, with Celebrity's rates comparable to those of Carnival and Royal Caribbean, you'll find a very wide range of folks aboard, those who appreciate the elegance of its ships and those who could care less. Clients who are more than price-motivated like Celebrity because, first, it's not Carnival, and second, because it offers a well-balanced cruise, with lots of activities and a glamorous, exciting atmosphere that's both refined and fun. Most passengers are couples in their 30s on up, with decent numbers of honeymooners and couples celebrating anniversaries, as well as families with children in summer and during the holidays.

COSTA CRUISES

200 South Park Rd., Suite 200, Hollywood, FL 33021-8541. ☎ **800/462-6782** or 954/266-5600. Fax 954/266-2100. www.costa.it.

THE LINE IN A NUTSHELL   Costa's Italian-flavored mid- and mega-size European-styled ships offer a moderately priced, festive, international experience—albeit a humble one in the food and service department.

THE EXPERIENCE   For years, Costa has played up its Italian heritage and history as the factor that primarily distinguishes it from its all-American competition, though today the line employs far fewer Italian crewmembers than in years past (mostly just the officers and maitre d's hail from Italy these days), and the new *CostaAtlantica,* designed by Carnival's Joe Farcus, is definitely a step into more mainstream American megaship territory.

Still, you'll find more pasta dishes on the menu than other lines offer, more opera singers among the entertainment offerings, and Italian-oriented activities like boccie ball. Plus, the line's strength in the Italian-American market definitely helps distinguish it from the Royal Caribbeans, Carnivals, and Norwegians of the world, and the number of Europeans sailing aboard (fewer in the Caribbean than on the line's Mediterranean sailings, but still significant at about 20%–30%) mean you get a passenger mix that's much more international than on most other lines, too. Unfortunately, Costa's disappointing food and dining service also separate it from its peers.

PASSENGER PROFILE   Costa attracts passengers of all ages who want lots of action and who deliberately avoid all-American megaships like those of Carnival. Costa passengers appreciate the line's Italian style and its sense of fun and cultural adventure (relatively speaking, of course). Italian-Americans are heavily represented aboard every Caribbean cruise. In the Caribbean, Costa appeals to retirees and young couples alike, although there are more passengers over 50 than under. Typically you won't see more than 40 or 50 kids on any one cruise except during holidays and school vacations. While about 80% to 90% of passengers are from North America, there's usually a healthy percent from Europe and South America as well.

DISNEY CRUISE LINE

210 Celebration Place, Suite 400, Celebration, FL 34747-4600. ℂ **800/951-3532** or 407/566-7000. Fax 407/566-7353. www.disneycruise.com

THE LINE IN A NUTSHELL   Though Carnival, Royal Caribbean, Celebrity, and Princess all devote significant attention to kids, it took Disney to create vessels where both kids and adults are really catered to equally, and with style. If you love Disney, you'll love these two floating theme parks; if not, there are cheaper cruises.

THE EXPERIENCE   Both classic and ultramodern, the line's two ships are like no others in the industry, designed to evoke the grand transatlantic liners but also boasting a handful of truly innovative features, including extra-large cabins for families, several restaurants through which passengers rotate on every cruise (one night your group may be in an Italian restaurant, the next night your group may be in an American restaurant and so on), fantastic Disney-inspired entertainment, separate adult pools and lounges, and the biggest kids' facilities at sea. In many ways, the experience is more Disney than it is cruise (for instance, there's no casino), but on the other hand, the ships are surprisingly elegant and well laid out, with Disney touches sprinkled around subtly, like fairy dust, amid the art deco and art nouveau design motifs. Head to toe, inside and out, these ships are a class act.

Disney is nothing if not organized, so its 3- and 4-day cruises aboard *Disney Wonder* are designed to be combined with a Disney theme park and hotel package to create a weeklong land/sea vacation. You can also book these shorter cruises (as well as *Disney Magic*'s weeklong cruises) separately.

PASSENGER PROFILE   Disney's ships attract a wide mix of passengers, from honeymooners to seniors, but naturally a large percentage is made up of young American families with children. Because of this, the overall age demographic tends to be younger than aboard many of the other mainstream ships, with many passengers in their 30s and early to mid-40s. There's a smallish number of foreign passengers as well.

HOLLAND AMERICA LINE

300 Elliott Ave. W., Seattle, WA 98119. ℂ **877-724-5425** or 206/281-3535. Fax 800/628-4855. www.hollandamerica.com.

THE LINE IN A NUTSHELL   Holland America has been in business since 1873, and has managed to hang on to more of its seafaring history and tradition than any other line today except Cunard. It offers a moderately priced, classic cruise experience that is casual, yet refined.

THE EXPERIENCE   Holland America consistently delivers a solid product, with old-world elegance at a fair price. Though the line has been retooling itself to attract younger passengers and families, it still caters mostly to older folks, and so generally it offers a more sedate and stately experience than other mainstream lines.

Aside from the new *Zuiderdaam* and *Oosterdam,* megaships which debut in December 2002 and June 2003, HAL's well-maintained vessels are midsize and cozy, and all have excellent (and remarkably similar) layouts that facilitate easy passenger movement. Decor on *Maasd,* and *Veendam* is stylish, classic, and, for the most part, understated, while the newer *Rotterdam, Amsterdam, Zaandam,* and *Volendam* are brighter and more colorful, yet still elegant. Throughout the public areas you'll find flowers that call to mind Holland's place in the floral trade, seafaring memorabilia that tells the story of Holland America Line's own history, and a sprinkling of Indonesian fabrics and woodcarvings (along with the mostly Indonesian and Filipino staff).

PASSENGER PROFILE   For years, HAL was known for catering to an almost exclusively older crowd, with most passengers in their 70s and up. And while you'll still mostly see older folks aboard, in the past several years the line has been revamping its image to attract younger passengers, and today about 40% of Caribbean guests are under age 55, with a few young families peppering the mix, especially in summers and during holiday weeks. Passengers tend to be amiable, low-key, and better educated than their equivalents aboard sister line Carnival, though they're a lot less affluent than passengers aboard luxury lines like Seabourn and Silversea.

NORWEGIAN CRUISE LINE

7665 Corporate Center Dr., Miami, FL 33126. ℂ **800/327-7030** or 305/436-4000. Fax 305/436-4126. www. ncl.com.

THE LINE IN A NUTSHELL   NCL makes its mark with its always-casual, open-seating dining, and while its older ships aren't perfect, its newer ones are much better. In fact, *Norwegian Sky, Norwegian Sun,* and *Norwegian Dawn* give the newest Royal Caribbean and Princess ships a run for their money.

THE EXPERIENCE   This is an exciting time for NCL. The company is now in a major expansion mode, launching four new ships in the span of about 3 years, and it continues to roll out exciting innovations, especially in the dining department. The 2,000-passenger *Norwegian Sky,* 1,960-passenger *Norwegian Sun* and *Norwegian Dawn,* and 2,244-passenger *Norwegian Star* represent the new, higher-quality NCL, while the line's four other midsize vintage-1980s vessels, carrying about 1,500 passengers each, represent its more budget-conscious past.

There's no doubt NCL is remaking itself, and quite impressively too. The line has quietly phased out its sports and music theme cruises, and in May 2000 it launched its "Freestyle Cruising" concept, a revolutionary ultraflexible dining program that appeals to people who don't like the regimentation and formality of traditional cruise dining. Now offered fleetwide, Freestyle means all restaurants on the ships operate with a casual dress code and have open seating between about 5:30 and 10pm every evening.

PASSENGER PROFILE   As a rule, NCL attracts a diverse lot, and passengers in general are younger, more price-conscious, and more active than those aboard lines such as HAL, Celebrity, and Princess. Typical NCL passengers are couples ages 25 to 60, including a fair number of honeymooners, plus families with kids during summers and holidays. (Kids under 2 sail free.) The atmosphere aboard all NCL vessels is informal and well-suited to the party-maker taking a first or second cruise.

PRINCESS CRUISES

24305 Town Center Dr., Santa Clarita, CA 91355. ℂ **800/PRINCESS** or 661/753-0000. Fax 661/259-3108. www.princesscruises.com.

THE LINE IN A NUTSHELL   Princess' megaship fleet offers a quality, mainstream cruise experience. Its newest ships are stylish, floating resorts with just the right combination of fun, glamour, and gentility for a pleasant and relaxing cruise.

THE EXPERIENCE   If you were to put Carnival, Royal Caribbean, Celebrity, and Holland America in a big bowl and mix them together, you'd come up with Princess. The Grand-class and Sun-class ships are less glitzy and frenzied than Carnival and Royal Caribbean; not quite as cutting-edge or witty as Celebrity's Millennium- and Century-class ships; and more youthful and entertaining than Holland America's near-megas. These ships appeal to a wide cross section of cruisers by offering lots of activities and touches of big-ship glamour, along with the kind of quiet nooks and calm spaces you find on smaller, more intimate vessels.

Aboard Princess you get a lot of bang (and choices) for your buck; the experience is attractively packaged, well executed, and a little bit looser than the traditional cruise line experience due to the line's "Personal Choice Dining" concept, in which some dining rooms offer open restaurant-style seating between 5:30 and midnight, while others stick to traditional early and late seatings.

PASSENGER PROFILE   In the past, most Princess passengers were middle-aged middle Americans, but as the line's older vessels are replaced by shiny new megaships, a broader representation of younger 30- and 40-somethings and their families are mixing with passengers in their 50s, 60s, and older. Overall, Princess passengers are not as rowdy and boisterous as those aboard Carnival and not as staid as those aboard Holland America. The Grand-class and Sun-class ships have extensive kids' facilities and are ideal for families. Their balance of formal and informal makes them perfect for a romantic vacation too. There's a lot going on, but also plenty of opportunities to do your own thing.

REGAL CRUISES

P.O. Box 1329, Palmetto, FL 34220. ℂ **800/270-7245** or 941/721-7300. Fax 941/723-0900. www.regal cruises.com.

THE LINE IN A NUTSHELL   Odd-man-out among the mainstream lines, Regal's single old ship isn't exactly regal, but ship buffs will appreciate the vestiges of classic decor and bargain shoppers will love the price.

THE EXPERIENCE   Regal Cruises offers 1- to 12-night itineraries at rock-bottom prices—less than $70 per person per day at times. Shorter cruises are party-hearty, while longer sailings are just the opposite. If you're on a tight budget and are looking for a small-scale Carnival-esque experience, this is a line to consider.

The 48-year-old *Regal Empress* (the line's only ship) keeps chugging along, and over the past several years has been the beneficiary of several well-thought-out renovations—improving her decor, adding a TV to every cabin, adding verandas to some of the suites, hanging classic art deco poster art in the public areas, and even introducing an Internet center—not bad for the old bird! Still,

Empress can't help showing her age (what can you expect? she's nearly half a century old) and is currently a blend of the best of the old days, some tacky early refurbishments, and the good intentions of today. There's more wood paneling than on most other ships in this chapter, but there's also Astroturf on the outside decks and no shortage of chintzy chrome and mirrors in the public rooms. Quirks and all, though, *Regal Empress* offers an unpretentious cruise with decent food and entertainment—especially considering her low prices. If you can afford it, book one of the suites or any of the Category 3 superior outside staterooms, and you'll have plenty of space to retire to if the crowds (big ones when the ship is fully booked) get to you.

PASSENGER PROFILE Passengers run the gamut from very young (children under age 2 sail free) to very old (since zillions of retirees live in the Clearwater/Tampa/St. Petersburg area). Caribbean cruises out of Port Manatee tend to be much more sedate than the raucous midsummer party cruises out of New York.

ROYAL CARIBBEAN INTERNATIONAL

1050 Caribbean Way, Miami, FL 33132. (C) **800/327-6700** or 305/539-6000. Fax 800/722-5329. www.royal caribbean.com.

THE LINE IN A NUTSHELL Cruises on these fun, activity-packed, glamorous (but not over-the-top glitzy) megaships offer great diversions, from solariums to huge kids' playrooms, and even miniature golf and rock-climbing on some ships.

THE EXPERIENCE Royal Caribbean offers some of the best-looking and best-designed (not to mention incredibly activity-packed) megaships in the biz, appealing to a wide range of people. Except for the older *Nordic Empress,* the company's vessels are all megaships with similar features such as multistory atria, mall-like shopping complexes, two-story dining rooms and showrooms, wide-open public areas and small cabins. There are lots of activities, a varied and well-executed entertainment repertoire, and enough glamour and glitz to keep things exciting, but not an excess that overwhelms the senses (except aboard the Voyager-class ships, where things can get to be overwhelming). Decor-wise, these ships are a shade or two toned down from the Carnival brood, and while the onboard experience is similar, the Royal Caribbean ships are less in-your-face than their Carnival counterparts. The new Radiance-class ships are the line's classiest to date, giving Royal Caribbean more of a Celebrity-style sophistication than a Vegas-style, party-on Carnival feel.

PASSENGER PROFILE You'll find all walks of life on a Royal Caribbean cruise: passengers in their 20s through 60s, mostly couples (a good number of them honeymooning) and some singles traveling with friends, but also lots of families—more than 200,000 kids sailed with Royal Caribbean in 2001. A shade more sophisticated than Carnival (at least in terms of ship decor), the line attracts passengers who consider it less glitzy and party-focused, though in reality the differences between the two are few. Overall, passengers are active, social, and looking for a good time, no matter what their age.

ROYAL OLYMPIC CRUISES

805 Third Ave., New York, NY, 10022-7513. (C) **800/872-6400** or 212/397-6400. Fax 888/662-6237. www. royalolympiccruises.com.

THE LINE IN A NUTSHELL This Greek line's ships generally stick to the Mediterranean, but its two newest vessels offer Caribbean, Panama Canal, and

Mexico/Central America cruises, plus sailings in South America. It's a little touch of Greece among the Caribbean's palms and white-sand beaches, and it provides a more destination- and learning-oriented experience than any of the other mainstream lines.

THE EXPERIENCE   Like mini versions of today's megaships, the high-speed, 840-passenger sister ships *Olympia Voyager* and *Olympia Explorer* offer a mega-ship-style variety of entertainment options, activities, and cabin choices, yet the ships stand apart with itineraries that visit remote ports, and onboard enrichment programs that are the best of any mainstream line in the Caribbean. The ships have a top speed approaching 30 knots (versus 22–24 for most megaships) and offer a more casual, low-key experience. Theme itineraries are offered throughout the year, including several that visit Mayan sites on an equinox, and others built around solar eclipses. "Mayaribbean" Maya-themed cruises depart weekly from Houston, visiting Mayan sites in Honduras, Belize, and Mexico's Yucatán peninsula, with archaeologists and historians aboard to lead discussions.

PASSENGER PROFILE   Over the years, Royal Olympic's passengers have primarily been well-traveled senior couples, many of whom have sailed with the line before. The line's new vessels are designed to attract a wider and generally younger group in the 35-to-55 age range. Summers and holidays, you'll find families with kids on board.

2 The Luxury Lines

On these top-shelf cruises, guests don't line up for a look at an ice sculpture or a slice of pepperoni pizza en route to St. Thomas or Nassau. Instead, they sip a '98 Bordeaux with their filet de boeuf in truffle sauce while sailing to Les Saintes or St. Barts. They order jumbo shrimp from the room service menu, and take indulgent baths in ritzy marble-furnished bathrooms. There are no midnight buffets, dancing waiters, belly-flop contests by the pool, assigned dinner seating (except on the Crystal ships), or many of the other typical cruise ship trappings. Instead, you'll find doting service, the best food and wine at sea, and a calm, elegant retreat to call home for a week or 2.

These cruise lines' ships are the the Ritz-Carlton Hotels of the sea. Mostly small and intimate, they're the sports cars of cruise ships and cater to discerning travelers who don't blink an eye at paying top dollar to be pampered with fine gourmet cuisine and spacious suites with walk-in closets. Formal nights see the vast majority of guests dressed in tuxedos and sparkling dresses and gowns, dining in elegant rooms with the finest linens, stemware, and china. (The exceptions to the rule of formal nights are the yachts of Windstar Cruises, which take a much more casual approach and feature a laid back decor.) Aboard all the lines, delicious French, Italian, and Asian cuisine often rivals that of respected shoreside restaurants and is served in high style by large staffs of doting, gracious waiters who know how to please. A full dinner can even be served to you in your cabin if you like. Though all these lines are pretty darn ritzy, you shouldn't expect the kind of five-star experience you'd get on land; none of these ultraluxury ships offer the level of service and cuisine you'd find at a Four Seasons or Ritz-Carlton hotel.

With the exception of the large Crystal ships, these high-end vessels tend to be small and intimate, carrying just a few hundred passengers. Most people attracted to these types of cruises are sophisticated, wealthy, relatively social, and used to the finer things in life. Extras are often included in the cruise rates. For instance, Silversea's and Seabourn's rates include unlimited wine, liquor, and beverages, along with tips, a stocked minibar, and one complimentary shore excursion per cruise. Radisson's rates include tips, wine with dinner, one-time stocked minibar, and unlimited soda and bottled water.

CUNARD

6100 Blue Lagoon Dr., Suite 400, Miami, FL 33126. © **800/5-CUNARD** or 305/463-3000. Fax 305/463-3010. www.cunardline.com.

THE LINE IN A NUTSHELL   Can you say "history"? Can you say "God Save the Queen"? Cunard, almost 165 years old at this writing, is a bona fide cultural icon, a tangible reminder of the days when Britannia really did rule the waves, and that is what sets this line apart. It's one of the most legendary lines around, but unfortunately offers only a handful of Caribbean cruises.

THE EXPERIENCE   Catering to a wealthy, well-traveled clientele, Cunard offers an onboard experience that's high-brow genteel British all the way, from the formal service to the decor, which pays tribute to England and to Cunard's long history through artwork and memorabilia.

Activities are relatively mellow, featuring enrichment lectures, walking tours of the ships' art collection, reading, and movies, and passengers participate at their own pace. Likewise, entertainment is low-key, featuring pianists, singers, string quartets, live dance bands, and lots of conversation and cocktails. Dining is a formal affair, and guests dress the part.

Cunard currently has two ships in its fleet, the classic British-flavored *Queen Elizabeth 2*, the only ship still offering regular transatlantic service, and the even more formal (and much smaller) European-style *Caronia*, which sails year-round from Southampton. *QE2* recalls the great ocean-liner days of decades ago— among other reasons, because it actually *was* built decades ago (in 1969). The ship is in great shape overall, but though Cunard diligently refurbishes her interiors, there's still a smattering of water-stained ceilings and a subtle mustiness on the lower decks.

PASSENGER PROFILE   In general, Cunard attracts a well-traveled, soft-spoken and heavily British crowd of passengers in their 50s and up, many of them repeaters who appreciate Cunard's old-fashioned virtues. This is more of a 4 o'clock tea crowd than an "in a hot tub with a bottle of tequila" crowd. That said, the few *QE2* Caribbean sailings draw a larger number of Yanks. Most passengers travel as couples, but there are also many widows and widowers as well as friends and relatives traveling together.

CRYSTAL CRUISES

2049 Century Park East, 14th Floor, Los Angeles, CA 90067. © **800/446-6620** or 310/785-9300. Fax 310/785-3891. www.crystalcruises.com.

THE LINE IN A NUTSHELL   Fine-tuned and fashionable, Crystal's pair of dream ships offer top-tier service and cuisine on vessels large enough to offer lots of outdoor deck space, generous fitness facilities, four restaurants, and over half a dozen bars and entertainment venues.

THE EXPERIENCE   Crystal boasts the two largest of the truly upscale ships in the industry. Carrying 940 passengers, they aren't huge, but they're big enough to offer much more than their high-end peers. You won't feel hemmed in and you likely won't be twiddling your thumbs from lack of stimulation. Service is excellent and cuisine is on par with Radisson Seven Seas, Silversea and

Seabourn; the line's Asian food is tops. Unlike Seabourn's small ships, which tend to be more calm and staid, Crystal's sociable California ethic and larger passenger capacity tend to keep things mingly, chatty, and active.

PASSENGER PROFILE Few other cruise lines attract as loyal a crop of repeat passengers, more than 50% of whom hail from affluent regions of California and most of whom step aboard for their second, third, or fourth Crystal cruise with a definite sense of how they want to spend their time on board. There's commonly a small contingent of passengers (about 15% of the mix) from the United Kingdom, Australia, Japan, Mexico, Europe, and South America. Most passengers are well-heeled couples, stylish but not particularly flamboyant, and over 55. A good number of passengers step up to Crystal from lines like Princess and Holland America. Passengers tend to be well traveled, although not particularly adventurous. There are rarely kids on board except during the holidays (and summers in Alaska), when you may see as many as 40.

RADISSON SEVEN SEAS CRUISES
600 Corporate Dr., Suite 410, Ft. Lauderdale, FL 33334. ℂ **800/285-1835.** Fax 402/501-5599. www.rssc. com.

THE LINE IN A NUTSHELL Radisson carries passengers in style and extreme comfort. Its brand of luxury is casually elegant and subtle, and its cuisine is among the best.

THE EXPERIENCE Radisson's ships are spacious, service is as good as it gets, and cuisine is some of the best at sea. In addition to their formal restaurants, all three ships have alternative, reservations-only restaurants specializing in northern Italian food. Even if what tickles your fancy isn't on the menu, the chef will prepare it for you.

These ships tend to be less stuffy and a bit more casual than Seabourn and Cunard. You can chuck your tux for the most part, although on formal nights they certainly aren't uncommon.

PASSENGER PROFILE This line appeals primarily to well-traveled and well-heeled passengers in their 50s and 60s, but younger passengers and honeymooners aren't unheard of. Many passengers are frequent cruisers who have also sailed on Seabourn and Crystal, or are taking a step up from Holland America. They have sophisticated tastes (and can do without inane activities like napkin-folding classes), and they appreciate a somewhat less formal ambiance—casual nights in the formal dining room see some passengers in polo shirts and jackets and others in nice T-shirts with jeans and sneakers.

SEABOURN CRUISE LINE
6100 Blue Lagoon Drive, Suite 400, Miami, FL 33126. ℂ **800/929-9595** or 305/463-3000, ext. 1273. Fax 305/463-3020. www.seabourn.com.

THE LINE IN A NUTSHELL Small and intimate, these quiet, comfortable mega-yachts lavish guests with personal attention and very fine cuisine.

THE EXPERIENCE Strictly upper-crust Seabourn caters to guests who are well mannered and prefer their fellow vacationers to be the same. Generally, they aren't into pool games and deck parties, preferring a good book and cocktail chatter, but maybe they'll go for recent enhancements like free minimassages on deck and soothing Eucalyptus oil baths drawn in suites upon request. We'll see . . . .

Due to the ships' small size, guests mingle easily and enjoy mellow pursuits like trivia games and presentations by guest lecturers. Because there are 157 crew members to just 208 guests (a higher ratio than almost any other line), service is very personal; staff members greet you by name from the moment you check in, and your wish is their command.

PASSENGER PROFILE   Seabourn's guests are well traveled seniors, mostly in their 60s and 70s, who are used to five-star treatment. The average household income here is in excess of $250,000, and many passengers have a net worth in the millions. You are likely to encounter former CEOs, lawyers, investment bankers, real estate tycoons, and entrepreneurs, plus lots of old-money folks. The majority of passengers are couples, and there are always a handful of singles as well, usually widows or widowers. A number of European and Australian guests usually spice up the mix, but no matter what their nationality, these are experienced globetrotting travelers. While some adult children and their parents travel together, don't expect to find children or even young adults on these ships. There is nothing to appeal to them, and the passengers prefer it that way.

SEADREAM YACHT CLUB

2601 South Bayshore Drive, Penthouse 1B, Coconut Grove, Florida 33133. © 800/707-4911 or 305/856-5622. Fax 305/856-7599. http://seadreamyachtclub.com.

THE LINE IN A NUTSHELL   Intimate cruise ships turned yachting vessels, SeaDream's two small ships deliver an upscale yet casual experience without the regimentation of traditional cruise itineraries and activities.

THE EXPERIENCE   SeaDream—a new line created by Seabourn founder Atle Brynestad with Seabourn's two *Sea Goddess* ships—will entice those who value impeccable service, a mellow atmosphere, and a good batch of Sevruga Malossol caviar. But the new line is seeking another kind of traveler as well: one who straddles a WaveRunner, bar hops in Monte Carlo, and enjoys a spontaneous mountain bike trek. But this isn't just the wealthy man's *Survivor* episode. Pampering is still a major focus, and the line's flexible itineraries and fluid daily schedules should appeal to landlubbers who are used to doing vacations at their own pace.

PASSENGER PROFILE   This new line targets affluent couples between the ages of 40 and 60 who have refined tastes but balk at the rigid structure of traditional cruise itineraries. SeaDream passengers are happy to strike up a game of backgammon beside the pool, or venture into town with the chef in search of the evening's special fish. They want top-notch service and gourmet food, but are secure enough to dispense with the stuffy atmosphere. At least that's the plan.

SILVERSEA CRUISES

110 E. Broward Blvd., Fort Lauderdale, FL 33301. © 800/722-9955. Fax 954/522-4499. www.silversea.com.

THE LINE IN A NUTSHELL   It doesn't get any better than free-flowing Moët & Chandon champagne and marble bathrooms stocked with wonderful Bulgari bath products. These gorgeous ships offer the best of everything.

THE EXPERIENCE   Fine-tuned and genteel, a Silversea cruise caters to guests who won't settle for anything but the best. The food and service are the best at sea, and the ships' Italian-style decor is warm and inviting. Nothing seems to have been forgotten in the creation of the plush Silversea fleet. Bed linens are Frette and tables are set with Christofle silver and Schott-Zwiesel crystal. These are dignified vessels for a dignified crowd that likes to dress for dinner. If you want the VIP treatment 24/7, this is your cruise line.

PASSENGER PROFILE While Silversea's typical passenger mix is 60-plus, shorter cruises and Caribbean sailings often skew the mix a tad younger, adding at least a handful of 30- and 40-something couples to the pot. Typically, about 85% of passengers are American and they're well-traveled, well-heeled, well-dressed, and not afraid to flaunt five-carat diamonds and gold Rolexes the size of Texas. Most guest are couples, though singles and small groups of friends traveling together are usually part of the scene too. Many have cruised with Silversea before, and they expect the best of everything.

WINDSTAR CRUISES

300 Elliott Ave. W., Seattle, WA 98119. (C) **800/258-7245** or 206/281-3535. Fax 206/281-0627. www.windstarcruises.com.

THE LINE IN A NUTSHELL The no-jackets-required policy on board Windstar's sleek vessels defines the line's casually elegant attitude. The small ships really do feel like private yachts—the atmosphere is down-to-earth, yet service and cuisine are first-class.

THE EXPERIENCE Windstar offers a truly unique cruise experience, giving passengers the delicious sensation of adventure aboard its fleet of four- and five-masted sailing ships, along with the ever-pleasant reality of first-class cuisine, service, and itineraries. This is no barefoot, rigging-pulling, paper-plates-in-lap, sleep-on-the-deck kind of cruise, but a refined yet down to earth yachtlike experience for a sophisticated, well-traveled crowd who wouldn't be comfortable on a big ship with throngs of other tourists.

On board, fine stained teak, brass details, and lots of navy-blue fabrics and carpeting lend a traditional nautical ambiance. While the ships' proud masts and white sails cut a traditional profile, they're also state-of-the-art, controlled by a computer so they can be furled or unfurled at the touch of a button. In the Caribbean, at least once per week, if at all possible, the captain shuts off the engines and moves by sail only, to give passengers a real taste of the sea. Under full sail, the calm tranquility is utterly blissful.

PASSENGER PROFILE People who expect high-caliber service and very high-quality cuisine but dislike the formality of the other high-end ships (as well as the mass-mentality of the megaships) are thrilled with Windstar. Overall, passengers are sophisticated, well-traveled, and unaffected, and want a somewhat adventurous, port-intensive Caribbean cruise, visiting islands like the Grenadines, the Tobago Cays, the British Virgin Islands, Belize, Honduras, and relatively isolated dependencies of Guadeloupe, such as Les Saintes. Most passengers are couples in their 30s to early 60s (with the average around 50), with a smattering of parents with adult children and some single friends traveling together. The line is not the best choice for first-timers, since it appeals to a specific sensibility, and it's definitely not a good choice for singles or families with children under 15 or 16.

3 Soft-Adventure Lines & Sailing Ships

These vessels are not your average cruise ships. All of them are small and intimate, carrying only 60 to 200 passengers, and they are often more adventure tour than they are conventional "cruise." Leave the jackets, ties, pumps, and pearls at home: These vessels are ultracasual and take passengers close up to nature, island culture, and the sea.

These ships generally visit a port every day, stopping at small, out-of-the-way ports that the big cruise ships would run aground trying to approach. Passengers on American Canadian Caribbean Line, Clipper, and Star Clippers are mostly well-traveled folks who are more concerned about learning, exploring, and getting to know the islands than they are about plush amenities and onboard activities, while passengers on Windjammer Barefoot Cruises are . . . well, they're looking for a good time. There may not be TVs in the cabins and you won't find a casino or bingo game on board, but you will find people who have booked this type of ship because they like to get to know their fellow passengers while learning something about the ports. Food will be relatively basic, and you won't find room service or midnight buffets. Don't expect doting service either, but do expect very personal attention, as crew and passengers get friendly fast.

Of the lines reviewed here, Clipper operates motorized coastal cruisers that are like B&Bs at sea, while ACCL offers a similar though much more spartan experience. Star Clippers and Windjammer both offer sailing ships, the former with a yachtlike vibe, the latter more like summer camp for adults.

AMERICAN CANADIAN CARIBBEAN LINE

P.O. Box 368, Warren, RI 02885. ℂ **800/556-7450** or 401/247-0955. Fax 401/247-2350. www.accl-small ships.com.

THE LINE IN A NUTSHELL   A family-owned New England line, ACCL operates tiny, no-frills ships that travel to offbeat places and attract a well-traveled, extremely casual and down-to-earth older crowd.

THE EXPERIENCE   ACCL's innovative and extremely informal small ships offer a cruise experience that gets passengers closer to the real life of the islands than is typical with the big-ship lines. Navigating hinterlands like the cays off the coast of Belize, remote out-islands in the Bahamas, and exotic islands near the Atlantic and Pacific mouths of the Panama Canal, the line focuses on encounters with indigenous cultures and exploring the natural wonders of the region. Many of ACCL's generally friendly, older passengers have sailed with the line before, and appreciate the ships' lack of glitz—which is putting it mildly. These ships are, in fact, about the most bare-bones you'll find, in amenities, services, and meals, and are the only ships featuring a BYOB policy.

PASSENGER PROFILE   These casual ships appeal to an unpretentious, sensible, early-to-bed crowd of mostly senior couples in their 60s through 80s, with the average age being 72. While some are physically fit, there are usually a few walking with canes and using hearing aids. Besides senior couples, there may be a few mother-daughter traveling pairs. All are attracted by the ships' casual atmosphere (wash-and-wear fabrics, durable windbreakers, and easy-to-care-for sportswear is about as fancy as these folks want to get). They want to avoid overrun Caribbean ports such as St. Thomas, and flee instead to isolated beaches and secluded havens where they can become quietly acquainted with regional cultures or comb the beaches. That said, passengers tend to be less adventurous than those on other small-ship lines, so ACCL doesn't offer hardcore activities like water-skiing and excursions in inflatable Zodiac boats.

CLIPPER CRUISE LINE

7711 Bonhomme Ave., St. Louis, MO 63105-1961. ℂ **800/325-0010** or 314/727-2929. Fax 800/727-6576. www.clippercruise.com.

THE LINE IN A NUTSHELL   Clipper's down-to-earth, comfortable small ships focus on offbeat ports of call, learning, and mingling with fellow passengers.

It's the ideal small-ship cruise for people who've tried Holland America or one of the other mainstream lines, and want a more intimate cruise experience.

THE EXPERIENCE   Clipper caters to mature, seasoned, easy-going, relatively affluent, well-traveled older passengers seeking a casual and educational vacation experience. You won't find any glitter, glitz, or Las Vegas–style gambling here; instead, you'll get to experience the natural world, history, and culture of the ports visited, courtesy of the naturalists who sail with every Caribbean sailing and the onboard historian who joins all Grenadines trips. A cruise director helps organize the days, answers questions, and assists passengers. Being small ships, the ambiance is intimate and conducive to establishing new friendships. On the downside, as with many other American-crewed small ships, cruise rates are not cheap.

The line's two primary Caribbean ships, *Nantucket Clipper* and *Yorktown Clipper,* are small and nicely appointed, with comfortable cabins, sizable lounges and dining rooms, and an overall relaxed feel. Like other small ships, they're able to access remote hideaways in the Southern Caribbean, the British Virgin Islands, and Central America, but they also suffer the typical problem of small ships: lack of stability. When a ship this size hits rough water, you'll know it. (Bring the Dramamine!)

PASSENGER PROFILE   The majority of Clipper passengers are well-traveled 45- to 75-year-old couples who are attracted by the casual intimacy of small ships and by the opportunity to learn something about the places they visit. Most are well educated though not academic, casual, and adventurous in the sense that they're up for a little snorkeling and hiking, but are happy to be able to get back to their comfortable cabins or have a nice drink in the lounge afterwards. Clipper attracts a remarkably high number of repeat passengers: On any given cruise, 40 percent or more of the passengers will have sailed with the line before. Many have also sailed with other small-ship lines, such as Lindblad Expeditions, Cruise West, and ACCL.

STAR CLIPPERS

4101 Salzedo Ave., Coral Gables, FL 33146. © **800/442-0550** or 305/442-0553. Fax 305/442-1611. www.star-clippers.com.

THE LINE IN A NUTSHELL   With the sails and rigging of classic clipper ships and some of the cushy amenities of modern megaships, a cruise on this line's 170- to 228-passenger ships offers adventure coupled with comfort.

THE EXPERIENCE   On Star Clippers, you'll have the best of two worlds. On the one hand, the ship offers comfortable, almost cushy public rooms and cabins. On the other, they espouse an unstructured, let-your-hair-down, hands-on ethic—you can climb the masts (with a harness, of course), pull in the sails, crawl into the bow netting, or chat with the captain on the open-air bridge.

On board, ducking under booms, stepping over coils of rope, leaning against railings just feet above the sea, and watching sailors work the winches are constant reminders that you're on a real working ship. Further, listening to the captain's daily talk about the next port of call, the history of sailing, or some other nautical subject, you'll feel like you're exploring some of the Caribbean's more remote stretches in a ship that really belongs here—an exotic ship for an exotic locale. In a sea of look-alike megaships, *Star Clipper* and new *Royal Clipper* stand out, recalling a romantic, swashbuckling era of ship travel.

PASSENGER PROFILE   Star Clippers unusual niche appeals to passengers who might recoil at the lethargy and/or sometimes forced enthusiasm of cruises aboard larger, more typical vessels. While you're likely to find a handful of late-20-something honeymoon-type couples, the majority of passengers are well-traveled couples in their late 40s to 60s, mostly active and intellectually curious professionals (such as executives, lawyers, and doctors) who appreciate the casual, sophisticated ambiance. With a nearly even mix of Europeans and North Americans on a typical Caribbean cruise, the international onboard flavor is as intriguing as the ship itself, with the sounds of English, German, and French mingling. Overall, the company reports a whopping 60% of passengers are repeaters back for another Star Clippers cruise.

WINDJAMMER BAREFOOT CRUISES

1759 Bay Rd., Miami Beach, FL 33139 (P.O. Box 190120, Miami Beach, FL 33119). ✆ 800/327-2601 or 305/672-6453. Fax 305/674-1219. www.windjammer.com.

THE LINE IN A NUTSHELL   Ultracasual and delightfully carefree, this eclectic fleet of cozy, rebuilt sailing ships (powered by both sails and engines) lures passengers into a fantasy world of pirates-and-rum-punch adventure.

THE EXPERIENCE   When you see that the captain is wearing shorts and shades and is barefoot like the rest of the laid-back crew, you'll realize Windjammer's vessels aren't your typical cruise ships. Their yards of sails, pointy bowsprits, chunky portholes, and generous use of wood create a swashbuckling storybook look, and while passengers don't have to fish for dinner or swab the decks, they are invited to help haul the sails, take a turn at the wheel, sleep out on deck whenever they please, and (with the captain's permission) crawl into the bow net. With few rules and lots of freedom, this is the closest thing you'll get to a real old-fashioned Caribbean adventure.

Making their way to off-the-beaten-track Caribbean ports of call, the ships are ultra-informal, and hokey yet endearing rituals make the trip feel like summer camp for adults. Add in the line's tremendous number of repeat passengers (and a few of its signature rum swizzle drinks) and you have a casual experience that's downright intimate.

PASSENGER PROFILE   Unlike some "all things to all people" cruise lines, Windjammer is for a particular kind of informal, fun-loving, down-to-earth, nutty, quirky, nonconformist passenger, and though some compare the experience to a continuous fraternity party, the passenger and age mix puts the lie to that description. From honeymooning couples in their 20s to grandparents in their seventies, the line attracts a broad range of adventurers who like to have fun and don't want anything resembling a highly regimented vacation. Passengers are pretty evenly divided between men and women, and 15% to 20% overall are single. Many passengers love the experience so much that they return again and again. Young children should probably not go (in fact, the line doesn't accept passengers under 6), nor should anyone prone to seasickness.

4 The European Lines

Down with McDonalds, baseball, and Budweiser, and helloooo baguettes, pickled herring, and sandals with socks. The lines described here don't cater primarily to Americans like the other lines in this chapter do; in fact, us Yanks will be in the minority for a change, but why not expand our horizons a little bit on vacation? Cruising with travelers from England, Austria, France, Spain, Holland, Sweden, Mexico, Brazil, Japan or wherever else, adds an exotic flavor to an otherwise typical Caribbean cruise.

The vessels here are midsize (or small, in the case of the Sea Cloud ships) and thus more intimate than the sprawling mainstream megaships, but they offer a similar balance of casual and formal, and a varied daily repertoire of activities and entertainment, from bridge tournaments to dancing lessons and Broadway-style song-and-dance revues. English is the first language of all these lines, but because of the stew of nationalities on board, activities may be translated into several languages, which of course adds time to the introduction of music acts, trivia games, and port talks. But you get used to it pretty fast. When it comes to shore excursions, there are usually separate buses for each language. Keep in mind that most Europeans speak some English—we're the ones who have embarrassingly limited language skills, not them.

In general, Europeans and South Americans tend to eat later and party into the wee hours, so dining hours may be adjusted accordingly. Casinos tend to be quieter, as Europeans tend not to be as gambling-crazy as Americans often are. European kids tend to be less segregated than their American brethren, following Mom and Dad into the casino, the disco, or even the steam room. While there may be a decent number of smokers on board, lounges and dining rooms do offer separate smoking and nonsmoking sections. Expect much of the entertainment to be more physical—magicians, acrobats, puppeteers, singers, and dancers rather than, say, comedians—so that speakers of many languages can appreciate it more easily.

FIRST EUROPEAN CRUISES

95 Madison Ave., Suite 609, New York, NY 10016. ℭ 888/983-8767 or 212/779-7168. Fax 212/779-0948. www.first-european.com.

THE LINE IN A NUTSHELL   Relatively new to cruising, First European is the U.S. arm of Europe-based Festival Cruises, founded in 1986 by George F. Poulides of the Greek Poulides shipping dynasty. Its fleet of six includes three attractive new ships all built since 1999, with the 1,566-passenger *European Vision* being the only one offering Caribbean cruises to the American market.

THE EXPERIENCE   First European Cruises came into being in 1997, and 2 years later the French-flagged *Mistral* debuted as the line's first new ship. While *Mistral* was an overall success, the larger *Vision* was able to improve upon her older sister's shortcomings, offering more cabin balconies; an Internet center; the latest toys, from a golf simulator to a climbing wall; and a casual buffet restaurant open 24 hours a day. There's also a main dining room and an intimate reservations-only restaurant. *Vision* also offers the same wonderful spa as *Mistral* does—one of the best at sea.

PASSENGER PROFILE   *European Vision* is a midsize melting pot of a ship, with no more than 10% to 20% of the passenger mix being North American (often less), and the rest mostly from Europe, but also South America and Asia. The international ambience is charming and exotic, and the sea of different languages you'll hear takes on almost musical proportions—though you may not feel quite as giddy about it when you're waiting for announcements and entertainment acts to be translated into three, four, or five languages (but you do get used to it).

MEDITERRANEAN SHIPPING CRUISES

420 Fifth Ave., New York, NY 10018. ℭ 800/666-9333 or 212/764-4800. Fax 212/764-1486. www.msc cruisesusa.com.

THE LINE IN A NUTSHELL   Mediterranean Shipping Cruises is an Italian company that operates primarily in Europe. *Melody,* the line's sole Caribbean ship, was built back in 1982 and sailed for years as one of Premier's family-oriented Big Red Boats, *Star/Ship Atlantic*. She offers a pair of low-priced, port-packed 11-night eastern and western Caribbean itineraries catering to Europeans and North Americans.

THE EXPERIENCE   To a point, the Italian roots of this line add a touch of European holiday to your Caribbean jaunt, but overall the experience is more bargain basement than continental class, with cuisine (for instance) that's a fairly standard mixture of international and Italian specialties. Activities on a typical cruise include bingo, bridge, dance lessons, arts and crafts, language classes, and gambling in the casino. You'll find wacky poolside games at the Riviera pool, but if you'd rather avoid the shenanigans, head aft to the quieter Calypso pool. A low-tech, low-key indoor/outdoor children's center offers a modest selection of activities and a small wading pool, but in general there are few efforts to segregate children into their own areas. Entertainment includes dancers, magicians, jugglers, and small-scale song-and-dance revues. Service is above average for a ship that operates these kind of inexpensive cruises.

PASSENGER PROFILE   On a typical Caribbean cruise, passengers are roughly half European (many of them younger, sometimes with children) and half North American (many of them older and a bit more conservative than the Europeans).

SEA CLOUD CRUISES

32-40 North Dean Street, Englewood, NJ 07631. © 888/732-2568 or 201/227-9404. Fax 206/227-9424. www.seacloud.com.

THE LINE IN A NUTSHELL   These sailing ships offer a deliciously exotic experience that will stay in the minds of small-ship lovers forever. *Sea Cloud I*, built in 1931, and *Sea Cloud II*, a modern replica of her older sister, attract a mixed European and American crowd that keeps things interesting.

THE EXPERIENCE   If grand living like the super-rich is what you want in your Caribbean jaunt, then *Sea Cloud I* and *II* are definitely worth considering. The 69-passenger *Sea Cloud I* was built as *Hussar* in 1931 by Wall Street tycoon Edward F. Hutton for his heiress wife Majorie Merriweather Post. No expense was spared in designing the four-masted sailing ship and her owners' cabins, which have been restored to their original grandeur, dripping with marble, gold detailing, and mahogany. Some of Mrs. Post's antique furniture remains. Though not a certified classic, *Sea Cloud II* is larger and includes an elegant lounge designed with rich mahogany woodwork, ornate ceiling moldings, leather club couches, and overstuffed bucket chairs.

Being small sailing ships, organized activities are few; it's the ships themselves that entertain. Plus, the ships are in port on all but one day of the cruise, visiting many less touristy islands like Les Saintes, Dominica, Bequia, Mayreau, Tobago, and St. Barts. There's a sailing class on every cruise, and sometimes a guest lecturer sails on board. Evenings, there's piano music and mingling over cocktails. Formal dinners are served on elegant candle-lit tables set with white linen, china and silver.

PASSENGER PROFILE   German-based Sea Cloud Cruises caters to a well-traveled clientele (mostly couples, though there are some singles and groups of friends) looking for a five-star sailing adventure. A typical Caribbean cruise draws about 30% to 40% American passengers, 20% German, 20% British, and the rest other Europeans.

Things to Know Before You Go

You've bought your ticket and you're getting ready to cruise. Here's the low-down on some details you need to think about before you go.

1 Passports & Visas

Good news in the convenience category: **Visas** are generally not required for American, Canadian, and European citizens visiting the Caribbean islands or ports in Mexico, though depending on the itinerary, you may be asked to fill out a tourist card or other form in the airplane, at the airport, or in the cruise terminal, especially if you're flying to a non-U.S. port to start your cruise. **Passports** aren't necessarily required by most Caribbean islands if your cruise departs from a U.S. port. Today's heightened security situation being what it is, however, we suggest that you carry your passport anyway, plus another photo ID. It speeds your way through Customs and Immigration and you never know when entry requirements can change. If you don't have a passport, you may also show proof of U.S. citizenship (such as a certified copy of your birth certificate, a Certificate of Naturalization, a Certificate of Citizenship, or a Report of Birth Abroad of a U.S. Citizen), plus a photo ID such as a driver's license. *Note that a driver's license is not acceptable as a sole form of identification; you'll need one of the documents listed above.* Your travel agent or a representative of your cruise line can help you determine if you need a passport for the islands you'll be visiting on your itinerary, and the documents your cruise line sends with your tickets will also provide information on what forms of ID you'll need to board the ship (most now require two forms). If your cruise departs from a non-U.S. port, you'll generally need a passport to fly to that country.

If you don't currently have a passport, the **State Department website** (www.travel.state.gov/passport_services.html) provides information on obtaining one. You can reach them via telephone at (℃ 202/647-4000. If you're leaving within a few weeks and need **expedited passport service,** here are the basics:

- **If this is your first passport,** your fastest option is to apply in person at 1 of the 14 passport centers located in major cities around the country, most of which operate by appointment only and are specifically for people traveling imminently (generally within 2 weeks). These centers are listed at www.travel.state.gov/agencies_list.html. You'll need to bring a completed passport application, ID, proof of citizenship (see list above), and two passport-size photos. To download an application, click on http://travel.state.gov/download_applications.html. You can also order an application over the phone at (℃ **900/225-5674** (35¢ per min. for automated information) or (℃ **888/362-8668** ($4.95 flat fee).
- **If you don't live near a passport center,** you can apply for expedited service at a local passport acceptance facility, located in post offices, courthouses,

> ## ⌒Tips Vaccinations Required?
>
> The Caribbean islands do not generally require inoculations against trop-
> ical diseases, although you might want to check out the **Centers for Dis-
> ease Control (CDC)** Caribbean travelers Web page (www.cdc.gov/travel/
> caribean.htm) to see what it suggests. In early 2002, for instance, the CDC
> advised travelers visiting rural areas of Trinidad and Tobago to be inocu-
> lated for yellow fever.

and so on, then follow up by sending your approved application to a passport center through overnight mail. To search for the facility nearest you,
click on http://visa.his.com.

- **If you need to renew an expired passport,** you can go to 1 of the 14 passport centers or send a renewal form by overnight mail. Click on http://
travel.state.gov/passport_renewal.html for information, downloadable
renewal forms and the address to send your completed forms to.

- **If you're really panicking,** contact a service like Travisa (www.travisa.com),
which is in the business of expediting passport and visa applications. It'll cost
in the neighborhood of $180 to $235 total (depending on how fast you need
your documents), and if it's your first passport you'll still have to go to a passport acceptance facility to show proof of citizenship and ID, but at least you'll
have experienced help in your corner. To be sure the expediting agency that
you contact is reputable, check with the Better Business Bureau
(www.bbb.org) or the American Society of Travel Agents (www.astanet.com).

Further information is available on the State Department website listed
above. You can also inquire at your local passport acceptance facility or call the
National Passport Information Center (© 888/362-8668 or 900/225-5674),
but be aware that the center charges for calls: a flat fee of $4.95 for the 888
number and 35 cents per minute for the 900. Fees for new passports are $60 for
adults and $40 for children. Renewals cost $40, and expedited service costs an
additional $35.

As you would before any trip abroad, make two photocopies of your documents and ID before leaving home. Take one set with you as a backup (keeping
it in a different piece of luggage from your originals) and keep one at home.

Each particular port of embarkation has its own process for handling your
papers. You may be asked to turn over your passport or proof of citizenship to
ship officials at the start of the cruise so that they can facilitate clearance procedures throughout the cruise. Your documents will then be returned to you at the
end of the trip.

All non-U.S. and non-Canadian citizens must have valid passports, alien-reg-
istration cards, and the requisite visas when boarding any cruise ship or aircraft
departing from and/or returning to American soil. Noncitizens also need to
present an ongoing or return ticket for an airline or cruise ship as proof that you
intend to remain on local shores only for a brief stay.

2 Money Matters

Know how they say cruises are all-inclusive vacations? They're lying. True, the
bulk of your vacation expenses are covered in your fare, but there are plenty of
extras that can really add up, including shore excursions, spa treatments, and

booze and soda. In this section, we'll go over the way monetary transactions are handled on board and in port.

ONBOARD CHARGE CARDS

Cruise ships operate on a cashless basis. Basically, this means you have a running tab and just have to sign for what you buy on board during your cruise and pay up at the end, usually with your credit card. Very, very convenient, yes—and also very, very easy to spend more than you would if you were doling out wads of cash each time. Shortly before or after embarkation, a purser or check-in clerk in the terminal or on board will issue you an **onboard charge card,** which on many ships these days also serves as your room key and as your ship ID, which you swipe through a scanner whenever you leave the ship and whenever you get back on after spending the day in port. On the last day of your cruise, an item-ized account of everything you've charged throughout the cruise will be slipped beneath your cabin door. If you agree with the charges, they'll be automatically billed to your credit-card account. If you'd rather pay in cash or if you dispute any charges, then you need to stop by the office of the ship's cashier or purser (where there's usually a long line, of course).

BRINGING CASH ASHORE

The cashless system works just fine on board, but remember: **You'll need cash in port.** Many people get so used to not carrying their wallets aboard the ship that they get off in port and find themselves without any money in their pock-ets. It's annoying to have to get back aboard to retrieve your cash, but can be a real pain in the butt if your ship is docked offshore and ferrying passengers back and forth by tender. You can put any shore excursions you sign up for on your room tab, and credit cards are accepted at most port shops (as are traveler's checks), but we do recommend having some real cash on hand, ideally in small denominations, to cover the cost of taxi rides, tips for tour leaders, or purchases from craft markets and street vendors.

For the most part, don't worry about exchanging money to **local currency,** since the good ole U.S. dollar is widely accepted in the Caribbean (at least in the tourist-savvy ports of call you're likely to visit) and is the legal currency of the U.S. Virgin Islands, the British Virgin Islands (oddly enough), and Puerto Rico. Even on more offbeat islands like Guadeloupe and Les Saintes, where they might prefer French francs, we've never had our U.S. dough turned away.

If you're running low on cash, there are **ATMs** in nearly every cruise port cov-ered in this guide, in some cruise terminals, and on board many of the mega-ships. Expect a hefty fee for using ATMs on board ship (like $5 in addition to what your bank charges you). If you're using a machine in a Caribbean port, remember that you'll probably get local currency rather than U.S. dollars, so don't withdraw more than you'll need. On American cruise lines, ATMs dis-pense dollars.

Many cruise lines, like Carnival and Royal Caribbean, will cash traveler's checks at the purser's desk. They will also sometimes cash personal checks of up to about $200 if issued in the U.S.; with an American Express card, you can typ-ically cash a check for up to $250. Currency information for specific islands is included in chapter 5, "The Ports of Call."

Gratuities for the crew are not normally included in the cruise rates, so you should reserve some cash so you can be generous at the end of your cruise. See "Tipping, Customs & Other End-of-Cruise Concerns" later in this chapter for guidelines.

3 Keeping in Touch While at Sea

Some people take a cruise because they're looking to get away from it all. If that's your intention, you have two choices: Take an adventure cruise or impose some self-restraint. That's because these days, it's almost as easy to communicate with the folks back home from a ship as it is to keep in touch from your home or office—though it's not cheap.

PHONING HOME

Aside from the adventure lines, almost all ships today have **direct-dial telephones** in their cabins. From most, you can call anywhere in the world via satellite, but it'll cost you between $4 and $15 a minute, with $8 or $9 being about average. It's cheaper by far to call home from a public telephone in port; we've listed where to find them close to the docks in the "Coming Ashore" sections of port reviews in chapter 5.

In addition to your cabin phone, each ship has a central phone number, fax number, and e-mail address, which you'll sometimes find in the cruise line's brochure and usually in the documents that you'll receive with your tickets. Distribute these to family members or friends in case there's an emergency at home, but advise them to contact you *only* in an emergency. It can't hurt to leave behind the number of the cruise line's headquarters or reservations department, too. Most ships also have Internet centers (see below), but you'll rack up a good-size bill if you log on often to check your messages.

INTERNET & E-MAIL AT SEA

Over the past several years, cruise lines have hustled to add computer rooms and Internet cafes to their ships to satiate Americans' growing desire to stay connected to home and work via e-mail, even while on vacation. At press time, most of the mainstream and luxury cruise lines offered computer access. The centers offer e-mail capabilities and Internet access, plus "Net cams" so that users can send vacation pictures of themselves to friends as digital postcards. State-of-the-art flat-screen monitors are popular. Many computer centers are open 24 hours.

Tips Seasickness Prevention & Maintenance

Fact of life: Water moves funny. Even longtime sailors sometimes suffer from seasickness in rough water. Over-the-counter remedies such as Dramamine and Bonine have proven effective in keeping the greens away, as have the TransDerm Scopolamine patch (placed behind the ear and available by prescription), seasickness bands (elastic wristbands that work through acupressure and are available in most pharmacies), and even good old-fashioned ginger.

If you're particularly worried, you should probably avoid small ships, which are more susceptible to the motion of the sea. Larger ships usually have stabilizers that help keep them on the straight and narrow, though even the largest ships can get jolted around if the weather gets really rough. If stability is a big issue for you, choose a cabin at midships on a middle deck, since it's the area least affected by the vessel's rocking and rolling in rough seas. Also, you might want to pick an itinerary with a lot of port calls and few or no days at sea—the fewer long stretches at sea, the less likely you'll be bothered by motion sickness.

E-mail services are usually available in one of two ways: either through temporary accounts that you set up once you're aboard ship (with rates averaging roughly $1–$3 per message) or through your home AOL, Earthlink, Hotmail, Yahoo, or other personal account, which you can access through the web. You may be charged a fee for sending each e-mail, even if you use your own account, since e-mails have to be batched out from the ship through a costly satellite hookup. Any way you slice it, though, e-mailing is loads cheaper than the per-minute expense of a phone call from ship to shore. Surfing the Internet will typically cost you about 50¢ to $1 a minute; though some lines (like Disney and Norwegian) offer a kind of all-you-can-eat package, charging a flat fee for unlimited use during the course of your cruise.

KEEPING ON TOP OF THE NEWS

Are you a CNN junkie? You can try to kick the habit during the course of your cruise, but if willpower fails, most ships do have the station as part of their regular TV lineup. Many ships also maintain the tradition of reprinting headline news stories pulled off the wire, printing them up and slipping them under passengers' doors daily.

4 Packing

One of the great things about cruising is that even though you'll be visiting several different countries during a typical weeklong itinerary, you'll only need to unpack once: You check into your cabin on day one, unpack, and settle in. The destinations come to you!

Just what do you need to pack, though? To some extent, that depends on the kind of cruise you're taking. Overall, though, cruise ship life mirrors life on land—and these days, for Americans especially, that mostly means casual. Here are some pointers.

DAYTIME CLOTHES

Across the board, casual daytime wear means shorts, T-shirts, bathing suits, and sundresses. Remember to bring a coverup and sandals if you want to go right from your deck chair to lunch in one of the restaurants or to an activity being held in a public room. When in port, the same dress code works, but be sure to respect local customs and err toward modesty (that is, something more than a skimpy bikini if you're straying from the beach area). You might want to bring a pair of aqua-socks (waterproof shoes) if you plan on doing any snorkeling or watersports in the ports (if you don't have them, many cruise lines will charge you about $5 to rent a pair; charging for aqua-socks is a moneymaker on some shore excursions too, such as to Jamaica's Dunn's River Falls, where they're necessary). Bring some good walking shoes so you can explore the islands as comfortably as possible.

If you plan on hitting the gym, don't forget sneakers and your workout clothes. And it can't hurt to bring along one pair of long casual pants and a long-sleeved sweatshirt (mostly to deal with air-conditioning), as well as a lightweight raincoat in case the weather turns dicey.

EVENING CLOTHES

As America as a whole gets more casual—witness "business casual" law offices and the whole baseball-cap-and-furs-wearing Park Avenue set—the cruise lines are responding by toning down or scrapping their dress codes.

Norwegian Cruise Line has pretty much ditched the concept of **formal nights** completely (though there's an "optional formal" captain's cocktail night when many people do choose to dress up, so you may see sequins and suits next to chinos and polo shirts). Other lines (Disney, for instance) have toned the definition of "formality" down to the point where a sports jacket is considered formal. However, most mainstream and luxury ships still have 2 traditional formal nights during any 7-night itinerary—usually the second night of the cruise for the captain's cocktail party and the second-to-last night of the cruise. Bring what you'd wear to a nice wedding: Men are encouraged to wear dark suits or tuxedos and women cocktail dresses, sequined jackets, gowns, or other fancy attire. If you just hate dressing up, women can get away with a blouse and a skirt or pants. And of course, accessories like jewelry and scarves can dress up an otherwise nondescript outfit. Most lines have tuxedos available for rent and rental information will be included with your tickets.

The other nights are much more casual, and are designated either **semiformal** (or informal) or **casual,** though lately many lines have done away with semiformal nights and just gone with a combination of formal and casual. Semiformal calls for suits or sports jackets for men and stylish dresses or pantsuits for women; casual nights call for chinos or dress pants and collared shirts for men, and dresses, skirts, or pantsuits for women.

In spite of the suggested dress codes, which are usually described in the back of a cruise line's brochure, you'll still find a wide variety of outfits being worn. Invariably, one person's "formal" is quite different from another's. So, like hemlines and everything else these days, almost anything goes. Passengers are asked not to wear baseball caps, shorts, and T-shirts for dinner in the formal dining rooms (though people inevitably do, and are rarely turned away), but pretty much every major line—Carnival, Celebrity, Costa, Holland America, NCL, Princess, and Royal Caribbean—now offers a **casual dining option** every night, where caps and shorts are the norm.

Despite the casual trend, you'll find there's usually a contingent of folks on board who like to get all decked out for dinner—including us. It's part of the fun; after all, how many chances do you get in your daily life to dress like you're in a Fred Astaire/Ginger Rogers movie? Plunk yourself down in a heavily trafficked lounge an hour or 2 before dinner and do some good old-fashioned people-watching. It's a veritable fashion show! If you bring your good jewelry, it's wise to keep it under lock and key when you're not wearing it. Most cabins these days have personal safes operated by a digital code, credit card, or, once in a while, a key lock. If your cabin doesn't have a safe (usually it's the older ships that don't), the ship's purser can hold onto your valuables.

Note that these fashion rules don't apply if you're sailing with ultracasual **small-ship lines** like Windjammer and American Canadian Caribbean, where shorts, T-shirts, and sandals can take you through the day and into the evening meals (although most people tend to dress up a tad more for dinner). Windstar and Star Clippers encourage a "smart casual" look, and have a no-jackets-required rule the entire week, through some men don sport jackets and women put on dresses for dinner. Similarly, passengers aboard Clipper Cruise Line go casual during the day and usually dress up a little a dinnertime.

SUNDRIES

Like hotel rooms, most cabins (especially aboard the newest and the most high-end ships) come with toiletries such as soap, shampoo, conditioner, and lotion, although you might still want to bring your own products—the ones provided often seem watered down. (If you forget to pack a personal effect or two, almost all ships have at least one small shop on board, selling items like razor blades, toothbrushes, sunscreen, film, and other items you may need, though prices can be steep.)

Most cabins also have **hair dryers,** but they tend to be weak, so don't expect miracles—if you have a lot of hair, bring your own. All ships reviewed in this book run on 110 AC current (many have both 110 and 220 outlets), so you won't need an adapter.

No need to pack a beach towel either, as almost all lines supply them on board. Bird watchers will want their binoculars and manuals, golfers their clubs (although they can always be rented at the courses), and snorkelers their gear (which can also be rented, usually through the cruise lines).

Aside from the small ships, most vessels have a **laundry service** on board and some **dry cleaning** too, with generally about a 24-hour turnaround time; there will be a price list in your cabin. Cleaning services tend not to be cheap—$1.50 to have one pair of socks washed and $3 for a T-shirt; dry-cleaning a suit will run about $9—so you might consider using the **self-service laundry rooms** on board some ships (Carnival, Crystal, Princess, and Holland America, among others) if you're planning to pack light and wear the same outfit several times.

If you like reading but don't want to lug three or four hefty novels on board, most ships of all sizes have **libraries** stocked with books and magazines—though of course the selection varies. Most ships also stock paperback bestsellers in their shops.

Lastly, remember to save room in your luggage (or bring an empty duffel bag or heavyweight shopping bag) for things you buy in port or in the ship's shops.

5 Tipping, Customs & Other End-of-Cruise Concerns

We know you don't want to hear about the end of your cruise before you've probably even gone, but it's best to be prepared. Here's a discussion of a few matters you'll have to take care of before heading back to home sweet home.

TIPPING

Most cruise lines pay their service staff low base wages with the understanding that the bulk of their income will come from tips. Each line has clear guidelines for gratuities, which are usually printed in your cruise documents and the daily schedule, and/or announced toward the end of the cruise. Traditionally, cabin stewards will leave little white envelopes (marked for cabin attendants, dining stewards, and waiters, along with suggested tipping percentages and amounts) in a spot where you'll be sure not to miss them. Today, however, more and more lines are automatically adding tips to each passenger's onboard account. Norwegian, Princess, and Carnival (on most ships at least) do it this way, with the amount adjustable if you request it at the purser's desk before the end of the cruise. Some lines, like Crystal, Star Clippers, and Windjammer, give you the option of paying cash directly to staff or adding gratuities on to your account. Some small lines pool the tips and divide them equitably among all crew. Ultra-luxury lines Silversea, Seabourn, and Radisson include tips in the cruise rates. Holland America and Windstar promote their "tipping not required" policies, but tipping really is expected.

Suggested tipping amounts vary slightly with the line and its degree of luxury. As a rule of thumb, however, each passenger should expect to tip about $3.50 per person per day for the cabin steward and the dining room waiter and about $2 for the dining room busboy. This adds up to about $9 per passenger (child or adult) per day—pretty close to what the lines that automatically add gratuities tack on ($10 per passenger, per day on Norwegian and Princess; $9.75 per passenger, per day on Carnival). Wine stewards and bartenders are usually rewarded with a 15% surcharge that's added onto a bill every time you sign it. Some lines suggest you tip the maitre d' about $5 per passenger for the week and slip another couple of bucks to the chief housekeeper, but it's your choice; if you've never even met these people, don't bother. Tipping the captain and officers is a no-no: They're on full salary.

On lines that follow traditional person-to-person gratuity policies, tip your dining steward and busboy during the cruise's final dinner, and leave your cabin steward his or her tip on the final morning, just before you debark. Tip spa personnel immediately after they work on you; 15% is standard. (Note that on Celebrity, Costa, Cunard, Holland America, NCL, and Windstar, Steiner spa personnel automatically add a tip to your account unless you indicate otherwise.)

DISEMBARKING

It's a good idea to begin repacking before dinner on your final night aboard, and be sure to fill out the luggage tags given to you, and attach them securely to each piece. You'll be asked to leave your luggage outside your cabin door before you retire that night (by midnight or so), after which deck hands will pick it up and spirit it away (*read:* toss it into elevators and bins to get it across the gangway to the terminal, so carry bottles of rum and other breakables off the ship yourself). At disembarkation, you'll find your bags waiting for you at the terminal, organized by the colored or numbered tags you attached. If you don't use this system, you'll have to lug your bags off yourself.

Ships normally arrive in port on the final day between 6 and 8am, and need at least 90 minutes to unload baggage and complete dockage formalities. That means no one disembarks much before 9am, and it can sometimes take until 10am before you're allowed to leave the ship, usually via assigned debarkation numbers. Have breakfast. Have coffee. Have patience.

In the cruise ship terminal, claim your luggage and then pass through customs before exiting. This normally entails handing the officer your filled-out declaration form as you breeze past, without even coming to a full stop. There are generally porters available in the terminals (to whom it's traditional to pay at least $1 per bag they carry), but you might have to haul your luggage through customs before you can get to them.

U.S. CUSTOMS

The U.S. government allows U.S. citizens $1,200 worth of duty-free imports every 30 days from the U.S. Virgin Islands; those who exceed their exemption are taxed at a 5% rate, rather than the normal 10%. The limit is $400 for the French islands of Guadeloupe and Martinique and $600 if you return directly from the following islands and countries: Antigua and Barbuda, Aruba, the Bahamas, Barbados, Belize, Costa Rica, Dominica, the Dominican Republic, Grenada, Guatemala, Haiti, Honduras, Jamaica, Montserrat, the Netherland Antilles (Curaçao, Bonaire, St. Martin, Saba, and St. Eustatius), Panama, St. Kitts and Nevis, St. Lucia, St. Vincent and the Grenadines, Trinidad and

Tobago, and the British Virgin Islands. If, for instance, your cruise stops in the U.S. Virgin Islands and the Bahamas, your total limit is $1,200 and no more than $600 of that amount can be from the Bahamas. If you visit only Puerto Rico, you don't have to go through customs at all, since it's an American commonwealth. Note that you must declare on your Customs form all gifts received during your stay abroad.

U.S. citizens or returning residents at least 21 years of age who are traveling directly or indirectly from the U.S. Virgin Islands are allowed to bring in 1,000 cigarettes free of duty. Duty-free limitations on articles from other countries are generally 1 liter of alcohol, 200 cigarettes (one carton), and 100 cigars (not Cuban). **Unsolicited gifts** can be mailed to friends and relatives on the U.S. mainland at the rate of $200 per day from the U.S. Virgin Islands or $100 per day from other islands. Unsolicited gifts of any value can be mailed from Puerto Rico. Most meat or meat products, fruit, plants, vegetables, or plant-derived products will be seized by U.S. Customs agents unless they're accompanied by an import license from a U.S. government agency.

Joint Customs declarations are possible for members of a family traveling together. For instance, if you're a husband and wife with two children, your exemptions in the U.S. Virgin Islands become duty-free up to $4,800.

Keep receipts for all purchases you make abroad. Sometimes merchants suggest making up a false receipt to undervalue your purchase, but be aware that you could be involved in a "sting" operation—the merchant might be an informer to U.S. Customs. It's unlikely, but possible.

We've found clearing customs in Florida to be a painless and speedy process, with Customs officials rarely asking for anything more than your filled-out Customs declaration form as they nod you through the door. Of course, better safe than sorry. It's prudent to carry proof that you purchased expensive cameras or jewelry on the U.S. mainland, before your trip. If you purchased such an item during an earlier trip abroad, you should carry proof that you have previously paid Customs duty on the item. Again, it's unlikely you'll need it, but it is possible.

To be on the safe side, if you use any medication containing controlled substances or requiring injection, carry an original prescription or note from your doctor.

For more specifics, visit the **U.S. Customs Service website** at www.customs. ustreas.gov. Citizens of the U.K. should visit the **U.K. Customs and Excise website** at www.hmce.gov.uk.

4

The Ports of Embarkation

Hands down, the busiest of the ports of embarkation is **Miami,** followed by Port Everglades in **Fort Lauderdale;** Port Canaveral at **Cape Canaveral,** directly east of Orlando; and **Tampa,** on Florida's west coast. **San Juan, Puerto Rico,** is both a major port of embarkation in the eastern Caribbean and a major port of call (see p. 232 for a review), while **New Orleans** is popular for ships sailing to Mexico and the western Caribbean. Ditto for the up-and-coming port at **Galveston, Texas,** one of the many alternative ports the cruise lines are using in their continual search to put their ships near U.S. population centers and to offer passengers other flight options—after all, there are only so many people that the lines can fly to and from Florida.

All of these ports are tourist destinations themselves, so most cruise lines now offer special deals to extend their passengers' vacation stays at the ports, either before or after their cruise. These packages, for 2, 3, or 4 days, often offer hotel and car-rental discounts, as well as sightseeing packages. Have your travel agent or cruise specialist check for the best deals.

In this chapter, we'll describe each port of embarkation, tell you how to get to it, and suggest things to see and do there, whether it's sightseeing, shopping, or hitting the beach. We'll also recommend a sampling of restaurants and places to stay. Note that **hotel prices** are winter rates for standard double rooms unless stated otherwise. Prices in the off-season will be lower. In addition to the hotels listed in this chapter, the following **motel chains** also have branches in all the mainland port cities unless noted otherwise:

- **Best Western,** © 800/780-7234; www.bestwestern.com
- **Clarion,** © 800/252-7466; www.clarioninn.com (no Galveston branch; Houston only)
- **Comfort Inn,** © 800/228-5150; www.comfortinn.com (no New Orleans branch)
- **Comfort Suites,** © 800/517-4000; www.comfortsuites.com (no Galveston branch; Houston only)
- **Courtyard by Marriott,** © 800/321-2211; www.courtyard.com (no Galveston branch; Houston only)
- **Days Inn,** © 800/544-8313; www.daysinn.com
- **Doubletree,** © 800/222-8733; www.doubletree.com
- **Econo Lodge,** © 800/553-2666; www.econolodge.com
- **Holiday Inn,** © 800/465-4329; www.holiday-inn.com
- **Howard Johnson,** © 800/406-1411; www.hojo.com (no Galveston branch; Houston only)
- **Motel 6,** © 800/466-8356; www.motel6.com (no Miami branch)
- **Quality Inn,** © 800/228-5151; www.qualityinn.com (no Galveston branch; Houston only)

All the ports in this chapter can be reached by train as well as by air and car. **Amtrak** (© **800/872-7245;**

www.amtrak.com) has a New York–Miami route that stops at Miami, Fort Lauderdale, and Orlando (for Cape Canaveral); a New York–Tampa route that stops at Orlando and Tampa; a Los Angeles–Orlando route that stops at Orlando, New Orleans, and Houston (for Galveston); and a route from Chicago to New Orleans.

For more information about each destination, check *Frommer's Florida, Frommer's South Florida, Frommer's New Orleans, Frommer's Texas* and *Frommer's Puerto Rico.*

1 Miami

It's the most Latin city in the U.S., with a hot-hot-hot club scene, sparkling beaches, crystal clear waters, and more palm fronds, glittering hotels, and red sports cars than you can shake a stick at, and on top of all that, Miami is also the undisputed cruise capital of the world. More cruise ships, especially super-size ones, berth here than anywhere else on earth, and more than three million cruise passengers pass through yearly. Not surprisingly, the city's facilities are extensive and state-of-the-art, and Miami International Airport is only 8 miles (13km) away, about a 15-minute drive.

Industry giants Carnival and Royal Caribbean both have long-term agreements with the port, and to accommodate the influx of new ships over the past few years, Miami has spent $76 million on major improvements to Terminals 3, 4, and 5, and added a 750-space parking facility.

GETTING TO MIAMI & THE PORT

The **Port of Miami** is at 1015 N. America Way, in central Miami. It's on Dodge Island, reached via a five-lane bridge from the downtown district. For information, call (C) **305/371-PORT** or head online to **www.metro-dade.com/portofmiami**.

BY PLANE **Miami International Airport** is about 8 miles (13km) west of downtown Miami and the port. If you've arranged air transportation and/or transfers through the cruise line, a cruise line rep will direct you to shuttle buses to the port. Taxis are also available; the fare is about $18. Some leading taxi companies include **Central Taxicab Service** ((C) **305/532-5555**), **Diamond Cab Company** ((C) **305/545-5555**), and **Metro Taxicab Company** ((C) **305/888-8888**).

You can also take a **no. 7 Metrobus** ((C) **305/770-3131**) for $1.25 from the airport to downtown Miami (the stop is at Miami Dade Community College), which will land you across the street from the bridge that leads to the port—not a good option if you're carrying luggage. **SuperShuttle** ((C) **305/871-2000**) charges about $9 to $18 per person, with two pieces of luggage ($2–$5 each additional piece), for a ride within Dade County, which includes the Port of Miami. Their vans operate 24 hours a day.

BY CAR The Florida Turnpike (a toll road) and Interstate 95 are the main arteries for those arriving from the north. Coming in from the northwest, take Interstate 75 or U.S. 27 to reach the center of Miami. Parking lots right at street level face the cruise terminals. Parking runs $8 per day. Porters can carry your luggage to the terminals.

EXPLORING MIAMI

A sizzling, multicultural mecca, Miami offers the best in cutting-edge restaurants, unusual attractions, entertainment, shopping, beaches, and the whole range of hotels, from luxury to boutique, kitschy to charming. South Beach is a people-watching paradise.

VISITOR INFORMATION   Contact the **Greater Miami Convention and Visitors Bureau,** 701 Brickell Ave., Suite 2700, Miami, FL 33131 (© **888/76-MIAMI** for brochures and 305/539-3034 for questions), or visit their website at www.tropicoolmiami.com.

GETTING AROUND   See "Getting to Miami & the Port," above, for taxi information. The meter starts at $1.50, and ticks up another $2 each mile and 30¢ for each additional minute, with standard flat-rate charges for frequently traveled routes. **Metromover** (© **305/770-3131**), a 4½-mile (7km) elevated line, circles downtown, stopping near important attractions and shopping and business districts. It runs daily from about 5am to midnight, and is fun if you've got time to kill. The fare is 25¢.

HITTING THE BEACH

A 300-foot (91m) wide sand beach runs for about 10 miles (16km) from the south of Miami Beach to Haulover Beach Park in the north. (For those of you who like to get an all-around tan, Haulover is a known nude beach.) Although most of this stretch is lined with a solid wall of hotels, beach access is plentiful, and you are free to frolic along the entire strip. A wooden boardwalk runs along the hotel side from 21st to 46th streets—about 1½ miles (2.5km).

There are lots of **public beaches** here, wide and well maintained, with life-guards, toilet facilities, concession stands, and metered parking (bring lots of quarters). Lifeguard-protected public beaches include 21st Street, at the begin-ning of the boardwalk; 35th Street, popular with an older crowd; 46th Street, next to the Fontainebleau Hilton; 53rd Street, a narrower, more sedate beach; 64th Street, one of the quietest strips around; and 72nd Street, a local old-timers' spot. On the southern tip of the beach is family favorite South Pointe Park, where you can watch the cruise ships. Lummus Park, in the center of the Art Deco district, is the best place for people-watching and model-spotting. The beach between 11th and 13th streets is popular with the gay crowd. The beach from 1st to 15th streets is popular with seniors.

In Key Biscayne, **Crandon Park,** 4000 Crandon Blvd. (© **305/361-5421**), is one of metropolitan Miami's finest white-sand beaches, stretching for some 3½ miles (5.5km). There are lifeguards, and you can rent a cabana with a shower and chairs for $20 per day. Saturday and Sunday the beach can be especially crowded. Parking nearby is $4 per car and $6 for campers, minivans, SUVs, and buses.

ATTRACTIONS

Miami's best attraction is a part of the city itself. Located at the southern end of Miami Beach below 20th Street, South Beach's **Art Deco district** is filled with outrageous and fanciful 1920s and 1930s architecture that shouldn't be missed (oh, and the characters strolling about in teeny-tiny beachwear are pretty inter-esting too). This treasure-trove, called "the Beach" or "SoBe," features more than 900 pastel, Pez-colored buildings in the Art Deco, Streamline Moderne, and Spanish Mediterranean Revival styles. The district stretches from 6th to 23rd streets, and from the Atlantic Ocean to Lennox Court. Ocean Drive boasts many of the premier Art Deco hotels.

Also in South Beach is the **Bass Museum of Art,** 2121 Park Ave. (© **305/ 673-7533;** www.bassmuseum.org), with a permanent collection of Old Masters,

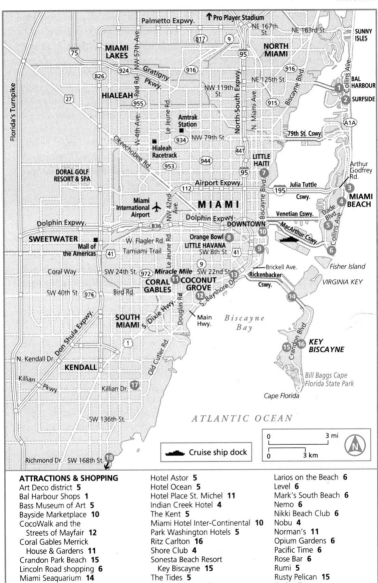

ATTRACTIONS & SHOPPING
Art Deco district **5**
Bal Harbour Shops **1**
Bass Museum of Art **5**
Bayside Marketplace **10**
CocoWalk and the
    Streets of Mayfair **12**
Coral Gables Merrick
    House & Gardens **11**
Crandon Park Beach **15**
Lincoln Road shopping **6**
Miami Seaquarium **14**
Miracle Mile **11**
Monkey Jungle **18**
Parrot Jungle and Gardens **17**
Vizcaya Museum & Gardens **13**

ACCOMMODATIONS
The Beach House Bal Harbour **2**
Biltmore Hotel **11**
The Delano **5**
The Eden Roc Renaissance Resort **3**
Fontainebleau Hilton **3**
The Hotel **6**

Hotel Astor **5**
Hotel Ocean **5**
Hotel Place St. Michel **11**
Indian Creek Hotel **4**
The Kent **5**
Miami Hotel Inter-Continental **10**
Park Washington Hotels **5**
Ritz Carlton **16**
Shore Club **4**
Sonesta Beach Resort
    Key Biscayne **15**
The Tides **5**
The Townhouse **5**
Wyndham Grand Bay Hotel **12**

DINING & NIGHTLIFE
Café Nostalgia **8**
Café Tu Tu Tango **12**
Casa Panza Restaurant **8**
ClubSpace **10**
crobar **6**
The Forge **3**
Joe's Stone Crab **6**
Joia **6**

Larios on the Beach **6**
Level **6**
Mark's South Beach **6**
Nemo **6**
Nikki Beach Club **6**
Nobu **4**
Norman's **11**
Opium Gardens **6**
Pacific Time **6**
Rose Bar **6**
Rumi **5**
Rusty Pelican **15**
Soyka **7**
Spris **6**
Sushi Samba **5**
Tantra **6**
Tobacco Road **9**
Tower Bar **4**
Van Dyke Cafe **6**
Versailles **8**

along with textiles, period furnishings, objets d'art, ecclesiastical artifacts, and sculpture. Rotating exhibits include pop art, fashion, and photography. The museum is open every day except Monday, from 10am to 5pm. Admission is $6 for adults, $4 seniors and students.

The adjoining **Coral Gables** and **Coconut Grove** neighborhoods are fun to visit for their architecture and ambience. In Coral Gables, the Old World meets the new as curving boulevards, sidewalks, plazas, fountains, and arched entrances evoke Seville. Today the area is an epicurean's Eden, boasting some of Miami's most renowned eateries as well as the University of Miami and the half-mile (1km) long **Miracle Mile,** a 5-block retail mecca (see "Shopping," below). You can even visit the boyhood home of George Merrick, the man who originally developed Coral Gables. The **Coral Gables Merrick House & Gardens,** 907 Coral Way (© **305/460-5361**), has been restored to its 1920s look and is filled with Merrick memorabilia. The house and garden are open for tours on Wednesday and Sunday between 1 and 4pm.

Coconut Grove, South Florida's oldest settlement, remains a village surrounded by the urban sprawl of Miami. It dates back to the early 1800s, when Bahamian seamen first sought to salvage treasure from the wrecked vessels stranded along the Great Florida Reef. Mostly people come here to shop, drink, dine, or simply walk around and explore. But don't miss the **Vizcaya Museum & Gardens,** 3251 S. Miami Ave. (© **305/250-9133;** www.vizcayamuseum. com), a spectacular 70-room Italian Renaissance–style villa. It is open every day except Christmas. The $10 admission fee includes a free guided tour.

THE ANIMAL PARKS   Just minutes from the Port of Miami in Key Biscayne, the **Miami Seaquarium,** 4400 Rickenbacker Causeway (© **305/361-5705;** http://miamiseaquarium.com), is a delight. Performing dolphins such as Flipper, TV's greatest sea mammal, perform along with "Lolita the Killer Whale." You can also see endangered manatees, sea lions, tropical-theme aquariums, and the gruesome shark feeding. It's open daily from 9:30am to 6pm. Admission is $22.95 for adults and $17.95 for children 3 to 9 (free for children under 3).

At **Monkey Jungle,** 14805 SW 216th St., Miami (© **305/235-1611;** www. monkeyjungle.com), the trick is that the visitors are caged and nearly 500 monkeys frolic in freedom and make fun of them. The most talented of these free-roaming primates perform shows daily for the amusement of their guests. The site also contains one of the richest fossil deposits in South Florida, with some 5,000 specimens. It's open daily from 9:30am to 5pm. Admission is $14.95 for adults, $9.95 for children 4 to 12, and free for children under 4.

In South Miami, **Parrot Jungle and Gardens,** 11000 SW 57th Ave. (© **305/669-7030;** www.parrotjungle.com), is actually a botanical garden, wildlife habitat, and bird sanctuary all rolled into one. Children can enjoy a petting zoo and a playground. It's open daily from 9:30am to 6pm. Admission is $15.95 for adults, $11.95 for children 3 to 10, and free for children under 3. *Note:* In late 2003, Parrot Jungle is scheduled to move to Watson Island, on MacArthur Causeway on I-395 between Miami and Miami Beach. Call before you go to double-check the park's location.

ORGANIZED TOURS

BY BOAT   From September through May, **Heritage Schooner Cruises** (© **305/442-9697;** www.heritageschooner.com) offers daily 2-hour jaunts at

1:30, 4, and 6:30pm aboard the 85-foot (26m) schooner *Heritage of Miami II*, departing from the Bayside Marketplace. Tickets cost $15 for adults and $10 for children under 12. On Friday, Saturday, and Sunday evenings, there are 1-hour tours at 8, 9, 10, and 11pm to see the lights of the city.

ON FOOT   An **Art Deco District Walking Tour,** sponsored by the Miami Design Preservation League (© **305/672-2014;** www.mdpl.org), leaves every Thursday at 6:30pm and Saturday at 10:30am from the Art Deco Welcome Center at 1001 Ocean Dr., South Beach. The 90-minute tour costs $15.

SHOPPING

Most cruise ship passengers shop right near the Port of Miami at **Bayside Marketplace,** 401 Biscayne Blvd. (© **305/577-3344;** www.baysidemarketplace. com), a mall with 150 specialty shops, street performers, live music, and some 20 eateries, including a Hard Rock Cafe and others serving everything from Nicaraguan to Italian food. Many have outdoor seating right along the bay for picturesque views of the yachts harbored there. It can be reached via regular shuttle service from the port or by walking over the Port Bridge.

A free shuttle from the Hotel Inter-Continental in downtown Miami takes you to the **Bal Harbour Shops** at 9700 Collins Ave. (© **305/866-0311;** www. balharbourshops.com). They're Miami's version of Rodeo Drive, housing big-name stores from Chanel and Prada to Lacoste and Neiman-Marcus (and Florida's largest Saks Fifth Ave.).

In South Beach, **Lincoln Road,** an 8-block pedestrian mall, runs between Washington Avenue and Alton Road, near the northern tier of the Art Deco district. It's filled with popular shops such as Gap and Banana Republic, interior-design stores, art galleries, and even vintage-clothing outlets, as well as coffeehouses, restaurants, and cafes. Despite the recent influx of commercial anchor stores, Lincoln Road still manages to maintain its funky, arty flair, attracting an eclectic, colorful crowd.

Coconut Grove, centered on Main Highway and Grand Avenue, is the heart of the city's boutique district and features two open-air shopping and entertainment complexes, **CocoWalk** (www.cocowalk.com) and the **Streets of Mayfair.**

In Coral Gables, **Miracle Mile,** actually a half-mile (1km) stretch of SW 22nd Street between Douglas and Le Jeune roads (aka 37th and 42nd aves.), features more than 150 shops.

For a change of pace from the fast-paced glitz of South Beach or the serene luxury of Coral Gables, head for **Little Havana,** where pre-Castro Cubans commingle with young artists who have begun to set up performance spaces in the area. It's located just west of downtown Miami on SW Eighth Street. In addition to authentic Cuban cuisine, the cafe Cubano culture is alive and well.

ACCOMMODATIONS

Thanks to the network of highways, you can stay virtually anywhere in Greater Miami and still be within 10 to 20 minutes of your ship.

DOWNTOWN   Set across the bay from the cruise ship piers, the Miami **Hotel Inter-Continental,** 100 Chopin Plaza (© **800/327-3005** or 305/577-1000; http://miami.interconti.com), is a bold triangular tower soaring 34 stories. Rates: $255 to $335.

SOUTH BEACH   The Art Deco, comfy-chic **Hotel Astor,** 956 Washington Ave. (© **800/270-4981** or 305/531-8081; www.hotelastor.com), originally built in 1936, reopened after a massive renovation in 1995. Rates: $150 to $800. The Astor is only 2 blocks from the beach, but if that's still too far for you, try the upscale **Hotel Ocean,** 1230–1238 Ocean Dr. (© **800/783-1725** or 305/672-2579; www.hotelocean.com). Rates: $200 to $280. If you're on a budget but want a cozy Deco feel, try the **Park Washington Hotels**—Park Washington, Belaire, Taft, and Kenmore—a group of small hotels run by Best Western, right next door to the Astor at 1020–1050 Washington Ave. (© **305/532-1930;** www.parkwashingtonresort.com). Rates: $135 and up. The **Delano,** 1685 Collins Ave. (© **800/555-5001** or 305/672-2000), is a sleek, post-modern, and self-consciously hip celebrity hot spot, but it's worth at least a peak. Rates: $325 to $810. **The Hotel,** 801 Collins Ave., at the corner of Collins and 8th Street (© **305/531-5796;** www.thehotelofsouthbeach.com), formerly known as The Tiffany Hotel until the folks behind the little blue box threatened to sue, is a Deco gem, as well as being the most fashionable hotel on South Beach, thanks to the whimsical interiors designed by haute couturier Todd Oldham. Rates: $195 to $345. The **Townhouse,** 150 20th St. (© **305/534-3800** or 877/534-3800; www.townhousehotel.com), is a funky newcomer with exercise bikes in the hallways and CD players and dataports in all rooms. Rates: $195 to $225. **The Kent,** 1131 Collins Ave. (© **800/688-7678** or 305/604-5068; www.islandoutpost.com/Kent) is part of Chris Blackwell's Island Outpost chain, and attracts a less upwardly mobile yet no less chic crowd of young, hip travelers. Rates: $160 to $295 suite. The trendy **Shore Club,** 1901 Collins Ave. (© **877/640-9500** or 305/695-3222; www.shoreclub.com), is where you'll find Miami's very first Nobu, the Japanese restaurant that took Manhattan by storm some years ago. Rates: $475 to $775.

MIAMI BEACH   At the **Indian Creek Hotel,** 2727 Indian Creek Dr., at 28th Street (© **800/491-2772** or 305/531-2727; www.indiancreekhotelmb.com), each room is an homage to the 1930s Art Deco age. Rates: $140 to $240. The **Eden Roc Renaissance Resort,** 4525 Collins Ave. (© **800/327-8337** or 305/531-0000; www.edenrocresort.com), and the **Fontainebleau Hilton,** next door at 4441 Collins Ave. (© **800/548-8886** or 305/538-2000; www.fontainebleau.hilton.com), are both popular, updated 1950s resorts evoking the bygone Rat Pack era, with spas, health clubs, outdoor swimming pools, and beach access. Rates: $300 to $360 and $290 to $460, respectively. **The Beach House Bal Harbour,** 9449 Collins Ave., in Surfside (© **305/535-8600** or 877/782-3557; www.rubellhotels.com/beach.html), brings a taste of Nantucket to Miami with soothing hues, comfortable furniture, oceanfront views, and a Ralph Lauren–decorated interior. Rates: $215 to $315.

COCONUT GROVE   Near Miami's City Hall and the Coconut Grove Marina, the **Wyndham Grand Bay Hotel,** 2669 S. Bayshore Dr. (© **800/327-2788** or 305/858-9600; www.wyndham.com/CoconutGrove), overlooks Biscayne Bay. Rates: $360 to $400 suite.

CORAL GABLES   The famous **Biltmore Hotel,** 1200 Anastasia Ave. (© **800/448-8355** or 305/445-1926; www.biltmorehotel.com), was restored a few years ago, but despite renovations, it exudes an old-world, stately glamour and is rumored to be haunted by ghosts of travel days past. Rates: $340 to $510. There's also the **Hotel Place St. Michel,** 162 Alcazar Ave. (© **800/848-HOTEL** or 305/444-1666; www.hotelplacestmichel.com), a three-story establishment reminiscent of an inn in provincial France. Rates: $165.

KEY BISCAYNE The **Sonesta Beach Resort Key Biscayne,** 350 Ocean Dr. (© **800/SONESTA** or 305/361-2021; www.sonesta.com/keybiscayne), offers relative isolation from the rest of congested Miami. Rates: $295 to $465. A new **Ritz-Carlton,** 455 Grand Bay Dr. (© **800/241-3333** or 305/365-4500; www. ritzcarlton.com), has opened on Key Biscayne, offering a to-die-for spa, not to mention oceanviews. Rates: $270 to $850 suite.

DINING

DOWNTOWN Up Biscayne Boulevard near the burgeoning Miami Design District is **Soyka,** 5556 NE Fourth Court (© **305/759-3117**), the hip down-town sibling of South Beach's News and Van Dyke cafes. Dinner main courses: $11 to $24.

SOUTH BEACH Join the celebs and models for pan-Asian cuisine at **Nemo,** 100 Collins Ave. (© **305/532-4550**). Dinner main courses: $22 to $36. Take time to stroll down the pedestrian mall on Lincoln Road, which offers art gal-leries, specialty shops, and several excellent outdoor cafes such as **Spris,** 731 Lin-coln Rd. (© **305/673-2020**), and the **Van Dyke Cafe,** 846 Lincoln Rd. (© **305/534-3600**). The standout culinary trendsetter on Lincoln Road, how-ever, is **Pacific Time,** 915 Lincoln Rd. (© **305/534-5979**), where you can enjoy a taste of the Pacific Rim with a deliciously modern South Beach twist. Dinner main courses: $20 to $32. The newest haute eateries-cum-lounges imported from New York (or at least inspired by its hot spots) include **Rumi,** 330 Lincoln Rd. (© **305/672-4353**), inspired by Lotus, Manhattan's restaurant of the moment, and oozing with lots of mirrors, mushy couches, and even a queen-size Murphy bed (dinner main courses $18–$30); **Sushi Samba,** 600 Lincoln Rd. (© **305/673-5337**), which features a delectable fusion of South American and Japanese cuisine (dinner main courses $14–$39; sushi priced by the piece); and **Nobu,** 1901 Collins Ave. (© **305/695-3232**), the now nearly legendary name in Nouvelle Japanese cuisine. Dinner main courses: $10 to $70.

At the legendary **Joe's Stone Crab,** 11 Washington Ave., between South Point Drive and 1st Avenue (© **305/673-0365**), about a ton of stone-crab claws are served daily during stone-crab season from October to May (the place is closed May 15–Oct 15), and people are kept waiting for up to 2 hours for a table. Crab prices vary depending on the market rate, but start around $20 per order. If the sky's the limit in the budget department, try **Mark's South Beach** in the Hotel Nash, 1120 Collins Ave. (© **305/604-9050**), for fine dishes such as slow-roasted salmon with horseradish. Dinner main courses: $22 to $43. Even if Glo-ria Estefan weren't co-owner of **Larios on the Beach,** 820 Ocean Dr. (© **305/ 532-9577**), the crowds would still flock to this bistro, which serves old-fashioned Cuban dishes such as *masitas de puerco* (fried pork chunks). Dinner main courses: $8 to $24.

COCONUT GROVE If you'd like to people-watch while you eat, head for **Café Tu Tu Tango,** 3015 Grand Ave., Suite 250 (© **305/529-2222**), on the sec-ond floor of CocoWalk. Designed to look like a disheveled artist's loft, it has original paintings (some half-finished) on easels or hanging from the walls. Din-ner main courses: $4 to $10.

CORAL GABLES **Norman's,** 21 Almeria Ave. (© **305/446-6767**), possibly the best restaurant in the entire city of Miami, is run by its namesake, Norman Van Aken, a James Beard award–winning chef and pioneer of New World and Floribbean cuisine. Dinner main courses: $26 to $38.

KEY BISCAYNE The surf and turf is routine at the **Rusty Pelican,** 3201 Rickenbacker Causeway (© **305/361-3818**), but it's worth coming for a drink and to catch the spectacular sunset view. Dinner main courses: $16 to $20.

LITTLE HAVANA One reason to visit Little Havana is to enjoy its excellent Hispanic cuisine. **Casa Panza Restaurant,** 1620 SW Eighth St. (© **305/643-5343**), a taste of old Seville in Little Havana, is a feast for the senses with flamenco dancers, tempting tapas, and a lively atmosphere that reels in crowds nightly. At 11pm, everyone, no matter what their religion, is given a candle to pray to La Virgen del Rocio, one of Seville's most revered saints—it's a party with piety! Dinner main courses: $13 to $14. Another place to check out is **Versailles,** 3555 SW Eighth St. (© **305/444-0240**), a late-night (open till 2am every night, 4am on Sat) palatial, mirrored diner serving all the Cuban mainstays in large and reasonably priced portions. Dinner main courses: $5 to $8.

MIAMI AFTER DARK

Miami nightlife is as varied as its population, and its sizzling nightlife is no stranger to A-list celebrities from Leonardo DiCaprio and Gwyneth Paltrow to Al Pacino, Sylvester Stallone, and Madonna. Look for the klieg lights to direct you to the hot spots of South Beach. While the blocks of Washington Avenue, Collins Avenue, and Ocean Drive are the main nightlife thoroughfares, you're more likely to spot a celebrity in a more off-the-beaten-path eatery such as **Tantra,** a grass-floored, Middle Eastern (aphrodisiac-inspired) eatery and late-night hangout at 1445 Pennsylvania Ave. (© **305/672-4765**); **Joia,** a popular, chic Italian eatery at 150 Ocean Dr. (© **305/674-8871**); or **The Forge,** 432 41st St. (© **305/538-8533**), an ornately decorated rococo-style steakhouse boasting one of the finest wine selections around.

Restaurants and bars are open late—usually until 5am. Also popular are the hotel bars, such as the Delano's **Rose Bar** and The Shore Club hotel's **Tower Bar.** Command central all hours of the night for the chic elite include the restaurants-cum-lounges **Rumi, Sushi Samba,** and **Nobu,** listed above in the "Dining" section.

As trends come and go, so do clubs, so before you head out for a decadent night of disco, make sure the place is still in business! At press time, some of the clubs at which to see, be seen, and, of course, dance, included **crobar,** 1445 Washington Ave. (© **305/531-5027**); **Level,** 1235 Washington Ave. (© **305/532-1525**); and **Opium Gardens,** 136 Collins Ave. (© **305/531-5535**), an open-air nightclub that's a magnet for the trendoid brass. For a Playboy Mansion–type scene by day, check out the **Nikki Beach Club,** 101 Ocean Dr. © **305/538-1111**), complete with tiki huts and teepees.

But South Beach isn't the only place for nightlife in Miami. Not too far from the Miami River is the city's oldest bar, **Tobacco Road,** 626 S. Miami Ave. (© **305/374-1198**), a gritty place that still attracts some of the city's storied, pre–Miami Vice natives. **ClubSpace,** 142 E. 11th St., at NE Second Avenue (© **305/372-9378**), occupies a very large warehouse in Downtown Miami and is vaguely reminiscent of a funky, SoHo-style dance palace. Down in Little Havana is **Café Nostalgia,** 2212 SW Eighth St. (© **305/541-2631**), where salsa is not a condiment but a way of life.

Other nocturnal options abound in **Coconut Grove** and **Coral Gables** and, slowly but surely, the downtown/Design District areas. Check the *Miami Herald, Miami New Times,* and **www.miami.citysearch.com** for specific events.

2 Fort Lauderdale

Fort Lauderdale's **Port Everglades** is the second-busiest cruise port in the world, drawing over 2.5 million cruise passengers in 2000. It boasts the deepest harbor on the eastern seaboard south of Norfolk, an ultramodern cruise ship terminal, and an easy access route to the Fort Lauderdale airport, less than a 5-minute drive away.

The port itself is fairly free of congestion, offering covered loading zones, drop-off and pickup staging, and curbside baggage handlers. Terminals are comfortable and safe, with seating areas, snack bars, lots of taxis, clean restrooms, and plenty of pay phones. Parking lots have recently been expanded to offer a total of 4,500 spaces.

GETTING TO FORT LAUDERDALE & THE PORT

Port Everglades is located about 23 miles (37km) north of Miami within the city boundaries of Fort Lauderdale, Hollywood, and Dania Beach. I-595 will take you right onto the grounds. For information, contact the **Port Everglades Authority** (© 954/523-3404; www.co.broward.fl.us/port.htm).

BY AIR   Small and extremely user-friendly, the **Fort Lauderdale/Hollywood International Airport** (© 954/359-6100) is less than 2 miles (3km) from Port Everglades (5 min. by bus or taxi), making this the easiest airport-to-cruise port trip in Florida. (Port Canaveral, by contrast, is about a 45-min. drive from the Orlando airport.) If you've booked air or transfers through the cruise line, a representative will show you to your shuttle after you land. If you haven't, taking a taxi to the port costs less than $10.

BY CAR   The port has three passenger entrances: Spangler Boulevard, an extension of State Road 84 East; Eisenhower Boulevard, running south from the 17th Street Causeway/Florida A1A; and Eller Drive, connecting directly with Interstate 595. Interstate 595 runs east-west, with connections to the Fort Lauderdale/Hollywood Airport, Interstate 95, State Road 7 (441), Florida's Turnpike, Sawgrass Expressway, and Interstate 75. Parking is available at the port in two large garages. The 2,500-space Northport Parking Garage, next to the Greater Fort Lauderdale/Broward County Convention Center, serves Terminals 1, 2, and 4. The 2,000-space Midport Parking Garage serves Terminals 18, 19, 21, 22, 24, 25, and 26. Garages are well lit, security patrolled, and designed to accommodate RVs and buses. The 24-hour parking fee is about $8.

EXPLORING FORT LAUDERDALE

Fort Lauderdale Beach, a 2-mile (3km) strip along Florida A1A, gained fame in the 1950s as a spring-break playground, popularized by the movie *Where the Boys Are.* But in the 1980s, partying college kids (who brought the city more mayhem than money) began to be less welcome as Fort Lauderdale sought to attract a more mainstream, affluent crowd, a task at which it has largely been successful.

In addition to miles of beautiful wide beaches, Fort Lauderdale has more than 300 miles (483km) of navigable natural waterways, in addition to innumerable artificial canals that permit thousands of residents to anchor boats in their backyards (and which has led to the city to be referred to as the "Venice of the Americas"). You can easily get on the water by renting a boat or hiring a private, moderately priced water taxi.

VISITOR INFORMATION   The **Greater Fort Lauderdale Convention & Visitors Bureau,** 1850 Eller Dr., Suite 303, Fort Lauderdale, FL 33316 (✆ **954/765-4466;** www.sunny.org), is an excellent resource, distributing a comprehensive guide on events and sightseeing in Broward County.

GETTING AROUND   For a taxi, call **Yellow Cab** (✆ **954/565-5400**). Rates start at $2.75 for the first mile and $2 for each additional mile. **Broward County Mass Transit** (✆ **954/357-8400**) runs bus service throughout the county. One-day passes are $2.50.

HITTING THE BEACH

Backed by an endless row of hotels and popular with visitors and locals alike, the **Fort Lauderdale Beach Promenade** underwent a $20 million renovation not long ago, and it looks marvelous. It's located along Atlantic Boulevard (Florida A1A), between SE 17th Street and Sunrise Boulevard. The fabled strip from *Where the Boys Are* is **Ocean Boulevard,** between Las Olas and Sunrise boulevards. On weekends, parking at the oceanside meters is difficult to find.

Fort Lauderdale Beach at the Howard Johnson is a perennial local favorite. A jetty bounds the beach on the south side, making it rather private, although the water gets a little choppy. High-school and college students share this area with an older crowd. One of the main beach entrances is at 4660 N. Ocean Dr. in Lauderdale by the Sea.

ATTRACTIONS

The Museum of Discovery & Science, 401 SW Second St. (✆ **954/467-6637;** www.mods.org), is an excellent interactive science museum with an IMAX theater. Check out the 52-foot (16m) tall "Great Gravity Clock" in the museum's atrium. Admission is $13 for adults, $11 for children, and $12 for seniors and students. It's open from 10am to 5pm Monday through Saturday; Sundays noon to 6pm.

The **Museum of Art,** 1 E. Las Olas Blvd. (✆ **954/763-6464;** www.museum ofart.org), is a truly terrific small museum whose permanent collection of 20th-century European and American art includes works by Picasso, Calder, Warhol, Mapplethorpe, Dalí, Stella, and William Glackens. African, South Pacific, Pre-Columbian, Native American, and Cuban art are also on display. Admission is $10 for adults, $5 for children over 12 and college students.

Bonnet House, 900 N. Birch Rd. (✆ **954/563-5393;** www.bonnethouse. org), a plantation-style home and 14-hectare (35-acre) estate, survives in the middle of an otherwise highly developed beachfront condominium area, offering a glimpse into the lives of Fort Lauderdale's pioneers. Seventy-five-minute guided tours are offered Wednesday through Friday at 10:30am, 11:30am, 12:30pm, and 1:30pm, Saturday and Sunday at 12:30, 1:15, 1:45, and 2:30pm. Plan to arrive at least 15 minutes before the tour's scheduled start time; cost is $9 adults, $8 seniors, $7 students, children under 6 free.

Butterfly World, Tradewinds Park South, 3600 W. Sample Rd., Coconut Creek, west of the Florida Turnpike (✆ **954/977-4400;** www.butterflyworld. com), cultivates more than 150 species. In the park's walk-through, screened-in aviary, visitors can watch newborn butterflies emerge from their cocoons and flutter around as they learn to fly. It's open from 9am to 5pm Monday through Saturday and 1 to 5pm Sunday. Admission is $13.95 adults, $8.95 kids 4 to 12, and free for kids under 4.

Fort Lauderdale

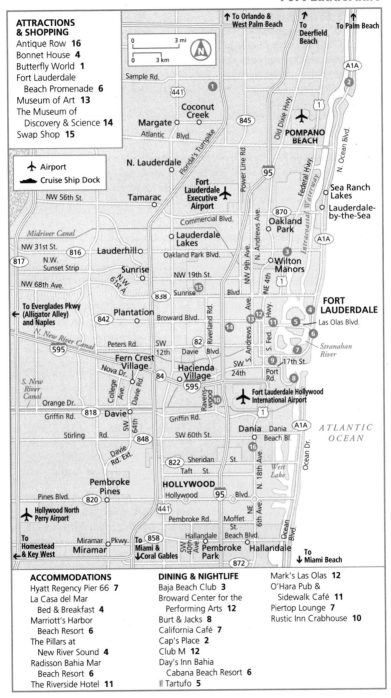

✈ Airport
⛴ Cruise Ship Dock

To Orlando &
West Palm Beach
To
Deerfield
Beach
To Palm Beach

A1A

Sample Rd.

441

Coconut
Creek

Margate

Atlantic   Blvd.

845

N. Ocean Blvd.

Old Dixie Hwy.

1

✈ POMPANO
BEACH

N. Lauderdale

Florida's Turnpike

Fort
Lauderdale
Executive
Airport

95

Power Line Rd.

Federal Hwy.

Sea Ranch
Lakes

Lauderdale-
by-the-Sea

Tamarac

Commercial Blvd.

870

Oakland
Park

A1A

Intracoastal Waterway

NW 56th St.

Midriver Canal

NW 31st St.   816

817   N.W.
Sunset Strip

NW 68th Ave.

Lauderhill

Lauderdale
Lakes

Oakland Park Blvd.

3
Wilton
Manors

NE 4th

N. Andrews Ave.

NW 9th Ave.

Sunrise

N.W.
61st A

NW 19th St.

838   Sunrise   Blvd.

15

FORT
LAUDERDALE

Las Olas Blvd.

To Everglades Pkwy
(Alligator Alley)
and Naples

N. New River Canal

595

Plantation

842

Broward Blvd.

Riverland Rd.

13 12
14   11
5

S. Andrews
Ave.

S. Fed.
Hwy.

6
7

Stranahan
River

Peters Rd.

Fern Crest
Village

Nova Dr.

84

SW
12th   Davie   Blvd.

82

Hacienda
Village

595

SW
24th

9   17th St.

Port
Rd.

8

S. New
River
Canal

Orange Dr.

College
Ave.

Davie Rd.

Griffin Rd.   818   Davie

SW
64th

Griffin Rd.

Ravenswood

10

Fort Lauderdale Hollywood
International Airport   ✈

1

Stirling   Rd.   848

Davie
Rd. Ext.

SW 60th St.

Dania   Dania   A1A
Beach Bl.

ATLANTIC
OCEAN

822   Sheridan   St.
Taft   St.

16

West
Lake

Ocean Dr.

Pembroke
Pines

820

Pines Blvd.

✈ Hollywood North
Perry Airport

HOLLYWOOD

Hollywood   95   Blvd.

441

Pembroke Rd.   Moffet
St.

NE
6th Ave.

N. 18th Ave.

To
Homestead
& Key West

Miramar   Pkwy.
Miramar

To
Miami &
Coral Gables

858

SW
40th
Ave

Hallandale
Beach   Beach Blvd.

Pembroke   Hallandale
Park

872

Ocean
Blvd.

To
Miami Beach

0   3 mi
0   3 km

ORGANIZED TOURS

BY BOAT   The Mississippi-style riverboat *Jungle Queen,* Bahia Mar Yacht Center, Florida A1A (© **954/462-5596;** www.junglequeen.com), is one of Fort Lauderdale's best-known attractions. Dinner cruises and 3-hour sightseeing tours take visitors up the New River past Millionaires' Row, Old Fort Lauderdale, the new downtown, and the Port Everglades cruise ship port. Call for prices and departure times.

Water Taxi of Fort Lauderdale, 651 Seabreeze Blvd. (© **954/467-6677;** www.watertaxi.com), operates a fleet of old port boats that offer taxi service on demand around this city of canals, carrying up to 72 passengers each. You can be picked up at your hotel and shuttled to the dozens of restaurants and bars on the route for the rest of the night. The service operates daily from 10am to midnight or 2am. The cost is $4 per person per trip, $5 for a full day. Opt for the all-day pass—it's worth it.

SHOPPING

Not counting the discount "fashion" stores on Hallandale Beach Boulevard, there are a few places visitors should know about, including **Antique Row,** a strip of U.S. 1 around North Dania Beach Boulevard (in Dania, about 1 mile/ 1.5km south of Fort Lauderdale/Hollywood International Airport) that holds about 200 antiques shops. Most shops are closed Sunday.

The **Swap Shop,** 3291 W. Sunrise Blvd. (© **954/791-SWAP;** www.florida swapshop.com), is one of the world's largest flea markets. In addition to endless acres of vendors, there is a mini-amusement park, a 13-screen drive-in movie theater, and even a free circus, complete with elephants, horse shows, high-wire acts, and clowns. It's open daily.

ACCOMMODATIONS

Fort Lauderdale Beach has a hotel or motel on nearly every block, and the selection ranges from run-down to luxurious.

Located very close to the port, the **Hyatt Regency Pier 66,** 2301 SE 17th St. (© **800/233-1234** or 954/525-6666; www.hyatt.com/usa/fort_lauderdale/ hotels), is a circular landmark with larger rooms than some equivalently priced hotels in town. Its famous Piertop Lounge, a revolving bar on its roof, is often filled with cruise ship patrons. Rates: $290.

Located just south of Fort Lauderdale's strip, **Marriott's Harbor Beach Resort,** 3030 Holiday Dr. (© **800/222-6543** or 954/525-4000; www.marriott harborbeach.com), is set on 6.5 hectares (16 acres) of beachfront property. All rooms have private balconies overlooking either the ocean or the Intracoastal Waterway. Rates: $260 to $430.

Radisson Bahia Mar Beach Resort, 801 Seabreeze Blvd. (© **800/327-8154** or 954/764-2233; www.radisson.com/ftlauderdalefl), is scattered over 42 acres (17 hectares) of seacoast. A four-story row of units is adjacent to Florida's largest marina. Rates: $89 to $184. The **Riverside Hotel,** 620 E. Las Olas Blvd. (© **800/325-3280** or 954/467-0671; www.riversidehotel.com), which opened in 1936, is a local favorite. Try for one of the ground-floor rooms, which have higher ceilings and more space. Rates: $180 to $370.

The Spanish Mediterranean–style **La Casa del Mar Bed & Breakfast,** 3003 Granada St. (© **800/739-0009** or 954/467-2037; www.lacasadelmar.com), has 10 individually furnished rooms and is only a block away from Fort Lauderdale Beach. Rates: $110 to $130. **The Pillars at New River Sound,** 111 N. Birch

Rd. (© **800/800-7666** or 954/467-9639; www.pillarshotel.com), is a small 23-room inn, the best of its size in the region. The clean and simple accommodations have very comfortable beds. Rates: $165 to $260. Call the **Fort Lauderdale Convention and Visitors Bureau** (© **954/765-4466;** www.sunny.org) for a copy of *Superior Small Lodgings,* a guide to other small accommodations in the area.

DINING

The only restaurant at Port Everglades itself, **Burt & Jacks,** at Berth 23 (© **954/522-2878;** www.burtandjacks.com), is a collaboration between actor Burt Reynolds and restaurateur Jack Jackson. As you sit at this elegant restaurant, you can watch the cruise ships and other boats pass by. A waiter will arrive with steaks, lobster, veal, pork chops, and more; you choose and your dish will arrive perfectly cooked. Reservations are required and so are jackets for men. Dinner main courses: $15 to $38.

California Café, at the Hyatt Pier 66 Hotel, 2301 SE 17th St. (© **954/728-3500**), serves brick-oven pizza and pasta dishes at affordable prices. Dinner main courses: $16 to $28.

Cap's Place, 2261 E. Sample Rd., in Lighthouse Point (© **954/941-0418;** www.capsplace.com), is a famous old-time seafood joint, offering good food at reasonable prices. The restaurant is on a peninsula; you get a ferry ride over (see their website for directions). Dolphin (not the mammal but a local saltwater fish also known as mahimahi) and grouper are popular and, like the other meat and pasta dishes here, can be prepared any way you want. Dinner main courses: $14 to $25.

Il Tartufo, 2400 E. Las Olas Blvd. (© **954/767-9190**), serves oven-roasted specialties and other Italian standards, plus a selection of fish baked in rock salt. Dinner main courses: $15 to $22.

Mark's Las Olas, 1032 E. Las Olas Blvd. (© **954/463-1000**), is the showcase of Miami restaurant mogul Mark Militello. The continental gourmet menu changes daily and might include Jamaican jerk chicken with fresh coconut salad or a superb sushi-quality tuna. Dinner main courses: $14 to $30.

Garlic crabs are the specialty at the **Rustic Inn Crabhouse,** 4331 Anglers Ave. (© **954/584-1637;** www.crabhouse.com), located west of the airport. This riverside dining choice has an open deck over the water. Dinner main courses: $10 to $19.

The restaurant and patio bar at the **Day's Inn Bahia Cabana Beach Resort,** 3001 Harbor Dr./Florida A1A (© **954/524-1555;** www.bahiacabanaresort.com), is charming and laid-back, serving inexpensive American-style dishes on a covered open-air deck overlooking Fort Lauderdale's largest marina; the Fort Lauderdale water taxi makes a stop here. Dinner main courses: 10 to $17.

FORT LAUDERDALE AFTER DARK

From the area's most famous bar, the revolving **Piertop Lounge,** in the Hyatt Regency at Pier 66 (© **954/525-6666**), you'll get a 360° panoramic view of Fort Lauderdale. The bar completes a revolution every 66 minutes. There is a dance floor and live music, including blues and jazz.

On weekends it's hard to get into **Club M,** 2037 Hollywood Blvd. (© **954/925-8396**), one of the area's busiest music bars, featuring a DJ and live bands on weekends playing blues, rock, and jazz.

O'Hara Pub & Sidewalk Café, 722 E. Las Olas Blvd. (© **954/524-1764**), is often packed with a trendy crowd who come to listen to live R&B, pop, blues, and jazz. Call their jazz hot line (© **954/524-2801**) to hear the lineup.

If you want to dance, try the **Baja Beach Club,** 3200 N. Federal Hwy. (© **954/563-8494**), perhaps the only dance club in the world that anchors an entire shopping mall.

The **Broward Center for the Performing Arts,** 201 SW Fifth Ave. (© **954/ 462-0222;** www.browardcenter.org), hosts top opera, symphony, dance, and Broadway productions. Call the 24-hour Arts Entertainment Hotline (© **954/ 357-5700**) for schedules and performers, or look for listings in the *Sun-Sentinel* or the *Miami Herald.*

3 Cape Canaveral & Cocoa Beach

Known as the "Space Coast" because of nearby Kennedy Space Center, the Cape Canaveral/Cocoa Beach area boasts 72 miles (116km) of beaches, plus fishing, golfing, surfing, and close proximity to Orlando's theme parks, only about an hour west—which is exactly why long-underutilized **Port Canaveral** is now busier than ever before, offering many 3- and 4-night cruise options, which are often sold as packages with pre- or post-cruise visits to the Orlando resorts.

Outside the port area, Cape Canaveral is . . . well, it's no Miami. Highways, strip malls, chain stores, and tracts of suburban homes predominate from the port area south into Cocoa Beach, where most of the hotels, restaurants, and beaches discussed here are located. The central areas of Cocoa Beach are mildly more interesting, with some great 1950s/1960s condo and hotel architecture, but stylish they're not.

GETTING TO CAPE CANAVERAL & THE PORT

Port Canaveral is located at the eastern end of the Bennett Causeway, just off State Highway 528 (the Bee Line Expressway), the direct route from Orlando. From the port, 528 turns sharply south and becomes Florida A1A, portions of which are known as Astronaut Boulevard and North Atlantic Avenue. For information about the port, contact the **Canaveral Port Authority** (© **888/ 767-8226** or 321/783-7831; www.portcanaveral.org).

BY AIR   The nearest airport is the **Orlando International Airport** (© **407/ 825-2001;** www.orlandoairports.net), a 45-mile (72km) drive from Port Canaveral via the S.R. 528 Bee Line Expressway. Cruise line representatives will meet you if you've booked air and/or transfers through the line. **Cocoa Beach Shuttle** (© **800/633-0427** or 321/784-3831) offers shuttle service between Orlando's airport and Port Canaveral; the trip costs $22 per person each way.

BY CAR   Port Canaveral and Cocoa Beach are about 45 miles (72km) east of Orlando and 186 miles (299km) north of Miami. They're accessible from virtually every interstate highway along the east coast. Most visitors arrive via Route 1, Interstate 95, or State Highway 528. At the port, park in the North Lots for north terminals nos. 5 and 10 and the South Lots for nos. 2, 3, or 4. Parking costs $7 a day.

EXPLORING CAPE CANAVERAL & COCOA BEACH

Port Canaveral probably wouldn't be on the cruise industry's radar if it weren't so close to Orlando, with most passengers shuttling directly from theme park to pier rather than spending any significant time here. Nevertheless, anyone interested in the space program or 1950s/1960s history should plan to arrive a

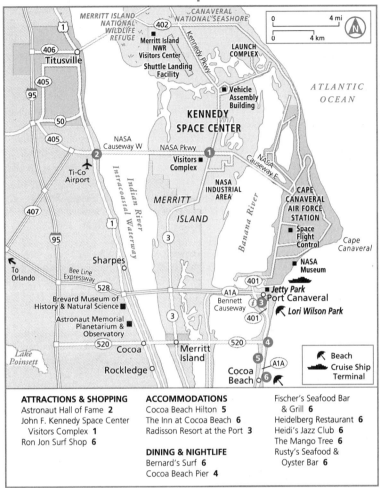

ATTRACTIONS & SHOPPING
Astronaut Hall of Fame **2**
John F. Kennedy Space Center
   Visitors Complex **1**
Ron Jon Surf Shop **6**

ACCOMMODATIONS
Cocoa Beach Hilton **5**
The Inn at Cocoa Beach **6**
Radisson Resort at the Port **3**

DINING & NIGHTLIFE
Bernard's Surf **6**
Cocoa Beach Pier **4**

Fischer's Seafood Bar
   & Grill **6**
Heidelberg Restaurant **6**
Heidi's Jazz Club **6**
The Mango Tree **6**
Rusty's Seafood &
   Oyster Bar **6**

day early (or stay a day after) to check out Kennedy Space Center and the Astronaut Hall of Fame.

VISITOR INFORMATION   Contact the **Florida Space Coast Office of Tourism,** 8810 Astronaut Blvd./Florida A1A, Suite 102, Cape Canaveral, FL 32920 (© **800/872-1969** or 321/868-1126; fax 321/868-1139; www.space-coast.com). Their office is in the Sheldon Cove building, right on the corner of Central Boulevard and Florida A1A, and is open Monday to Friday from 8am to 5pm.

GETTING AROUND   For taxis, call **Comfort Travel** (© **800/567-6139** or 321/784-8294) or **Brevard Yellow Cab** (© **321/723-1234**).

THE ORLANDO THEME PARKS
All it took was a sprinkle of pixie dust in the 1970s to begin the almost-magical transformation of Orlando from a large swath of swampland into the most visited tourist destination in the world. Today it's home to three giants—Walt

Disney World, Universal Orlando, and SeaWorld—whose local offerings include seven of the eight most popular theme parks in the United States.

Many cruises from Port Canaveral are sold as land-sea packages that include park stays, but if you decide to visit Orlando before or after your cruise, it's essential to plan ahead. Otherwise, the number of attractions begging for your time and the hyper-commercial atmosphere can put a serious dent in your psyche as well as your wallet and stamina. Even if you had 2 weeks, it wouldn't be long enough to hit everything, so try to tamp down the urge to do everything in Walt Disney World and then some. Stay selective, stay sane. That's our motto.

It would take a significant portion of this *book* to detail everything to do in Orlando, but we list some basic information on the major theme parks below. If you plan to spend a considerable amount of time here, we suggest picking up a copy of *Frommer's Walt Disney World® & Orlando.*

VISITOR INFORMATION   For information about **Walt Disney World**—including vacation brochures and videos—write or call Walt Disney World, Box 10000, Lake Buena Vista, FL 32830-1000 (✆ **407/934-7639** or 407/824-2222; www.disneyworld.com).

For information about **Universal Orlando,** call ✆ **800/837-2273** or 407/363-8000, surf over to **www.universalorlando.com**, or write to **Universal Orlando,** 1000 Universal Studios Plaza, Orlando, FL 32819.

You can obtain SeaWorld information online at **www.seaworld.com**.

WALT DISNEY WORLD
Walt Disney World is the umbrella above four theme parks: the **Magic Kingdom, Epcot, Disney–MGM Studios,** and **Animal Kingdom,** which drew almost 40 million guests despite an economic decline in 2001, according to *Amusement Business* magazine. Besides its theme parks, Disney has an assortment of other venues, including three water parks, several entertainment venues, and a number of shopping spots.

TICKET PRICES   At press time, **1-day/one-park tickets,** for admission to the Magic Kingdom, Epcot, Animal Kingdom, or Disney–MGM, are $48 for adults, $38 for children 3 to 9. And those prices don't include Orlando's 6% sales tax. (Ouch!) Discounted multiday, multipark passes are available; many Disney cruise packages include these passes.

OPERATING HOURS   Park hours vary and are influenced by special events and the economy. So call ahead or go to **www.disneyworld.com** to check. Generally, expect Animal Kingdom to be open 8 or 9am to 5 or 6pm; Epcot to be open 10am to 9pm; and Magic Kingdom and Disney–MGM to be open 9am to 5 or 6pm. All may open or close earlier or later.

The Parks
MAGIC KINGDOM   The most popular theme park on the planet, it offers 40 attractions, plus restaurants and shops, in a 43-hectare (107-acre) package. Its symbol, Cinderella Castle, forms the hub of a wheel whose spokes reach to seven "lands" that simulate everything from an Amazonian jungle to Colonial America. If you're traveling with little kids, this is *the* place to go.

EPCOT   This 105-hectare (260-acre) park (the acronym stands for Experimental Prototype Community of Tomorrow) has two sections. **Future World** is centered on Epcot's icon, a giant geosphere that looks like a big golf ball. Major corporations sponsor the park's 10 themed areas, and the focus is on discovery, scientific achievements, and tomorrow's technologies in areas running from energy to undersea exploration. The **World Showcase** is a community of 11 miniaturized nations surrounding a 16-hectare (40-acre) lagoon. All of these "countries" have indigenous architecture, landscaping, restaurants, and shops; and cultural facets are explored in art exhibits, dance or other live performances, and innovative films. This park definitely appeals more to adults; but it has few thrill rides, so if that's a requirement, go elsewhere. *Note:* Hiking through this park will often exhaust even the fittest person—some folks say Epcot really stands for "Every Person Comes Out Tired"—so we recommend splitting your visit over 2 days.

DISNEY–MGM STUDIOS   You'll probably spy the Earful Tower—a water tower outfitted with gigantic mouse ears—before you enter this park, which Disney bills as "the Hollywood that never was and always will be." Once inside, you'll find pulse-quickening rides such as the **Rock 'n' Roller Coaster** and **Twilight Zone of Terror,** and movie- and TV-themed shows such as **Jim Henson's Muppet*Vision 3D.** This 45-hectare (110-acre) park has some of the best street performing anywhere. Both adults and kids will love it, and best of all, it can comfortably be done in 1 day.

ANIMAL KINGDOM   This 202-hectare (500-acre) park opened in 1998 and combines animals, elaborate landscapes, and a handful of rides to create yet another reason that many guests don't venture outside Disney World. Animal Kingdom ranks with Tampa's Busch Gardens (see "Tampa," later in this chapter) as one of the top two critter parks in Florida. It's a conservation venue as much as an attraction, so it's easy for most of the animals to escape your eyes here (unlike at Busch). And though the thrill rides are better at Busch, Animal Kingdom has much better shows, such as **Tarzan Rocks!** and **Legend of the Lion King.** The park is good for both adults and children and can be done in a single outing, but if you come on a hot summer day, come early or it's unlikely you'll see many of the primo animals, who are smart enough to seek shade.

UNIVERSAL ORLANDO

Universal Orlando is the No. 1 contender to Walt Disney World in the ongoing, "anything you can do we can do better," knock-down-drag-out battle between the Magic Mickster and the Orlando area's wannabes. Although it's a distant second when it comes to attendance numbers, it's unquestionably the champion at entertaining teenagers and the older members of the thrill-ride crowd.

In addition to its original park, **Universal Studios Florida,** it has added a second theme park, **Islands of Adventure,** plus an entertainment district and several resorts.

TICKET PRICES   A **1-day/one-park ticket** costs $49.95 (plus 6% sales tax) for adults, $40.95 for children 3 to 9. A 2-day, two-park unlimited-access Escape Pass is $84.95 for adults, $81.95 for children 3 to 9; a 3-day, two-park pass is $104.95 for adults, $96.95 for children 3 to 9. Discount passes are usually included in Universal cruise packages.

OPERATING HOURS   The parks are open 365 days a year, generally from 9am to 6pm, though often later, especially in summer and around holidays, when they're sometimes open until 9pm. The best bet is to call before you go so that you're not caught by surprise.

The Parks

UNIVERSAL STUDIOS FLORIDA   Even with fast-paced, grown-up rides such as **Back to the Future: The Ride, Terminator,** and **Men in Black Alien Attack,** Universal Studios Florida is fun for kids. And as a plus, it's a working motion-picture and TV studio, so occasionally filming is being done at Nickelodeon's sound stages or elsewhere in the park. **Hanna-Barbera characters** such as Yogi Bear, Scooby Doo, and Fred Flintstone are usually on hand to greet visitors, as is a talented group of actors portraying a wide range of other characters. You can do the park in a day, although you'll be a tad breathless when you get to the finish line.

ISLANDS OF ADVENTURE   This 45-hectare (110-acre) theme park opened in 1999 and it is, bar none, *the* Orlando theme park for thrill-ride junkies. Sporting themed areas as varied as Dr. Seuss, Jurassic Park, and Marvel comics, the park successfully combines both nostalgia and state-of-the-art technology. Roller coasters roar above pedestrian walkways and water rides slice through the park. **The Amazing Adventures of Spider-Man** is a 3-D track ride that is arguably the best all-around attraction in Orlando; the **Jurassic Park River Adventure's** 70-foot (21m) drop scared creator Steven Spielberg into jumping ship before going over; and **Dueling Dragons** draws more raves from coaster crazies than any other in Orlando. Unless it's the height of high season, the park can be done in a day. It is not, however, a park for families with young kids: *9 of the park's 14 major rides have height restrictions.* If, however, you have teens, or are an adrenaline junkie, this is definitely the place for you.

SEAWORLD

TICKET PRICES   A **1-day ticket** costs $49.95 for ages 10 and over, $40.95 for children 3 to 9, plus 6% sales tax.

OPERATING HOURS   The park is usually open 9am to at least 6pm, and later during summer and holidays when there are additional shows at night.

A 81-hectare (200-acre) marine-life park, **SeaWorld** (✆ **407/351-3600;** www.seaworld.com), explores the deep in a format that combines conservation awareness with entertainment. While that's what Disney is attempting at Animal Kingdom, the message here is subtle and a more inherent part of the experience.

Shamu, a killer whale, is the star of the park, which also has several other Orcas, including some babies. The pace is much more laid-back than that of Universal or Disney, and it's a good way to take a day off from trudging through the frenzied parks. SeaWorld is easily toured in a single day and is appropriate for everyone from small children to adults. Though **Journey to Atlantis** and **Kraken** are pretty high-tech coasters, SeaWorld can't compete with the wonders of Walt's World or Universal. But those parks don't let you discover the crushed-velvet texture of a stingray or the song of the sea lions.

SPACE COAST ATTRACTIONS

JOHN F. KENNEDY SPACE CENTER   Set amid 150,000 acres (60,702 hectares) of marshy wetlands favored by birds, reptiles, and amphibians, the Kennedy Space Center (✆ **321/449-4444;** www.kennedyspacecenter.com) is where astronauts left for the moon in 1969, where the shuttles have lifted off since 1981, and where America's components of the International Space Station are sent into orbit. Even if you've never really considered yourself a science or space buff, you can't help but be impressed by the achievements the place represents.

Security restrictions mean that most of the center is off-limits, but the **Visitors Complex** is designed to offer a glimpse of the works, with real NASA spacecraft; exhibits; hands-on activities for kids; a daily Q&A with a real astronaut; IMAX movies; a Space Shuttle mock-up; a Launch Status Center where presentations are given on current shuttle missions; an outdoor rocket garden displaying now-obsolete Redstone, Atlas, Saturn, and Titan rockets; and more. There are also the obligatory gift shop and several ridiculously pricey stops where you can grab a bite. Plan to eat before or after your visit.

Some visitors stick to the visitor center, but for a more complete insight into the space age, take the **bus tour** of the larger complex. Buses depart at 15-minute intervals; but the wait to get aboard can easily take an hour or more, so figure this into your planning. In the past, buses have stopped at three sites around the complex, with visitors allowed to spend as much time at each as they liked before catching the next bus back, but at press time new security restrictions had put Launch Complex 39 and the International Space Station Center off-limits, leaving only one stop still open to the public—the **Apollo/Saturn V Center.** Here, visitors experience a narrated simulation of the Apollo 8 launch while looking into an actual Mission Control room that was used for the mission. Following the show, visitors enter an enormous hall where an entire Apollo Saturn V rocket is on display, held up horizontally by huge metal supports. Numerous exhibits cover various aspects of the Apollo program, and a lunar module hangs from the ceiling above the snack bar.

Kennedy Space Center is accessible via State Highway 405, just off U.S. 1. The visitor complex is open daily (except Christmas and certain launch days) from 9am to 5:30pm. The last tour departs at 2:15pm. Admission is $26 adults, $16 children 3 to 11. Parking at the visitor center is free. Be sure to pick up a map at the visitor center, and expect to spend most of the day on-site to best experience the place.

ASTRONAUT HALL OF FAME   Less than 6 miles (10km) west of Kennedy Space Center on State Highway 405, near the intersection with U.S. 1, the Astronaut Hall of Fame (© **321/269-6100;** www.astronauts.org) is a satellite attraction founded by the Space Camp Foundation and the astronauts who flew NASA's Mercury missions, and focuses on the heroic human element of the space program. Film presentations introduce visitors to the origins of rocketry and to the sheer power of the rockets themselves; displays of personal memorabilia offer insight into the astronauts' lives; and displays of NASA memorabilia are just plain awesome: actual Mission Control terminals at which you can sit to access interactive information; Jim Lovell's logbook from Gemini VII; and, most mind-blowing of all, the actual Apollo 14 command module *Kitty Hawk,* whose plaque bears the inscription "This spacecraft flew to the moon and back January 31-February 9, 1971." Nuff said.

But let's get down to brass tacks. The Astronaut Hall of Fame offers one main thing Kennedy Space Center doesn't: the chance to pretend you're an astronaut through various simulations. In the **G-force simulator,** two wannabe spacemen at a time are strapped tightly into pods at opposite ends of what looks like a giant barbell, which then begins whirling on its axis so fast that your cheeks start to flap, just like in the movies. A film projected in the pod simulates a high-speed test flight. Just across the room, the **3D 360 simulator** takes a group of passengers on a simulated shuttle flight from Earth to the new International Space Station, along the way pitching you backward, forward, sideways, and upside-down. At the **Walk on the Moon simulator,** visitors are strapped into a harness, which is then counterbalanced to their weight so that they can bounce around as if weightless, doing their "one small step for man" imitation. Next door, the **Mission to Mars simulator** bumps you over the surface of the red planet in a rover. Not bad, but of the group it's the simulator to skip if you've got limited time. Now, the warnings: Simulators are off-limits to folks under 48 inches, which is okay since smaller kids would probably freak out anyway. Also, if you tend to get motion sickness, you'll probably want to avoid everything except the weightlessness simulation. Lastly, on the off-chance you're there on a slow day, be sure to allow at least a few minutes between simulations, even if you've got a cast-iron constitution. Trust us on this one.

The center is open daily except Christmas from 9am to 5pm, though guests are not admitted after 4pm. Admission is $13.95 for adults, $12.95 for seniors, $9.95 for kids 6 to 12, and free for children 5 and under.

HITTING THE BEACH

Though the Cape Canaveral/Cocoa Beach area doesn't have the spectacular beach culture of Miami, it doesn't lack for pleasant coastline. The following beaches (or "parks" in the local lingo) are located within an easy drive of the port area.

Closest to the cruise ship port and actually part of the larger port complex, the clean, nicely landscaped **Jetty Park,** 400 E. Jetty Rd., is the most elaborate and possibly the nicest of the local beaches, perched at a point from which the whole expanse of the Cape Canaveral/Cocoa Beach coastline stretches away to the south. It's some view. A massive stone jetty juts seaward as protection for the mouth of Port Canaveral, and alongside is an elevated platform from which fishermen dangle their lines right into the surf. A snack bar, bathrooms, showers, picnic facilities, a children's playground, and fishing and beach equipment rental are available. Parking costs $3 per car and $7 per RV for overnight stays. Follow the signs after entering the port area, near where State Road 528 and Florida A1A intersect.

A series of beaches are accessible (and generally signposted) off Florida A1A heading south from the port. The **Cocoa Beach Pier** area, off Florida A1A at Meade Avenue, is a great surfing spot with volleyball, an open-air bar, and a party atmosphere, while **Lori Wilson Park,** farther south at 1500 N. Atlantic Ave., is another nicely landscaped area on the order of Jetty Park, with bathrooms and showers, a rustic boardwalk with some shaded picnic areas and benches, a nature center, and The Hammock, a quarter-mile (0.5km) boardwalk nature trail that winds through ferns, twisted trees, and other *Jurassic Park*–looking foliage, while butterflies flutter by and spiders eye them from their webs. Parking is free.

SHOPPING

Let's be unkind: You could shop here, but why bother? The offerings in Cape Canaveral and Cocoa Beach are mostly the kind of national mall shops that you've probably got at home, so save your energy and dollars for the Caribbean. An exception—as much for the experience as for the goods—is the **Ron Jon Surf Shop,** 4151 N. Atlantic Ave./Florida A1A (© **321/799-8888;** www.ron jons.com/locations/cocoabeach.htm). Inside the pink and green, South Beach– looking Art Deco building is enough au courant beachwear to transform you and a good-size army into surfer dudes in no time flat. The store also rents beach bikes, body boards, surfboards, kayaks, beach chairs, and other equipment by the hour, day, or week. It's open 24 hours a day, 365 days a year.

ACCOMMODATIONS

Only a 5-minute drive from the port, **Radisson Resort at the Port,** 8701 Astronaut Blvd./Florida A1A (*(C* **800/333-3333** or 321/784-0000; www.radisson.com/capecanaveralfl), offers comfortable rooms and very comfortable two-room suites that are a great option for families, featuring a kitchenette with microwave, fridge, and place settings; living room with sofa bed and giant TV, and bedroom with a Jacuzzi and second giant TV. The great jungle-motif front courtyard has a large amoeba-shaped pool and a second courtyard has tennis courts. Cruise passengers who are arriving by car can leave their vehicles free in the hotel's lot during their cruise and take the free Radisson shuttle to and from the port. Rates: $109 rooms; $129 suites.

At the other end of the spectrum, **The Inn at Cocoa Beach,** 4300 Ocean Beach Blvd., just off Florida A1A behind the Ron Jon Surf Shop (*(C* **800/343-5307** or 321/799-3460; www.theinnatcocoabeach.com), is almost entirely couples-oriented, presenting itself as more of a personalized inn than a traditional hotel. Almost all of its 50 comfortable, B&B-style rooms face the ocean, with rocking chairs on their balconies and king- or queen-size beds, TVs, and large bathrooms. A bar off the lobby operates on the honor system (just sign for what you take), and a lobby dog and six tropical birds in cages around the property add to the homey, low-key atmosphere. Rates: $135 to $250.

Located near Lori Wilson Park on Florida A1A (and, for you '60s TV fans, near a street called I Dream of Jeannie Lane), the **Cocoa Beach Hilton,** 1550 N. Atlantic Ave./Florida A1A (*(C* **800/526-2609** or 321/799-0003; www.cocoabeachhilton.com), is the most upscale of the beachfront mainstream hotels, though it's more like a downtown business hotel that's been transplanted to the seashore. Rooms are spacious but have smallish picture windows only; none offers a balcony. Rates: $79 to $179.

DINING

In the heart of Cocoa Beach, the Fischer Family restaurants, **Bernard's Surf** (*(C* **321/783-2401;** www.bernardssurf.com), **Fischer's Seafood Bar & Grill** (*(C* **321/783-2401;** www.fischersseafood.com), and **Rusty's Seafood & Oyster Bar** (*(C* **321/783-2033;** www.rustysseafood.com), are all bunched up together at 2 S. Atlantic Ave., at Minuteman Causeway Road. At Bernard's, opened in 1948, photos testify to the many astronauts—and Russian cosmonauts too—who have celebrated their safe return to Earth with the restaurant's steak and seafood, the latter provided by the Fischer family's own boats. Fischer's Seafood Bar & Grill is a *Cheers*-like lounge popular with the locals, serving fried combo platters, shrimp and crab claw meat, and the like. Rusty's is another casual option, with spicy seafood gumbo, raw or steamed oysters, burgers and sandwiches, pasta, and so on. There's another Rusty's branch on the south side of Port Canaveral harbor, at 628 Glen Cheek Dr. (*(C* **321/783-2033**), serving the same menu but with views of the fishing boats and cruise ships heading in and out of the port. Bernard's main courses $14 to $35; Fischer's main courses $9 to $16, sandwiches and salads $4 to $8; Rusty's main courses $10 to $20, sandwiches and salads $4 to $9.

The Mango Tree, 118 N. Atlantic Ave./Florida A1A, between N. 1st and N. 2nd streets (*(C* **321/799-0513**), is the most beautiful and sophisticated restaurant in Cocoa Beach, serving gourmet seafood, pasta, chicken, and continental dishes in a plantation-home atmosphere. Dinner main courses: $13 to $30.

In downtown Cocoa Beach, the **Heidelberg Restaurant,** 7 N. Orlando Ave./ Florida A1A at the Minuteman Causeway (🕿 **321/783-6806**), serves German and Continental cuisine such as beef filet Stroganoff, filet steak a la Madagaskar, roast duck, sauerbraten, and grilled loin pork chops in a middling-elegant atmosphere. The adjoining Heidi's Jazz Club (see "Port Canaveral After Dark," below) has music nightly except Mondays. Dinner main courses: $15 to $21.

PORT CANAVERAL AFTER DARK

The Cocoa Beach Pier, 401 Meade Ave., off Florida A1A a half mile (1km) north of State Road 520 (🕿 **321/783-7549;** www.cocoabeachpier.com), juts out 800 feet (244m) over the Atlantic, offering a casual beer-and-fruity-drinks atmosphere, an open-air bar with live music most nights, an ice-cream shop, restaurants, and an arcade (plus beach equipment rentals and volleyball right next door on the sand).

At the Heidelberg Restaurant (see "Dining," above), **Heidi's Jazz Club,** 7 N. Orlando Ave./Florida A1A at the Minuteman Causeway (🕿 **321/783-4559;** www.heidisjazzclub.com), offers live jazz and blues Tuesday through Sunday, with featured performers on selected Friday and Saturday evenings and an open jam session Sundays at 7pm. See their website for a schedule of performances.

4 Tampa

Tampa was a sleepy port until Cuban immigrants founded Ybor City's cigar industry in the 1880s. A few years later, Henry B. Plant built a railroad to carry tourists into town and constructed his garish Tampa Bay Hotel (now the Henry B. Plant Museum). During the Spanish-American War, Teddy Roosevelt trained his Rough Riders here and walked the Ybor City streets with Cuban revolutionary José Marti. A land boom in the 1920s gave the city its charming, Victorian-style Hyde Park suburb (now a gentrified area, just across the Hillsborough River from downtown), and the go-go 1980s and 1990s brought skyscrapers, a convention center, a performing-arts center, and lots of shopping and dining options to the downtown area.

On the western shore of Tampa Bay, **St. Petersburg** is the picturesque and pleasant flip side of Tampa's busy business, industrial, and shipping life. Originally conceived and built primarily for tourists and wintering snowbirds, it's got a nice downtown area, some quality museums, and a few good restaurants.

The **Port of Tampa** is set amid a complicated network of channels and harbors near historic Ybor City and its deepwater Ybor Channel. Ships sailing from here head primarily to the western Caribbean, the Yucatán, and Central America.

GETTING TO TAMPA & THE PORT

The **Garrison Seaport Cruise Terminal** is located at 1101 Channelside Dr. (🕿 **813/905-5044;** www.tampaport.com).

BY AIR   **Tampa International Airport** (🕿 **813/870-8700**) lies 5 miles (8km) west of downtown Tampa, near the junction of Florida 60 and Memorial Highway. If you haven't arranged transfers with the cruise line, the port is an easy 15-minute taxi ride away; the fare is $17 per person via **Central Florida Limo** (🕿 **813/396-3730**). **Travel Ways** (🕿 **800/888-1428**) also runs a bus service, which costs $16 per person from the airport to Garrison Terminal.

BY CAR   Tampa lies 188 miles (303km) southwest of Jacksonville, 50 miles (80km) north of Sarasota, and 245 miles (394km) northwest of Miami. From

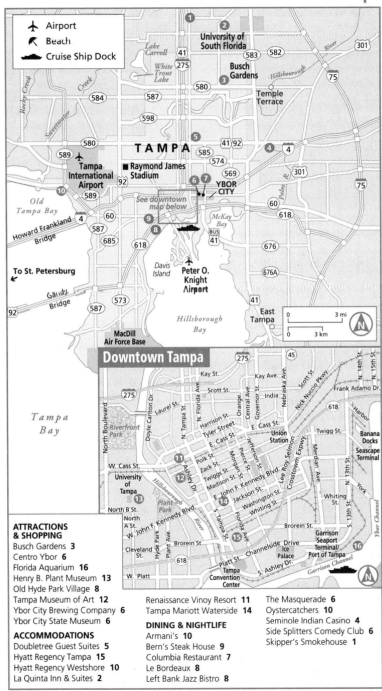

- ✈ Airport
- ⚓ Beach
- ⛴ Cruise Ship Dock

University of South Florida
Lake Carroll
Busch Gardens
White Trout Lake
Temple Terrace
Rocky Creek
Sweetwater Creek
Hillsborough River
TAMPA
Tampa International Airport
■ Raymond James Stadium
YBOR CITY
Old Tampa Bay
See downtown map below
McKay Bay
Howard Frankland Bridge
To St. Petersburg
Gandy Bridge
Davis Island
Peter O. Knight Airport
Hillsborough Bay
East Tampa
MacDill Air Force Base

0   3 mi
0   3 km

Downtown Tampa

Tampa Bay
Riverfront Park
North Boulevard
Union Station
Banana Docks
Seascape Terminal
University of Tampa
Plant Park
Frank Adamo Dr.

ATTRACTIONS & SHOPPING
Busch Gardens **3**
Centro Ybor **6**
Florida Aquarium **16**
Henry B. Plant Museum **13**
Old Hyde Park Village **8**
Tampa Museum of Art **12**
Ybor City Brewing Company **6**
Ybor City State Museum **6**

ACCOMMODATIONS
Doubletree Guest Suites **5**
Hyatt Regency Tampa **15**
Hyatt Regency Westshore **10**
La Quinta Inn & Suites **2**

Renaissance Vinoy Resort **11**
Tampa Mariott Waterside **14**

DINING & NIGHTLIFE
Armani's **10**
Bern's Steak House **9**
Columbia Restaurant **7**
Le Bordeaux **8**
Left Bank Jazz Bistro **8**

The Masquerade **6**
Oystercatchers **10**
Seminole Indian Casino **4**
Side Splitters Comedy Club **6**
Skipper's Smokehouse **1**

Garrison Seaport Terminal/ Port of Tampa
Tampa Convention Center
Ybor Channel
Garrison Channel

I-75 and I-4: To Terminals 2 and 6 take I-4 West to Exit 1 (Ybor City), go South on 21st Street, then turn right on Adamo Drive (Hwy. 60) and then left on Channelside Drive; for Terminal 7 go south on 21st Street (21st St. merges with 22nd St. after crossing Adamo Dr.), turn right on Maritime Boulevard, and then go left on Guy N. Verger to Hooker's Point. From Tampa International Airport: To Terminals 2 and 6, follow signs to I-275 North, go to I-4 East and then to Exit 1 (Ybor City), go South on 21st Street, turn right on Adamo Drive (Hwy. 60), and then turn left on Channelside Drive; for Terminal 7, use directions from I-75 above. The port has ample parking (at $8 per day), with good security.

EXPLORING TAMPA

Tampa is best explored by car, as only the commercial district can be covered on foot. If you want to go to the beach, you'll have to head to neighboring St. Petersburg.

VISITOR INFORMATION Contact the **Tampa/Hillsborough Convention and Visitors Association,** Inc. (THCVA), 400 N. Tampa St., Suite 1010, Tampa, FL 33602 (© **800/44-TAMPA** or 813/223-2752; www.visittampabay. com). You can also stop by the **Tampa Bay Visitor Information Center,** 3601 E. Busch Blvd. (© **813/985-3601**), north of downtown in the Busch Gardens area.

GETTING AROUND Taxis in Tampa do not normally cruise the streets for fares; instead, they line up at public loading places, such as the airport, cruise terminal, and major hotels. **Yellow Cab** (© **813/253-0121**) or **United Cab** (© **813/253-2424** or 813/251-5555) charge about $1.75 per mile.

The **Hillsborough Area Regional Transit/HARTline** (© **813/254-HART**) provides regularly scheduled bus service between downtown Tampa and the suburbs. Fares are $1.15 for local services and $1.50 for express routes; exact change is required.

ATTRACTIONS

BUSCH GARDENS Yes, admission prices are high, but Busch Gardens remains Tampa Bay's most popular attraction. The 136-hectare (335-acre) family entertainment park, at 3000 E. Busch Blvd. (© **888/800-5447** or 813/ 987-5171; www.buschgardens.com), features thrill rides, animal habitats, live entertainment, shops, restaurants, and games. The park's zoo ranks among the best in the country, with nearly 3,400 animals.

Montu, the world's tallest and longest inverted roller coaster, is part of **Egypt,** the park's ninth themed area, which also includes a replica of King Tutankhamen's tomb and a sand-dig area for kids. **Timbuktu** is a replica of an ancient desert trading center, complete with African craftspeople at work. It also features a sandstorm ride, Dolphin theater with daily shows, a boat-swing ride, a roller coaster, and a video-game arcade. **Morocco,** a walled city with exotic architecture, has Moroccan craft demonstrations and a sultan's tent with snake charmers. **The Congo** features white-water raft rides; Kumba, the largest steel roller coaster in the southeastern United States; and Claw Island, a display of rare white Bengal tigers in a natural setting.

Rhino Rally is the newest addition. It's an off-road adventure in 16-passenger "Ralliers," or Land Rovers, that travel a bumpy course that allows views of Asian elephants, buffalo, antelope, and more. Hang onto your hat when a flash flood whisks away the bridge—and your vehicle.

The Serengeti Plain is an open area with more than 500 African animals roaming in herds. This 32-hectare (80-acre) natural grassy veldt can be viewed from the tram ride, the Trans-Veldt Railway, or the Skyride. **Nairobi** is home to a natural habitat for various species of gorillas and chimpanzees, a baby-animal nursery, a petting zoo, reptile displays, and Curiosity Caverns, where visitors can observe animals active at night. **Bird Gardens,** the original core of Busch Gardens, offers rich foliage, lagoons, and a free-flight aviary holding hundreds of exotic birds, including golden and American bald eagles, hawks, owls, and falcons. This area also features Land of the Dragons, a children's adventure.

Crown Colony, a multilevel restaurant overlooking the Serengeti plains, is the home of a team of Clydesdale horses, as well as the Anheuser-Busch hospitality center. **Akbar's Adventure Tours,** which offers a flight simulator, is located here.

To get to the Gardens, take Interstate 275 northeast of downtown to Busch Boulevard (Exit 33), and go east 2 miles (3km) to the entrance on 40th Street (McKinley Ave.). Admission is $49.95 for adults and $40.95 for kids 3 to 9 (plus 6% tax). Parking is $7. Park hours are at least 10am to 6pm; hours are extended during summer. See the website for opening and closing times.

OTHER ATTRACTIONS   Only steps from the Garrison Seaport Center, the **Florida Aquarium** (© 813/273-4000; www.flaquarium.net) celebrates the role of water in the development and maintenance of Florida's topography and ecosystems, with more than 10,000 aquatic plants and animals. An overriding theme follows a drop of water as it bubbles through Florida limestone and winds its way to the sea. Admission is $15 for ages 13 and older, $12 for seniors, and $10 for children 5 to 12.

Thirteen silver minarets and distinctive Moorish architecture make the stunning **Henry B. Plant Museum,** 401 W. Kennedy Blvd. (© **813/254-1891;** www.plantmuseum.com), the focal point of the Tampa skyline. This National Historic Landmark, built in 1891 as the Tampa Bay Hotel, is filled with European and Oriental furnishings and decorative arts from the original hotel collection.

Ybor City is only about a mile or so from the cruise ship docks. It's Tampa's historic Latin enclave and one of only three national historic districts in Florida. Once known as the cigar capital of the world, Ybor offers a charming slice of the past with its Spanish architecture, antique street lamps, wrought-iron balconies, ornate grillwork, and renovated cigar factories. Stroll along Seventh Avenue, the main artery (closed to traffic at night), where you'll find cigar shops, boutiques, nightclubs, and the famous 100-year-old **Columbia Restaurant** (see "Dining," below).

The **Ybor City State Museum,** 1818 9th Ave., between 18th and 19th streets (© **813/247-6323;** www.ybormuseum.org), is primarily devoted to the area's cigar history, with a collection of cigar labels, cigar memorabilia, and works by local artisans. Admission is $2 per person. The museum is open daily from 9am to 5pm.

At **Centro Ybor,** a shopping/entertainment complex between 7th and 8th avenues and 16th and 17th streets (© **813/241-4545;** www.thecentroybor.com), you'll find a multiscreen cinema, several restaurants, a comedy club, a large open-air bar, a bunch of typical mall-type stores, and GameWorks, a high-tech entertainment center designed by Steven Spielberg's Dreamworks and

Universal Studios. The Ybor City Chamber of Commerce has its **Cigar Museum & Visitor Center** here (on 8th Ave. next to Centro Espanol).

The permanent collection of the **Tampa Museum of Art,** 600 N. Ashley Dr. (℡ 813/274-8130; www.tampamuseum.com), is especially strong in ancient Greek, Etruscan, and Roman artifacts, as well as 20th-century art. The museum grounds, fronting the Hillsborough River, contain a sculpture garden and a decorative fountain. It's open 10am to 5pm Tuesday to Saturday (till 8pm on Thurs), and 1 to 5pm on Sunday. Admission is $5 adults, $4 seniors, free for kids under 6.

ORGANIZED TOURS

BY BUS   Swiss Chalet Tours, 3601 E. Busch Blvd. (℡ 813/985-3601), operates guided tours of Tampa, Ybor City, and the surrounding region. Four-hour (10am–2pm) tours run on Monday and Thursday, and cost $40 for adults, $35 for children. Seven-hour tours (10am–5pm) cost $70 for adults and $45 for children.

ON FOOT   Ybor City walking tours are available through the **Ybor City State Museum** (see "Other Attractions," above). Tours are $2 for ages 6 and older.

HITTING THE BEACH

You have to start at **St. Petersburg,** across the bay, for a north-to-south string of interconnected white sandy shores. Most beaches have restrooms, refreshment stands, and picnic areas. You can either park on the street at meters (usually 25¢ for each half-hr.) or at one of the four major parking lots located from north to south at **Sand Key Park** in Clearwater, beside Gulf Boulevard (also known as Rte. 699), just south of the Clearwater Pass Bridge; **Redington Shores Beach Park,** beside Gulf Boulevard at 182nd Street; **Treasure Island Park,** on Gulf Boulevard just north of 108th Avenue; and **St. Pete Beach Park,** beside Gulf Boulevard at 46th Street.

SHOPPING

On and around Seventh Avenue in Ybor City, you'll find lots of **cigar stores** selling handmade stogies, as well as a variety of interesting boutiques and shops.

Some 60 upscale shops, plus restaurants and movie theaters, are located at **Old Hyde Park Village,** an outdoor, European-style market at Swann and Dakota avenues near Bayshore Boulevard (℡ 813/251-3500; http://oldhyde parkvillage.com). There's nothing particularly "Tampa" about it, but if you need a new Brooks Brothers suit or Ann Taylor dress for your cruise, it'll do.

ACCOMMODATIONS

TAMPA   There are two Tampa Hyatts. The **Hyatt Regency Westshore,** 6200 Courtney Campbell Causeway (℡ 800/233-1234 or 813/874-1234; www. westshore.hyatt.com), sits in a 14-hectare (35-acre) wildlife preserve at the Tampa end of the long causeway traversing Tampa Bay, about 2 miles (3km) from the airport and 8 miles (13km) from downtown. In addition to regular rooms and suites, 45 Spanish-style town houses/villas are set about a half mile (1km) from the main hotel building. Rates: $149 to $305. The **Hyatt Regency Tampa,** Two Tampa City Center at 211 N. Tampa St. (℡ 800/233-1234 or 813/225-1234; www.hyatt.com), sits in Tampa's commercial center and caters mostly to the corporate crowd. Rates: $199 to $270. The other big downtown hotel, the **Tampa Marriott Waterside,** 400 N. Florida Ave., at Ice Palace Drive

(© **800/228-9290** or 813/221-4900; fax 813/221-0923; www.marriotthotels. com), opened in 2000. About half of the rooms have balconies overlooking the bay or city (the best views are high up on the south side). Rates: $159 to $264.

La Quinta Inn & Suites, 3701 E. Fowler Ave. (© **800/687-6667** or 813/ 910-7500; fax 813/910-7600; www.laquinta.com), is a motel with a pinch of upscale. Rooms have coffeemakers and dataports, and the place is located only 1½ miles (2.5km) from Busch Gardens. Rates: $84.99 to $124.

ST. PETERSBURG   Overlooking Tampa Bay, the **Renaissance Vinoy Resort,** 501 Fifth Ave. NE, at Beach Drive (© **800/HOTELS1** or 737/894-1000; www. renaissancehotels.com), is the grande dame of the region's hotels. Built as the grand Vinoy Park in 1925, this elegant Spanish-style establishment reopened in 1992 after a meticulous $93 million restoration. Many of the guest rooms offer lovely views of the bay. Accommodations in the new wing ("The Tower") are slightly larger than those in the hotel's original core. Rates: $320 to $390.

DINING

On the 14th floor of the Hyatt Regency Westshore Hotel, **Armani's,** 6200 Courtney Campbell Causeway (© **813/207-6800**), is a stylish northern Italian restaurant with a panoramic view of the city skyline and the bay. Jackets are required. Dinner main courses: $18 to $35. At **Bern's Steak House,** 1208 S. Howard Ave. (© **813/251-2421**), the steaks are close to perfect. You order according to thickness and weight. Dinner main courses: $17 to $60. Located in a converted home, the romantic **Le Bordeaux,** 1502 S. Howard Ave. (© **813/254-4387**), presents some of the region's best French food at reasonable prices. The menu changes seasonally. Part of the establishment is the lounge-style **Left Bank Jazz Bistro,** featuring live jazz Monday to Friday from 5:30 to 8pm. Dinner main courses: $16 to $27.

In Ybor City, the nearly 100-year-old **Columbia Restaurant,** 2117 Seventh Ave. E., between 21st and 22nd streets (© **813/248-4961**), occupies an attractive tile-sheathed building that fills an entire city block, about a mile from the cruise docks. The aura is pre-Castro Cuba. The simpler your dish is, the better it's likely to be. Filet mignons, roasted pork, and the black beans, yellow rice, and plantains are flavorful and well prepared. Flamenco shows begin on the dance floor Monday through Saturday at 7:30pm. Dinner main courses: $12 to $23.

The best fish in Tampa is served at **Oystercatchers,** in the Hyatt Regency Westshore Hotel complex, 6200 Courtney Campbell Causeway (© **813/207-6815**). Pick the fish you want from a glass-fronted buffet or enjoy mesquite-grilled steaks, chicken rollatini, and shellfish. Dinner main courses: $20 to $30.

TAMPA AFTER DARK

Nightfall transforms **Ybor City,** Tampa's century-old Latin Quarter, into a hotbed of music, ethnic food, poetry readings, and after-midnight coffee and dessert. Seventh Avenue, one of its main arteries, is closed to all but pedestrian traffic Wednesday through Saturday evenings. **The Masquerade,** 1503 E. Seventh Ave. (© **813/247-3319**), set in a 1940s movie palace, is just one of the many nightclubs that pepper the streets here. Other options include **Side Splitters Comedy Club,** 12938 N. Dale Mabry Hwy. (© **813/960-1197**), which features stand-up pros most nights of the week. There's a $6 to $8 cover.

In North Tampa, **Skipper's Smokehouse,** 910 Skipper Rd., at the corner of Nebraska Avenue (© **813/971-0666;** www.skipperssmokehouse.com), is a favorite evening spot, with an all-purpose restaurant and bar (with oysters and fresh shellfish sold by the dozen and half-dozen) and live music back in the Skipper Dome, a sprawling deck sheltered by a canopy of oak trees.

Northeast of town, at Exit 5 off I-4, the **Seminole Indian Casino,** 5223 N. Orient Rd., at Hillsborough Road (© **800/282-7016** or 813/621-1302; www. casino-tampa.com), is open 24 hours every day of the year, with poker, bingo, and slots.

For more on Tampa nightlife, the Tampa/Hillsborough Arts Council maintains **Artsline** (© **813/229-ARTS**), a 24-hour information service about current and upcoming cultural events.

5 New Orleans

New Orleans may be best known as a world-class party town, but by some yardsticks it's also the busiest seaport in the nation, visited by thousands of cargo vessels transporting grains, ores, machinery, and building supplies, as well as by a number of cruise ships bound for ports in the western Caribbean, including Cancún, Playa del Carmen, and Cozumel. You can watch the parade of cargo ships pass by you as you steam downriver to the ocean, against the backdrop of Louisiana's Mississippi River delta.

GETTING TO NEW ORLEANS & ITS PORT

The **Julia Street Cruise Ship Terminal** sits at the foot of Julia Street on the Mississippi River, in the Central Business District, a 10-minute walk or a short streetcar or taxi ride away from the edge of the French Quarter. For information, call the **Port of New Orleans** at © **504/522-2551** or check out **www.portno. com**.

BY AIR   New Orleans International Airport (© **504/464-0831**) is about 15 miles (24km) northwest of the port. Cruise line representatives meet all passengers who have booked transfers through the line. For those who haven't, a taxi to the port costs about $24 and takes about 20 minutes. **Airport Shuttle** (© **504/592-0555** or 866/596-2699) runs vans at 10- to 12-minute intervals from outside the airport's baggage claim to the port and other points in town. It costs $10 per passenger each way; it's free for children under 6.

BY CAR   Take I-10 downtown. Take the Tchoupitoulas/St. Peters Street exit, the last one before you cross the Mississippi. Stay to the right, and head toward the New Orleans Convention Center. Turn right onto Convention Center Boulevard, then left onto Henderson Street, which will take you to Port of New Orleans Place. Turn left and continue on to the Cruise Ship Terminal. You can park your car in long-term parking at the port, but only for blocks of 7 days. Reserve parking through your cruise line. You must present a boarding pass or ticket before parking.

EXPLORING NEW ORLEANS

The **French Quarter** is the oldest part of the city and still the most popular for sightseeing. Many visitors never leave its confines, but by venturing outside the Quarter you'll be able to feel the pulse of the city's commerce, see river activities that keep the city alive, stroll through spacious parks, drive or walk by the impressive homes of the **Garden District,** and get a firsthand view of the bayou/lake connection that explains why New Orleans grew up here in the first place.

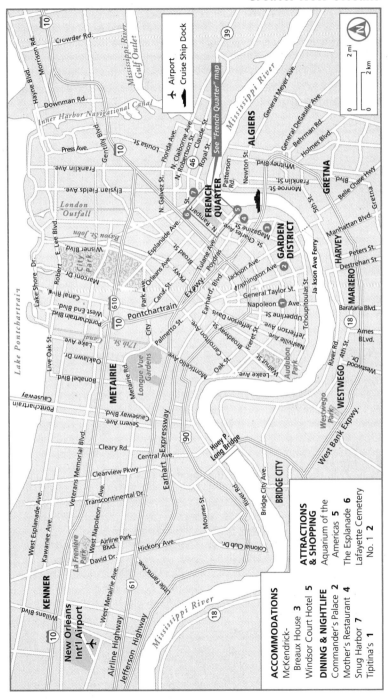

Greater New Orleans

Airport
Cruise Ship Dock

See "French Quarter" map

2 mi
2 km

ALGIERS

GRETNA

HARVEY

MARRERO

WESTWEGO

BRIDGE CITY

METAIRIE

KENNER

New Orleans Int'l Airport

FRENCH QUARTER

GARDEN DISTRICT

Lake Pontchartrain

Mississippi River

Mississippi River Gulf Outlet

Inner Harbor Navigational Canal

London Outfall

City Park

Bayou St. John

Audubon Park

Westwego Park

Longue Vue Gardens

La Frenière Park

Huey P. Long Bridge

Crowder Rd.
Morrison Rd.
Hayne Blvd.
Downman Rd.
Press Ave.
Gentilly Blvd.
Franklin Ave.
Elysian Fields Ave.
Florida Ave.
N. Claiborne Ave.
N. Robertson St.
Claude St.
Royal St.
Louisa St.
Esplanade Ave.
N. Galvez St.
Broad St.
N. Rampart St.
St. Claude Ave.
Magazine St.
St. Charles Ave.
E. Lee Blvd.
Wisner Blvd.
Marconi Dr.
Robert
Canal Blvd.
Lake Shore Dr.
West End Blvd.
Pontchartrain Blvd.
Park Ave.
Orleans Ave.
Tulane
Poydras
Canal St.
City
Jackson Ave.
Washington Ave.
General Taylor St.
Napoleon Ave.
Upperline St.
Jefferson Ave.
Nashville Ave.
Tchoupitoulas St.
St. Jefferson Davis
Earhart Blvd.
Broad St.
Freret
Carrollton Ave.
Palmetto St.
Monticello Ave.
Oak St.
Leake Ave.
Walnut St.
Broadway
Live Oak St.
Oaklawn Dr.
Lake Ave.
Bonabel Blvd.
Metairie Rd.
Causeway Blvd.
Severn Ave.
Cleary Rd.
Central Ave.
Clearview Pkwy.
Transcontinental Dr.
Veterans Memorial Blvd.
West Esplanade Ave.
Kawanee Ave.
West Napoleon Ave.
Airline Park Blvd.
Hickory Ave.
David Dr.
Mounes St.
Colonial Club Dr.
Little Farms Ave.
West Metairie Ave.
Williams Blvd.
Airline Highway
Jefferson Highway
17th St. Canal
610
Pontchartrain Expwy.
Earhart Expressway
West Bank Expwy.
Bridge City Ave.
River Rd.
Colonial Club Dr.
Causeway
Pontchartrain

General Meyer Ave.
General DeGaulle Ave.
Behrman Blvd.
Holmes Blvd.
Whitney Blvd.
Patterson Rd.
Newton St.
Monroe St.
Franklin St.
5th St.
Belle Chase Hwy.
Blvd.
Gretna Blvd.
Manhattan Blvd.
Peters St.
Destrehan Ave.
4th St.
Barataria Blvd.
Ames Blvd.
River Rd.
Westwood Dr.

10 39 46 10 610 10 90 18 61 18

ACCOMMODATIONS
McKendrick-
Breaux House **3**
Windsor Court Hotel **5**

DINING & NIGHTLIFE
Commander's Palace **2**
Mother's Restaurant **4**
Snug Harbor **7**
Tipitina's **1**

ATTRACTIONS & SHOPPING
Aquarium of the
Americas **5**
The Esplanade **6**
Lafayette Cemetery
No. 1 **2**

VISITOR INFORMATION   Contact the **Greater New Orleans Convention and Visitors Bureau,** 1520 Sugar Bowl Dr., New Orleans, LA 70112 (© **504/ 566-5011;** www.neworleanscvb.com), for brochures, pamphlets, and information. In New Orleans, the **New Orleans Welcoming Center** is located at 529 St. Ann St. in the French Quarter (© **800/672-6124**).

GETTING AROUND   Taxis are plentiful. If you're not near a taxi stand, call **United Cabs** (© **504/522-9771**) and a car will come in 5 to 10 minutes. The meter begins at $2.50 (plus $1 for each additional person), and charges $1.20 per mile after the initial $2.50 fee.

Streetcar lines run the length of St. Charles Avenue. The nostalgic wooden cars operate 24 hours a day and cost $1.25 per ride (you must have exact change). A transfer from streetcar to bus costs 25¢. You board at the corner of Canal and Carondelet streets in the French Quarter, or at intervals along St. Charles. A **VisiTour Pass,** which gives you unlimited rides on all streetcar and bus lines, sells for $5 for 1 day, $12 for 3 days. You can buy passes through hotel information counters and certain retail stores; you'll find a list at **www.regional transit.org/location.html**.

Where the trolleys don't run, a **city bus** will. For route information, call © **504/248-3900** or pick up a map at the **Greater New Orleans Convention and Visitors Bureau** or the **New Orleans Welcoming Center** (addresses above). Most buses charge $1.25 per ride (plus 25¢ for a transfer), although some express buses charge $1.50.

The **Vieux Carré Minibus** takes you to French Quarter sights. The route is posted along Canal and Bourbon streets. The minibus operates weekdays between 5am and 6:30pm, weekends 8am to 6:30pm, and costs $1.25.

From Jackson Square (at Decatur St.), you can take a 2¼-mile (3.5km), 30-minute **horse-drawn carriage** ride through the French Quarter. **Royal Carriage Tour Co.** (© **504/943-8820**) offers group tours for $10 per person in open-topped surreys suitable for up to eight passengers at a time, daily from 9am to midnight. Private rides for up to four passengers in a Cinderella carriage go for $50 a pop.

ATTRACTIONS

At the well-designed **Aquarium of the Americas,** 1 Canal St., at the Mississippi River (© **800/774-7394** or 504/861-2537), a 400,000-gallon tank holds a kaleidoscope of species from the deep waters of the nearby Gulf of Mexico. Admission is $13.50 for adults, $6.50 for children under 12; open 9:30am to 6pm Sunday through Thursday, 9:30am to 7pm Friday and Saturday.

Incorporating seven historic buildings connected by a brick courtyard, the **Historic New Orleans Collection,** 533 Royal St., between St. Louis and Toulouse (© **504/523-4662**), evokes New Orleans of 200 years ago. The oldest building in the complex escaped the tragic fire of 1794. The others hold exhibitions about Louisiana's culture and history. All are open from 10am to 4:30pm daily. Admission is free.

Founded in 1950, the **New Orleans Pharmacy Museum,** 514 Chartres St., at St. Louis (© **504/565-8027;** www.pharmacymuseum.org), is just what the name implies. In 1823, the first licensed pharmacist in the United States, Louis J. Dufilho, Jr., opened an apothecary shop here. Today you'll find old apothecary bottles, voodoo potions, pill tile, and suppository molds, as well as the old glass cosmetics counter and a jar of leeches, in case you feel the need to be bled.

The French Quarter

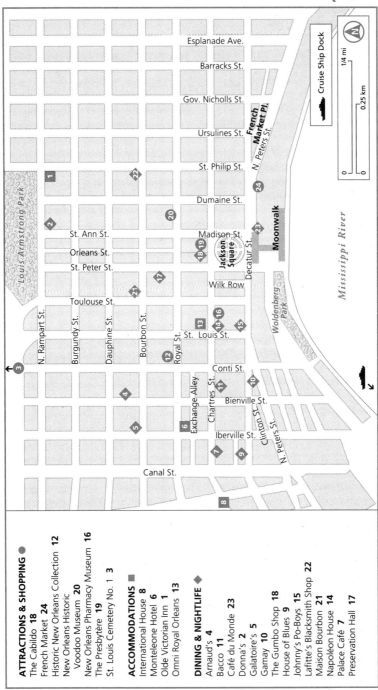

Esplanade Ave.
Barracks St.
Gov. Nicholls St.
Ursulines St.
St. Philip St.
Dumaine St.
St. Ann St.
Orleans St.
St. Peter St.
Toulouse St.
St. Louis St.
Conti St.
Bienville St.
Iberville St.
Canal St.
Madison St.

Louis Armstrong Park
French Market Pl.
N. Peters St.
Jackson Square
Moonwalk
Wilk Row
Woldenberg Park
Mississippi River
Decatur St.
N. Rampart St.
Burgundy St.
Dauphine St.
Bourbon St.
Royal St.
Chartres St.
Exchange Alley
Clinton St.
N. Peters St.

Cruise Ship Dock

1/4 mi
0.25 km
0
0

ATTRACTIONS & SHOPPING ●
The Cabildo **18**
French Market **24**
Historic New Orleans Collection **12**
New Orleans Historic
Voodoo Museum **20**
New Orleans Pharmacy Museum **16**
The Presbytère **19**
St. Louis Cemetery No. 1 **3**

ACCOMMODATIONS ■
International House **8**
Monteleone Hotel **6**
Olde Victorian Inn **1**
Omni Royal Orleans **13**

DINING & NIGHTLIFE ◆
Arnaud's **4**
Bacco **11**
Café du Monde **23**
Donna's **2**
Galatoire's **5**
Gamay **10**
The Gumbo Shop **18**
House of Blues **9**
Johnny's Po-Boys **15**
Lafitte's Blacksmith Shop **22**
Maison Bourbon **21**
Napoléon House **14**
Palace Café **7**
Preservation Hall **17**

It's open Tuesday through Sunday 10am to 5pm; admission $2 adults, $1 seniors and students, free for children under 12.

Constructed from 1795 to 1799 as the Spanish government seat in New Orleans, **The Cabildo,** 701 Chartres St., at Jackson Square (© **800/568-6968** or 504/568-6968), was the site of the signing of the Louisiana Purchase transfer. It's now the center of the Louisiana State Museum's facilities in the French Quarter, with a multiroom exhibition that traces the history of Louisiana from exploration through Reconstruction, covering all aspects of life, including antebellum music, mourning and burial customs, immigrants, and the changing roles of women in the South. It's open Tuesday through Sunday 9am to 5pm; admission $5 adults, $4 students and seniors, free for children under 13.

Also on Jackson Square, **The Presbytère,** 751 Chartres St. (© **800/568-6968** or 504/568-6968), was planned as housing for the clergy but is now a Mardi Gras museum that traces the history of the annual event, with everything from elaborate Mardi Gras Indian costumes to Rex Queen jewelry from the turn of the century on display. A re-creation of a float allows you to pretend you are throwing beads to a crowd on a screen in front of you. It's open Tuesday through Sunday 9am to 5pm; admission $5 adults, $4 seniors and students, free for children under 13.

The collections of the **New Orleans Historic Voodoo Museum,** 724 Dumaine St., at Bourbon (© **504/523-7685** or 504/522-5223), celebrate the occult and the mixture of African and Catholic rituals first brought to New Orleans by slaves from Hispaniola. A gift shop and voodoo parlor are stocked with apothecary ingredients, and the staff can provide you with psychic services. Admission is $7 for adults; $5.50 for college students, military personnel, and seniors; $4.50 for high-school kids; and $3.50 for grade-school children. It's open daily from 10am to 8pm. A new location at 217 North Peter's St. contains a collection of more contemporary voodoo artifacts.

While we're on the subject of the undead, there's the issue of New Orleans' cemeteries: Since the city is prone to flooding, bodies have been interred aboveground since its earliest days, in sometimes very elaborate tombs that are definitely worth a visit. **St. Louis Cemetery No. 1,** Basin St. between Conti and St. Louis streets, at the top of the French Quarter, is the oldest extant cemetery (1789) and the most iconic. The acid-dropping scene from *Easy Rider* was shot here, prompting the city to declare that no film would ever, ever, *ever* be shot again in one of its cemeteries. In the Garden District, **Lafayette Cemetery No. 1,** 1427 Sixth St., right across the street from Commander's Palace Restaurant, is another old cemetery that's been beautifully restored. Though both of these cemeteries are usually full of visitors during the day, you should exercise caution when touring, as they've seen some crime over the years.

ORGANIZED TOURS

ON FOOT   There are a lot of tours offered in New Orleans, but **Historic New Orleans Walking Tours** (© **504/947-2120**) is the place to go for authenticity, offering tours of the French Quarter, the Garden District (including Lafayette Cemetery), and a cemetery and voodoo tour. Prices are about $10 to $14 per person.

A daily guided **voodoo-and-cemetery walking tour** of the French Quarter departs from the original **New Orleans Historic Voodoo Museum,** 724 Dumaine St., led by a folk historian and acclaimed storyteller who calls herself Bloody Mary (© **504/486-2080**). The walking tours are all $22 and include museum admission.

BY BUS **Gray Line,** 1 Toulouse St. (*©* **800/535-7786** or 504/587-0861), offers a 2-hour bus tour that gives a fast overview of the city. Tours cost $24 for adults and $12 for children, and require advance booking.

SHOPPING

Despite what you may think while making your first walk down Bourbon Street, there's more to New Orleans shopping than tourist traps selling cheap T-shirts, alligator snow globes, and other souvenir items—although there are plenty of those too (most of them with an absolutely mind-boggling selection of hot sauces). The city's antiques stores are especially good.

On Decatur Street across from Jackson Square, **The French Market** has shops selling candy, cookware, fashion, crafts, toys, New Orleans memorabilia, and candles. There is a lot of kitsch, but there are some good buys mixed in; and it's always fun to stroll through and grab a few beignets at Café du Monde (see "Snacks & Sweets," below). It's open from 10am to 6pm; Café du Monde is open 24 hours.

From Camp Street down to the river on **Julia Street,** you'll find many of the city's best contemporary art galleries. Of course, some of the works are a bit pricey, but there are good deals to be had if you're collecting, and fine art to be seen if you're not.

Magazine Street is the Garden District's premier shopping street, with more than 140 shops among the 19th-century brick storefronts and cottages. You'll find antiques, art galleries, boutiques, crafts, and more. The greatest concentration of stores is between Felicity and Washington streets, but if you're so inclined, you could shop your way from here all the way to Audubon Park, hopping over the dry patches on the city bus. Be sure to pick up a copy of *Shopper's Dream,* a free guide and map to most of the stores. It's available all along the street.

ACCOMMODATIONS

In the Garden District, the **McKendrick-Breaux House,** 1474 Magazine St. (*©* **888/570-1700** or 504/586-1700), was built at the end of the Civil War by a wealthy plumber and Scottish immigrant, and today is one of the best guesthouses for value. It's been completely restored to its original charm, with each room furnished with antiques, family collectibles, and fresh flowers. Rates: $125 to $195.

In the Central Business District, just outside the French Quarter and close to the cruise ship terminal, the **International House,** 221 Camp St., just west of Canal (*©* **800/633-5770** or 504/553-9550; fax 504/200-6532; www.ihhotel. com), is a very modern, minimalist hotel that was constructed in an old beaux arts bank building. Rooms are simple with high ceilings, ceiling fans, very contemporary bathrooms, dataports, CD players with CDs, and photos and knickknacks that remind you you're in New Orleans. It's all corridors and dark and chic. Rates: $180 to $289.

About 7 blocks from the cruise ship terminal is the atmospheric **Monteleone Hotel,** 214 Royal St., between Iberville and Bienville (*©* **800/535-9595** or 504/523-3341; fax 504/528-1019; www.hotelmonteleone.com), the oldest hotel in the city and also the largest hotel in the French Quarter—because of its size you can almost always get a reservation here, even when other places are booked. Everyone who stays here loves it, probably because its staff is among the most helpful in town. Decor and floor layouts are slightly different in each of the rooms, so ask to see a few different ones. Rates: $140 to $225.

Three streets from Bourbon in the French Quarter, the **Olde Victorian Inn,** 914 N. Rampart St. (© **800/725-2446** or 504/522-2446; www.oldevictorian inn.com), was formerly known as P. J. Holbrook's, and is now owned by Keith and Andre West-Harrison (and their four dogs and one cat), who have retained the former decor and menu. It's a beautifully restored 1840s home, with antiques and reproductions. Some rooms have balconies, and most have fireplaces. The inn can arrange wedding packages that include a service in its courtyard; you can head off for your honeymoon cruise from there! Rates: $120 to $175.

The **Omni Royal Orleans,** 621 St. Louis St., between Royal and Chartres (© **800/843-6664** or 504/529-5333; fax 504/529-7037; www.omnihotels. com), is a most elegant hotel located smack in the center of the Quarter. The lobby is a small sea of marble, and the rooms are sizable and elegant, full of muted tones and plush furniture, with windows that let you look dreamily out over the Quarter. Service varies, but can be exceptional. Rates: $169 to $259.

In the Central Business District, the **Windsor Court Hotel,** 300 Gravier St. (© **800/262-2662** or 504/523-6000; fax 504/596-4749; www.windsorcourt hotel.com), was named Best Hotel in North America by *Condé Nast Traveler,* so feel free to hold it to a high standard. Accommodations are exceptionally spacious and classy, with large bay windows or a private balcony overlooking the river or the city. Downstairs, two corridors display original 17th-, 18th-, and 19th-century art, and there's a plush reading area with an international newspaper rack on the second floor. Rates: $290 to $400.

DINING

Essentially, New Orleans is one giant restaurant. In 1997, a U.S. survey named it "the fattest city in the country," which makes sense once you've tasted what's being whipped up at 3 or 4 or 8 or 40 of the city's best restaurants. We've profiled many of the best below. Most of them are in the French Quarter.

In business since 1918 and still mighty fine, the legendary **Arnaud's,** 813 Bienville St. (© **504/523-5433**), is set up in three interconnected, once-private houses from the 1700s, and its three Belle Epoque dining rooms are lush with Edwardian embellishments. Menu items include snapper or trout topped with crabmeat, filet mignon, shrimp Arnaud, oysters stewed in cream, roasted duck a l'orange, and classic Bananas Foster. Dinner main courses: $17 to $28.

Bacco, 310 Chartres St., between Bienville and Conti (© **504/522-2426**), a great New Orleans bistro, has an elegant setting with pink faux-marble floors and Venetian chandeliers. You can feast on wood-fired pizzas, regional seafood, and such specialties as black truffle fettuccini and lobster ravioli. Dinner main courses: $19 to $25

Galatoire's, 209 Bourbon St., at Iberville (© **504/525-2021**), feels like a bistro in turn-of-the-20th-century Paris, and is one of the city's most legendary places—one of the ones where the locals go for a good meal. Menu items include trout (meunière or amandine), rémoulade of shrimp, oysters en brochette, a savory Creole-style bouillabaisse, and a good eggplant stuffed with a purée of seafood. Dinner main courses: $14 to $22.

Gamay, in the Bienville House hotel, 320 Decatur St., at Conti (© **504/299-8800**), serves contemporary Creole cuisine in a formal setting. Entrees include the gigantic almond-crusted soft-shell crab with garlic shrimp and saffron pasta, and a Gulf fish of the day. Dinner main courses: $18 to $28.

The Gumbo Shop, 630 St. Peter St., at Chartres (© **504/525-1486**), is a cheap and convenient place to get solid, classic Creole food. The menu reads like a textbook list of traditional local food: red beans and rice, shrimp Creole, craw-fish étouffée. The seafood gumbo with okra is a meal in itself, and do try the jambalaya. Dinner main courses: $6 to $15.

Johnny's Po-Boys, 511 St. Louis St., between Chartres and Decatur (© **504/ 524-8129**), serves pretty much anything you can think of on huge hunks of French bread, including fried seafood (the classic), deli meats, cheese omelets, ham and eggs, and the recommended vegetarian selection: the French Fry po' boy. All items are under $8.

Not far outside the Quarter, **Mother's Restaurant,** 401 Poydras St., at Tchoupitoulas (© **504/523-9656**), has long lines and zero atmosphere, but wow, those po' boys. Customers have been flocking here since 1938 for home-made biscuits and red-bean omelets at breakfast, po' boys at lunch, and soft-shell crabs and jambalaya at dinner. Everything's between $2 and $17.

Napoléon House, 500 Chartres St. (© **504/524-9752**), at the corner of St. Louis Street, would have been the home of the lieutenant himself if some locals' wild plan to bring him here to live out his exile had panned out. A landmark 1797 building with an incredible atmosphere, the place is a hangout for drink-ing and good times, but also serves food. The specialty is Italian muffuletta, with ham, Genoa salami, pastrami, Swiss cheese, and provolone. Dinner main courses: $5 to $20.

Right on the border of the French Quarter, the open kitchen at **Palace Café,** 605 Canal St., at Chartres (© **504/523-1661**), serves contemporary Creole food with a big emphasis on seafood: catfish pecan meunière, andouille-crusted fish of the day, and lots more. Don't miss the white chocolate bread pudding. Dinner main courses: $11 to $25.

Outside the Quarter, at the corner of Washington Avenue and Coliseum Street in the Garden District, **Commander's Palace,** 1403 Washington Ave. (© **504/899-8221**), still reigns as one of the finest dining choices not only in New Orleans, but in the whole United States—the James Beard Foundation voted it the country's best restaurant in 1996. The cuisine is haute Creole. Try anything with shrimp or crawfish, or the Mississippi quail, or . . . oh, just try anything! Dinner main courses: $29 to $32.

SNACKS & SWEETS

Café du Monde, 800 Decatur St., right on the river (© **504/581-2914**), is basi-cally a 24-hour coffee shop that specializes in beignets, a square, really yummy French doughnut–type thing, hot and covered in powdered sugar. It's a great spot for people-watching, but if you don't want to wait for a table, you can always get a bag of beignets to go. Grab *lots* of napkins. Handi-Wipes would be a good idea too.

NEW ORLEANS AFTER DARK

Life in "The Big Easy" is conducive to all manner of nighttime entertainment, usually raucous. There's a reason why jazz was born in this town.

Do what most people do: Start at one end of **Bourbon Street** (say, around Iberville), walk down to the other end, and then turn around and do it again. Along the way, you'll hear R&B, blues, and jazz pouring out of dozens of bars, be beckoned by touts from the numerous strip clubs, and see one tiny little storefront stall after another sporting hand-lettered signs that say OUR BEER IS CHEAPER THAN NEXT DOOR. It's a scene. Bacchanalian? Yes. Will you spend time in Purgatory for it? Maybe, but it's loads of fun. Grab yourself a big $2 beer or one of the famous rum-based Hurricanes—preferably in a yard-long green plastic cup shaped like a Roswell alien—and join the party.

Most of the places in this section have a cover charge that varies depending on who's performing; some are free.

Preservation Hall, 726 St. Peter St., just off Bourbon (© **504/522-2841** during the day, 504/523-8939 after 8pm; www.preservationhall.com), is a deliberately shabby little hall with very few places to sit and no air-conditioning. Nonetheless, people usually pack the place to see the house band, a bunch of mostly older musicians who have been at this for eons. Don't request "When the Saints Go Marching In" 'cause the band won't play it—even classics get to be old smelly hats when you've played them 45,000 times. There's a $5 admission fee.

Close by, **Maison Bourbon,** 641 Bourbon St. (© **504/522-8818**), presents authentic and often fantastic Dixieland and traditional jazz. Stepping into the brick-walled room, or even just peering in from the street, takes you away from the mayhem outside. There's a one-drink minimum.

Lafitte's Blacksmith Shop, 941 Bourbon St. (© **504/523-0066**), is a French Quarter pub housed in an 18th-century Creole blacksmith shop that looks like only faith keeps it standing. Tennessee Williams used to hang out here.

If you're looking to get away from the Bourbon scene and hear some real brass-band jazz, head up to **Donna's,** 800 N. Rampart St., at the top of St. Ann Street (© **504/596-6914;** www.donnasbarandgrill.com). There's no better place to hear the authentic sound that made New Orleans famous. The cover varies, but is always reasonable.

Jazz, blues, and Dixieland pour out of the nostalgia-laden bar and concert hall **Tipitina's,** way out in the Uptown neighborhood at 501 Napoleon Ave. (© **504/891-8477;** www.tipitinas.com).

House of Blues, 225 Decatur St. (© **504/529-2583**), is one of the city's largest live-music venues. You stand and move among the several bars that pepper the club. There's also a restaurant.

One block beyond Esplanade, on the periphery of the French Quarter, **Snug Harbor,** 626 Frenchman St. (© **504/949-0696;** www.snugjazz.com), is a jazz bistro, a classic spot to hear modern jazz in a cozy setting. Sometimes R&B combos and blues are added to the program. There's a full dinner menu.

6 Galveston

Since the September 11, 2001, terrorist attacks, cruise lines have stepped up their search for additional homeports that will allow more Americans to drive to their ships rather than fly (in the process easing flight congestion to the big cruise ports of Miami and Ft. Lauderdale). This is old news, though, to Galveston, Texas, an island some 50 miles (80km) south of Houston, just off the mainland, which was already being developed as a promising alternative option for Caribbean-bound megaships. Ships departing from Galveston can reach the open sea in about 30 minutes, compared to several hours of lag time from the Port of Houston—which, like New Orleans, sits inland, on the edge of the Houston Ship Channel, above Galveston Bay. (The Port of Houston does have one advantage: It's closer to the airports. It takes 45 to 90 minutes to travel between the Port of Galveston and the airports, depending upon which airport you're using. Currently, Royal Olympic Cruises' *Olympia Voyager* is sailing out of Houston to the western Caribbean.)

The Port of Galveston offers one 132,000-square-foot (12,263 sq. m) cruise ship terminal. It was originally a cargo dock dating back to 1927, and in 1990 was renovated and converted into a cruise ship terminal, then refurbished and enhanced again to the tune of $10.6 million in 2000 when Carnival's *Celebration* moved there year-round. Carnival's *Jubilee* and Royal Caribbean's *Rhapsody of the Seas* are also now sailing out of Galveston to the western Caribbean year-round. Within walking distance of the terminal is the historic **Strand District,** Galveston's revitalized downtown, with shops, art galleries, museums, and eateries lining its quaint brick streets.

GETTING TO GALVESTON & THE PORT

The **Texas Cruise Ship Terminal** at the Port of Galveston is at Harborside Drive and 25th Street, on Galveston Island. It's reached via I-45 south from Houston. For information, call © **409/766-6113** or check out **www.portofgalveston. com** or **www.galveston.com.**

BY PLANE   You'll fly into one of two Houston airports: **William P. Hobby Airport** (south of downtown Houston, and about 31 miles/50km, or a 45-min. drive from the terminal) or **George Bush Intercontinental Airport** (just north of downtown Houston, and about 54 miles/87km, or an 80-min. drive from the terminal). Bush is the larger airport and it's international. If you've arranged air transportation and/or transfers through the cruise line, a cruise line representative will direct you to shuttle buses that take you to the port. Taxis are also available. **United Cab** (© 713/699-0000) charges $75 per carload to Hobby Airport and $119 to George Bush Intercontinental Airport. The following taxi companies provide service from the port to the airports only (not the other way around): **Busy Bee** (© 409/762-6666) for $65 to Hobby Airport and $90 to George Bush (each additional passenger is $5); **Quality Cab** (© **409/765-5555**) for $60 to Hobby and $110 to Bush; and **Yellow Cab Company** (© **409/763-3333**) for $60 to Hobby and $95 to Bush.

Just the Ticket transportation service (© **409/762-6622**) is a shuttle service operating 15-passenger vans and charging $45 per person between Hobby Airport and the port, and $70 per person between George Bush Intercontinental and the port. Discounts are offered for groups of five or more. **Galveston Limousine Service** (© **800/640-4826** or 409/744-5466) provides the same service, charging $25 per person to/from Hobby and $30 to/from Bush. Round-trip rates are $40 and $50, respectively. Both companies require reservations.

BY CAR   I-45 is the main artery for those arriving from the north. To get to the terminal, follow I-45 South to Exit 1C (at Harborside Dr./Hwy. 275); it's the first exit after the causeway. Turn left (east) onto Harborside Drive and continue for about 5 miles (8km) to the cruise terminal.

PARKING   Long-term parking at the port is $40 for a 4-night cruise, $45 for a 5-night cruise, and $60 for a 7-night cruise. The lots are one-third mile (0.5km) from the cruise ship terminal, and shuttle buses transport passengers between the lots and the terminal, where porters are available to carry luggage.

7 San Juan, Puerto Rico

In addition to being the embarkation port for a number of ships, San Juan is also a major port of call, so see "Puerto Rico," in chapter 5, for information on this city.

5

The Ports of Call

Here's the good news: There are no lousy Caribbean islands. Sure, depending on your likes and dislikes, you'll appreciate certain islands more than others. Some—like Key West, St. Thomas, and Nassau—are much more overrun with tourists than others, but then again, these islands appeal to shoppers, with their large variety of stores and bustling main streets. Others—Virgin Gorda, St. John, Jost Van Dyke, and Les Saintes, for instance—are quieter and more natural, and will appeal to those who are looking to walk along a deserted beach or take a drive along a lonely, winding road in the midst of pristine tropical foliage. Prices are high at some ports—like Bermuda, the U.S. Virgin Islands, St. Barts, St. Martin, and Aruba—and low at others—like Cozumel, Jamaica,

and the Grenadines. But no matter what you're preferences are, you'll want to make the most of the limited time you have in the ports.

Choosing activities to participate in aboard ship is one thing, but when the ship pulls up to a port of call, figuring out how to make the most of your limited time on land is a tougher endeavor. Should you take an organized tour or go off on your own? And just what are the best shore excursions? Where are the best beaches? Where's the shopping? Any good restaurants or bars nearby?

We'll answer all those questions and more, as we take you to 36 ports of call, mainly in the Caribbean, but also including the Bahamas, Mexico's Yucatán Peninsula, the Panama Canal, and Key West.

1 Port Strategies & Tips

SHORE EXCURSIONS VS. GOING IT ON YOUR OWN

The shore excursions offered by the cruise lines can be a wonderful and carefree way to get to know the islands, offering everything from island tours and snorkeling and sailing excursions (often with a rum-punch party theme) to more physically challenging pursuits like bicycle tours, hiking, kayaking, and horseback riding. But do you really *need* to sign up for them? The answer is, not everywhere. At some ports—Aruba, Curaçao, St. Thomas, St. Martin, Puerto Rico, Grand Cayman, and Grenada, for instance—your best bet is doing it on your own. So, in the following section, we'll advise you on which islands are good bets for solo exploring; tell you whether you should go it on foot or by taxi, motor scooter, ferry, or other form of transportation; and detail the best sights to see. One downside to exploring independently is that you'll be forgoing the kind of narrative you'd get from a guide, and may miss out on some of the historical, cultural, and other nuances of a particular island. On the other hand, you may find your own fascinating details, things that an organized tour might pass over. See the following page for a chart rating various aspects of each island—dining, shopping, activities close to the port, beaches and watersports. This is a good tool for deciding which ports interest you at a glance.

Tips **Booking Shore Excursions Early**

If you want to arrange a private custom-designed excursion for your family or group of friends, or just want to save a little money on a snorkeling trip in Cozumel, Florida-based **Port Promotions** (www. shoreexcursions. com) organizes shore excursions and allows you to book them online as late as a week before your cruise. You'll get a confirmation via email. Port Promotions often uses the same tour companies that the cruise lines do, though groups tend to be smaller and rates for Caribbean tours are about 10% cheaper. If you change your mind before the excursion, you can e-mail or call Port Promotions to get a refund.

In other ports, touring on your own could be an inefficient use of your time, entailing lots of hassles and planning, maybe costing more, and possibly incurring some risk (because of poor roads or driving conditions, for instance). In these cases, the shore excursions offered by the cruise lines are the way to go. Under each port review we'll describe the best excursions available.

Keep in mind that **shore excursion prices** vary from line to line, even for the exact same tour; the prices we've listed are typical and are adult rates; children's rates for many excursions are also offered, so just ask. Also note that some cruise lines may not offer all these tours, while others may offer even more. Note also that in some cases the excursions fill up fast, especially on the megaships, so don't dawdle in signing up. When you receive your cruise documents, or at the latest when you board the ship, you'll get a pamphlet with a listing of the excursions offered for your itinerary. Look it over, make your selections, and sign up on the first or second day of your cruise. In some cases, if a tour offered by your ship is booked up, you can try to book it independently once you get to port. The popular Atlantis submarine tour, for example—offered at Grand Cayman, Nassau, St. Thomas, and other islands—usually has an office/agent in the cruise terminals or nearby. If there's an excursion you absolutely can't miss, and you don't want to risk getting left out of, there are a few ways to book excursions before you sail. A company called **Port Promotions,** in Plantation, Florida, is now allowing travel agents and passengers to book shore excursions online (see box below for contact information). A few cruise lines have similar services—at press time, Royal Caribbean, Celebrity, and Princess offered pre-booking of shore excursions on their websites (www.royalcaribbean.com, www.celebritycruises.com, and www. princess.com) or via the printed forms sent with your cruise documents. Disney also allows guests to pre-book excursions by phone or fax.

If you want to **rent a car** in port, make reservations in advance. **Avis** (© **800/ 331-1212;** www.avis.com), **Budget** (© **800/472-3325;** www.drivebudget. com), and **Hertz** (© **800/654-3001;** www.hertz.com) all have offices on most of the Caribbean islands in this chapter; **Dollar** (© **800/800-4000;** www. dollar.com) and **National** (© **800/227-7368;** www.nationalcar.com) are less well represented in the region. See "Getting Around" in the individual port listings to see which companies have offices there. Also note that in certain ports we advise against renting at all.

DOCKING, DOLLARS & OTHER PORT DETAILS

ARRIVING IN PORT Most cruise ships arrive in port sometime before 10am, though this will vary slightly from line to line and port to port. If you're a U.S. citizen, you'll rarely have to clear Customs or Immigration, because your ship's purser has your passport or other ID and will have done all the paperwork for you. When local officials give the word, you just go ashore. Often, you can walk down the gangway right onto the pier, but if you're on a large cruise ship and the port isn't big enough, your ship will anchor offshore and ferry passengers to land via a small boat called a tender. In either case, you might have to wait in line to get ashore, but the wait will be longer if you have to tender in. Once ashore, even if you've come by tender, you aren't stuck there—tenders run back and forth on a regular basis, so you can return to the ship at any time for lunch, a nap, or whatever. Tenders all look pretty much alike, so you might be confused as to which one's heading to your ship, but officers are on duty to check your ID and make sure you get to the right boat.

SCHEDULING YOUR TIME ASHORE   All shore excursions are carefully organized to coincide with your time in port. If you're going it on your own, you can count on finding taxi drivers at the pier when your ship docks. In most cases it's a good idea to arrange with the driver to pick you up at a certain time to bring you back to the port. In most ports you can also rent a car, moped/scooter, or bicycle to get around.

CUSTOM EXCURSIONS   If you want to do something special in port— find a special restaurant for lunch or do some scuba diving, golf, tennis, horseback riding, or fishing—your best bet is doing a little research before you go—starting with this book. The smaller lines, whether high-end or adventure, will usually help you organize custom excursions, but you'll have less luck on the larger ships. While it can't hurt to talk with your cruise director or shore excursion manager beforehand, keep in mind that they'll most likely just tell you to sign up for one of their organized excursions and won't have the time or ability to help you arrange personal and private tours. For liability reasons, the excursion staff on many ships, especially the megas, are strongly discouraged from even making recommendations for bicycle rentals, scooters, etc.: If you fall off your bike and break your leg on an excursion not organized by the ship, cruise lines don't want to be held responsible.

Less formally, it can't hurt to ask your waiter, masseuse, or bartender about their favorite beaches, watering holes, and other things to do in port: Since they're often there week after week, they may know the islands you're visiting quite well.

It goes without saying that if you arrive at a port of call and find the harbor filled with ships, you can expect the shops, restaurants, beaches, and everything else to be crowded. For that reason, if you plan to arrange excursions on your own, try to make reservations early—either before your trip or at least before you land in port—since facilities and tours might be filled by passengers from other cruise ships or by land-based vacationers.

CALLING HOME   Prices for calling home from a cruise ship are sky high (anywhere from $4–$15 a min.), so it's a better idea to call from land, when you're in port. Most phones in port will take any phone card, but for some phones you'll need to purchase a local calling card from a vendor in port. We've included information on where to find phones in all the port reviews. Country codes are as follows: United States and Canada, 1; Australia, 61; New Zealand, 64; the United Kingdom, 44; and the Republic of Ireland, 353. Another option is using your ship's Internet center to keep in touch with folks at home via e-mail. It'll still cost you, but not nearly as much as you'll spend on phone calls. You'll also find Internet centers close to the docks in some ports.

Port	Review on Page	Overall Experience	Shore Excursions	Activities Close to Port	Beaches & Water Sports	Shopping	Dining/Bars
Antigua	p. 79	4	3	4	5	2	4
Aruba	p. 86	5	3	4	5	4	4
Bahamas: Nassau	p. 94	4	3	4	4	3	3
Bahamas: Freeport	p. 102	3	2	2	3	3	3
Barbados	p. 107	4	3	3	3	3	3
Belize	p. 114	4	5	2	4	2	3
Bequia	p. 121	4	2	4	4	2	4
Bonaire	p. 127	3	4	3	5	2	3
British Virgin Islands: Tortola	p. 136	4	3	3	3	2	3
British Virgin Islands: Virgin Gorda	p. 141	5	3	4	4	2	3
Cozumel (Mexico)	p. 146	4	5	4	2	4	3
Curaçao	p. 153	4	3	4	2	3	3
Dominica	p. 159	3	4	3	2	3	3
Grand Cayman	p. 167	5	5	4	5	4	3
Grenada	p. 171	5	3	4	3	3	3
Guadeloupe	p. 177	4	4	5	4	4	5
Jamaica: Ocho Rios	p. 186	4	5	4	3	2	3
Jamaica: Montego Bay	p. 191	4	5	4	3	3	3
Key West	p. 195	4	4	5	2	3	4
Les Saintes	p. 207	4	2	5	3	2	3
Martinique	p. 212	4	3	3	4	3	3
Nevis	p. 222	4	1	4	4	2	2
Playa del Carmen (Mexico)	p. 152	4	5	3	3	2	3
Puerto Rico	p. 228	5	2	5	3	4	4
St. Barts	p. 245	4	3	4	4	4	3
St. Croix	p. 250	4	4	4	4	5	3
St. John	p. 288	4	3	4	4	2	2
St. Kitts	p. 258	3	3	1	3	2	3
St. Lucia	p. 264	4	4	3	4	2	3
St. Martin	p. 272	4	3	4	4	4	4
St. Thomas	p. 278	4	4	4	4	5	3
Trinidad	p. 294	2	2	1	2	2	3
Tobago	p. 296	4	3	1	4	2	2

Frommer's Ratings: Caribbean Ports of Call

Ratings Guide: 1 = ★   2 = ★ ★   3 = ★ ★ ★   4 = ★ ★ ★ ★   5 = ★ ★ ★ ★ ★

5 stars is the highest rating.

Tips **Don't Forget Cash When Going Ashore**

It's happened to both of us and it's happened to our friends, so it can happen to you, too: After a few days of living cash-free aboard ship, it doesn't even cross your mind to grab the greenbacks when you're going ashore. You get there and realize you're penniless. It's soooo frustrating, especially if you've had to take a tender in from offshore. Don't let it happen to you.

DUTY-FREE SHOPPING The savings on duty-free merchandise can range from as little as 5% to as much as 50%. Unless there's a special sale being offered, many products carry comparable price tags from island to island. If you have particular goods you're thinking of buying duty-free, it pays to check prices at your local discount retailer before you leave home, so you'll know whether or not you're really getting a bargain. (Note that the U.S. dollar is widely accepted throughout the islands as well as in Bermuda, so even though we've listed each island's official local currency, there's rarely a need to exchange U.S. dollars. Credit cards and traveler's checks are also widely accepted.)

AVOIDING PROHIBITED MERCHANDISE You may be eyeing that gorgeous piece of **black-coral jewelry,** but did you know that it's illegal to bring many products made from coral and other marine animals back to the United States, because of laws prohibiting trade in endangered species? Remember, corals aren't rocks: They're living animals—a single branch of coral contains thousands of tiny coral animals, called polyps. The shopkeeper selling it won't tell you that, of course, and it may in fact be legal for him to sell it. Nonetheless, you will be in violation of U.S. and international law if you bring these items back to the States. If caught, you could face stiff penalties and have your treasured mementos confiscated.

Sea turtles, too, are highly endangered, and sea horses, while not yet protected by laws, are currently threatened with extinction. The best way to appreciate, remember and protect all of these natural beauties is with an underwater camera on a snorkeling expedition.

REBOARDING Most passengers start heading back to the ship around 4pm or not much later than 5. By 6 you're often sailing off to your next destination. In some cases—for instance, in Nassau, New Orleans, Key West, and the British Virgin Islands (for the smaller ships)—the ship may stay in port until after midnight so that passengers can stay ashore and enjoy the island's nightlife. When actually walking back aboard, you'll generally have to present your shipboard ID and another ID as well, except aboard some of the smaller ships.

If a shore excursion runs late, the ship will be held until the excursion's participants are back on board. It occasionally happens, though, that a passenger goes off on his or her own, has a little too much fun, and misses the boat. If it happens to you, don't panic: The cruise line's port agent (whose offices will be at or close to the pier) will be able to get you back aboard, though it'll cost you—you'll either have to charter a boat or pay for a flight to the next port of call.

THE CRUISE LINES' PRIVATE ISLANDS

Royal Caribbean, Princess, Disney, Holland America, Norwegian, and Costa all have private islands (or patches of islands) in the Bahamas that are included as a port of call on many of their Caribbean and Bahamas itineraries and are off-limits to anyone but the line's passengers. While completely lacking in any Caribbean culture, they do offer cruisers a guaranteed beach day with all the trimmings.

2 A Brief History of the Caribbean

Caribbean history reads like a Hollywood blockbuster—brutal conquests, devastating plagues, swashbuckling pirates, new frontiers, monumental sea battles, slave insurrections, and violent revolutions. Grab your popcorn.

PRE-COLUMBIAN CULTURES Every schoolchild learns that in 1492 Columbus sailed the ocean blue. He was a johnny-come-lately, of course—people lived in the Caribbean for hundreds, even thousands of years before Europeans arrived. Three major groups, all originally from South America, were there when Columbus arrived.

The least advanced of the native peoples, the **Ciboney,** were probably the first to arrive. Living primarily in rock shelters and caves, they formed small family groups, hunted turtles and reptiles, and collected shellfish, wild fruits, and herbs. Their rudimentary tools were made of stone.

The more advanced **Arawak** and **Carib** peoples had frequent contact with each other and shared many of the same material technologies. They farmed, hunted, and fished, and used similar methods to construct canoes, build huts, weave cloth, and make pottery. Both peoples cultivated root plants—yucca, yams, arrowroot, peanuts, peppers, and gourds—and seed crops like maize, beans, and squash. Pineapple and guava, shellfish, fish, iguanas, birds, and snakes provided additional sustenance. Men generally hunted and fished, while women farmed, cooked, wove cloth, and made household pottery and baskets.

The Arawak, by all accounts, were peaceful, gentle, and friendly. Women enjoyed considerable status, religion was based on the belief that spirits inhabited both humans and natural objects, and islands were divided into provinces ruled by chiefs.

Carib authority was less centralized. Independent villages were presided over by village chiefs, who came together to elect war chiefs for each island. Men lived together in communal houses and kept their wives, who they treated as servants, in separate huts. Because they resisted Spain's efforts to enslave them, the Carib were vilified as bloodthirsty savages by the Spanish. In fact, the word "cannibal" comes from the Spanish name for the tribe—*caribal.* There is no evidence that the Carib practiced cannibalism—the Spanish may have made the claim to justify their assault on the tribe. The Carib were more aggressive than the Arawak, who were frequently on the receiving end of Carib raids. However, when the French and English settled the Lesser Antilles (most of the Caribbean islands except Cuba, Jamaica and Hispaniolia) in the 1630s, the Carib were friendly and provided food for the starving adventurers—they became violent only after the Europeans attacked them

EUROPEAN "DISCOVERY" OF THE ISLANDS On October 12, 1492, Columbus became the first European to reach the New World, landing on Watling's Island in the Bahamas. This exploratory first voyage was followed in 1493 by a second and much larger expedition to establish a permanent foothold on the islands. On his second expedition, along with 1,500 men, Columbus brought horses, sheep, cattle, and hogs, as well as plants grown in Europe such as wheat, barley, grapes, and sugarcane. Landing first on Dominica, the fleet passed through and named the islands of the Lesser Antilles before arriving in Hispaniola (where Haiti and the Dominican Republic are located) in November 1494. Before returning to Spain, Columbus sighted Jamaica and explored Cuba.

ENSLAVEMENT OF THE INDIANS   The Spanish crown distributed land on the islands to individual settlers, who were expected to cultivate it for four years. In return, they received the use of the property in perpetuity. By the time Columbus returned on his third voyage in 1498, the system had been distorted considerably, with Indian communities forced to work the land as slave laborers. Without this slave system, the colonial economies certainly would have failed. The Spanish not only enslaved the local population, but eventually, if unintentionally, almost completely obliterated it by bringing in diseases that the native islanders had no immunity to.

DISEASE & DECIMATION   Prior to the 15th century, the peoples of Europe and Africa rarely mingled, and the indigenous peoples of the Americas existed in total isolation. Consequently, a distinctive disease environment developed on each continent. Until the Europeans and Africans arrived, a host of illnesses—among them smallpox, measles, typhus, yellow fever, malaria, and tuberculosis—were unknown in the New World. The native peoples had no natural immunity to these diseases, and when exposed to them, they died in staggering numbers. In 1492, as many as six million Arawak and Carib Indians lived in the Caribbean. Within twenty years, almost all were dead. Europeans and African slaves gave each other diseases as well, and as many as a third of both groups died during their first two years on the islands.

GOLD FEVER   The Spanish were interested in only one thing in the New World: gold. Wherever gold was found, settlers rushed in, but the meager gold sources on any given island was quickly exhausted. Undaunted, the Spanish would move on to another island, with Indian slaves in tow. Eventually, they searched farther, into Mexico, Panama, and Peru, where they hit the jackpot: the unparalleled treasures of the Aztec and Inca.

Once the enormous value of the gold and silver in Mexico and Peru became clear, the Spanish ignored the Antilles except as a source of slaves. King Ferdinand authorized slaving expeditions to the Lesser Antilles and the Curaçao group in 1511. By 1520, the northern (or Leeward) islands from the Virgins to Barbuda (located next to Antigua), except for Saint Kitts and Nevis, were depopulated. The inhabitants of the Curaçao group, Barbados, Saint Lucia, and Tobago were also forcibly removed, and on the remaining islands, the Carib retreated to the mountainous interiors, where they resisted would-be enslavers with considerable skill.

TREASURE SHIPS & PIRATES   Aside from providing slaves, the islands remained important because Spanish treasure fleets had to pass by them on their way from Mexico and Peru to Seville, the sole port in Spain authorized to receive the gold, silver, and other riches from the New World. Rulers of other European states, envious of Spain's wealth, encouraged their subjects to plunder Spanish ships. Piracy became an accepted business, and thousands of buccaneer ships, sailing from ports in France, Britain, and the Netherlands, attacked Spanish ships, as well as ports in the Caribbean and along the coast of Central America. **Sir Francis Drake** took the greatest booty, capturing an entire year's yield of Peruvian silver in 1573. To protect its treasure fleets from pirates, Spain closed its American empire to outside trade, forbidding its American colonies from trading with any other European powers. Spain also limited ocean crossings to

Europe—only two heavily guarded convoys made the trip each year. While great forts were built on gold- and silver-loaded islands along the fleet route, other island settlements remained unprotected, and had to fend for themselves when buccaneers came onto their shores to help themselves to food, water and any other supplies that they needed on their long journey. Spain's focus on Peru and Mexico precluded state development of the Caribbean colonies, and for three centuries, most inhabitants of the forgotten islands earned modest livings as farmers and ranchers.

COLONISTS FROM NORTHERN EUROPE   The British, French, and Dutch established permanent colonies on the islands in the 1620s, initially concentrating on the smaller, still unoccupied islands of the eastern Caribbean, and moving west into the Greater Antilles (Cuba, Jamaica and Hispaniola) after 1650. The success of these efforts often depended on events in Europe, and islands, like chips in a poker game, often changed hands during wars on the Continent. Governments, more interested in European affairs and with no money to spend on colonial development, played only a limited role in the initial settlement and economic development of the islands. Individual adventurers, often acting for groups of merchants, established the first Dutch, French, and British colonies. Governments gave adventurers exclusive licenses to exploit specific areas in return for a share of the profit.

In 1618, the Dutch began to challenge Spanish control of the Caribbean by establishing their own colonies and trade in the region. During the 17th century, the Netherlands led all other European nations in manufacturing, commerce, and finance capitalism, and it soon dominated trade with the Far East, Africa, and the Caribbean. The **Dutch West India Company,** chartered in 1621, had a state-granted 25-year monopoly in the Americas. Between 1625 and 1635, Dutch maritime forces changed the balance of power in the Caribbean, making it possible for Dutch traders to control most of the region's commerce for decades. The Dutch established colonies on Sint Maarten, Saint Eustatius, Saba, Curaçao, Aruba, and Bonaire. Eventually the Dutch West India Company's fortunes waned and its monopoly expired after investors became displeased by the venture's profits. Individual traders then moved in to fill the void. The **Dutch West India Company** reorganized to focus on the trade in West African slaves and goods to Caribbean colonies settled and controlled by other European powers.

New waves of British and French marauders followed the Dutch to the Caribbean. Tropical products such as **tobacco** and **sugar** were fetching high prices in Europe, and few investments at home promised comparable profits. The prospect of economic gain was the primary lure, but adventurers, fame-seekers, and religious nationalists had their own motives for going to the Caribbean. The British and French claimed many of the same islands, but speaking in very general terms, the British settled St. Kitts, Barbados, Nevis, Antigua, Montserrat, Anguilla, the British Virgin Islands, and Jamaica, while the French established colonies on Guadeloupe, Martinique, Saint Christophe (the French name for St. Kitts), and what is today Haiti. The Danish (St. Thomas, St. John, and St. Croix) and Swedish (St. Barts) came later and in much smaller numbers.

ENORMOUS SUGAR PROFITS   The Caribbean enjoyed relative peace and prosperity for much of the 1700s, and the region's economy—especially the sugar industry—grew rapidly. During the 18th century, the islands produced 80% to 90% of the sugar consumed in Western Europe. Demand encouraged planters to develop large-scale plantations and ushered in a new era of slavery. Profits and associated tax revenues convinced British and French politicians that both sugar and slavery were essential to their national economies.

SLAVERY ON AN UNPRECEDENTED SCALE   Economically, socially, and politically, slavery dominated the sugar islands to an extent never matched in human history. By the 1750s, almost nine out of ten people on all the islands where sugar was grown were slaves. Conditions were brutal: Heat, disease, and backbreaking work killed slaves before they could reproduce and sugar estates could operate only by constantly importing enormous numbers of new slaves from Africa. Except for the Spanish, all the colonial powers supported and were directly involved in the slave trade. The genocide began even before the human cargo from Africa arrived on the islands. The trip across the Atlantic—the Middle Passage, as it was known—claimed the lives of millions. Shackled together, subsisting on tainted water and food of minimal nutritional value, and exposed to disease, 20% of the slaves died aboard ship. As many as another third, already weakened by confinement and malnutrition, perished in their first few years on the islands. And three out of four babies born to slaves died before the age of five.

ENGLAND & FRANCE COMPETE FOR DOMINANCE   From 1740, Great Britain and France fought throughout the world to gain commercial and colonial supremacy. The Caribbean was a major theater of battle, but the struggle was worldwide in scope, affecting Europe, North America, Africa, and India as well. Caribbean islands, often used as bargaining chips, changed flags frequently as the balance of world power shifted between France and England. But the swing of the pendulum affected Caribbean societies and economies only superficially. Battles were fought by soldiers, not civilians. Crops and plantations were largely unscathed, and planters essentially maintained power over island politics regardless of which flag happened to be flying at any particular time. Slaves, of course, remained slaves whether an island was designated as British or French.

Islands held by both sides were vulnerable to attack, as neither side was willing to spend the huge sums needed to protect them. The British maintained two permanent ports in the region; France had none, electing instead to send ships from Europe for specific purposes. The French fleets arrived fresh from the dockyard and in good shape, while the British ships quickly rotted under the tropical conditions. Once they arrived in the region, however, the French fleets quickly ran out of food, while British ships obtained provisions from their permanent naval stations. Disease also played a role: Any victory had to be won almost immediately, as a long siege led to staggering death rates from illnesses.

SLAVE RESISTANCE   During the height of the slave era, blacks outnumbered whites ten to one on most islands. Individual slaves frequently ran away, and groups of slaves planned escapes and uprisings. Slaves rebelled much more frequently in the Caribbean than in the United States, and thousands joined in widespread insurrection on dozens of occasions, destroying plantations and killing slave owners. But only the 1791 revolt on Saint-Domingue (now Haiti), led by **Toussaint L'Ouverture,** culminated in permanent liberation, with the establishment of an independent Haiti in 1804. On other islands, maroons— escaped slaves who banded together and formed their own independent communities—sought refuge in mountains and areas of dense brush and broken terrain. But as planters cut down forests to create new cane estates, maroons fled to Dominica and Saint Vincent, two lush, mountainous islands designated as

Carib territory. Escaped slaves on the flatter, drier islands had no hiding places at all.

ABOLITION OF SLAVERY & INFLUX OF INDENTURED SERVANTS

Slavery dominated every facet of life in the Caribbean islands—it made sugar plantations possible, shaped social and familial relations, and dominated the laws and politics of the region. The abolition of slavery, therefore, represented a cataclysmic change in island life. In 1833, pressured by more frequent slave rebellions, and by the large segment of the British population who increasingly found slavery morally repugnant, cruel, and economically inefficient, England permanently ended slavery in its Caribbean colonies. Inspired by the success of British abolitionists, French intellectuals pressed for emancipation, winning the fight in 1848. The Dutch abolished slavery in 1863. Many freed slaves moved off the plantations to squat on vacant land, and the loss of free labor temporarily crippled sugar production. To fill the labor void, planters recruited indentured workers (who labored under contract), primarily from India, but also from China, Indochina, and Africa's west coast.

INDEPENDENCE & ECONOMIC CHALLENGES

At the end of the 19th century, the United States succeeded the European powers as the main economic and political force in the Caribbean. Under the centralized political systems in place until the 1950s, laws governing the region continued to be made in London, Paris, and the Hague, but after almost a century of economic decline on the islands, it was American capital that provided the means to rebuild the sugar, coffee, and banana industries. And American military power, protecting American commercial interests in the region, intervened in Cuba, Haiti, and the Dominican Republic.

In the years between the two world wars, island-wide political movements developed, paving the way for independence. Since World War II, some islands have become integral parts of larger nations with constitutional arrangements that give their peoples management of local affairs. Puerto Rico and the Virgin Islands entered into relationships with the United States, the French Antilles were integrated into France, and the Dutch West Indies became an autonomous part of the Kingdom of the Netherlands. The major British colonies have become totally independent states, while smaller islands remaining within the British sphere enjoy home rule.

The Caribbean islands have different languages, political systems, and cultural traditions, but all face similar economic problems as they search for new sources of income to replace the declining sugar industry. Tourism is now the region's main business.

3 Antigua

Though it's the largest of the British Leeward Islands, Antigua (pronounced On-TEE-*gah,* not An-TEE-*gwa*) is still only 23km (14 miles) long and 18km (11 miles) wide, and offers little of the polish or glitz of some Caribbean islands. And that's its greatest asset: serenity. Nice, relaxing beaches are close to port; **St. John's,** the main town, is sleepy and undemanding; and the locals, usually friendly, sometimes wary, are easygoing. Sure, there are things to do, but nothing will raise your blood pressure. Close to port, you can shop lazily in historic, restored warehouses that now feature boutiques and restaurants; spend half an hour or so at a museum to get a sense of Antigua's past; or climb a gentle hill to the massive cathedral overlooking town. Not all of St. John's is charming, but the town is full of cobblestone sidewalks, weather-beaten wooden houses, and louvered Caribbean verandas. The island's British accent is another plus. Antigua has been independent since 1981, but the U.K. legacy lives on: Driving is on the left, half of the tourists are subjects of the queen, every little village has an Anglican church, and the island's greatest passion is for the sport of cricket.

Away from St. John's, the rolling, rustic island boasts important historic sites and lots of pretty beaches. On the southern coast, **Nelson's Dockyard,** once Britain's main naval station in the Lesser Antilles, is now a well-maintained national park. Tucked away in the arid, grassy interior, **Betty's Hope,** with its picturesque windmills, conjures up Antigua's sugar plantation past. And the **Wallings Conservation Area,** in the island's southwestern, volcanic section, is the best example of the moist forests that covered Antigua before Europeans cleared the land for agriculture.

Antigua cashed in on sugar and cotton production for years. Today tourism is the main industry. Most Antiguans are descendants of African slaves brought over centuries ago to labor in the fields. People of European, Asian, and Middle Eastern extraction are also represented in the population of 68,000.

COMING ASHORE   Most cruise ships dock at **Heritage Quay** (pronounced *key*) in St. John's, the island's capital and only town of any size. Heritage Quay and the adjacent **Redcliffe Quay** are the main shopping areas, but duty-free stores, restaurants, taxis, and other services can be found in the surrounding blocks as well. When several ships are in port, some dock at the **Deep Water Harbour Terminal,** 1.5km (a mile) from St. John's. From there, you can either walk or take a short taxi ride into town. A handful of smaller vessels drop anchor at English Harbour, on the south coast.

Credit-card phone booths can be found on the dock, at both quays, and at Deep Water Harbour. If you want a more comfortable, air-conditioned place to make calls, try the Kinko's-like **Parcel Plus** (© 268/462-4854) at 14 Redcliffe St. (in Redcliffe Quay), where you can also check your e-mail ($3 for 15 min.). **Cable & Wireless** (© 268/480-4237), on the corner of Long and Thames streets, sells prepaid phone cards for as little as $4.

You'll find **ATMs** at both quays and at the corner of Thames and St. Mary streets.

LANGUAGE   Antigua is a former British colony, so the official language is **English,** often spoken with a musical West Indian lilt.

CURRENCY   Although the **Eastern Caribbean dollar** (EC$2.70 = $1 U.S.; EC$1 = 37¢ U.S.) is Antigua's official currency, the U.S. dollar is readily accepted by most shopkeepers and cab drivers, and almost all businesses post their prices in U.S. currency. Prices quoted in this section are in U.S. dollars. Credit cards and traveler's checks are accepted by most tourist-oriented businesses as well.

INFORMATION   The **Antigua and Barbuda Department of Tourism,** at Nevis Street and Friendly Alley in St. John's (© 268/462-0480), is open Monday through Friday from 8am to 4:30pm. Before you leave home, contact the Department of Tourism's New York office (© 888/268-4227 or 212/541-4117; www.interknowledge.com/antigua-barbuda).

CALLING FROM THE U.S.   When calling Antigua from the U.S., simply dial "1" before the numbers listed throughout this section.

GETTING AROUND

BY TAXI Taxis meet every cruise ship. Although meters are nonexistent, rates are fixed by the government, and are posted at the taxi stand at the end of Heritage Quay's pedestrian mall. From the cruise ship dock, it's $10 to Dickenson Bay, $20 to Betty's Hope, $22 to Nelson's Dockyard, and $25 to Devil's Bridge. Settle on a fare (and the currency) before hopping in. Drivers often double as tour guides: For this added service, expect to pay about $20 per hour for up to four people, with a 2-hour minimum. Tip between 10% and 15% for all rides.

BY BUS Buses are cheap (little more than $1 to almost anywhere on the island), but service is erratic. The privately operated vehicles, mostly 12-seat vans (all have license plates beginning with "A" or "B"), run from early morning until about 6pm. If you're adventurous and want to chew the fat with Antiguan villagers, give it a whirl.

There are two bus stations in St. John's: East Bus Station, on Independence Avenue, serves the north and east; West Bus Station, near St. John's market, is the terminus for routes to the south and west (and English Harbour).

BY RENTAL CAR Driving is on the left side. Most roads are decent, but some are narrow and chock-full of potholes. Inadequate signage is a problem island-wide. On the bright side, you'll never have to worry about traffic jams. **Avis, Budget, Hertz,** and **National** all operate on the island. Your valid driver's license and a local temporary driving permit ($20, available from all rental agencies) are required.

Frommer's Favorite Antigua Experiences

Sand, Sun & Sloth: It's your choice: A bustling, social strand or a tranquil, private refuge. Either is within easy reach of the dock. (See "Beaches," below.)

Salt, Sailors & Swashbucklers: Nelson's Dockyard, on Antigua's southern coast, is a must for history buffs. Colonial forts guard the narrow passage into the protected harbor where the British, beginning in the 1700s, maintained their most important naval station in the Lesser Antilles. Like a Caribbean version of Colonial Williamsburg, the national park, with its many restored buildings, evokes another era. (See "On Your Own: Beyond the Port Area," below.)

SHORE EXCURSIONS OFFERED BY THE CRUISE LINES

Four-Wheel-Drive Island Tour ($55–$64, 3 hr.): Tour the island's only remaining rain forest via a four-wheel-drive vehicle, and stop at the ruins of forts, sugar mills, and plantation houses. The excursion includes beach time.

Nelson's Dockyard at English Harbour ($37–$39, 3 hr.): After traversing the island's hilly countryside, you'll visit the site of the planet's last surviving, working Georgian dockyard. Many colonial buildings still stand, including forts, residences, and barracks, and several have been converted into restaurants, hotels, shops, and museums. The sea vistas are impressive.

Catamaran Tour ($39–$49, 3 hr.): Sail along the coast with time to swim, sunbathe, and snorkel. Lunch and equipment are included.

Jolly Roger Cruise ($33–$39, 4 hr.): Aboard this wooden "pirate ship," you can take in some of the island's coastal sights, snorkel, dance on the poop deck, limbo, and walk the plank. Drinks and buffet lunch are included.

EXCURSIONS OFFERED BY LOCAL AGENCIES

Catamaran Cruises: Kokomo Cat Cruises (© 268/462-7245) and **Wadadli Cats** (© 268/462-4792) offer different all-day catamaran cruises every day except Monday. Prices, which include an open bar, buffet lunch, and snorkeling equipment, range from $60 to $90 (children under 12 half-price, under 2 free). Check, though, to make sure you'll be back in time to reboard your cruise ship before it leaves.

Miscellaneous Tours: Several reputable operators offer outback eco-adventures, Jeep safaris, kayak and snorkeling excursions, and bus tours of the island. Prices range, and discounts for children under 12 are common. Inquire at **Antigua Destination Planners** (© 268/463-1944), **Paradise Island Tours** (© 268/462-7280), and **Wadadli Island Tours** (© 268/773-0367).

ON YOUR OWN: WITHIN WALKING DISTANCE

St. John's has a number of attractions that can be easily reached on foot. To your right, just as you pass through immigration formalities, **Redcliffe Quay** is Antigua's most interesting shopping complex. Most of the sugar, coffee, and tobacco produced on the island in years past was stored in the warehouses here, and before slavery was abolished on the island in 1834, the area witnessed slave auctions. The restored buildings, with their stone foundations, wooden-slat sidings, colorful shutters, and red corrugated metal roofs, now house an array of boutiques and restaurants. For more local color, turn right (south) once you've reached Market Street and walk 5 blocks to the **Public Market.** The roof of the enclosed structure casts a strange color on the vendors' wares below, but it's still the best place to sample locally produced fruits and vegetables or to pick up some Antiguan pottery or baskets. It's at its most animated early in the morning, especially on Fridays and Saturdays. Across the street, next to the West Bus Station, fishermen hawk their catch every morning at the waterfront **Fish Market.** Chances are slim that you'll buy anything here, but stop by for the salty and sometimes saucy scene. Next retrace your steps on Market Street, walking north to the intersection of Long Street, where you'll find the **Museum of Antigua and Barbuda** (© 268/462-4930). Although not the plushest exhibition space in the Caribbean, the museum traces the history of the nation from its geological birth to the present day. Housed in a former courthouse, a neo-Classical structure built in 1750, its exhibits include pre-Columbian tools and artifacts, a replica of an Arawak wattle-and-daub hut, African-Caribbean pottery, and sections dedicated to the island's naval, sugar, and slavery eras. It's open Monday to Friday from 8:30am to 4pm; Saturday from 10am to 2pm. Admission is free, but a donation of $2 is requested. A couple of blocks uphill from the museum, bordered by Church, Long, and Newgate streets, **St. John's Anglican Cathedral** (© 268/462-4686) dominates St. John's skyline with its 70-foot-high, aluminum-capped twin spires. The original St. John's, a simple wooden structure built in 1681, was replaced in 1720 by a brick building, which was destroyed during an 1843 earthquake. Upon its completion in 1847, the present baroque structure was not universally appreciated: Ecclesiastical architects criticized it as being like "a pagan temple with two dumpy pepperpot towers." The cavernous interior is entirely encased in pitch pine, a construction method intended to secure the building from hurricanes and earthquakes.

ON YOUR OWN: BEYOND THE PORT AREA

One of the major historical attractions of the eastern Caribbean, **Nelson's Dockyard National Park** (© 268/460-1379) lies 18km (11 miles) southeast of St. John's, alongside one of the world's best-protected natural harbors. English ships used the site as a refuge from hurricanes as early as 1671, and the dockyard played a major role during the 18th century, an era of privateers, pirates, and great sea battles. Admiral Nelson's headquarters from 1784 to 1787, the restored dockyard today remains the only Georgian naval base still in use. At its heart, the **Dockyard Museum** (© 268/460-8181), housed in a former Naval Officers' House built in 1855, traces the history of the site from its beginning as a British Navy stronghold to its development as a national park and yachting center. Nautical memorabilia compose much of the display. Uphill and east of the Dockyard, the **Dow's Hill Interpretation Center** (© 268/460-2777) features an entertaining 20-minute multimedia overview of Antiguan history and an observation platform that affords a 360-degree view of the park. Farther uphill, Palladian arches mark the **Blockhouse,** a military fortification built in 1787 that included officers' quarters and a powder magazine. For an eagle's-eye view of English Harbour, continue to the hill's summit, to the **Shirley Heights Lookout** (© 268/460-1785). Fortified to defend the precious cargo in the harbor below, Fort Shirley's barracks, arched walkways, batteries, and powder magazines are scattered around the hilltop. The Lookout, with its view of the French island of Guadeloupe, was the main signal station used to warn of approaching hostile ships.

The grounds of the national park, which represent 10% of Antigua's total land area, are well worth exploring. Bordered on one side by sandy beaches, the park is blanketed in cactus, tamarind, cinnamon, and turpentine trees, and mangroves that shelter African cattle egrets. An array of **nature trails,** which take anywhere from 30 minutes to 5 hours to walk, meander through the vegetation and offer vistas of the coast. One trail climbs to **Fort Berkeley,** built in 1704 to protect the harbor's entrance. Admission, which is $3 for adults (children under 12 are free), covers the Dockyard, the Dockyard Museum, Dow's Hill Interpretation Center, the Blockhouse, Shirley Heights, and the rest of the park. The complex is open daily from 9am to 5pm, and is within walking distance of cruise ships that dock at English Harbor. Free guided tours of the dockyard last 15 to 20 minutes; tipping is discretionary.

To see what's billed as the only operational 18th-century sugar mill in the Caribbean, visit **Betty's Hope,** not far from Pares village on the island's east side (© 268/462-1469). On-site are twin mills, the remnants of a boiling house, and a small visitor center, which opens its doors Tuesday through Saturday from 10am till 4pm. Gardeners should be able to spot golden seal bushes, neem trees, and wild tamarinds on the rolling hills. Serene cows saunter lazily on the grounds. Not far from Betty's Hope, on the extreme eastern tip of the island, **Devil's Bridge** is one Antigua's most picturesque natural wonders. Over the centuries, powerful Atlantic breakers, gathering strength over the course of their 4,828km (3,000-mile) run from Africa, have carved out a natural arch in the limestone coastline and created blowholes through which the surf spurts skyward at high tide.

Another option for nature lovers, **Wallings Conservation Area** (© 268/462-1007) is Antigua's largest remaining tract of tropical rain forest. Located in the southwest, this lush wilderness area features three hiking trails and numerous opportunities to spot some of Antigua's nonhuman inhabitants: birds (purple-throated caribs, Antillean crested hummingbirds, broadwinged hawks), mammals (mongooses, bats), amphibians (tree frogs), and reptiles (lizards, snakes). Vegetation includes strangler fig, hog plum, black loblolly, mango, and silk cotton trees, as well as numerous epiphytes. If you've spent your day at Nelson's Dockyard, pass through the area on the way back to your ship via the circular **Fig Tree Drive.** Although full of potholes in places, this is the island's most scenic drive. It wends through the tropical forest, passing fishing villages, frisky goats, and old sugar mills along the way.

SHOPPING

Most shops of interest in St. John's are clustered in Heritage Quay and Redcliffe Quay, and on St. Mary's Street, all within easy walking distance of the cruise ship docks. Duty-free items include English woolens and linens, as well as local pottery, straw work, and rum.

Redcliffe Quay, to your right as you pass through customs, was a slave-trading and warehouse district before abolition. Tastefully renovated, it now contains interesting specialty shops, including **Jacaranda** on Redcliffe Street (© 268/462-1888), which sells batik clothing, spices, and Caribbean art; **The Goldsmitty** on Redcliffe Street (© 268/462-4601), which offers handmade gold jewelry; and **The Map Shop** on St. Mary's Street (© 268/462-3993), which stocks old and new map prints, sea charts, and Caribbean literature.

Located at the cruise dock, **Heritage Quay** is a run-of-the-mill shopping center with 40 duty-free shops and a vendors' hall.

The best place to find authentic Caribbean souvenirs in the Nelson's Dock-yard area is **Sofa** (© **268/463-0610**), which is housed in a renovated shed in Falmouth Harbour. The eclectic collection of handmade, mostly local products here includes hot sauces, arts and crafts, housewares, and garden items.

BEACHES
Antiguans claim that the island is home to 365 beaches, one for each day of the year. True or not, all of them are public, and quite a few are spectacular.

Closest to St. John's, **Fort James Beach,** located 5 minutes and a $7 cab fare from the cruise dock, is popular with both locals and tourists. The cordoned area is always safe, but farther from shore, undercurrents are occasionally strong. Volleyball and cricket are daily happenings. You can rent umbrellas and beach chairs, and the open-air restaurant/bar allows you to spend every minute outdoors. For a change of pace, hike up the hill to explore the authentically derelict ruins of **Fort James,** which once protected St. John's harbor. Another restaurant/bar at the summit offers splendid views of the area.

A bit farther north, a $10 cab ride from the dock, the 1km (half-mile) long beach at **Dickenson Bay** is the island's most bustling strand, with numerous hotels, restaurants, and watersports. It's the place to watch people, try out some watersports equipment, or just bake in a social environment. The water is calm, drinking and eating options abound, and chairs and umbrellas are available for rent.

Pleasant, picturesque spots on the less-developed southwest coast include unspoiled **Darkwood Beach** and nearby **Turner's Beach.** Showers, snorkeling equipment, and chairs are available. Restaurants serve fresh seafood, while bars keep you hydrated.

If you crave complete peace and quiet, head to Antigua's most beautiful beach, at **Half Moon Bay.** Isolated at the island's southeast extreme, this expanse is virtually undeveloped. Waves at the beach's center are great for bodysurfing, while the quieter eastern side is better for children and snorkeling. There's a restaurant and bar near the parking lot.

SPORTS
GOLF   The 18-hole, par-70 **Cedar Valley Golf Club,** Friar's Hill Road (© **268/462-0161**), is a 5-minute, $10 taxi ride from the cruise dock. The 5,616m (6,142-yd.) golf course has panoramic views of the northern coast. Greens fees for 18 holes and use of a cart are $65. Club rental is $15.

SCUBA DIVING & SNORKELING   Antigua's dive sites include reefs, wall drops, caves, and shipwrecks. To arrange a dive contact **Dive Antigua,** at the north end of Dickenson Bay (© **268/462-3483**). A two-tank dive is $72. Reef snorkeling is $26.

WATERSPORTS   Tony's Watersports (© **268/462-6326**) and **Sea Sports** (© **268/462-3355**), both located at Dickenson Bay Beach, offer a full range of watersports equipment. Prices are negotiable depending on season and demand, but sample fares for jet skis are $35 per half hour, for water-skiing $25 per lap, and for tubing $25.

WINDSURFING   Windsurfing Antigua Watersports (© **268/461-9463**), also at Dickenson Bay Beach, specializes in 2-hour introductory lessons ($60) that are limited to four people. Experienced wind sailors can rent a full rig for the day at $50, or for half a day at $40. The operation also rents Sunfish ($20 per hr.), kayaks ($10 per hr.), and snorkel gear ($10 for the day).

GREAT LOCAL RESTAURANTS & BARS

Lunch menus on the island focus on West Indian cuisine, but you can get sandwiches, salads, and burgers as well. Antigua's **local beer** is Wadadli, the island's Carib name. The **local rum** is Cavalier.

There's no better place to watch the street life of St. John's than the second-floor wraparound veranda at **Hemingway's,** on St. Mary's Street (© **268/462-2763**). Across from Heritage Quay, on the main road leading from the dock, it serves tasty salads, sandwiches, burgers, seafood, and refreshing tropical drinks. The cheerful **Redcliffe Tavern,** in Redcliffe Quay on Redcliffe Street (© **268/461-4557**), occupies a rustic, 250-year-old warehouse and offers tables interspersed with gargantuan machinery from old factories, printing houses, and pumping stations. Lunch entrees include pineapple stuffed with crab and spicy jerk chicken with plantains, as well as salads, soups, and sandwiches. Across Redcliffe Street but slightly closer to the waterfront, **Commissioner Grill** (© **268/462-1883**) is sunny and colorful. One of the few eateries in town that's open on Sunday, its menu features West Indian specialties at moderate prices. If you've opted to spend all day at the beach, your best bet at Dickenson Bay is **Coconut Beach Restaurant** (© **268/462-1538**), a quiet, open-air beachside refuge at the strand's southern extreme, complete with palm trees and superb seafood.

If you're in English Harbour, stop for a lunch break at the rustic **Admiral's Inn,** in Nelson's Dockyard (© **268/460-1027**). Built in 1788, this restored brick building originally stored barrels of pitch, turpentine, and lead used to repair ships. The menu changes daily but usually features pumpkin soup and main courses such as local red snapper, grilled steak, and lobster.

4 Aruba

More of a desert island than a rain forest, Aruba has unwaveringly sunny skies, warm temperatures, and cooling breezes, along with some of the best beaches in the Caribbean—or in the world, for that matter: miles of white sugary sand; turquoise and aqua seas; warm, gentle surf; and plenty of space.

If you tire of lolling on the beach, there are scuba diving, snorkeling, great windsurfing, and all the other watersports you expect from a sun-and-sea vacation. On land, you can golf, ride a horse, or drive an all-terrain vehicle over the island's wild-and-woolly outback. Away from the beach, Aruba's full of cactus, iguanas, and strange boulder formations. Contrasting sharply with the southern shoreline's beaches, the north coast features craggy limestone cliffs, sand dunes, and crashing breakers.

Focused on shopping? The concentration of stores and malls in Oranjestad, the island's capital, is as impressive as any in the Caribbean. In between purchases, try your luck at one of the island's dozen **casinos;** two are just steps away from your ship. Or maybe grab a bite to eat: Unlike the so-so fare found in most of the Caribbean, Aruba's culinary offerings are diverse, inventive, and often outstanding.

Aruba's still part of the Netherlands, so there's a Dutch influence, which adds a nice European flavor. There are a few small museums, and some centuries-old indigenous rock glyphs and paintings, but nobody comes to Aruba for culture or history.

Only 32km (20 miles) long and 9.5km (6 miles) across at its widest point, the island is slightly larger than Washington, D.C. It's the westernmost of the Dutch ABC islands—Aruba, Bonaire, and Curaçao—and lies less than 32km (20 miles)

north of Venezuela. Aruba's capital and largest city, **Oranjestad,** is on the island's southern coast and pretty far to the west.

The Arubans are as friendly as can be. With little history of racial or cultural conflicts, locals have no cause for animosity. And everybody speaks English, as well as Dutch, Spanish, and Papiamento, the local patois.

COMING ASHORE Cruise ships arrive at the **Aruba Port Authority,** a modern terminal with a tourist information booth, phones, ATMs, and plenty of shops. From the pier it's a 5-minute walk to the **shopping districts** of downtown Oranjestad.

LANGUAGE The official language is **Dutch,** but nearly everybody speaks **English.** The language of the street is often **Papiamento,** a patois that combines various European, African, and indigenous American languages. **Spanish** is also widely spoken.

Frommer's Favorite Aruba Experiences

Pretend You're Neil Armstrong: Alien boulders and stark terrain mark Aruba's northern coast, making you feel like a visitor to the moon. The roads are unpaved but easy to navigate in an all-terrain vehicle. You can stop at a lighthouse, an old chapel, and the ruins of a gold-smelting factory, but the major attractions are supplied by nature. (See "Shore Excursions Offered by the Cruise Lines," below, and "On Your Own: Touring by Rental Jeep," below)

Make Like Captain Nemo: Submerge 45m (150 ft.) beneath the sea in a modern submarine to marvel at nature's underwater splendor. (See "Shore Excursions Offered by the Cruise Lines," below.)

CURRENCY   The **Aruba florin (AFl)** is the official currency, but U.S. dollars are as widely accepted; and most items and services are priced in both currencies. Traveler's checks and major credit cards are almost universally accepted as well. The exchange rate is relatively stable at about 1.77 AFl to U.S.$1 (1 AFl = 56¢ U.S.). Prices quoted in this section are in U.S. dollars.

INFORMATION   For information, go to the **Aruba Tourism Authority,** 172 L. G. Smith Blvd., Oranjestad (© **297/8-23777;** www.aruba.com). It's open Monday to Saturday from 9am to 5pm.

CALLING FROM THE U.S.   When calling Aruba from the U.S., dial the international access code (011) before the numbers listed in this section.

GETTING AROUND

BY RENTAL CAR   Excellent roads connect major tourist attractions, and all the major rental companies accept valid U.S. or Canadian driver's licenses. Rent a four-wheel-drive vehicle for the rough roads in the outback. **Avis, Budget, Dollar, Hertz,** and **National** all have offices here.

BY MOTORCYCLE OR BIKE   Scooters and motorcycles are impractical unless you plan to stick to paved roads. They're available at **George's Cycle Center,** L.G. Smith Blvd. 136 (© **297/8-25975**) Scooters rent for $30 per day, while motorcycles go for $45 up to $100 for a Harley. You can rent mountain bikes at **Semver Cycle Rental,** Noord 22 (© **297/8-66851**), where rates start at $25 per day.

BY TAXI   Taxis line up at the dock to take you wherever you want to go. Cabs don't have meters, but fares are fixed; and every driver has a copy of the official rate schedule. Ask the fare before getting in the car. The dispatch office number is © **297/8-22116.** The fare from the cruise terminal to the beach resorts is $6 to $8. Tip between 15% and 20%. Most drivers speak good English and are eager to give you a tour of the island. Expect to pay $35 per hour for a maximum of four passengers.

BY BUS   Aruba has good daily bus service beginning at 6am. Same-day round-trip fare between the beach hotels and Oranjestad is $2; a one-way ride is $1.15. Have exact change. The bus terminal is across the street from the cruise terminal on L. G. Smith Boulevard.

SHORE EXCURSIONS OFFERED BY THE CRUISE LINES

Four-Wheel-Drive Backcountry Aruba Tour ($54, 4 hr.): Just like the solo tour described in "On Your Own: Within Walking Distance," below, but this version does the tour in a convoy of four-passenger sports utility vehicles, with you behind the wheel and in radio contact with your guide. A stop is made for lunch and swimming.

Atlantis Submarine Journey ($74 adults, $37 children 4–16, 2 hr.): If you loved Captain Nemo and *20,000 Leagues Under the Sea,* don't miss your chance to cruise 45m (150 ft.) below the sea in a submarine. During the gentle descent, you'll pass by scuba divers, coral reefs, shipwrecks, and hundreds of curious sergeant majors, damselfish, parrotfish, and angelfish.

Aruba Bus Tour ($26, 3 hr.): This air-conditioned bus tour rolls along part of Aruba's wild and woolly windward coastline to the Natural Bridge (a rocky "bridge" cut by the sea and wind) and the Casibari rock formations, as well as along Aruba's hotel strip.

ON YOUR OWN: WITHIN WALKING DISTANCE

Aruba's capital has a sunny Caribbean demeanor, with Dutch colonial buildings painted in vivid colors. The main thoroughfare, **Lloyd G. Smith Boulevard,** runs along the waterfront and is crowded with marinas, shopping malls, restaurants, and bars. **Caya G. F. Betico Croes,** or Main Street, is another major shopping venue running roughly parallel to the waterfront several blocks inland. The harbor is packed with fishing boats and schooners docked next to stalls, where vendors hawk fruits, vegetables, and fish. On the other side of the Seaport Marketplace shopping mall, **Queen Wilhelmina Park,** named after one of Holland's longest-reigning monarchs, features manicured lawns, views of colorful fishing boats, and luxuriant tropical vegetation. If you're looking for a little culture, Oranjestad has a handful of museums that are worth a bit of your time. Squeezed between St. Franciscus Roman Catholic Church and the parish rectory, the small **Archaeological Museum of Aruba,** J. E. Irausquinplein 2A (© **297/8-28979**), highlights the island's Amerindian heritage, with pottery vessels, shell and stone tools, burial urns, and skulls and bones on display. (Free admission. Open Mon–Fri 8am–noon and 1–4pm.) To defend the island against pirates, the Dutch erected **Fort Zoutman** in 1796. In 1867, **Willem III Tower,** named after the then-reigning Dutch monarch, was added. Since 1992, the complex has housed the modest **Museo Arubano,** Zoutmanstraat z/n (© **297/8-26099**), which displays prehistoric Amerindian artifacts and remnants from the Dutch colonial period. (Admission $1.25. Open Mon–Fri 9am–noon and 1–4pm.) The small **Numismatic Museum of Aruba,** Zuidstraat 7, 1 block northeast of Fort Zoutman (© **297/8-28831**), looks unpromising from the outside, but its meticulous, homemade exhibits tell the history of the world through coins. Dedicated numismatists can spend the better part of the morning perusing the 35,000 different specimens from more than 400 countries, but anyone with a passing interest in coins or history will appreciate this labor of love. (Free admission; donations appreciated. Open Mon–Fri 7:30am–3:30pm.)

ON YOUR OWN: TOURING BY RENTAL JEEP

The best way to see Aruba's desertlike terrain is to rent a four-wheel-drive vehicle. Car-rental companies have maps highlighting the best routes to reach the attractions. Here's one popular route.

Following the system of roads that traces the perimeter of the island, start clockwise from Oranjestad. Drive past the hotel strip, toward the island's north-westernmost point. Here, the **California Lighthouse** affords sweeping 360° views of spectacular scenery—gentle sand dunes, rocky coral shoreline, and tur-bulent waves. The picturesque lighthouse gets its name from the *California,* a passenger ship that sank off the nearby coast in 1916. The story that this vessel was the only ship to have heard (and ignored) the *Titanic's* distress signal is malarkey. (In fact, the *Californian* [with a final "n"] of *Titanic* infamy was tor-pedoed by a German submarine off the coast of Greece in 1915.) From here on, your adventure will take you into the island's moonlike terrain, past heaps of giant boulders and barren rocky coastline. The well-maintained road that links the hotel strip with Oranjestad deteriorates abruptly into a band of rubble, and the calm, turquoise sea turns rough and rowdy.

By the time you reach the **Alto Vista Chapel,** about 8km (5 miles) from the lighthouse, chances are you'll already be coated with red dust. Don't let that stop you from peeking inside the quaint pale-yellow church that was built in 1750 and renovated 200 years later. Radiating serenity from its cactus-studded perch overlooking the sea, the chapel, Aruba's first, was built by native Indians and Spanish settlers before the island had its own priest. Farther along the northern coast, you'll approach the hulking ruins of the **Bushiribana Gold Smelter.** Built in 1872, its massive stone walls are remnants of Aruba's gold-mining 19th cen-tury. Climb the multitiered interior for impressive sea views. Too bad the walls have been marred with artless graffiti.

Within view of the smelter, **Natural Bridge** is Aruba's most photographed attraction. Rising 7.5m (25 ft.) above the sea and spanning 30m (100 ft.) of rock-strewn waters, this limestone arch has been carved out over the centuries by the relentless pounding of the surf. Because the bridge acts as a buffer between the sandy beach and open ocean, many people come to swim and pic-nic. Next, head toward the center of the island and the bizarre **Ayó and Casi-bari rock formations.** Looking like something out of *The Flintstones,* the gargantuan Ayó rocks served Aruba's early inhabitants as a dwelling or religious site. The reddish-brown petroglyphs on the boulders suggest mystical signifi-cance. Although the Casibari boulders weigh several tons each, they look freshly scattered by some cyclopean dice-roller. Look for the formations that resemble birds and dragons, or climb the trail to the top of the highest rock mound for a panorama of the area.

Farther east, back along the northern coast, **Arikok National Park,** Aruba's showcase ecological preserve, sprawls over roughly 20% of the island. Its premier attractions are a series of caves that punctuate the cliff sides of the area's mesas. The most popular, **Fontein Cave,** has brownish-red drawings left by Amerindi-ans and graffiti etched by early European settlers. Stalagmites and stalactites here look like human heads and bison; park rangers stationed at the cave will point them out. The hole is an important roosting place for long-tongued bats, which nap in the damp inner sanctum. Nearby **Quadirikiri Cave** boasts two large chambers with roof openings that allow sunlight in, making flashlights unnec-essary. Hundreds of small bats use the 100-foot-long tunnel to reach their nests deeper in the cave. You'll need a flashlight to explore the 300-foot-long passage-way of **Baranca Sunu,** another cave in the area commonly known as the Tun-nel of Love because of its heart-shaped entrance. Helmets and lights can be rented at the entrance for $6.

Heading southeast toward Aruba's behemoth oil refinery, you'll eventually come to **Baby Beach,** at the island's easternmost point. Like a great big bathtub, this shallow bowl of warm turquoise water is protected by an almost complete circle of rock, and is a great place for a dip after a sweaty day behind the wheel.

SHOPPING

Although Aruba boasts plenty of shopping, don't expect prices to be fabulously cut-rate: The days of Caribbean bargains are waning. Nevertheless, the island's low 3.3% duty can make prices on items such as jewelry and fragrances attractive. What's more, there's no sales tax.

Because the island is part of the Netherlands, **Dutch goods** such as Delft porcelain, chocolate, and cheese are especially good buys. Items from **Indonesia,** another former Dutch colony, are reasonably priced too. **Skin and hair-care products** made from locally produced aloe are also popular and practical. If you're looking for **big-ticket items,** Aruba offers the usual array of watches, cameras, gold and diamond jewelry, Cuban cigars, premium liquor, English and German china, porcelain, French and American fragrances, and crystal.

Aruba's retail activity centers on Oranjestad. About 1km (a half mile) long, **Caya G. F. Betico Croes,** better known as Main Street, is the city's major shopping venue. Downtown also teems with several contiguous shopping malls that stretch for several blocks along the harbor front. **Seaport Mall** and **Seaport Marketplace** feature more than 130 stores, two casinos, 20 restaurants and cafes, and a movie theater. Just down the road, **Royal Plaza Mall** is chock-full of popular restaurants and generally upscale boutiques.

BEACHES

All of Aruba's beaches are public, but chairs and shade huts are hotel property. If you use them, expect to be charged.

Palm Beach, home of Aruba's glamorous high-rise hotels, is the best spot for people-watching. This stretch of white sand is also great for swimming, sunbathing, sailing, fishing, and snorkeling. It can get crowded, and with two piers and numerous watersports operators, it's also busier and noisier than Aruba's other beaches.

Separated from Palm Beach by a limestone outcrop, **Eagle Beach** stretches as far as the eye can see. The sugar-white sand and gentle surf are ideal for swimming, and although the nearby hotels offer watersports and beach activities, the ambience is relaxed and quiet. A couple of bars punctuate the expansive strand, and shaded picnic areas are provided for the public.

Baby Beach, at Aruba's easternmost tip, is a prime destination for families with young children. The protection of rock breakwaters makes this shallow bowl of warm turquoise water perfect for inexperienced swimmers. Giant sea grape bushes offer protection from the sun. There are a refreshment stand and washrooms, but no other facilities.

SPORTS

SCUBA DIVING & SNORKELING   Aruba is no Bonaire, but it still offers enough coral reefs, marine life, and wreck diving to keep scuba divers and snorkelers busy. The best snorkeling sites are around Malmok Beach and Boca Catalina, where the water is calm and shallow, and marine life is plentiful. Dive sites stretch along the entire southern coast, but most divers head for the German freighter *Antilla,* which was scuttled during World War II off the island's northwestern tip, near Palm Beach. The island's largest watersports operators,

Pelican Adventures (☎ 297/8-72302) and **Red Sail Sports** (☎ 297/8-61603), offer sailing, windsurfing, and water-skiing in addition to snorkeling and scuba diving. Two-tank dives are $55 to $65; one-tank dives are $35 to $40. Snorkelers on dive boats pay $25 (equipment included), but an array of multistop, snorkeling-only cruises are also offered, starting at $30.

WINDSURFING Aruba's world-class windsurfing conditions attract wind sailors from around the world. **Malmok Beach** is the island's most popular windsurfing spot. Sailed by novices and pros alike, it has slightly gusty offshore winds, minimal current, and moderate chop. **Boca Grandi,** on the extreme eastern coast, is for advanced wave sailors only. Most windsurfing operations are clustered around Malmok Beach, where equipment averages $35 for 2 hours, $45 for half a day, and $60 for a full day. Two-hour beginner lessons with equipment are $50. Operators include **Aruba Boardsailing Productions** (☎ 297/8-63940) and **Roger's Windsurf Place** (☎ 297/8-61918).

GAMBLING

Aruba boasts 11 casinos, most of them casually elegant. Slot machines gear up at 10am; table games such as baccarat, blackjack, poker, roulette, and craps can start as early as noon; and bingo starts in the afternoon.

Two casinos are steps from the dock. At the Aruba Sonesta Beach Resort, the **Crystal Casino,** L. G. Smith Blvd. 82 (☎ 297/8-36000), is Aruba's only 24-hour casino and probably its most elegant. In addition to slots and an array of table games, it features a race and sports book room with a satellite linkup and wagering based on Las Vegas odds. The **Seaport Casino,** L. G. Smith Blvd. 9 (☎ 297/8-35027), also in downtown Oranjestad, fits in well with the surrounding shopping mall; you might think it's just another store.

GREAT LOCAL RESTAURANTS & BARS

For a crash course in Caribbean cooking, head for **Boonoonoonoos,** Wilhelminastraat 18-A (☎ 297/8-31888). Located in an old Aruban town house, this cozy spot's menu reads like a culinary travelogue. Try the Jamaican jerk ribs, or curried chicken Trinidad.

Opulence and first-rate French cuisine make **Chez Mathilde,** Havenstraat 23 (☎ 297/8-34968), the perfect choice for special occasions. Main courses include pan-fried trout, curry mushroom chicken, wild boar, and ostrich. It's pricey, but you deserve it.

Hip and happy **Cuba's Cookin',** Wilhelminastraat 27 (☎ 297/8-80627), serves flavorful Cuban dishes expertly prepared. Kid-friendly **Waterfront Crabhouse,** Seaport Market, L. G. Smith Boulevard (☎ 297/8-35858), offers grilled-cheese sandwiches and "psketti." The more sophisticated adult fare includes red snapper, Maine lobster, and crab.

5 Bahamas: Nassau & Freeport

Technically, the 700 islands of the Bahamas aren't in the Caribbean—they're in the Atlantic Ocean, just north of the Caribbean and less than 160km (100 miles) from Miami. Because they're an important port of call on the cruise ship circuit and part of the West Indies, though, they're almost always lumped together with their island neighbors to the south.

If you're a seasoned cruiser, chances are you've been to the Bahamas already and might prefer an itinerary that includes more far-flung ports, but if you're

Nassau

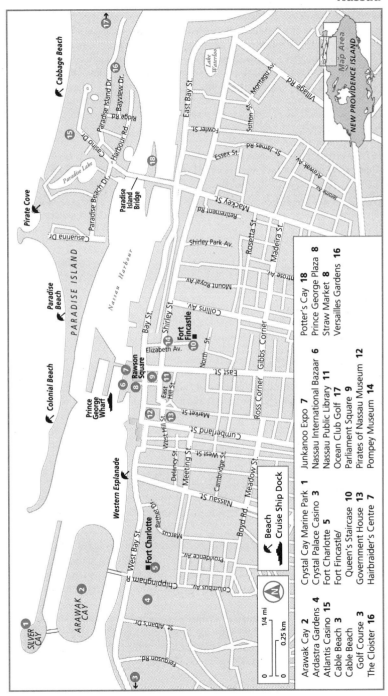

Arawak Cay **2**
Ardastra Gardens **4**
Atlantis Casino **15**
Cable Beach **3**
Cable Beach
  Golf Course **3**
The Cloister **16**

Crystal Cay Marine Park **1**
Crystal Palace Casino **3**
Fort Charlotte **5**
Fort Fincastle/
  Queen's Staircase **10**
Government House **13**
Hairbraider's Centre **7**

Junkanoo Expo **7**
Nassau International Bazaar **6**
Nassau Public Library **11**
Ocean Club Golf **17**
Parliament Square **9**
Pirates of Nassau Museum **12**
Pompey Museum **14**

Potter's Cay **18**
Prince George Plaza **8**
Straw Market **8**
Versailles Gardens **16**

Beach
Cruise Ship Dock

1/4 mi
0.25 km

new to the region, the Bahamas are a great introduction, with everything you'd expect from a fun-in-the-sun vacation—postcard-perfect beaches, a full range of water activities, and warm temperatures year-round. There's a well-developed tourist infrastructure—things work here—and economic conditions are the envy of most other West Indian islands; so you won't see the kind of poverty that plagues some Caribbean islands. In many ways, the Bahamas isn't much different from, say, some parts of Florida, but if you're looking for something on the exotic side, you'll be able to see colonial sights, British influences, and West Indian color too—you'll know right away you're not in Kansas anymore.

The Bahamas became an independent commonwealth of Great Britain in 1973. Tourism and offshore banking account for the islands' current prosperity. About 85% of Bahamians are descended from African slaves; people of European extraction make up most of the rest of the population.

LANGUAGE   **English** is the official language of the Bahamas. Most people in the tourism industry speak a standard American version of the language at work. You'll also hear an island lilt and a vocabulary that reflects British, Arawak, and African influences.

CURRENCY   The Bahamas' legal tender is the **Bahamian dollar** (B$1), whose value is always the same as that of the U.S. dollar. Both currencies are accepted everywhere on the islands, and most stores accept traveler's checks and major credit cards.

CALLING FROM THE U.S.   Calling the Bahamas from the United States is as simple as phoning between states: Just dial "1" before the numbers listed throughout this section.

NASSAU

Located 298km (185 miles) southeast of Miami, Nassau is the cultural, social, political, and economic center of the Bahamas. With its beaches, shopping, resorts, casinos, historic landmarks, and water and land activities, it's also the island chain's most visited destination—one million travelers a year make their way to the town, and Nassau is one of the world's busiest cruise ship ports. The Nassau/Paradise Island area comprises two separate islands. Nassau is on the northeastern shore of the 34km (21-mile) long island of New Providence, while tiny Paradise Island, linked to New Providence by bridges, protects Nassau harbor for a 5km (3-mile) stretch. Although the area accounts for only 2% of the nation's land area, its 175,000 residents represent 60% of the Bahamian population.

COMING ASHORE   The cruise ships dock at Prince George Wharf in the center of town, near Rawson Square and adjacent to the main shopping areas. Your best bet for making long-distance phone calls is the Bahamas Telecommunications (BATELCO) phone center on East Street, about 4 blocks inland from Rawson Square.

INFORMATION   The **Tourism Office** is located in the British Colonial Hilton, 1 Bay St. (© **242/322-7500**), and is open Monday through Friday 9am to 5:30pm. A smaller booth at Rawson Square is near the dock. For information before you go, call the Tourist Office in the U.S. (© **800/4-BAHAMAS;** www. bahamas.com).

GETTING AROUND

Unless you hire a horse-drawn carriage, the only way to see old Nassau is on foot. The major attractions and stores are pretty concentrated, so walking is the

Frommer's Favorite Nassau Experiences

Gorging on Fresh Conch at Arawak Cay: The small man-made island across the West Bay Street shore has the freshest conch around. For a true island experience, wash it down with the local cocktail—coconut water, milk, and gin. (See "Great Local Restaurants & Bars," later in this chapter.)

Taking a Walk Through Colonial History: Nassau has numerous forts, government buildings, and private establishments that keep the flavor of the islands' colonial past alive. Shops and boutiques abut the historic attractions, so you can get some culture and feed your shopping addiction at the same time. (See "On Your Own: Within Walking Distance," below.)

most convenient mode of transportation anyway. If you're really fit, you can even trek over to Cable Beach or Paradise Island.

BY TAXI   Practical for longer trips, taxis are required to have working meters, but some drivers insist on flat rates. The initial meter fare is $2, and each additional quarter-mile for the first two passengers is 30¢; for third and fourth passengers, add $2 each to the meter reading. There's also a surcharge for luggage stowed in the trunk. Tip your driver 15%. You can hire a five-passenger cab at $23 to $25 per hour. Taxis can be hailed on the street or taken from stands. Radio cabs can be ordered at © **242/323-5111.**

BY JITNEY   Jitneys, medium-size buses that travel set routes throughout the city, are the least expensive means of transport. The fare is 75¢ for adults, 50¢ for children, and exact change is required. Buses operate from early in the morning until about 8pm.

BY FERRY   Ferries run from the end of Casuarina Drive on Paradise Island across the harbor to Rawson Square for $2 per person. Water taxis also operate during the day between Paradise Island and Prince George Wharf for $3 per person.

BY HORSE-DRAWN CARRIAGE   Horse-drawn surreys are the regal (if touristy) way to see Nassau. Agree on a price before you start. The average charge for a 20- to 25-minute tour is $10 per person. The maximum load is two adults plus one child under the age of 12 (or three small adults—if you've been spending too much time at the ship's buffet, you don't qualify). The colorfully painted surreys are available daily from 9am to 4:30pm, except when the horses rest—usually from 1 to 3pm May through October, 1 to 2pm November through April. You'll find surreys in front of the cruise port building.

BY MOTOR SCOOTER/MOPED   To rent a motor scooter, contact **Ursa Investment,** Prince George Wharf (© **242/326-8329**). Mopeds run about $20 an hour or $50 for a full day.

BY RENTAL CAR   Most vehicles have left-hand steering, and driving is British style. If you're used to driving on the right, it may take some time to adjust. Thankfully, traffic is seldom heavy except downtown near the port. Rental-car license plates carry the letters "SD" (which stands for "suicide driver" according to joking Bahamians). **Avis, Budget, Dollar,** and **Hertz** all have offices here.

SHORE EXCURSIONS OFFERED BY THE CRUISE LINES

It's easy to get around Nassau via taxi or foot, so you can do a lot on your own. Cruise lines typically offer a variety of excursions, though, including the ones described below.

Heart of Nassau and Ardastra Gardens ($25, 2½ hr.): After touring Bay Street, the main shopping district, you'll witness Ardastra Gardens' marching flamingo review. Other stops include the Queen's Staircase and Fort Charlotte.

Fort Fincastle ($21, 2 hr.): Visit the Queen's Staircase and see some of Nassau's most beautiful homes. Then cross the bridge to Paradise Island for a tour of the Cloister and Versailles Gardens.

Crystal Cay ($21, 3 hr.): One of the country's most popular attractions, the Crystal Cay Marine Park features a network of aquariums, an underwater observation tower, landscaped parks, lounges, and a restaurant. The tour is more expensive if you rent snorkeling equipment.

EXCURSIONS OFFERED BY LOCAL AGENCIES

Goombay Guided Walking Tours: These 45-minute tours, arranged by the Ministry of Tourism (© **242/326-9772**), leave from the Tourist Information Booth on Rawson Square, usually at 10am, 11:30am, 1pm, 2:30pm, and 3:45pm daily. Make reservations in advance. The tours include descriptions of some of the city's oldest buildings, with information on Nassau's history, customs, and traditions. The cost is $12 for adults, $2 for children under 12.

Scuba Diving, Sea Scootering & Shark Dives: Unpretentious and friendly **Nassau Scuba Centre,** Coral Harbour (© **242/362-1964;** www.nassau-scuba-centre.com), offers transportation to and from Prince Georges Wharf for cruise ship visitors, with dives at 9am and 1pm. Two-tank dives run about $70; snorkeling is $30, including equipment. For certified divers, shark dives allow you to either watch a divemaster feed sharks ($115) or don a chain-mail shark suit and feed them yourself (for a hefty $399). **Stuart Cove's Dive Bahamas,** Southwest Bay Street, South Ocean (© **800/879-9832** in the U.S., or 242/362-4171; www.dive-bahamas.com), offers more options, including "scenic underwater bubbles" that allow nondivers to move about underwater without scuba equipment on scooters ($69). The operation can be a mob scene, though, and the service is less personal than that at Nassau Scuba. Reserve ahead with both operations.

Walking on the Ocean Floor: If you loved Captain Nemo and *20,000 Leagues Under the Sea,* you won't want to miss **Hartley's Undersea Walk,** East Bay Street (© **242/393-8234**). As part of a 3½-hour yacht cruise, you'll don a breathing helmet and spend about 20 minutes walking along the ocean bottom through a "garden" of tropical fish, sponges, and other undersea life. You don't have to be able to swim, and you can wear your glasses; but some people find the high-pitched pinging noise annoying. Ships depart from the Nassau Yacht Haven Tuesday through Saturday at 9:30am and 1:30pm. The whole experience is $150 per person.

Yacht Cruises: Located at the Paradise Island Bridge, **Nassau Cruises** (© **242/363-3577**) has three luxurious yachts that head for the secluded beaches of Blue Lagoon Island, 6.5km (4 miles) east of Paradise Island. The boats leave daily at

10 and 11:30am and return at 1:30, 3, and 4:30pm. A day pass ($20 for adults and $10 for children) covers the boat ride only. An all-inclusive day pass ($50 for adults and $25 for children) includes transportation to the dock, the boat ride, lunch, two daiquiris for adults, and all nonmotorized watersports.

ON YOUR OWN: WITHIN WALKING DISTANCE

Walking is the best way to see the major sites of Nassau and to get a feel for the city's character and history. Start at Prince George Wharf, where your ship is docked.

As you exit from the cruise ship wharf into the main port area, aggressive hawkers will encourage you to have your hair braided at the **Hairbraider's Centre.** This government-sponsored open-air pavilion attracts braiding experts from all over the island. If you're looking for a Bo Derek look, here's your chance. If you're not, a simple "no thanks" keeps the touts at bay.

Just across Bay Street from Rawson Square (inland from the wharf), the flamingo-pink government buildings of **Parliament Square** were constructed in 1815. The House of Assembly, old colonial Secretary's Office, and Supreme Court flank a statue of Queen Victoria, while a bust on the north side of the square honors Sir Milo B. Butler, the Bahamas' first governor-general.

Built as a prison in 1798, the **Nassau Public Library,** located a block inland from Parliament Square, facing Shirley Street, is one of the city's oldest buildings and surely one of the more interesting libraries anywhere. Its octagonal shape was copied from a munitions storage facility, and the decidedly unpenitentiary pink paint was added after 1889, when the building reopened as a library. The books, historical prints, colonial documents, and Arawak Indian artifacts are kept in former cells.

Slaves carved the **Queen's Staircase** out of a solid limestone cliff in 1793. Originally designed as an escape route for soldiers at Fort Fincastle, each step now represents a year in Queen Victoria's 65-year reign. Lush plants and a waterfall stand guard over the staircase, which is located a few blocks up from the library on East Street and leads to **Fort Fincastle,** Elizabeth Avenue (© 242/ 322-2442), built in 1793 by Lord Dunmore, the royal governor. An elevator climbs a 126-foot-high water tower, where you can look down on the arrowhead-shaped fort. Walk around on your own or hire a guide. (*Note:* You may find some of them aggressive.)

Walking downhill from Fort Fincastle and back toward the waterfront, turn left on East Hill Street past Market Street. On the left stands **Government House,** the official residence of the governor-general, built in 1801. Tropical foliage lines the grounds leading to the colonial mansion, and a statue of Columbus stands over the hillside steps. This one's for kids, but young-at-heart parents may also enjoy the corny **Pirates of Nassau museum** at King and George streets, downhill from Government House (© 242/356-3759). Step aboard an embattled pirate ship and come face-to-face with Captain Teach and his fearsome crew as they guide you through the age of piracy in the lawless Nassau of 1716. It's open 9am to 5pm Monday through Saturday, and admission is a steep $15 for adults—only worth it if you're with kids, as each adult may bring two children free; each additional child is $8.

On Bay Street, about a block closer to the waterfront than the Pirates of Nassau, is the **Straw Market,** which burned to the ground in 2001 but at press time was expected to reopen soon on the same spot (vendors were temporarily relocated just 1 block farther along Bay St.). Some of the items sold at the stalls here are authentic, but much of what you see comes from Asia. There are better places to get the real thing (see "Shopping," below), but enjoy the scene anyway. Hours are roughly 7:30am to 7pm.

The modest **Pompey Museum,** which was located adjacent to the Straw Market (and should return once the buildings are reconstructed), is temporarily displayed at the Bahamas Historical Society, on the corner of Elizabeth Avenue and Shirley Street (*©* **242/393-2175**). Displays recount the story of Bahamian slavery, abolition, and emancipation through artifacts, historical documents, and drawings. It's open Monday through Friday 10am to 4pm, Saturday 10am to noon. Admission is $1 for adults, 50¢ for children.

If you're up for more walking, **Potter's Cay,** under the Paradise Island Bridge, provides more market color. Sloops from the less populated Out Islands bring in their fresh catch. Freshly grown herbs and vegetables are also sold, along with limes, papayas, pineapples, and bananas. Stalls sell conch in several forms: raw and marinated in lime juice, as spicy deep-fried fritters, and in salad and soup.

ON YOUR OWN: BEYOND THE PORT AREA

About 1.5km (a mile) west of downtown Nassau, just off West Bay Street, **Fort Charlotte** covers more than 40 hilltop hectares (100 acres). The Bahamas' largest fort, it offers impressive views of Paradise Island, Nassau, and the harbor. The complex, constructed in 1788, features a moat, dungeons, underground passageways, and 42 cannons.

Parading pink flamingos are the main attraction at the lush, 5-acre **Ardastra Gardens,** Chippingham Road, about 1.5km (a mile) west of downtown Nassau (*©* **242/323-5806**). The graceful birds obey the drillmaster's orders, and with their long-legged precision and discipline, they give the Rockettes a run for their money. The performances, accompanied by informative commentary, are presented daily at 11am, 2pm, and 4pm. Other exotic wildlife—boa constrictors, honey bears, macaws, and capuchin monkeys—are less talented but fascinating in their own right. Paths meander through tropical foliage that's sure to enchant gardeners. Guided tours are given Monday to Saturday at 10:15am and 3:15pm. The $20 admission fee includes a T-shirt, a free drink, and round-trip transportation.

Crystal Cay Marine Park, on Silver Cay off West Bay Street, between downtown Nassau and Cable Beach (*©* **242/328-1036**), has a network of aquariums, landscaped parks, lounges, a gift shop, and a restaurant, but its outstanding feature is the underwater observation tower. A spiral staircase descends 6m (20 ft.) below the surface of the water, providing views of coral, stingrays, sea turtles, Caribbean sharks, and other sea life in their natural habitat. The tower also rises 30m (100 ft.) above the water to two viewing decks. Nature trails with lush tropical foliage, waterfalls, and wildlife add to the setting. The park is a 10-minute ferry ride from the Prince George Wharf. Adult admission is $16; kids pay $11. (*Note:* If the sea is turbulent, visibility may be compromised.)

The Cloister, on Ocean Club Drive on Paradise Island (*©* **242/363-3000**), is part of a monastery built in the 13th century by French monks. In the 1920s, William Randolph Hearst bought it, had it disassembled, and moved it from France to his estate in San Simeon, California. The stones were stored for years because no one knew how to properly reassemble them. In 1962, Huntington Hartford, the A&P grocery store heir and developer of Paradise Island, bought the structure from Hearst and hired a sculptor to reconstruct it on the island. It's quite an anomaly on tropical Paradise Island, but it's a serene spot. The adjacent

Versailles Gardens feature formal vistas, tropical flowers, and classic bronze and marble statuary. There is no admission fee.

The mythical lost city of Atlantis submerged under Bahamian waters? Sure, it sounds hokey, and all the grandiloquent hype makes you want to hate the place; but **The Dig** and **Marine Habitat** at the Atlantis Paradise Island megaresort actually end up exceeding expectations. Drawing on age-old myths of the lost city, The Dig is a fantastic world of faux ancient ruins flooded by the sea. The interconnected passageways, boulevards, and chambers, now inhabited by piranhas, hammerhead sharks, stingrays, and morays, are visible through huge glass windows. Purported to be the largest man-made marine habitat in the world— "second only to Mother Nature"—the resort's sprawling 11-million-gallon lagoon system boasts more than 200 sea species and 50,000 individual creatures. Tickets for the guided "Discovery Tour," available at the resort's guest services desks, are $25 for adults, $19 for children under 12. (*Note:* This tour does not include use of the resort's beach or water slide, which are reserved for guests only.) For information, call ✆ **242/363-3000** or check out **www.atlantis.com**.

GAMBLING

If you think your ship's casino is as good as most land-based facilities, you haven't been to the impressive, 100,000-square-foot **Atlantis Casino** in the Atlantis Paradise Island megaresort (✆ **242/363-3000**), the largest gaming and entertainment complex in the Caribbean. Two astounding glass sculptures, the *Temple of the Sun* and the *Temple of the Moon,* anchor the vast facility and tie in with the resort's Lost City of Atlantis theme. Open 24 hours a day, the casino boasts almost 1,000 slot machines and 78 gaming tables for baccarat, roulette, craps, blackjack, and Caribbean stud poker. Unlike most other casinos, the Atlantis makes no attempt to hide what's going on outside: Huge windows provide panoramas of the adjacent marina and lagoons.

The 35,000-square-foot **Crystal Palace Casino,** West Bay Street, Cable Beach (✆ **242/327-6200**), screams 1980s with its pink and purple rainbow decor. The only casino on New Providence Island, it's part of the Nassau Marriott Resort. Despite tough competition from the Atlantis Casino, it stacks up well against most other casinos in the Caribbean, with 700 slot machines and more than 60 gaming tables. The oval-shaped bar extends onto the gaming floor, and the lounge offers live entertainment. It's open Sunday to Thursday from 10am to 4am, Friday and Saturday 24 hours.

Taxis will take you to either casino from the cruise pier.

SHOPPING

In 1992, the Bahamas abolished import duties on 11 luxury-good categories, including china, crystal, fine linens, jewelry, leather goods, photographic equipment, watches, and fragrances. Even so, you can end up spending more on an item in the Bahamas than you would at home. True bargains are rare, as is finding much that's really worth buying. The principal shopping area is **Bay Street** and the adjacent blocks, which are almost the first things you see when you leave your ship. Here you'll find duty-free luxury-goods stores, such as Colombian Emeralds and Solomon's Mines, plus hundreds of others selling T-shirts, tourist gimcracks, duty-free booze and cigars, and recordings of junkanoo music.

In the crowded aisles of the **Straw Market** on Bay Street, between Market Range and Navy Lion Road, you can watch craftspeople weave and plait straw hats, handbags, dolls, place mats, and other items, but be aware that many of the items aren't of the best quality; in fact, much of it has been imported from Asia. Welcome to the global market, folks! It's tourist central, so most shop-keepers are willing to bargain, though some won't budge. If you want a really beautiful handmade straw work, walk a few blocks to **The Plait Lady,** at Victoria and Bay streets. The merchandise here is vastly superior to what's peddled in the Straw Market, and it's 100% Bahamian-made. Both **Island Tings,** Bay Street between East Street and Elizabeth Avenue, and **Seagrape,** West Bay Street at the Travelers' Rest restaurant (10 min. west of Cable Beach by car), offer Bahamian arts and crafts, Junkanoo masks, and jewelry.

The tired-looking **Nassau International Bazaar,** running from Bay Street to the waterfront near Prince George Wharf, has 30 shops that sell goods from around the globe. The stores at **Prince George Plaza,** Bay Street, sell designer merchandise and are often crowded.

Marlborough Antiques, across the street from the Hilton British Colonial on Marlborough Street, has an eclectic and interesting collection of antiques and books.

Bahamas Rum Cake Factory, at 602 E. Bay St., carries an array of Bahamian food products, including hot sauces, spices, and the eponymous dessert, which you can buy as they come out of the oven. If you can't get enough of the local rum, try a milkshake with a shot. And if you get home and want more, you can arrange worldwide cake delivery through their website, **www.bahamasrumcake factory.com**.

BEACHES

On New Providence Island, sun worshippers make the pilgrimage to **Cable Beach,** which offers various watersports and easy access to shops, a casino, bars, and restaurants. The beach stretches for 6.5km (4 miles), and the waters can change quickly from rough to calm and clear. It's 8km (5 miles) from the port—a $10 taxi ride or 75¢ via the No. 10 bus.

More convenient for cruise ship passengers but inferior to Cable Beach, the **Western Esplanade** sweeps westward from the Hilton British Colonial hotel. Facilities include restrooms, changing facilities, and a snack bar. In the months preceding Junkanoo, local bands practice their carnival routines here.

Paradise Beach on Paradise Island is a ferry ride away from Prince George Wharf (see "Getting Around," earlier in this chapter). The price of admission ($3 for adults, $1 for children) includes use of a shower and locker. An extra $10 deposit is required for towels. Paradise Island has a number of smaller beaches as well, including **Pirate's Cove Beach** and **Cabbage Beach.** Bordered by casuarinas, palms, and sea grapes, Cabbage Beach's broad sands stretch for 3km (2 miles) but it's likely to be crowded with guests of the nearby resorts. Tranquility seekers find something approaching solitude on the northwestern end, accessible by boat or foot only.

SPORTS

GOLF **South Ocean Golf Course,** Southwest Bay Road (© **242/362-4391**), is the best course on New Providence Island and one of the best in the Bahamas. Located 30 minutes from Nassau, this 18-hole, 6,133m (6,707-yd.), par-72 beauty has some first-rate holes with a backdrop of trees, shrubs, ravines, and undulating hills. Although not as challenging, the 6,437m (7,040-yd.), par-72 **Cable Beach Golf Course,** Cable Beach, West Bay Road (© **242/327-6000**), has lakes and ponds tucked picturesquely throughout, and the length encourages strong hitters to shave strokes with long, well-placed drives.

The 18-hole, 6,492m (7,100-yd.), par-72 PGA course at the **Ocean Club** (*€* **242/363-6680**) on Paradise Island was designed by Tom Weiskopf and hosts the Michael Jordan Celebrity Invitational. The visually intimidating par-4 seventh hole has water down the right side off the tee and the added difficulty of prevailing left-to-right winds. Hole 12 features wetlands and a panorama of the Atlantic, while the 17th plays entirely along the beach.

All the courses offer club and other equipment rental. Expect greens fees for 18 holes to run $100 or more.

GREAT LOCAL RESTAURANTS & BARS

Conch, Bahamian "rock lobster," and boiled fish are local specialties; pigeon peas and rice are popular side dishes. The **local beer** is Kalik, and Nassau's **local rum** is Bacardi.

ON ARAWAK CAY   You'll get all the conch you can eat on **Arawak Cay,** a small man-made island across West Bay Street from Ardastra Gardens and Fort Charlotte. Join the locals in sampling conch with hot sauce, and wash it down with a coconut-water-and-gin cocktail. Gorging on the cay is a local tradition and a real Bahamian experience.

IN NASSAU   If you want fancy, **Graycliff Restaurant,** West Hill Street, next to Government House (*€* **242/322-2796**), is one of the most elegant restaurants in the West Indies. It was built in the 1740s by a former privateer and became Nassau's first inn in 1844, and during the American Civil War its cellar served as a jail for war prisoners. Polly Leach, a friend of Al Capone, owned the house some time later, as did Lord and Lady Dudley, friends of the Duke and Duchess of Windsor. Royalty and celebrities have eaten in the elegant surroundings for decades, enjoying its extensive wine list and hand-rolled cigars. The continental lunches and dinners (jacket required) are expensive, but worth it if you've squirreled away for a really special meal. Call ahead for reservations.

Much more modest, **Bahamian Kitchen,** Trinity Place, off Market Street, next to Trinity Church (*€* **242/325-0702**), is one of the best places for good, down-home Bahamian food at modest prices. Specialties include lobster Bahamian style, fried red snapper, and curried chicken.

Near Ardastra Gardens, **The Shoal,** Nassau Street (*€* **242/323-4400**), is another local favorite and a featured restaurant in the Ministry of Tourism's "Real Taste of the Bahamas" program, which highlights independent establishments that serve indigenous cuisine. Every cab driver knows the place, which really hops on Sunday mornings. Try the boiled fish breakfast.

Café Matisse, on Bank Lane at Bay Street, behind Parliament Square (*€* **242/356-7012**), is set in an old colonial home and features antique tile floors, Matisse prints, and a serene outdoor courtyard. The extensive menu includes seafood, pastas, and pizzas. It's an unbeatable respite from shopping and sightseeing in downtown Nassau.

ON PARADISE ISLAND   Among the 30-plus pricey restaurants and bars in the **Atlantis Paradise Island,** on Casino Drive (*€* **242/363-3000**), two merit special mention. **Seagrapes** serves an affordable buffet of tropical foods, with a special emphasis on Cuban, Caribbean, and Cajun dishes. **Five Twins,** just off the casino floor, features an elegantly minimalist sushi and satay bar. The lighting is soothingly dim, and the black-and-white marble floor complements the black lacquer dinnerware and scarlet napkins. Don't pass up the tropical-fruit soup dessert.

FREEPORT/LUCAYA

Freeport/Lucaya on Grand Bahama Island (often referred to as GBI) is the second most popular destination in the Bahamas. Technically, Freeport is the land-locked section of town while adjacent Lucaya hugs the waterfront. Originally intended as two separate developments, the two have grown together over the years, and though they offer none of Nassau's colonial charm, they do offer plenty of sun, surf, golf, tennis, and watersports—though the frenzy of the gam-bling and shopping scenes here might be too much for some visitors.

It wasn't until the 19th century that the first permanent settlers arrived on the island. Most earned a living as fishermen or by harvesting timber. GBI remained sparsely populated until 1955, when American developer Wallace Groves joined British industrialist Sir Charles Hayward to build the tax-free city of Freeport for tourism and manufacturing. Today, tourism remains the lifeblood of the island's 50,000 residents.

COMING ASHORE   On Grand Bahama Island, your ship docks at a dreary port in the middle of nowhere, a $10 taxi ride from Freeport and the International Bazaar, center of most of the action.

CALLING HOME FROM THE BAHAMAS   There are long-distance phones in the port terminal.

INFORMATION   Information is available from the **Grand Bahama Tourism Board,** International Bazaar in Freeport (© **800/823-3136** or 242/352-8044). Another information booth is located at Port Lucaya (© **242/373-8988**). It's open from 9am to 5:30pm Monday to Saturday. For information before you go, call the **Bahamas Tourism Board** in New York (© **800/4-BAHAMAS**) or visit the website at **www.bahamas.com**.

GETTING AROUND

Once you get to Freeport by taxi, you can explore the center of town on foot. If you want to make excursions to the west or east ends of the island, your best bet is to rent a car.

BY TAXI   The government sets taxi rates, which start at $2 and increase 30¢ for each additional quarter-mile. Cabs wait at the dock, or you can call **Freeport Taxi Company** (© **242/352-6666**) or **Grand Bahama Taxi Union** (© **242/ 352-7101**).

BY RENTAL CAR   Roads are good on GBI, and traffic is light. Remember, though, that driving is on the left side. **Avis, Budget, Dollar,** and **Hertz** all have offices here.

BY MOTOR SCOOTER OR BICYCLE   You can rent scooters or bicycles at the major hotels such as **The Resort at Bahamia,** West Sunrise Highway (© **242/350-7000**). A two-seat scooter requires a $100 deposit and rents for about $40 a day; bicycles require a $50 deposit and cost about $12 for a half day, $20 for a full day.

BY BUS   Public bus service runs from the International Bazaar to downtown Freeport and from the Pub on the Mall to the Lucaya area. The typical fare is 75¢ to $1.

SHORE EXCURSIONS OFFERED BY THE CRUISE LINES

Snorkel Adventure ($29–$35, 3 hr.): It's a standard snorkeling excursion, let-ting you swim with the fishes and explore coral formations.

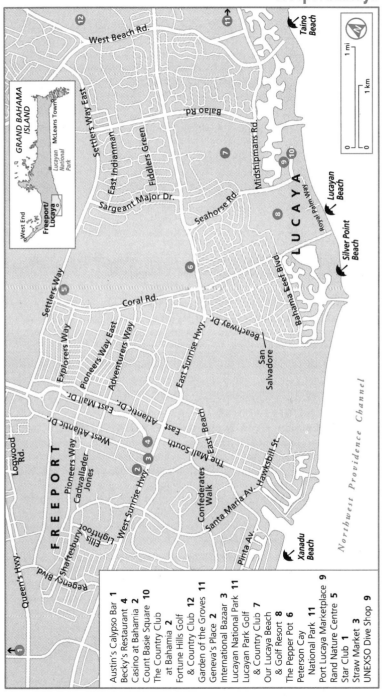

West Beach Rd.

Taino Beach

1 mi

1 km

GRAND BAHAMA ISLAND

McLeans Town

Lucayan National Park

West End

Freeport/Lucaya

Settlers Way East

Balao Rd.

East Indianman

Fiddlers Green

Sargeant Major Dr.

Seahorse Rd.

Midshipmans Rd.

L U C A Y A

Lucayan Beach

Silver Point Beach

Royal Palm Way

Settlers Way

Coral Rd.

Explorers Way

Pioneers Way East

Adventurers Way

East Sunrise Hwy.

Beachway Dr.

San Salvadore

Bahama Reef Blvd.

East Mall Dr.

West Atlantic Dr.

Pioneers Way

East Atlantic Dr.

The Mall South

East Beach

Confederates Walk

Santa Maria Av.

Hawksbill St.

Pinta Av.

Cadwallader Jones

Logwood Rd.

F R E E P O R T

Ellis

Lightroot

Shaftesbury

Regency Blvd.

Queen's Hwy.

Xanadu Beach

Northwest Providence Channel

Austin's Calypso Bar **1**
Becky's Restaurant **4**
Casino at Bahamia **2**
Count Basie Square **10**
The Country Club
  at Bahamia **2**
Fortune Hills Golf
  & Country Club **12**
Garden of the Groves **11**
Geneva's Place **2**
International Bazaar **3**
Lucayan National Park **11**
Lucayan Park Golf
  & Country Club **7**
Our Lucaya Beach
  & Golf Resort **8**
The Pepper Pot **6**
Peterson Cay
  National Park **11**
Port Lucaya Marketplace **9**
Rand Nature Centre **5**
Star Club **1**
Straw Market **3**
UNEXSO Dive Shop **9**

Frommer's Favorite Freeport/Lucaya Experiences

Touring Lucayan National Park: About 19km (12 miles) from Lucaya, this park boasts one of the loveliest beaches on Grand Bahama, as well as caves, mangroves, and nature walks through various ecological zones. (See "Shore Excursions Offered by the Cruise Lines," below.)

Visiting the Star Club: Built in the 1940s, this gem has hosted many famous guests over the years. A salty old joint, it's now the island's only after-hours bar and a watering hole Ernest Hemingway would have loved. (See "Great Local Restaurants & Bars," below.)

Glass Bottom Boat Tour ($23, 3 hr.): Departing from Port Lucaya Marketplace, this trip allows you to view coral reefs without getting your feet wet. Divers feed the fish below as you watch.

Sanctuary Bay Dolphin Encounter ($75, 3¼ hr.): Pat a dolphin on the nose! On this excursion you can watch, touch, and photograph Flipper, or at least one of his relatives. See the UNEXSO information below for more elaborate dolphin excursions you can arrange on your own.

Kayaking Nature Adventure ($70, 6 hr.): Visit a protected island creek, kayak through a mangrove forest, explore the island's caves, and take a guided nature walk into Lucayan National Park. The excursion includes lunch and beach time.

Lucayan Beach Experience ($46, 6 hr.): The Lucayan Beach resort complex has facilities for pool volleyball, basketball, beach bowling, and body painting. The cost includes lunch. But $46 to go to the beach? C'mon.

EXCURSIONS OFFERED BY LOCAL AGENCIES

Kayak & Bike Tours: Kayak Nature Tours (© 242/373-2485) offers three worthwhile and recommended excursions suitable for cruisers. The first, to Lucayan National Park, features sea kayaking through mangroves, a nature hike, a stop at two caves, and a swim and picnic at Gold Rock Beach ($69, 6 hr.). The second, to Peterson Cay National Park, includes sea kayaking to the small offshore cay, guided snorkeling, beach time, and lunch ($69, 5 hr.). The other features a 5-hour bicycle ride on a historic trail through nature. Frequent stops, snacks, and a swim are included ($69). Guides on each of the tours are personable, informative, and professional.

Scuba, Snorkeling, Shark Dives & Dolphin Swims: In the Bahamas, reef diving takes a backseat to theme park–style "adventure" programs, including shark-feeding dives and swim-with-dolphins adventures. One of the premier diving and snorkeling facilities in the Caribbean, the **Underwater Explorers Society (UNEXSO),** at Lucaya Beach (© 800/992-3483 or 242/373-1244; www.unexso.com), offers reef, shark, and wreck dives. Two-tank reef dives are $70, shark dives are $89, 3-hour learn-to-dive courses are $99, and snorkeling trips are $29 adults, $15 children under 12. Premier snorkeling sites include Paradise Cove and Deadman's Reef. UNEXSO also allows divers to swim alongside dolphins in the open ocean. Several different programs are available. The **Close Encounter** ($59, children under 5 free) allows guests to observe the sea mammals from an observation deck while listening to an informative presentation.

Later, you can wade into the waist-high water and touch the creatures. The highlight of the **Swim with the Dolphins** experience ($139, minimum age 12, under 16 must be accompanied by an adult) is swimming alongside the animals in protected waters after a briefing on dolphin behavior. The open-ocean **Snorkel with the Dolphins** program ($159, minimum age 12, under 16 must be accompanied by an adult) allows you to dive with bottlenose dolphins in shallow waters. These programs are popular, so advance reservations are a must.

Party/Snorkel Cruises: Superior Watersports in Freeport (© 242/373-7863) offers daily 5-hour beach party/snorkeling cruises that include equipment, lunch, and unlimited rum punch ($59 for adults, $39 for children 2–12). **Paradise Watersports,** at the Xanadu Beach Resort and Marina (© 242/352-2887), offers a snorkeling cruise that transports passengers on a 48-foot catamaran to a coral reef ($30 adults, $15 children under 12) and a glass-bottom boat ride ($25 adults, $15 children under 12).

ON YOUR OWN: BEYOND THE PORT AREA

There's nothing of note within walking distance of the port. You must take a cab over to Freeport/Lucaya for all attractions.

One of the island's prime attractions, the 5-hectare (12-acre) **Garden of the Groves,** was once the private meditation garden of Freeport's founder, Wallace Groves. The tranquil park features waterfalls, flowering shrubs, about 10,000 trees, tropical birds, Bahamian raccoons, Vietnamese pot-bellied pigs, and West African pygmy goats. The serene hilltop chapel overlooking the pond is a popular place for exchanging vows. It's located at the intersection of Midshipman Road and Magellan Drive, Freeport (© 242/373-5668), and is open Monday through Saturday from 9am to 4pm, Sunday 10am to 4pm; $9.95 for adults, $6.95 for ages 3 to 10.

About a kilometer (a couple of miles) east of downtown Freeport, the 100-acre **Rand Nature Centre** serves as the regional headquarters of the Bahamas National Trust. Pineland nature trails meander past native flora and wild birds, including the Bahama parrot and the island's only flock of West Indian flamingos. Other highlights include native animal displays (don't miss the boa constrictors), a replica of a Lucayan Indian village, an education center, and a gift shop. It's located on East Settlers Way, Freeport (© 242/352-5438), and is open Monday through Saturday, 9am to 4pm; $5 for adults, $3 for ages 5 to 12.

Peterson Cay National Park, approximately 24km (15 miles) east of Freeport and 1km (half a mile) offshore, is accessible by boat only. Coral reefs ringing the tiny island make for great snorkeling and diving, and the serene location is perfect for a picnic. For information, contact the Rand Nature Centre (© 242/352-5438).

If your ship's in port late, don't miss the free nightly concert at **Count Basie Square,** in the center of Port Lucaya's waterfront restaurant-and-shopping complex. The legendary jazz bandleader who lends his name to the square had a home on Grand Bahama, and today the square's vine-covered bandstand attracts steel-drum bands, small Junkanoo groups, and gospel singers.

SHOPPING

The **International Bazaar,** at East Mall Drive and East Sunrise Highway, next to the Casino at Bahamia, is pure 1960s Bahamian kitsch, and though relentlessly cheerful, it's a little long in the tooth. Each area of the 4-hectare (10-acre), 100-shop complex attempts to capture the ambience of a different region of the globe.

Stereotypes abound. You'll find Japanese items in the "Ginza," sidewalk cafes on the "Left Bank," silk saris in "India," woodcarvings and dashikis in "Africa," serapes and piñatas in "Spain," and everything from high-end luxury goods to T-shirts throughout. Some items here run about 40% less than in the United States, though certainly not all. Buses marked INTERNATIONAL BAZAAR deliver passengers to the center's much-photographed Torii Gate, a Japanese symbol of welcome.

The **Straw Market,** beside the International Bazaar, features items with a Bahamian touch—baskets, hats, handbags, and place mats. Quality varies, so look around before buying your souvenirs.

The **Port Lucaya Marketplace,** on Seahorse Road near the UNEXSO Dive Shop, is a 2½-hectare (6-acre) shopping-and-dining complex much like the International Bazaar. Steel-drum bands and strolling musicians add to the festive atmosphere. Many of the restaurants and shops overlook a 50-slip marina, and the boardwalk along the water is ideal for watching the dolphins at **UNEXSO** (www.unexso.com), which has a dive shop if you're in need of wet suits, underwater cameras, or more prosaic items such as swimsuits, sunglasses, and hats.

BEACHES
Grand Bahama Island has huge stretches of white-sand beaches. **Xanadu Beach,** immediately east of Freeport at the Xanadu Beach Resort, is the premier stretch in the Freeport area, offering most watersports equipment. It can get crowded at times. **Taíno Beach, Churchill Beach,** and **Fortune Beach** are all conveniently located on the Lucaya oceanfront. A 20-minute ride east of Lucaya, **Gold Rock Beach** may be the island's best. Secluded in Lucayan National Park, it has barbecue pits, picnic tables, and a spectacular low tide. **Barbary Beach,** slightly closer to Lucaya, is great for seashell hunters, and in May and June white spider lilies in the area bloom spectacularly.

SPORTS
GOLF With more links than any other island in the Bahamas, Grand Bahama is becoming a prime golf destination. **The Country Club at Bahamia,** The Mall South (© 242/352-6721), has two championship courses. The Emerald Course has plenty of trees along the fairways, as well as an abundance of water hazards and bunkers. Its toughest hole is the ninth, a par-5 with 498m (545 yd.) from the blue tees to the hole. The Ruby Course has a total of 6,172m (6,750 yd.) if played from the championship tees.

Our Lucaya Beach & Golf Resort, Royal Palm Way, F-42500, Lucaya (© 242/373-2002), also has two courses. The Lucayan course, designed by Dick Wilson, features well-protected elevated greens, fairways lined with tropical foliage, and doglegs. The par-72 links-style Reef course, designed by Robert Trent Jones, Jr., is 6,337m (6,930 yd.) from the championship tees, with water traps on 13 of 18 holes.

The course at **Lucayan Park Golf & Country Club,** at Lucaya Beach (© 242/373-1066), was recently made over and is known for its entrance and a hanging boulder sculpture. Greens are fast, and there are a couple of par-5 holes more than 457m (500 yd.) long. Total distance from the blue tees is 6,240m (6,824 yd.); par is 72.

Fortune Hills Golf & Country Club, Richmond Park, Lucaya (© 242/373-4500), was designed as an 18-hole course, but the back nine were never completed. You can replay the front nine for a total of 6,324m (6,916 yd.) from the blue tees; par is 72.

You can rent clubs and other equipment from all of GBI's golf courses. Greens fees for 18 holes during winter months range from $40 (Fortune Hills) to $90 (The Country Club at Bahamia and Our Lucaya). Prices drop as much as 50% during the summer.

WATERSPORTS   Paradise Watersports, at the Xanadu Beach Resort and Marina (✆ **242/352-2887**), rents paddle-boats ($8 for 30 min.) and offers water-skiing ($20 for 30 min.) and parasailing ($40).

GAMBLING
The 20,000-square-foot **Casino at Bahamia,** on the Mall at West Sunrise Highway (✆ **242/350-7000**), offers gaming, dining, and live entertainment. The exterior looks like a Moroccan palace—a fanciful Kismet sort of conceit that's perfect next to the kitsch of the International Bazaar. Serious gamblers appreciate the variety of games: full-service sports book, double odds, craps, blackjack, minibaccarat, roulette, Caribbean stud poker, big six wheel, and hundreds of slots and poker video games. The facility's $10 million facelift was completed in late 2001.

GREAT LOCAL RESTAURANTS & BARS
The most popular **Bahamian beer** is Kalik. Bahamian Hammerhead, another brand, is brewed on Grand Bahama. GBI's **local rums** include Don Lorenzo and Ricardo.

If you'd like a taste of the Bahamas the way they used to be, head for the **Star Club,** on Bayshore Road, on the island's west end (✆ **242/346-6207**). Built in the 1940s, the Star was Grand Bahama's first hotel, and over the years it's hosted many famous guests. The joint's still run by the family of the late Austin Henry Grant, Jr., a former Bahamian senator and West End legend. You can order Bahamian chicken in the bag, burgers, fish and chips, or "fresh sexy" conch prepared as chowder, fritters, and salads. But come for the good times, not the food. Next door, **Austin's Calypso Bar** is a colorful old dive if ever there was one.

At Freeport Harbor, near the cruise ship dock, **Pier 1** (✆ **242/352-6674**) serves clam chowder, fresh oysters, baby shark, sand crabs, a fresh fish of the day, and more in several dining rooms. There's also a nice high-ceilinged bar. **Geneva's Place,** East Mall Drive and Kipling Lane (✆ **242/352-5085**), offers traditional Bahamian meals. It's one of the best places to sample conch, whether it be stewed, cracked, or fried, or part of a savory conch chowder. **The Pepper Pot,** East Sunrise Highway at Coral Road (✆ **242/373-7655**), a 5-minute drive east of the International Bazaar in a tiny shopping mall, serves takeout portions of the best carrot cake on the island, as well as a savory conch chowder, fish, pork chops, chicken souse (a traditional soup), cracked conch, sandwiches, and hamburgers. **Becky's Restaurant,** at the International Bazaar, East Sunrise Highway (✆ **242/352-8717**), offers authentic Bahamian cuisine prepared in the time-tested style of the Out Islands. Try the souse, stewed fish, and johnnycakes.

6 Barbados
No port of call in the southern Caribbean can compete with Barbados when it comes to natural beauty, attractions, and fine dining. With all it offers, you'll think the island is much bigger than it is. But what really put Barbados on world tourist maps is its seemingly endless stretches of pink and white sandy beaches, among the best in the entire Caribbean Basin.

Frommer's Favorite Barbados Experiences

Renting a Car for a Barbados Road Trip: Seventeenth-century churches, tropical flowers, snorkeling, great views, and more are just a rental-car ride away. (See "On Your Own: Beyond the Port Area," below.)

Visiting Gun Hill Signal Station: If you've got less time, hire a taxi or rent a car and go to Gun Hill for panoramic views of the island. (See "On Your Own: Beyond the Port Area," below.)

Taking a Submarine Trip: Sightseeing submarines make several dives daily. (See "Shore Excursions Offered by the Cruise Lines," below.)

This Atlantic outpost was one of the most staunchly loyal members of the British Commonwealth for over 300 years, and although it gained its independence in 1966, Britishisms still remain—the accent is British, driving is on the left, cricket is a popular sport, and Queen Elizabeth II is still officially the head of state.

Originally operated on a plantation economy that made its aristocracy rich, the island is the most easterly in the Caribbean, floating in the mid-Atlantic like a great coral reef. Topography varies from rolling hills and savage waves on the eastern (Atlantic) coast to densely populated flatlands, rows of hotels and apartments, and sheltered beaches in the southwest.

The people in Barbados are called Bajans, and you'll see this term used everywhere.

COMING ASHORE   The cruise ship pier, a short drive from Bridgetown, the capital, is one of the best docking facilities in the southern Caribbean. You can walk right into the modern cruise ship terminal, which has car rentals, taxi services, sightseeing tours, and a tourist information office, plus shops and scads of vendors (see "Shopping," below).

If you want to go into Bridgetown, about 1.5km (a mile) from the port, instead of to the beach, you can take a hot, dusty walk of at least 30 minutes, or catch a taxi. The one-way fare ranges from $4 on up. There's also a bus running until noon for $1.

There's a huge phone center in the terminal where you can make credit-card calls to the U.S. and other international destinations. You'll also find fax facilities and phone cards and stamps for sale.

LANGUAGE   **English** is spoken with an island lilt.

CURRENCY   The Barbados dollar (BD$) is the official currency, and is available in $100, $20, $10, and $5 notes and $1, 25¢, and 10¢ silver coins, plus 5¢ and 1¢ copper coins. The exchange rate is BD$1.90 to U.S.$1 (BD$1 = 53¢ U.S.). Unless otherwise specified, prices in this section are given in U.S. dollars. Most stores take traveler's checks or U.S. dollars, so don't bother to convert them if you're here for only a day.

INFORMATION   The Barbados Tourism Authority is on Harbour Road (P.O. Box 242), Bridgetown, Barbados, W.I. (© **888/BARBADOS** or 246/427-2623; www.barbados.org). Its cruise terminal office, which is very well run, is always open when a cruise ship is in port.

Barbados

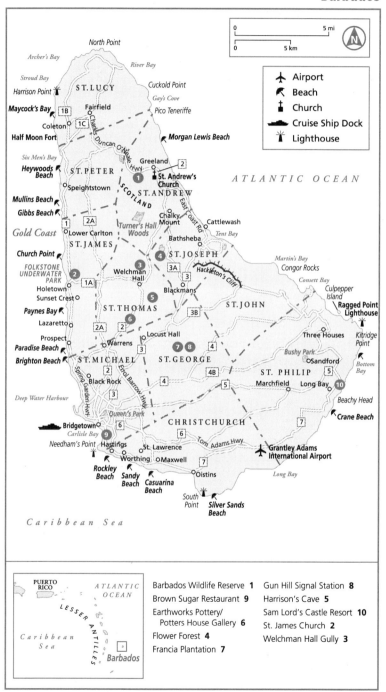

0 _____ **5 mi**
0 _____ **5 km**

✈ Airport
🏄 Beach
⛪ Church
🚢 Cruise Ship Dock
🗼 Lighthouse

North Point
Archer's Bay
Stroud Bay
River Bay
Harrison Point
Maycock's Bay
1B
Fairfield
Coleton
1C
Half Moon Fort
Cuckold Point
Gay's Cove
Pico Teneriffe
Morgan Lewis Beach

ST. LUCY

Six Men's Bay
Heywoods Beach
ST. PETER
Speightstown
Greeland
2
St. Andrew's Church
St. Andrew's Church
ATLANTIC OCEAN

ST. ANDREW

Mullins Beach
Gibbs Beach
1
2A
Turner's Hall Woods
Chalky Mount
Cattlewash
Gold Coast
Lower Carlton
Bathsheba
Tent Bay
ST. JAMES
Church Point
FOLKSTONE UNDERWATER PARK
4 ST. JOSEPH
Martin's Bay
Congor Racks
2
3
Welchman Hall
3A
3
Hackleton's Cliff
Consett Bay
Culpepper Island
Ragged Point Lighthouse
Holetown
Sunset Crest
1A
Blackmans
5
ST. JOHN
Paynes Bay
Lazaretto
ST. THOMAS
6
3B
Prospect
2A
2
Locust Hall
Three Houses
Kitridge Point
Warrens
7 **8**
4
Bushy Park
Bottom Bay
Paradise Beach
Brighton Beach
ST. MICHAEL
3
ST. GEORGE
Sandford
ST. PHILIP
5
2
4B
Black Rock
3
4
5
Marchfield
Long Bay
10
Deep Water Harbour
Queen's Park
Beachy Head
Bridgetown
6
CHRISTCHURCH
Crane Beach
Carlisle Bay
9
6
7
Needham's Point
Hastings
St. Lawrence
Tom Adams Hwy.
Grantley Adams International Airport
Rockley Beach
Worthing
Maxwell
7
Sandy Beach
Casuarina Beach
Oistins
Long Bay
South Point
Silver Sands Beach

Caribbean Sea

PUERTO RICO
ATLANTIC OCEAN
LESSER ANTILLES
Caribbean Sea
Barbados

Barbados Wildlife Reserve **1**
Brown Sugar Restaurant **9**
Earthworks Pottery/ Potters House Gallery **6**
Flower Forest **4**
Francia Plantation **7**
Gun Hill Signal Station **8**
Harrison's Cave **5**
Sam Lord's Castle Resort **10**
St. James Church **2**
Welchman Hall Gully **3**

109

CALLING FROM THE U.S.   When calling Barbados from the United States, you need only dial a "1" before the telephone numbers listed here.

GETTING AROUND

BY TAXI   Taxis are not metered, but their rates are fixed by the government. Even so, drivers may try to get more money out of you, so make sure you settle on the rate before getting in. Taxis are identified by the letter *Z* on their license plates, and you'll find them just outside of the terminal.

BY BUS   Blue-and-yellow public buses fan out from Bridgetown every 20 minutes or so onto the major routes; their destinations are marked on the front. Buses going south and east leave from Fairchild Street, and those going north and west depart from Lower Green and the Princess Alice Highway. Fares are about BD$1.50 (75¢ U.S.) and exact change is required.

Privately owned minibuses run shorter distances and travel more frequently. These bright yellow buses display destinations on the bottom-left corner of the windshield. In Bridgetown, board at River Road, Temple Yard, and Probyn Street. Fare is about BD$1.50 (75¢ U.S.).

BY RENTAL CAR   While it's a good way to see the island if you've got an adventurous streak and an easygoing attitude, before you decide to rent a car, keep in mind that driving is on the left side of the road and the signs are totally inadequate (boy, could we tell you stories!). **Hertz** has an office here. Rental cars all have an *H* on their license plates (meaning "hired"), so everyone will know you're a tourist.

SHORE EXCURSIONS OFFERED BY THE CRUISE LINES

It's not easy to get around Barbados quickly and conveniently, so a shore excursion is a good idea here.

Harrison's Cave ($37–$54, 3–4 hr.): Most cruise lines offer a tour to Harrison's Cave in the center of the island (see "On Your Own: Beyond the Port Area," below, for details).

Atlantis Submarine Adventure ($83–$89, 2 hr.): *Atlantis* transports passengers through Barbados's undersea world, where you can watch the fishies and other colorful marine life through 28-inch windows.

Barbados Highlights Bus Tour ($29–$38, 3 hr.): Tours take passengers by bus to Gun Hill Signal Station, St. John's Church, and Sam Lord's Castle Resort (see "On Your Own: Beyond the Port Area," below, for details).

TOURING THROUGH LOCAL OPERATORS

Island Tours/Eco Tours: Since most cruise lines don't really offer a comprehensive island tour, many passengers deal with one of the local tour companies. **Bajan Tours,** Glenayre, Locust Hall, St. George (© **800/550-6288,** ext. 2225 from the U.S., or 246/437-9389; www.funbarbados.com/Tours/bajantrs.cfm), offers an island tour that leaves between 8:30 and 9am and returns to the ship before departure. It covers all the island's highlights. On Friday they conduct a heritage tour, focusing mainly on the island's major plantations and museums. On Tuesday and Wednesday they offer an Eco Tour, which takes in the natural beauty of the island. Call ahead for information and to reserve a spot. The cost is generally around $56 per person.

Taxi Tours: If you can afford it, touring by taxi is far more relaxing than the standardized bus tour. Nearly all Bajan taxi drivers are familiar with their island

and like to show off their knowledge to visitors. The standard rate is about $20 per hour per taxi (for one to four passengers). You might want to try contacting taxi owner/driver **Aaron Francis** (© **246/431-9059**). He's a gem—friendly, reliable, and knowledgeable.

ON YOUR OWN: WITHIN WALKING DISTANCE

About the only thing you can walk to is the cruise terminal. The modern, pleasant complex has an array of duty-free shops and retail stores, plus many vendors selling arts and crafts, jewelry, liquor, china, crystal, electronics, perfume, and leather goods.

ON YOUR OWN: BEYOND THE PORT AREA

We don't recommend wasting too much time in Bridgetown—it's hot, dry, and dusty, and the honking horns of traffic jams only add to its woes. So, unless you want to go shopping, you should spend your time exploring all the beauty the island has to offer instead. The tourist office in the cruise terminal is very helpful if you want to go somewhere on your own.

Welchman Hall Gully, St. Thomas (Hwy. 2 from Bridgetown; © **246/438-6671**), is a lush tropical garden owned by the Barbados National Trust. It's 13km (8 miles) from the port (reachable by bus) and features some plants that were here when the English settlers landed in 1627.

All cruise ship excursions visit **Harrison's Cave,** Welchman Hall, St. Thomas (© **246/438-6640**), Barbados's top tourist attraction. Here you can see a beautiful underground world from aboard an electric tram and trailer. Admission is $13 for adults and $6 for children. If you'd like to go on your own, a taxi ride takes about 30 minutes and costs just under $25.

About 1.5km (a mile) from Harrison's Cave is the **Flower Forest,** Richmond Plantation, St. Joseph (© **246/433-8152**). This old sugar plantation stands 255m (850 ft.) above sea level near the western edge of the "Scotland district," in one of the most scenic parts of Barbados. The forest is 19km (12 miles) from the cruise terminal; one-way taxi fare is about $15 and the entrance fee is $8.

A fine home still owned and occupied by descendants of the original owner, the **Francia Plantation,** St. George (© **246/429-0474**), stands on a wooded hillside overlooking the St. George Valley, about 16km (10 miles) from the port. You can explore several rooms. It's open 10am to 4pm Monday through Sunday. Admission is $5 for adults, $2.50 for children. One-way taxi fare is about $20.

Built in 1818, the **Gun Hill Signal Station,** Highway 4 (© **246/429-1358**), one of two such stations owned and operated by the Barbados National Trust, is strategically placed on the highland of St. George and commands a wonderful panoramic view from east to west. It's 19km (12 miles) from the port; the one-way taxi ride costs about $15, and the entrance fee is $4.60. It's open Monday through Saturday, 9am to 5pm.

Sam Lord's Castle Resort, Long Bay, St. Philip (© **246/423-7350**), was built in 1820 by one of Barbados's most notorious scoundrels, Samuel Hall Lord. Legend says he made his money by luring ships onto the jagged, hard-to-detect rocks of Cobbler's Reef and then "salvaging" the wreckage. You can explore the architecturally acclaimed centerpiece of this luxury resort, which has a private sandy beach. It's a $12 taxi ride from the cruise terminal. It's open Monday through Saturday 10am to 5pm. Admission is $7.50.

If it's wildlife you want, head for the **Barbados Wildlife Reserve** (© **246/422-8826**), in St. Peter Parish on the northern end of the island. It's not exactly

Animal Kingdom, but on this 4-acre site you'll see turtles, rabbits, iguanas, peacocks, green monkeys, and a caged python.

Maybe it's the party life you crave. If so, don't miss the **Mount Gay Rum Tour** in Bridgetown (© **246/425-9066;** www.mountgay.com). You'll get a 45-minute soup-to-nuts introduction about rum in an air-conditioned rum shop (they say, of all the rum shops on the island, it's the only one with A/C). The tour costs $6 per person.

SHOPPING

The shopping-mall–size **cruise terminal** contains duty-free shops, retail stores, a convenience store, and a plethora of vendors selling arts and crafts, jewelry, liquor, china, crystal, electronics, perfume, and leather goods. Vendors sell great local hot sauce, as well as yummy Punch de Crème (you can get a free sample before buying), a creamy rum drink. For rum cake, an island specialty, the family-owned **Calypso Island Bakery** has a shop in the terminal (© **246/426-1702**). The shrink-wrapped cakes last up to 6 months and make great gifts. In general, though, you'll find a wider selection of stuff to buy and better prices in Bridgetown—last time we were there, T-shirts in the terminal were going for $15 apiece, a roll of film was $5, and a liter of J&B (yellow label) was anywhere from $10.75 to $15.15.

Good **duty-free** buys include cameras, watches, crystal, gold jewelry, bone china, cosmetics and perfumes, and liquor (including locally produced Barbados rum and liqueurs), along with tobacco products and British-made cashmere sweaters, tweeds, and sportswear. **Cave Shepherd,** Broad Street, Bridgetown (© **246/431-2121**), is the largest department store on Barbados and the best place to shop for tax-free merchandise.

Among Barbados **handcrafts,** you'll find lots of black-coral jewelry, but beware—because black coral is endangered, it's illegal to bring it back to the United States. We suggest looking, but not buying. Local clay potters turn out different products, some based on designs centuries old. Check out the **Potters House Gallery** (© **246/425-3463**) and **Earthworks Pottery** (© **246/425-0223;** www.barbados.org/shops/earthworks), both on Edghill Heights, in St. Thomas parish. Crafts include wall hangings made from grasses and dried flowers, straw mats, baskets, and bags with raffia embroidery. Bajan leatherwork includes handbags, belts, and sandals.

In Bridgetown, standout stores include **Articrafts,** on Broad Street, for Bajan arts and crafts, straw work, handbags, and bamboo items; and **Colours of De Caribbean** (© **246/436-8522**), at the Waterfront Marina, for tropical clothing, jewelry, and decorative objects.

BEACHES

Beaches on the island's western side—the luxury resort area called the Gold Coast—are far preferable to those on the surf-pounded Atlantic side, *which are dangerous for swimming.* The government requires that there be access to all beaches, via roads along the property line or through the hotel entrance, so all Barbados beaches are open to the public, even those in front of the big resort hotels and private homes.

ON THE WEST COAST (GOLD COAST)   Take your pick of the west-coast beaches, which are about a 15-minute, $8 taxi ride from the cruise terminal. **Payne's Bay,** with access from the Coach House (© **246/432-1163**) or Daphne's Restaurant (© **246/432-2731**), is a good beach for watersports, especially snorkeling. There's a parking area here. This beach can get rather crowded, but the beautiful bay makes it worth it. Directly south of Payne's Bay, at Fresh Water Bay, is a trio of fine beaches: **Brighton Beach, Brandon's Beach,** and **Paradise Beach.**

Church Point lies north of St. James Church, opening onto Heron Bay, site of the Colony Club Hotel (© **246/422-2335**). Although this beach can get crowded, it's one of the most scenic bays in Barbados, and the swimming is ideal. Retreat under some shade trees when you've had enough sun. You can also order drinks at the Colony Club's beach terrace.

Snorkelers in particular seek out the glassy blue waters by **Mullins Beach.** There are some shady areas, and you can park on the main road. Order food and drink at the Mullins Beach Bar (© **246/422-1878**).

ON THE SOUTH COAST   Depending on traffic, south-coast beaches are usually easy to reach from the cruise terminal. Figure on about an $8 taxi fare. **Sandy Beach,** reached from the parking lot on the Worthing main road, has tranquil waters opening onto a lagoon. This is a family favorite, with lots of screaming and yelling, especially on weekends. Food and drink are sold here.

Windsurfers are particularly fond of the trade winds that sweep across **Casuarina Beach** even on the hottest summer days. Access is from Maxwell Coast Road, across the property of Casuarina Beach Hotel (© **246/428-3600**). This is one of the wider beaches on Barbados. The hotel has food and drink.

Silver Sands Beach is to the east of the town of Oistins, near the very southernmost point of Barbados, directly east of South Point Lighthouse and near the Silver Rock Resort (© **246/428-2866**). This white sandy beach is a favorite with many Bajans, who probably want to keep it a secret from as many visitors as possible. (Tough luck, Bajans!) Windsurfing is good here, but not as good as at Casuarina Beach. You can buy drinks at Silver Rock Resort's bar, called Jibboms (© **246/428-2866**).

ON THE SOUTHEAST COAST   The southeast coast is known for its big waves, especially at **Crane Beach,** a white sandy stretch backed by cliffs and palms that often appears in travel-magazine articles about Barbados. The Crane Beach Hotel (© **246/423-6220**) towers above it from the cliffs, and Prince Andrew owns a house here. The beach offers excellent bodysurfing, but this is real ocean swimming, not the calm Caribbean, so be careful. At $20 from the cruise pier, the one-way taxi fare is relatively steep, so try to share the ride with other cruise passengers.

SPORTS

GOLF   The 18-hole, par-72 championship course at the west coast's **Sandy Lane Golf Club,** St. James (© **246/432-1311;** www.sandylane.com), is open to all. Greens fees are $220 in winter and $165 in summer for 18 holes, or $60 in winter and summer for 9 holes. Carts and caddies are available. Make reservations the day before you arrive in Barbados or before you leave home. The course is a 20- to 25-minute taxi ride from the cruise terminal. The one-way fare is about $20.

WINDSURFING   Experts say that Barbados windsurfing is as good as any this side of Hawaii. In fact, it's a very big business between November and April, when thousands of windsurfers from all over the world come here. **Silver Sands** is rated the best spot in the Caribbean for advanced windsurfing (skill rating 5 to 6). **Barbados Windsurfing Club,** at the Silver Sands Resort in Christ

Church (☎ **246/428-6001**), gives lessons and rents boards. To reach the club, take a taxi from the cruise terminal; it's an $18 one-way fare.

GREAT LOCAL RESTAURANTS & BARS

Two tips for you: Be sure to try the tasty local delicacy, flying fish (you can even get it in burger form), and, because this is a British-flavored island, the custom in restaurants is that you won't get your bill until you ask for it.

The Rusty Pelican, in downtown Bridgetown overlooking the Careenage, has great atmosphere and Bajan flying fish to boot. Also in town, try **Mustors** (☎ **246/426-5175**), on McGregor Street. It's a favorite with locals and serves authentic Barbadian lunch fare. For pub grub, try the hopping **Whistling Frog Pub** (☎ **246/420-5021**), located at Time Out at the Gap Hotel, next to the Turtle Beach Resort.

 Brown Sugar, Aquatic Gap (off Bay St.), St. Michael, just below Bridgetown on Carlisle Bay (☎ **246/426-7684;** www.brownsugarrestaurant.com), is an alfresco restaurant in a turn-of-the-century bungalow. The chefs prepare some of the tastiest Bajan specialties on the island. Of the main dishes, Creole-broiled pepper chicken is popular, as are the stuffed crab backs. There's a great lunch buffet for less than $20 per person.

7 Belize

Located on the northeastern tip of Central America, bordering Mexico on the north, Guatemala to the west and south, and the Caribbean to the east, Belize combines Central American and Caribbean cultures, offering both ancient Mayan ruins and a 56m (185-ft.) coral reef that runs the entire length of the country—it's the largest in the western hemisphere and the second largest in the world, supporting a tremendous number of patch reefs, shoals, and more than 1,000 islands called cayes (pronounced "keys"), the largest and most populous being Ambergris Caye. (Both Ambergris Caye and Caye Caulker are popular with visitors, offering a barefoot informality.) The country is noted for its eco-friendly philosophy and, unlike many other Caribbean countries, is serious in its dedication to conservation: One-fifth of Belize's total landmass is dedicated as nature reserves, and 7,770 square km (3,000 sq. miles) of its waters are protected as well.

 Previously known as British Honduras, Belize gained its independence from England in 1981. It has a parliamentary democracy and is a member of the British Commonwealth. Belmopan is the capital, but **Belize City** is the economic center of the country. Trying to choose which natural or man-made wonder to explore will be the most stress you'll feel in this very laid-back, diverse, stable, and English-speaking nation, whose population of about 216,000 comprises Creoles, Garifuna (Black Carib Indians), Mestizos (a mix of Spanish and Indian), Spanish, Maya, English, Mennonites, Lebanese, Chinese, and Eastern Indians. The country has the highest concentration of **Mayan sites** among all Central American nations, including Altun Ha, Caracol, Cerros, Lamanai, Lubaantun, Xunantunich, and also nearby Tikal in Guatemala. During the classic period (A.D. 250–900), there were a million Maya in Belize, and although the civilization began to decline after A.D. 900, some Mayan centers were occupied until contact with the Spanish in the 1500s. Today, Belize has joined with El Salvador, Guatemala, Honduras, and Mexico to establish *Mundo Maya* (World of the Maya), a program dedicated to the preservation of Mayan culture.

Belize

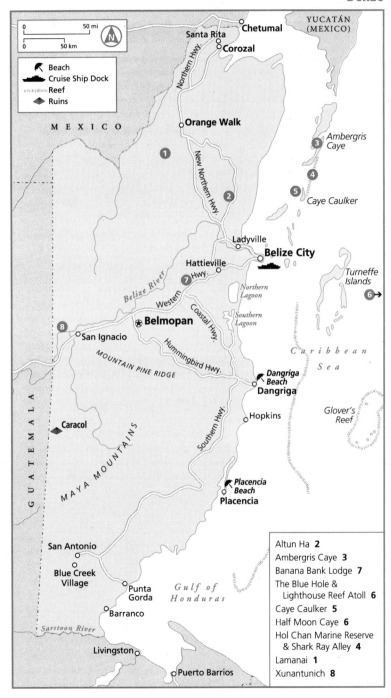

Scale: 50 mi / 50 km

Legend:
- Beach
- Cruise Ship Dock
- Reef
- Ruins

YUCATÁN (MEXICO)

Chetumal
Santa Rita
Corozal
Orange Walk
MEXICO
Ambergris Caye **3**
4
5 Caye Caulker
Ladyville
Belize City
Hattieville
Northern Lagoon
Southern Lagoon
Turneffe Islands **6** →
Belize River
Western Hwy.
Coastal Hwy.
Belmopan
San Ignacio
MOUNTAIN PINE RIDGE
Hummingbird Hwy.
Caribbean Sea
Dangriga Beach
Dangriga
Hopkins
Glover's Reef
Caracol
MAYA MOUNTAINS
Southern Hwy.
Placencia Beach
Placencia
San Antonio
Blue Creek Village
Punta Gorda
Gulf of Honduras
Barranco
Sarstoon River
Livingston
Puerto Barrios
GUATEMALA
Northern Hwy.
New Northern Hwy.
1
2
7
8

Altun Ha **2**
Ambergris Caye **3**
Banana Bank Lodge **7**
The Blue Hole &
  Lighthouse Reef Atoll **6**
Caye Caulker **5**
Half Moon Caye **6**
Hol Chan Marine Reserve
  & Shark Ray Alley **4**
Lamanai **1**
Xunantunich **8**

Frommer's Favorite Belize Experiences

Visiting Lamanai: Satisfying to both the archaeology buff and the wildlife enthusiast, a visit to this Mayan site gives you both land and water experiences. How can you pass up wonderful photo ops and howler monkeys? (See "Shore Excursions Offered by the Cruise Lines," below.)

Snorkeling or Diving at Hol Chan Marine Reserve & Shark Ray Alley: The reef is what it's all about when it comes to the waters of Belize: Friendly fish and playful stingrays make for an extremely memorable day. (See "Shore Excursions Offered by the Cruise Lines," below.)

Going Horseback Riding: Whether you're an experienced rider or have always wanted to give it a try, Banana Bank Ranch is definitely the place to go. (See "Excursions Offered by Local Agencies," below.)

Tubing in Caves: Glide down the Caves Branch River in an inner tube while wearing miner-style flashlight headbands. (See "Shore Excursions Offered by the Cruise Lines," below.)

The country gained dubious celebrity status in recent years as the setting for reality TV show *Temptation Island* (even though it's not, in fact, an island), but adventurous travelers have been vacationing here for years. It's only in the past several years, as Belize has gradually developed its tourism infrastructure, that cruise lines have added the country to their ever-expanding itineraries. Although Belize is a year-round destination, the waters are especially clear from April to June, and the dry season, lasting from February to May, coincides nicely with the cruise high season.

COMING ASHORE A new multimillion-dollar 5,000-square-foot pier opened in Belize City in October 2001. While big ships still can't pull alongside because of shallow waters and must tender in passengers from anchorages offshore (a 20- to 30-min. trip each way), the spiffy pier area now offers a new shopping complex, with restaurants, tourist information, and even a tranquil Mayan-themed courtyard. Smaller ships, like Windstar's, skip Belize City completely and anchor offshore from the cayes and other parts of the mainland, such as Dangriga.

LANGUAGE **English** is the official language of Belize, although **Spanish,** Creole, Garifuna, and Mayan are spoken throughout the country as well.

CURRENCY The **Belize Dollar** (BZ) has a fixed exchange rate of BZ$2 to U.S.$1 (U.S.$1 = BZ50¢), so even after a few too many rum punches, you won't have to take out your calculator here. Most establishments, as well as taxis and vendors on the street, take U.S. dollars, and most places take credit cards too. In especially touristy areas, just be sure to ask if the price quoted is in U.S. or BZ dollars.

INFORMATION If you want information before you leave home, contact the **Belize Tourism Board** (© 800/624-0686 or 2-31913; www.travel belize.org) or the **Belize Tourism Industry Association** (© 2-75717). The **Belize Audubon Society** (© 2-34987) also has a huge presence, in not only

America Online Keyword: Travel

Booked seat 6A, open return.

Rented red 4-wheel drive.

Reserved cabin, no running water.

Discovered space.

With over 700 airlines, 50,000 hotels, 50 rental car companies and
5,000 cruise and vacation packages, you can create the perfect get-
away for you. Choose the car, the room, even the ground you walk on.

Travelocity.com
A Sabre Company
Go Virtually Anywhere.

Book your air, hotel, and transportation all in one place.

Hotel or hostel? Cruise or canoe? Car?
Plane? Camel? Wherever you're going,
visit Yahoo! Travel and get total control
over your arrangements. Even choose
your seat assignment. So. One hump
or two? travel.yahoo.com

powered by
COMPAQ.

YAHOO!
Travel

bird-watching but all areas of nature conservation, and manages many of the country's reserves.

CALLING FROM THE U.S.   To make a call from the U.S. to Belize, dial the international access code (011), the country code (501), and then the number of the establishment.

GETTING AROUND

BY TAXI   Taxis are available at the pier, in town, and in resort areas, and are easily recognized by their green license plates. Although there are no meters on the taxis, the drivers do charge somewhat standard fares, but it's always important to find out what your fare will be prior to hiring a taxi.

BY WATER TAXI   At the **Marine Terminal** in Belize City (© **2-31969**) there's water-taxi service to Ambergris Caye, Caye Caulker, and various other cayes. Boats leave at 9am, 10:30am, noon, and 3pm. The ride from Belize City to San Pedro, the main town on Ambergris Caye, is approximately 80 minutes and costs $45 round-trip.

BY PLANE   Local airlines **Tropic Air** (© **800/422-3435** or 2-62012; www. tropicair.com) and **Maya Island Air** (© **800/225-6732** or 2-62435; www.maya airways.com) offer hourly flights to Ambergris Caye, Caye Caulker, Placencia, and Dangriga. The flight to Ambergris Caye takes approximately 20 minutes, and, because you fly so low, you get a breathtaking view of the surrounding cayes and atolls. Keep your eyes open for stingrays and dolphins swimming below you. Flights leave from Belize City to San Pedro approximately every 90 minutes until 5pm and cost approximately $94 round-trip. The term *puddle jumper* really applies here: The planes can be as small as six-seaters and you may even get to sit next to the pilot.

BY RENTAL CAR   Not recommended. Although most of the major roads and highways are paved, there are lots of patches in need of repair, which makes for a very bumpy ride.

SHORE EXCURSIONS OFFERED BY THE CRUISE LINES

Lamanai ($82, 7½ hr.): Lamanai is one of the largest ceremonial centers in Belize. In the original Mayan language, its name means "submerged crocodile," and you will see various crocodile carvings throughout the site. Starting with a 45-minute drive up the Northern Highway to Tower Hill, you'll board a riverboat and head up the New River. Along the way, through the mangroves, your guide will point out crocodiles basking in the sun, a variety of birds (including jacanas and hawks), delicate water lilies, and other exotic flowers such as black orchids. You'll pass local fisherman and, surprisingly, Mennonite farms—Mennonites from Canada and Mexico began arriving in Belize in 1958 in search of land and a more isolated and simple life, and today their community numbers around 7,000. Landing at the Lamanai grounds, you'll have lunch and then tour the series of temples. There are more than 700 structures, most of them still buried beneath mounds of earth. For a view above the thick jungle, you can climb some of the temples—look in the trees for toucans and spider monkeys playing or napping. You won't mistake the roar of the howler monkey. Your guide may tell you about the red gumbo-limbo tree, whose bark becomes a shade of red and then peels off—it's jokingly referred to as the tourist tree. There's a small archaeological museum on the site, as well as a few stands to buy souvenirs.

Altun Ha ($80, 6½ hr.): Meaning "water of the rock," Altun Ha is a relatively small site of temples and tombs that was rediscovered in 1957 during expansion of the Northern Highway. This is one of the most extensively excavated sites and was an important trading post during the classical Mayan period. Many treasures were found here, including a carved jade head representing Kinish Ahau, the Mayan sun god. It has become one of the country's national symbols, and is depicted on the nation's currency. The tour includes lunch, and there's a small gift shop on-site.

Xunantunich ($80–$92, 8 hr.): This site, near the Guatemalan border and overlooking the Mopan River, was a major ceremonial center during the classic Mayan period. After crossing the river by hand-cranked ferry, you can explore six major plazas surrounded by more than 25 temples and palaces, including "El Castillo" (the castle), the largest of the temples. Be sure to climb to the top—it's well worth it for the amazing panoramic view. There's also a new visitor's center with old excavation photos, a scale model, and a few exhibits and souvenir shops. Afterwards, you'll head to San Ignacio for lunch and enjoy a marimba band.

Hol Chan Marine Reserve & Shark Ray Alley ($70, 8 hr.): You'll head north for an hour-long speedboat ride to Hol Chan (Mayan for "little channel"), 6.4km (4 miles) southeast of San Pedro on Ambergris Caye, snorkel the reef for about an hour, and then head off to the Shark Ray Alley dive site, about 5 minutes away, where you'll see and pet dozens of southern stingrays and nurse sharks. Guides bring goodies for them to eat, and they stick around till the food is gone. Remember to bring a disposable underwater camera—if you're going to pet a stingray, you may as well capture it on film! Lunch is on San Pedro, and you can find yourself a rum punch, go shopping, or just hang out at the beach.

Cave Tubing ($75, 6½ hr.): On arriving at Jaguar Paw, you take a 45-minute hike down a jungle trail where your guide will point out various plants and trees used by the ancient Maya for medicinal purposes. When you get to the cave, your guide will hand out flashlights and inner tubes and set you afloat, propelled by the current, through the cave system. On several occasions, you'll emerge into the sunlight before entering another cave. The float lasts about 2 hours, after which you'll have lunch. Bring a change of clothes.

Belize City Tour ($30–$38, 3 hr.): It's hardly one of the most exciting tours and definitely not a great way to see the natural side of Belize, but if you want to do something quick and easy, this is the tour. It will give you a feel for the city, its colonial architecture, and its culture through a visit to the Belize Maritime Museum and Terminal, the Government House Museum, and St. John's Cathedral, built in 1812, making it the oldest Anglican cathedral in Central America. Around lunchtime, the Mennonite farmers and craftsman are out selling their handmade furniture. Their denim overalls, checked shirts, and straw cowboy hats make them easily recognizable.

EXCURSIONS OFFERED BY LOCAL AGENCIES

Taxi Tours: Generally, the excursions offered by the cruise lines are the way to go in Belize, but if you crave a more personalized experience, you can hire a taxi driver who doubles as a guide (make sure you tell them you want a guide before getting into the taxi and negotiating a price). Tour guides must be licensed by the Belize Tourism Board and are recognizable with a photo ID. Of the many operators, one of the larger ones is **Discovery Expeditions** (© 2-30748), which offers a wide variety of tours all around the country and can arrange custom tours. For a tour of Belize City, try to snag Lasalle Tillet of **S&L Travel & Tours** (*©* **2-77593**). Everyone in town seems to know him, and you'll enjoy his cheerful and insightful information.

Horseback Tours: Banana Bank Lodge (*©* **81-2020;** www.bananabank. com), located in Belmopan, about an hour's drive from the pier, offers 7-hour tours through the jungle, plains, and riverbank. Larger-than-life cowboy-owner John Carr greets each of his guests personally and makes your riding experience a memorable one. The $85 per-person cost includes a delicious traditional lunch and a tour of the grounds. Well-trained horses are matched to each rider's ability.

Fishing Excursions: Belize is a fishing mecca, with an abundance of game fish that guarantees excellent sport. The estuaries, inlets, and mouths to the many rivers are known for their tarpon, snook, and jacks; the lagoons and grass flats are known for the bonefish, permit, and barracuda; the coral reefs support grouper, snapper, jacks, and barracuda; and the deeper waters offshore are home to sailfish, marlin, bonito, and pompano. One of the largest operations is the **Belize River Lodge** (*©* **888/275-4843;** www.belizeriverlodge.com), which offers a day-fishing package that includes lunch and drinks ($350 for up to two guests). A favorite local fishing guide is **Richard Young, Jr.** (*©* **2-74385**). Most guides and boatmen speak English.

ON YOUR OWN: WITHIN WALKING DISTANCE

Belize City is the hub of the country but doesn't boast the country's major attractions. The historic **harbor district** right around the pier is small and quaint. You'll find a few restaurants, and the **Baron Bliss Park and Lighthouse** is just a short stroll away. After sailing from Portugal, the eponymous baron arrived sick with food poisoning, and remained aboard his yacht for 2 months while local fisherman and administrators treated him kindly and taught him about Belize. He died soon after, but not before changing his will and leaving $2 million to Belize in a trust fund. That money made possible the building of the Bliss Institute Library and Museum and a number of health clinics and markets around the country, as well as helping with the Belize City water system. The baron is considered Belize's greatest benefactor, and Baron Bliss Day, a national holiday, is celebrated on March 9.

Outside the immediate port area, much of the rest of the city is run down and poor, with narrow, crowded streets and many old colonial structures that are in need of repair. However, since tourism is an important industry in Belize, the country is making an effort to spruce up the city and reduce crime, instituting a squad of Tourism Police to patrol popular tourist areas. Its officers are dressed in brown uniforms.

ON YOUR OWN: BEYOND THE PORT AREA

A 20-minute flight will get you to **Ambergris Caye,** the largest of Belize's 200 offshore islands and the inspiration for the Madonna song "La Isla Bonita." You know, "last night I dreamt of San Pedro . . . tropical island breeze . . . all of nature wild and free . . . blah blah blah"? The thing is, she got it about right. They have a motto here: "No shoes, No shirt . . . No problem," and that's really true. Everyone drives around in golf carts, and you can too (for about U.S.$35 for an afternoon, from rental places located along the main streets and near the little airport). Once in San Pedro (the island's main town), the beach is akin to the main street, offering plenty of shopping, restaurants, bars, and watersports.

Slightly smaller **Caye Caulker** is Belize's second most popular caye, and is even more laid back, with plenty of beachfront restaurant and bars. Despite the growth of tourism, the island retains a small village feel, with a distinct cultural flavor not found in areas with large-scale tourist development. Almost all the businesses are locally owned and you rarely see vehicles larger than golf carts on the streets. You can just hang out on the beach or dive into some watersports, including snorkeling, scuba, fishing, kayaking, windsurfing, sailing, manatee watching, and birding.

Back in Belize City, the **Princess Hotel-Casino** is located a couple of kilometers (a mile or two) from the cruise pier on Newtown Barricks Road (© **800/ 770-4354** or 501/2-32670); it's about 10 minutes and $5 by taxi from the pier.

SHOPPING

In general, the best buys in Belize are wooden and slate carvings, Mayan calendars, pottery, ceramics, and furniture made by the Mennonites. Near the Radisson Pier, you'll find the **National Handicrafts Sales Centre** (© **2-33833**) specializing in locally made mahogany bowls and assorted other carvings and artwork. **Marie Sharp's hot sauces and jams** seem to be served everywhere and can be purchased to take home. On Ambergris Caye, you'll find a variety of slightly more upscale gift shops, and the excursion sites all have goods available.

BEACHES

Compared to many other islands in the Caribbean, the beaches of Belize are neither the biggest nor the widest, but they are relaxing, with very clear water. Areas that offer the best beach sunbathing are in the cayes, including Ambergris Caye, Caye Caulker, Tobacco Caye, Dangriga, and Placencia. There are no beaches near Belize City.

SPORTS

WATERSPORTS   If you don't opt for one of your ship's dive excursions, local dive shops can customize an experience as well. **Hugh Parkey's Belize Dive Connection** (© **888/223-5403** or 2-34526; www.belizediving.com) is conveniently located on the Radisson Pier and offers day scuba dives and snorkel trips with a yummy lunch catered by the Fort Street Restaurant. In San Pedro, **Aqua Dives** (© **800/641-2994** or 26-3415; www.aquadives.com) is located on the beachfront and can plan a diving or snorkeling adventure.

In the center of **Lighthouse Reef Atoll,** about 80km (50 miles) due east of Belize City, the "Blue Hole" was originally a cave. The roof fell in some 10,000 years ago as the land receded into the sea, leaving an almost perfectly circular hole 300m (1,000 ft.) in diameter and 124m (412 ft.) deep. Popularized by a Jacques Cousteau television special, it's become the most famous dive site in all Belize. **Half Moon Caye,** located at the southeast corner of Lighthouse Reef Atoll, was the first reserve to be established by the Natural Parks System Act of 1981, which specifically protected the Red-footed Booby bird and its rookery. Some 98 other species of birds have been recorded on the Caye.

One of the newest national parks in Belize is **Laughing Bird Caye,** located 21km (13 miles) southeast of Placencia Village in the Stann Creek District. Although the caye was named for the original large number of laughing gulls, the birds have virtually abandoned their rookery because of excessive human encroachment. Since Laughing Bird caye is a shelf atoll with deep channels, the scuba-diving and snorkeling opportunities are outstanding.

Many dive excursions include a barbecue lunch on **Goff's Caye.** Part of the Central Main Reef, it's a popular dive site itself.

GREAT LOCAL RESTAURANTS & BARS

The **local beer** is Belikan, and you can order it most anywhere. If you visit Altun Ha you'll recognize the site as the beer's logo (or vice versa).

IN BELIZE CITY Around the pier you'll find several pleasant restaurants within walking distance. You can stroll to The Great House Hotel at 13 Cork St. and find **The Smokey Mermaid** (② 2-34759), situated in a lovely mango-tree-shaded patio garden. One of their specialties is the yucca-crusted snapper with a fruity salsa topping. For dessert, be sure to try their coconut pie. The **Fort Street Restaurant,** 4 Fort St. (② 2-30116), has a delicious lunch menu and a very friendly staff. **Chateau Caribbean,** 6 Marine Parade (② 2-30800), offers Caribbean and Asian specialties. At the **Radisson Hotel** (② 2-33333) you have several dining choices either inside or on their deck outside overlooking the Caribbean.

IN SAN PEDRO, AMBERGRIS CAYE Most of the restaurants and bars here are on the beach, so you can just stroll along and stop at whatever place strikes your fancy.

ON CAYE CAULKER Caye Caulker has about 25 restaurants, also mostly on the beach, offering Belizean and international cuisine, including fresh seafood. Lobster, conch, and red snapper are seasonal specialties.

FARTHER OUT Heading west of Belize City, the very rustic **Cheers Bar & Restaurant** (② 1-49311) is kind of in the middle of nowhere on the Western Highway at mile 31 (about 3km/2 miles from The Belize Zoo and 26km/16 miles from Banana Bank Lodge), but the food is good, it has a nice outdoor patio, and it's frequented by tourists and locals. Leave behind a memento T-shirt to say you were here—there are dozens of them from all over the world. Still farther west, you'll find **Eva's Restaurant** at 22 Burns St., San Ignacio, about 5km (3 miles) from Xunantunich (② 9-22267). For warm hospitality, **La Palapa Restaurant,** Mayaland Villas, right off the highway in San Ignacio, about 3km (2 miles) from Xunantunich (② 9-23506), offers an outdoor, patio-style lunch setting.

8 Bequia

Bequia (meaning "Island of the Cloud" in the original Carib, and inexplicably pronounced *beck*-wee) is the largest island in the St. Vincent Grenadines, with a population of around 5,000. Sun-drenched, windswept, peaceful, and green (though arid), it's a popular stop for small-ship lines such as Clipper, ACCL, Star Clippers, Windjammer, and the more upscale Seabourn, SeaDream, and Windstar, which join the many yachts in Admiralty Bay throughout the yachting season.

Very much a tourism-oriented island, Bequia is nevertheless anything but touristy. You'll find a few of the requisite cheesy gift shops in the main town, **Port Elizabeth,** but none of the typical cruise port giants such as Little Switzerland. Instead, the town offers one of the most attractive port settings in the Caribbean, with restaurants, cozy bars, a produce market, and craft shops strung out along and around the **Belmont Walkway,** a path that skirts so close to the calm bay waters that at high tide you have to skip across rocks to avoid getting your feet wet. Many ships spend the night here or make late departures, allowing passengers to take in the nightlife.

The island's rich seafaring tradition manifests itself in fishing, sailing, boat building (though most handmade boats you'll see are scale models made for the yachting set), and even whaling, though this is whaling of more of a token, almost ritualistic sort—only about one whale is taken in any given year.

COMING ASHORE   Ships dock right in the center of the island's main town, Port Elizabeth, a stone's throw from the restaurants, bars, and shops that line the waterfront.

LANGUAGE   The official and daily-use language is **English.**

CURRENCY   The **Eastern Caribbean dollar** (EC$2.70 = $1 U.S.; EC$1 = 37¢ U.S.) is used on Bequia; however, U.S. dollars are accepted by all businesses. It's always a good idea to ask if you're not sure which currency a price tag refers to. Rates quoted in this section are given in U.S. dollars.

INFORMATION   There's a small tourist information booth right on the beach by the cruise dock, but frankly, you can almost see everything there is to do from the same spot. It's a pretty small island. For information before you go, contact the **Bequia Tourist Association** (✆ **784/458-3286;** www.bequia sweet.com) or the St. Vincent & The Grenadines Department of Tourism (✆ **212/687-4981** in the U.S., or 784/457-1502; www.svgtourism.com).

CALLING FROM THE U.S.   To place a call to Bequia you need only dial a "1" before the numbers listed in this section.

GETTING AROUND
Ships dock right in Port Elizabeth, putting you within walking distance of all the town sights. The popular Princess Margaret Beach is within walking distance as well.

 Frommer's Favorite Bequia Experiences

Strolling Along the Belmont Walkway: In the evenings, this walkway at water's edge makes for a terrifically romantic stroll as you make your way from one nightspot to the next. You might even pick up the company of one of the friendly port dogs, who seem more interested in companionship than panhandling. (See "On Your Own: Within Walking Distance," below.)

Visiting Brother King's Old Hegg Turtle Sanctuary: Wanna see baby turtles? This is your place. You'll see hundreds of the critters in the main swimming pool and in their own little private cubbyholes, and hear about the sanctuary's conservation efforts. Donations are gladly accepted. (See "On Your Own: Beyond the Port Area," below.)

Visiting the Lower Bay & Princess Margaret Beach: South of Port Elizabeth, this stretch of sand is frequently described by cruisers as "the best beach I've ever experienced." It's a little chunk of paradise, backed by waving palms and fronted by yachts bobbing at anchor in the distance. (See "Beaches," below.)

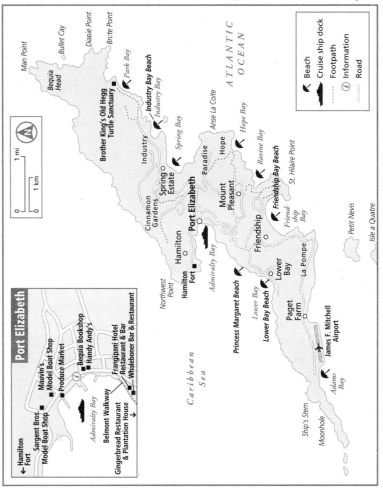

BY TAXI   You'll find plenty of taxis lined up right at the cruise dock to take you around the island. The fare is approximately $20 per hour, or $5 per person per hour for groups of more than four.

BY MINIBUS   The entire island of Bequia is served by a fleet of small, unofficial dollar-cab minibuses that cruise regular routes, picking up passengers when flagged down (there are also some obvious bus stops scattered around). Tell the driver where you want to go and he'll tell you a price.

BY RENTAL CAR   Rentals are available at **Handy Andy's Rentals,** on the Main Road in Port Elizabeth, to the right of the dock if you're facing inland (✆ **784/458-3722;** fax 784/457-3402). Day rental of a small golf-cart–type vehicle is $65. A Jeep Wrangler rents for $75. **Phil's Car Rental** (✆ **784/458-3304**), located at the cruise ship dock, has Geo Trackers and Suzuki Sidekicks for rent at $52 per day.

BY MOTORCYCLE/BICYCLE   **Handy Andy's** (see above) also rents Honda 250XR motorbikes for $45 and Mongoose mountain bikes for $20.

SHORE EXCURSIONS OFFERED BY THE CRUISE LINES

Bequia is very much a "relax and have a drink" kind of island, rather than one with a lot of definable, tourable attractions. Aside from a standard island tour, most excursions offered are sailing trips around the island and to neighboring Mustique and Tobago Cays.

Island Tour ($35, 3 hr.): The typical island tour is by taxi, meaning you can arrange one easily once you get ashore if your ship doesn't offer one officially. Tours generally visit beautiful Industry Bay on the island's east coast, the Old Hegg Turtle Sanctuary, and a model-boat shop, and at some point stop for a complementary drink in Spring Bay.

Sail & Snorkel Catamaran Trip ($85, 5–6 hr.): This is your typical booze cruise, though moderation is suggested if you're going to do any snorkeling. The trip sails around Bequia's coast, where you'll see the "Moonhole," a residential community set among odd rock formations, as well as the old whaling station on Petit Nevis, a small island off the coast.

Sailing Excursion to Mustique ($85, 7–8 hr.): Sail aboard a schooner to exclusive (read: rich people own it) Mustique, just southeast of Bequia, for strolling, shopping, snorkeling, or simply lying on the beach. Complimentary drinks are included aboard ship. A shorter version of this tour travels between islands by powerboat rather than sailing ship—less romantic, but speedier ($65, 3–4 hr.).

ON YOUR OWN: WITHIN WALKING DISTANCE

In theory, almost the entire island of Bequia is within walking distance, but only for serious walkers. We decided to test this theory out by walking from Port Elizabeth first to Hamilton Fort, just north of town, then backtracking through the port and down to the tiny old whaling village of **Paget Farm,** near the airport on Bequia's southern tip. As the crow flies it's not much of a distance, but curving roads and hilly terrain made it a real journey that took about 4 to 5 hours round-trip, with no significant stops. If your ship is in port late and you're in good shape, it's a great way to see the island (including lovely Friendship Bay, on the east coast) and meet some of the local people along the way. Bring water.

For those wanting something less strenuous, strolling around Port Elizabeth itself is close to idyllic. The **Belmont Walkway** runs south from the docks right at the water's edge (meaning at high tide parts of it are actually under a few in. of water), fronting many restaurants, shops, and bars. In the evenings this area is particularly romantic.

Heading north from the docks along the Main Road you'll find a homey **produce market** that also stocks some tourist items. Across the street, **Mauvin's Model Boat Shop** (② 784/458-3669) is one of the most visible reminders of the island's boat-building tradition, though now the money seems to lie in crafting scale models of real boats for sale to the yachting crowd. Farther along the Main Road, **Sargent Bros. Model Boat Shop** (② 784/458-3344) is a larger shop offering the same type of merchandise. The workshop is a little more accessible here, so you can easily see the craftsmen creating their wares (all the work is done by hand; no power tools are employed at all), and see models in various stages of construction. At both shops, the models are amazing, lovingly constructed, and signed by the craftsman—and they're not what you'd call cheap:

Tips Use Your Ship's Facilities

Since Bequia is an extremely dry island and is very conscious of water conservation, it has few public washrooms. You'd be well advised to use your
ship's bathroom facilities before coming ashore.

Prices start around $100 for a tiny model, and can go up as high as $10,000 for
something really fabulous.

If you continue walking along the Main Road, you'll pass through an area
with many boating supply stores and a few bars and food stands obviously
geared to the local fishing and sailing trades. It's a quiet, pretty walk, even
though it may well be the most "industrial" part of the island. Eventually you'll
come upon a concrete walkway hanging above the water along the coast. From
here the going gets rough—many sections of the walkway have been cracked and
heaved drastically off-kilter by hurricanes, and it's patched here and there with
planks and other makeshift materials. At the end of the walkway the road starts
curving uphill and inland through a quiet residential area, and thus all the way
up to **Hamilton Fort,** perched above Admiralty Bay and offering a lovely view
of Port Elizabeth, though that's about all it offers—a few tiny fragments of battlements and five plugged canons are all that remain of the old fort. A taxi can
take you here as well by another route, if you want to avoid the walk (a good
idea unless you're in decent shape and very sure-footed).

ON YOUR OWN: BEYOND THE PORT AREA

At Park Beach on the island's northeast coast, 3km (2 miles) east of Port Elizabeth, **Brother King's Old Hegg Turtle Sanctuary** (© 784/458-3596) offers a
chance to see conservation in action. Founded in 1995 by the eponymous King
and dedicated to raising and releasing Hawksbill turtle hatchlings, the sanctuary
is a real labor of love. A main concrete swimming pool and small plastic kiddy
pools allow maturing hatchlings to socialize. Brother King and his assistants are
on hand to tell you about their conservation efforts, and will gladly accept donations to help keep the place going.

Aside from this and the activities in Port Elizabeth, most of the island's other
attractions are beaches, so turn to that section, below.

SHOPPING

You'll find most shopping worth doing within walking distance of the docks in
Port Elizabeth. Heading south from the pier, one of the first businesses you'll
come to is the **Bequia Bookshop** (© 784/458-3905), selling books on the
island's and region's culture and history, books of poetry and prose by local
authors, yachting guides, and a selection of other fiction and nonfiction titles,
as well as truly beautiful scrimshaw pocket knives, pendants, money clips, necklaces, and pins, all made from polished camel bone rather than the traditional
whale bone. Presumably, camels are not yet endangered.

Sam McDowell, the artist who creates these scrimshaw items, opens his
Banana Patch Studio for visitors by appointment. Located in the little village
of Paget Farm on the southern part of the island, near the airport, the studio displays Sam's scrimshaw and whaling-themed paintings, as well as his wife Donna's
shellwork. Call or fax © 784/458-3865 for an appointment.

A Quiet Day on Union Island

Some small ships stop for a day at quiet, tranquil (very quiet, very tranquil) Union Island, the southernmost port of entry in the St. Vincent
Grenadines. Think of your stop here as a "recovery day" rather than a
whiz-bang exciting day in port: There are few facilities (none whatso-
ever in Chatham Bay, where ships usually tender passengers to land),
few people, and few opportunities to do anything more than swim,
snorkel, and do a little beachcombing. You'll likely see hundreds of
conch-shell pieces along the beach, since a number of local fishermen
are based here. (You can always tell if the conch was naturally thrown
up on the beach or caught, since those caught have a small gash in the
shell—the method the fishermen use to sever the muscle by which the
conch beast holds onto its shell home.) Some enterprising fishermen
set out the best shells they find on small tables, offering them to
tourists for a couple bucks—you miss out on the personal thrill of finding them yourself, but they're some mighty nice shells.

   Snorkeling is decent in Chatham Bay, though the waters don't yield
the diversity you'll see elsewhere in the eastern Caribbean.

There are several generic gift shops farther along, some fronting off the Belmont Walkway, including **Solana's,** for Caribelle batiks, T-shirts, and so on, and
The Crab Hole (© 784/458-3290), for batiks and jewelry.

   Heading in the other direction, north from the docks, you'll find the two
model-boat shops described above, as well as a couple of open-air souvenir/crafts
stalls, a produce market, and **Kennie's Music Shop** (© 784/458-3748), for
island sounds on CD and cassette.

BEACHES
Beaches are one of the big draws on Bequia, and all are open to the public. Tops
on the list is **Princess Margaret Beach,** a golden-sand stretch lying just south of
Port Elizabeth. To get there, take the Belmont Walkway to its end; from there,
take the dirt path over the hill. **Lower Bay beach** is a little farther down along
the same stretch of coast.

   On the northeast coast, the beach at **Industry Bay** is, despite its name,
windswept and gorgeous, a scene straight out of a romance novel. Trees on the
hills surrounding the bay grow up to a certain height and then level out, growing sideways due to the constant wind off the Atlantic. The small, three-room
Crescent Beach Hotel (© 784/458-3748) lies along this stretch, in case you
want to come back after your cruise and stay a while. Along the southeast coast
is **Friendship Bay,** an area that draws many European visitors.

   There are no clothing-optional beaches on Bequia. Also, do not under any
circumstances pick or eat the small green apples you'll see growing in some
spots. These are manchineel, and are extremely poisonous.

SPORTS
Besides walking (see above) and biking (mountain bikes are available to rent
from Handy Andy's Rentals right by the cruise dock), the sports here, like the

rest of life on the island, center around the water. **Dive Bequia** (© **784/458-3504;** www.dive-bequia.com) and **Bequia Dive Adventure** (© **784/458-3247**), located along Belmont Walkway, right by the docks, specialize in diving and snorkeling.

GREAT LOCAL RESTAURANTS & BARS

The coastal stretch along the Belmont Walkway is chockablock with restaurants and bars. The local beer of St. Vincent and the Grenadines is Hairoun, which is decent but not up to the level of St. Lucia's Piton. The local rum is Sunset.

The **Frangipani Hotel Restaurant and Bar** (© **784/458-3255**) is right on the water along the walkway. Lunch (served 10am–5pm) includes sandwiches, salads, and seafood platters. Dinner specialties include conch chowder, baked chicken with rice-and-coconut stuffing, and an array of fresh fish. On Thursday nights the bar hosts an excellent steel band. It's a lovely scene, with yachters, locals, cruisers from ships that have stayed late in port, and a coterie of friendly local dogs, all getting to know one another over drinks (the dogs usually have water) or settling down for the restaurant's special barbecue.

Farther along the walkway, the **Whaleboner Bar & Restaurant** (© **784/458-3233**) serves a nice thin-crust pizza (with toppings such as lobster, shrimp, and generic "fish"), sandwiches, fish and chips, and cold beer, either indoors or at tables in their shaded, oceanview front yard. It's a perfect casual resting-up spot after walking around the island.

The **Gingerbread Restaurant & Bar,** also right along the waterfront (© **784/458-3800**), has a beautiful balcony dining room that's open throughout the day, and its downstairs cafe serves coffee, tea, and Italian ice cream at outside tables. **Plantation House** (© **784/458-3425**), farther along still, is the premier dining spot on the island, and serves informal lunches between noon and 2:30pm. Service and cuisine are both first-rate. Reservations are recommended.

9 Bonaire

Ever wonder what's going on under all that water you've been cruising on for days? There's no better place to find out than the island of Bonaire—"Divers Paradise," as the slogan on the island's license plates says. Avid divers have flocked to this unspoiled treasure for years for its pristine waters, stunning coral reefs (which encircle the island just feet from shore), and vibrant marine life— it's simply one of the best places in the Caribbean for diving and snorkeling.

The island also offers other adventure activities such as mountain biking, kayaking, and windsurfing, but if these options sound too strenuous, why not just marvel at the sun-basking iguanas, fluorescent lora parrots, blue-tailed lizards, wild donkeys, graceful flamingos, and feral goats? As for flora, you're likely to see more cacti in Bonaire than anywhere outside of the deserts of Mexico and the Southwest. Sprawling bushes of exotic succulents and permanently windswept divi-divi trees also abound. If you'd rather join the iguanas and just bake in the sun, Bonaire's beaches are intimate and uncrowded. In fact, the entire island is cozy and manageable. In no time at all, you'll feel it's your very own private resort.

Relying on your high-school French, you might think Bonaire ("good air") is a French island. It's not. Located 80km (50 miles) north of Venezuela and 48km (30 miles) west of Curaçao, this untrampled, boomerang-shaped refuge—39km (24 miles) long and 5km to 11km (3–7 miles) wide, large enough to require a motorized vehicle if you want to explore, but small enough that you won't get lost—is the "B" of the ABC Netherlands Antilles chain (Aruba and Curaçao are the "A" and the "C"). The name "Bonaire" actually comes from the Caiquetio word "bonay," which means "low country."

The Caiquetios, members of the Arawak tribe who sailed from the coast of Venezuela a thousand years ago, were Bonaire's first human inhabitants. Europeans arrived 500 years later, in 1499, when Alonso de Ojeda and Amerigo Vespucci claimed the island for Spain. The Spanish enslaved the indigenous people and moved them to other Caribbean islands. Later, the Europeans used the island to raise cows, goats, horses, and donkeys. The Dutch gained control in the 1630s, and on the back of African slave labor, Bonaire became an important salt producer.

With the discovery of oil in Venezuela early in the 20th century, Aruba and Curaçao became refining centers, and Bonaire, too, got a piece of the pie. Tourism, the island's major industry today, developed after World War II, when Bonaire won self-rule from the Netherlands (though it remains a Dutch protectorate). The people of Bonaire are a mix of African, Dutch, and South American ancestries. You'll also meet expatriates from the U.S., Britain, and Australia.

COMING ASHORE   Cruise ships dock in the port of **Kralendijk** (*Crawl*-endike), the island's capital, commercial center, and largest town (pop. about 2,500). The dock leads to Wilhelmina Park, a pleasant public space named after a former Dutch queen. **Queen Beatrix Way,** the brick-paved path along the waterfront, is lined with open-air restaurants and bars. Most of the town's shopping is a block inland on **Kaya Grandi.**

Your best bet for making **long-distance phone calls** is the 24-hour central phone company office (Telbo) at Kaya Libertador Simón Bolívar 8.

LANGUAGE   Almost everyone in Bonaire speaks **English,** which, along with **Dutch,** is a required course in the local schools. **Papiamentu** is the local patois and language of the street, a rich blend of Dutch, Spanish, Portuguese, French, English, Caribbean Indian, and several African languages. Given the island's proximity to Venezuela, you're likely to hear **Spanish** as well.

CURRENCY   Bonaire's official currency is the Netherlands Antilles florin (NAf), also known as the guilder (exchange rate: 1.78 florins = U.S.$1; NAf1 = U.S.56¢). Each florin is divisible by 100 cents. Don't waste your time exchanging money, though, since the U.S. dollar is as widely accepted as the local currency. Prices quoted in this section are in U.S. dollars. Change may be a mixture of dollars and florins. If you need cash, there are several **ATMs** along Kaya Grandi. Traveler's checks and credit cards are widely accepted.

INFORMATION   The **Tourism Corporation Bonaire** is located at Kaya Grandi 2 in Kralendijk (✆ **599/717-8322** or 599/717-8649; fax 599/717-8408; usa@TourismBonaire.com).

CALLING FROM THE U.S.   When calling Bonaire from the United States, dial the international access code (011) before the numbers listed in this section.

GETTING AROUND

BY RENTAL CAR   Highway signs are in Dutch, and sometimes English, with easy-to-understand international symbols. Driving is on the right, the same as in the States and most of Europe. A valid driver's license is acceptable for renting and driving a car. **Avis, Budget, Hertz,** and **National** all have offices here.

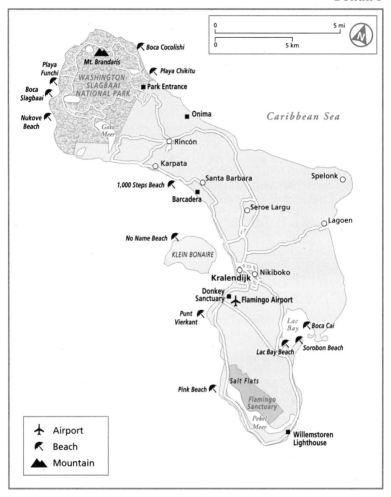

Map Legend:
- **Airport**
- **Beach**
- **Mountain**

Locations shown on map: Boca Cocolishi, Playa Funchi, Mt. Brandaris, Playa Chikitu, WASHINGTON-SLAGBAAI NATIONAL PARK, Park Entrance, Boca Slagbaai, Nukove Beach, Onima, *Caribbean Sea*, Goto Meer, Rincón, Karpata, Spelonk, 1,000 Steps Beach, Santa Barbara, Barcadera, Seroe Largu, Lagoen, No Name Beach, KLEIN BONAIRE, Kralendijk, Nikiboko, Donkey Sanctuary, Flamingo Airport, Punt Vierkant, Lac Bay, Boca Cai, Lac Bay Beach, Sorobon Beach, Pink Beach, Salt Flats, Flamingo Sanctuary, Pekel Meer, Willemstoren Lighthouse

BY TAXI   Taxis greet cruise ship passengers at the pier. Although the cars are unmetered, the government establishes rates, and drivers should produce a price list upon request. Most cabs can be hired for a tour of the island, with as many as four passengers allowed to go along for the ride. Negotiate a price before leaving, but expect to pay about $25 per hour. You can get more information from the **Taxi Central Dispatch office** (© **599/717-8100**).

BY SCOOTER OR MOPED   If you plan to stick relatively close to the port area, scooters and mopeds are practical, open-air alternatives. They can be rented from **Hot Shot Scooters,** Kaya Bonaire 4C (© **599/717-7166**), or **Macho! Scooter Rentals** at the Plaza Resort Bonaire, J. A. Abraham Blvd. 80 (© **599/ 717-2500**). Mopeds are about $18 a day; two-seat scooters run about $38.

BY BICYCLE   For getting around town or exploring the nearby coast, try bicycling. The coastal terrain is essentially flat, but the sun can be brutal even before noon. Plan your excursion as early in the day as possible. **Cycle Bonaire,**

Kaya L. D. Gerharts 11D (© **599/717-7558**), rents 21-speed mountain bikes ($15–$20) and arranges half- ($40) and full-day ($55) tours.

SHORE EXCURSIONS OFFERED BY THE CRUISE LINES

Scuba Excursion for Certified Divers ($69, 3 hr.): Dive in the island's famous Bonaire Marine Park.

Bike Tour ($64, 3–4 hr.): This scenic ride along mostly flat and downhill terrain affords riders views of Bonaire's many species of birds, cacti, and other flora and fauna, including pink flamingos. The ride takes you along the island's northern shoreline.

Snorkeling ($39–$69, 3 hr.): The snorkeling off the coast of Bonaire is some of the best you'll find in the Caribbean. A variety of snorkeling tours include spending time at "No Name Beach," Ebo's Reef, and Karel's Hills, all located off the shore of uninhabited Klein Bonaire.

ON YOUR OWN: WITHIN WALKING DISTANCE

You can walk the length of **Kralendijk** in an hour or less. It's a sleepy town, but its residents like it that way, thank you. The **tourist office,** Kaya Grandi 2, has walking-tour maps, but because Bonaire has always been off the beaten track, Kralendijk's highlights are modest and few. You'll probably want to stroll along the seafront with its views and restaurants, and along **Kaya Grandi,** the island's major shopping district. Just south of the town dock is **Fort Oranje,** a tiny fortress that has a cannon dating from the time of Napoleon. The town has some charming Dutch Caribbean architecture—gabled roofs you might see in Amsterdam, but in cheerful Caribbean colors, especially sunny ochre and terra cotta. If your ship arrives early enough, you can visit the **waterfront produce market.**

ON YOUR OWN: BEYOND THE PORT AREA

As a day visitor, you'll probably choose to explore either the northern or southern part of the island. The coastal road north of Kralendijk is said to be one of the most beautiful in the Antilles. Turquoise, azure, and cobalt waters stretch to the horizon on your left, while pink-coral and black-volcanic cliffs loom on your right. Towering cacti, intimate coastal coves, strange rock formations, and panoramic vistas add to the beauty. The north also boasts Washington-Slagbaai National Park, an impressive, 13,500-acre preserve that occupies the northwestern portion of the island, and Rincon, Bonaire's "other" town and oldest settlement.

NORTH OF KRALENDIJK   Soon after leaving Kralendijk, on the coast road, across from the Bonaire Caribbean Club, you'll find **Barcadera,** an old cave once used to trap goats. Take the stone steps down to the cave and examine the stalactites.

Just past the Radio Nederland towers, **1,000 Steps Beach** and dive site offers lovely views: picturesque coves, craggy coastline, and tropical waters of changing hues. Actually, there are only 67 steps; it just feels like a thousand if you're schlepping dive gear.

At the Kaya Karpata intersection, you'll see a mustard-colored building on your right. It's what's left of the aloe-processing facilities of **Landhuis Karpata,** a 100-year-old former plantation. The modest exhibits here explain the cultivation, harvesting, and processing of aloe, once a major export crop.

Thirty or 40 arduous minutes after turning right on Kaya Karpata, you'll arrive in **Rincon,** the original Spanish settlement on the island, founded in

Frommer's Favorite Bonaire Experiences

Scuba Diving: Diving in Bonaire is said to be easier than anywhere else on Earth. The island's leeward coast has more than 80 dive sites, and whether you're diving from a boat or right from shore, you'll see spectacular coral formations and as many types of fish as anywhere in the Caribbean. If you're not certified to dive, you can take a half-day resort course to see firsthand what divers rave about. If you'd rather just stick to snorkeling, abundant marine life is perfectly visible just beneath the crystal-clear water.

Mountain Biking Along the Western Coast: Bike along the coast on a road carved through lava and limestone, and bordered with cactus. The road north from the island's capital and main town, Kralendijk, is relatively flat and passes several uncrowded beaches—perfect for cooling off. If you're looking for more of a challenge, pedal uphill to Bonaire's oldest town, Rincon. (See "Shore Excursions Offered by the Cruise Lines," above.)

Exploring Washington-Slagbaai National Park: This preserve is home to a variety of exotic wildlife and vegetation and offers spectacular coastal views. At times, the towering cacti, iguanas, and thousands of jittery lizards make you think you're in Arizona, but the humidity, flamingos, and beaches make it clear you're not. (See "On Your Own: Beyond the Port Area," below.)

Making New Friends at the Donkey Sanctuary: Miss your pooch back home? Why not lavish your love on some deserving surrogates? Donkeys were first brought to Bonaire centuries ago as beasts of burden; when more efficient modes of transport replaced them, many reverted to feral ways in the outback. More than 40 of them, most of them orphaned or injured by cars, call this oasis near the airport home, and greet you as you enter the gate, accompanying you around the tidy, brightly colored grounds. After recuperation and rehabilitation, they're returned to the wild. If you're moved by the animals' unconditional affection, you can adopt one; as a new parent, you'll receive photos and letters from your adoptee twice a year. The sanctuary is located at Punt Vierkant 5, just south of the airport in Kralendijk (© 599/95-607-607), and is open Tuesday through Sunday from 10am to 4pm. There's no admission charge, but donations are appreciated. The souvenir shop has donkey shirts, donkey bags, and donkey art.

1527. The town eventually became the home of African slaves who worked the island's plantations and salt pans. Nestled in a valley away from either coast, Rincon was hidden from marauding pirates, who plagued the Caribbean for decades. Today, the quiet and picturesque village is home to Bonaire's oldest church, a handsome ochre-and-white structure, and to **Prisca's,** an island institution serving the best local ice cream. Try the rum raisin, peanut, pistachio, or ponche crema (a little like eggnog). The shop is located in a pistachio-colored building on Kaya Komkomber (that's Papiamentu for "cucumber").

The pride of Bonaire, located on the island's northern tip, **Washington-Slag-baai National Park** is one of the Caribbean's first national parks. Formerly two separate plantations that produced aloe and charcoal and raised goats, it now showcases the island's geology, animals, and vegetation. The park boasts more than 190 species of birds; thousands of kadushi, yatu, and prickly pear cactus; and herds of wild goats, foraging donkeys, flocks of flamingos, and what seems like billions of lizards. The scenery includes stark, desertlike hills, quiet beaches, secluded caverns, and wave-battered cliffs. You have two options: Either take the shorter 24km (15-mile) route around the park, marked with green arrows, or take the longer 35km (22-mile) track, marked with yellow arrows. You'll have plenty of opportunities to hike, swim, or snorkel either way. Admission is $10 for adults, $2 for children under 15, and the park is open from 8am to 5pm daily except for major holidays; last entry is at 3pm. Guide booklets and maps are available at the gate, where there's also a small museum. The unpaved roads are well marked and safe, but rugged; jeeps trump small cars.

On your way back to Kralendijk, take the Kaminda Onima, which traces the island's northeastern coast to **Onima,** the site of 500-year-old Caiquetio Indian inscriptions. Some of the red and brown drawings depict turtles and rain; others appear to have religious significance. You should be able to recognize snakes, human hands, and the sun among the roughly 75 inscriptions.

Before returning to Kralendijk, call on **Sherman Gibbs.** You'll find his monument to the beauty of common objects on Kaminda Tras di Montaña, the road leading back to Kralendijk. Eccentric is one way to describe Mr. Gibbs; genius is another. If you're familiar with the Watts Tower in Los Angeles, you know "junk" can be transformed into something beautiful. Sherman, who's as gentle as his pet iguanas, combines old detergent bottles, boat motors, buoys, car seats, and just about anything else that strikes his fancy to create a wondrously happy sanctuary. The wind and old fan blades power his TV.

SOUTH OF KRALENDIJK   Just minutes south of town, dazzlingly bright salt pyramids dominate the horizon. These hills, looking more like alpine snowdrifts than sodium mounds, are created when seawater is forced into lakes by the tide and then evaporates, leaving crystallized salt behind. Farther from the road, abandoned saltworks have been set aside as a **flamingo sanctuary.** Bonaire is one of the world's few nesting places for pink flamingos, a species that until recently was seriously threatened by extinction. Thanks to the reserve, the island's flamingo population during the breeding season now swells to roughly 10,000, rivaling the island's human population of 14,000. The sanctuary is completely off-limits to the public because the birds are extremely wary of humans and disturbances of any kind. But even from the road you can spot a pink haze on the horizon, and with binoculars you can see the graceful birds feeding in the briny pink-and-purple waters.

At the island's southern tip, restored slave huts stand as monuments to the inhumanity of the island's slave era. Each hut, no bigger than a large doghouse, provided crude nighttime shelter for slaves brought from Africa by the Dutch West Indies Company to cut dyewood, cultivate maize, and harvest solar salt. On Friday afternoons, the slaves trekked 7 hours in the oppressive heat to their homes and families in Rincon for the weekend, returning to the salt pans on Sunday evenings.

Located on the eastern side of the island's southern tip, the classically picturesque **Willemstoren Lighthouse,** Bonaire's first, was built in 1837. It's fully automated today and usually closed to visitors, but its magnificent setting is the real draw. Odd little bundles of driftwood, bleached coral, and rocks in the area look like something out of *The Blair Witch Project*, but they're actually constructed by fishermen to mark where boats have been left.

A few minutes up the east coast is **Lac Bay,** a lagoon that's every bit as tranquil as the nearby windward sea is furious. The calm, shallow waters and steady breezes make the area ideal for windsurfing, and various fish come here to hatch their young. Deep inside the lagoon, mangrove trees with Edward Scissorhands roots lunge out of the water. If it weren't for the relentlessly cheerful sun, they might seem sinister. Wild donkeys, goats, and flamingos pepper the countryside along the way.

SHOPPING

Don't expect to be caught up in a duty-free frenzy in Bonaire. You'll be able to hit every store in Kralendijk before lunch, and you'll probably find greater selections and prices at other ports. The island is a great place to buy certain items, though. Consider top-of-the-line **dive watches** and **underwater cameras.** Or how about jewelry with marine themes?

You'll find most shops on **Kaya Grandi,** on the adjacent streets, or in small malls. For Tag-Heuer dive watches, Cuban cigars, Lladró porcelain, Daum crystal, and Kosta Boda glass, try **Littman Jewelers** at Kaya Grandi 33. In the centrally located Harborside Mall, **Little Holland** has silk neckties, Nautica menswear, blue Delft porcelain, and an even more impressive array of Cuban cigars. If you're an aficionado, you'll love the shop's climate-controlled cigar room with its Montecristos, H. Upmanns, Romeo & Julietas, and Cohibas. **Sparky's,** in the same mall, carries perfume and other cosmetics, including Lancôme, Esteé Lauder, Chanel, Calvin Klein, and Ralph Lauren. **Maharaj Gifthouse,** at Kaya Grandi 21, has jewelry, gifts, and more blue Delft porcelain. **Boolchand's,** at Kaya Grandi 19, has a peculiarly wide range of items, including underwater cameras, electronic goods, watches, sunglasses, and shoes.

Benetton, at Kaya Grandi 49, has smart casual wear at discounts of 20% to 30%. If batik shirts, bathing suits, or souvenir T-shirts are what you want, try **Best Buddies,** Kaya Grandi 32; **Boutique Vita,** Kaya Grandi 16; **Bye-Bye Bonaire,** Harborside Mall; or **Island Fashions,** Kaya Grandi 5.

Probably the best place for dressier women's clothing, including Hermès scarves, Oscar de la Renta resort wear, and Kenneth Cole shoes, is **The Shop at Harbour Village** at Kaya Gobernador N. Debrot 72. You can also find sunglasses, jewelry, and perfume with Cartier, Fendi, Donna Karan, and Givenchy labels.

On a hot day, nothing beats the frozen-food section at **Cultimara Supermarket,** Kaya L. D. Gerharts 13. The store offers free coffee, a wide assortment of Dutch cheeses and chocolates, straight-from-the-oven breads and pastries, and various products from the Caribbean, Europe, South America, and the United States.

BEACHES

Bonaire's beaches are narrow and full of coral, but they're clean, intimate, and uncrowded. Swimming on the tranquil, leeward coast is never a problem, but the east coast is rough and dangerous. **Pink Beach,** south of Kralendijk, is the island's best strand. Aptly named, the sand here turns a rosy hue as the sun sets. No refreshment stands or equipment rentals mar the panoramic setting, so bring your own drinks and towels. Bring sun protection too: The few palm trees offer little shade. The southern end has less exposed rock. Crowded with Bonaireans on weekends, it's yours alone during the week.

The water at **Lac Bay Beach** is only a third to a half meter (1 to 2 ft.) deep, making it especially popular with families. In a protected area of Bonaire's southeast coast, it boasts windsurfing concessions and snack bars. Trees provide shade. Across the bay, white-sand **Sorobon Beach** is the island's only nude beach. It's part of the Sorobon Beach Resort, which means that as a nonguest, you'll pay for the privilege of disrobing.

North of Kralendijk, **Nukove Beach** is a small white-sand cove carved out of a limestone cliff. A narrow sand channel cuts through an otherwise impenetrable wall of elkhorn coral, giving divers and snorkelers access to the sea.

Washington-Slagbaai National Park boasts a number of beaches. **Boca Slagbaai,** once a plantation harbor, draws snorkelers and picnickers. A 19th-century building has toilets, showers, and a snack bar. Be careful venturing into the water barefoot, though: The coral bottom can be sharp. The island's northernmost beach, **Boca Cocolishi,** is a perfect spot to picnic. The calm, shallow basin is good for snorkeling, but stay close to shore. Algae makes the water purplish, and the sand, formed by coral and mollusk shells, is black. At **Playa Chikitu,** the water is treacherous but the cove, sand dunes, and crashing waves are secluded and beautiful. On one side of **Playa Funchi,** flamingos nest in the lagoon; on the other, there's excellent snorkeling.

Klein Bonaire, the small island about 1.5km (less than a mile) west of Kralendijk, boasts **No Name Beach,** which features a 274m (300-yd.) white-sand strip. The finger, brain, and mustard hill corals are patrolled by parrotfish and yellowtail snappers, attracting snorkelers and divers. There are no facilities or shade.

SPORTS

KAYAKING   For a peaceful, relaxing time, kayak through the mangroves in Lac Bay. Proceed at your own pace in the calm waters, but take time to observe the hundreds of baby fish and the bizarre tree roots. Bring protection from the sun and the ravenous mosquitoes. Divers and snorkelers can tow a lightweight sea kayak behind them as they explore the waters of the leeward coast. Guided trips and kayak rentals are available from **Discover Bonaire,** Kaya Gobernador N. Debrot 79 (© **599/717-5252**), and, in Sorobon, from **Jibe City** (© **599/ 717-5233**). A half-day guided tour through the mangroves is $45, including a guide, kayak, and transportation. Kayak rental alone is $20 for half a day, $25 for a two-seater.

MOUNTAIN BIKING   Bonaire has miles of roads, paved and unpaved, flat and hilly. The truly athletic can even follow goat paths. Take water, a map, a wide-brimmed hat, and plenty of sunscreen. Discover Bonaire (see above) conducts guided bike tours through the kunuku (outback) and Washington-Slagbaai Park.

SCUBA DIVING & SNORKELING   Bonaire has 80 dive sites and a rich marine ecosystem that includes brain, elkhorn, staghorn, mountainous star, gorgonian, and black coral; anemones, sea cucumbers, and sea sponges; parrotfish, surgeonfish, angelfish, groupers, blennies, frogfish, and yellowtails; and morays and sea snakes. Dive shops are numerous and highly professional. Expect to pay $45 to $50 for a one-tank dive (equipment extra) and $100 for an introductory resort course (equipment included). **Great Adventures at Harbour Village,** Kaya Gobernador N. Debrot 72 (© **800/868-7477** in the U.S. and Canada, or 599/717-7500), is the island's poshest operation, upscale but unpretentious and friendly. In addition to two of the island's most beautiful boats, it boasts a first-class photo shop where you can rent underwater still and video cameras. **Sand Dollar Dive & Photo,** Kaya Gobernador N. Debrot 77 (© **599/717-5433**), is popular with return visitors and offers comparable services. The resort's "Sand Penny" children's program is a godsend for parents who want to dive without worrying about the kids. **Habitat Dive Center,** Kaya Gobernador N. Debrot 103 (© **800/327-6709** in the U.S., or 599/717-8290), attracts diving fanatics, including disciples of Captain Don Stewart, an island icon and the driving force behind the Bonaire Marine Park. The full-service shop includes a photo shop and lab and equipment repair.

Thanks to shallow-water coral reefs, snorkelers can enjoy Bonaire's awesome marine environment, too. The island's **Guided Snorkeling Program** includes a slide-show introduction to reef fishes, corals, and sponges; an in-water demonstration of snorkeling skills; and a guided tour of one of several sites. The cost is $25 per person. Equipment rental is about $10 more. You can arrange a tour through any of the dive shops listed above or through **Buddy Dive Resort,** Kaya Gobernador N. Debrot 85 (© **800/934-DIVE** in the U.S., or 599/717-5080); **Bon Bini Divers,** at the Lions Dive Hotel Bonaire, Kaya Gobernador N. Debrot 90 (© **800/327-5424** in the U.S., or 599/717-5425); **Carib Inn,** J. A. Abraham Boulevard (© **599/717-8819**); or **Dive Inn,** Kaya C. E. B. Hellmund 27 (© **599/717-8761**).

WINDSURFING Shallow waters, steady breezes, and protection from choppy waters make Lac Bay perfect for beginners and pros. Sorobon has two equipment-rental centers: **Jibe City** (© **599/717-5233**) and **Bonaire Windsurf Place** (© **599/717-2288**). Boards and sails are $45 for half a day, $60 for a full day. Beginner's lessons are $45, including equipment.

GREAT LOCAL RESTAURANTS & BARS

Kralendijk offers a variety of culinary options at generally reasonable prices. One of Bonaire's most popular restaurants, **Capriccio,** Kaya Isla Riba 1 (© **599/717-7230**), serves impeccably fresh Northern Italian cuisine on the harbor front. Originally from Padua and Milan, the restaurateurs offer savory salads, homemade pastas, straight-from-the-oven focaccia, thin-crust pizzas, and more substantial fare such as mahimahi braised in onion, olives, and sun-dried tomatoes, and braised duck in port wine sauce. **Zeezicht Seaside Restaurant,** Kaya Jan N. E. Craane 12 (© **599/717-8434**), is a local favorite, also on the downtown waterfront. Seviche, conch sandwiches, and a gumbo of conch, fish, shrimp, and oysters are on the menu, and mermaids, fishing nets, and pirates adorn the walls. To sample traditional Bonairean food in an unpretentious setting, try **Bon Awa,** Kaya Nikiboko Zuid 8 (© **599/717-5157**), with its outside tables, killer hot sauce, and outstanding homemade ice cream.

10 The British Virgin Islands: Tortola & Virgin Gorda

With small bays and hidden coves that were once havens for pirates, the BVIs are among the world's loveliest cruising regions, consisting of some 40 islands located in the northeastern corner of the Caribbean, about 97km (60 miles) east of Puerto Rico. Only Tortola, Virgin Gorda, and Jost Van Dyke are of significant size. The other islets, most of them tiny rocks and cays, have names such as Fallen Jerusalem and Ginger. Norman Island is said to have been the prototype for Robert Louis Stevenson's Treasure Island, and Blackbeard inspired a famous ditty by marooning 15 pirates and a bottle of rum on the rocky cay known as Dead-man Bay. Yo-ho-ho.

Columbus came this way in 1493, but the British Virgins apparently made little impression on him. Although the Spanish and Dutch contested it, Tortola was officially annexed by the English in 1672. Today, these islands are a British colony, with their own elected government and a population of about 17,000.

The vegetation is varied and depends on the rainfall. Palms and mangos grow in profusion in some parts, while other places are arid and studded with cacti.

Smaller cruise lines such as Seabourn, Windstar, and Windjammer Barefoot Cruises call at Tortola and the more scenic Virgin Gorda and Jost Van Dyke. Unlike port calls at St. Thomas and other major ports, visits here are less bound by rigid scheduling.

LANGUAGE **English** is spoken here.

CURRENCY The **U.S. dollar** is the legal currency, much to the surprise of arriving Brits who find no one willing to accept their pounds.

CALLING FROM THE U.S. When calling the BVIs from the United States, you need only dial a "1" before the numbers listed here.

TORTOLA

Road Town, the colony's capital, sits about midway along the southern shore of 62 square km (24-sq.-mile) Tortola. Once a sleepy village, it's become a bustling center since **Wickhams Cay,** a 70-acre landfill development and marina, brought in a massive yacht-chartering business.

The island's entire southern coast is characterized by rugged mountain peaks. On the northern coast are beautiful bays with white sandy beaches, banana trees, mangoes, and clusters of palms.

If your ship isn't scheduled to visit Virgin Gorda but you want to, you can catch a boat, ferry, or launch here and be on the island in no time, since it's only a 19km (12-mile) trip.

COMING ASHORE Visiting cruise ships anchor at **Wickhams Cay 1** in Road Town. You'll be brought ashore by tender and let off a pleasant 5-minute walk from Main Street. You should have no trouble finding your way around town.

INFORMATION The **BVI Tourist Board** office is on Wickhams Cay 1 in the Akara Building and is open Monday to Friday from 8:30am to 4:30pm (© **284/494-3134**). You can pick up a copy of the Welcome Tourist Guide here. For info before you go, log on to **www.britishvirginislands.com**.

GETTING AROUND

BY TAXI Open-air and sedan-style taxis meet every arriving cruise ship. To call a taxi in Road Town, call the **BVI Taxi Association** (© **284/494-2322**) or **Wheatley's** (© **284/494-3357**). Two other local taxi services, **Quality Taxi** (© **284/494-8397**) and the **Waterfront Taxi Association** (© **284/494-3456**), are within walking distance of the cruise pier.

BY BUS **Scato's Bus Service** (© **284/494-2365**) picks up passengers (mostly locals) who hail it down. Fares for a trek across the island are about $1 to $4.

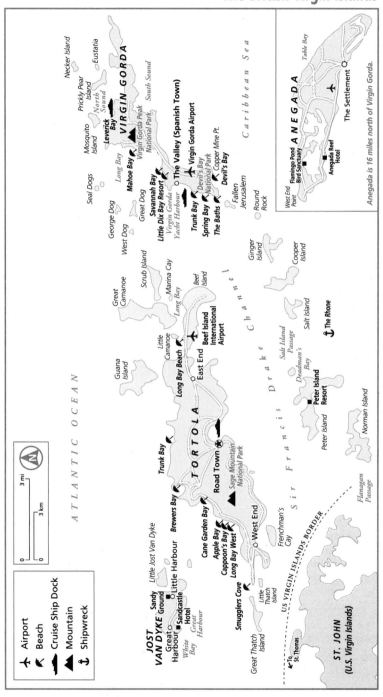

The British Virgin Islands

ATLANTIC OCEAN

Caribbean Sea

JOST VAN DYKE
Little Jost Van Dyke
Sandy Ground
Great Harbour
Little Harbour
Sandcastle Hotel
White Bay
Great Harbour
Little Thatch Island
Great Thatch Island

Airport
Beach
Cruise Ship Dock
Mountain
Shipwreck

3 mi
3 km
0

N

Smugglers Cove
Long Bay West
Cappoon's Bay
Apple Bay
Cane Garden Bay
Brewers Bay
West End
Frenchman's Cay
Trunk Bay
Road Town
Sage Mountain National Park
TORTOLA
Long Bay Beach
East End
Long Bay
Little Camanoe
Great Camanoe
Guana Island
Scrub Island
Marina Cay
Beef Island
Beef Island International Airport

US VIRGIN ISLANDS BORDER
To St. Thomas
ST. JOHN
(U.S. Virgin Islands)
Flanagan Passage

Sir Francis Drake Channel

Norman Island
Peter Island
Peter Island Resort
Deadman's Bay
Salt Island Passage
Salt Island
⚓ The Rhone
Cooper Island
Ginger Island
Round Rock
Fallen Jerusalem
Copper Mine Pt.
Devil's Bay
The Baths
Spring Bay
Trunk Bay
Devil's Bay National Park
Virgin Gorda Yacht Harbour
Little Dix Bay Resort
Savannah Bay
The Valley (Spanish Town)
Virgin Gorda Airport
Mahoe Bay
VIRGIN GORDA
Virgin Gorda Peak National Park
Leverick Bay
Long Bay
Mosquito Island
North Sound
South Sound
Prickly Pear Island
Necker Island
Eustatia

Great Dog
George Dog
West Dog
Seal Dogs

Table Bay
ANEGADA
The Settlement
Flamingo Pond Bird Sanctuary
Anegada Reef Hotel
West End Point

Anegada is 16 miles north of Virgin Gorda.

137

Frommer's Favorite Tortola Experiences

Visiting Bomba's Surfside Shack: The oldest, most memorable bar on Tortola may not look like much, but it's the best party on the island. (See "Great Local Restaurants & Bars," below.)

Spending a Day at Cane Garden Bay: It's the best beach on the island, with palm trees, sand, and a great local restaurant (shack) for lunch and drinks. (See "Beaches," below.)

Hiking Up Sage Mountain: It's one of the best ways to learn about Tortola's natural character. Organized shore excursions usually include hiking trips to the 1,780-foot peak, beginning with a ride along mountain roads in an open-air safari bus.

Taking an Island Tour: Open-air safari buses take you on a scenic journey around the extremely hilly island. Take your ship's organized tour (see "Shore Excursions Offered by the Cruise Lines," below), or take a 2- to 3-hour taxi tour from the pier, with beach stops, for about $15 per person.

BY RENTAL CAR   We don't recommend driving here, as the roads are bad and driving is on the left. But if you're intent on it, **Budget** and **Hertz** have offices here.

SHORE EXCURSIONS OFFERED BY THE CRUISE LINES

Island Tour ($30–$34, 3½ hr.): Hop on an open-air safari bus and embark on a scenic journey around the island. You'll enjoy some panoramic views and good photo ops, and end with a stop at Cane Garden Bay Beach for swimming, sunbathing, and just plain old relaxing.

Mount Sage & Cane Garden Bay tour ($34, 4 hr.): Start with a hike up Sage Mountain and end with a 1½-hour stop at Cane Garden Bay beach.

Lambert Beach Resort ($20, 5 hr.): After a drive along the lovely north and south coasts, you'll spend an afternoon at the Lambert Beach Resort, where you'll find a bar and the casual Turtle's Restaurant.

EXCURSIONS OFFERED BY LOCAL AGENCIES

Bus Tours/Snorkeling/Glass-Bottom Boat Tours: Since the shore excursions here are very modest, you might consider calling **Travel Plan Tours,** Romasco Place, Wickham's Cay, Road Town (© **284/494-2872**), which will take one to three people on a 3-hour guided tour of the island (about $23 a person), a snorkeling excursion (about $28 a person), or an all-day catamaran sailing excursion ($85 including lunch).

Taxi Tours: You can take a 2- to 3-hour taxi tour for about $45 for up to three people. For a taxi in Road Town, call © **284/494-2322.**

ON YOUR OWN: WITHIN WALKING DISTANCE

Besides the handful of shops on Main and Upper Main streets in Road Town, there's also a **Botanic Garden** (© **284/494-4557**) right in the middle of town, across from the police station. It's open daily from 8am to 6pm and features a wide variety of flowers and plants, including a section on medicinal plants.

ON YOUR OWN: BEYOND THE PORT AREA

You have mainly nature to look at on Tortola. The big attraction is **Mount Sage National Park,** which rises to 1,780 feet (the highest point in the BVIs and USVIs) and covers 37 hectares (92 acres). It was established in 1964 to protect those remnants of Tortola's original forests not burned or cleared during its plantation era, and is both the oldest national park in the British Virgin Islands and the best present-day example of the territory's native moist forests. You'll find a lush forest of mango, papaya, breadfruit, and coconut trees; many of the plants and trees are labeled, and there are also birchberry, mountain guava, and guavaberry trees here, all of which have edible fruit. This is a great place to enjoy a picnic while overlooking neighboring islets and cays. Any taxi driver can take you to the mountain. Before going, stop at the **tourist office** (see above) and pick up a brochure with a map and an outline of the park's trails. The two main hikes are the Rain Forest Trail and the Mahogany Forest Trail. For a quiet beach day, head to **Smuggler's Cove,** a secluded, picture-perfect spot with white sand and calm turquoise water. *Note:* At press time there is no fee for park admission, but the BVI National Trust plans to implement one soon, possibly by the end of 2002. Call ✆ **284/494-2069** or 284/494-6177 for more information.

SHOPPING

Shopping on Tortola is a minor activity compared to other Caribbean ports. Only British goods are imported without duty, and they are the best buys, especially English china. You'll also find West Indian art, terra-cotta pottery, wicker and rattan home furnishings, Mexican glassware, dhurrie rugs, baskets, and ceramics. Most stores are on Main Street in Road Town.

Some good shops to visit include **Pusser's Company Store,** Main Street, Road Town (✆ **284/494-2467**), for Pusser's rum, fine nautical artifacts, and a selection of Pusser's sports and travel clothing and upmarket gift items. The **Sunny Caribee Herb and Spice Company,** also on Main Street (✆ **284/494-2178**), is a good spot for Caribbean spices, seasonings, teas, condiments, and handcrafts. You can buy two world-famous specialties here: West Indian Hangover Cure and Arawak Love Potion.

BEACHES

Most of the beaches are a 20-minute taxi ride from the cruise dock. Figure on about $15 per person one way (some will charge less, about $5 per person if you've got a group), but discuss it with the driver before setting out. You can also ask him to pick you up at a designated time.

The finest beach is at **Cane Garden Bay,** which compares favorably to the famous Magens Bay Beach on the north shore of St. Thomas. It's on the northwest side of the island, across the mountains from Road Town, but it's worth the effort to get there, and is so special you might take a taxi here in the morning and not head back to your cruise ship until departure time. Plan to have lunch here at **Rhymer's** (✆ **284/495-4639**), where the chef will cook some conch or whelk, or perhaps some barbecue spareribs. The beach bar and restaurant is open daily from 8am to 9pm, serving breakfast, lunch, and dinner, with main courses ranging from $15 to $25. Showers are available, and Rhymer's rents towels.

Surfers like **Apple Bay,** also on the northwest side, but you'll have to watch out for sharks (no joke: on a recent trip a friend saw one while surfing, and its dorsal fins were visible from the shore). A hotel here called **Sebastians** (✆ **284/495-4212**) caters to the surfing crowd that visits in January and February, but the beach is ideal year-round. **Brewers Bay,** site of a campground, is on the northwest shore near Cane Garden Bay and is good for beach strolling and swimming. Both snorkelers and surfers come here. **Smugglers Cove** (sometimes known as Lower Belmont Bay) is a wide crescent of white sand wrapped around calm, sky-blue water, located at the extreme western end of Tortola, opposite the offshore island of Great Thatch and very close to St. John's in the U.S. Virgin Islands. Snorkelers also like this beach.

SPORTS
SCUBA DIVING *Skin Diver* magazine has called the wreckage of the RMS *Rhône,* which sank in 1867 near the western point of Salt Island, the world's most fantastic shipwreck dive. It teems with marine life and coral formations, and was featured in the motion picture *The Deep. Chikuzen,* a 270-foot steel-hulled refrigerator ship that sank off the island's east end in 1981, is another intriguing dive site off Tortola, although it's no *Rhône.* The hull, still intact under about 24m (80 ft.) of water, is now home to a vast array of tropical fish, including yellowtail, barracuda, black-tip sharks, octopus, and drum fish. **Baskin in the Sun** (© 800/233-7938 in the U.S., or 284/494-2858; www. baskininthesun.com), a PADI five-star facility on Tortola, is a good choice for divers. It has three locations: at the Prospect Reef Resort, near Road Town; at Soper's Hole, on Tortola's West End; and on Peter's Island. Baskin's most popular trip is the supervised half-day scuba diving, which caters to beginners, but there are trips for more advanced levels as well. A full-day two-tank dive is $85; a half-day is $65 (equipment rental is $10 a day). Daily excursions are scheduled to the *Rhône,* as well as Painted Walls (an underwater canyon formed of brightly colored coral and sponges), and the Indians (four pinnacle rocks sticking out of the water, which divers follow up to 60 ft. below the surface). **Underwater Safaris** (© 800/537-7032 in the U.S., or 284/494-3235) can take you to all the best sites. It offers a complete PADI and NAUI training facility and is associated with The Moorings yacht charter company. Underwater Safaris' Road Town office is a 5-minute, $4 taxi ride from the docks.

GREAT LOCAL RESTAURANTS & BARS
On Cappoon's Bay, **Bomba's Surfside Shack** (© 284/495-4148) is the oldest, most memorable bar on Tortola, sitting on a 20-foot-wide strip of unpromising coastline near the West End. It's the "junk palace" of the island, covered with Day-Glo graffiti and laced with wire and rejected odds and ends of plywood, driftwood, and abandoned rubber tires. They must've spent their decorating budget on the sound system, which thumps mightily. The Sunday- and Wednesday-night barbecues are about $10 per person. It's open daily from 10am to midnight (or later, depending on business).

Standing on the waterfront across from the ferry dock, **Pusser's Road Town Pub** (© 284/494-3897) serves Caribbean fare, English pub grub, and good pizzas. The drink to have here is the famous Pusser's Rum, the same blend of five West Indian rums that the Royal Navy served to its men for more than 300 years. Honestly, it's not the world's greatest rum, but sometimes you just have to do things for the experience. **Capriccio di Mare,** Waterfront Drive (© 284/ 494-5369), is the most authentic-looking Italian cafe in the Virgin Islands, serving fresh pastas with succulent sauces, well-stuffed sandwiches, and great pizza. For a fine roti (curries wrapped in flat bread) sans atmosphere—it's sparsely furnished and not too attractive—try **Roti Palace** (© 284/494-4196), in Road

Town. **Callaloo,** at the Prospect Reef Resort (𝒞 **284/494-3311**), is very romantic if it's a balmy day and the tropical breezes are blowing. Begin with the conch fritters or shrimp cocktail, and don't pass on the house salad, which has a zesty papaya dressing. Main dishes include fresh fish. At **Pusser's Landing,** Frenchman's Cay, on the West End (𝒞 **284/495-4554**), you can enjoy grilled fish such as mahimahi, or West Indian roast chicken. Try the mango soufflé for dessert. **Quito's Gazebo** (𝒞 **284/495-4837**), on Cane Garden Bay, is owned by local recording star Quito Rhymer. It's a good place for West Indian fish dishes; Quito performs Thursday to Sunday and Tuesday.

VIRGIN GORDA

Instead of visiting Tortola, some small cruise ships put in at lovely Virgin Gorda, famous for its boulder-strewn beach known as **The Baths.** The second-largest island in the colony, it got its name ("Fat Virgin") from Christopher Columbus, who thought the mountain framing it looked like a protruding stomach. At 16km (10 miles) long and 3km (2 miles) wide, the island is about 19km (12 miles) east of Road Town, so it's easy to take a ferry or boat here if your ship only visits Tortola.

The island was a fairly desolate agricultural community until Little Dix Bay Hotel opened here in the early 1960s. Other major hotels followed, but privacy and solitude still reign supreme on Virgin Gorda.

COMING ASHORE   Virgin Gorda doesn't have a pier or landing facilities to suit any of the large ships. Most vessels anchor and send small craft ashore, disembarking passengers at **Leverick Bay.** Many others dock beside the pier in Road Town on Tortola and then send tenders across the channel to Virgin Gorda. A limited number of taxis are usually available at Leverick Bay.

GETTING AROUND   The best way to see the island is to call **Andy Flax** at the Fischers Cove Beach Hotel (𝒞 **284/495-5252**). He runs the Virgin Gorda Tours Association, which gives island tours for about $40 per couple. They'll pick you up at the dock if you give them 24-hour notice. **Taxis** are available in limited numbers at Leverick Bay (if you can get one) and will take visitors to Spanish Town (about 20 min. away) or to The Baths and area beaches for about $5 per person each way.

 Frommer's Favorite Virgin Gorda Experiences

Visiting The Baths: House-size boulders and clear waters make for excellent swimming and snorkeling in a fabulous setting. (See "Beaches" and "Shore Excursions Offered by the Cruise Lines," both below.)

Spending a Beach Day in Spring Bay or Trunk Bay: Located near The Baths, Spring Bay has one of the best beaches on the island, with white sand, clear water, and good snorkeling. Trunk Bay, a wide sand beach that can be reached by boat or via a rough path from Spring Bay, is another good bet. (See "Beaches," below.)

Taking an Island Tour: Open-air safari buses do a good job of showing guests this beautiful island. (See "Shore Excursions Offered by the Cruise Lines," below.)

SHORE EXCURSIONS OFFERED BY THE CRUISE LINES

The Baths Excursion ($38, 3–4 hr.): All cruise lines stopping here offer this trip. (See "Beaches," below, for details.)

Island Tour ($42, 3–4 hr.): The open-air safari buses do a good job of showing guests this beautiful island. You'll get views of the sea, the entire erratically shaped island, and Tortola and St. Thomas too as you head across the island from Leverick Bay via North Sound Road, ascending at least partway up 1,370-foot Gorda Peak. Some tours stop at the base of the mountain, from which a local guide walks visitors through the national park to the peak, where visitors can mount an observation deck and snap photos. After, visitors reboard their bus for a drive to the quaint capital, called Spanish Town. Tours usually include a stop at Copper Mine Point, where visitors can view the ruins of a 19th-century copper mine.

ON YOUR OWN: WITHIN WALKING DISTANCE

The **watersports center** in Leverick Bay rents two- and four-person dinghies starting at $40 per half day, and snorkeling equipment for $5 per day. Visitors can also hire a water taxi here to visit **Bitter End Yacht Club** (✆ 284/494-2746; www.beyc.com) in the North Sound area, for a lobster lunch or for a little windsurfing or sailing. The taxis pick up guests at Bitter End for the trip back; a round-trip fare costs $25 per person. There's also a local branch of the BVI's famous **Pusser's Company Store,** which includes a gift shop, restaurant, and bar.

ON YOUR OWN: BEYOND THE PORT AREA

The **Virgin Gorda Yacht Harbour** is a taxi ride away from the Leverick Bay pier, and has several restaurants, shops, a bank, and the local office of the BVI Tourist Board. You might also consider cabbing it to the glamorous **Little Dix Bay Resort** (✆ 284/495-5555), established by Laurence Rockefeller in 1965, to enjoy a lunch buffet at an outdoor pavilion that shows off Virgin Gorda's beautiful hills, bays, and sky.

SHOPPING

Souvenirs and locally produced artwork are available right in Leverick Bay, where most of the island's shopping is located. The **Palm Tree Gallery** (✆ 284/495-7479) carries jewelry, artwork, books, postcards, and other souvenirs.

Stores in the Yacht Harbour area include **DIVE BVI** (✆ 284/495-5513), which sells diving equipment and offers diving instructions for all ability levels; **Margo's Jewelry Boutique** (✆ 284/495-5237), which sells handcrafted gold and silver items; **Virgin Gorda Craft Shop** (✆ 284/495-5137), featuring locally made items; and **Wine Cellar** (✆ 284/495-5250), which offers oven-baked French bread and pastries, cookies, and sandwiches. The **Blue Banana Boutique** (✆ 284/495-6633), also in the Yacht Harbour area, sells women's swimwear and beachwear.

BEACHES

The major reason cruise ships come to Virgin Gorda is to visit **The Baths,** where geologists believe ice-age eruptions caused house-size boulders to topple onto one another to form the saltwater grottoes we see today. The pools around The Baths are excellent for swimming and snorkeling (equipment can be rented on the beach), and a crawl between and among the boulders, which in places are very cavelike, is more than a little bit fun. There's a cafe just above the beach for

A Slice of Paradise: Jost Van Dyke

Covering only 10 square km (4 sq. miles), mountainous Jost Van Dyke is truly an offbeat, rarely visited retreat—unless you count the small yachts dotting the Great Harbour. There's no cruise pier, so passengers are shuttled ashore via tender. Small-ship lines such as Windjammer Barefoot Cruises will sometimes throw an afternoon beach party on the beach at White Bay, with the crew lugging ashore a picnic lunch for a leisurely afternoon of eating, drinking, and swimming. If your ship stays late, don't miss a trip to **Foxy's** (© 284/495-9258; www.foxy sbvi.com), a well-known watering hole at the far end of the Great Harbour that's popular with the yachting set as well as locals. It's your classic island beach bar, with music pounding and drinks flowing into the wee hours.

a quick snack or a cool drink before heading back to the ship. **Devil's Bay** is a great beach near The Baths, and is usually less crowded.

Also near The Baths is **Spring Bay,** one of the best of the island's beaches, with white sand, clear water, and good snorkeling. Nearby is **The Crawl,** a natural pool formed by rocks that's great for novice snorkelers; a marked path leads there from Spring Bay. **Trunk Bay** is a wide sand beach that can be reached by boat or via a rough path from Spring Bay. **Savannah Bay** is a sandy stretch north of the yacht harbor, and **Mahoe Bay,** at the Mango Bay Resort (© 284/495-5672), has a gently curving beach and vivid blue water.

Devil's Bay National Park can be reached by a trail from The Baths. The walk to the secluded coral-sand beach takes about 15 minutes through a natural setting of boulders and dry coastal vegetation.

SPORTS
WATERSPORTS   Kilbrides Sunchaser Scuba, at the Bitter End Resort at North Sound (© 800/932-4286 in the U.S., or 284/495-9638; www.sunchaser scuba.com), offers diving at more than 20 BVI sites, including the wreck of the RMS *Rhône.* You can purchase a video of your dive.

GREAT LOCAL RESTAURANTS & BARS
At the end of the waterfront shopping plaza in Spanish Town, **Bath and Turtle Pub,** Virgin Gorda Yacht Harbour (© 284/495-5239), is the island's most popular bar and pub. You can join the regulars over midmorning guava coladas or peach daiquiris and order fried fish fingers, nachos, very spicy chili, pizzas, Reubens or tuna melts, steak, lobster, and daily seafood specials such as conch fritters. **Mad Dog** (© 284/495-5830) is a hot-dog stop near The Baths that also serves BLTs, beer, and frozen piña coladas.

11 Cozumel & The Yucatán Peninsula
Some days the heaps of cruise ships (try 10-plus) visiting this very popular cruise port make the port town of **San Miguel** on the island of Cozumel seem more like Times Square than the sleepy, refreshingly gritty Mexican port town it once was. San Miguel has developed at a faster rate in the past few years than just

about any other Caribbean port on the map, so if you haven't been there in a while, you may not recognize the place. Still, crowds and white, shiny, Miami-wannabe boutiques aside, Cozumel's allure remains its proximity to the ancient Mayan ruins at **Tulum** and **Chichén-Itzá** on the mainland of the Yucatán Peninsula. To see the ruins, you must take a rocky 45-minute ferry ride between Cozumel and Playa del Carmen, on the mainland, though a few cruise ships call directly on Playa del Carmen (anchoring just offshore) or nearby **Calica,** where there's a pier. At press time, Carnival was developing a new port and pier called the **Port of Cancun** at Xcaret, just down the road from Playa del Carmen. Besides the ruins, the island's beaches are a big draw, along with diving and shopping for silver jewelry and local handicrafts (and T-shirts from that notorious beer pit, Carlos 'n Charlie's).

LANGUAGE **Spanish** is the tongue of the land, although **English** is spoken in most places that cater to tourists.

CURRENCY The Mexican currency is the nuevo peso (new peso). Its symbol is the "$" sign, but it's hardly the equivalent of the U.S. dollar—the exchange rate is about $8.70 pesos to U.S.$1 ($1 peso = about 11¢). The main tourist stores gladly accept U.S. dollars, credit cards, and traveler's checks, but if you want to change money, there are many banks within a block or so of the Muelle Fiscal pier.

CALLING FROM THE U.S. When calling from the U.S., you need to dial the international access code (011) and 52 before the numbers listed here.

MAYAN RUINS ON THE MAINLAND

Because all of the sites listed here are quite far from the cruise piers, most cruise passengers visit them as part of shore excursions. Admission to the sites is included in the excursion price.

The largest and most fabled of the Yucatán ruins, **Chichén-Itzá** was founded in A.D. 445 by the Mayans and later inhabited by the conquering Toltecs of central Mexico. Two centuries later, it was mysteriously abandoned. After lying

---

 Alternate Yucatán Ports

While Cozumel gets the most traffic by far, a handful of other Yucatán ports have entered the scene, including **Mahahual** (just over 161km/100 miles south of Playa del Carmen), which is often referred to as **Costa Maya** by the cruise lines and is not to be confused with Riviera Maya, which stretches between Cancun and Tulum; technically Costa Maya is the region between Mahahual and Xcalak near the border with Belize. Millions of dollars have been invested in a pier and an oceanfront shopping and restaurant complex, and Princess, Royal Caribbean, Regal, Carnival, and Norwegian are among the lines that visit the port. The Mayan ruins of nearby Chetumal, Oxtankah, and Chakchoben are the draw, along with silky white beaches, and diving and snorkeling at the Chincorro, Mexico's largest coral atoll. Other Yucatán ports of call include **Progreso,** on the Gulf coast of the Yucatán, where the Mayan ruins and colonial architecture of nearby Merida are the big draw.

The Yucatán's Upper Caribbean Coast

← To Progreso

El Cuyo

Holbox

Isla Holbox

Isla Contoy

RÍO LAGARTOS
NATURE RESERVE

Chiquilá

Isla Mujeres

Punta Sam

Cancún

QUINTANA ROO
STATE

Buenaventura

Puerto
Juárez

Isla Cancun

YUCATÁN
STATE

180

■ Croco-Cun

■ Jardín
Botanico

Puerto
Morelos

180
D

180
D

180
D

Nuevo Xcan

307

To Valladolid
& Chichén Itzá
←

180

Punta
Bete

Chemax

Xcaret
Calica

Playa del
Carmen

San Gervasio

◆ San
Gervasio

Pamul

◆ Cobá

Xpuha

Puerto Aventuras

San Miguel
de Cozumel

Akumal

*Yalku
Lagoon*

Xel-ha Lagoon
National Park

El Cedral

ISLA DE
COZUMEL

Tancah

Chankanaab
Nature Park

Tulum

Chunyaxche

◆ Muyil

Caribbean Sea

Boca Paila

Chumpón

Vigia Chíco

Punta Allen

| 0 | | 25 mi |

| 0 | | 25 km |

N

*Peninsula
Vigia Grande*

*Bahia de la
Ascensión*

Felipe Carrillo
Puerto

SIAN KA'AN
BIOSPHERE RESERVE

To Chetumal
↓ & Costa Maya

✈ Airport

⬛ Cruise Ship Dock

- - - - Ferry Route

ııııı Reef

◆ Ruins

dormant for 2 more centuries, the site was resettled and enjoyed prosperity again until the early 13th century, when it was once more relinquished to the surrounding jungle. The area covers 18 square km (7 sq. miles), so you can see only a fraction of it on a day trip.

The best known of Chichén-Itzá's ruins is the pyramid **Castillo of Kukulkán,** which is actually an astronomical clock designed to mark the vernal and autumnal equinoxes and the summer and winter solstices. A total of 365 steps, one for each day of the year, ascend to the top platform. During each equinox, light striking the pyramid gives the illusion of a giant snake slithering down the steps to join its gigantic stone head mounted at the base. The government began restoration of the site in the 1920s, and today it houses a museum, a restaurant, and a few shops.

About 130km (80 miles) south of Cancún and about a 30-minute drive from Playa del Carmen, the walled city of **Tulum** is the single most visited Mayan ruin. It was the only Mayan city built on the coast and the only one inhabited when the Spanish conquistadors arrived in the 1500s. From its dramatic perch atop seaside cliffs, you can see wonderful panoramic views of the Caribbean. Tulum consists of 60 individual structures. As with Chichén-Itzá, its most prominent feature is a pyramid topped with a temple to Kukulkán, the primary Mayan/Olmec god. Other important structures include the Temple of the Frescoes, the Temple of the Descending God, the House of Columns, and the House of the Cenote, which is a well. There's also a sliver of silky beach amidst the site, so bring your bathing suit for a quick refreshing dip.

A 35-minute drive northwest of Tulum puts you at **Cobá,** site of one of the most important city-states in the Mayan empire. Cobá flourished from A.D. 300 to 1000, with its population numbering perhaps as many as 40,000. Excavation work began in 1972, but archaeologists estimate that only 5% of this dead city has yet been uncovered. The site lies on four lakes. Its 32 primitive hectares (81 acres) provide excellent exploration opportunities for the hiker. Cobá's pyramid, Nohoch Mul, is the tallest in the Yucatán.

COZUMEL

The ancient Mayans, who lived here for 12 centuries, would be shocked by the million cruise passengers who now visit Cozumel each year. Their presence has greatly changed San Miguel, the only town, which now has fast-food joints and a Hard Rock Cafe. Development, however, hasn't touched much of the island's natural beauty. Ashore, away from San Miguel, you'll see abundant wildlife, including armadillos, brightly colored tropical birds, and lizards. Offshore, the government has set aside 32km (20 miles) of coral reefs as an underwater national park, including the stunning Palancar Reef, the world's second-largest natural coral formation.

COMING ASHORE   Gone are the days of anchoring offshore, as there are now three piers for cruise ships to call on. The newest is **Punta Langosta,** right in the center of San Miguel, which puts you just steps from the shops, restaurants, and cafes across the street. Other ships pull alongside the well-accoutered **International Pier** (3km/2 miles south of San Miguel) or at the **Puerto Maya pier** (another mile or so farther south), both a $4 to $5 taxi ride from town or a 30- to 45-minute walk from the heart of San Miguel. The beaches are close to the International Pier.

You can make telephone calls in Cozumel from the Punta Langosta pier or from the Global Communications phone center on the International Pier, for a

Frommer's Favorite Cozumel Experiences

Visiting the Mayan Ruins at Chichén-Itzá or Tulum: Chichén-Itzá is the largest and most fabled of the Yucatán ruins—and the flight there, in a small plane, only adds to the experience. Tulum is perched dramatically above the ocean (and in the middle of "iguana central"—they're everywhere), and tours there often include a stop at the beautiful Xel-Ha Lagoon for some swimming. (See "Mayan Ruins on the Mainland," above, and "Shore Excursions," below.)

Renting a Motor Scooter: You can easily see most of the island this way, including its wild and natural side. (See "On Your Own: Beyond the Port Area," below.)

Signing Up for a Jeep Trek: Explore Cozumel's jungles and sandy back roads on a fun self-drive caravan-style adventure, and then stop at a beach for lunch and swimming. (See "Shore Excursions," below.)

few bucks a minute, or from a kiosk inside the terminal. Keep in mind, there are often lines for the phones. In town, try the **Calling Station,** Avenida Rafael Melgar 27 (© **987/2-1417**), at the corner of Calle 3 in San Miguel, 3 blocks from Muelle Fiscal.

INFORMATION   The **Tourism Office,** Plaza del Sol (© **987/2-7563**), distributes the *Vacation Guide to Cozumel* and *Cozumel Island's Restaurant Guide;* both have island maps. It's open Monday to Friday from 8am to 2:30pm. For info before you go, call © **800/44-MEXICO** or click on **www.visitmexico.com.**

GETTING AROUND
The town of San Miguel is so small you can walk anywhere you want to go. Essentially, there's only one road in Cozumel—it starts at the northern tip of the island, hugs the western shoreline, and then loops around the southern tip and returns to the capital.

If you're driving in Cozumel, it's helpful to know that the roads parallel to the sea are called avenues, and these have the right of way. The ones running from the sea are called streets, and you have to stop at each avenue to give way.

BY TAXI   Taxi service is available 24 hours a day. Call © **987/2-0236.** Cabs are relatively inexpensive, but since it's customary here to overcharge cruise ship passengers, settle on a fare before getting in—the better you bargain, the cheaper the taxi ride. The average fare from San Miguel to most major resorts and beaches is about $8; between the International terminal and downtown it's about $5. More distant island rides cost $12 and up.

BY RENTAL CAR   If you want to drive yourself, four-wheel-drive vehicles or open-air jeeps are the best rental choice. **Avis, Budget,** and **Hertz** all have offices here. **Rent-a-Car,** Avenida 5A at Calle 2 N. (© **800/527-0700** in the U.S., or 987/2-0903), 2 blocks from the pier at Muelle Fiscal, rents both. A four-door economy car rents for about $35 a day, with a Geo Tracker going for $80 and up. *Note:* Most rental cars in the Caribbean have manual transmissions, so if you need an automatic, be sure to specify that when renting.

BY MOPED Mopeds are a popular means of getting about despite heavy traffic, hidden stop signs, potholed roads, and a high accident rate. The best and most convenient rentals are at **Auto Rent** (© **987/2-0844**) in the Hotel Ceiba, a block from the pier at Muelle Fiscal. The cost is about $30 per day, including helmet rental; Mexican law requires that you wear a helmet.

BY FERRY A number of passenger ferries link Cozumel with Playa del Carmen. The most comfortable are the big speedboats and water-jet catamaran run by **Aviomar** (© **987/2-0477**). They operate Monday to Saturday from 8am to 8pm, Sunday from 9am to 1pm. The trip takes 25 minutes. All the ferries have ticket booths at the main pier. One-way fares cost about $8 per person. You'll get a ferry schedule when you buy your ticket.

SHORE EXCURSIONS

It's easier to see the ruins at Chichén-Itzá, Tulum, and Cobá from Playa del Carmen, because it's on the mainland and therefore closer to the ruins sites. Many ships en route to Cozumel pause in Playa del Carmen to drop off passengers who have signed up for ruins tours. After the tours, passengers either take a ferry back to the ship in Cozumel or, if the tour is by plane, get dropped off at the airport in Cozumel, near downtown. See "Mayan Ruins on the Mainland," above, for details about the ruins. If your ship is not dropping passengers off at Playa del Carmen (many don't), then keep in mind that shuttling back and forth via ferry or tender will add another hour or two to your schedule. If you're more interested in a lazy, relaxing day (and your ship doesn't go to Playa del Carmen), you may want to just hang out in Cozumel.

Chichén-Itzá Excursion ($220–$240, 6–7 hr.): Founded in A.D. 445, Chichén-Itzá is the largest and most fabled of the Yucatán ruins—and you can even climb up its tallest pyramid for wonderful views of the ancient city, much of which is still covered in foliage and earth. You'll take a 45-minute flight each way on 10- to 20-seater aircraft. The flight there is almost as interesting as the ruins. This tour may leave from Playa del Carmen. (*Note:* It can get hot. Bring plenty of water.)

The Mayan Ruins of Tulum & Xel-ha ($63–$74 adults, $33–$59 kids, 6–7 hr.): This is a very worthwhile experience. The ruins of this walled city are all the more spectacular because they're located on a cliff, dramatically perched above the ocean. This tour often includes an hour or two stop at the Xel-Ha Lagoon, a beautiful and natural setting for swimming (in this case, the tour is 7–8 hr. long and costs another $20 or so). The tour leaves from Playa del Carmen.

Jeep Trek ($68–$74, 4–6 hr.): Hop in a four-seat Jeep, draw straws to see who gets to drive, and explore the natural side of Cozumel, its jungle mangroves and sandy back roads. Much of the roller coaster–like route is off-road, and the Jeeps travel in a convoy. Included is a visit to the La Palma ruin, where the goddess Ixchel is said to still grant wishes (you make them with your eyes closed, facing the sea), and a stop at a lovely secluded beach for swimming and a picnic lunch of tasty Mexican fare.

Horseback-Riding Tours ($71, 3–4 hr.): Worthwhile horseback-riding tours offer a chance to see Cozumel's landscape, but although they tout visits to Mayan ruins, don't get your hopes up—there's little more than a few refrigerator-size rocks here and there on Cozumel. The tour includes a guide who discusses Mayan culture and customs while exploring the inside of a cave where the Mayans gathered for ceremonial meetings. A bus transports riders to a ranch, where the ride begins; on the trip back to the ship, guests are served free and refreshingly colllllld Mexican beer, as is the case on just about all bus excursions in Mexico.

ON YOUR OWN: WITHIN WALKING DISTANCE

For walkers, the classic grid layout makes getting around the town of San Miguel easy. Directly across from the downtown tender docks, the main square—**Plaza del Sol** (also called la plaza or el parque)—is excellent for people-watching. **Avenida Rafael Melgar,** the principal street along the waterfront, runs along the western shore of the island, site of the best resorts and beaches. Most of the shops and restaurants are on Rafael Melgar, although many well-stocked duty-free shops line the Malecón, the seaside promenade.

Only 3 blocks from Muelle Fiscal on Agenda Rafael Melgar between Calles 4 and 6 N., the **Museo de la Isla de Cozumel** (© 987/2-1434) has two floors of exhibits displayed in what was Cozumel's first luxury hotel. Exhibits start in the pre-Hispanic times and continue through the colonial era to the present. Included are many swords and nautical artifacts; one of the displays showcases endangered species. The highlight is a reproduction of a Mayan house. It's open daily from 10am to 6pm, and sometimes later; admission is $3.

ON YOUR OWN: BEYOND THE PORT AREA

You can rent a motor scooter and zip around most of the island, including its wild and natural side. Stop for lunch at a beachside open-air seafood restaurant for some grilled fish and a cool drink. Scooters can be rented from several out-fits, including Auto Rent (see "By Moped," above).

Outside of San Miguel is the **Chankanaab Nature Park,** where a saltwater lagoon, offshore reefs, and underwater caves have been turned into an archaeo-logical park, botanical garden, and wildlife sanctuary. More than 10 countries have contributed seedlings and cuttings. Some 60 species of marine life occupy the lagoon, including sea turtles. Reproductions of Mayan dwellings are scat-tered throughout the park. There's also a wide white-sand beach with thatch umbrellas and a changing area with lockers and showers. Both scuba divers and snorkelers enjoy examining the sunken ship offshore (there are four dive shops here). The park also has a restaurant and snack stand. It's all located at Carretera Sur, Kilometer 9 (no phone). It's open daily from 9am to 5pm. Admission is $7, free for children 9 and under. The 10-minute taxi ride from the pier at Muelle Fiscal costs about $5.

Mayan ruins on Cozumel are very minor compared to those on the mainland. **El Cedral** lies 3km (2 miles) inland at the turnoff at kilometer 17.5, east of Playa San Francisco. It's the island's oldest structure, with traces of original Mayan wall paintings. The Spanish tore much of it down, and the U.S. Army nearly finished the job when it built an airfield here in World War II. Little remains now except a Mayan arch and a few small ruins covered in heavy growth. Guides at the site will show you around for a fee.

Another meager ruin is at **San Gervasio,** reached by driving west across the island to the army air base, and then turning right and continuing north 6.5km (4 miles) to San Gervasio. This was once a ceremonial center and capital of Cozumel. The Mayans dedicated the area to Ixchel, the fertility goddess. The ruins cost $3.50 to visit, plus $1 for entrance to the access road. For $12, guides will show people what's left, including several broken columns and lintels. It's open daily from 8am to 5pm.

SHOPPING

You can walk from the tender pier at Muelle Fiscal to the best shops in San Miguel (they start right across the street from the new Punta Langosta pier, and are 3km–5km/2–3 miles by taxi or foot from the International and Puerto Maya cruise ship piers). Because of the influx of cruise ship passengers, prices are relatively high here, but you can and should bargain. Silver jewelry is big business, and it's generally sold by weight. You can find some nice pieces, but again, don't expect much of a bargain. **Ultra Femme,** Avenida Rafael Melgar 341 (© 987/872-0025), is one of the most important jewelers in Cozumel, and the exclusive distributor of Rolex watches on the Mexican Riviera. **Rachat & Romero,** Avenida Rafael Melgar 101 (© 987/2-0571), has a wide variety of loose stones, which they can mount while you wait.

There are wall-to-wall shops along the waterfront in San Miguel for all manner of souvenirs. Also, shops line the perimeter of Plaza del Sol, adjacent to the downtown ferry pier (a quarter-mile or so north of the Punta Langosta pier), and several shopping arcades are accessible from the plaza, including the pleasant, tree-lined **Plaza Confetti** and the peach-painted **Villa Mar complex,** with several good silver jewelry shops.

Agencia Publicaciones Gracia, Avenida 5A, a block from Muelle Fiscal, is Cozumel's best source for English-language books, guidebooks, newspapers, and magazines. **Casablanca,** Avenida Rafael Melgar 33 (located in front of the International Pier), has a fine selection of Mexican jewelry and loose stones, plus a well-chosen collection of Mexican crafts. **Gordon Gilchrist,** Studio 1, Avenida 25 S. 981 at Calle 15 S., produces Cozumel's finest etchings of local Mayan sites. **Unicornio,** 5 Avenida Sur 2 (© 987/872-0171), 2 blocks from Muelle Fiscal, has Mexican handcrafts.

If you're docking at the International Pier, there are a bunch of nice shops in the terminal, selling everything from Mexican blankets to jewelry, T-shirts, and handcrafts of all kinds. Again, prices aren't cheap—a roll of film went for $9 at the terminal last time we were there.

BEACHES

Cozumel's best powdery white-sand beach, **Playa San Francisco,** stretches for some 5km (3 miles) along the southwestern shoreline. It was once one of the most idyllic beaches in Mexico, but resort development is threatening to destroy its old character. You can rent equipment for watersports here, or have lunch at one of the many palapa restaurants and bars on the shoreline. There's no admission to the beach, and it's about a $10 taxi ride south of San Miguel's downtown pier. If you land at the International Pier, you're practically at the beach already.

Playa del Sol, about 1.5km (a mile) south of Playa del San Francisco, is a fine beach but has a big reputation, so it's likely to be wall-to-wall with your fellow cruisers. **Playa Bonita** (sometimes called "Punta Chiqueros") is one of the least crowded beaches, but it lies on the east (windward) side of the island and is difficult to reach unless you rent a vehicle or throw yourself at the mercy of a taxi driver. It sits in a moon-shaped cove sheltered from the Caribbean Sea by an off-shore reef. Waves are only moderate, the sand is powdery, and the water is clear.

You may want to consider **Parque Chankanaab,** a parklike beach area lined with thatched umbrellas and contoured plastic chaise longues. While the water is rough here and not ideal for swimming, the beach and scenery are very nice and the place is popular with locals. Admission is $7, and you can swim with dolphins (for a fee, of course) or rent snorkeling equipment. There's also a restaurant and bar. This beach is about a 15-minute, $8 taxi ride from the downtown pier.

If you don't want to go far, there are two hotel beaches a stone's throw north of the International Pier (facing the water, they're on the right) that welcome day visitors. **Le Ceiba** charges $5 per person for the day and includes one tropical drink, and the **Crown Paradise sol Caribe** charges $22 per person for the day (9am–5pm), which includes a drink and lunch.

SPORTS

SCUBA DIVING   Jacques Cousteau did much to extol the glory of Cozumel for scuba divers, discovering black coral in profusion, plus hundreds of species of rainbow-hued tropical fish. Underwater visibility can reach 75m (250 ft.). All this gives Cozumel some of the best diving in the Caribbean. Cruisers might want to confine their adventures to the finest spot, **Palancar Reef.** Lying about 1.5km (a mile) offshore, this fabulous water world features gigantic elephant-ear sponges and black and red coral, as well as deep caves, canyons, and tunnels. It's a favorite of divers from all over the world. The best scuba outfitters are **Aqua Safari,** Avenida Rafael Melgar at Calle 5, next to the Vista del Mar Hotel (© 987/2-0101; www.aquasafari.com), and **Diving Adventures,** Calle 51 Sur no. 2, near the corner of Avenida Rafael Melgar (© 888/3-38-03-88 from the U.S., or 987/2-3009; www.divingadventures.net).

SNORKELING   The shallow reefs at Playa San Francisco and Chankanaab Bay are among the best snorkeling spots. You'll see a world of sea creatures parading by, everything from parrotfish to conch. The best outfitter is **Cozumel Snorkeling Center,** Calle Primera Sur (© 987/2-0539), which offers a 3-hour snorkeling tour ($35 per person), including all equipment and refreshments. They can also arrange parasailing. You can also just rent snorkeling equipment at Chankanaab.

GREAT LOCAL RESTAURANTS & BARS

The **local beer** is Sol. On a hot day, a quart bottle of the stuff is manna from heaven.

The new **Carlos 'n Charlie's,** Avenida Rafael Melgar 11, right across from the new Punta Langosta pier (© 987/2-0191; www.carlosn-charlies.com), is Mexico's equivalent of the Hard Rock Cafe, but much wilder. Though moved into more sterile Houlihan's-style digs in a brand-new whitewashed mall, the music still blares and dancing tourists pound back yard-long glasses of beers as if they're going out of style—just like they did at the old sawdust-covered Carlos 'n Charlie's that once roared just down the road. Many a cruise passenger has stumbled back from this place clutching a souvenir glass as though it were the Holy Grail—dubious proof of a visit to Mexico. People come here for good times and the spicy, tasty ribs. You can dine surprisingly well on Yucatán specialties and the best chicken and beef fajitas in Cozumel.

Another party spot is the **Hard Rock Cozumel** itself, at Avenida Rafael Melgar 2A (© 529/872-5273; www.hardrock.com), which serves the hard stuff as well as burgers and grilled beef or chicken fajitas. Yet another is the **Fat Tuesday,** at the end of the International Pier (© 987/2-5130), where you'll find lots of crewmembers on their day or night off (you can even hear their revelry from the ship). Join the fun and guzzle a 16-ounce margarita for $5 a pop or a 24-ounce version for $7. A half block from the pier, **Las Palmeras,** Avenida Rafael Melgar (© 987/2-0532), is ideal for casual eating. If you arrive in time, it serves one of the best breakfasts in town; for lunch, it offers tempting seafood dishes or Mexican specialties.

Right in front of the in-town cruise dock, **Café del Puerto,** Avenida Rafael Melgar 3, is a local favorite. The kitchen bridges the gap between Mexico and Europe with such dishes as a superbly prepared mustard steak flambé, a succulent lobster, and Yucatán chicken wrapped in banana leaves. Also on the main drag in town are **Lobster's Cove** (© **987/2-4022**) and **Las Palmeras** (© **987/ 2-0532**), just across from the downtown pier, both offering tasty seafood and Mexican dishes. Just north of the ferry pier, **El Capi Navegante,** Avenida 10A Sur 312 at Calles 3 and 4, 5 blocks from Muelle Fiscal (© **987/2-1730**), offers the freshest fish in San Miguel, as well as a great lobster soufflé. **La Choza,** Calle Rosada Salas 198 at Avenida 10A Sur, 2 blocks from the Muelle Fiscal pier (© **987/2-0958**), offers real local cooking that's a favorite of the town's savvy foodies.

PLAYA DEL CARMEN

Some cruise ships spend a day at Cozumel and then another at Playa del Carmen, but most drop off passengers here for tours to Tulum and Chichén-Itzá and then head on to spend the day tied up at Cozumel.

The famed white-sand beach here was relatively untouched by tourists not many years ago, but today the pleasure-seeking hordes have replaced the Indian families who used to gather coconuts for copra (dried coconut meat). Shops have sprung up like weeds, but if you can tolerate the crowds, the snorkeling is still excellent over the offshore reefs. Turtle watching is another local pastime.

Avenida Juárez in Playa del Carmen is the principal business zone for the Tulum-Cancún corridor. Part of Avenida 5 running parallel to the beach has been closed to traffic, forming a good promenade. Most visitors at some point head for **Rincón del Sol,** a tree-filled courtyard built in the colonial Mexican style. It has the best collection of handcraft shops in the area, some of which offer goods of excellent quality—much better than the junky souvenirs peddled elsewhere.

COMING ASHORE   Some cruise ships anchor offshore or at the pier of Cozumel, then send passengers over to Playa del Carmen by tender. Others dock at the new **Puerto Calica Cruise Pier,** 13km (8 miles) south of Playa del Carmen. Taxis meet each arriving ship, and drivers transport visitors into the center of Playa del Carmen.

GETTING AROUND
BY TAXI   Taxis are readily available to take you anywhere, but you can walk to the center of town, to the beach, and to most major shops.

Frommer's Favorite Playa del Carmen Experiences

Taking a Tour of Tulum or Chichén-Itzá: Both of the tours described in the Cozumel section, under "Shore Excursions," above, are also offered here.

Spending a Day in Xel-ha: You'll find yourself floating around the lagoon on an inner tube without a care in the world.

BY RENTAL CAR   If you decide to rent a car for the day, **Avis, Budget, Hertz,** and **National** all have offices here.

SHORE EXCURSIONS

Most visitors head for the Mayan ruins the moment they reach shore (see "Shore Excursions" in the Cozumel section, above).

Xcaret Ecological Park ($72, 8 hr.): Lying 6.4km (4 miles) south of Playa del Carmen on the coast, Xcaret (pronounced "*Ish*-car-et") is a 250-acre ecological theme park where many visitors spend their entire day. It's a great place, with Mayan ruins scattered about the lushly landscaped area. Visitors can put on life jackets for an underwater river ride, which takes them through currents running throughout a series of caves. You can also snorkel through—something we highly recommend—as well as swim with dolphins (though it costs extra). There are a botanical garden and a dive shop on the grounds.

ON YOUR OWN: WITHIN WALKING DISTANCE

You can walk to the center of town, to the beach, and to the small shopping district.

ON YOUR OWN: BEYOND THE PORT AREA

Other than the beach and shopping, the only major attractions are Xcaret and Xel-ha (both open daily). The easiest way to get to either is to sign up for your ship's organized excursion (see above), which includes transportation; otherwise, you'll have to get ferry tickets on your own to get between Cozumel and Playa del Carmen. If you come independently of a tour, general admission for **Xcaret** (© 988/3-0654; www.xcaretcancun.com) is a steep $39 for adults, $24 for children 5 to 11 (free for kids 4 and under). The **Xel-Ha eco park** (© 987/5-4070; www.xel-ha.com.mx), just a few miles farther south of Xcaret (and pronounced "Shell ha"), features a sprawling natural lagoon filled with sparkling blue-green water and surrounded by lush foliage. The use of inner tubes and snorkeling gear is included in the admission price, and you can spend a great couple of hours wending your way from one end of the snaking body of calm water to the other, accompanied by schools of tropical fish. Xel-Ha has dolphins too, along with shops, restaurants, and lots of beach chairs. Admission is $25 for adults and $13 for kids. Buses from Playa del Carmen come here frequently; a taxi costs about $5 one way.

GREAT LOCAL RESTAURANTS & BARS

El Chino, Calle 4, Avenida 15 (© 987/3-0015), is a pristine restaurant known locally for its regional Yucatán specialties, as well as standard dishes from throughout Mexico. **El Tacolote,** Avenida Juárez (© 987/3-1363), specializes in fresh seafood and the best grilled meats in town, brought to your table fresh from the broiler on a charcoal pan to keep the food warm.

If you want to stay in the thick of things, there's a **Señor Frog's** (© 987/3-09-30), right at the ferry pier for all the beer and shots you can stomach.

12 Curaçao

As you sail into the harbor of Willemstad, be sure to look for the quaint "floating bridge," the Queen Emma pontoon bridge, which swings aside to open the narrow channel. Welcome to Curaçao, the largest and most populous of the Netherlands Antilles, just 56km (35 miles) north of the Venezuelan coast.

Curaçao was first discovered by the Spanish around 1499, but in 1634, the Dutch came and prospered. Because much of the island's surface is an arid desert, the settlers ruled out farming and instead developed Curaçao into one of the Dutch Empire's busiest trading posts. In 1915, when the Royal Dutch/Shell Company built one of the world's largest oil refineries to process crude from Venezuela, workers from 50 countries poured onto the island, and today it remains a melting pot, its population descended from a curious mixture of bloodlines, including African, Dutch, Venezuelan, and Pakistani. The oil refineries went into decline after the war, and by the 1980s tourism had begun to develop, leading to the building of many new hotels. Today the island still retains a Dutch flavor, especially in Willemsted, whose harbor is bordered by rows of picture-postcard, pastel-colored gabled Dutch-colonial houses. While these structures give Willemstad a storybook appearance, the rest of the island looks like the American Southwest, its desertlike landscape dotted with three-pronged cacti, spiny-leafed aloes, and divi-divi trees bent by trade winds.

COMING ASHORE   Cruise ships dock in Willemstad at a $9 million megapier just beyond the Queen Emma pontoon bridge, which leads to the duty-free shopping sector and the famous floating market. It's a 5- to 10-minute walk from here to the center of town, or you can take a taxi from the stand. Rumor has it that a private developer plans to build a shopping/entertainment complex in the adjacent historic fort. The town itself is easy to navigate on foot. Most of it can be explored in 2 or 3 hours, leaving plenty of time for beaches or watersports. Although the ship terminal has a duty-free shop, save your serious shopping for Willemstad. There's a phone center at the cruise terminal.

LANGUAGE   **Dutch, Spanish,** and **English** are spoken on Curaçao, along with **Papiamento,** a patois that combines the three major tongues with Amerindian and African dialects.

CURRENCY   The official currency is the **Netherlands Antillean florin** (NAf), also called a guilder, which is divided into 100 cents (NAf$1.73 = U.S.$1; NAf1 = U.S.58¢). Canadian and U.S. dollars are accepted for purchases, so there's no need to change money. Unless otherwise noted, prices in this section are given in U.S. dollars.

INFORMATION   For visitor information, go to the **Curaçao Tourist Board,** Pietermaai (© **599/9-4616000**). It's open Monday to Friday from 8am to 5pm. For information before you go, contact the Tourism Department in New York (© **800/445-8266** or 800/328-7222; www.Curacao-tourism.com).

CALLING FROM THE U.S.   When calling Curaçao from the United States, you need to dial the international access code (011) before the numbers listed here.

GETTING AROUND

BY TAXI   Taxis don't have meters, so settle on a fare before getting in. Drivers are supposed to carry an official tariff sheet. Generally, there's no need to tip. The best place to get a taxi is on the Otrabands side of the floating bridge, or call © **599/9-8690747**. Up to four passengers can share the price of an island tour by taxi, which costs about $30 per hour.

BY BUS   A fleet of DAF yellow buses operates from Wilhelmina Plein, near the shopping center, and runs to most parts of Curaçao. You can hail a bus at any designated bus stop.

Noordpunt

Westpunt Westpunt
Boca Tabla

Playa Abao

Knip Bay

Playa Lagun St. Christoffelberg

CHRISTOFFEL NATIONAL PARK

Santa Cruz

Caribbean Sea

Santa Marta Bay Soto Barber

St. Willibrordus

Daaibooi

Boca St. Marie

Boca Hato

Curaçao International Airport

Hato Caves
Julianadorp

Fort St. Michiel

Brienvengat

Blauwbaai

Curaçao Museum
Emmastad

Caribbean Sea

Piscadera Bay

Santa Catarina

St. Anna Bay

Santa Rosa

St. Joris Bay

WILLEMSTAD

Seaquarium

Punda

Princess Beach Resort & Casino

Montagne

Jan Thiel Bay

Spanish Water

Santa Barbara Beach

Curaçao Underwater Park

Punt Kanon Lighthouse

Ostpunt

0   5 mi

0   5 km

BY RENTAL CAR   Driving is on the right on paved roads. **Avis, Budget,** and **Hertz** all have offices here.

SHORE EXCURSIONS OFFERED BY THE CRUISE LINES

Many excursions aren't really worth the price here—you can easily see the town on your own and hop a taxi to the few attractions on the island outside of Willemstad (see "Getting Around," above).

Hato Caves/Curaçao Liqueur Tour ($30, 3 hr.): After a short bus ride to the caves and a walking tour through the grottoes, stalactites, and petroglyphs, the tour takes passengers to an old plantation house for a look around, and then to Curaçao Liqueur Factory for a tour and a sample of the popular liqueur, which is made from Laraha orange peels.

Countryside Bus Tour ($31, 2–3 hr.): This excursion takes you via bus to sights such as the Westpunt, Mount Christoffel, the towering cacti, and the rolling

Frommer's Favorite Curaçao Experiences

Visiting Christoffel National Park: Hike up the 371m (1,237 ft.) St. Christoffelberg, passing cacti, iguanas, wild goats, many species of birds, and ancient Arawak paintings along the way. There's also 32km (20 miles) of roads, so you can see the park by car. (See "On Your Own: Beyond the Port Area," below.)

Gazing Into the Mirrored Waters of Hato Cave: Stalagmites and stalactites are mirrored in a mystical underground lake in these caves, whose limestone formations were created by water seeping through the coral. (See "On Your Own: Beyond the Port Area," below.)

Take the Hato Caves/Curaçao Liqueur Tour: This is a neat combination. A short bus ride gets you to the caves, and then to a plantation house and the liqueur factory for a tour. (See "Shore Excursions Offered by the Cruise Lines," above.)

hills topped by landhuizen (plantation houses) built more than 3 centuries ago. You'll also stop at a beach, the Curaçao Seaquarium, and Chobolobo, an old colonial mansion where the original Curaçao liqueur is still distilled.

ON YOUR OWN: WITHIN WALKING DISTANCE

Willemstad is the major attraction here, and you can see it on foot. After years of restoration, the town's historic center and the island's natural harbor, Schottegat, have been inscribed on UNESCO's World Heritage List. Be sure to watch the **Queen Emma pontoon bridge** move. It's motorized and a man actually drives it to the side of the harbor every so often so that ships and boats can pass through the channel. It's the coolest thing to see.

A statue of **Pedro Luis Brion** dominates the square known as **Brionplein,** at the Otrabanda end of the Queen Emma pontoon bridge. Born in Curaçao in 1782, Brion became the island's favorite son and best-known war hero. He was an admiral of the fleet under Simón Bolívar and fought for the independence of Venezuela and Colombia.

Fort Amsterdam, site of the Governor's Palace and the 1769 Dutch Reformed church, has the task of guarding the waterfront. The church still has a British cannonball embedded in it. The arches leading to the fort were tunneled under the official residence of the governor. A corner of the fort stands at the intersection of Breedestraat and Handelskade, the starting point for a plunge into the island's major shopping district.

A few minutes' walk from the pontoon bridge, at the north end of Handelskade, is the **Floating Market,** where scores of schooners tie up alongside the canal. Boats arrive here from Venezuela and Colombia, and from other West Indian islands, to sell tropical fruits and vegetables, as well as handcrafts. The modern market under its vast concrete cap has not diminished the fun of watching the activity here. Either arrive early or stay late to view these marine merchants setting up or storing their wares.

Between the I. H. (Sha) Capriles Kade and Fort Amsterdam, at the corner of Columbusstraat and Hanchi di Snoa, is the **Mikve Israel-Emanuel Synagogue.**

Dating from 1651, the Jewish congregation was the first in the New World. Next door, the **Jewish Cultural Historical Museum,** Kuiperstraat 26-28 (© **599/9-4611633**), is housed in two buildings dating from 1728. They were the rabbi's residence and the mikvah (bath) for religious purification purposes. Entry is through the synagogue and admission is $3.

You can walk from the Queen Emma pontoon bridge to the **Curaçao Museum,** Van Leeuwenhoekstraat (© **599/9-4626051**). The building, constructed in 1853 by the Royal Dutch Army as a military hospital, has been carefully restored and furnished with paintings, objets d'art, and antique furniture, and houses a large collection from the Caiquetio tribes. On the museum grounds is an art gallery for temporary exhibitions of both local and international art.

ON YOUR OWN: BEYOND THE PORT AREA

Cacti, bromeliads, rare orchids, iguanas, donkeys, wild goats, and many species of birds thrive in the 4,500-acre **Christoffel National Park** (© **599/9-864-0363**), located about a 45-minute taxi or car ride from the capital near the northwestern tip of Curaçao. The park rises from flat, arid countryside to 1,230-foot-high St. Christoffelberg, the tallest point in the Dutch Leewards. Along the way are ancient Arawak paintings and the **Piedra di Monton,** a rock heap piled by African slaves who cleared this former plantation. Legend says slaves could climb to the top of the rock pile, jump off, and fly back home across the Atlantic to Africa. If they had ever tasted a grain of salt, however, they would crash to their deaths. The park has 32km (20 miles) of one-way trail-like roads. The shortest is about 8km (5 miles) long, but takes about 40 minutes to drive because of its rough terrain. One of several hiking trails goes to the top of St. Christoffelberg. It takes about 1½ hours to walk to the summit (come early in the morning before it gets hot). There's also a museum in an old storehouse left over from plantation days. The park is open Monday to Saturday from 8am to 4pm and on Sunday from 6am to 3pm, and guided tours are available. Admission is $10 per person.

The **Curaçao Seaquarium,** off Dr. Martin Luther King Boulevard (© **599/9-4616666**), displays more than 400 species of fish, crabs, anemones, and other invertebrates, sponges, and coral. In the "shark and animal encounter," divers, snorkelers, and experienced swimmers are able to feed, film, and photograph sharks, stingrays, lobsters, tarpons, parrotfish, and other marine life in a controlled environment. Nonswimmers can see the underwater life from a 14m (46-ft.) semisubmersible observatory. Curaçao's only full-facility, white-sand, palm-shaded beach is on the Seaquarium grounds. Admission is $13 for adults and $7.25 for children 2 to 14. Hours are Monday through Sunday, 8:30am to 4:30pm.

Stalagmites and stalactites are mirrored in a mystical underground lake in **Hato Caves,** F. D. Rosseveltweg (© **599/9-8680379**). Long ago, geological forces uplifted this limestone terrace, which was originally a coral reef. The limestone formations were created over thousands of years by water seeping through the coral. After crossing the lake, you enter two caverns known as "The Cathedral" and La Ventana ("The Window"), where you'll see samples of ancient Indian petroglyphs. The caves are open daily from 10am to 4pm, and professional local guides take visitors through every hour. Admission is $6.50 for adults, $5 for children 4 to 11, and free for kids 3 and under.

SHOPPING

Curaçao is a shopper's paradise, with some 200 stores lining Heerenstraat, Breedestraat, and other streets in the 5-block district called the **Punda.** Many shops occupy the town's old Dutch houses.

The island is famous for its 5-pound "wheelers" of Gouda and Edam cheese. Look for good buys on wooden shoes, French perfumes, Dutch blue Delft souvenirs, finely woven Italian silks, Japanese and German cameras, jewelry, silver, Swiss watches, linens, leather goods, liquor, and island-made rum and liqueurs, especially Curaçao liqueur, some of which has a distinctive blue color. Some stores also offer good buys on intricate lacework imported from everywhere between Portugal and China. If you're a street shopper and want something colorful, consider a carving or flamboyant painting from Haiti or the Dominican Republic; both are hawked by street vendors at any of the main plazas.

Suggested shops include **Bamali,** Breedestraat 2 (© **599/9-461-2258**), for Indonesian-influenced clothing (mostly for women); **Gandelman Jewelers,** Breedestraat 35, Punda (© **599/9-461-1854**), for a large selection of fine jewelry as well as Curaçaoan gold pieces; and **Curaçao Creations,** Schrijnwerkerstraat 14 (© **599/9-462-4516**), for Curaçao handcrafts.

BEACHES

Curaçao has some 38 beaches, ranging from hotel sand patches to secluded coves. The seawater remains an almost-constant 76°F year-round, with good underwater visibility, but beaches here just aren't as good as others in the region. Taxi drivers waiting at the cruise dock will take you to any of the beaches, but you'll have to negotiate a fare. To be on the safe side, arrange to have your driver pick you up at a certain time and take you back to the cruise dock.

The **Curaçao Seaquarium** has the island's only full-facility, white-sand, palm-shaded beach, but you'll have to pay the full aquarium admission to get in (see "On Your Own: Beyond the Port Area," above). The rest of the beaches here are public.

A good beach on the eastern side of the island is **Santa Barbara Beach,** on land owned by a mining company between the open sea and the island's primary watersports and recreational area, known as Spanish Water. You'll also find Table Mountain and an old phosphate mine. The natural beach has pure-white sand and calm water. A buoy line protects swimmers from boats, and there are restrooms, changing rooms, a snack bar, and a terrace. You can rent water bicycles and small motorboats. It's open daily from 8am to 6pm. The beach has access to the **Curaçao Underwater Park** (© **599/9-462-4242**), which stretches from the Princess Beach Resort to the eastern tip of Curaçao and includes some of the island's finest reefs.

Daaibooi is a good beach about 30 minutes from town, in the Willibrordus area on the west side of Curaçao. It's free, but there are no changing facilities.

Blauwbaai (Blue Bay) is the largest and most frequented beach on Curaçao, with enough white sand for everybody. Along with showers and changing facilities, there are plenty of shady places to retreat from the noonday sun. To reach it, take the road that goes past the **Holiday Beach Hotel & Casino** (© **599/9-462-5400**), heading in the direction of Juliandorp. Follow the sign that tells you to bear left for Blauwbaai and the fishing village of San Michiel.

Westpunt is known for its gigantic cliffs and the Sunday divers who jump from them into the ocean below. This public beach is on the northwestern tip of the island. **Knip Bay,** just south of Westpunt, has beautiful turquoise waters.

On weekends, live music and dancing make the beach a lively place. Changing facilities and refreshments are available. **Playa Abao,** with crystal turquoise water, is situated at the northern tip of the island.

Warning: Beware of stepping on the hard spines of sea urchins, which are sometimes found in these waters. While not fatal, their spines can cause several days of real discomfort. For temporary first aid, try the local remedies of vinegar or lime juice.

GREAT LOCAL RESTAURANTS & BARS

Curaçao's **local beer** is the very Dutch Amstel. The **local drink** is Curaçao liqueur, some of which has a distinctive blue color.

De Taveerne, Landhuis Groot Davelaar, Sileña, northeast of the Downtown Punda area (© **599/9-7370669**), is actually two restaurants: a French restaurant at street level and a less formal brasserie serving inexpensive international food on its second floor. If you're hot, dusty, and in a hurry, your best bet might be to order a platter of food in the brasserie. **Golden Star,** Socratesstraat 2, at the corner of Dr. Hugenholtzweg and Dr. Maalweg, southeast of Willemstad (© **599/9-4654795**), is the best place to go on the island for criollo, or local food. It's inland from the coast road leading southeast from St. Anna Bay, 8 minutes by taxi from the cruise dock. **La Pergola,** in the Waterfront Arches, Waterfort Straat (© **599/9-4613482**), is an Italian restaurant where the menu items change virtually every day. **Rijstaffel Indonesia and Holland Club Bar,** Mercuriusstraat 13, Salinja (© **599/9-4612999**), is the best place on the island to sample the Indonesian rijstaffel, the traditional "rice table" with all the zesty side dishes. You'll need a taxi to get to this villa in the suburbs near Salinja, near the **Princess Beach Resort & Casino** (© **599/9736-7888**) southeast of Willemstad.

13 Dominica

First things first. It's pronounced "Dome-ee-*nee*-ka," not "Doe-*min*-i-ka." And it has nothing to do with the Dominican Republic. The Commonwealth of Dominica is an independent country, and English, not Spanish, is the official language. The only Spanish commonly understood in Dominica is *mal encaminado a Santo Domingo* ("accidentally sent to the Dominican Republic"), the phrase stamped on the many letters that make it to their proper destination only after an erroneous but common detour.

To be sure, Dominica has some rough edges. The island is poor, so don't expect luxury or up-to-the-minute technology around every corner, and not everything man-made is as beautiful as nature's handiwork. Balancing this, though, is the fact that Dominica is the most lush and mountainous island in the eastern Caribbean. About 47km (29 miles) long and 26km (16 miles) wide, and lying between the French islands of Guadeloupe and Martinique, smack-dab in the center of the arc formed by the Antilles, it's blessed with astonishing natural wonders—crystal-pure rivers (one for every day of the year, they say), dramatic waterfalls, volcanic lakes (one gurgles and boils from the heat and tumult in the earth below), and foliage as gargantuan as any H. G. Wells ever imagined on Venus. Volcanic coral reefs, every bit as biologically complex as the rain forests onshore, ring the island, and a bit farther from land, whales mate and calve.

Much of Dominica's beauty is accessible to even the most sedentary visitor. Sitting in a rowboat, you can glide up a river through swampland crowded with mangroves and exotic birds, and impressive waterfalls are minutes from paved roads. You can also wend through astonishingly verdant rain forests along undemanding nature trails.

The island's people—primarily descendants of the West Africans brought over to work the plantations, plus some descendants of Europeans and Indians—are another great natural resource. Friendly and proud of their national independence, Dominica's 72,000 citizens remain, for the most part, unchanged by tourism. Don't be surprised when you're greeted with a smile and an "OK," the island's equivalent of "hi." Unfortunately, in Roseau, the main city, drug dealers offering to sell you some of the local weed may also greet you—tourism might be a still-developing industry here, but some others are obviously a little further along.

One portion of the island's population has immeasurable ethnological significance: Concentrated in a territory in the northeast, Dominica's approximately 3,000 Carib Indians are the last remaining descendants of the people who dominated the region when Europeans arrived.

COMING ASHORE   Dominica has two cruise ship ports. The most frequented is in the heart of **Roseau,** the country's capital and largest town. The other is near the northwestern town of **Portsmouth.** Banks, restaurants, a market, a tourism office, and the recommended Dominica Museum line the road opposite Roseau's harbor. Portsmouth's port has a tourist welcome center (with an auditorium for speakers and films), shops, and instant access to Fort Shirley and Cabrits National Park.

LANGUAGE   **English** is Dominica's official language. Almost everyone speaks **Creole** as well, a patois that combines elements of French, English, and African language. Dominica's Creole is similar to those spoken on the neighboring French islands of Guadeloupe and Martinique.

CURRENCY   The **Eastern Caribbean dollar** (EC$2.70 = U.S.$1; EC$1 = U.S.37¢) is Dominica's official currency, but U.S. dollars are accepted almost everywhere. You're likely to receive change in the local currency. Several **ATMs** in Roseau, including one at the port, dispense both U.S. and EC dollars. Credit cards and traveler's checks are widely accepted.

INFORMATION   Dominica's **Division of Tourism** operates branches at the Roseau and Portsmouth cruise ship berths (the Roseau office is located a block from the waterfront at the old post office building on Dame M. E. Charles Blvd.). For information before you leave home, contact the **Dominica Tourist Office** (© **212/949-1711;** www.ndcdominica.dm/travel.htm). Several island businesses, including restaurants, tour operators, and other service providers, have joined forces to create another site, **www.delphis.dm/home.htm**, which has scores of links and helpful information.

CALLING FROM THE U.S.   When calling Dominica from the United States, simply dial "1" before the numbers listed here.

GETTING AROUND
BY RENTAL CAR   Dominica's road system is extensive and relatively well maintained considering the frequent torrential rains; but driving is on the left side, and passage through the mountains can be harrowing. You need a valid driver's license and a Dominican driver's permit, which costs about $10 and is available through rental agencies. Don't get annoyed when other drivers sound their horns; honking usually indicates an oncoming vehicle (especially at sharp curves)

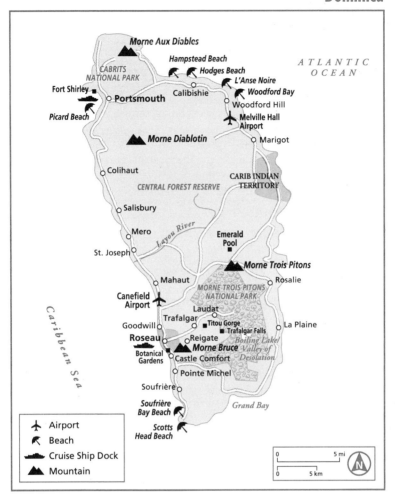

A map of Dominica showing:

Legend:
- ✈ Airport
- ↞ Beach
- ⛴ Cruise Ship Dock
- ⛰ Mountain

Locations shown: Morne Aux Diables, Hampstead Beach, Hodges Beach, L'Anse Noire, Woodford Bay, CABRITS NATIONAL PARK, Calibishie, Woodford Hill, Fort Shirley, Portsmouth, Melville Hall Airport, Picard Beach, Morne Diablotin, Marigot, Colihaut, CENTRAL FOREST RESERVE, CARIB INDIAN TERRITORY, Salisbury, Mero, Emerald Pool, St. Joseph, Layou River, Morne Trois Pitons, Mahaut, Rosalie, Canefield Airport, MORNE TROIS PITONS NATIONAL PARK, Laudat, Trafalgar, Goodwill, Titou Gorge, Trafalgar Falls, La Plaine, Roseau, Reigate, Boiling Lake, Morne Bruce, Valley of Desolation, Botanical Gardens, Castle Comfort, Pointe Michel, Soufrière, Grand Bay, Soufrière Bay Beach, Scotts Head Beach. ATLANTIC OCEAN, Caribbean Sea.

---

or is meant as a friendly greeting. **Avis, Budget,** and **Hertz** all have offices here, as do the local agencies **Valley Car Rentals,** with offices in both Roseau and Portsmouth (℃ **767/448-3233** Roseau, 767/445-5252 Portsmouth), and **Garraway Rent-a-Car,** in downtown Roseau at 17 Old St. (℃ **767/448-2891**).

BY TAXI Taxis and public minivans are designated by license plates that begin with the letters *H* or *HA*. Fleets of both await cruise ship passengers at the Roseau and Portsmouth docks. Drivers are generally knowledgeable about sites and history, and the standard sightseeing rate is $18 per hour for up to four people. The vehicles are unmetered, so negotiate a price in advance and make sure everyone's talking about the same currency. You can get more information from the **Dominica Taxi Association** (℃ **767/449-8533**). **Mally's Tour and Taxi Service** (℃ **767/448-3114**) and **Julius John's** (℃ **767/449-1968**) are two reputable operators.

Frommer's Favorite Dominica Experiences

Hiking to the Emerald Pool: A 15-minute walk through a gorgeous forest brings you to this primeval pool, where you can swim or just take in the beauty of the picture-perfect waterfall, the moss-covered boulders, and the sunlight streaming through branches high overhead. (See "Shore Excursions Offered by the Cruise Lines," below.)

Paddling Up the Indian River: Minutes from Portsmouth, the gentle Indian River drains into the Caribbean from its source in the foothills of the island's tallest mountain, 4,747-foot high Morne Diablotin. As a boatman paddles you up the twisting river, you'll pass through swampland that features giant palms and mango trees with serpentine roots. (See "Shore Excursions Offered by the Cruise Lines," below.)

Experiencing Carib Culture: Along a rugged portion of Dominica's northeastern coast, the 3,700-acre Carib Territory is home to the world's last surviving Carib Indians. The Caribs today live like most other rural islanders—growing bananas and coconuts, fishing, and operating small shops—but their sturdy baskets of dyed and woven larouma reeds and their wooden canoes carved from the trunks of massive gommier trees are evidence of the people's links to the past. A traditional big house, called the Karbet, serves as a cultural and entertainment center. If you're lucky, you'll witness a performance of the Karifuna Cultural Group, whose youthful members are dedicated to the regeneration of Carib spirit and culture. (See "Shore Excursions Offered by the Cruise Lines," below.)

Exploring Fort Shirley/Cabrits National Park: On Dominica's northwestern coast, right by the cruise ship port of Portsmouth, the 260-acre Cabrits National Park combines stunning mountain scenery, tropical deciduous forest and swampland, volcanic-sand beaches, coral reefs, and the romance of an 18th-century fort. (See "On Your Own: Within Walking Distance," below.)

SHORE EXCURSIONS OFFERED BY THE CRUISE LINES

Trafalgar Falls and Emerald Pool Nature Tour ($40, 4 hr.): Drive to Morne Bruce for a panoramic view of Roseau and learn about local flora and fauna at the Botanical Gardens. Proceed to a lookout point for a majestic view of Trafalgar Falls. After refreshment at a nearby restaurant, drive to the Emerald Pool, where, after a 15-minute trail walk, you can swim in a natural pool surrounded by moss-covered boulders at the base of a picture-perfect waterfall.

Roseau and Indian River Tour ($40, 5 hr.): Drive through Roseau and fishing villages along the island's western coast to the town of Portsmouth. Embark on wooden canoes for a guided tour of the Indian River. Ferns, lianas, and reeds cluster between the trees, forming a cool green tunnel of foliage. You'll spot herons, bananaquits, and the occasional iguana. Land crabs shuffle between the roots, and fish occasionally pop out of the water. The relaxing trip features informative commentary by your boatman and a brief stop at a rain-forest refreshment stand for a beer or soda, where you can also pick up a fish or bird fashioned origami style from reed. Cruise lines often offer this excursion, but if you're in Portsmouth, locals with boats are everywhere trying to drum up business (the actual ride upstream is only about a mile or so), so you can skip the middleman and hop in one for about $20 a person (or whatever you can negotiate).

Carib Indian Territory ($51, 5 hr.): Drive to the Carib Territory, where the tribe's chief will acquaint you with Carib history. Attend a performance by the Karifuna Cultural Group and view local crafts.

Champagne Scuba Dive ($51, 3 hr.): Certified divers can dive the reef named for the bubbles produced by an underwater geothermal vent. Observe corals, fishes, and other marine life. Equipment is included.

D'Auchamps Gardens and Museum ($36, 3 hr.): Walk through an impressive collection of exotic plants and flowers and learn about their uses and origins. Along a marked trail through this old coffee estate you'll see cacao, avocado, breadfruit, and citrus trees, as well as heliconias, orchids, and other spectacular blooms from around the world. View Trafalgar Falls and a variety of birds. Learn about Dominica's history at the museum.

EXCURSIONS OFFERED BY LOCAL AGENCIES

Nature Tours: Dominica has several excellent tour operators who know the island's many features and intricate terrain like the backs of their hands. One truly outstanding and highly recommended operation is **Ken's Hinterland Adventure Tours,** Fort Young Hotel, Victoria St., Roseau (✆ 767/448-4850), which offers tours that focus on botany, natural history, bird-watching, and whale-watching; more vigorous tours focus on activities such as river hiking, waterfall stalking, or mountain climbing. **Dominica Tours** (✆ 767/448-2638) is another good choice.

Carib Indian Excursions: For trips through the Carib Territory, you might want to make arrangements with **NICE** (Native Indigenous Carib Excursions; ✆ 767/448-2489). You can't miss with the firsthand knowledge of Carib traditions offered by NICE's operator, former Carib chief Irvince Auguiste.

See "Sports," below, for information on scuba, snorkeling, and kayaking trips.

ON YOUR OWN: WITHIN WALKING DISTANCE

IN ROSEAU In the early 18th century, the French chose to build their largest settlement at what is now Roseau because the area has the largest expanse of flat land on the leeward coast and was well supplied with fresh water from the nearby Roseau River. The town's name comes from the river reeds (*roseaux* in French) that grow profusely around the estuary. As you come ashore, you'll see the **Dominica Museum,** which faces the bay front. Housed in an old market house dating from 1810, the museum's permanent exhibit provides a clear and interesting overview of the island's geology, history, archaeology, economy, and culture. The displays on pre-Columbian peoples, the slave trade, and the Fighting Maroons—slaves who resisted their white slave owners and established their own communities—are particularly informative. The museum is open Monday to Friday from 9am to 4pm, Saturday from 9am to noon; admission is $2.

Directly behind the museum is the **Old Market Square.** Vendors of vegetables, fruits, and other merchandise have crowded this cobbled square for centuries, and over the years the location has also witnessed slave auctions, executions, and political meetings and rallies. Today it offers primarily handcrafts and souvenirs. The **Public Market Place** at the mouth of the Roseau

River, to your left as you leave the ship, is the Old Market Square's successor as the town's center of commercial activity. It's most colorful on Saturday mornings, when farmers and country vendors from the hills artfully display their fruits, vegetables, root crops, and flowers across the courtyards, sidewalks, and stalls of the marketplace.

It took more than 100 years to build the **Roseau Cathedral of Our Lady of Fair Heaven,** on Virgin Lane. Made of cut volcanic stone in the Gothic-Romanesque revival style, it was finally completed in 1916. The original funds to build the church were raised from levies on French planters, and Caribs erected the first wooden ceiling frame. Convicts on Devil's Island built the pulpit, and one of the stained-glass windows is dedicated to Christopher Columbus. The **Methodist Church** stands next door to the Cathedral on land that once belonged to Catholics who later converted to Methodism. The Protestant church's location and the "conversion" of the land caused such discomfort in the late 1800s that a street riot ensued. Things are calmer today.

On the eastern edge of Roseau, the **Botanical Gardens** lie at the base of Morne Bruce, the mountain overlooking the town. The gardens were established at the end of the 19th century to encourage crop diversification and to provide farmers with correctly propagated seedlings. London's Kew Gardens provided exotic plants collected from every corner of the tropical world, and experiments conducted to see what would grow in Dominica revealed that everything does. Unfortunately, in 1979 Hurricane David destroyed many of the garden's oldest trees. One arboreal victim, an African baobab, still pins the bus it crushed, a monument to the power of the storm. At the garden's aviary you can see sisserou and jacko parrots, part of a captive-breeding program designed to increase the ranks of these endangered species.

IN PORTSMOUTH   The cruise ship dock at Portsmouth leads directly to 104-hectare (260-acre) **Cabrits National Park,** which combines stunning mountain scenery, tropical deciduous forest and swampland, volcanic sand beaches, coral reefs, and the romance of 18th-century **Fort Shirley** overlooking the town and Prince Rupert's Bay. Previous visitors to the area include Christopher Columbus, Sir Francis Drake, Admiral Horatio Nelson, and John Smith, who stopped here on his way to Virginia, where he founded Jamestown. Fort Shirley and more than 50 other major structures compose one of the West Indies' most impressive and historic military complexes. Admission is $2.

ON YOUR OWN: BEYOND THE PORT AREAS

Approximately 15 to 20 minutes by car from Roseau, **Trafalgar Falls** is actually two separate falls referred to as the mother and the father falls. The cascading white torrents dazzle in the sunlight before pummeling black lava boulders below. The surrounding foliage comes in innumerable shades of green. To reach the brisk water of the natural pool at the base of the falls, you'll have to step gingerly along slippery rocks, so the nonballetic shouldn't attempt the climb. The constant mist that tingles the entire area beats any spa treatment. The rainbows are perpetual.

Titou Gorge, near the village of Laudat, offers an exhilarating swimming experience. Wending through the narrow volcanic gorge, you struggle against the cool current like a salmon swimming upstream to spawn. The sheer black walls enclosing the gorge loom 6m (20 ft.) above. At first, they seem sinister, but worn smooth by the water, they're ultimately womblike rather than menacing. Rock outcrops and a small cave provide interludes from the water flow, and eventually you reach the small but thundering waterfall that feeds the torrent. **Emerald Pool** sits deep in the rain forest not far from the center of the island. After walking 15 minutes along a relatively easy trail shaded by majestic trees, you reach a 15m (50-ft.) waterfall that crashes into the pool, named for the moss-covered boulders that enclose it. You can splash in the refreshing water if you like, floating on your back to see the thick rain-forest canopy and bright blue sky above you.

About 6.5km (4 miles) from Portsmouth, in the midst of orange, grapefruit, and banana groves, the **Syndicate Nature Trail** provides an excellent introduction to tropical rain forests. The easy loop trail meanders through a stunningly rich ecosystem that features exotic trees such as the lwoyé kaka, and the chantannyé.

Hard-core masochists have an easy choice—the forced march through the **Valley of Desolation** to **Boiling Lake.** Experienced guides say this all-day hike is like spending hours on a maximally resistant Stairmaster; one ex-Marine drill sergeant, a master of understatement, referred to it as "arduous." No joke, the trek is part of the Dominican army's basic training (of course, you won't have to carry one of your colleagues along the way). Why would any sane person endure this hell? To breathe in the harsh, sulfuric fumes that have killed all but the hardiest vegetation? Because the idea of baking a potato in the steam rising from the earth is irresistible? Maybe to feel the thrill that comes with the risk that you might break through the thin crust that separates you from hot lava? Or could it be the final destination, the 21m-wide (70-ft.-wide) cauldron of bubbling, slate-blue water of unknown depth? Don't even think of taking a dip in this flooded fumarole: The water temperature ranges from 180° to 197°F. Can we sign you up?

SHOPPING

In addition to the usual duty-free items—jewelry, watches, perfumes, and other luxury goods—Dominica offers handcrafts and art not obtainable anywhere else, most notably **Carib Indian baskets** made of dyed larouma reeds and balizier (heliconia) leaves. Designs for these items originated in Venezuela's Orinoco River valley and have been handed down from generation to generation since long before the time of Columbus. Dominican designs and materials are similar to those made today in the Orinoco valley—amazing considering that there's been no interaction between the two peoples for more than 500 years. The Carib basket you buy, therefore, is more than a souvenir; it's a link to the pre-Columbian Caribbean. You can buy Carib crafts directly from the craftspeople in the Carib Territory or at various outlets in Roseau. A small, 12-inch basket will cost about $10, and you can get a bell-shaped model about 22 inches high for $30 or $35. **Floor mats** made from vertiver grass are another Dominican specialty.

At **Tropicrafts,** at the corner of Queen Mary Street and Turkey Lane in Roseau (© **767/448-2747**), you can watch local women weave grass mats with designs as varied and complex as those you made as a child with your Spirograph. The large store also stocks Carib baskets, locally made soaps and toiletries, rums, jellies, condiments, woodcarvings, and masks made from the trunks of giant fougère ferns. The **Rainforest Shop,** at 12 Old St. in Roseau (© **767/448-8834**), is dedicated to the preservation of Dominica's ecosystem and offers colorful hand-painted items made from recycled materials such as oil drums, coconut shells, and newspapers. The **Crazy Banana,** at 17 Castle St. (no phone), features Dominican arts and crafts, including straw and ceramic items, as well as jewelry and Cuban cigars. For unique and sometimes whimsical objects, try **Balisier's** (no phone) at 35 Great George St. Local artist Hilroy Fingal transforms throwaway items such as aluminum cans, perfume bottles, rocks, and coconut shells into things of beauty. His aesthetic is a little like Keith Haring's and every bit as fun. **Caribana,** at 31 Cork St. (☎ 767/448-7340), is one of the island's oldest craft shops. It offers items as varied as furniture, home accessories, jewelry, books, and skin-care products, and also serves as a showcase for local painters and sculptors and as a gathering place for the local arts community. **Frontline Cooperative,** at 78 Queen Mary St. (☎ 767/448-8664), specializes in books about Caribbean peoples, issues, and cooking.

BEACHES

If your sole focus is beaches, you'll likely find Dominica disappointing. Much of the seacoast is rocky, and many sandy beaches have dark, volcanic sand. But there are golden sand beaches as well, primarily on the northern coast. Head for **Woodford Bay, L'Ance Tortue, Pointe Baptiste,** or **Hampstead Beach;** all have white sand, palm trees, and azure waters protected by reefs or windswept headlands.

SPORTS

FISHING   Dominica is a prime destination for anglers looking to catch marlin, wahoo, yellowfin tuna, or dorado. The island's numerous rivers flow into the Caribbean, providing an abundance of bait fish, including bonito, jacks, and small tuna that attract bigger deepwater species. You can drop your line in the water a mere 15 minutes from the dock. **Rainbow Sportfishing** (☎ 767/448-8650) operates a 10m (32-ft.) Sea Ray, while **Gamefishing Dominica** (☎ 888/CASTAWAYS in the U.S., or 767/449-6638) has two boats, a 10m (34-ft.) Luhrs and a 8½m (28-ft.) Pacemaker. Coastline fishing prices start at $50 per person, with a four-passenger minimum. Deep-water half-day excursions are $450 for up to six anglers.

SCUBA DIVING   Dominica's lush, beautiful scenery above water is echoed underwater in the surrounding Caribbean and Atlantic. Although the island is drained by hundreds of rivers and streams, the jagged volcanic underseascape prevents runoff sediment from clouding the water. Visibility ranges from 18m (60 ft.) to more than 30m (100 ft.). Most local dive operations surpass international standards set by PADI, NAUI, and SSI, and small, uncrowded excursions are the norm. **Dive Dominica** (☎ 888/262-6611 in the U.S., or 767/448-2188) is perhaps the island's best operator. Single-tank boat dives run about $50. First-time dives with instruction run about $100 to $125.

SNORKELING   Dominica offers almost 30 top-notch snorkeling areas, including the popular Champagne site. Snorkelers can join a dive-boat party, participate in special snorkel excursions, or explore the coast in a sea kayak, periodically jumping overboard for a look below. The calm water on the island's leeward side is perfect for viewing the riotous colors of sponges, the corals, and the 190-plus fish species native to the area. Offshore snorkeling and equipment rental can be arranged through the dive operator listed above. Prices start at approximately $25.

GREAT LOCAL RESTAURANTS & BARS

Seafood, local root vegetables referred to as "provisions," and Creole recipes are among the highlights of Dominican cuisine. Crapaud ("mountain chicken" in

English, though it's really mountain frog) is the national delicacy. For a **local beer,** try Kubuli; for a **local rum,** try Soca or Macoucherie.

IN ROSEAU Try **La Robe Créole,** 3 Victoria St. (© 767/448-2896), which gets top marks for its callaloo soup (made from the spinachlike leaves of a local vegetable called dasheen, plus coconut), lobster and conch crepes, and mango chutney. The decor features heavy stone walls, solid ladder-back chairs, and colorful madras tablecloths. **Guiyave,** 15 Cork St. (© 767/448-2930), an airy restaurant on the second floor of a pistachio-colored wood-frame house, features steamed fish, conch, octopus, and spareribs. Take a table on the veranda and cool off with one of the fresh-squeezed juices. How about soursop, tamarind, sorrel, cherry, or strawberry? The downstairs takeout counter offers chicken patties, spicy rotis, and delectable tarts and cakes. The **Sutton Grille,** 25 Old St. (© 767/449-8700), in the Sutton Place Hotel, boasts an airy dining area ensconced in 100-year-old stone walls. You can choose a table a few steps up from the bustle of downtown Roseau or one set back from the action. The menu, a veritable primer of Creole and other West Indian cookery, also offers a generous sprinkling of international and vegetarian dishes.

IN PORTSMOUTH If you disembark in Portsmouth, get a table at the **Coconut Beach Restaurant** at Picard Beach (© 767/445-5393). It overlooks the Caribbean and the twin peaks of Cabrits National Park across Prince Rupert's Bay. The fresh seafood and Creole dishes taste even better with the tang of salt in the air. The **Purple Turtle** (© 767/445-5296) is closer to the dock and features lobster and crayfish, as well as lighter fare such as rotis, sandwiches, and salads.

14 Grand Cayman

Grand Cayman is the largest of the Cayman Islands, a British colony 772km (480 miles) due south of Miami (Cayman Brac and Little Cayman are the others). It's the top of an underwater mountain, whose side—known as the **Cayman Wall**—plummets straight down for 150m (500 ft.) before becoming a steep slope that falls away for 1,800m (6,000 ft.) to the ocean floor.

Despite its "grand" name, the island is only 35km (22 miles) long and 13km (8 miles) across at its widest point. Flat, relatively unattractive, and full of scrubland and swamp, Grand Cayman and its sister islands nevertheless boast more than their share of upscale, expensive private homes and condos, owned by millionaire expatriates from all over who come because of the tiny nation's lenient tax and banking laws. (Enron, the poster child of shady business dealings, reportedly had more than 690 different subsidiaries here to help it avoid paying U.S. taxes.)

Grand Cayman is also popular because of its laid-back civility—so civil that ships aren't allowed to visit on Sunday. **George Town** is the colony's capital and its commercial hub, and many hotels line the sands of the nation's most famous sunspot, **Seven Mile Beach.** Scuba divers and snorkelers come for the coral reefs and other formations that lie sometimes within swimming distance of the shoreline.

COMING ASHORE Cruise ships anchor off George Town and ferry their passengers to a pier on Harbour Drive. The short tender ride can be choppy, but the landing point couldn't be more convenient: You're let off right in the heart of the shopping district. There's a **tourist information booth** at the pier, and taxis line up to meet cruise ship passengers. There's a phone center for credit-card calls on Shedden Road, right in downtown.

LANGUAGE **English** is the official language of the islands.

CURRENCY The legal tender is the Cayman Islands dollar (CI80¢ = U.S.$1; CI1 = U.S.$1.25), but U.S. dollars are commonly accepted. Be sure to note which currency price tags refer to before making a purchase. Prices in this section are given in U.S. dollars.

INFORMATION The **Department of Tourism** is in the Pavilion Building, Cricket Square (P.O. Box 67), George Town, Grand Cayman, BWI (© **800/ 346-3313** or 345/949-0623). It's open Monday to Friday from 9am to 5pm. To get info before you go, contact the **Grand Caymans Tourism Board** in New York (© **212/682-5582;** www.caymanislands.ky).

CALLING FROM THE U.S. When calling Grand Cayman from the U.S., you need only dial a "1" before the numbers listed here.

GETTING AROUND

BY TAXI Taxi fares are fixed; typical one-way fares range from $12 to $20. **Holiday Taxi** (© **345/947-1066**) offers 24-hour service.

BY RENTAL CAR The roads are good by Caribbean standards, so driving around is relatively easy, as long as you remember to drive on the left side of the road. **Avis, Budget, Dollar,** and **Hertz** all have offices here.

BY MOTOR SCOOTER OR BICYCLE The terrain is relatively flat, so motor scooters and bicycles are another way to get around. **Soto Scooters Ltd.,** Seven Mile Beach (© **345/945-4465**), at Coconut Place, offers Honda Elite scooters for about $30 daily, and bicycles for $15 daily.

SHORE EXCURSIONS OFFERED BY THE CRUISE LINES

Nearly all the shore excursions here are underwater adventures, which you can book through your cruise ship or on your own.

Stingray City ($39–$49, 2–3 hr.): The waters off Grand Cayman are home to Stingray City, one of the world's most unusual underwater attractions. Set in the very shallow, sun-flooded waters of North Sound, about 3km (2 miles) east of the island's northwestern tip, the site was discovered in the mid-1980s when local fishermen cleaned their catch and dumped the offal overboard. They noticed scores of stingrays (which usually eat marine crabs) feeding on the debris, a phenomenon that quickly attracted local divers and marine zoologists.

 Frommer's Favorite Grand Cayman Experiences

Swimming with Stingrays: At Stingray City, you can hop into the water with dozens of these weird-looking but gentle sea creatures, which will swim right into your arms, like dogs. (See "Shore Excursions Offered by the Cruise Lines," above.)

Taking In the Scene on Seven Mile Beach: Grand Cayman's famed stretch of sand is known for its watersports and its translucent aquamarine waters. (See "Beaches," below.)

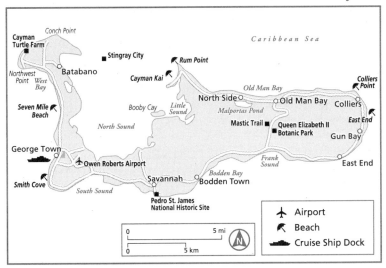

Today, anywhere from 30 to 100 relatively tame stingrays hover in the waters around the site for their daily handouts from hordes of snorkelers (often hundreds of cruise passengers at a time, so don't be surprised if they're not hungry). Stingrays are terribly gentle creatures, and love to have their bellies rubbed, but they possess viciously barbed stingers capable of inflicting painful damage to anyone mistreating them. Never try to grab one by the tail. As long as you don't, you can feed and pet these velvet-skinned creatures without incident. Some tours include a quick island tour, including a stop at the Cayman Turtle Farm and a town called Hell (to look at some interesting rock formations and, of course, buy a T-shirt with that great Hell logo). The island tour and Stingray City excursion usually runs about 3 hours.

Atlantis Submarine Excursion ($76, 1½ hr.): A 45-minute ride in the submarine is usually offered. The "Atlantis Expedition" dive visits the Cayman Wall; the "Atlantis Discovery" lasts 40 minutes and introduces viewers to the marine life of the Caymans.

Island Tour via Bicycle ($60, 3 hr.): A great way to really get a feel for an island—and get some exercise—is via bicycle. You pick up your touring mountain bike at the Beach Club Colony Hotel (© **345/949-8100**), ride along the coastline for views of Seven Mile Beach, and then journey inland en route to the north side of the island to ride along the coast again.

EXCURSIONS OFFERED BY LOCAL AGENCIES

Stingray City: If the tours on your ship get booked, about half a dozen entrepreneurs lead expeditions to Stingray City, and there are usually a few tour agents waiting around the terminal in George Town to snare cruise passengers as they debark. One well-known outfit is **Treasure Island Divers** (© **800/872-7552** from the U.S. or 345/949-4456; www.tidivers.com), which charges $30 per person.

Taxi Tours: If you want to see the island, you can grab a taxi in port and take a tour. Taxis should cost about $40 per hour and can hold up to five people. A

3-hour tour covers all the sights in a leisurely fashion. Make sure to stop in the town called Hell and send a postcard home.

ON YOUR OWN: WITHIN WALKING DISTANCE

In George Town, **Cayman Islands National Museum,** Harbour Drive (✆ 345/ 949-8368; www.museum.ky), is housed in a veranda-fronted building that once served as the island's courthouse. Exhibits include Caymanian artifacts collected by Ira Thompson (beginning in the 1930s), and other items relating to the natural, social, and cultural history of the Caymans. There are a gift shop, theater, and cafe; a $5 donation is requested.

ON YOUR OWN: BEYOND THE PORT AREA

The only green-sea-turtle farm of its kind in the world, **Cayman Turtle Farm,** Northwest Point (✆ 345/949-3894; www.turtle.ky), is the island's most popular land-based tourist attraction. Once a multitude of turtles lived in the waters surrounding the Cayman Islands, but today these creatures are an endangered species. The turtle farm's purpose is twofold: to replenish the waters with hatchlings and yearling turtles and, at the other end of the spectrum, to provide the local market with edible turtle meat. You can peer into 100 circular concrete tanks containing turtles ranging in size from 6 ounces to 600 pounds, or sample turtle dishes at a snack bar and restaurant. The farm is open from 8:30am to 5pm. Admission is $6 for adults, $3 for children 6 to 12.

On 26 hectares (65 acres) of rugged wooded land, **Queen Elizabeth II Botanic Park,** off Frank Sound Road, North Side (✆ 345/947-9462), offers visitors a 1-hour walk along a short (1.5km/¾-mile) trail through wetlands, swamps, dry thicket, and mahogany trees. You might spot hickatees (the freshwater turtles found only on the Caymans and in Cuba), the rare Grand Cayman parrot, or the anole lizard with its cobalt-blue throat pouch. There are six rest stations along the trail, plus a visitor center and a canteen. There are also a heritage garden, a floral garden, and a lake.

The **Mastic Trail,** west of Frank Sound Road, is a restored 200-year-old footpath through a 2-million-year-old woodland area in the heart of the island. Named for the majestic mastic tree, the trail showcases the reserve's natural attractions, including a native mangrove swamp, traditional agriculture, and an ancient woodland area. You can follow the 3km (2-mile) trail on your own, but we recommend taking a 3-hour guided tour. Call ✆ **345/945-6588** to make a reservation. The trail, adjacent to the Botanical Park, is about a 45-minute drive from George Town.

SHOPPING

There's duty-free shopping here for silver, china, crystal, Irish linens, and British woolen goods, but we've found most prices to be similar to those in the United States. You'll also find cigar shops and international chains such as Coach, the leather-goods store. Please don't succumb and purchase turtle or black-coral products. You'll see them everywhere, but it's illegal to bring them back into the United States and most other Western nations.

Some standout shops include **Artifacts Ltd.,** Harbour Drive, on the harbor front, across from the landing dock (✆ 345/949-2442), for back issues of Cayman stamps; **The Jewelry Centre,** Fort Street (✆ 345/949-0070), one of the largest jewelry stores in the Caymans; and the **Kennedy Gallery** West Shore Centre (✆ 345/949-8077), specializing in watercolors by local artists.

BEACHES

Grand Cayman's **Seven Mile Beach,** which begins north of George Town, an easy taxi ride from the cruise dock, has sparkling white sands with a backdrop of Australian pines. The beach is really about 9km (5½ miles) long, but who are we to quibble with tradition? It's lined with condominiums and plush resorts, and is known for its array of watersports and its translucent aquamarine waters. The average water temperature is a balmy 80°F.

SPORTS

SCUBA DIVING & SNORKELING   Coral reefs and other formations encircle the island and are filled with marine life. It's easy to dive close to shore, so boats aren't necessary; but plenty of boats and scuba facilities are available, as well as many dive shops renting scuba gear to certified divers. The best dive operation is **Bob Soto's Reef Divers,** P.O. Box 1801, Grand Cayman, BWI (✆ **800/262-7686** for reservations, or 345/949-2022; www.bobsotosdiving. com), with full-service dive shops at Treasure Island, the Scuba Centre on North Church Street, and Soto's Coconut in the Coconut Place Shopping Centre. There are full-day resort courses as well as excursions for experienced divers daily on the west, north, and south walls, plus shore diving from the Scuba Centre. The staff is helpful and highly professional.

GREAT LOCAL RESTAURANTS & BARS

A favorite **local beer** is Stingray, and a favorite **local rum** is Tortuga.

Abanks' Club Paradise, on Harbour Drive (✆ **345/945-1444**), is less than a kilometer (less than a half-mile) walk south of the pier. It's a great open-air seaside cafe for a sandwich, chicken fingers, and a couple of cool Stingray beers or a frozen drink. **Cracked Conch by the Sea,** West Bay Road, near Turtle Bay Farm (✆ **345/945-5217**), serves some of the island's freshest seafood, including the inevitable conch, plus meat dishes such as beef, jerk pork, and spicy combinations of chicken. The **Crow's Nest Restaurant,** South Sound, on the southwesternmost tip of the island, a 4-minute drive from George Town (✆ **345/949-9366**), is one of those places that evokes the Caribbean "the way it used to be." There's no pretense here—you get good, honest Caribbean cookery, including grilled seafood, at great prices. Many dishes are spicy, especially their signature appetizer—fiery coconut shrimp.

The Wreck on the Rocks, North Church Street, near the beginning of West Bay Road (✆ **345/949-6163**), has a loyal clientele and is divided into an amusingly decorated pub and a Caribbean-inspired dining room open to a view of the harbor. In the pub, you can order such British staples as fish and chips or cottage pie. **Ottmar's Restaurant and Lounge,** West Bay Road (✆ **345/945-5879**), is one of the island's top restaurants, offering such dishes as Bavarian cucumber soup; bouillabaisse; French pepper steak; Wiener schnitzel; and chicken Trinidad, stuffed with grapes, nuts, and apples rolled in coconut flakes, sautéed golden brown, and served in orange-butter sauce.

15 Grenada

The southernmost nation of the British Windwards, Grenada (Gre-*nay*-dah) is one of the lushest in the Caribbean. Called the "Spice Island," it has extravagant fertility—a result of the gentle climate and volcanic soil—that produces more spices than anywhere else in the world: clove, cinnamon, mace, cocoa, tonka beans, ginger, and a third of the world's supply of nutmeg. The beaches are white and sandy, and the populace (a mixture of English expatriates and islanders of African descent) is friendly. Once a British Crown Colony but now independent, the island nation also incorporates two smaller islands: Carriacou and Petite Martinique, neither of which has many tourist facilities.

St. George's, the country's capital, is one of the most colorful ports in the West Indies. Nearly landlocked in the deep crater of a long-dead volcano, and flanked by old forts, it reminds many visitors of Portofino, Italy. Here you'll see some of the most charming Georgian colonial buildings in the Caribbean, many with red tile roofs (the tiles were brought by European trade ships as ballast) and pastel walls. Churches dot the hillside of the harbor. Frangipani and flamboyant trees add even more color.

Crisscrossed by nature trails, Grenada's interior is a jungle of palms, oleander, bougainvillea, purple and red hibiscus, crimson anthurium, bananas, breadfruit, bird song, ferns, and palms. The island's lush tropical scenery and natural bounty attract visitors who want to snorkel, sail, fish, hike on jungle paths, or loll the day away on the 3km (2-mile) white-sand **Grand Anse Beach,** one of the best in the Caribbean.

COMING ASHORE Ships either dock at a pier right in St. George's or anchor in the much-photographed harbor and send their passengers to the pier by tender. A **tourist information center** at the pier dispenses island data. The Carenage (St. George's main street) is only a short walk away from the pier; a taxi into the center of town costs about $3. To get to Grand Anse, you can take a regular taxi or a water taxi (see "Getting Around," below).

You'll find a pair of credit-card phones for international calls inside the small cruise terminal and two more just outside of it. There are six more London-style red phone booths midway around the Carenage, less than a half-mile from the terminal.

 Frommer's Favorite Grenada Experiences

Hiking to the Seven Sisters Waterfall: A hearty walk along a muddy path that winds through the thick, pristine jungle. At the end of the approximately 1.5km (mile-long) trail there's a set of beautiful waterfalls. You can even jump from the tops of two of them into the pools below. (See "Shore Excursions Offered by the Cruise Lines," below.)

Visiting Levera National Park: With beaches, coral reefs, a mangrove swamp, a lake, and a bird sanctuary, this is a paradise for hikers, swimmers, and snorkelers alike. (See "On Your Own: Beyond the Port Area," below.)

Taking the Rain-Forest & Grand Etang Lake Tour: Take a bus to an extinct volcanic crater some 522m (1,740 ft.) above sea level. On the way, drive through rain forests and stop at a spice estate. (See "Shore Excursions Offered by the Cruise Lines," below.)

Picnicking at Annandale Falls: A 15m (50-ft.) cascade is the perfect backdrop for a picnic among tropical flora—and you can swim in the falls afterward. (See "On Your Own: Beyond the Port Area," below.)

LANGUAGE **English** is commonly spoken on this island. **Creole English,** a mixture of African, English, and French, is spoken informally by the majority.

CURRENCY The official currency is the **Eastern Caribbean dollar** (EC$2.70 = U.S.$1; EC$1 = U.S.37¢). Always determine which dollars—EC or U.S.—you're talking about when discussing a price. Credit cards and traveler's checks are commonly accepted in tourist areas. Unless otherwise specified, all prices in this section are given in U.S. dollars.

INFORMATION Go to the **Grenada Board of Tourism,** on the Carenage in St. George's (© **800/927-9554** or 473/440-2279), for maps and general information. It's open Monday to Friday from 8am to 4pm. To get information before you go, contact the **Grenada Tourism Board** in New York (© **212/687-9554;** www.grenadagrenadines.com).

CALLING FROM THE U.S. When calling Grenada from the United States, you need only dial a "1" before the numbers listed here.

GETTING AROUND

St. George's can easily be explored on foot, although parts of the town are steep as the streets rise up from the harbor.

BY TAXI Taxi fares are set by the government. Most cruisers take a cab from the pier to somewhere near St. George's. You can also tap most taxi drivers as a guide for a day's sightseeing. The charge is about $15 per hour, but be sure to negotiate a price before setting out, and make sure you're both talking about the same currency. From the pier to Grand Anse Beach is about $10 per carload.

BY MINIVAN Minivans, used mostly by locals, charge EC$1 to EC$6 (37¢–U.S.$2.20). Most minivans depart from Market Square or from the Esplanade area of St. George's. The most popular run is between St. George's and Grand Anse Beach.

BY WATER TAXI Water taxis are an ideal way to get around the harbor and to Grand Anse Beach (the round-trip fare is about $4) or from one end of the Carenage to the other (for another $2). Look for them on the Carenage by the cruise ship welcome center.

BY RENTAL CAR We don't recommend driving here, as the roads are very narrow and winding.

SHORE EXCURSIONS OFFERED BY THE CRUISE LINES
Because of Grenada's lush landscape, we recommend spending at least a few hours touring its interior, one of the most scenic in the West Indies.

Hike to Seven Sisters Waterfalls ($35, 4 hr.): After a mile-or-so walk along a muddy path in the lush Grand Etang rain forest, passengers are free to take a swim in the natural pools or hop off the edge of the cascading waterfalls. It's gorgeous and lots of fun. Don't forget to wear your bathing suit and maybe a pair of Teva-type sandals.

Rain Forest/Grand Etang Lake Tour ($33–$37, 3 hr.): This is a great way to experience Grenada's lush, cool, dripping-wet tropical interior. Via bus, you travel past the red-tiled roofs of St. George's en route to the bright blue Grand Etang Lake, within an extinct volcanic crater some 570m (1,900 ft.) above sea level. On the way, you drive through rain forests and stop at a spice estate. Some tours include a visit to the Annandale Falls.

Island Bus Tour ($33, 3 hr.): Typical scenic island tours take you through the highlights of the interior and along the coast, including Grand Anse Beach. Along the way you get to see the most luxuriant part of Grenada's rain forest, a nutmeg-processing station, a sugar factory, and many small hamlets. Many cruise lines also book a tour ($27, 2 hr.) that explores St. George's historical sites and forts before taking you to some of the island's natural highlights, including a private garden where some 500 species of island plants and flowers are cultivated.

Party Cruises ($33, 3 hr.): Party cruises are popular here, with no shortage of rum and reggae music. The cost includes rum punch, sodas, a beach stop, and sometimes snorkeling.

ON YOUR OWN: WITHIN WALKING DISTANCE
In St. George's, you can visit the **Grenada National Museum,** at the corner of Young and Monckton streets (© **473/440-3725**), set in the foundations of an old French army barracks and prison built in 1704. Small but interesting, it houses ancient petroglyphs and other archaeological finds, a rum still, and various Grenada memorabilia, including the island's first telegraph and two notable bathtubs: the wooden barrel used by the fort's prisoners and the carved marble tub used by Joséphine Bonaparte during her adolescence on Martinique. The most comprehensive exhibit illuminates the native culture of Grenada. The museum is open 9am to 4:30pm Monday to Friday, and 10am to 1pm Saturday; admission is $2 for adults and 50¢ for children.

If you're up for a good hike, walk around the historical Carenage from the cruise terminal and head up to **Fort George,** built in 1705 by the French and originally called Fort Royal. (You can pick up a rudimentary walking-tour map from the cruise terminal to help you find interesting sites along the way.) While the fort ruins and the 200- to 300-year-old canons are worth taking a peek at, it's the 360° panoramic views of the entire harbor area that are most spectacular, taking in your ship, the sea, and many of the red-tile-roofed buildings dotting the island. Don't forget your camera! Before or after a visit to the fort, be sure to walk along **Church Street** (which leads right to the fort) as far as St. Johns or Juille Street. Along the way, you'll see lots of quaint 18th- and 19th-century architecture framed by brilliant flowering plants; examples of Grenada's sedan porches, open-ended porches originally used as porte cocheres to keep residents dry when going between house and carriage; **St. Andrew's Presbyterian Church,** built in 1831 with the help of the Freemasons; **St. George's Anglican Church** (✆ 473/ 440-2436), built in 1825 by the British; the **Houses of Parliament;** and the **Roman Catholic Cathedral,** rebuilt in 1884 (the tower dates back to 1818).

ON YOUR OWN: BEYOND THE PORT AREA

You can take a taxi up Richmond Hill to **Fort Frederick** (✆ 473/440-6158), which the French began in 1779. The British retook the island in 1783 and completed the fort in 1791. From its battlements you'll have a panoramic view of the harbor and the yacht marina.

Don't miss the mountains northeast of St. George's. If you don't have much time, **Annandale Falls,** a tropical wonderland where a 50-foot-high cascade drops into a basin, is just a 15-minute drive away, on the outskirts of the **Grand Etang Forest Reserve.** The overall beauty is almost Tahitian. You can have a picnic surrounded by liana vines, elephant ears, and other tropical flora and spices. Annandale Falls Centre offers gift items, handcrafts, and samples of the island's indigenous spices. Nearby, a trail leads to the falls, where you can enjoy a refreshing swim. If you've got more time and want a less crowded spot, the even better **Seven Sisters Waterfalls** is farther into Grand Etang, an approximately 30-minute drive and then a mile or so hike along a muddy trail. It's well worth the trip and you'll really get a feel for the power and beauty of the tropical forest here. The falls themselves are lovely and you can even climb to the top and jump off into the pool below. Be careful, though: It's awfully slippery on those rocks. If you want to skip the jumping you can still enjoy a relaxing swim in the cool water after the sweaty hike.

Opened in 1994, 180-hectare (450-acre) **Levera National Park** has several white sandy beaches for swimming and snorkeling, although the surf is rough. Offshore are coral reefs and sea-grass beds. Inland, the park contains a mangrove swamp, a lake, and a bird sanctuary—perhaps you'll see a rare tropical parrot. It's a hiker's paradise. The interpretation center (✆ 473/442-1018) is open Monday to Friday from 8am to 4pm, Saturday from 10am to 4pm, and Sunday from 9am to 5pm. About 24km (15 miles) from the harbor, the park can be reached by taxi, bus, or water taxi.

SHOPPING

The local stores sell luxury imports, mainly from England, at prices that are not quite down at duty-free level. This is no grand Caribbean merchandise mart, so if you're cruising on to such islands as Aruba, St. Martin, or St. Thomas, you might want to postpone serious purchases. On the other hand, you can find some fine local handcrafts, gifts, and art here.

Spice vendors besiege you wherever you go, including just outside of the cruise terminal. If you're not interested, a polite "I just bought some from another vendor" usually works. But you really should take at least a few samples home with you. The spices here are fresher and better than any you're likely to find in your local supermarket, so nearly everybody comes home with a hand-woven basket full of them. Nutmeg products are especially popular. The Grenadians use every part of the nutmeg: They make the outer fruit into a tasty liqueur and a rich jam, and grind the orange membrane around the nut into a different spice called mace. You'll also see the outer shells used as gravel to cover trails and parking lots. **Arawak Islands,** Upper Belmont Road, has different fragrances distilled from such island plants as frangipani, wild lilies, cinnamon, nutmeg, and cloves. You'll also find body oils, soaps, an all-natural insect repellent that some clients insist is the most effective (and safest) they're ever used, and some mighty fine hot sauce. We regretted not buying more the last time we were there, but then we found their mail-order website (**www.arawak-islands.com**).

Some worthwhile shops include **Art Fabrik,** Young Street (© 473/440-0568), for batik shirts, shifts, shorts, skirts, T-shirts, and the like; **Creation Arts & Crafts,** the Carenage (© 473/440-0570), for off-island handcrafts (from Venezuela, Sint Maarten, and Cuba); **Sea Change Bookstore** (© 473/440-3402), the Carenage, for recent British and American newspapers; **Spice Island Perfumes,** the Carenage ((© 473/440-2006), for perfumes made from the natural extracts of local herbs and spices; and **Tikal,** Young Street (© 473/440-2310), for handcrafts from Grenada and around the world.

BEACHES

Grenada's **Grand Anse Beach,** with its 3km (2 miles) of wide sugar-white sands, is one of the best beaches in the Caribbean, with calm waters and a great view of St. George's to make the scene complete. There are several restaurants beachside, (see "Great Local Restaurants & Bars," below), and you can also join a banana-boat ride or rent a Sunfish sailboat. From the port, it's about a 10-minute, $10 taxi ride, although you can also take a water taxi from the pier for only $4 round-trip.

SPORTS

SCUBA DIVING & SNORKELING Grenada offers an underwater world rich in submarine gardens, exotic fish, and coral formations. Visibility is often up to 36m (120 ft.). Off the coast is the wreck of the nearly 180m (600-ft.) ocean liner *Bianca C.* Novice divers should stick to the west coast; the more experienced might search out the sites along the rougher Atlantic side. **Sanvic's Watersports,** directly on the beach in the Grenada Grand Beach Resort, Grand Anse Beach (© 473/444-4371, ext. 638), is the premier scuba-diving outfit, offering snorkeling trips, and will pick you up at the pier in a courtesy bus and bring you back to the cruise ship later. American-run **Eco-Dive,** at Coyaba Beach Resort on Grand Anse Beach (© 473/444-4129; www.scubadivegrenada.com), gives Sanvic's serious competition, offering scuba diving and snorkeling jaunts to reefs and shipwrecks teeming with marine life. Diving instruction is available. (*Note:* Grenada doesn't have a decompression chamber. In the event of an emergency, divers must be taken to the facilities on Barbados or Trinidad.)

GREAT LOCAL RESTAURANTS & BARS

A favorite **local beer** is Carib; a favorite **local rum** is Clarkecourt.

Your last chance to enjoy food from old-time island recipes, many now fading from cultural memory, may be at **The Plantation House** (aka **the Betty**

Mascoll Morne Fendue Plantation House), at St. Patrick's (© **473/442-9330**), 40km (25 miles) north of St. George's. The house was built in 1912 of chiseled river rocks held together by a mixture of lime and molasses. Betty Mascoll was born that same year and lived here right up until her recent death. You dine as an upper-class family did in the 1920s. Lunch is likely to include a yam-and-sweet-potato casserole or curried chicken with lots of island-grown spices. The most famous dish is the legendary pepper-pot stew, which includes pork and oxtail, tenderized by the juice of grated cassava. The new proprietor, Dr. Jean Thompson, and the veteran staff need time to prepare, so it's imperative to call ahead. They serve a fixed-price lunch Monday to Saturday from 12:30 to 3pm.

The Nutmeg, the Carenage, located right on the harbor over the Sea Change Shop (© **473/440-2539**), is a casual hangout for the yachting set and a favorite with expatriates and visitors. The menu is extensive.

Rudolf's, the Carenage (© **473/440-2241**), serves great steak, flying fish, and mahimahi, and prepares conch and shrimp in several different ways.

16 Guadeloupe

Take the things you love about France—sophistication, great food, and an appreciation of the good things in life—add the best of the Caribbean—nice beaches, a relaxed pace, and warm, friendly people—and combine with efficiency and modern convenience. Voilà! Guadeloupe. And once you leave the crowded, narrow streets of Pointe-à-Pitre, the commercial center and main port, you'll see that the island is more developed and modern than many others in the region.

Guadeloupe's **Creole cuisine,** a mélange of French culinary expertise, African cooking, and Caribbean ingredients, is reason enough to get off the ship, regardless of how much you're enjoying the food on board. And if **shopping** is your favorite sport, you'll have ample opportunity to stock up on French perfumes, clothes, and other luxury products. For the more adventurous, there are a volcano, scuba diving, surfing, and hiking to spectacular mountain waterfalls. Of course, you can always work on your tan at one of the island's many beaches. Or maybe you just want to sit at a sidewalk cafe, sip your espresso while glancing through a copy of *Le Monde,* and watch the world go by.

Guadeloupe, the political entity, is an overseas region of France that includes the islands of St. Barthélemy (St. Barts), St. Martin, Les Saintes, La Désirade, Marie-Galante, and Guadeloupe itself. The name Guadeloupe, however, usually refers to two contiguous islands—Basse-Terre and Grande-Terre—separated by a narrow seawater channel, the Rivière Salée. Nestled between Antigua and Dominica, these two islands are shaped like a 1,373 square km (530-sq.-mile) butterfly. The eastern wing, the limestone island of Grande-Terre, is known for its white-sand beaches, rolling hills, sugarcane fields, and resort areas. Pointe-à-Pitre, your port of debarkation, is here. The butterfly's larger, volcanic western wing, Basse-Terre, is dominated by the National Park of Guadeloupe, a mountainous rain forest replete with waterfalls and La Soufrière, a brooding, still occasionally troublesome volcano. The capital of Guadeloupe, also called Basse-Terre, is at the southern tip of this western wing.

Almost half of Guadeloupe's population of 410,000 is under the age of 20. About 80% of Guadeloupeans are descended from African slaves, with people of European and East Indian ancestry making up most of the remaining 20%. Today, sugar and rum are the island's main exports.

COMING ASHORE Cruise ships dock at the modern **Centre Saint-John Perse,** adjacent to downtown Pointe-à-Pitre, Grande-Terre's main city. The terminal has shops, restaurants, cafes, a small tourist office, and phones.

LANGUAGE **French** is the official language, but you'll often hear islanders speaking a local **Creole** among themselves. Don't expect to get too far with only English unless you're at one of the busier tourist areas. Bring a phrase book. Guadeloupeans are nice people; meet them halfway.

CURRENCY Guadeloupe is an overseas region of France, so the **Euro** (€) is now the official currency (exchange rate: €1 = U.S.90¢; $1 = €1.10). There are numerous **ATMs** (*distributeur de billets*) in downtown Pointe-à-Pitre. You'll have no trouble using your credit cards.

INFORMATION The main **tourist office** (Office du Tourisme) in Pointe-à-Pitre is at 5 Square de la Banque, a 5-minute walk from the port (© **590/82-09-30**), and is open Monday to Friday from 8am to 5pm, Saturday 8am to noon. If you want information before you leave home, contact the **Guadeloupe Tourist Office** in New Jersey (© **732/302-1223;** www.frenchcaribbean.com).

CALLING FROM THE U.S. When calling Guadeloupe from the United States, dial the international access code (011) and 590 before the numbers listed in this section. The numbers listed already have a 590 prefix, but that's not the same 590: You have to dial 590 twice (bureaucracy in France is just as inscrutable as anywhere). **Telecartes** phone cards make local and international calls easier and less expensive. They're sold at post offices and other outlets marked TELECARTE EN VENTE ICI and are used in phone booths (marked TELECOM) found all over. Many phones accept Visa, MasterCard, and other credit cards for long-distance calls.

 Frommer's Favorite Guadeloupe Experiences

Climbing a Volcano: Draped in thousands of banana trees and other lush foliage, La Soufrière rises 1,440m (4,800 ft.) above the surrounding sea and dominates the island of Basse-Terre. You can drive to a parking area at La Savane à Mulets, then hike the final 465m (1,500 ft.)—2 arduous hours—right to the mouth of the volcano. (See "On Your Own: Beyond the Port Area," below.)

Touring Grande-Terre's Atlantic Coast: Drive out to Grande-Terre's eastern extreme, La Pointe des Châteaux, to watch the Atlantic and Caribbean vent their fury on the rocky shore. Continue up the coast to La Porte d'Enfer and La Pointe de la Grande Vigie for splendid views of limestone cliffs and sparkling aquamarine waters. (See "On Your Own: Beyond the Port Area," below.)

Soaking Up the French-Caribbean Ambience: Walk the streets of Pointe-à-Pitre. Browse through the stores and maybe buy some perfume or "thigh-reducing cream" from one of the upscale pharmacies (look for the neon green cross). Pick up a newspaper, find a shady table at a sidewalk cafe, order a cold, fresh fruit juice, and luxuriate in your blessed life.

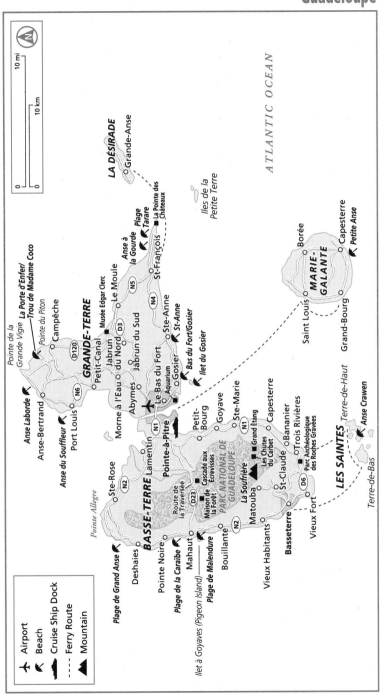

Legend:
- ✈ Airport
- 🏖 Beach
- ⚓ Cruise Ship Dock
- - - - Ferry Route
- ▲ Mountain

ATLANTIC OCEAN

LA DÉSIRADE
Grande-Anse

Îles de la Petite Terre

GRANDE-TERRE
Pointe de la Grande Vigie
La Porte d'Enfer/Trou de Madame Coco
Pointe du Piton
Campêche
Anse Laborde
Anse-Bertrand
Anse du Souffleur
Port Louis
Musée Edgar Clerc
Le Moule
Petit-Canal
Jabrun du Nord
Jabrun du Sud
Morne-à-l'Eau
Abymes
Le Bas du Fort
Aquarium
Gosier
Bas du Fort/Gosier
Îlet du Gosier
Ste-Anne
Anse à la Gourde
Plage Tarare
St-François
La Pointe des Châteaux

N6
D120
D3
N5
N4

Pointe Allegre
Ste-Rose
Deshaies
Pointe Noire
Plage de Grand Anse
Plage de la Caraïbe
Mahaut
Plage de Malendure
Bouillante
Vieux Habitants
Îlet à Goyaves (Pigeon Island)

BASSE-TERRE
Lamentin
Pointe-à-Pitre
Petit-Bourg
Goyave
Ste-Marie
Capesterre
Grand Étang
Bananier
Trois Rivières
Parc Archéologique des Roches Gravées
Capesterre
Route de la Traversée
Maison de la Forêt
Cascade aux Écrevisses
PARC NATIONAL DE GUADELOUPE
La Souffrière
Les Chutes du Carbet
St-Claude
Matouba
Basseterre
Vieux Fort

N1
N2
D23
N1
D6
N2

MARIE-GALANTE
Borée
Capesterre
Petite Anse
Saint Louis
Grand-Bourg

LES SAINTES
Terre-de-Haut
Anse Crawen
Terre-de-Bas

0   10 mi
0   10 km
N

GETTING AROUND

BY TAXI   Metered taxis await cruise passengers at the Pointe-à-Pitre pier. Rates are regulated, but they can be expensive, especially on Sundays and holidays, when fares are 40% higher. Taxis can be hired for private tours, but you'll have a hard time finding a driver who speaks English. Negotiate a price before setting out, and make sure all terms are clear to avoid an unpleasant scene later. One recommended driver is **Alain Narcisse,** an enthusiastic, knowledgeable, English-speaking guide who offers tours of Grande-Terre, northern Basse-Terre, and southern Basse-Terre. He's often booked, so make arrangements in advance by calling © **590/35-27-29** or 590/83-24-79. General **radio cab dispatch numbers** include © **590/20-74-74,** 590/82-96-69, and 590/83-09-55.

BY MOTOR SCOOTER   Motorbikes are available in Pointe-à-Pitre at **Vespa Sun** (© **590/91-30-36**) and **Moto Guadeloupe** (© **590/82-12-50**). Expect to pay about $30 a day, including insurance and a deposit of roughly $150 (credit cards are accepted).

BY BUS   Buses are inexpensive, comfortable, and efficient. Almost all play zouk, an upbeat local music (at reasonable decibel levels), and some have videos. Signs (*arrêt-bus*) indicate bus stops, but you can wave down a driver anywhere along the road. Pay the driver or the conductor as you get off. The fare from Pointe-à-Pitre to Gosier is just over $1.

BY RENTAL CAR   Guadeloupe's road system is one of the best in the Caribbean, and traffic regulations and road signs are the same as elsewhere in France. Driving is on the right. Reserve a car before leaving home, especially during the high season. **Avis, Budget, Hertz,** and **National** all have offices on the island. Your valid driver's license from home will be honored. Almost all rentals have standard transmissions. Be forewarned that Guadeloupeans are skillful but aggressive drivers; don't tarry in the passing lane.

SHORE EXCURSIONS OFFERED BY THE CRUISE LINES

Carbet Falls ($40, 4 hr.): After driving through the banana plantations and rain forests of Basse-Terre's south side, hike 30 minutes to picturesque Carbet Falls, where you're free to swim in the refreshing water. Wear sturdy walking shoes.

Pigeon Island ($50, 4½ hr.): First pass through Guadeloupe's National Park, a lush and mountainous tropical rain forest, on the Route de la Traversée. At Pigeon Island, board a glass-bottom boat for a 90-minute ride around a beautiful coral reef now designated the Cousteau Underwater Reserve. Marvel at the numerous fish, corals, and other marine life.

EXCURSIONS OFFERED BY LOCAL AGENCIES

Hiking Tours: Basse-Terre's **Parc National** has 322km (200 miles) of well-marked trails. Some meander through tropical rain forests to waterfalls and mountain pools; others focus on La Soufrière volcano, geology, animals, and vegetation. The **Bureau des Guides de Moyenne Montagne** (© **590/81-24-83**) offers a range of guided tours. Easy 1-hour hikes cost around $10; a 4-hour climb up La Soufrière is about $60. Free maps and brochures in English can be obtained from the **National Park Office,** Habitation Beausoleil, Montéran, Boite Postal 13, St-Claude 97120 (© **590/80-24-25**).

Snorkeling Tours: To snorkel in the Cousteau Underwater Reserve, contact **Nautilus** (© **590/98-89-08**) or **Aquarus** (© **590/98-87-30**), both located at the Bouillante town dock, south of Malendure. They make guided tours in glass-bottom boats several times daily; at least 15 minutes is reserved for snorkeling and refreshments (about 90 min., $15–$25).

ON YOUR OWN: WITHIN WALKING DISTANCE

The little trolley that meets cruise ship passengers at the port is supposed to provide hassle-free transportation around Pointe-à-Pitre. Unfortunately, it's no match for the city's traffic and narrow roads. Unless you enjoy traffic jams, walk. It's a better way to browse, shop, and visit the museums.

Pointe-à-Pitre's narrow streets and congested sidewalks are bustling with activity, and its markets are among the Caribbean's most colorful. The largest, **Marché St. Antoine,** at the corner of Rues Frébault and Peynier, is well known for its playful, sassy vendors, who sell tropical produce and spices in madras bags. **Marché de la Darse,** on the waterfront at the foot of Place de la Banque, offers exotic fruits, vegetables, and souvenirs. The **Place Gourbeyre Flower Market,** next to the cathedral, is ablaze with tropical blooms, including roses de porcelaine and alpinias. Lined with royal palms, scarlet flamboyants, and travelers palms, the renovated **Place de la Victoire** commemorates Victor Hugues' defeat of the English in 1794. It's the largest public space in town and is bordered with restaurants and cafes. The nearby **Cathedral of St-Pierre and St-Paul,** built in 1871, has an iron framework designed to withstand earthquakes and hurricanes. Three churches destroyed by successive earthquakes form its foundation. The **Musée Municipal Saint-John Perse,** 9 Rue de Nozières, near the corner of Rue Achille-René Boisneuf (© **590/90-01-92**), chronicles the life of native son Alexis Léger, who won the Nobel Prize for literature under the nom de plume "Saint-John Perse" in 1960. The museum is housed in one of the city's most beautifully restored colonial mansions, an urban chalet that features ornate friezes, voluted consoles, and wrought-iron galleries. Open windows allow breezes into the main parlor, which is furnished with bourgeois furniture. In addition to many of the poet's personal effects, the museum boasts photographs documenting Guadeloupean life from the turn of the century through the 1930s; you can buy postcards of some of them in the museum gift shop. The museum is open Monday to Friday from 9am to 5pm, Saturday 8:30am to 12:30pm. Admission is about $2 for adults, half price for students.

The **Musée Schoelcher,** 24 Rue Peynier (© **590/82-08-04**), tells the story of Victor Schoelcher, the key figure in the move to abolish slavery in Guadeloupe. The powerful exhibit, housed in a renovated mansion, includes a slave-ship model, a miniature guillotine, china from Bordeaux with scenes from *Uncle Tom's Cabin,* and racist caricatures published in Parisian journals. Particularly moving is an 1845 census document that lists slaves as nothing more than plantation animals. It's open Monday to Friday from 9am to 5pm; admission is $1.50, half that for students and children.

ON YOUR OWN: BEYOND THE PORT AREA

Guadeloupe is too large to tour in 1 day. You'll have to choose among Grande-Terre, northern Basse-Terre, and southern Basse-Terre.

GRANDE-TERRE

The **Aquarium de la Guadeloupe,** near the Bas du Fort Marina just east of Pointe-à-Pitre (© **590/90-92-38**), is compact but has an impressive collection of exotic fish, corals, and sponges from the Caribbean and the Pacific. Come face-to-face with hugging sea horses, sleeping nurse sharks, and graceful sea turtles. Don't miss the polka-dot grouper known as *mérou de Grace Kelly.*

Explanatory markers are in both French and English. The souvenir shop sells hand-painted folk art, jewelry, and fish- and sea-themed trinkets and T-shirts. It's open daily from 9am to 7pm; admission is about $5.50 for adults, $2.75 for children under 12.

La Pointe des Châteaux (Castle Point), at Grande-Terre's easternmost point, is an impressive seascape spectacle. Angry Atlantic waves bash black limestone rocks and jagged cliffs with a roughness reminiscent of Brittany's Finistère coast or England's Land's End. Follow the path leading to the point where the land falls off abruptly to the ocean for the best views of the island of La Désirade.

Farther north, **La Porte d'Enfer** is a quaint little cove and beach protected from the furious Atlantic by an outcrop of limestone cliffs. The name means "Hell's Gate," but swimming close to shore in the turquoise water is usually safe. Don't venture out too far, though; the next cove, **Le Trou de Madame Coco** (Madame Coco's hole), is where (according to legend) the sea stole Madame Coco and her parasol as she promenaded along the edge. **La Pointe de la Grande Vigie,** at the northernmost tip of the island, has paths that lead to the edge of spectacular cliffs with dramatic views of Porte de l'Enfer and, on a clear day, the island of Antigua. Cacti and other succulents grow everywhere.

Along the northern coasts of Grande-Terre and Basse-Terre, **La Réserve Naturelle du Grand Cul-de-Sac Marin** is one of the Caribbean's largest marine reserves.

BASSE-TERRE

Basse-Terre's greatest attraction is the **Parc National de la Guadeloupe,** 29,600 hectares (74,000 acres) of tropical rain forests, mountains, waterfalls, and ponds. UNESCO designated the park a World Biosphere Reserve in 1992. Its 322km (200 miles) of well-marked trails make it one of the best places for hiking in the entire Caribbean. Pick up information and maps at park entrances. Thirty minutes from Pointe-à-Pitre, **La Maison de la Forêt** (Forest House; closed Mon) lies on the Route de la Traversée, which bisects the park, and is the starting point for easy walking tours of the surrounding mountainous rain forest. English-language trail guides describe the plant and animal life. Nearby, the **Cascade aux Ecrevisses** (Crayfish Falls), a slippery 10-minute walk from the roadside, is nice for a cooling dip. To the south, the steep hike to the three falls of **Les Chutes du Carbet** (Carbet Falls) is among Guadeloupe's most beautiful excursions (one of the falls drops 65 ft., the second 360 ft., the third 410 ft.). The middle fall, the most dramatic, is the easiest to reach. On the way up, you'll pass **Le Grand Etang** (the Great Pond), a volcanic lake surrounded by tree-size ferns, giant vining philodendrons, wild bananas, orchids, anthuriums, and pineapples.

The park's single greatest feature is the still-simmering volcano **La Soufrière,** rising to 1,440m (4,800 ft.) and flanked by banana plantations and lush vegetation. In 1975, ashes, mud, billowing smoke, and tremors proved that the volcano is still active, and today you can smell sulfurous fumes and feel the heat through the soil as steam spews from the fumaroles. The summit is like another planet: Steam rises from two active craters, large rocks form improbable shapes, and roars from the earth make it difficult to hear your companions. Go with an experienced guide (see "Hiking Tours" under "Excursions Offered by Local Agencies," above). On your way down, don't miss **La Maison du Volcan,** the volcanology museum in St-Claude.

Gardeners should save a couple of hours to visit the **Domaine de Valombreuse** (© **590/95-50-50**), a 2½-hectare (6-acre) floral park with exotic birds, spice gardens, and 300 species of tropical flowers. Created in 1990, and close to the town of Petit Bourg, the park has a riverside restaurant and a superior gift shop. It's open daily from 9am to 6pm; admission is about $6 for adults, $3.50 for children under 12.

Parc Archéologique des Roches Gravées, on Basse-Terre's southern coast in the town of Trois-Rivières (© **590/92-91-88**), has the West Indies' largest collection of Arawak Indian petroglyphs. The animal and human images etched on boulders date from between A.D. 300 and 400. Paths and stone stairways meander through the tranquil grounds, which include avocado, banana, cocoa, coffee, guava, and papaya trees. Explanatory brochures are in French and English. It's open daily from 8:30am to 4:30pm; admission is about $1.50.

SHOPPING

Parlez-vous Chanel? Hermès? Saint Laurent? Baccarat? If you do, you'll find that Guadeloupe has good buys on almost anything French—scarves, perfumes, cosmetics, crystal, and other luxury goods—and many stores offer 20% discounts on items purchased with foreign currency, traveler's checks, or credit cards. You can also find local **handcrafted items,** madras cloth, spices, and rum at any of the local markets.

Right at Pointe-à-Pitre's port, the **Centre Saint-John Perse** has about 20 shops that frequently offer lower prices than can be found elsewhere in town. **L'Artisan Parfumeur** sells French and American perfumes, as well as tropical scents. **Suzanne Moulin** features original African-inspired jewelry and crafts. **Jean-Louis Padel** specializes in gold jewelry. If you're looking for beach and resort wear, stop by **Vanilla Boutique** and **Brasil Tropique.** For something a little more provocative, look through the delicate lingerie at **Soph't.**

Rue Frébault, directly in front of the port, is one of the best shopping streets for duty-free items. **Rosébleu,** 5 Rue Frébault, offers china, crystal, and silver from Christoffle, Kosta Boda, and other high-end manufacturers. **Phoenicia,** 8 Rue Frébault and 121 bis Rue Frébault (© **590/83-50-36** and 590/82-25-75), has large selections of French perfumes and cosmetics. For men's and women's fashions, as well as for cosmetics and perfumes, browse through **Vendôme,** 8–10 Rue Frébault. Across the street at the intersection of Rues Frébault and Delgrès, **Geneviève Lethu** (© **590/21-22-49**) is a French version of Williams-Sonoma, with everything for preparing and serving food. If you find yourself overdosing on froufrou, duck into **Tati,** France's answer to Kmart. It's at the intersection of Rues Frébault and Abbé Grégoire (© **590/89-46-00**). This venerable old department-store chain, famous for its anti-fashion pink-plaid shopping bags, is great for inexpensive basics.

The French Antilles are where the beguine began, so if you're in the market for French Antillean music or French-language books, there are a couple of large book and music stores across from each other on Rue Schoelcher: **Librairie Antillaise** at no. 41 (© **590/82-19-96**) and **Librairie Général** at no. 46 (© **590/82-17-70**). Each has a small selection of English-language books as well.

BEACHES

Beaches on Grande-Terre's southern coast have soft white sand. Those on the Atlantic coast have wilder water and are less crowded. The convenient **Bas du Fort/Gosier** hotel area has mostly man-made strips of sand with rows of beach chairs, watersports shops, and beach bars. Changing facilities and chairs are available for a nominal fee. The tiny, uninhabited **Ilet Gosier,** across Gosier Bay, is a quieter option popular with those who want to bare it all. You can take a fishing boat to the island from Gosier's waterfront. The wide strip of white sand at **Ste-Anne,** about 30 minutes from Pointe-à-Pitre, is lined with shops and food stands. **Plage Tarare,** just before the tip of Pointe des Châteaux, is the most popular nude beach.

On Basse-Terre, the **Plage de Grande Anse** is a long expanse of ochre sand. A pleasant walk north from Deshaies, it offers changing facilities, watersports, boutiques, and outdoor snack bars. Farther south, the gray expanse of **Plage de Malendure** is alive with restaurants, bars, and open-air boutiques. It's the departure point for snorkeling and scuba trips to the Cousteau Reserve off Pigeon Island.

SPORTS
SNORKELING   Beachside stands at virtually all the resorts on Grande-Terre's southern coast rent snorkeling equipment for about $8 a day. The St-François reef and the Ilet de Gosier are especially recommended.

GREAT LOCAL RESTAURANTS & BARS
Many restaurants change their hours from time to time and from season to season, so call in advance for reservations and exact hours. Most, but not all, restaurants accept major credit cards.

The **local beer** is Corsaire, while Bonka is the **local coffee. Local rums** come in a variety of flavors—bois bandé, shrubb (orange and vanilla), lemon—and are painstakingly nurtured at small rum estates such as Séverin, Longueteau, Damoiseau, Bologne, and Montebello. Local producers compare their slow, time-honored process to that used to make cognac.

ON GRANDE-TERRE
Chez Violetta-La Créole, Perinette, in Gosier (℃ **590/84-36-80**), was established by the late Violetta Chaville, the island's legendary high priestess of Creole cookery. Her brother continues the family tradition, serving stuffed crabs, cod fritters, and conch fricassee. It's open daily from noon to 3:30pm.

Chez Monia at 4 Rue Victor Hugues, off of Rue Nozières in Pointe-à-Pitre, serves ice cream that is pure heaven in the midday heat. Flavors (*aromes*) include pear, lemon, kiwi, guava, and champagne. Three scoops in a homemade waffle cone costs about $2. Street vendors also offer superior ice cream, usually flavored with fresh vanilla and coconut, straight from their hand-cranked machines.

ON BASSE-TERRE
In Deshaies, Lucienne Salcède's family has run **Le Karacoli** (℃ **590/28-41-17**), one of Guadeloupe's best seaside restaurants, for almost 30 years. Sit on the beachfront terrace in the shadow of almond and palm trees and let the waves hypnotize you. In the distance, the island of Montserrat is visible. Try a rum aperitif or two, then bliss out on cod fritters, stuffed christophine, and avocado féroce before moving on to Creole lobster or conch. It's open daily from noon to 2pm; closed the entire month of September. Reservations are imperative on weekends.

17 Jamaica

A favorite of North American honeymooners, Jamaica is a mountainous island 145km (90 miles) south of Cuba and about 161km (100 miles) west of Haiti. It's the third largest of the Caribbean islands, with some 11,396 square km (4,400 sq. miles) of predominantly green terrain, a mountain ridge peaking at 2,220m (7,400 ft.) above sea level and, on the north coast, many beautiful white-sand beaches rimming the clear blue sea.

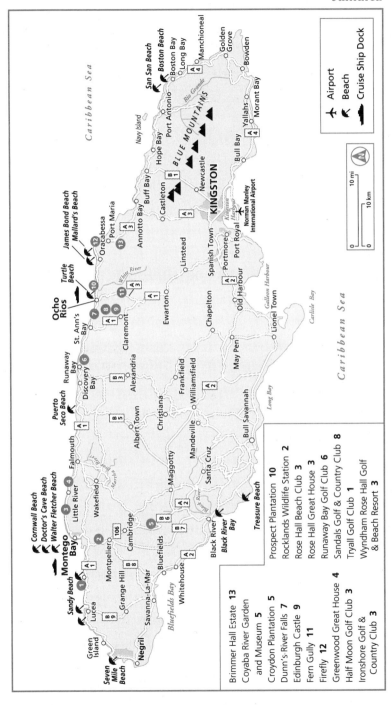

Jamaica

Legend:
- ✈ Airport
- ⌂ Beach
- ⚓ Cruise Ship Dock

Caribbean Sea

Caribbean Sea

Places and features:

Sandy Beach • Cornwall Beach • Doctor's Cave Beach • Walter Fletcher Beach
Montego Bay • Negril • Seven Mile Beach • Green Island • Lucea • Grange Hill • Savanna-La-Mar • Montpelier • Whitehouse • Bluefields • Cambridge • Wakefield • Little River • Falmouth • Maggotty • Santa Cruz • Bluefields Bay • Black River • Black River Bay • Treasure Beach • Bull Savannah • Williamsfield • Mandeville • Christiana • Albert Town • Frankfield • Alexandria • Claremont • St. Ann's Bay • Runaway Bay • Discovery Bay • Puerto Seco Beach • Turtle Beach • Ocho Rios • Oracabessa • Port Maria • James Bond Beach • Mallard's Beach • San San Beach • Boston Beach • Boston Bay • Long Bay • Manchioneal • Golden Grove • Bowden • Morant Bay • Yallahs • Bull Bay • Newcastle • Kingston • Norman Manley International Airport • Port Royal • Spanish Town • Portmore • Old Harbour • Lionel Town • May Pen • Chapelton • Ewarton • Linstead • Annotto Bay • Castleton • Buff Bay • Hope Bay • Port Antonio • Navy Island • Hope Bay

Rio Grande • White River • BLUE MOUNTAINS • Kingston Harbour • Galleon Harbour • Carlile Bay • Long Bay

Numbered locations:

- Brimmer Hall Estate **13**
- Coyaba River Garden and Museum **5**
- Croydon Plantation **5**
- Dunn's River Falls **7**
- Edinburgh Castle **9**
- Fern Gully **11**
- Firefly **12**
- Greenwood Great House **4**
- Half Moon Golf Club **3**
- Ironshore Golf & Country Club **3**
- Prospect Plantation **10**
- Rocklands Wildlife Station **2**
- Rose Hall Beach Club **3**
- Rose Hall Great House **3**
- Runaway Bay Golf Club **6**
- Sandals Golf & Country Club **8**
- Tryall Golf Club **1**
- Wyndham Rose Hall Golf & Beach Resort **3**

One of the most densely populated nations in the Caribbean, with a vivid sense of its own identity, Jamaica has a history rooted in the plantation economy and some of the most impassioned politics in the Western Hemisphere, all of which leads to a sometimes turbulent day-to-day reality. You've probably heard, for instance, that the island's vendors and hawkers can be pushy and the locals not always the most welcoming to tourists, and while there's some truth to this, we've had nothing but positive experiences on many visits to Jamaica. So, keep an open mind.

Most cruise ships dock at **Ocho Rios** on the lush northern coast, although more and more are opting to call at the city of **Montego Bay** ("Mo Bay"), 108km (67 miles) to the west. These ports offer comparable attractions and some of the same shopping possibilities. Don't try to do both ports in one day, however, since the 4-hour round-trip ride leaves time for only superficial visits to each.

LANGUAGE   The official language is **English,** but most Jamaicans speak a richly nuanced patois that's primarily derived from English but includes elements of African, Spanish, Arawak, French, Chinese, Portuguese, and East Indian languages.

CURRENCY   The unit of currency is the **Jamaican dollar,** designated by the same symbol as the U.S. dollar ($). For clarity, we use the symbol J$ to denote prices in Jamaican dollars. The exchange rate is usually U.S.$1 = J$42; J$1 = U.S.2¢. Visitors can pay in U.S. dollars, but always find out if a price is being quoted in Jamaican or U.S. dollars—there's a big difference!

INFORMATION   To get info before you go, call the **Jamaica Tourist Office** in New York (© **800/233-4582** or 212/856-9727; www.jamaica-travel.com). Information booths in the ports are discussed below.

CALLING FROM THE U.S.   When calling Jamaica from the United States, you need only dial a "1" before the numbers listed here.

OCHO RIOS

Once a small banana and fishing port, Ocho Rios is now Jamaica's cruise ship capital, welcoming a couple of ships every day during high season. Though the area has some of the Caribbean's most fabled resorts, and Dunn's River is just a 5-minute taxi ride away, the town itself is not much to see, despite there being a few outdoor local markets within walking distance. Don't expect to shop in the markets without a lot of hassle and a lot of very pushy hawking of merchandise—some of which is likely to be ganja, the locally grown marijuana. (Remember, it may be readily available, but it's still illegal.) In recent years the government has been making an effort to keep things saner around the markets, employing a veritable army of blue-uniformed "resort patrol" officers on bikes to help keep order.

COMING ASHORE   Most cruise ships dock at the port of Ocho Rios, near Dunn's River Falls. Only 1.5km (a mile) away is one of the most important shopping areas, Ocean Village Shopping Centre. The route to this shopping center from the cruise ship pier is called the "turtle walk" and is marked. There are bathrooms and a telephone center at the terminal.

INFORMATION   You'll find **tourist board offices** at the Ocean Village Shopping Centre in Ocho Rios (© **876/974-2582**), open Monday to Friday from 9am to 5pm. There's also a small information stand right at the dock.

Frommer's Favorite Ocho Rios Experiences

Tubing on the White River: Offered by most cruise lines, this trip is just a downright fantastic experience. (See "Shore Excursions Offered by the Cruise Lines," below.)

Riding Horseback Through the Surf: An excursion by horseback includes a ride along the beach and through the surf. (See "Shore Excursions Offered by the Cruise Lines," below.)

Riding a Mountain Bike to Dunn's River Falls: This excursion takes you to the top of a mountain, where you hop on your mountain bike and soar downhill to the falls. (See "Shore Excursions Offered by the Cruise Lines," below.)

GETTING AROUND

BY TAXI   Taxis are your best means of transport, but always agree on a fare before you get in. Your best and safest bet is to get a taxi from the pier; there will be lots of them waiting. Taxis licensed by the government display **JTB** decals, indicating that they're official Jamaican Tourist Board taxis. All others are gypsy cabs, which you should avoid. Taxi dispatchers are at the pier and fixed rates are posted. Otherwise, if you're getting into a taxi from somewhere else on the island, always agree to the price first.

BY RENTAL CAR   We don't recommend renting a car here.

SHORE EXCURSIONS OFFERED BY THE CRUISE LINES

Dunn's River Falls Tour ($44, 4 hr.): These falls cascade 180m (600 ft.) to the beach and are the most visited attraction in Jamaica, which means they're hopelessly overcrowded when a lot of cruise ships are in port (the hordes thin out in the afternoon, though, so consider hopping a taxi there yourself later in the day). Tourists are allowed to climb the falls, and it's a ball to slip and slide your way up with the hundreds of others, forming a human chain of sorts. Don't forget your waterproof camera and your aqua-socks. (If you do, most cruise lines will rent you aqua-socks for an extra $5.) This tour also visits Shaw Park Botanical Gardens, Fern Gully, and other local attractions, with time allocated for shopping. Wear a bathing suit under your clothes.

River Tubing Safari ($59, 6 hr.): This is one of the best excursions we've ever taken. After a scenic 30-minute van ride deep into the pristine jungles, the group of 20 or so passengers and a couple of guides get into the White River, sit back into big black inner tubes (they have wooden boards covering the bottom so your butt doesn't get scraped on the rocks), and begin the 5km (3-mile) glide downriver, passing by gorgeous, towering bamboo trees and other lush foliage. It's sometimes peaceful and sometimes exhilarating—especially when you hit the rapids! (If your ship doesn't offer this tour—at press time, only a few did—you can contact the operator directly, and they'll try to get you on a trip: **Safari Tours Jamaica,** P.O. Box 142, Ocho Rios, Jamaica (✆ **876/795-0482;** fax 876/974-3382; safari@cwjamaica.com.)

Chukka Cove Horseback-Riding Excursion ($79, 3 hr.): Riders will love this trip. After a 45-minute ride from the stables through fields you'll gallop along

> ⎛ **Tips** **Cruise Booze**
>
> If you step inside the small cruise "terminal" in Ocho Rios, you'll find a shop called Cruise Booze, which sets up a tasting station where you can sample a ton of different rums, including a 150-proof white rum.

the beach and take your horse bareback into the surf for a thrilling ride. *Tip:* Take the morning ride and your horse is bound to be more energetic. (Also, if you book directly with Chukka Cove [© **876/972-2506**], the same tour, including transportation there and back, is only $55. The Chukka folks also offer a 3-hr. mountain-biking tour; after being driven up picturesque Lillyfield Mountain, you glide down the 11km/7-mile route, drinking in the scenery along the way.)

Dunn's River Falls Mountain-Biking Trek ($61–$69, 4 hr.): After you're driven up to the summit of 1,500-foot-high Murphy Hill, above Ocho Rios, strap on your helmet, hop on your mountain bike, and enjoy a mostly downhill ride through the natural limestone and ferns, passing the eight springs that form Dunn's River Falls. Once at the bottom, you'll have time to climb the falls before heading back to the ship.

Countryside/Plantation Bus Tour ($54, 5 hr.): This tour includes a drive through the Jamaican countryside to Brimmer Hall Plantation, a working plantation property with a Great House and tropical crops, such as bananas and pimiento. On the way back, you pass the estates once occupied by Noël Coward and Ian Fleming. Often a stop at Dunn's River Falls is tacked onto the end of the tour. Another variation on this tour ($40, 4–5 hr.) stops at the Prospect Plantation instead of Brimmer Hall.

Snorkeling Excursion ($31, 2 hr.): A coral reef near the cruise pier is one of the best places in the area for snorkeling, with panoramic underwater visibility. You can also take a 1-hour cruise on a glass-bottom boat for a look at underwater Jamaica ($39).

Martha Brae River Rafting ($50, 5 hr.): This tour, in 30-foot, two-seat bamboo rafts, is traditionally one of the most heavily booked excursions from both Ocho Rios and Montego Bay. However, most people find it disappointing. We'd recommend the tubing and bicycling excursions instead.

ON YOUR OWN: WITHIN WALKING DISTANCE
Aside from some markets (see "Shopping," below), there's little to do close to the docks.

ON YOUR OWN: BEYOND THE PORT AREA
South of Ocho Rios, **Fern Gully** was originally a riverbed. Today, the main A3 road winds some 210m (700 ft.) through a rain forest filled with wild ferns, hardwood trees, and lianas. For the botanist, there are hundreds of varieties of ferns; for the less plant-minded, roadside stands sell fruits and vegetables, carved-wood souvenirs, and basketwork. The road runs for about 6.5km (4 miles).

Near Lydford, southwest of Ocho Rios, are the remains of **Edinburgh Castle.** This was the lair of one of Jamaica's most infamous murderers, a Scot named Lewis Hutchinson who used to shoot passersby and toss their bodies into a deep pit. The authorities got wind of his activities, and although he tried to escape by canoe, he was captured by the navy and hanged. Rather proud of his achievements (evidence of at least 43 murders was found), he left £100 and instructions for a memorial to be built. It never was, but the 1763 castle ruins remain. To get to Lydford, take the A3 south until you reach a small intersection directly north of Walkers Wood, and then follow the signposts west.

The 1817 **Brimmer Hall Estate,** Port Maria, St. Mary's (© 876/994-2309), 34km (21 miles) east of Ocho Rios, is a working plantation where you're driven around in a tractor-drawn jitney to see the tropical fruit trees and coffee plants. Knowledgeable guides tell you about the processes necessary to produce the fine fruits of the island. Afterward, you can relax beside the pool and sample a wide variety of drinks, including an interesting one called "Wow!" The **Plantation Tour Eating House** offers typical Jamaican dishes for lunch. There's also a souvenir shop with a good selection of ceramics, art, straw goods, woodcarvings, rums, liqueurs, and cigars. Tours run daily if there are enough people. Hours are 7am to 5pm daily. Admission is $15 for adults, $7.50 for children, free for kids under 5.

About 1.5km (1 mile) from the center of Ocho Rios, at an elevation of 126m (420 ft.), **Coyaba River Garden and Museum,** Shaw Park Road (© 876/974-6235; www.coyabagardens.com), was built on the grounds of the former Shaw Park plantation. The Spanish-style museum displays artifacts from the Arawak, Spanish, and English settlements in the area. The gardens are filled with native flora, a cut-stone courtyard, and fountains. It's open daily from 8am to 5pm. Admission is $4.50 for adults, $2.25 for children.

At the 180m (600-ft.) **Dunn's River Falls,** on the A3 (© 876/974-2857), you can relax on the beach, splash in the waters at the bottom of the falls, or climb with a guide to the top and drop into the cool pools higher up between the cascades of water. The beach restaurant provides snacks and drinks, and dressing rooms are available. If you're planning to climb the falls, wear aquasocks or sneakers to protect your feet from the sharp rocks and to prevent slipping. At the prettiest part of Dunn's River Falls, known as the Laughing Waters, scenes were shot for the James Bond classics *Dr. No* and *Live and Let Die.*

About 5km (3 miles) east of Ocho Rios along the A3, adjoining the 18-hole Prospect Mini Golf Course, the working **Prospect Plantation** (© 876/994-1058) is often a shore-excursion stop. On your leisurely ride by covered jitney, you'll readily see why this section of Jamaica is called "the garden parish of the island." You'll see pimiento (allspice), banana, cassava, sugarcane, coffee, cocoa, coconut, pineapple, and the famous leucaena "Tree of Life"—plus, for what it's worth, Jamaica's first hydroelectric plant. Horseback riding is available on three

---

Tips **Insider Tip: A 1-Day Cultural Exchange**

The Jamaica Tourist Board's **Meet the People program** offers a neat way to learn about this country by spending time in the company of its people. And it's free! The JTB matches you with a local person or family who shares the same interest you do, even if that happens to be ornithology. Together you can, say, spend an afternoon at the beach, attend a church service, or share a meal or picnic. You might even do an afternoon of golf or basketball and a beer. Your kids will be introduced to Jamaican playmates. Nearly 1,000 Jamaican families are registered hosts, and are eager to share their perspectives of Jamaica. Contact the tourist board at © 800/Jamaica or jamaicatrv@aol.com to arrange this in advance of your visit.

scenic trails. The rides vary from 1 to 2¼ hours; you'll need to book a horse at least an hour in advance. Rates are $20 per person per hour.

Firefly, Grants Pen, 32km (20 miles) east of Ocho Rios above Oracabessa (© **876/725-0920**), was the home of Sir Noël Coward and his longtime companion, Graham Payn, who, as executor of Coward's estate, donated it to the Jamaica National Heritage Trust. The recently restored house is as it was on the day Sir Noël died in 1973.

SHOPPING

Shopping in Ocho Rios is not as good as in Montego Bay and other ports, but if your money's burning a hole in your pocket, you can wander around the **Ocho Rios Craft Park,** opposite the Ocean Village Shopping Centre off Main Street. Some 150 stalls stock hats, handbags, place mats, woodcarvings, and paintings, plus the usual T-shirts and jewelry. More luxurious items can be found at **Soni's Plaza,** on Main Street, and the **Taj Mahal** (© **876/974-6455**), located opposite the pier and looking like the Mini-Me of the original. **Coconut Grove Shopping Plaza** is a collection of low-slung shops linked by walkways and shrubs. The merchandise consists mainly of local craft items. **Island Plaza shopping complex,** right in the heart of Ocho Rios, has paintings by local artists, local handmade crafts (be prepared to do some haggling), carvings, ceramics, and even kitchenware, plus T-shirts, of course. At all of these places, prepare yourself for aggressive selling and fierce haggling. Every vendor asks too much for an item at first, which gives them the leeway to negotiate the price.

To find local crafts or art without the hassle of the markets, head for **Beautiful Memories,** 9 Island Plaza (© **876/974-2374**), which has a limited but representative sampling of Jamaican art, as well as local crafts, pottery, woodwork, and hand-embroidered items. We generally ignore hotel gift shops, but the **Jamaica Inn Gift Shop** in the Jamaica Inn, Main Street (© **876/974-2514**), is better than most, selling everything from Blue Mountain coffee to Walkers Wood products, and even guava jelly and jerk seasoning. If you're lucky, you'll find marmalade from an old family recipe, plus Upton Pimento Dram, a unique liqueur flavored with Jamaican allspice.

If you'd like to flee the hustle and bustle of the Ocho Rios bazaars completely, take a taxi to **Harmony Hall** (© **876/975-4222**), Tower Isle, on the A3, 6.4km (4 miles) east of Ocho Rios. One of Jamaica's Great Houses, the restored house is now a gallery selling paintings and other works by Jamaican artists. The arts and crafts here are of high quality—not the usual junky assortment you might find at the beach.

At press time, **Island Village** (www.islandjamaica.com), a new entertainment and shopping complex developed by Island Records' Chris Blackwell, had recently opened at the western end of Ocho Rios, between Reynolds Pier and Turtle Beach. Attractions include the ReggaeXplosion museum, a casino, an outdoor concert venue and indoor theater, shopping, and a branch of Jimmy Buffett's Margaritaville.

BEACHES

Mallards Beach, at the Renaissance Jamaica Grand Resort (© **876/974-2201**) on Main Street, is shared by hotel guests and cruise ship passengers and tends to be overcrowded. Locals may steer you to the good and less-crowded **Turtle Beach,** southwest of Mallards. You might also want to check out the big **James Bond Beach** in Oracabessa, at the east end of Ocho Rios.

> **Tips   Deal or No Deal?**
>
> Some so-called duty-free prices are indeed lower than stateside prices, but then the Jamaican government hits you with a 15% "General Consumption Tax." Buyers beware.

SPORTS

GOLF   SuperClubs' 18-hole, par-72 **Runaway Bay Golf Club,** at Runaway Beach near Ocho Rios on the north coast (© 876/973-7319), is one of the better courses in the area, although it's nowhere near the courses at Montego Bay. Call ahead to book tee times. Winter greens fees are about $80 plus $14 for the mandatory caddy. Players can rent carts and clubs. The 18-hole, par-71 **Sandals Golf & Country Club** at Ocho Rios (© 876/975-0119) is also open to the public, charging $70 for 9 holes and $100 for 18. The course lies about 210m (700 ft.) above sea level. To get there from the center of Ocho Rios, travel along the main bypass for 3km (2 miles) until Mile End Road; turn right at the Texaco station there, and drive for 8km (5 miles).

GREAT LOCAL RESTAURANTS & BARS

The favorite **local beer** is Red Stripe; a favorite **local rum** is Appleton.

Ocho Rios Jerk Centre, on DaCosta Drive (© 876/974-2549), serves up lip-smacking jerk pork and chicken. Don't expect anything fancy; just come for platters of meat. For a special lunch out, **Almond Tree Restaurant,** 83 Main St., in the Hibiscus Lodge Hotel, 3 blocks from the Ocho Rios Mall (© 876/974-2813), is a two-tiered patio restaurant overlooking the Caribbean, with a tree growing through its roof. Lobster thermidor is the most delectable item on the menu. **Evita's Italian Restaurant,** Eden Bower Road, 5 minutes south of Ocho Rios (© 876/974-2333), is run by a flamboyant Italian and is the premier Italian restaurant in Ocho Rios. It serves pastas and excellent fish dishes, as well as unique choices such as jerk spaghetti and pasta Viagra (don't ask). Lunch with drinks runs about $20. The casual **Little Pub Restaurant,** 59 Main St. (© 876/974-2324), is an indoor-outdoor pub serving grilled kingfish, stewed snapper, barbecued chicken, the inevitable and overpriced lobster, and other items. **Parkway Restaurant,** 60 DaCosta Dr. (© 876/974-2667), couldn't be plainer or less pretentious, but it's always packed with hungry diners chowing down on Jamaican-style chicken, curried goat, sirloin steak, lobster, fillet of red snapper and other seafood, and, to top it off, banana cream pie.

There are probably more great rum bars on Jamaica than churches. Among the best is **Bibi Bips,** 93 Main St. (© 876/974-8759).

MONTEGO BAY

Montego Bay is sometimes less of a hassle than the port at Ocho Rios, and has better beaches, shopping, and restaurants, as well as some of the best golf courses in the Caribbean, superior even to those on Puerto Rico and the Bahamas. Like Ocho Rios, Montego Bay has its crime, traffic, and annoyance, but there's much more to see and do here.

There's little of interest in the town itself except shopping, although the good stuff in the environs is easily reached by taxi or shore excursion. Getting around from place to place is one of the major difficulties here. Whatever you want to visit seems to be in yet another direction.

Frommer's Favorite Montego Bay Experiences

In addition to these, our favorite shore excursions from Ocho Rios are also offered from Montego Bay.

Visiting Rocklands Wildlife Station: This is the place to go if you want to have a Jamaican doctor bird perch on your finger or feed small doves and finches from your hand. (See "On Your Own: Beyond the Port Area," below.)

Spend a Day at the Rose Hall Beach Club: With a secluded beach, crystal-clear water, a full restaurant, two beach bars, live entertainment, and more, it's well worth the $8 admission. (See "Beaches," below.)

COMING ASHORE   Montego Bay has a modern cruise dock with lots of conveniences, including duty-free stores, telephones, tourist information, and plenty of taxis to meet all ships.

INFORMATION   You'll find the **tourist board offices** at Cornwall Beach, St. James (© **876/952-4425**), open Monday to Friday from 9am to 5pm.

GETTING AROUND
BY TAXI   If you don't book a shore excursion, a taxi is the way to get around. See "Getting Around" under "Ocho Rios," earlier, for taxi information, as the same conditions apply to Mo Bay.

SHORE EXCURSIONS OFFERED BY THE CRUISE LINES
In addition to the tour listed below, most of those listed under Ocho Rios are also offered from Montego Bay.

Croydon Plantation Tour ($55, 4–5 hr.): Forty kilometers (25 miles) from Montego Bay, the plantation can be visited on a half-day tour on Tuesday, Wednesday, and Friday. Included in the price are round-trip transportation from the dock, a tour of the plantation, a fruit tasting in season (featuring pineapple and a variety of other tropical fruits), and a barbecued chicken lunch.

ON YOUR OWN: WITHIN WALKING DISTANCE
There's nothing really. You'll have to take a taxi to the town for shopping or sign up for an excursion.

ON YOUR OWN: BEYOND THE PORT AREA
These attractions can be reached by taxi from the cruise dock.

The most famous Great House in Jamaica is the legendary **Rose Hall Great House,** Rose Hall Highway (© **876/953-2323**), located 14km (9 miles) east of Montego Bay along the coast road. The house was built about 2 centuries ago by John Palmer, and gained notoriety from the doings of "Infamous Annie" Palmer, wife of the builder's grandnephew, who supposedly dabbled in witchcraft and took slaves as lovers, killing them when they bored her. Annie also was said to have murdered several of her husbands while they slept, and eventually suffered the same fate herself. The house, now privately owned, has been restored. **Annie's Pub** sits on the ground floor. The house is open daily from 9am to 5:15pm; admission is a steep $15 for adults, $10 for children under 12.

On a hillside perch 23km (14 miles) east of Montego Bay and 11km (7 miles) west of Falmouth, **Greenwood Great House,** on the A1 (② **876/953-1077**), is even more interesting to some than Rose Hall. Erected in the early 19th century, the Georgian-style building was from 1780 to 1800 the residence of Richard Barrett, a relative of Elizabeth Barrett Browning. On display are the family's library, portraits of the family, and rare musical instruments. Open from 9am to 6pm daily; admission is $12 for adults and $6 for children under 12.

It's a unique experience to have a Jamaican doctor bird perch on your finger to drink syrup, or to feed small doves and finches from your hand, or simply to watch dozens of birds flying in for the evening at **Rocklands Wildlife Station,** Anchovy, St. James (② **876/952-2009**). Lisa Salmon, known as the "Bird Lady of Anchovy," established this sanctuary. It's perfect for nature lovers and bird-watchers, but don't take children 5 and under, as they tend to worry the birds. Rocklands is about 1.5km (a mile) outside Anchovy on the road from Montego Bay. It's open daily from 9am to 5pm, and charges $8 admission for adults and $4 for children age 5 to 12.

SHOPPING

The main shopping areas are at **Montego Freeport,** within easy walking distance of the pier; **City Centre,** where most of the duty-free shops are, aside from those at the large hotels; and **Holiday Village Shopping Centre.**

Old Fort Craft Park, a shopping complex with nearly 200 vendors licensed by the Jamaica Tourist Board, fronts Howard Cooke Boulevard up from Gloucester Avenue in the heart of Montego Bay, on the site of Fort Montego. With a varied assortment of handcrafts, this is browsing country. You'll see a selection of wall hangings, hand-woven straw items, and hand-carved wood sculptures, and you can also get your hair braided. Vendors can be extremely aggressive, so be prepared for some major hassles, as well as some serious negotiation. Persistent bargaining on your part will lead to substantial discounts.

You can find the best selection of handmade Jamaican souvenirs at the **Crafts Market,** near Harbour Street in downtown Montego Bay. Straw hats and bags, wooden platters, straw baskets, musical instruments, beads, carved objects, and toys are all available here. That "jipijapa" hat will come in handy if you're going to be out in the island sun.

Ambiente Art Gallery, 9 Fort St. (② **876/952-7919**), stocks local artwork. At **Blue Mountain Gems Workshop,** at the Holiday Village Shopping Centre (② **876/953-2338**), you can take a tour of the workshops to see the process from raw stone to the finished product available for purchase later. **Klass Kraft Leather Sandals,** 44 Fort St. (② **876/952-5782**), offers sandals and leather accessories made on location.

Half Moon Plaza, set on the coastal road about 13km (8 miles) east of Montego Bay's commercial center, is an upscale minimall located at one of the region's most elegant hotels, the Half Moon Club (② **876/953-2211**).

BEACHES

Cornwall Beach is a long stretch of white-sand beach with dressing cabanas. Daily admission is about $2 for adults, $1 for children. A bar and cafeteria serve refreshments.

Doctor's Cave Beach (② **876/952-2566**), on Gloucester Avenue across from the Doctor's Cave Beach Hotel (② **876/952-4355; www.doctorscave.com**), helped launch Mo Bay as a resort in the 1940s. Admission to the beach is about

$3 for adults, half price for children up to 12. Dressing rooms, chairs, umbrellas, and rafts are available.

One of the premier beaches of Jamaica, **Walter Fletcher Beach,** in the heart of Mo Bay, is noted for its tranquil waters, which make it a particular favorite for families with children. Changing rooms are available, and lifeguards are on duty. There's also a restaurant for lunch. The beach is open daily, with an admission price of about $1 for adults, half price for children.

You may want to skip the public beaches and head for the **Rose Hall Beach Club** (© 876/680-0969), lying on the main road 18km (11 miles) east of Montego Bay. It sits on 1km (half a mile) of secure, secluded, white sandy beach, with crystal-clear water. The club offers a full restaurant, two beach bars, a covered pavilion, an open-air dance area, showers, restrooms, and changing facilities, plus beach volleyball courts, various beach games, and a full watersports activities program. There's also live entertainment. The club is open daily from 9am to 5pm; admission fees are about $6 for adults, $3 for children under 12.

SPORTS

GOLF   **Wyndham Rose Hall Golf & Beach Resort,** Rose Hall (© 876/953-2650), has a noted 18-hole, par-71 course with an unusual and challenging seaside and mountain layout. The 90m-high (300-ft.-high) 13th tee offers a rare panoramic view of the sea, and the 15th green is next to a 12m (40-ft.) waterfall, once featured in a James Bond movie. A fully stocked pro shop, a clubhouse, and a professional staff are among the amenities. Greens fees are $125.

The excellent, regal 18-hole, par-72 course at the **Tryall Club** (© 876/956-5660; www.tryallclub.com), 19km (12 miles) from Montego Bay, has often been the site of major golf tournaments, including the Jamaica Classic Annual and the Johnnie Walker Tournament. Greens fees are $115, plus $18 for a mandatory caddy.

Half Moon, at Rose Hall (© 876/953-2560; www.halfmoon-resort.com/golf), features an 18-hole, par-72 championship course designed by Robert Trent Jones, Sr. Greens fees are $130 plus $17 for a mandatory caddy.

Ironshore Golf & Country Club, Ironshore, St. James, Montego Bay (© 876/953-3681), a well-known, 18-hole, par-72 course, is privately owned but open to the public. Greens fees are $130 plus $17 for a mandatory caddy.

HORSEBACK RIDING   The best horseback riding is offered by the helpful staff at the **Rocky Point Riding Stables,** at the Half Moon Club, Rose Hall, Montego Bay (© 876/953-2286). The stables, built in the colonial Caribbean style in 1992, are the most beautiful in Jamaica.

RAFTING   **Mountain Valley Rafting,** 31 Gloucester Ave. (© 876/956-4920), offers excursions on the Great River, departing from the Lethe Plantation, about 16km (10 miles) south of Montego Bay. Bamboo rafts are designed for two, with a raised dais to sit on. In some cases, a small child can accompany two adults on the same raft, although you should exercise caution when doing so. A half-day experience includes transportation to and from the pier, an hour's rafting, lunch, a garden tour of the Lethe property, and a taste of Jamaican liqueur.

WATERSPORTS   **Seaworld Resorts Ltd.,** Cariblue Hotel, Rose Hall Main Road (© 876/953-2180), operates scuba diving, deep-sea fishing jaunts, sailing, windsurfing, and many other watersports. Its scuba dives go to offshore coral reefs that are among the most spectacular in the Caribbean. There are three

PADI-certified dive guides, one dive boat, and all the necessary equipment for inexperienced or certified divers.

GREAT LOCAL RESTAURANTS & BARS

The Pork Pit, 27 Gloucester Ave., near Walter Fletcher Beach (© **876/952-1046**), is the best place to go for the famous Jamaican jerk pork and jerk chicken. Many beachgoers come over here for a big lunch. Picnic tables encircle the building, and everything is open-air and informal. Order half a pound of jerk meat with a baked yam or baked potato and a bottle of Red Stripe beer. Prices are very reasonable.

The Native Restaurant, Gloucester Avenue (© **876/979-2769**), continues to win converts with such appetizers as jerk reggae chicken, ackee and saltfish (an acquired taste), smoked marlin, and steamed fish. The boonoonoonoos, billed as "A Taste of Jamaica," is a big platter with a little bit of everything, including meats and several kinds of fish and vegetables.

18 Key West

No other port of call offers such a sweeping choice of fine dining, easy-to-reach attractions, street entertainment, and roguish bars as does this heavy-drinking, fun-loving town at the very end of the fabled Florida Keys. It's America's southernmost city, located at Mile Marker 0, where U.S. Route 1 begins, but it feels more like a colorful Caribbean outpost mixed with a dash of New Orleans.

You have only a day, so flee the busy cruise docks and touristy **Duval Street** for a walk through hidden and more secluded byways, such as **Olivia** or **William streets.** Or you might want to spend your day playing golf or going diving or snorkeling.

COMING ASHORE   Ships dock at **Mallory Square,** Old Town's most important plaza, or at nearby **Truman Annex,** a 5-minute stroll away. Both are on the Gulf of Mexico side of the island, and virtually everything is at your doorstep, including the two main arteries, Duval Street and Whitehead Street, each filled with shops, bars, restaurants, and the town's most important attractions.

LANGUAGE   Speak **English** here. You're in the U.S. of A., remember.

CURRENCY   U.S. dollars are used here.

INFORMATION   The **Greater Key West Chamber of Commerce,** 402 Wall St. (© **305/294-5988;** www.keywestchamber.org), lies near the cruise ship docks, and answers questions about local activities, distributes free maps, and helps arrange tours and fishing trips. *Pelican Path* is a free walking guide that

 Frommer's Favorite Key West Experiences

Viewing the Sunset from Mallory Dock: More than just a sunset, it's a daily carnival. If your ship is in port late enough, don't miss it. (See "On Your Own: Within Walking Distance," below.)

Taking a Catamaran Party Cruise: The popular Fury catamarans take passengers snorkeling and then back to shore, with music, booze, and a good time. (See "Shore Excursions Offered by the Cruise Lines," below.)

documents the history and architecture of Old Town, and *Solares Hill's Walking and Biking Guide to Old Key West* contains a bunch of walking tours. To get info before you go, contact the **Tourism Board** (© 800/733-5397; www.seekeys. com).

GETTING AROUND

The island is only 4 miles (6.5km) long and 2 miles (3km) wide, so getting around is easy. Hundreds of people who live here own bicycles instead of cars. The most popular sights, including the Hemingway House, the recently restored bright red brick Custom's House, and the Harry S Truman Little White House, are within walking distance of the cruise docks, so you're hardly dependent on public transportation unless you want to go to the beaches on the island's Atlantic side.

BY TAXI   Island taxis operate around the clock, but are small and not suited for sightseeing tours. They will, however, take you to the beach and arrange to pick you up at a certain time. You can call one of four services: **Florida Keys Taxi** (© 305/294-2227), **Maxi-Taxi Sun Cab System** (© 305/294-2222), **Pink Cabs** (© 305/296-6666), and **Island Transportation Services** (© 305/296-1800). Prices are uniform; the meter starts at about $1.75 and adds 35¢ per quarter-mile.

BY TRAM   The **Conch Tour Train** (© 305/294-5161; www.conchtourtrain. com) is a narrated 90-minute tour that takes you up and down all the most interesting streets and offers commentary on 100 local sites, giving you lots of lore about the town. It's the best way to see lots of Key West in a short time. The depot is located at Mallory Square near the cruise ship docks. Trains depart every 30 minutes. Most ships sell this as an excursion, but you can also do it on your own; departures are daily from 9am to 4:30pm and cost $20 for adults, $10 for children ages 4 to 12 (3 and under free). The trip has only one stop where passengers can get on and off (at the Historic Seaport). If you want more flexibility, try the **Old Town Trolley** (© 305/296-6688; www.trolleytours.com). It's less popular than the Conch Tour Train, but it lets you get off and explore a particular attraction, and then reboard another of its trains later. Professional guides spin tall tales about Key West throughout the 90-minute route. The trolleys operate 7 days a week from 9am to 4:30pm, with departures every 30 minutes from convenient spots throughout town. You can board the trolley near the cruise docks (look for signposts). Tours cost about $20 for adults, $10 for children ages 4 to 12, and are free for children under 4.

BY MOTOR SCOOTER OR BICYCLE   One of the largest and best places to rent a bicycle or motorbike is **Keys Moped and Scooter Rental,** 523 Truman Ave., about a block off Duval Street (© 305/294-0399). Cruise ship passengers might opt for a 3-hour motor-scooter rental for about $12, the 9am to 5pm rental for $18, or the all day (24-hr.) rental for $23. One-speed, big-wheeled "beach cruiser" bicycles with soft seats and big baskets for toting beachwear rent for about $4 for 8 hours.

BY BUS   The cheapest way to see the island is by bus, which costs only about 75¢ for adults and 35¢ for senior citizens and children 6 years and older (kids 5 and under ride free).

BY RENTAL CAR   Walking or cycling is better than renting a car here, but if you do want to rent, **Avis, Budget, Dollar,** and **Hertz** all have offices here, as

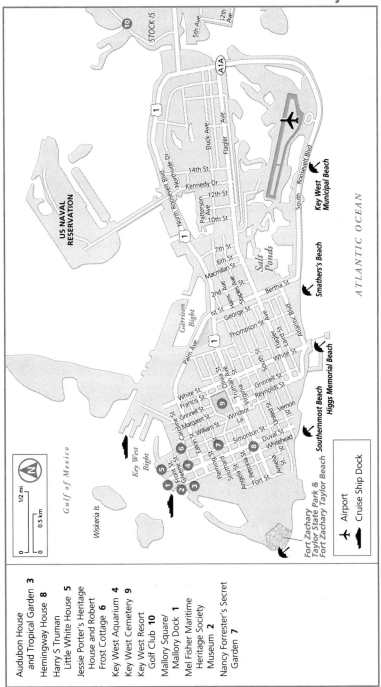

Audubon House
and Tropical Garden **3**
Hemingway House **8**
Harry S Truman
Little White House **5**
Jessie Porter's Heritage
House and Robert
Frost Cottage **6**
Key West Aquarium **4**
Key West Cemetery **9**
Key West Resort
Golf Club **10**
Mallory Square/
Mallory Dock **1**
Mel Fisher Maritime
Heritage Society
Museum **2**
Nancy Forrester's Secret
Garden **7**

do **Tropical Rent-a-Car,** 1300 Duval St. (© **305/294-8136**), and **Enterprise Rent-a-Car,** 2834 N. Roosevelt Blvd. (© **800/325-8007** or 305/292-0220; www.enterprise.com). If you're visiting in winter, make reservations at least a week in advance.

SHORE EXCURSIONS OFFERED BY THE CRUISE LINES
In Key West, it's definitely not necessary to take an organized excursion since everything is so accessible by foot or tram. If you like the services of a guide, most lines offer walking tours. Also, the trams and trolleys discussed above have running narratives about Key West history and culture. Here are a couple of other popular options.

Catamaran Party Cruises ($40, 3 hr.): The popular Fury catamarans take passengers to a reef for some snorkeling and then finish the trip back to shore with music, booze, and a good time. You can also book these trips on your own (© **800/994-8898** or 305/294-8899; www.furycat.com). Their sunset sail is an option if your ship will be in port late ($30, 2 hr.).

Guided Bike Tour ($25, 2 hr.): Get the lowdown on Key West's multifaceted history and quirky culture while peddling along a 2½-mile (4km) route.

EXCURSIONS OFFERED BY LOCAL AGENCIES
Glass-Bottomed Boat Tours: The MV *Discovery* (© **800/262-0099** or 305/ 293-0099; www.discoveryunderseatours.com), a 23m (78-ft.) motor craft, has 20 large viewing windows (angled at 45°) set below the water line to allow passengers to view reef life in comfort from below deck. Two-hour tours depart daily at 10:30am, 1:30pm, and sunset from Land's End Village & Marina at the western end of Margaret Street, a 6-block walk from the cruise ship docks. The cost is about $25, $30 for the sunset tour.

ON YOUR OWN: WITHIN WALKING DISTANCE
If the lines aren't too long, you'll want to see the Harry S Truman Little White House and the Hemingway House, but don't feel obligated. If you want to see and capture the real-life mood and charm of Key West in a short time, leave the most-visited attractions to your fellow cruise ship passengers and head for the others mentioned below. All are an easy walk from the docks.

Audubon House and Tropical Garden, 205 Whitehead St., at Green Street (© **305/294-2116** or 877/281-2473; www.audubonhouse.com), is dedicated to the 1832 Key West sojourn of the famous naturalist John James Audubon. The ornithologist didn't live in this three-story building, but it's filled with his engravings. The main reason to visit is to see how wealthy sailors lived in Key West in the 19th century, and the lush tropical gardens surrounding the house are worth the price of admission.

The **Harry S Truman Little White House,** 111 Front St. (© **305/294-9911;** www.trumanlittlewhitehouse.com), the president's vacation home, is part of the 41-hectare (103-acre) Truman Annex near the cruise ship docks. The small house, which takes less than an hour to visit, affords a glimpse of a president at play.

There may be long lines at the **Hemingway House,** 907 Whitehead St. (© **305/294-1575**), where "Papa" lived with his second wife, Pauline. Here, in the studio annex, Hemingway finished *For Whom the Bell Tolls* and *A Farewell to Arms,* among others. Hemingway had some 50 polydactyl (many-toed) cats, whose descendants still live on the grounds.

Jessie Porter Newton, known as "Miss Jessie" to her friends, was the grande dame of Key West, inviting the celebrities of her day to her house, including

Tennessee Williams and her girlhood friend Gloria Swanson, as well as family friend Robert Frost, who stayed in a cottage out back. Today, you can wander the grounds, look at the antique-filled rooms, and inspect her mementos and the exotic treasures collected by six generations of the Porter family at **Jessie Porter's Heritage House and Robert Frost Cottage,** 410 Caroline St. (© **305/296-3573**).

On the waterfront at Mallory Square, the **Key West Aquarium,** 1 Whitehead St. (© **305/296-2051;** www.keywestaquarium.com), in operation since 1932, was the first tourist attraction built in the Florida Keys. The aquarium's special feature is a "touch tank" where you can feel a horseshoe crab, sea squirt, sea urchin, starfish, and, of course, conch, the town's mascot and symbol. It's worth taking a tour, as the guides are both knowledgeable and entertaining—and you'll get to pet a shark, if that's your idea of a good time.

The **Key West Cemetery** (© **305/292-6718**), 21 prime acres (8.5 hectares) in the heart of the historic district, is the island's foremost offbeat attraction. The main entrance is at Margaret Street and Passover Lane. Stone-encased caskets rest on top of the earth because graves dug into the ground would hit the water table. There's also a touch of humor here: One gravestone proclaims "I Told You I Was Sick" and another says "At Least I Know Where He Is Sleeping Tonight." To get a better scoop on what you'll be seeing, print out the cemetery tour at **www.key west.com/cemetery.html** before you go.

The late treasure hunter Mel Fisher used to wear heavy gold necklaces, which he liked to say were worth a king's ransom. He wasn't exaggerating. After long and risky dives, Fisher and his associates plucked more than $400 million in gold and silver from the shipwrecked Spanish galleons *Santa Margarita* and *Nuestra Señora de Atocha,* which were lost on hurricane-tossed seas some 350 years ago. Now this extraordinary long-lost Spanish treasure—jewelry, doubloons, and silver and gold bullion—is displayed at the **Mel Fisher Maritime Heritage Society Museum,** near the docks at 200 Greene St. (© **305/294-2633;** www.melfisher.org).

Nancy Forrester's Secret Garden, 1 Free School Lane, off Simonton between Southard and Fleming streets (© **305/294-0015**), is the most lavish and verdant garden in town. Some 150 species of palms and thousands of species of other plants, including orchids, climbing vines, and ground covers, are planted here, creating a blanket of lush, tropical magic. It's a 20-minute walk from the docks, near Key West's highest point, Solares Hill. Pick up a sandwich at a deli and picnic at tables in the garden. Admission is $6 per person; hours are 10am to 5pm daily.

If your ship leaves late enough, you can take in a unique local celebration: **viewing the sunset from Mallory Dock.** Sunset watching is good fun all over the world, but in Key West it's been turned into a carnival-like, almost pagan celebration. People from all over begin to crowd Mallory Square even before the sun starts to fall, bringing the place alive with entertainment—everything from string bands to a unicyclist wriggling free of a straitjacket to a juggler tossing around machetes and flaming sticks. The main entertainment, however, is that massive fireball falling out of view, a sight that's always greeted with hysterical applause.

ON YOUR OWN: BEYOND THE PORT AREA

Nothin'. That's the beauty of Key West: Everything worthwhile is accessible by foot.

SHOPPING

Within a 12-block radius of Old Town, you'll find mostly tawdry and outrageously overpriced merchandise, but if you're in the market for some Key West kitsch, this is the neighborhood for you. Shopping by cruise ship passengers has become a joke among Key West locals, but that's their problem. We say be proud of your flamingo snow globe and floppy straw hat. What else says "vacation" better?

Among the less-kitschy alternatives, a few standouts are located much farther along **Duval Street,** the main drag leading to the Atlantic, and on hidden back streets. You can reach all these stores from the cruise ship docks in a 15- to 20-minute stroll.

Haitian Art Company, 600 Frances St. (© **305/296-8932**), claims to inventory the largest collection of Haitian paintings in the United States. Prices range from $15 to $5,000. **Key West Aloe, Inc.,** 524 Front St. or 540 Greene St. (© **305/294-5592**), is aloe, aloe, and more aloe; the shop's inventory includes shaving cream, aftershave lotion, sunburn ointments, and fragrances for men and women based on tropical essences such as hibiscus, frangipani, and white ginger. **Key West Hand Print Fashions and Fabrics,** 201 Simonton St. (© **305/292-8951**), sells bold, tropical prints—hand-printed scarves with coordinated handbags and rack after rack of busily patterned sundresses and cocktail dresses that will make you look jaunty on deck. **Key West Island Bookstore,** 513 Fleming St. (© **305/294-2904**), is well stocked with books on Key West and has Florida's largest collection of works by and about Hemingway. In the rear is a rare-book section where you may want to browse, if not buy.

BEACHES

Beaches are not too compelling here. Most are man-made, often with imported Bahamian or mainland Florida sand. Those mentioned below are free and open to the public daily from 7am to 11pm. There are few facilities, just locals hawking beach umbrellas, food, and drinks.

Fort Zachary Taylor State Beach (© **305/292-6883**) is the best and the closest to the cruise ship docks, a 12-minute walk away. This 20-hectare (51-acre) man-made beach is adjacent to historic Fort Taylor, once known as Fort Forgotten because it was buried under tons of sand. The beach is fine for sunbathing and picnicking and is suitable for snorkeling. To get there, go through the gates leading into **Truman Annex** (© **305/292-6713**). Watering holes near one end of the beach include the raffish **Green Parrot Bar** (© **305/294-6133**) and **Meteore Smokehouse Barbecue** (© **305/294-5602**).

Higgs Memorial Beach lies a 25-minute walk from the harbor near the end of White Street, one of the main east-west arteries. You'll find lots of sand, picnic tables sheltered from the sun, and fewer of your fellow cruise ship passengers. **Smathers Beach,** named in honor of one of Florida's most colorful former senators, is the longest (about 1½ miles/2.5km), most isolated, and least accessorized in town. Unfortunately, it's about a $10 one-way taxi ride from the cruise docks. The beach borders South Roosevelt Boulevard. There's no shade here.

SPORTS

FISHING   As Hemingway, an avid fisherman, would attest, the waters off the Florida Keys are some of the world's finest fishing grounds. You can follow in his wake aboard the 40-foot *Linda D III* and *Linda D IV* (© **800/299-9798** or 305/296-9798; www.charterboatlindad.com), which offer the best deep-sea fishing here. Arrangements should be made a week or so before you're due in port. Full-day charters for up to 6 people $675, half-day $450. Full-day shared charters $165 per person, half-day $110. Make arrangements as far in advance as possible.

GOLF Redesigned in 1982 by architect Rees Jones, the 18-hole, par-70 **Key West Resort Golf Club,** 6450 E. Junior College Rd. (© **305/294-5232;** www. keywestgolf.com), lies 6 miles (9.5km) from the cruise docks, near the southern tip of neighboring Stock Island. It features a challenging terrain of coral rock, sand traps, mangrove swamp, and pines. Greens fees are $140, including a golf cart. The course is a 10- to 15-minute, $15 taxi ride from the dock each way.

SCUBA DIVING The largest dive outfitter is **Captain's Corner,** 125 Ann St., half a block from the dock (© **305/296-8865;** www.captainscorner.com). The five-star PADI operation has 11 instructors, a well-trained staff, and an 18m (60-ft.) dive boat that was used by Timothy "James Bond" Dalton during the filming of *License to Kill.* To reach the departure point, walk to the end of Green Street.

GREAT LOCAL RESTAURANTS & BARS

RESTAURANTS All the restaurants listed below are within an easy 5- to 15-minute walk of the docks. Several "raw bars" near the dock area offer seafood, including oysters and clams, although the king here is conch—served grilled, ground into burgers, made into chowder, fried in batter as fritters, or served raw in a conch salad. Even if you don't have lunch, at least sample the local favorites: a slice of Key lime pie with a Cuban coffee. The pie's unique flavor comes from the juice and minced rind of the local, piquant Key lime.

Cruise ship passengers on a return visit to Key West often ask for "The Rose Tattoo," a historic old restaurant named for the Tennessee Williams film partially shot on the island. The restaurant is now the **Bagatelle,** 115 Duval St., at Front Street (© **305/296-6609**), one of Key West's finest. Look for daily specials or stick to the chef's better dishes, such as conch ceviche (thinly sliced raw conch marinated in lime juice and herbs). **Blue Heaven,** 729 Thomas St. (© **305/296-8666**), is a dive that serves some of the best food in town, including fresh local fish, most often grouper or red snapper. Their hot and spicy jerk chicken is as fine as that served in Jamaica. **Camille's,** 1202 Simonton St., at Catherine Street (© **305/296-4811**), is an unpretentious, hip cafe that serves the best breakfast in town and has the best lunch value. Try a sandwich made from the catch of the day, served on fresh bread, and finish off with some of their great Key lime pie. **El Siboney,** 900 Catherine St. (© **305/296-4184**), is the place for time-tested Cuban favorites such as ropa vieja, roast pork with garlic and tart sour oranges, and paella Valenciana.

Half Shell Raw Bar, Land's End Marina, at the foot of Margaret Street (© **305/294-7496**), is Key West's original raw bar, offering fresh fish, oysters, and shrimp direct from its own fish market. To be honest, though, we prefer the food at **Turtle Kraals Wildlife Bar & Grill,** Land's End Village, at the foot of Margaret Street (© **305/294-2640**). Try the tender Florida lobster, spicy conch chowder, or perfectly cooked fresh fish (often dolphinfish with pineapple salsa or baked stuffed grouper with mango crabmeat stuffing).

Pepe's Café & Steak House, 806 Caroline St., between William and Margaret streets (© **305/294-7192**), is the oldest eating-house in the Florida Keys, established in 1909. Diners eat under slow-moving paddle fans at tables or dark pine booths with high backs. At lunch (served noon–4pm), choose from zesty homemade chili, perfectly baked oysters, fish sandwiches, and Pepe's deservedly famous steak sandwiches.

If something cool would go down better than a full meal, check out the **Flamingo Crossing** ice-cream shop, 1105 Duval St., at Virginia Street (© **305/ 296-6124**).

BARS   Key West is a bar town, and since many ships stay in town late, you'll likely have an opportunity to do some carousing. Most places recommended below offer fast food to go with their drinks. The food isn't the best on the island, but usually arrives shortly after you order it, which suits most rushed cruise ship passengers just fine. Try some of the favorite **local beer,** Hog's Breath, or some of the favorite **local rum,** Key West Gold (even though it's a cheat—it isn't actually made on the island).

Heavily patronized by cruise ship passengers, **Captain Tony's Saloon,** 428 Greene St. (© **305/294-1838**), is the oldest active bar in Florida, and is tacky as hell. The 1851 building was the original Sloppy Joe's, a rough-and-tumble fisherman's saloon. Hemingway drank here from 1933 to 1937, and Jimmy Buffett got his start here before opening his own bar and going on to musical glory. The name refers to Capt. Tony Tarracino, a former Key West mayor and rugged man of the sea who owned the place until 1988.

The current **Sloppy Joe's,** 201 Duval St. (© **305/294-5717**), is the most touristy bar in Key West, visited by almost all cruise ship passengers, even those who don't normally go to bars. It aggressively plays up its association with Hemingway, although the bar stood on Greene Street back then (see above). Marine flags decorate the ceiling, and its ambience and decor evoke a Havana bar from the 1930s.

Jimmy Buffett's Margaritaville, 500 Duval St. (© **305/296-3070**), is the third most popular Key West bar with cruise ship passengers. Buffett is the hometown boy done good, and his cafe, naturally, is decorated with pictures of himself. And, yes, it sells T-shirts and Margaritaville memorabilia in a shop off the dining room. His margaritas are without competition, but then they'd have to be, wouldn't they?

Open-air and very laid-back, the **Hog's Breath Saloon,** 400 Front St. (© **305/296-HOGG**), near the cruise docks, has been a Key West tradition since 1976. Drinking is a sport here, especially among the fishermen who come in after a day chasing the big one. Live entertainment is offered from 1pm to 2am.

For a real local hangout within an easy walk of the cruise ship docks, head to **Schooner Wharf,** 202 William St., Key West Bight (© **305/292-9520**), the most robust and hard-drinking bar in Key West, drawing primarily a young crowd, many of whom work in the tourist industry or on the local fishing boats.

19 Les Saintes

You want charming? The eight islets of Les Saintes (pronounced "lay sant") are irresistibly so: pastel-colored gingerbread houses with tropical gardens, sugarloaf hills that slope down to miniature beaches, and picturesque bays with pelicans, sailboats, and turquoise water. Only two of the islands in this French archipelago off the southern coast of Guadeloupe are inhabited: Terre-de-Bas and its more populous neighbor, Terre-de-Haut (more populous, in this case, meaning it has about 1,700 inhabitants). Terre-de-Haut (pronounced "t'air d'oh"), with only one village—the straightforwardly named Le Bourg ("town")—is the destination of most visitors. Some say it's what Saint-Tropez was like before Brigitte Bardot. For a U.S. point of reference, think Fire Island, Provincetown, Martha's Vineyard, or Sausalito with a French-Caribbean twist. Nautical and quaint are the watchwords.

Les Saintes

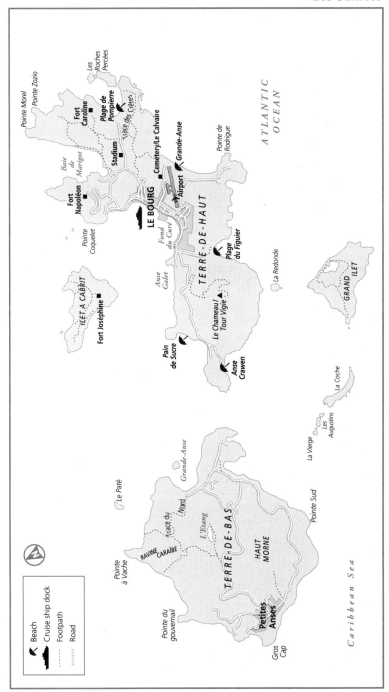

But Les Saintes, also known as Iles des Saintes, isn't a fantasy park built to look enchanting. Although tourism is important to the island's economy, most people here still make their living from the sea. Les Saintois, as the locals are called, are widely regarded as the best fishermen in the Antilles, and it's this underlying saltiness that keeps the place from being cloyingly sweet.

Christopher Columbus was the first European to sight the islands, on November 4, 1493. To commemorate the Feast of All Saints, he named the islands Los Santos. He didn't bother to go ashore, though. The arid, rocky terrain seemed unsuitable for agriculture, and Carib Indians, who had already proved fierce on other islands, made their presence known.

Europeans didn't seriously attempt to settle the islands until 1648, when the French established a colony to monitor ships passing through the channel between Les Saintes and the more important French colony of Guadeloupe to the north. Carib Indian attacks forced abandonment of the original settlement, but a permanent French presence followed in 1652. Reflecting its strategic significance, Les Saintes became known as the Gibraltar of the West Indies.

In the 17th and 18th centuries, the archipelago witnessed the French and English battle for supremacy of the seas. In 1666, the English took possession of Terre-de-Haut Bay, but within days a terrible storm wiped out their fleet. A week later, on August 15, the French and their Carib Indian allies forced the English to surrender, an event that is still celebrated annually. More than a hundred years later, in 1782, the English had their revenge, decisively defeating the French in the Battle of Les Saintes. Control of the islands didn't revert to France until the signing of the second Treaty of Paris in 1815. To deter any further aggression, the French constructed forts on a couple of the islands, but no violence ensued; and the bastions never fired a shot.

Terre-de-Haut's poor soil precluded the production of sugarcane, a lucrative business on Guadeloupe. Consequently, slaves from Africa were never brought here. The colonists, primarily from the French coastal regions of Brittany, Normandy, and Poitou, turned to the sea for their livelihood. Today their fair-haired, blue-eyed descendants are the primary residents of the island. Motorboats have all but replaced the traditional sailboats (*santois*), and *salakos,* the bamboo-and-cloth hats that resemble Chinese parasols, are harder and harder to find. You can still see colorful fishing nets drying along the waterfront, though.

Terre-de-Bas, more fertile than its sister isle, is home primarily to descendants of African slaves, who worked that island's sugarcane, cotton, and pepper fields. Coffee grown there was served at Napoleon's table.

COMING ASHORE   Cruise ships dock at **Le Bourg** in Terre-de-Haut. The village has two main streets, both parallel to the bay and lined with cafes, restaurants, and souvenir shops. **Telephones** at the dock require a télécarte, a prepaid phone card sold at the post office (a 10-min. walk from the dock; take a right) and other outlets marked TELECARTE EN VENTE ICI. Some phones now accept U.S. calling cards or major credit cards for long-distance calls.

LANGUAGE   The official language is **French,** but many islanders speak **Creole** with each other. Few locals feel comfortable with English, though, so take the opportunity to practice your high-school French. Most everyone is helpful and friendly, especially if you smile and make an effort.

CURRENCY   Les Saintes is part of the larger archipelago of Guadeloupe, an overseas region of France, so the **Euro** (€) is now the official currency (exchange rate: €1 = U.S.90¢; $1 = €1.10). Notes are denominated in 500, 200, 100, 50,

---

Fun Fact Tormented by Love? Have a Pastry

As you leave your ship, you'll spot local women selling Les Saintes' signature sweet, tartlets known as *tourments d'amour* (love's torments). Legend has it that young maidens baked these flaky-crusted, coconut-filled treats to present to their betrotheds as they returned from lengthy fishing expeditions. From time to time, the cruel and heartless sea claimed the life of a beloved, leaving a teary-eyed damsel at the dock with nothing but her pain and pastry. Is it the suffering that makes the tourments d'amour so tasty?

20, 10, and 5 euros; coins come in 1 and 2 euro and 50, 20, 10, 5, 2, and 1 cent denominations. You can withdraw euros from the **ATM** next to the tourism office (see "Information" below).

INFORMATION   If you take a right on the main road after you leave the ship, you'll see signs for the **tourism office** (OFFICE DU TOURISME). It's less than a 5-minute walk. Most printed information available here is in French, but the maps are helpful even if you don't understand the lingo. For info before you go, contact the Tourism Board in the United States (© **410/286-8310;** www.french caribbean.com).

CALLING FROM THE U.S.   When calling Les Saintes from the U.S., dial the international access code (011) and 590 before the numbers listed here. Yes, the numbers listed here already begin with 590, but an effort by the French telephone authorities to standardize procedures requires that you dial those three digits twice. Really.

GETTING AROUND

If you're reasonably fit, there's no reason you can't walk wherever you want to go. If you're the type who runs 8km (5 miles) a day, you can hike up Le Chameau, traipse around Fort Napoléon, head over to Plage de Pompierre, and complete the Trace des Crêtes, with time for a meal or swim before returning to the ship.

BY TAXI   The island has a handful of minivans that serve as taxis. Each seats six to eight passengers, and most drivers offer 3-hour tours of the island for about $40 (be aware, though, that fluent English is not widely spoken). You'll find the cabs parked directly in front of the cruise ship dock.

BY SCOOTER   Terre-de-Haut is less than 6.5km (4 miles) long and less than 3km (2 miles) wide. Aside from tourist vans and the occasional private car, four-wheeled vehicles are rare (at last count, there were fewer than three dozen). Scooters rule the roads. Scores of them await you just off the dock along Le Bourg's main road. Expect to pay about $35 for a two-seater for the day. A $500 deposit (credit cards accepted) is required.

BY BICYCLE   You can rent bicycles for between $15 and $20 along Le Bourg's main road. The island is hilly, though. You'd do better to rent a scooter or walk.

SHORE EXCURSIONS OFFERED BY THE CRUISE LINES

Don't expect any. This is a wander-around-at-your-own pace kind of place. See "Sports," below, for scuba, snorkeling, and fishing excursions you can arrange through local agencies.

ON YOUR OWN: WITHIN WALKING DISTANCE

Everything is within walking distance of the dock. **Fort Napoléon** looms over Le Bourg's picturesque bay. The French started building this stone bastion after they regained Les Saintes from the British in 1815 but didn't complete it until 1867. Today it houses engaging, detailed exhibits that cover the entire history of the islands, including life before Columbus, European expansion into the New World, early French settlements, the Battle of Les Saintes, and the development of the fishing industry. You can wander through barracks, dungeons, and the grounds, which feature an impressive array of cacti and succulents. Keep an eye out for the resident iguanas (the locals have given them such names as Victor Hugo and Voltaire), as well as harmless snakes and turtledoves. Pick up the English-language brochure that describes the vegetation when you purchase your admission ticket; adult admission is about $2.80, children under 12 pay $1.40. For 80¢, you can rent a cassette that provides excellent English commentary as you walk through the museum. The fort is open a brief 3½ hours a day, from 9am to 12:30pm, so make it your first destination.

On the hill that leads to Fort Napoléon, visit **Jerome Hoff,** a fourth-generation Santois of Alsatian ancestry who paints religious icons in a heartfelt but slightly disturbing style. He has the wild-eyed air of a John the Baptist, but he's a gentle man, retired now, who loves to talk about his 50 years of singing in the church choir. You can't miss his modest home and studio—they're surrounded by numerous quirky signs that feature colorful saints and passionate prayers.

On the route to the tourism office and the ATM, you'll pass Le Bourg's **stone church.** It's humble, but worth the couple of minutes it takes to peek inside.

If you're up for some hiking, the **Trace des Crêtes trail** traces the spine of one of Terre-de-Haut's hills just north of the airport and offers remarkable views of beaches, cliffs, and neighboring islands. Although clearly marked, the path is rocky and challenging—you have an advantage if you're part goat. Wear sunscreen and bring water.

Be sure to stop for a few minutes at the **cemetery** next to the airport. You'll notice several graves adorned with conch shells, which signify a sea-related death. On Saturday nights, refrigerator-size speakers are brought in, makeshift food stands are set up, and the cemetery becomes a huge open-air disco. In the same vicinity, **Le Calvaire** is a giant Christ statue at the summit of a hill; numerous steps ascend to great panoramas.

Chameau means camel in French, and with a bit of imagination you can see that **Le Chameau,** the highest point on Terre-de-Haut, looks sort of like the hump of a dromedary. The concrete road to the 300m (1,000-ft.) summit is off-limits to all motorized vehicles, and, mercifully, it's shaded much of the way. After 30 to 60 minutes of arduous climbing, you're rewarded with spectacular views of the entire archipelago, Guadeloupe, and Dominica. **Tour Vigie,** a military lookout dating from the time of Napoleon, crowns the mountain; unfortunately, it's usually locked.

SHOPPING

Little boutiques that sell beachwear, T-shirts, jewelry, and knickknacks line the streets. Stop by Pascal Foy's **Kaz an Nou Gallery** behind the church. You can watch him make Cases Creoles, miniature carved wooden Creole houses in candy colors. They're becoming collector's items. **Galerie Martine Cotten,** at the foot of the dock, features the work of an artist originally from Brittany who celebrates the natural beauty and fishing traditions of Les Saintes. Beyond the

Frommer's Favorite Les Saintes Experiences

Meandering Around Fort Napoléon: The French built this impressive stone fortification after they regained Les Saintes in 1815, and today it houses engaging, detailed exhibits covering the entire history of the islands. (See "On Your Own: Within Walking Distance," above.)

Trekking to the Top of Le Chameau: The highest point on Terre-de-Haut, Le Chameau is located in the southern part of the island and offers a tough (though shaded) 30- to 60-minute climb, for which you're rewarded with spectacular views. (See "On Your Own: Within Walking Distance," above.)

Sunbathing on Picture-Perfect Pompierre Beach: No beach on Terre-de-Haut is nicer than Plage de Pompierre, located only a 15-minute walk from the dock. (See "Beaches," below.)

town hall, **Ultramarine** is a tiny cottage where you can buy unusual dolls, clothes, T-shirts, and handcrafted items from France, Haiti, and Africa. **Galerie Marchande Seaside,** a group of shops situated around a patio, is just up the street after you turn right from the pier. Art, gifts, antiques, jewelry, lace, beachwear, and ice cream are available.

BEACHES
Beaches with golden sand are tucked away in almost all of the island's coves. Calm, crescent-shaped **Plage de Pompierre** (sometimes spelled Pont Pierre) is shaded by sea-grape bushes, as well as almond and palm trees. A 15-minute walk from the dock, it boasts soft white sand, shade from coconut palms, and quiet seclusion. The gentle water in the cliff-encircled cove is a stunning aquamarine. Because the bay is a nature preserve, fishing and anchoring are prohibited. It's the island's most popular sunbathing spot, so your best bet is to go early or late.

Secluded on the western coast, **Anse Crawen** is the unofficial nudist beach. Nudity is officially banned, but enforcement is sporadic and fines are inconsistent—anywhere from $20 to $100-plus, which makes the whole deal look like a police-sanctioned scam. You'll probably see nude bodies on other beaches too; they're usually found next to the signs that forbid nude bathing. **Grande Anse,** near the airfield, is large, but there's no shade, and the rough surf has a strong undertow. Although swimming is discouraged, the cliffs at either end of the beach and the powerful breakers make for a dramatic seascape. The usually deserted **Figuier,** on the southern coast, has excellent snorkeling.

SPORTS
FISHING   Going out to sea with a local fisherman is one way to experience Les Saintes' nautical heritage. Most of the local sailors will be delighted to take you out, if you can communicate well enough to negotiate a price. Most fishermen are stationed next to the cruise ship dock; just follow the waterfront to the fishing boats.

SCUBA, SNORKELING & OTHER WATERSPORTS   For scuba diving and snorkeling, go to **La Dive Bouteille Centre Nautique des Saintes** (© 590/99-54-25; www.divebouteille.com) at the Plage de la Colline west of town past

---

Tips **The Goats of Love**

Don't leave anything unattended while swimming at Plage de Pompierre. Savvy goats hide out in the scrub behind the beach, patiently scoping out the action. Once you go into the water, they'll make a beeline for your unattended picnic basket and treat themselves to anything edible. They're especially fond of those tourments d'amour you just bought at the dock. Who's crying now?

---

the market, or **UCPA** (© **590/99-54-94**), on the other side of Fort Napoléon hill in Marigot Bay. One-tank dives run about $40. Both also rent sea kayaks and windsurfing equipment.

GREAT LOCAL RESTAURANTS & BARS

Virtually every restaurant in Terre-de-Haut offers seafood that couldn't be fresher, and many feature Creole dishes. A local favorite is smoked kingfish (*thazard fumé*). **L'Auberge Les Petits Saints aux Anarcadiers** (© **590/99-50-99**) is a hillside veranda restaurant overlooking the bay. On Route de Rodrigue, it boasts a tropical garden and countless antiques. The terrace restaurant at the **Hôtel Bois Joli** (© **590/99-50-38**), on the island's western tip, offers a view of Pain de Sucre, Les Saintes' petite version of Rio de Janeiro's Sugarloaf Mountain, and is fringed with palm trees. For pasta, pizza, or salad, try **La Saladerie's** seaside terrace on the way to Fort Napoléon. **Le Génois** (© **590/99-53-01**), yet another waterfront option (30m/100 ft. from the dock; turn left), is popular with yachties, who can dock right at the restaurant. The salads here are named after legendary sailboats, while the pizzas pay tribute to local beaches. **Café de la Marine** (© **590/99-53-78**), on the bay and main street, serves thin-crusted pizzas and seafood. One of the island's best bakeries (*boulangeries*), **Le Fournil de Jimmy** (© **590/99-88-12**), is on the same square as the town hall, across from the tourist office. If you stop in at the right time, you can get a crusty baguette hot from the oven. If you'd rather have something cold, try one of the Italian gelati at **Tropico Gelato.** Turn right off the dock; it's a couple of storefronts down on your right.

20 Martinique

Fairy-tale romance and horrific disaster: Who could resist such an enticing combination? As if being the birthplace and childhood home of Empress Joséphine, sweetheart and wife of Napoleon, weren't enough, Martinique mesmerizes with the epic tragedy that befell St. Pierre one fair day in 1902: bustling cosmopolitan capital one minute, devastated volcanic graveyard of 30,000 souls the next. Love and death make quite a one-two punch, but they're just the hook. Look a bit deeper to appreciate Martinique's subtler attractions—quaint seaside villages, colonial ruins, and captivatingly beautiful rain forests and beaches.

"Madiana," or "island of flowers," was the Carib name for the island, and hibiscus, bougainvillea, and bird of paradise grow in lush profusion alongside mango, pineapple, banana, and papaya. Like Guadeloupe and St. Barts, Martinique is as French as Bordeaux, and you'll find everything from baguettes to Balenciaga here. But with African and New World roots forever entwined, Créole cuisine and traditions continue to flourish.

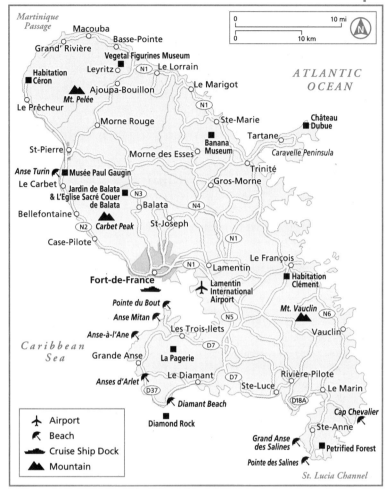

Martinique Passage

Macouba
Basse-Pointe
Grand' Rivière
Vegetal Figurines Museum
Le Lorrain
Leyritz
Habitation Céron
N1
Ajoupa-Bouillon
Le Marigot
Mt. Pelée
Le Prêcheur
Morne Rouge
Ste-Marie
N1
Château Dubuc
St-Pierre
Banana Museum
Morne des Esses
Tartane
Caravelle Peninsula
Anse Turin
Musée Paul Gaugin
Trinité
Le Carbet
Gros-Morne
Jardin de Balata & L'Eglise Sacré Couer de Balata
N3
Balata
N4
Bellefontaine
Carbet Peak
St-Joseph
N2
Case-Pilote
N1
Fort-de-France
N1
Lamentin
Le François
Lamentin International Airport
Habitation Clément
Pointe du Bout
Anse Mitan
N5
Mt. Vauclin
N6
Anse-à-l'Ane
Les Trois-Ilets
Vauclin
Caribbean Sea
Grande Anse
D7
La Pagerie
Anses d'Arlet
Le Diamant
D7
Rivière-Pilote
Le Marin
D37
Ste-Luce
D18A
Diamant Beach
Cap Chevalier
Diamond Rock
Ste-Anne
Grand Anse des Salines
Petrified Forest
Pointe des Salines

ATLANTIC OCEAN

St. Lucia Channel

✈ Airport
🏹 Beach
🚢 Cruise Ship Dock
🏔 Mountain

0   10 mi
0   10 km

About 80km (50 miles) long and 35km (22 miles) wide, the island features a diverse topography. Rain forests drape the volcanic mountains of the north; small, rounded hills and enclosed valleys mark the central plain; and white-sand beaches ring the arid, flat south.

Martinique's first inhabitants, Stone Age hunter-gatherers, probably arrived 4,000 years ago. These proto-Martinicans were long gone by 100 B.C. when the more sophisticated Arawaks settled the island. Caribs, who annihilated the Arawaks by A.D. 700, still lived on Martinique in 1502, when Columbus arrived and waxed rhapsodic: "This is the most wonderful, the most fertile, the sweetest, the most equable, the most charming land in the world." The gold-seeking Spaniards were less impressed and never colonized the island. That was left to the French, who arrived in 1635. After systematically killing or driving off the Caribs, the French began importing slaves from Africa to work the sugar fields. Enduring more than a hundred years of bondage, the slaves were liberated after the French Revolution in 1789, but the reprieve was brief: Napoleon reinstated slavery, and the chains and manacles weren't permanently broken until 1848. During the 18th and 19th centuries, France and England constantly vied for European preeminence, and the islands of the Caribbean became pawns in a game of geopolitical chess. As a result, Martinique was twice briefly occupied by the British. After abolition, indentured servants from India added to the cultural mix. In 1902, the eruption of Mount Pelée destroyed St. Pierre, the island's commercial and cultural capital, and power shifted south to Fort-de-France. In 1946, Martinique became an overseas department of France, and in 1974, it achieved regional status—the French minister of the interior appoints a prefect, but the island's citizens elect representatives to the national legislature in Paris and the regional legislature in Fort-de-France.

Most of Martinique's 380,000 residents are descendants of African slaves, but others of European, Asian, and Middle Eastern ancestry add to the melting pot. Attesting to the generally amicable relations among the various peoples, every shade of skin color is represented.

COMING ASHORE Most cruise ships dock in the heart of Fort-de-France, at the **Pointe Simon Cruise Dock,** which has quays for two large vessels. Because Martinique is a popular port of call, ships also dock at the Passenger Terminal at the **main harbor,** a cargo port on the north side of the bay, a $10 cab ride from the center of town.

If you want to check your e-mail, go to **Le Web Cyber Café,** upstairs at 4 Rue Blénac (© **596/70-31-62**), where being online will set you back about $3.50 for 15 minutes—cheaper than aboard ship. It's open every day except Sunday, starting at 9am. Ask for an American keyboard unless you're familiar with the substantially different character placement on French keyboards.

LANGUAGE **French** is Martinique's official language, but you can get by with English at most restaurants and tourist sites. You'll also hear the island patois, **Créole,** on the street. Because many of the island's service employees work hard to improve their English, cruisers who speak no French find Martinique easier to navigate than Guadeloupe, the other big French Caribbean island. Ask for English-language brochures and commentaries when sightseeing; most sites have them.

CURRENCY Martinique is an overseas region of France, so the **Euro** (€) is now the official currency (exchange rate: €1 = U.S.90¢; U.S.$1 = €1.10). Notes are denominated in 500, 200, 100, 50, 20, 10, and 5 euros; coins come in 1 and 2 euro and 50, 20, 10, 5, 2, and 1 cent denominations. There are numerous **ATMs** (*distributeur de billets*) in downtown Fort-de-France, and you'll have no trouble using your credit cards and traveler's checks. You can change money at **Change Caraïbe** (© **596/60-28-40**), 4 Rue Ernest Deproge, on the waterfront, or 1 block inland at **Change Point Change** (© **596/63-80-33**), 14 Rue Victor Hugo.

INFORMATION The **Office du Tourisme,** on Boulevard Alfassa, on the waterfront in downtown Fort-de-France (© **596/63-79-60**), is open Monday through Friday 8am to 5pm, and Saturday from 8am to noon. For info before you go, contact the Martinique Promotion Bureau in the U.S. (© **800/391-4909;** www.martinique.org).

CALLING FROM THE U.S. When calling Martinique from the U.S., dial the international access code (011) and 596 before the numbers listed here. The numbers listed here already begin with 596, but an effort by the French telephone authorities to standardize procedures requires that you dial those three digits twice.

GETTING AROUND

BY TAXI Travel by taxi is convenient but expensive. Few cabs are metered, so agree on a price before getting in. Taxis wait for ships at the cruise pier, and several English-speaking drivers give tours of the island for roughly $40 an hour for up to four passengers. For a radio taxi, call © **596/63-63-62.**

BY BUS For trips beyond Fort-de-France, collective taxi-minibuses are a cheap but iffy alternative. These privately owned minivans (look for the TC sign) generally seat eight and have flexible routes and unpredictable schedules. Often crowded and sometimes less than comfortable, they're widely used by adventurous tourists nonetheless, particularly those who speak some French. The reason? Price: A one-way ride to Grande Anse des Salines beach is about $5. Vans leave from a parking lot at Pointe Simon, in the heart of Fort-de-France.

BY RENTAL CAR Martinique's size and myriad attractions make renting a car especially worthwhile. Roads are in excellent condition and almost always scenic. You need a valid driver's license and must be at least 21. **Avis, Budget, Hertz,** and **National** all have offices here.

BY FERRY To reach La Pagerie (Empress Joséphine's birthplace), the island's golf course, horseback-riding stables, and the resort area of Pointe du Bout, take one of the blue ferries operated by **Somatour** (© **596/73-05-53**) from Quai d'Esnambuc, east of the cruise dock, in Fort-de-France. The trip across the bay takes 15 minutes, and round-trip tickets are $6 per person. Boats leave at least once an hour.

SHORE EXCURSIONS OFFERED BY THE CRUISE LINES

Golf at the Country Club of Martinique ($115, 6 hr.): The 18-hole, par-71 course in Trois Ilets, designed by Robert Trent Jones, is both challenging and picturesque, with 6,072m (6,640 yd.) of twisting fairways and fast greens. Transportation, greens fees (for 18 holes), and a golf cart are included; lunch is not. (See "Sports," later in this section, for more details on the course.)

St. Pierre and Rain Forest Drive ($59, 4 hr.): Drive through Martinique's lush rain forest, visit a butterfly farm and botanical park among the ruins of the island's first sugar plantation, and then explore the ruins of St. Pierre, devastated by Mount Pelée's eruption in 1902. On the drive back to Fort-de-France, make a quick stop at the church of Balata, a replica of Paris's Sacred Heart (Sacré Coeur) Basilica.

Martinique Snorkeling ($49, 2½ hr.): Across the bay from Fort-de-France, the reef at Anse Dufour offers excellent snorkeling for experts and novices. The reef is filled with marine animals, including French grunts, blackbar soldierfish, and silversides. Snorkeling equipment is provided, as are professional instruction, supervision, and transportation.

EXCURSIONS OFFERED BY LOCAL AGENCIES

Adventure Excursions & Hiking: Martinique's lush, mountainous northern half provides myriad adventure opportunities. **Aventures Tropicales** (© **596/ 64-58-49**), based in Fort-de-France, is the island's premier adventure tour operator, offering canyoning and river-crossing in a tropical rain forest, kayaking through mangroves to uninhabited islands, hiking up Mount Pelée, and a 4WD tour through rivers, rain forests, and banana plantations. Prices vary depending on activity but generally range from $35 to $45, and some excursions require a minimum number of participants. Make arrangements before arriving on the

Frommer's Favorite Martinique Experiences

Touring "Pompeii of the Caribbean": Mount Pelée erupted in 1902, killing all but one of St. Pierre's 30,000 residents. See the havoc this not-yet-dormant volcano wreaked on the town's church, theater, and other buildings, and view smaller relics at the volcano museum. (See "On Your Own: Beyond the Port Area," below.)

Traveling Back to the 17th Century: The estate ruins at Habitation Céron, near the island's northern Caribbean coast, are enormously evocative of early colonial times, when sugar was king. The old stone plantation buildings are covered with moss, and the wild gardens abound with lush vegetation and singing birds. (See "On Your Own: Beyond the Port Area," below.)

island. **Syndicat d'Initiative,** Grand Rivière (② 596/55-72-74), will guide you on the island's most popular hike, a 19km (12-mile), 6-hour trek through the forest reserve between Le Prêcheur, the northernmost town on Martinique's Caribbean coast, and Grand Rivière, a fishing village on the northern Atlantic tip of the island. Walking's the only way to get from one town to the other: No roads connect them. The trail encompasses dry and tropically humid forests, rivers, waterfalls, and unspoiled beaches. Advance arrangements are required, and the hike is limited to healthy, experienced trekkers. The $35 fee includes a professional guide, lunch, and drinks.

Horseback Treks: Pros and novices are both accommodated on morning horseback rides offered by **Ranch Jack,** Morne Habitué, Trois Ilets (② 596/68-37-69). The daily promenades pass over hills, through fields, and onto beaches, as guides provide a running commentary on the history, fauna, and botany of the island. Transportation to and from the cruise dock can be arranged. The price of a half-day excursion with refreshments is about $45.

See "Sports," later in this section, for **scuba and snorkeling.**

ON YOUR OWN: WITHIN WALKING DISTANCE
Fort-de-France is a bustling, cosmopolitan town with 100,000 residents and an unmistakable French air. Part New Orleans, part French Riviera, it's full of ochre buildings, ornate wrought-iron balconies, cascading flowers, and tall palm trees. The town's narrow streets, cluttered with boutiques and cafes, climb from the bowl of the sea to the surrounding hills, forming a great urban amphitheater. There's plenty here to keep you busy.

At the eastern end of downtown, **La Savane** is a broad formal park with palms, mangoes, and manicured lawns, perfect for a promenade or rest in the shade. Its most famous feature is the **Statue of Empress Joséphine,** carved in 1858 by Vital Dubray. Like a variation on the Venus de Milo, this white marble empress is headless: Napoleon's Little Créole was unceremoniously decapitated and doused with red paint in 1995 by locals who remembered her role in reinstating slavery on the island in the early 1800s.

Across the street at 21 Rue de la Liberté, the **Bibliothèque Schoelcher** (Schoelcher Library; ② 596/70-26-67) is one of Fort-de-France's great Belle Epoque buildings. Named in honor of Victor Schoelcher, one of France's most influential abolitionists, this elaborate structure, designed by French architect Henri Pick, was first displayed at the 1889 Paris Exposition. Four years later, the red-and-blue Romanesque portal, Egyptian lotus-petal columns, iron-and-glass cupola, and multicolored tiles were dismantled and then reassembled piece by piece at the present site. The interior light, mosaics, and tile floor are glorious. The proud repository of Schoelcher's 10,000-volume book collection, as well as an impressive archive of colonization, slavery, and emancipation documents, it's open Monday through Saturday. There's no admission charge.

Another Henri Pick masterpiece, **St. Louis Cathedral,** on Rue Victor Schoelcher at Rue Blénac (© 596/73-59-78), was built in 1895. A contemporary of Gustave Eiffel (of Eiffel Tower fame), Pick used massive iron beams to support the walls, ceiling, and spire. A grand example of Industrial Revolution architecture, it's been likened to a Catholic railway station. The organ, stained-glass windows, and ornamented interior walls are well worth a look and can be viewed every morning except Saturday.

Built in 1640, **Fort St. Louis,** Boulevard Alfassa (© 596/60-54-59), dominates the rocky promontory east of La Savane. A noteworthy example of 17th- and 18th-century military architecture, it first defended Fort-de-France in 1674 against Dutch invaders; beginning in 1762, it was the site of numerous battles between French and English forces. Today, the bastion remains the French navy's headquarters in the Caribbean. Guided tours leave daily every 30 minutes beginning at 9:30am. Bring a picture ID. The entrance fee, payable in dollars, is $5 for adults, $2.50 for students.

The best of Fort-de-France's many museums, the **Musée Départemental Archéologie Precolombienne Préhistoire,** 9 Rue de la Liberté (© 596/71-57-05), traces 2,000 years of Martinique's pre-Columbian past with more than a thousand relics from the Arawak and Carib cultures. Spread over three floors, the detailed exhibits document various pottery and tool styles, burial practices, agricultural methods, social and religious customs, and changes that occurred after the arrival of Europeans. Across the street from La Savane, it's open Monday to Friday from 8am to 5pm, and Saturday from 9am to noon. Admission is about $3 for adults, $2 for students, and 75¢ for children. The tiny gift stand sells pottery reproductions.

A less established museum, the **Musée du Carnaval** (© 596/73-49-07), next to the cruise terminal on Rue des Gabares, focuses on the history, costumes, and traditions of Martinique's unique version of Carnaval—pajama parades, drag marriages, junkyard jump-ups, and decorated jalopies, to name a few. English-speaking guides help you navigate the tiny museum, which is open Tuesday through Friday from 9am to 4pm, and on Saturday from 9am to noon. Admission is about $3 for adults, $2 for students, and 75¢ for kids under 12.

ON YOUR OWN: BEYOND THE PORT AREA

Martinique is much too large to tackle in a single day. You'll have to make some tough choices about which of its many museums, plantations, floral parks, and natural wonders to visit. Here are three suggested itineraries for the day.

NORTH OF FORT-DE-FRANCE; CARIBBEAN COAST Less than 8km (5 miles) north of Fort-de-France, on the scenic Route de la Trace (Rte. N3), **L'Eglise Sacré Coeur de Balata** overlooks the capital and its bay. This quiet village church is anything but typical: Built in 1924, it's a one-fifth–scale replica of the wedding-cake–pretty Sacré Coeur Basilica that crowns Montmartre in Paris.

Rather than the white stone of the Paris original, this unintentionally whimsical copy uses gray freestone.

Martinique's Carib name, Madiana, means "island of flowers." To see what the Caribs were talking about, stroll through the **Jardin de Balata** (© **596/64-48-73**). Just minutes north of the Sacré Coeur church, this lush, Edenic garden showcases 200 species of plants, trees, and tropical flowers, including towering ferns, lotuses, alpinias, porcelain roses, anthuriums, and heliconias. The hillside oasis, which boasts resident hummingbirds, frogs, and lizards, is open daily from 9am to 5pm. Admission is about $6 for adults, $2.50 for kids under 12.

Yes, it's hot outside, but things could be worse. One of Martinique's must-see attractions, the village of **St. Pierre** on the northwest coast, was the cultural and economic capital of Martinique until 8am on May 8, 1902, when Mount Pelée, the hulking volcano that dominates the northern tip of the island, exploded in fire and lava. Three minutes later, all but 1 of St. Pierre's 30,000 inhabitants had been incinerated, buried in ash and lava, or asphyxiated by poisonous gas. The town once hailed as the "Paris of the Antilles" and the "Pearl of the West Indies" because of its beautiful buildings, imposing residences, and lively theaters suddenly became "the Pompeii of the Caribbean." It never regained its splendor, and today it's no more than a sleepy fishing village, home to fewer than 5,000 souls. Ruins of a church, theater, and other buildings punctuate the town, memorials to St. Pierre's former glory and the horrific fury of Pelée. In lieu of walking from one ruin to another, you can hop on the rubber-wheeled trolley known as the **Cyparis Express,** which departs from the Musée Volcanologique (see below). The 50-minute tours operate Monday to Friday from 10:30am to 1pm and from 2:30 to 7pm, departing once an hour, more or less. The fee is about $7 for adults, half that for kids. (The trolley is named in honor of Cyparis, a prisoner locked behind thick cell walls, who was the sole human to survive the eruption. Found in his dungeon 4 days after the disaster, he later toured with P. T. Barnum's circus, showing his burn scars to curious folks around North America.)

The town's touristic potential hasn't been grotesquely exploited: Aside from the ruins, the only other point of interest is the **Musée Volcanologique,** Rue Victor Hugo (© **596/78-15-16**). Founded by American volcanologist Franck A. Perret, this one-room exhibit traces the story of the cataclysm through pictures and relics excavated from the debris, including petrified spaghetti, lava-encrusted teapots, twisted musical instruments, a human skull, and distorted clocks that stopped at the hour of destruction. Open daily from 9am to 5pm, it charges adults about $1.50; children under 8 enter free.

Part sugar-plantation ruins, part tropical paradise, **Habitation Céron** (© **596/52-94-53**) is the most evocative of Martinique's historical agricultural sites. This sprawling 17th-century estate, 15 minutes north of St. Pierre, is almost as wild and tranquil as the surrounding rain forest, but its verdigris cisterns, moss-covered stone buildings, and archaic, still functioning water mill are all haunted with the ghosts of a time when sugar was king, slaves toiled in the heat, and French colonists lived in languid comfort. Traversed by a rushing stream that's still harnessed to operate the mill, the immense grounds feature centuries-old trees, exuberant foliage that cascades down hillsides, and a variety of birds, including hawks, quail doves, hummingbirds, and bananaquits. Aside from its importance as Martinique's first sugar plantation, Céron is historically significant because Madame de Maintenon, who secretly wed France's King Louis XIV in the late 1600s, lived in the area for several years. The site is open daily from 9:30am to 5pm. Self-guided tours of the estate cost $5.50. The on-site restaurant, housed in former slave quarters, serves crayfish, octopus, and other seafood.

A few miles south of St. Pierre, **Le Carbet** is where Columbus landed in 1502, the first French settlers arrived in 1635, and the French painter Paul Gauguin lived for 5 months in 1887. Too ill to return to France after a failed quest for "noble savages" in Panama, the artist wrote that "only in Martinique was I able to feel truly myself." An unassuming museum devoted to Gauguin and his Martinican works, the **Musée Paul Gauguin,** Anse Turin (© 596/78-22-66), sits not far from the hut the painter once occupied. It boasts no original paintings, but it does have reproductions of the dozen pictures he composed on the island, precursors of his later, more famous Tahitian works. Other items on display include biographical texts and whiny, self-pitying letters he wrote to his wife back in France. Other exhibits include Créole costumes and contemporary island art. The museum has extensive English commentary and is open daily from 9am to 5:30pm. Admission is about $3 for adults, 75¢ for children under 10, and free for those under 8.

NORTH OF FORT-DE-FRANCE; ATLANTIC COAST   Looking for decorating ideas? **Habitation Clément** (© 596/54-62-07), a beautifully maintained 19th-century Créole estate, features room after room of West and East Indian colonial furniture. The stately home itself, with Antillean louvered windows, beamed ceilings, and hardwood and painted-tile floors, exemplifies the comfort enjoyed by bourgeois landowners during the plantation era. The furniture is better than you'll see in an episode of *Antiques Roadshow.* Styles range from Martinican colonial to Louis XV, Louis Phillipe, and William IV. Don't miss the soaring locust-wood bedposts carved with lotus motifs or the mahogany roll-top desk. Just outside the Atlantic coast town of Le François, due east of Fort-de-France, the estate is open daily from 9am to 6pm. Admission is $6.50 for adults, $3.75 for kids under 12, and includes self-guided tours of the home, the on-site rum distillery, and the surrounding gardens.

Like a lonely exile, **Château Dubuc** (© 596/58-09-00) stands at the eastern tip of the Presqu'île de la Caravelle, a craggy peninsula that juts eastward into the Atlantic Ocean, just south of La Trinité. In 1657, 18-year-old Pierre Dubuc left Normandy to fight Caribs in Martinique. For his valiant service, the French crown awarded him the remarkably isolated peninsula. First settled in 1671, the land was cultivated with sugar cane, but its greater value was as a depot for illicit trade in slaves and contraband. Devastating hurricanes and battles with the English hastened the abandonment of the estate in 1770. Today, the plantation ruins are most interesting for their antiquity (they're the oldest on the island) and location, high above the protected waters of Treasure Bay. Admission to the ruins and tiny museum, which are open daily from 8:30am to 6pm, is $2.25 for adults, 75¢ for children. If you have time, descend the well-marked trail to the calm, deserted beach below. The entire area is protected as a nature reserve.

Given a choice, simians skip the historical ruins and swing on over to the **Banana Museum,** farther up the coast just outside Ste. Marie (© 596/69-45-52). Few visitors have the patience to read all the information displayed here (ask for the mercifully abbreviated English guide), but you'll learn interesting tidbits that are sure to make you a hit at the next cocktail party: Did you know that banana trees grow up to 9m (30 ft.) a year? That they're actually giant ferns, not trees? That one variety has purple-and-green zebra-striped leaves? Armed with your new-found intelligence, stroll along the meandering pathway through a functioning banana plantation, view old Créole shacks, and get acquainted with some living examples of the plant's many varieties. The museum is open daily from 9am to 5pm (to 1pm on Sun during the low season). Admission is $4.50 for adults, $2.25 for kids under 12.

After the mentally taxing exhibits of the Banana Museum, you may just want to veg out. The offbeat **Vegetal Figurines Museum** is just the place to do it. Tucked away in a room behind the front desk of the **Hotel Plantation de Leyritz** near Basse Pointe (© **596/78-53-92**), this strange collection features 70 human figures made from fruit peels, wild mushrooms, flower petals, leaves, and almost any other plant material imaginable. A poor man's Madame Tussaud's, the museum's masterworks include Marie Antoinette, Queen Elizabeth, flappers, and angels, each half a meter (a couple of feet) tall. The sheer ingenuity of the artist is sure to make any craft-lover gaga. How do you make vegetal stiletto heels, fans, wings, and parasols look so convincing? And what attitudes these dolls have! With the drop-dead chic of a runway model, they're downright intimidating. But wait, they're just dead plants. This palace of quirkiness is open daily from 8am to 6pm, and it's free.

SOUTH OF FORT-DE-FRANCE Marie Josèphe Rose Tascher de la Pagerie was born in 1763 in the quaint little village of **Trois Ilets,** across the bay from Fort-de-France. As Joséphine, she became the wife of Napoleon Bonaparte in 1796 and Empress of France in 1804. Although reviled by some historians as ruthless and selfish, she's revered by some on Martinique as having been uncommonly gracious. Others, however, blame her for Napoleon's reintroduction of slavery. A small museum, the **Musée de la Pagerie** (© **596/68-33-06**), sits in the former estate kitchen building, where Joséphine gossiped with her slaves. Displays include the bed that she slept in until she departed for France at age 16, portraits of her and of Napoleon, invitations to Parisian balls, bills attesting to her extravagance as the empress, and letters, the most notable being a passionate missive from lovelorn Napoleon. The plantation house itself was destroyed in a hurricane, but the kitchen and partially restored ruins of the sugar mill and church remain (the latter is in the village itself). The museum is open Tuesday through Sunday from 9am to 5:30pm, and an English-speaking guide is usually on hand. Admission is about $3 for adults, 75¢ for children under 16. The nearby **Parc des Floralies** (© **596/68-34-50**) displays more than a hundred species of flowers, trees, and greenery, as well as aviaries housing exotic birds. It's open from 8:30am to 5pm Monday through Friday, and from 9:30am to 5:30pm on weekends. Admission is just over $2 for adults, about 85¢ for kids.

Diamond Rock, a craggy multifaceted protrusion in the bay south of Trois Ilets, not only resembles a diamond, but was once the jewel in the crown of the British Caribbean fleet. The British and French fought on so many fronts during the early 19th century that ships were sometimes in short supply. Only one ship was assigned to blockade the ports of Martinique, St. Pierre in the north and Fort-de-France in the south. Short of ships but not imagination, the British proclaimed Diamond Rock a man-of-war and proceeded to equip the islet with guns. No temporary gesture, it remained in service for 2 years. Birds have replaced Brits as the primary residents. On a misty day, the rock looks more like the Loch Ness Monster emerging from the depths than a diamond.

Just east of Diamond Rock, the **Anse Caffard Memorial** commemorates the 46 slaves who perished in an 1830 shipwreck just off the coast. The memorial's 15 human figures, with heads bowed and shoulders slumped, look out from the lonely, grass-covered hillside to the sea and Diamond Rock below. Grouped in triangular formation, signifying the Europe-Africa-America slave-trade axis, the somber white stones are reminiscent of the huge stone heads of Easter Island and every bit as haunting.

You'll have passed through a number of quaint coastal villages by this time but none sweeter than **Ste. Luce.** Absurdly picturesque with its blindingly white stucco walls, red-tile roofs, turquoise sea, and multicolored fishing boats, this town is pure sun-drenched maritime serenity. Swim or snorkel off the small, pleasant beach, meditate on horizon-dominating Diamond Rock, or check out the village boutiques and cafes. For an unhurried taste of French island life, this as good a place as any to spend the day.

If you spell vacation b-e-a-c-h and have no desire to soak up French ambience, cut to the chase and head for Martinique's best strand, **Grande Anse des Salines.** Stretching as far as the eye can sea, these white sands are at the island's southern tip, about an hour from Fort-de-France (see "Beaches," below).

SHOPPING

Martinique offers a good selection of French luxury items—perfumes, fashionable clothing, luggage, crystal, and dinnerware—at prices that can be as much as 30% to 40% lower than those in the States. Unfortunately, because some luxury goods, including jewelry, are subject to a hefty value-added tax, the savings are ultimately less compelling. Paying in dollar-denominated traveler's checks or credit cards is sometimes good for a 20% discount. The main shopping district in Fort-de-France is bounded by Rue Ernest Deproge (on the waterfront), La Savane, Rue Lamartine, and Rue de la République, with Rue Victor Hugo being the single most important stretch. Martinican goods, such as rum, Créole jewelry, madras fabric, folk paintings, and hand-woven baskets, are good buys and more representative of the island. The **open-air market** in La Savane, at Rue de la Liberté and Rue Ernest Deproge, has the best selection of these items. For sheer Caribbean color, stroll through the enclosed **vegetable and fruit market** on Rue Isambert near Rue Blénac; built in 1901, it's another work of architect Henri Pick. Stores generally open at 9am and close at 5pm; most close for lunch, usually between 1 and 3pm. On Saturdays, shops are open in the morning only; on Sundays virtually all are closed.

Duty-free divas invariably make **Roger Albert,** 7 Rue Victor Hugo (© 596/71-71-71), their first stop. This well-known outlet frequently has the best buys on French perfume, china, and crystal. **Cadet-Daniel,** 72 Rue Antoine Siger (© 596/71-41-48), is its chief competitor. Compare and save.

Centre des Métiers d'Art, Rue Ernest Deproge (© 596/70-25-01), near the tourist office, is one of the best arts-and-crafts stores in Martinique. Pass over the junk and focus on the more accomplished handmade items, including ceramics, painted fabrics, and patchwork quilts.

The French consider libations an art, and aficionados consider Martinican rum among the world's finest. **La Case à Rhum** (© 596/73-73-20), in the Galerie Marchande, 5 Rue de la Liberté, stocks all the local brands and allows sample nips to help you decide which bottle to buy. (FYI: White rum ferments in stainless-steel vats; golden rum is aged for at least a year in large oak casks; and old dark rum, which can be as satisfying as Cognac or Armagnac, ages in small oak casks for at least 3 years.)

If you find yourself across the bay in Pointe du Bout, stop by **La Belle Matadore,** Immeuble Vermeil Marina (midway between the La Pagerie Hôtel and the Méridien Hotel). This boutique takes the history and tradition of Créole jewelry seriously, and virtually every piece for sale replicates designs developed during slave days by *matadores* (prostitutes), midwives, and slaves.

Love to shop but hate the heat? Halfway between Fort-de-France and the Lamentin airport, and less than 20 minutes from the cruise dock by cab, **La Galleria** is Martinique's largest shopping mall. In air-conditioned, suburban comfort, you can browse through about a hundred clothing shops—Benetton, La Perla, Lacoste—shoe boutiques, department stores, and perfumeries (including a branch of Roger Albert). There are also a handful of cafes, a bakery or two selling Martinican and French pastries, and several ATMs. Open every day except Sunday, the mall opens at 9am.

BEACHES

Serious beach bunnies hop south of Fort-de-France to **Grand Anse des Salines,** widely regarded as Martinique's nicest strand. At the island's extreme southern tip, about an hour from the capital by car, it features coconut palm trees, views of Diamond Rock, and white sand that seems to go on for miles. During summer holidays and weekends, it's busy with families and children, but during the week, it's often quiet and uncrowded. Beachside stands offer refreshment. To get to the island's main **gay beach,** turn right at the entrance to Grand Anse des Salines and drive to the far end of the parking lot, near the sign for Petite Anse des Salines. Follow the path through the woods and then veer left till you find the quiet section with the good-looking guys.

Conveniently located across the bay from Fort-de-France, **Pointe du Bout** is Martinique's most lavish resort area. Aside from a marina and a variety of watersports, the area has some modest man-made white-sand beaches. The sandy, natural beaches at nearby **Anse Mitan** and **Anses d'Arlet** are popular with both swimmers and snorkelers.

Beaches north of Fort-de-France have mostly gray (they like to call it silver) volcanic sand. The best of the bunch is **Anse Turin,** just to the side of the main Caribbean coastal road, between St. Pierre and Le Carbet. Extremely popular with locals and shaded by palms, it's where Gauguin swam when he called the island home.

Martinique has no legal nudist beaches, but toplessness is as common here as anywhere in France. As a rule, public beaches lack changing cabins or showers, but hotel lockers and changing cabanas can be used by nonguests for a charge.

SPORTS

GOLF When Robert Trent Jones, Sr., designed **Golf de la Martinique** (✆ **596/68-32-81**) in 1976, he chose a picturesque, historic site: the seaside hills neighboring La Pagerie, the birthplace of Empress Joséphine. Thirty-two kilometers (20 miles) from Fort-de-France, this good, tough, 18-hole, 6,072m (6,640-yd.), par-71 course features emerald hills, swaying palms, constant vistas of the turquoise sea, and, thankfully, year-round trade winds that help keep things cool. The par-5 12th, with a dogleg to the right, is the most difficult hole. The fairway here is narrow, the green is long, and the wind, especially between December and April, is tricky. The 15th and 16th require shots over sea inlets. Facilities include a pro shop, a golf academy, a bar, a restaurant, and tennis courts. English-speaking pros are at your service. Greens fees and cart rental run about $75 for 18 holes, $40 for 9. A set of clubs is another $15.

SCUBA DIVING & SNORKELING Favorite dives in the coastal waters off Martinique include the caves and walls of Diamond Rock and the dozen ships sunk by the 1902 volcanic eruption at St. Pierre (the most popular wreck, the metal-hulled *Roraima,* was made famous by Jacques Cousteau and rests on a slant in 45m/150 ft. of water). For cruisers, the most convenient dive operators

Once, Twice, Three Times a Lady?

Everything is up-to-date in Martinique, so chances of seeing women in full traditional Créole garb are slim. You might run into someone wearing one of the colorful headscarves, though. If you do, count the number of knots in the cloth. One means she's single, two means she's engaged, and three means she's married. Four signifies that she's married but wouldn't necessarily let that stop her from having a good time.

are across the bay from Fort-de-France in Pointe du Bout. **Espace Plongée,** at the Hôtel Méridien (© **596/66-01-79**), and **Planète Bleue** (© **596/66-08-79**), based at the Pointe du Bout marina, are among the island's best operators. If you want to dive around St. Pierre, try **UCPA** (© **596/78-21-03**). Single-tank dives with all equipment run about $40. The waters of Pointe du Bout and nearby Anse Mitan and Anse Dufour are popular with snorkelers, as are the small bays of Sainte Anne and Anses d'Arlet on the southwest coast. Snorkeling equipment from on-site vendors runs about $10.

GREAT LOCAL RESTAURANTS & BARS

Hey, it's France: Expect great food. More than any other island in the French West Indies, Martinique gives French and Créole cuisine equal billing. If you're on a mission to sample the booze of every port of call, Martinique's **local beer** is Lorraine; Clement, De Paz, and Saint James are among the island's best **rums.** Too early in the day for demon rum? Slake your thirst with Didier, the Caribbean's only naturally carbonated spring water.

IN FORT-DE-FRANCE A small, elegant restaurant located in a beautiful 19th-century mansion in the hills above Fort-de-France, **La Belle Epoque,** Route de Didier (© **596/64-41-19**), serves exquisite classic French cuisine. The fixed-price lunch special, which includes an appetizer, a main course, and dessert, is a steal, costing less than $25. Enhanced by the languid, colonial atmosphere, the seafood ravioli in wine and lobster sauce and rum shrimp flambé are memorable. **Le Planteur,** 1 Rue de la Liberté, across the street from La Savane in the heart of town (© **596/63-17-45**), offers views of the park and bay. Try the flavorful cassoulet of minced conch or the seafood stew in cream sauce.

AT POINTE DU BOUT Just minutes by car from the resorts of Pointe du Bout, **La Villa Créole,** Anse Mitan (© **596/66-05-53**), serves down-home Créole staples such as *accras de morue* (codfish beignets), *boudin Créole* (Créole blood sausage), and *féroces* (avocado, codfish, and manioc hushpuppies). Don't leave your garden table without indulging in the chocolate fondant with bittersweet chocolate and pear sauce. The nearby **Au Poisson d'Or,** Anse Mitan (© **596/66-01-80**), a rustic roadside eatery, offers more Créole choices such as grilled conch in coconut milk and stewed shrimp.

NEAR ST. PIERRE Fifteen minutes north of St. Pierre, **Habitation Céron,** Anse Céron, Le Prêcheur (© **596/52-94-53**), a 17th-century sugar estate, offers Créole crayfish freshly harvested from the on-site farm. Fish, octopus, and vegetables straight from the garden are also served at the open-air, riverside tables. A few miles south of St. Pierre, on the beach in Le Carbet, **Le Trou Crabe,** Le

Coin (© **596/78-04-34**), serves grilled kingfish, vanilla crayfish, and a full repertoire of Créole treats. The giant aquarium and resident shark are sure to enthrall the kids.

BASSE POINTE If you opt for a day on Martinique's Atlantic coast, treat yourself to the artistry of one of the island's premiere old-style female Créole chefs. **Chez Mally,** Route de la Côte Atlantique, Basse Pointe (© **596/78-51-18**), operates from a modest house along the main road in the center of town. Grandmotherly Mally Edjam (increasingly with assistance from friends) is usually busy in the kitchen turning out delicacies, such as spicy stuffed land crab and a Créole version of pork curry.

21 Nevis

Off the beaten tourist track, south of St. Martin and north of Guadeloupe, Nevis is the junior partner in the combined Federation of St. Kitts and Nevis, which gained self-government from Britain in 1967 and became a totally independent nation in 1983. It's a stormy marriage, though: Nevis's 1998 referendum for separation from its larger partner failed by the slimmest of margins.

Though smaller than St. Kitts and lacking a major historical site like Brimstone Hill Fortress, Nevis is nevertheless the more appealing and upbeat of the two islands. When viewed from its sister island, about 3km (2 miles) away, Nevis appears to be a perfect cone, rising gradually to a height of 970m (3,232 ft.). Columbus first sighted the island in 1493, naming it Las Nieves, Spanish for "snows," because its peak reminded him of the Pyrenees. Settled by the British in 1628, the island became a prosperous sugar-growing island as well as the most popular spa island of the 18th century, when people flocked in from other West Indian islands to visit its hot mineral springs. Nevis's two most famous historical residents were **Admiral Horatio Nelson,** who married a local woman here in 1787, and **Alexander Hamilton,** who was born here and went on to find fame as a drafter of the American Federalist Papers, as George Washington's treasury secretary, and as Aaron Burr's unfortunate dueling partner. Today, the island's capital city, **Charlestown,** has a lovely mixture of port-town exuberance and small-town charm, and the popular **Pinney's Beach** is just a knockout.

COMING ASHORE Only small ships call on Nevis, docking right in the center of Charlestown and/or dropping anchor off the coast of Pinney's Bay Beach.

LANGUAGE **English** is the language of both islands.

CURRENCY The local currency is the **Eastern Caribbean dollar** (U.S.$1 = EC$2.70; EC$1 = U.S.37¢). Many shops and restaurants quote prices in U.S. dollars. Always determine which currency locals are talking about. We've used U.S.-dollar prices in this section.

INFORMATION There's a small tourist board office on Main Street, near the docks. If you want to collect additional information ahead of time, contact the tourist board office in the U.S. (© **866/55-NEVIS** or 212/535-1234; www.nevisisland.com).

CALLING FROM THE U.S. When calling St. Kitts or Nevis from the United States, you need dial only a "1" before the numbers listed here.

GETTING AROUND

BY TAXI The entirety of Charlestown is accessible on foot, but if you want to visit Pinney's Beach or elsewhere on the island, you can hop a taxi in

The map shows Nevis with the following labeled locations:

To St. Kitts · The Narrows · Newcastle Airport · Newcastle · Newcastle Beach · Mosquito Bay · Long Haul Bay · Oualie Beach · Fort Ashby · Cotton Ground · Pinney's Beach · Eden Brown Estate · Huggins Bay · ATLANTIC OCEAN · Nevis Peak · Charlestown · New River · Caribbean Cove · Hermitage Village · Bath · Fig Tree · White Bay · Montpelier · Gingerland · Botanical Garden · White Bay Beach · Saddle Hill · Indian Castle Beach · Caribbean Sea

Charlestown inset: Nevis Handcraft Cooperative Society · Jews' Burial Ground · Grove Park Cricket Ground · Governor's House · Government Rd · Pemberton Gift Shop · Police · Nelson Museum · Happy Hill Alley · Main St · Prince William St · Court House & Library · Craddock Rd · Chapel St · Island Rd · Alexander Hamilton Birthplace · Island Hopper · Prince Charles St · Cotton Ginnery · Market · Nevis Philatelic Bureau · Gallows Bay

Legend:
- ✈ Airport
- 🏖 Beach
- 🚢 Cruise Ship Dock
- ▲ Mountain

Charlestown. The cost to Pinney's is about $5.50. Taxi drivers double as guides on Nevis, so if you want to take a general tour of the island, negotiate a price with your driver.

BY RENTAL CAR   Because driving is on the left side in Nevis and most of the worthwhile sites are within walking distance or easily reached by taxi, we don't recommend renting a car here.

SHORE EXCURSIONS OFFERED BY THE CRUISE LINES

Few organized excursions are offered on Nevis. Some of the small-ship lines offer a day at Pinney's Beach as part of their regular visit, and might also offer hiking and snorkeling options, but the island is so small and easy to negotiate on your own that excursions aren't really necessary. If you want some local commentary, you can hire a taxi driver to give you an island tour. (See "Getting Around," above.)

ON YOUR OWN: WITHIN WALKING DISTANCE

If your ship docks in Charlestown, you're dead center of a perfect walking-tour opportunity. Charlestown is a lovely little place, laid back in somewhat the same manner as St. John, but with some of the really rural character of sister island St. Kitts.

If you head left from the docks and walk a little ways (maybe 0.5km/a quarter-mile) along Main Street, you'll come to the **Alexander Hamilton Birthplace**

Frommer's Favorite Nevis Experiences

Wandering Around Charlestown: The capital city is a fine place to wander around on your own, visiting the birthplace of American statesman Alexander Hamilton, the small but appealing Nelson Museum, and the 17th-century Jewish cemetery; poking your head into some of the small shops; or greeting the goats and chickens that wander past, evidently taking their own walking tours. (See "On Your Own: Within Walking Distance," below.)

Taking Some Downtime on Pinney's Beach: Lounge back, have a beer, take a swim in the reef-protected waters, do a little snorkeling, or engage in some beachcombing. Talk about relaxation. (See "Beaches," below.)

(© 869/469-5786; www.nevis-nhcs.org/nevishistory.html), where the road curves just before the turnoff to Island Road. It's a rustic little two-level house set right on the coastline. On the first floor is the **Museum of Nevis History** and gift shop (admission $2, $1 children under 12), but in all honesty you'll do just as well to skip it and just appreciate the outside, taking a moment to read the historic plaque. Far be it from us to take a couple bucks out of the island's economy, though, so if you're feeling philanthropic, drop your two bucks and then head on for the rest of your walk.

Backtracking along Main Street, you'll pass several serviceable if unremarkable shops (see "Shopping," below). Keep walking through the center of town, saying "hi" to the occasional mama goat and kids you'll pass, and then turn left onto Government Road. One block up on the left, you'll find the **Jews' Burial Ground,** with graves from 1684 to 1768. Stones left atop the graves attest to the visitors who have been there before you to pay their respects. When we were there, the dead were being entertained with reggae music coming from the doorway of a shop across the street, while a breeze stirred the few trees on the property. All in all, not a bad resting spot.

Backtrack to Main Street, turn left, and continue on past the Grove Park Cricket Ground, bearing left when the road forks. Head up the hill (where you'll see first an abandoned hotel and then several buildings standing alone on the hill to your right), and then turn at the first right, which will bring you back behind those buildings, the first of which is the inaccessible Government House and the second of which is the **Nelson Museum** (© 869/469-0408; www.nevis-nhcs. org/nelsonmuseum.html). A very small, very homemade kind of place, it's nevertheless an interesting and evocative spot, and well worth the $2 admission ($1 for children 12 and under). The museum traces the history of Admiral Horatio Nelson's career enforcing England's Navigation Acts in the Caribbean, and also houses artifacts from Nevis's Carib, Arawak, and Aceramic peoples; a small display on Nevis today; and a number of wonderful clay artworks, including a replica of the old "Coolie Man's Store," by local artist Gustage "Bush Tea" Williams. The timeline of Nelson's Caribbean career includes ship models, ceramic and bronze Nelson figures, paintings of his battles and other scenes, a scrap from the Union Jack under which the admiral was standing when he was shot, a miniature of his casket, and an actual ticket to his funeral, with wax seal.

A tiny birdcage with wood enclosing box bears the inscription "In a number of letters written to Fanny Nisbet [Nelson's wife], Nelson mentioned his search for a traveling birdcage. This bird cage, though not the one Nelson finally procured, is from that period." Museum hours are 8am to 4pm Monday through Friday, Saturday 9am to noon.

Once back outside, amble slowly off in the same direction you were going (right from the gate). Keep bearing right and you'll eventually be back on Main Street, in plenty of time to do a little shopping or stop into one of the local bars or restaurants.

ON YOUR OWN: BEYOND THE PORT AREA

The 3-hectare (8-acre) **Botanical Garden of Nevis** (© 869/469-3509) is located 5km (3 miles) south of Charlestown on the Montpelier Estate. There are several gardens, including a tropical rain-forest conservatory, a rose and vine garden, a cactus garden, a tropical fruit garden, and an orchid garden. Fountains, ponds, and re-creations of Mayan sculptures dot the grounds, which are open Monday through Saturday 9:30am to 4pm. Admission is $9 adults, $4 children. There's a restaurant and gift shop on-site.

On the east coast, about 30 minutes from Charlestown and within close proximity of Butlers Village, the **Eden Brown Estate** is said to be haunted. Once it was the home of a wealthy planter whose daughter's husband-to-be was killed in a duel at the prenuptial feast. The mansion was then closed and left to the ravages of nature. A solid gray stone still stands. Only the most adventurous, they say, come here on a moonlit night (so it's a good thing you have an excuse—your ship is bound to sail before sunset).

SHOPPING

Nevis is not a shopping hub on the order of St. Thomas or even the much more laid-back St. John. In fact, it's no kind of shopping hub at all. Still, there are a few shops worth poking your head into, all of them along Main Street, right in the port area.

Island Hopper, on Main, 1 block north of Prince Charles Street (© 869/469-0893), is the best shop in town for visitors, stocking a huge selection of batik clothing. The **Nevis Handcraft Cooperative Society,** at the corner of Main and Prince Charles streets (© 869/469-1746), is pretty sparse, but does carry some folklorically bottled hot sauces and guava jellies, as well as some low-quality craft items. **Pemberton Gift Shop,** across Main Street from Island Hopper (© 869/469-5668), is also sparse, but has a selection of T-shirts, gift items, and a shelf of CSR (Cane Spirit Rothschild), the local cane sugar liquor. **Jerveren's Fashions,** in the Cotton Ginnery complex right at the pier (© 869/469-0062), has a decent selection of T-shirts and gifts.

For stamp collectors, the **Nevis Philatelic Bureau** at the Head Post Office, on Market Street next to the public market, 1 block south and 1 block east of the docks (© 869/469-5535), has a range of Nevis stamps.

BEACHES

The name to know on Nevis is **Pinney's Beach,** located north of Charlestown. A lovely spot for swimming, snorkeling, beachcombing, or just sitting back and watching the pelicans divebomb into the surf, it's home to the Four Seasons resort, reopened in late 2000 after being obliterated by 1999's Hurricane Lenny. As a counterpoint to conspicuous luxury, the rickety **Sunshine's Bar and Grill**

(© 869/469-5817), "Home of the Killer Bee," sits right on the beach, offering beer and other refreshments along with the aforementioned Bee, a "killer" drink.

GREAT LOCAL RESTAURANTS & BARS

A nice place to eat in Charleston is **Eddy's Bar & Restaurant,** on Main Street (© 869/469-5958), which sits on an upper floor and offers good sandwiches, steaks, and seafood, as well as a nice balcony's-eye view of the slowly bustling town below. **Cotton House Restaurant and Bar** (© 869/469-0305), on the second floor of the Cotton House complex, right by the cruise dock, is nothing fancy, but is a pleasant place to grab a snack and a beer in the shade.

22 Panama

The Panama Canal is an awesome feat of engineering and human effort. Construction began in 1880 and wasn't completed until 1914, at the expense of thousands of lives, and the vast majority of the original structure and equipment is still in use. Transiting the canal, which links the Atlantic Ocean with the Pacific, is a thrill for anyone even vaguely interested in engineering or history.

Passing through the canal takes about 8 hours from start to finish, and is a fascinating procedure—the route is about 80km (50 miles) long and includes passage through three main locks, which, through gravity alone, raise ships over Central America and down again on the other side. Between the locks, ships pass through artificially created lakes such as the massive Gatun Lake, 26m (85 ft.) above sea level. It often costs ships about $100,000 to pass through, with fees based on each ship's weight. Your ship will line up in the morning, mostly with cargo ships, to await its turn through the canal. While transiting, there will be a running narration of history and facts about the canal by an expert who's brought on board for the day.

Cruises that include a canal crossing are generally 10 to 14 nights long, with popular routes between Florida and Acapulco, visiting a handful of Caribbean and Mexican ports and a few ports in Central America along the way, including Panama's San Blas Islands, Costa Rica's Puerto Caldera, and Guatemala's Puerto Quetzal.

COLON

In compliance with a treaty signed between the United States and Panama in 1977, canal operations passed from U.S. to Panamanian hands at the stroke of midnight on December 31, 1999. Not only did the transition go smoothly, but the canal changeover spurred government agencies and private developers in Panama to expand the canal zone's tourism infrastructure—not simply trying to attract as many ships as possible, but developing new attractions at the canal's Atlantic entrance to lure cruise passengers off their ships and into Panama's interior on shore excursions and for pre- and post-cruise stays. Even ships not transiting the canal are being wooed, with a long-term goal of making the city of Colon a homeport for cruise ships sailing to the southern Caribbean.

The linchpin project in the new canal-area developments is **Colon 2000,** a $45 million private port development that opened in October 2000 in Colon City, near the canal's Caribbean entrance, and that is capable of handling any size cruise vessel—even the 100,000-ton-plus ships that are too large to pass through the canal. Colon 2000's developer, Corporacion de Costas Tropicales, has created a tour company, **Adventuras 2000** (www.colon2000.com/aventours.html), which offers a series of shore excursions highlighting Panama's history, culture, and diverse natural attractions (see "Excursions Offered by the

Cruise Lines" below). The project has opened many new jobs to locals, who are being trained as bilingual tour guides, drivers, and so on.

Colon 2000's glass-and-marble terminal building has a large lounge, an Internet cafe, a huge duty-free shopping mall (part of the Colon Free Zone, the second largest tax-free zone in the world), restaurants, and craft shops. The entire complex is surrounded by landscaped parkland and is adjacent to a Radisson hotel that's scheduled to open in late 2002. Unfortunately, the town surrounding the splashy new development remains depressed. So there's no question passengers calling here should book an organized tour.

Princess, Holland America, and Royal Caribbean were some of the first lines to include Colon 2000 as a port of call on some Panama Canal itineraries. It doesn't hurt that they're getting incentives by the Panamanian government: Panama has hedged its bets by establishing a 5-year program that pays cruise ships $2.50 to $12 per passenger for calls at any Panamanian port. The incentives grow as the passenger count rises, and additional incentives are offered to lines that register their ships in Panama.

Another new development in Colon, the Cristobal Cruise Terminal (Pier 6), offers piers for two ships of any size and has a duty-free shopping area, restaurants, and telephones. A rail line here, connecting Colon and the capital of Panama City, is in the planning stages.

EXCURSIONS OFFERED BY THE CRUISE LINES

The following excursions represent a sampling of those offered from Colon:

Emberá Indian Village Tour ($87, 3½ hr.): Today, Panama's Emberá Indians live much as they did in the early 16th century, when their first tourist—Vasco

Nunez de Balboa, who "discovered" the Pacific Ocean—came through. You'll travel by dugout canoe up the Cargres River, visit the Emberá village, witness a performance of traditional dance, and (surprise, surprise) have an opportunity to purchase handcrafts.

Fort San Lorenzo & Gutun Locks ($65, 4½–6 hr.): Visit the late 16th-century Fort San Lorenzo, built at the entrance to the Chagres River to protect the riches Spain was busily pillaging from the area. The tour also visits the Gutun Locks, where you'll learn about the history of the Canal.

Kayaking the Canal ($75, 3¾ hr.): From Colon, you'll travel to Sol Melina, where you'll spend about 1 hour kayaking amid the plant life, mammals, and birds, then head by bus to the Gutun Locks for a look at the Canal's workings.

Panama City Tour ($75, 4½–6 hr.): Visit the ruins of Old Panama, founded in 1519 by Pedro Arias Davila and destroyed in 1671 by the pirate Sir Henry Morgan; head to Colonial Panama, built to replace the original capital; and then visit the Miraflores Locks for a look at the Canal.

The Pirates Trail ($43, 4 hr.): Founded in 1597, Portobelo was a trading town through which passed the gold from Pizarro's plunder of Peru, which made it a frequent target of British pirates, including William Parker, Sir Henry Morgan, and Edward Vernon. On this tour, you'll visit Fort San Geronimo, Fort San Felipe, the Customs House, and the Black Christ Church; learn about the area's history; and then get a view of the Canal from the Gutun Locks.

PORTS ALONG THE CANAL ROUTE

The **San Blas Islands** are a beautiful archipelago and home to the Kuna Indians, whose women are well known for their colorful, hand-embroidered stitching. If you get a chance to go ashore, the tiny women, dressed in their traditional *molas* (bright, intricately appliquéd blouses), sell all manner of this textile art in square blocks and strips, all of which are known as molas and make great pillow covers or wall hangings. They cost about $5 to $10 each, but don't try to bargain too much—these gals will only go so low before standing firm. When your ship anchors offshore at the islands, be prepared for throngs of Kunas to emerge from the far-off distance, paddling (or, in a few cases, motoring) their dugout canoes up to the ship, where they will spend the entire day calling for money or anything else ship passengers toss overboard. The Kuna seem to enjoy diving overboard to retrieve coins thrown to them, but, of course, it's a sad sight, too, watching entire families so needy. Makes you feel really guilty for rolling in on that fancy cruise ship of yours.

In Costa Rica, many ships call at **Puerto Caldera** on the Pacific side or **Puerto Limón** on the Atlantic side. While there's nothing to see from either cargo port, both are great jumping-off points for tours that all visiting ships offer of the country's lush, beautiful rain forests, which are alive with some 850 species of birds, 200 species of mammals, 9,000 species of flowering plants, and about 35,000 species of insects. After a scenic bus ride, tours will take you on a nature walk through the forest.

In Guatemala, most Panama Canal–bound ships call at **Puerto Quetzal,** on the Pacific coast; a few may call at **Santo Tomas** on the Caribbean side. Both are used as gateways to Guatemala's spectacular Mayan ruins at Tikal. They're the country's most famous attractions and are considered the most spectacular yet discovered, with more than 3,000 temples, pyramids, and other buildings of the ancient civilization—some of them dating as far back as A.D. 300—nestled in a thick, surreal jungle setting. Excursions here are neither cheap nor easy—a 10-hour tour involves buses, walking, and a 1-hour flight, and costs about $500—but the journey is well worth the effort. Excursions to the less-spectacular Mayan sites in Honduras are also offered from Puerto Quetzal, as are several overland tours of Guatemala's interior.

23 Puerto Rico

San Juan, the capital of Puerto Rico, has the busiest ocean terminal in the West Indies and is one of the cruise trade's most important ports. While cruise groups, by their sheer size, can overwhelm many ports of call, San Juan absorbs cruise passengers with ease. The San Juan metropolitan area, home to about a third of Puerto Rico's four million people, is one of the largest and most sophisticated urban centers in the Caribbean, offering all the amenities of a modern major city: great shopping, interesting neighborhoods, beautiful people, excellent restaurants, glamorous bars and nightclubs, and fine museums. It also offers some of the drawbacks: traffic, crowded sidewalks, and, in some areas, crime (avoid the La Perla neighborhood, along the north-central edge of Old San Juan).

Founded in 1521 by Spanish conquistador **Juan Ponce de León,** the city is one of the oldest in the New World. The cobblestone streets of the hilly old section of the city (**Old San Juan,** the ancient walled city on San Juan Island) are lined with brightly painted colonial townhouses, ancient churches, intimate parks, and sun-drenched plazas. Like the pyramids of Egypt and the Great Wall of China, Old San Juan's Spanish colonial forts and city walls are United Nations World Heritage Sites. Another attraction is the people: Puerto Ricans are warm, quick to laugh, and proud of their multicultural heritage, a distinct blend of Amerindian, Spanish, African, and American influences that is present in the culture of the island, from salsa music to Puerto Rican cuisine.

San Juan's shopping ranks among the Caribbean's best, and the city's historic sites, beaches, gambling, and other diversions make it, overall, the number-one port of call in the region. You'll find some of the Caribbean's best restaurants here, as well as sprawling beaches with high-rise luxury hotels reminiscent of those in Miami.

Old San Juan is the prime tourist haunt, but there's much more to the metropolitan area. Other interesting neighborhoods include **Santurce,** linked with San Juan Island by a causeway; **Condado,** a strip of beachfront hotels, restaurants, casinos, and nightclubs on a peninsula stretching from San Juan Island to Santurce; **Hato Rey,** the business center; **Río Piedras;** site of the University of Puerto Rico; and **Bayamón,** an industrial and residential quarter. **Isla Verde,** another resort zone, is connected to the rest of San Juan by an isthmus.

Puerto Rico has been inhabited since about 3000 B.C., when the earliest people arrived from Florida or Central America. Around A.D. 100, Arawak Indians from South America reached the island. Over the next 1,400 years, Puerto Rico went through many cultural phases. Eventually, the island became home to the Caribbean's most advanced indigenous people, the *Taínos.* In 1493, Christopher Columbus landed on the island, and within 50 years, the native population was decimated by forced labor, malnutrition, Western diseases, and warfare with the Spanish.

Puerto Rico remained part of Spain's empire for 4 centuries. Positioned at the gateway to the Caribbean, Puerto Rico was vital to the protection of Spain's lucrative trade with its Mexican and South American colonies, and it was the site of major battles against the British and the Dutch in 1595, 1598, and 1625. In nonmilitary matters, however, Puerto Rico remained a neglected backwater, and most islanders, including slaves brought from Africa, lived much as the Taínos had before them. Piracy and trade in contraband became big business during the 18th century, and Puerto Rico began to develop its own distinct national identity, fueled by the emergence of large plantations. Spanish rule ended in 1898, when the island was ceded to the United States in the wake of the Spanish-American War. In 1917, Puerto Ricans became U.S. citizens, and in 1952 the island became a semiautonomous commonwealth of the United States. In the last referendum on statehood, in 1998, slightly more Puerto Ricans voted for maintaining the status quo than for joining the union; a small fraction favored independence.

COMING ASHORE   Cruise ships dock on the historic Old San Juan peninsula, a short walk from the Plaza de la Marina, Old San Juan's main bus station, and most of the Old Town's historic treasures. A small **tourist information center** is located next to credit-card phones on Plaza de la Marina, just in front of Pier 1; the information center is open 9am to 5:30pm Thursday and Friday, 9am to 8pm Saturday through Wednesday.

During periods of heavy volume—Saturday and Sunday in midwinter, when as many as 10 cruise ships dock on the same day—additional, less convenient piers are used. You'll need motorized transit (a taxi or a van supplied by the cruise line as part of the shore-excursion program) to get to the Old Town from these docks. For information about the port, contact the **Port of San Juan,** P.O. 362829, San Juan, PR 00936-2829 (© **787/723-2260**).

LANGUAGE   **Spanish** is the native tongue, but most people in the tourism industry also speak **English.** The farther you venture from San Juan, the more likely it is you'll have to practice your Spanish.

CURRENCY   Puerto Rico is part of the United States, so the **U.S. dollar** is the coin of the realm. Canadian currency is accepted, albeit reluctantly, by some of San Juan's bigger hotels. Credit cards and traveler's checks are widely accepted.

Frommer's Favorite San Juan Experiences

Strolling Through Historic Old San Juan: Meander through block after block of narrow cobblestone streets lined with centuries-old Spanish colonial architecture. There's enough here to keep you busy for 2 or 3 days, so you'll have to pick and choose from among the many historical sites, museums, churches, plazas, and forts. (See "Shore Excursions Offered by the Cruise Lines" and "Walking Tour: Old San Juan," both below.)

Hiking Through El Yunque National Forest: One of Puerto Rico's most popular attractions, El Yunque covers 11200 hectares (28,000 acres) and receives up to 200 inches of rain per year. There are 240 different tropical trees, more than 50 orchid species, 150 varieties of ferns, 68 types of birds, and millions of tiny *coquí* tree frogs. You can hike, picnic, and swim in mountain streams. (See "Shore Excursions Offered by the Cruise Lines," below.)

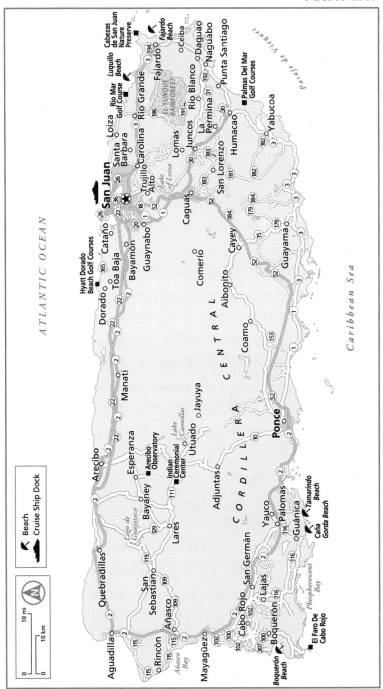

INFORMATION   For advice and maps, drop by the **Tourist Information Center** at La Casita, near Pier 1 (© **787/721-2400**). For info before you go, contact the Puerto Rico Tourism Company (© **800/223-6530;** www. prtourism.com).

CALLING FROM THE U.S.   Calling Puerto Rico from the continental United States is as simple as dialing between U.S. states: Just dial "1" before the numbers listed here.

GETTING AROUND

Driving in congested San Juan is frustrating, and parking in some areas is impossible. You're better off walking around the Old Town. Take buses or taxis to Condado, Ocean Park, and Isla Verde.

BY TAXI   Taxis operated by the **Public Service Commission** (PSC) are metered in San Juan, but the fare structure between major tourism zones is standardized. The set rates from the cruise ship piers are $6 to Old San Juan, $10 to Condado, and $16 to Isla Verde. You can also hire a taxi for an hour for $20. If a meter's used, the initial charge is $1, plus 10¢ for each additional one-thirteenth of a mile and 50¢ for each suitcase. The minimum fare is $3. After 10pm, there's a night charge (add $1 to the meter reading). For phone numbers of taxi companies, look in the Yellow Pages or call the PSC (© **787/756-1919**).

BY TROLLEY   When you tire of walking around Old San Juan, board one of the free trolleys. They depart from Plaza de la Marina and Piers 2 and 4, but you can hop on anywhere along the route.

BY BUS   The Metropolitan Bus Authority operates extensive bus service in the greater San Juan area. Bus stops are marked by signs that read PARADA, and terminals are in the dock area and at Plaza de Colón in Old San Juan. Buses use special lanes and proceed against the flow of traffic, so they're quicker than other vehicles during rush hour. Metrobus I runs between Old San Juan and Río Piedras, with stops in the Santurce shopping areas, the Hato Rey financial district, and the University of Puerto Rico and nearby market area. The A5 connects Old San Juan to Condado, Ocean Park, and Isla Verde. A typical fare is 25¢ to 50¢. For additional route and schedule information, call © **787/250-6064.**

BY RENTAL CAR   Puerto Rico has expressways and thousands of miles of other paved roads, so travel by car is pretty effortless, except in metropolitan San Juan, where traffic can be heavy and nightmarish—the 500-year-old streets in the old town just weren't built with cars in mind. Driving is on the right side of the road, and all other U.S. rules apply. Signs are in Spanish, though, and the metric system is used for distance markers (km rather than miles) and at gas stations (l instead of gal.); confusingly enough, speed limits are posted in miles per hour. **Avis, Budget, Dollar,** and **Hertz** all have offices here.

SHORE EXCURSIONS OFFERED BY THE CRUISE LINES

Don't bother with organized shore excursions if it's Old San Juan you want to see—it's easy enough to get around on your own. On the other hand, if you prefer a guide or want to explore somewhere farther afield, an organized tour may be a good idea.

Old San Juan Walking Tour ($30, 2 hr.): Visit El Morro, the most dramatic of the city's military fortifications, as well as other historic sites including Casa Blanca, the Ballajá Barracks, San José Church, and San Juan Cathedral. The tour ends at Capilla del Cristo, near the Old Town's main shopping area.

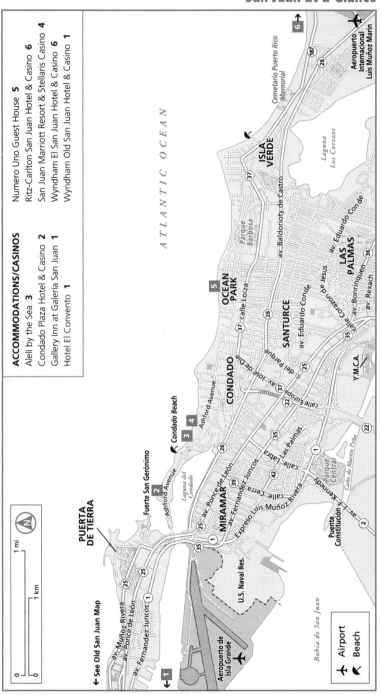

San Juan at a Glance

ACCOMMODATIONS/CASINOS

Aleli by the Sea **3**
Condado Plaza Hotel & Casino **2**
Gallery Inn at Galería San Juan **1**
Hotel El Convento **1**

Numero Uno Guest House **5**
Ritz-Carlton San Juan Hotel & Casino **6**
San Juan Marriott Resort & Stellaris Casino **4**
Wyndham El San Juan Hotel & Casino **6**
Wyndham Old San Juan Hotel & Casino **1**

← See Old San Juan Map

PUERTA
DE TIERRA

ATLANTIC OCEAN

Fuerte San Gerónimo

Condado Beach

Laguna del
Condado

Ashford Avenue

CONDADO

OCEAN
PARK

calle Loiza

SANTURCE

Parque
Barbosa

ISLA
VERDE

Laguna
Los Corozos

Cementario Puerto Rico
Memorial

Aeropuerto
Internacional
Luis Muñoz Marín

LAS
PALMAS

Y.M.C.A.

MIRAMAR

Parque
Central

Calle de Martín Peña

Puente
Constitución

U.S. Naval Res.

Bahía de San Juan

Aeropuerto de
Isla Grande

✈ Airport
↙ Beach

0 — 1 mi
0 — 1 km

231

San Juan as a Port of Embarkation

Puerto Rico is the number-one port of embarkation in the Caribbean, with more than 1.2 million visitors embarking on 700 cruises every year from here. Most cruise lines have packages that include hotel rooms on the island.

GETTING TO SAN JUAN & THE PORT   Luis Muñoz Marín International Airport (© 787/791-1014) is on the city's east side, about 12km (7½ miles) from the port. Taxi fares from the airport are fixed at $8 to Isla Verde, $12 to Condado and Ocean Park, and $16 to Old San Juan and the cruise ships. The ride to the port takes at least 30 minutes—longer if traffic is heavy, and it often is.

ACCOMMODATIONS   In Old San Juan   The quietly elegant **Hotel El Convento,** 100 Calle del Cristo (© 800/468-2779 or 787/723-9020; www.elconvento.com), is Puerto Rico's most famous lodging. A former Carmelite convent, it offers large rooms, many with views of the Old Town. Rates: $315 to $375 winter; $180 to $240 summer. **Wyndham Old San Juan Hotel & Casino,** 100 Brumbaugh St. (© 800/996-3426 or 787/721 5100; www.wyndham.com/OldSanJuan), is on the waterfront across the street from the cruise ship docks. Rooms are comfortable, and Old San Juan is a step away. Rates: $315 to $365. On Old San Juan's highest hill, with a sweeping view of the sea, **Gallery Inn at Galería San Juan,** 204–206 Calle Norzagaray (© 787/722-1808; www.thegalleryinn.com), was the home of a Spanish aristocrat in the 1700s. Many of the rooms open to patios, fountains, and gardens. Art is everywhere, contributing to the hotel's cultured, contemplative, bohemian ambience. Rates: $145 to $350.

In Condado   The original high-rise, high-glamour section of modern San Juan, Condado boasts numerous hotels, restaurants, and night-clubs. Among its best hotels are the **Condado Plaza Hotel & Casino,** 999 Ashford Ave. (© 800/468-8588 or 787/721-1000; www.condadoplaza.com; rates: $340–$490), and the **San Juan Marriott Resort & Stellaris Casino,** 1309 Ashford Ave. (© 800/981-8546 or 787/722-7000; www.marriott.com/marriott/SJUPR; rates: $325–$430). **Alelí by the Sea,** 1125 Sea View St., a block off Ashford Avenue (© 787/725-5313), is a small, charming option on the beach. Rooms are basic but clean; the big draws are the sound of the surf just outside your window and the rates—about $55 to $90.

Motels in Condado include the **Comfort Inn,** 1 Mariano Ramirez Bages, off Ashford Avenue at Joffre Street, Condado (© 787/724-4160; www.choicecaribbean.com), where rates are $89, and **San Juan Days Inn-Condado Lagoon Hotel,** 6 Clemenceau St., Ashford Avenue to

El Yunque Rain Forest ($27, 4–5 hr.): Get acquainted with one of Puerto Rico's premier natural wonders. After arriving at Baño Grande, a natural swimming hole, hike half an hour along the Camimitillo trail and see parrot nests, giant ferns, orchids, and palms. Listen for the song of Puerto Rico's national symbol,

Mariano Ramirez Street, then 2 blocks ((✆ **787/721-0170; www.the.days inn.com/sanjuan08830**), where rates are also $89.

In Ocean Park   Conveniently located between Condado and Isla Verde, and more a neighborhood than a tourist zone, Ocean Park is a favorite of gay travelers. **Numero Uno Guest House,** 1 Calle Santa Ana ((✆ **787/ 727-5482**), a tranquil guesthouse on the beach above Pamela's restaurant (see "Great Local Restaurants & Bars," later in this section) welcomes both gay and straight guests. The recently renovated rooms, some with beach views, are airy and bright. There are no TVs, but this gem is for people who'd rather listen to crashing waves than CNN. Rates: $85 to $185.

In Isla Verde   Similar to Condado in atmosphere and abundance of hotels, but more recently developed, Isla Verde has a number of dazzlingly deluxe resort complexes, including the **Wyndham El San Juan Hotel & Casino,** 6063 Isla Verde Ave. ((✆ **800/468-2818,** or 787/791-1000; www.wyndham.com/Resorts/SJUES; rates: $395–$595), and the **Ritz-Carlton San Juan Hotel & Casino,** 6961 Rte. 187 ((✆ **800/241-3333** or 787/ 253-1700; www.ritzcarlton.com; rates: $519–$710). At the other end of the spectrum, motels include the **Howard Johnson Carolina,** 4820 Isla Verde Ave. ((✆ **787/728-1300; www.the.hojo.com/carolinasanjuan 09692**), which has rooms from $100 to $125.

SAN JUAN AFTER DARK   The San Juan club scene is hot. In general, people get pretty dressed up, so forget about T-shirts or shorts. **Babylon,** in the Wyndham El San Juan Hotel & Casino, 6063 Isla Verde Ave. ((✆ **787/791-1000**), attracts a rich and beautiful crowd, as well as hundreds of wannabes. On weekends, you may wait 2 hours to get in. For dance action in the Old Town, head for **Club Lazer,** 251 Calle del Cruz ((✆ **787/725-7581**), where you can dance the night away to the sounds of salsa and merengue. In Condado, **Club Millennium,** in the Condado Plaza Hotel, 999 Ashford Ave. ((✆ **787/722-1900**), draws disco devotees and features a cigar bar on the side. San Juan's exuberant gay scene is easily the Caribbean's best, and no club in town surpasses the energy of **Eros,** 1257 Avenida Ponce de León, in Santurce ((✆ **787/722-1131**). Also in Santurce, you'll find the enduringly popular lesbian bar, **Cups,** 1708 Calle San Mateo ((✆ **787/268-3570**).

For a mellow experience and a sophisticated atmosphere, try **Carli Café Concierto,** in old San Juan on Plazoleta Rafael Carríon ((✆ **787/725-4927**), a bistro offering live piano and jazz music. **Palm Court** in the Wyndham El San Juan Hotel & Casino, 6063 Isla Verde Ave. ((✆ **787/791-1000**), has a giant chandelier and an intricate, wood-paneled ceiling, and is probably the island's most glamorous meeting place.

the tiny coquí tree frog. After a short stop at an interpretive station, proceed to Yohaku observation tower and Coca waterfall.

Tropical Horseback Riding ($69, 3½ hr.): Meet your horse, briefly learn the ropes, and then ride down a beautiful beach. Take a quick swim during the refreshment stop.

Bioluminescence Bay Kayak Tour ($65, 4½ hr.): Ride to Las Cabezas de San Juan Natural Reserve, at Puerto Rico's northeasternmost point. Under the light of the stars, paddle down mangrove-lined channels and watch the water glow as billions of single-celled organisms light up as they sense the movement of your boat.

Bacardi Rum Distillery Tour ($19, 2 hr.): Learn about the Puerto Rican sugar and rum industries. Watch giant fermenting tanks transform sugar cane into rum, and then follow the liquor from vat to barrel to bottle. Taste the finished product.

EXCURSIONS OFFERED BY LOCAL AGENCIES

If you're staying in a hotel before or after your cruise, book tours at the tour desk. Otherwise try **Rico Suntours,** 176 Calle San Jorge, San Juan (© 787/ 722-2080), or **Castillo Tours & Travel Services,** 2413 Calle Laurel, Punta La Marias, Santurce (© 787/791-6195 or 787/726-5752). For serious adventure, rock climbing, rappelling, cave exploring, or canyoneering, your best bet is **Aventuras Tierra Adentro,** 268-A Avenida Piñero, Río Piedras (© 787/ 766-0470).

WALKING TOUR   OLD SAN JUAN

The streets are narrow and teeming with traffic, but strolling through Old San Juan is like walking through 5 centuries of history. More than 400 Spanish colonial buildings from the 16th and 17th centuries, many featuring intricate wrought-iron balconies with lush hanging plants, have been lovingly restored here. The streets' blue paving stones were used originally as ballast by ships crossing the ocean from Spain. Although Old San Juan is a National Historic Zone, it's as vibrant today as it ever has been. Block after block, you'll find shops, cafes, museums, plazas, people, and pigeons. The crowds thin out by late afternoon, so linger around to experience Old San Juan's more sedate charms.

Begin your adventure near the post office, amid the taxis, buses, and urban hubbub of:

❶ Plaza de la Marina

The Plaza is a small park that overlooks San Juan Bay, which was one of the New World's most important harbors for trading and for military protection. Walking west from the plaza, you'll come to San Juan's showcase promenade, El Paseo de la Princesa. This renovated 19th-century walkway traces the ancient city walls past heroic statues, gurgling fountains, and landscaped gardens.

Proceed along the Paseo to:

❷ La Princesa

This gray-and-white building on the right served as one of the Caribbean's most notorious prisons for centuries.

Today it houses contemporary Puerto Rican art exhibits and the offices of the Puerto Rico Tourism Company.

Continue walking westward to the fountain near the sea's edge. Turn right and follow the promenade as it skirts the base of the:

❸ City Wall

The wall was completed in the 1700s and once formed part of the New World's most impregnable defenses against enemy invaders and pirates. Marvel at the immensity, antiquity, and engineering genius of the wall, which on average is 12m (40 ft.) high and 6m (20 ft.) thick.

Follow the promenade until you reach the:

❹ San Juan Gate

The Gate stands at Calle San Juan and Recinto del Oeste. Turn right through the portal. The gate was built in 1635 and served as the main entrance into San Juan. Today, it's the only remaining passage through the wall into the city.

Turn right at the first street and walk uphill along Calle Recinto del Oeste to the wrought-iron gates of:

❺ La Fortaleza

Also known as Santa Catalina Palace, La Fortaleza is the residence of Puerto Rico's governor. Although it initially served military purposes, it's the oldest executive mansion in continuous use in the Western Hemisphere (construction began in 1533). Over the past 4 centuries, numerous additions and alterations have been made, resulting in the current amalgam of marble, mahogany, and stained glass. The architectural pastiche includes medieval, baroque, gothic, neoclassical, and Moorish elements. English-language tours are given Monday through Friday (except holidays) every hour on the hour (except noon) from 9am to 3pm.

Now retrace your steps along Calle Recinto del Oeste, downhill to Caleta de San Juan. The colonial house at number 51, on the northeast corner, is the:

❻ Felisa Rincón de Gautier Museum

This is the former home of one of San Juan's most popular mayors. An organizer of the city's women and other dispossessed, Fela, as her many admirers called her, swept into power in 1946 and led the city for 22 years. The first woman in the Western Hemisphere to be the chief executive of a major city, she was the brains behind Head Start, the preschool program for low-income children. Watch the short English-language documentary of her life, tour the modest rooms of her home, and view some of the hundreds of pictures of Madame Mayor with the world's celebrities (✆ 787/723-1897; free admission;

open weekdays, except holidays, 9am–4pm).

Walking back to Calle Recinto del Oeste, turn right and proceed 1 block to Caleta de las Monjas. Fork left to a panoramic view and a modern statue marking the center of:

❼ Plazuela de la Rogativa

According to local legend, the British, while besieging San Juan in 1797, misidentified the flaming torches of a rogativa, or religious procession, as Spanish reinforcements. Frightened by the display, the would-be invaders hastily retreated. Statues in this plaza memorialize the event.

Continue westward, parallel to the city wall, passing through a pair of urn-topped gateposts. The road will fork. Bear to the right and continue climbing the steep cobblestone-covered ramp to its top. Walk westward across the field toward the neoclassical gateway leading to the:

❽ Castillo de San Felipe del Morro ("El Morro")

This castle, whose treasury and strategic position were for centuries the envy of both Europe and the Caribbean, was where Spanish Puerto Rico defended itself against the navies of Great Britain, France, and Holland, as well as hundreds of pirate ships. First built in 1540, and substantially enhanced in 1787, the fortress was part of a comprehensive defense network. The six-level complex rises 42m (140 ft.) above the sea on a rocky promontory. You can spend the better part of the morning exploring its labyrinth of dungeons, barracks, towers, ramps, and tunnels on your own. Check out the small, air-conditioned military museum and the gift shop. Both El Morro and San Cristóbal (see below) are managed by the U.S. National Park Service, which provides continuous video presentations and scheduled guided tours in English. (It's at the western end of Calle Norzagaray, ✆ 787/729-6960; $2 for adults, $1 for ages 13–17 and over 62, children free; open daily 9am–5pm. Save your ticket stub, which gets you admission to Fort San Cristóbal, below.)

Retrace your steps through the treeless field to Calle del Morro, then walk uphill to the small plaza at the top of the street. On the right is:

⑨ Casa Blanca

Though it was his family home, Juan Ponce de León, the conquistador and Puerto Rico's first governor, never actually lived here: While the structure was being built, he was off looking for the Fountain of Youth, ironically dying (from battle wounds) along the way, in 1521. The city's oldest fort, Casa Blanca was San Juan's only defense against attacks until La Fortaleza was completed in 1533. Today, it features a small museum illustrating Indian life and 16th- and 17th-century colonial family life. The garden and fountains in back are a tranquil respite from the streets. (1 Calle de San Sebastián, ✆ 787/724-5477; $1 for adults, 50¢ for children and senior citizens; open daily Tues–Sat 9am–5pm, except for an hour at noon.)

Exit through the front entrance and walk downhill, retracing your steps for a half block, then head toward the massive tangerine-colored building on your right, the:

⑩ Cuartel de Ballajá

These former military barracks once housed 1,000 Spanish soldiers and their families. Built between 1854 and 1864, the complex is the last and largest military building erected by Spain in the Western Hemisphere. The three-story quadrangular structure, constructed in a sober neoclassical style, has long arcades that enclose a large patio once used as a parade ground. Today, the building's second floor is home to the **Museo de las Americas** (Museum of the Americas), which showcases Caribbean as well as North, Central, and South American cultures. The popular arts exhibits focus on housing and furniture styles, handcrafts, tools, musical instruments, toys, clothing, and religious objects. The carved wooden saints (*santos*) are especially interesting. (Cuartel de Ballajá; ✆ 787/724-5052; free admission; open Tues–Fri 10am–4pm, Sat and Sun 11am–5pm; guided tours at 10:30am, 1:30, and 2:30pm.)

Exit through the barracks' eastern door, where you'll immediately spot the dramatic and modern:

⑪ Plaza del Quinto Centenario (Quincentennial Plaza)

This plaza is dominated by a large, totem pole–like column that commemorates the 500th anniversary of Columbus's arrival.

Now, walk a short block southeast to the borders of:

⑫ Plaza de San José

This plaza features a statue of Juan Ponce de León cast from an English cannon captured during a 1797 naval battle. Three sites around this square are worth visiting. Built in 1532, the **Iglesia de San José** is where Ponce de León's descendants worshipped. Despite being looted over the years, the church, on the plaza's north side, still has several treasures, including a carved crucifix presented to Ponce de León, paintings by Puerto Rican 18th-century master José Campéche, and works by Francisco Oller, who painted in the late 1800s and early 1900s. A 15th-century Flemish work in the Chapel of Belém is venerated by many who believe it works miracles (✆ 787/725-7501; free admission; open Mon–Wed and Fri 7am–3pm, Sat 8am–1pm). The **Museo Pablo Casals** (✆ 787/723-9185; $1 for adults, 50¢ for children under 12; open Tues–Sat 9:30am–4:30pm) honors the Spanish-born cellist who adopted Puerto Rico as his home (his mother and wife were Puerto Rican). Original manuscripts of Casals' music, his cello, and his piano are displayed in the main hall. The video library upstairs archives many of his performances. Casals'

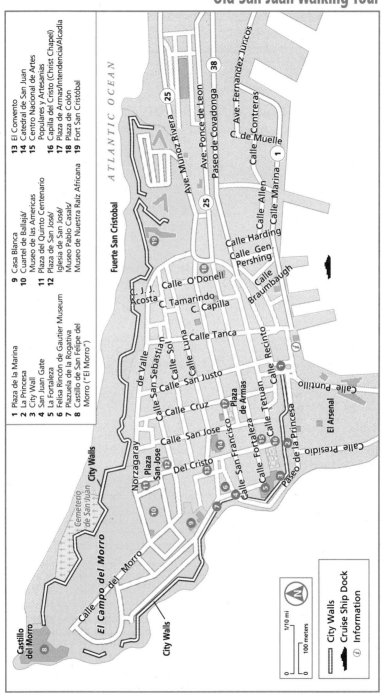

1 Plaza de la Marina
2 La Princesa
3 City Wall
4 San Juan Gate
5 La Fortaleza
6 Felisa Rincón de Gautier Museum
7 Plazuela de la Rogativa
8 Castillo de San Felipe del Morro ("El Morro")

9 Casa Blanca
10 Cuartel de Ballajá/ Museo de las Americas
11 Plaza del Quinto Centenario
12 Plaza de San José/ Iglesia de San José/ Museo Pablo Casals/ Museo de Nuestra Raíz Africana

13 El Convento
14 Catedral de San Juan
15 Centro Nacional de Artes Populares y Artesanias
16 Capilla del Cristo (Christ Chapel)
17 Plaza de Armas/Intendencia/Alcadia
18 Plaza de Colón
19 Fort San Cristóbal

City Walls
Cruise Ship Dock
ⓘ **Information**

1/10 mi
100 meters

ATLANTIC OCEAN

Castillo del Morro

El Campo del Morro

Cementerio de San Juan

City Walls

Fuerte San Cristóbal

Ave. Muñoz Rivera
Ave. Ponce de Leon
Paseo de Covadonga
Ave. Fernandez Juncos
C. de Muelle
Calle Contreras
Calle Marina
Calle Allen
Calle Harding
Calle Gen. Pershing
Calle Braumbaugh
Calle O'Donell
C. Tamarindo
C. Capilla
C. J. J. Acosta
Calle Tanca
Calle Recinto
Calle Puntillo
de Valle
Calle San Sebastián
Calle Sol
Calle Luna
Calle San Justo
Calle Cruz
Calle San Jose
Calle San Francisco
Calle Fortaleza
Calle Tetuan
Plaza de Armas
Paseo de la Princesa
Del Cristo
Norzagaray
Plaza San Jose
El Arsenal
Calle Presidio
Calle del Morro
City Walls

237

legacy on the island includes the annual Casals Music Festival and the Puerto Rico Symphony Orchestra. The **Museo de Nuestra Raíz Africana** (Museum of Our African Roots) compactly and ingeniously chronicles the history of Africans in Puerto Rico. Various exhibits trace the slave experience and focus on African contributions to local music, dance, clothing, art, cuisine, religion, and language. Placards are in Spanish, but the exhibits are fascinating and often self-explanatory (© 787/724-0700, ext. 4239; free admission; open Tues–Sat 9:30am–5pm, Sun 11am–5pm).

Exiting from the plaza's southwestern corner, walk downhill along one of the capital's oldest and best-known streets, Calle del Cristo. Two blocks down, on the north side of shady Plaza de las Monjas, look for:

⓭ El Convento

The New World's first Carmelite convent, El Convento opened in 1651 with 30-foot-thick walls designed to withstand hurricanes and enemy attacks. The building remained a convent for 250 years, but fell on hard times early in the 20th century and served as a dance hall and flophouse. Today, the beautifully restored building is the Hotel El Convento, possibly Puerto Rico's most elegant hotel.

Across the street from El Convento stands the island's most famous church, the:

⓮ Catedral de San Juan

The original thatch-roofed, wooden cathedral, built in the early 1520s, was destroyed by a hurricane in 1529. Reconstruction in 1540 added a circular staircase and vaulted Gothic ceilings, but most of the current church was built in the 1800s. Look for the tomb of Ponce de León and the wax-encased mummy of St. Pio, a Roman martyr (153 Calle del Cristo; © 787/722-0861; free admission; open weekdays 8:30am–4pm).

Now walk 2 blocks south along Calle del Cristo, through one of the Caribbean's most attractive shopping districts. After passing Calle La Fortaleza, look on your left for the:

⓯ Centro Nacional de Artes Populares y Artesanias

Operated by the Institute of Puerto Rican Culture, this center displays a collection of the island's folk arts and crafts (253 Calle del Cristo; © 787/722-0621; free admission; open Mon–Sat 9am–5pm).

Continue to the southernmost tip of Calle del Cristo (just a few steps away) to the wrought-iron gates that surround a chapel no bigger than a newspaper kiosk, the:

⓰ Capilla del Cristo (Christ Chapel)

Legend has it that in 1753 a young rider lost control of his horse in a race down Calle del Cristo during the feast of St. John the Baptist and plunged over the steep precipice at the street's end. A witness to the tragedy promised to build a chapel if the young man's life was saved. Records maintain that the horseman died, but lore contends otherwise. In another version of the story, the horseman, after himself praying to God while falling over the cliff, survived to build the chapel. The delicate silver altar here can be seen through glass doors (free admission; open Mon, Wed, and Fri 10:30am–3:30pm).

Retrace your steps about a block north along the Calle del Cristo, then turn right on Calle Fortaleza. One block later, take a left onto Calle San José, then proceed another block to the capital's liveliest square, the:

⓱ Plaza de Armas

This broad, open plaza has lots of pigeons, several old men playing dominos, office workers and shoppers basking in the sun, and a 19th-century statue representing the four seasons. Originally used for military drills, the plaza now hosts folk dances and concerts on weekends. The neoclassical **Intendencia** (which houses offices of the U.S. State Department) and the Alcadía (San Juan's City Hall) flank the square.

Walk eastward along the plaza's northern border, Calle San Francisco, for 4 blocks until you reach another square:

⑱ Plaza de Colón

This park is notable for its statue of Cristóbal Colón (Christopher Columbus). Bronze plaques at the monument's base commemorate episodes in the explorer's life.

Finally, walk to the plaza's northeast corner, where Calle San Francisco meets Boulevard del Valle. Turn left and follow the signs to:

⑲ Fort San Cristóbal

Built in 1634 (and expanded in the 1770s), this fortress rises more than 45m (150 ft.) above the sea. A complex maze of tunnels and moats connects the central fort with wave after wave of outlying posts. Don't miss the **Garita del Diablo** (the Devil's Sentry Box), a lonely post at the edge of the sea where, legend has it, the devil himself snatched away solitary sentinels. (The Fort is uphill from Plaza de Colón on Calle Norzagaray. ℂ 787/ 729-6960; $2 for adults, $1 for ages 13–17 and over 62, and children are free. Note that your ticket stub from El Morro is good for admission here. Open daily 9am–5pm.)

CASINOS

Casinos are one of San Juan's biggest draws, and most large hotels have one. They're generally open daily from noon to 4am, but some never close. Dress, usually informal during the day, becomes impressive in the evenings. The **Casino at the Ritz-Carlton,** 6961 State Rd., Isla Verde (ℂ **787/253-1700**), is the largest in Puerto Rico. Combining elegant 1940s decor with tropical fabrics and patterns, it's one of the plushest entertainment complexes in the Caribbean. The **San Juan Grand Beach Hotel & Casino,** 187 Isla Verde Ave. (ℂ **800/ 443-2009** or 787/791-6100), is another elegant place to rendezvous. One of its Murano glass chandeliers is "longer than a bowling alley." Most convenient for cruise ship passengers, the **Wyndham Old San Juan Hotel & Casino,** 100 Brumbaugh St. (ℂ **787/721-5100**), is directly across from Pier 3 and often bustling.

BEACHES

Puerto Rico is ringed by hundreds of miles of sandy beaches, and you won't have to leave San Juan to play in the surf. Perhaps the most famous beach in the Caribbean, **Condado Beach,** at the western end of Ashford Avenue, is the backyard playground of Condado's resort hotels. A favorite of families, it can get pretty crowded in winter. The beaches of **Isla Verde,** behind the hotels and condominiums along Isla Verde Avenue, are less rocky and are excellent for people-watching. If you're looking for a more picturesque, sedate scene, head to **Ocean Park,** north of McLeary Street. The waters here are sometimes choppy, but they're still swimmable. Popular with college students on weekends, the beach is also very gay-friendly. Condado Beach, Isla Verde, and Ocean Park all have white sand, palm trees, ocean breezes, beautiful bodies, and ample eating and drinking options. Snorkeling gear and other watersports equipment is available to rent.

If you're anxious to get out of the city, **Luquillo Beach,** about 48km (30 miles) east of San Juan, near the town of Luquillo, stretches along a vast coconut grove. Coral reefs protect the clear lagoon from the fierce Atlantic, and a "Sea Without Barriers" facility caters to people with physical disabilities. Be aware, however, that some sections of the beach aren't as well maintained as they once were.

All *balnearios*—government-run beaches with dressing rooms, showers, lifeguards, snack bars, and parking—are open to the public; there's a nominal charge for lockers and showers. Public beaches are closed on Mondays. However, if Monday is a holiday, the beaches will be open that day but closed the next. Hours are 9am to 5pm in winter, 9am to 6pm during the off-season. If you find a secluded spot, be vigilant about your surroundings: Solitude is nice, but there's safety in numbers.

SPORTS

DEEP-SEA FISHING Many say that Captain Mike Benitez, who's chartered boats out of San Juan for more than 40 years, sets the standard by which other deep-sea-fishing captains are judged. Contact him at **Mike Benitez Marine Services,** P.O. Box 9066541, Puerto de Tierra, San Juan, PR 00906-6541 (© 787/ 723-2292; www.mikebenitezfishing.com). **Captain Bill Burleson,** P.O. Box 8270, Humacao, PR 00792 (© 787/850-7442), operates charters off the southeast coast. For both companies, expect to pay a little under $500 for a half-day excursion (up to six anglers).

GOLF Puerto Rico is a golfer's dream, but you'll need to sign up for a ship excursion or rent a car to reach the major courses from San Juan. With 72 holes, **Hyatt Dorado Beach Resort & Country Club** (© 787/796-8961 or 787/ 796-8916; www.hyatt.com) offers the greatest concentration of golf in the Caribbean. All four 18-hole courses at the Hyatt's Regency Cerromar and Dorado Beach properties here were designed by Robert Trent Jones, Sr. Jack Nicklaus ranks the fourth hole at the Dorado Beach East course as one of the 10 best-designed holes in the world. The **Doral Resort at Palmas del Mar** (© 800/725-6273 or 787/852-6000; www.palmasdelmar.com), 72km (45 miles) east of San Juan, has two courses: the par-72 Palm course designed by Gary Player and the newer 18-hole Flamboyan course designed by Rees Jones. The **Westin Rio Mar Country Club** (© 787/888-8811; www.westinriomar. com), 32km (20 miles) away from San Juan in Rio Grande, also has two 18-hole courses, one designed by Tom and George Fazio, the other by Greg Norman.

Greens fees for 18 holes range from $110 at the Hyatt Cerromar North Course to $175 at both Westin courses and at the Hyatt Dorado East Course. Club rental for 18 holes is between $35 and $50. During the off-peak summer months, prices drop about 30% at some courses.

SCUBA DIVING & SNORKELING Puerto Rico offers excellent diving and snorkeling, but the best sites aren't within easy reach of San Juan. **Caribe Aquatic Adventures,** P.O. Box 9024278, San Juan Station, San Juan 00902 (© 787/724-1882; www.caribeaquaticadventure.com), will take you to good diving and snorkeling sites around the capital or near Fajardo on the northeast coast. Caribe operates out of the Radisson Normandie Hotel (Av. Muñoz-Rivera, at the corner of Calle Los Rasales in Puerta de Tierra). A local reef dive is $50. Much more interesting trips to Fajardo (which include a picnic) require a minimum of three passengers (for $405—two dives for $135 per person; snorkelers pay $85).

WINDSURFING, KITEBOARDING & JET-SKIING The most popular windsurfing beach in the San Juan area is Puntas las Marias, between Isla Verde and Ocean Park. You can rent equipment and take lessons from nearby **Velauno,** 2430 Calle Loiza (© 866/778-3521 or 787/728-8716). Boards and a complete rig are $75 per day; 4-hour beginner lessons are $150. Velauno also offers kiteboarding—windsurfing powered by a large kite rather than sails. A 1-hour introductory course is $49. Two-hour kite-control classes are $100. Another popular place for windsurfing is along the beachfront of the Hyatt Resorts at Dorado, about 48km (30 miles) west of San Juan. **Penfield Island Adventures** (© 787/ **796-1234,** ext. 3768, or 787/796-2188), at the Hyatt Regency Cerromar, rents windsurfing equipment, jet skis, kayaks, and sailboats.

SHOPPING
San Juan has some great bargains—prices are often even lower than those in St. Thomas—and U.S. citizens pay no duty on items bought in Puerto Rico. Every tourist zone offers ample shopping opportunities, but the streets of the Old Town, especially **Calle San Francisco** and **Calle del Cristo,** are the major venues. Generally, shopping hours are 8am to 6pm from Monday to Thursday and Saturday, 8am to 9pm on Friday, and 11am to 5pm Sunday for some stores, though most are closed. **Local handcrafts** can be good buys, including santos (hand-carved wooden religious figures), needlework, straw work, hammocks, guayabera shirts (loose-fitting shirts), papier-mâché masks, and paintings and sculptures by local artists.

El Alcazar, 103 Calle San José, has the largest collection of antique furniture, silver, and art objects in the Caribbean. You'll need help to wade through the massive inventory, though—it fills several buildings. Smaller but still impressive, **Olé,** 105 Calle Fortaleza, has antique santos, coins, and silver. It's also the place to get a custom-fitted Panama hat. **Puerto Rican Arts & Crafts,** 204 Calle Fortaleza, has authentic handcrafts, including papier-mâché carnival masks from the town of Ponce. **José E. Alegria & Associates,** 152–154 Calle del Cristo, is half antiques shop, half gift arcade, while **Galería Botello,** 208 Calle del Cristo, once the home of late Puerto Rican artist Angel Botello, sells his paintings and sculptures, as well as antique santos.

Old San Juan's best book and music store, **Cronopios,** is at 255 Calle San José. Most books are in Spanish, but there are plenty in English too. Looking for Puerto Rican novels? Try *The House on the Lagoon,* by Rosario Ferré, or *The Renunciation,* by Edgardo Rodríguez Julia. And pick up some salsa CDs while you're browsing.

If your T-shirt or shot-glass collection is incomplete, the **Hard Rock Cafe** is at 253 Recinto Sur, and the **Harley-Davidson Boutique** is near the Wyndham Old San Juan Hotel, across from Pier 3.

Designer outlet shops include London Fog, 156 Calle del Cristo; Polo Ralph Lauren, 201 Calle del Cristo; Coach, 158 Calle del Cristo; and Tommy Hilfiger, 206 Calle del Cristo.

GREAT LOCAL RESTAURANTS & BARS
San Juan has some of the best restaurants in the Caribbean and a variety of cuisines that only a major city can offer. A favorite **local beer** is Medalla. The most famous **local rum** is Bacardi (pronounced bah-carrrr-*dee*), in all of its varieties; Don Q is also popular.

In Old San Juan, **Amadeus,** 106 Calle San Sebastián (© 787/722-8635), offers nouvelle Caribbean dishes and features an intimate courtyard in back. **El Patio de Sam,** practically next door at 102 Calle San Sebastián (© 787/ **723-1149**), is a popular gathering spot for expatriates, journalists, and shopkeepers. The unpretentious **La Bombonera,** 259 Calle San Francisco (© 787/ **722-0658**), famous for its homemade Puerto Rican meals and 1940s diner atmosphere, has attracted the island's literati and Old San Juan families for decades. San Juan's trailblazing nuevo Latino bistro, **Parrot Club,** 363 Calle Fortaleza (© 787/725-7370), blends Spanish, Taíno, and African cuisines.

In Condado, **Miró Marisquería Catalana,** 76 Condado Ave. (© 787/723-9593), serves seafood and traditional Catalonian dishes. Not far away, **Ajili Mójili,** 1052 Ashford Ave. (© 787/725-9195), serves some of the island's best upmarket Puerto Rican cuisine.

For stylish but relaxed beachfront dining and sublime Caribbean delicacies, no place beats **Pamela's,** 1 Calle Santa Ana (© 787/726-5010), in Ocean Park. You'll savor every bite.

24 St. Barthélemy (St. Barts)

Chic, sophisticated St. Barthélemy—St. Barts to everyone in the know—is internationally renowned as one of the ritziest refuges in the Caribbean, rivaled only by Mustique as the preferred island retreat of the rich and famous. From early fans Nureyev, Baryshnikov, and Buffett to later enthusiasts Mick Jagger, Princess Di, Calvin Klein, Madonna, and Naomi Campbell, the glitterati who've played here form a veritable Who's Who of fabulousness. Despite its transformation over the past couple of decades into a celebrity hot spot, St. Barts retains its charm, serenity, natural beauty, and Gallic flavor. Just 24km (15 miles) from St. Martin and politically part of Guadeloupe, the island's 13 square km (8 sq. miles) of dramatic hills and pristine white-sand beaches are decidedly French, like a peaceful slice of the Côte d'Azur transplanted in the Caribbean. The roller-coaster terrain, strict zoning and construction laws, and a local consensus that stratospheric pricing is the surest way to maintain exclusivity protect the island from massive development that would certainly change its character.

First inhabited about 3,000 years ago by Ciboney Indians, then later by Arawaks (A.D. 200) and Caribs (A.D. 1000), St. Barts was first spotted by Europeans in 1496, when Christopher Columbus named the island after his baby brother, Bartolemeo. Finding no gold, the single-minded Spanish moved on. Nothing much happened until 1648, when 60 Frenchmen from St. Kitts colonized the hills. Caribs massacred these settlers 8 years later, bringing the colonial experiment to a quick end. In 1674, Huguenots from Brittany and Normandy claimed the island. In no time, St. Barts's strategic position, natural harbor, and numerous bays and anchorages made it a haven for French buccaneers who plundered Spanish galleons. In 1784, King Louis XVI traded the island to Sweden for free port rights in the Swedish town of Goteborg. Delighted to have a colony in the New World, the Swedes built forts, houses, and roads, walled off pastures, and brought law and order. Renaming the main town Gustavia to honor their king, they declared St. Barts a free port, spurring unprecedented development. But with changing trade routes, hurricanes, droughts, disease, and, finally, a fire that destroyed Gustavia, the colony faltered. Sweden transferred St. Barts back to France in 1878, with the stipulation that it remain a free port. Over the next hundred years, the island's economy centered on fishing and small-scale agriculture (the rugged, volcanic hills precluded a plantation economy). It wasn't until the 1980s that St. Barts began to impress jet-setting tourists. Later, tax breaks for French nationals fueled investment in tourism.

In sharp contrast to most Caribbean islands, where descendants of African slaves form the majority, St. Barts's 7,000 year-round residents are primarily of French ancestry, mostly from Brittany and Normandy. Many affluent Americans and Europeans have villas on the island, some living in the Caribbean year-round, others making seasonal visits.

COMING ASHORE Cruise ships anchor off Gustavia, the main town, and ferry passengers to the dollhouse-size harbor and town via tenders. Phones and ATMs are in the immediate vicinity of the harbor. The post office (or PTT), which also serves as a telecommunications center, is located at the back corner of the harbor opposite the dock. You can check your e-mail at the second-floor offices of **Centre @lizes** (📞 **590/29-89-89**), on Rue de la République, a few blocks to the right of the dock. Access to the Internet is about 12¢ a minute. Be sure to ask for an American keyboard: The position of letters on French keyboards is significantly different.

LANGUAGE **French** is the official language, but virtually everyone speaks **English** as well.

CURRENCY St. Barts is part of the French overseas region of Guadeloupe, so the **Euro** (€) is now the official currency (exchange rate: €1 = U.S.90¢; $1 = €1.10). Notes are denominated in 500, 200, 100, 50, 20, 10, and 5 euros; coins come in 1 and 2 euro and 50, 20, 10, 5, 2, and 1 cent denominations. Prices mentioned in this section are in dollars. You'll have no trouble using credit cards and traveler's checks.

INFORMATION The **Office Municipal du Tourisme** (📞 **590/27-87-27**), adjacent to the dock on Quai Général de Gaulle, is open Monday from 8:30am to 12:30pm; Tuesday through Friday from 8am to noon and from 2 to 5pm; and

> ⸜Tips⸝ **Caveat Emptor**
>
> Many locals argue that the tranquility and charm that bring St. Barts's loyal repeat visitors back to the island time and time again are under siege. The increasing number of cruise ship passengers has created controversy and resistance. Shops in the main town of Gustavia have been known to close when large cruise ships anchor off the harbor, and many shop owners who stay open complain that their regular, free-spending clientele stays away when cruisers are in town. Harsher critics compare the influx of cruise ships to the opening of a Wal-Mart on Fifth Avenue. Most Caribbean islands depend on cruise tourism, but on St. Barts, where quiet, affluent stayover guests spend exponentially more than cruisers, only shipping agents, taxi drivers, and a handful of T-shirt vendors favor development of the island as a port of call.
>
> Intimidated? Offended? Relax. Few locals are overtly hostile and most respond to smiles and human warmth. Respect the low-key elegance that makes St. Barts special, maintain a low profile, and enjoy the pleasures of the island's outstanding beaches and restaurants.

Saturday from 9am to noon. For information before you go, get on the horn to Maison de la France in the U.S. (© 212/838-7800; www.st-barths.com).

CALLING FROM THE U.S. When calling St. Barts from the United States, dial the international access code (011) and 590 before the numbers listed here, which *also* begin with 590. That's right: If you want to make a connection, you have to dial 590 twice. It's just one of those oddities that make the world go round.

GETTING AROUND

BY TAXI Taxis meet cruise ships at Gustavia's harbor. Because the island is so small, no destination is too distant. Consequently, fares seem reasonable. Dial © 590/27-66-31 for service if you don't spot a cab. The fare is about $3.50 for rides up to 5 minutes; each additional 3 minutes is another $2.80.

BY RENTAL CAR If you love adventure, rent an open-sided Mini-Moke (a jeep–golf cart hybrid) or Suzuki Samurai: Zipping up and down St. Barts's jagged, picturesque hills is more thrilling than riding most amusement-park rides. Roads are in excellent condition, and local drivers are alert and competent, but tend to drive aggressively. Automatic transmissions are in short supply, so reserve in advance: If you're not already adept at using a stick shift, St. Barts is not the place to learn. **Budget** and **Avis** have offices here, as does **Europcar** (© 590/27-74-34). The island has only two gas stations: one near the airport, the other in Lorient. Both are closed on Sundays, but the airport station has a pump that accepts credit cards any time of day, any day of the week.

BY MOTOR SCOOTER Terrified by winding roads and speeding drivers, mothers on St. Barts are loath to let their kids ride scooters. Few bikes have the power to make it up the steep hills anyway. If you have a death wish, go ahead and rent a motorbike or scooter from **Meca Moto** (© 590/52-92-49), Rue du Général de Gaulle, or **Tropic'all Rent** (© 590/27-64-76), Rue du Roi Oscar II, both in Gustavia. Expect to pay about $30 for the day, mandatory helmet included. A $200 deposit or credit-card imprint is required.

SHORE EXCURSIONS OFFERED BY THE CRUISE LINES

Minibus Island Tour ($25, 1½ hr.): This brief excursion highlights the island's natural beauty and beaches. Stops include Gustavia, the port and main town; St. Jean, one of the more popular beaches and shopping areas; Grand Cul de Sac, the lagoon and beach favored by windsurfers; and Corossol, a tiny fishing village where the traditions of St. Barts survive.

ON YOUR OWN: WITHIN WALKING DISTANCE

Aside from shopping, eating, and hanging out in sidewalk cafes, cruisers sticking close to port can visit Gustavia's modest points of interest. **St. Bartholomew's Church,** Rue Samuel Fahlberg, dates from the 1850s and features limestone and volcanic stone walls, as well as imported pitch pine pews. Its tiny Anglican, English-speaking congregation is an anomaly on this overwhelmingly French Catholic island.

Evidence of St. Barts's faint but lingering Swedish presence, the **Wall House,** Rue Duquesne, is a staid, stone building near the harbor's mouth, across from the dock. Once a Swedish home, the structure was rebuilt after fire devastated it (and much of Gustavia) in 1852. Since 1989, it's housed the **Municipal Museum** (© 590/29-71-55), an unfocused but respectable introduction to the history, sociology, ethnology, economy, and ecology of the island. The most interesting items include Amerindian artifacts, rustic farm furnishings, clothing used by early French settlers, and photos documenting hurricane devastation. Admission for persons over 12 is $2; the exhibits are open Monday 2:30 to 6pm, Tuesday through Friday 8:30am to 12:30pm and 2:30 to 6pm, and Saturday 9am to 1pm.

ON YOUR OWN: BEYOND THE PORT AREA

Visiting the tiny fishing village of **Corossol** is a vibrant way to experience the St. Barts of the past. About 10 minutes by taxi from the dock, this quaint, totally un-chic hamlet is home to traditional folk who still live off the sea. It's your best bet for spotting women in traditional 17th-century bonnets and for watching roadside vendors weave items from palm fronds. On the town's waterfront, about 30m (100 ft.) to the left of the road from Gustavia, the **Inter Oceans Museum** (© 590/27-62-97) catalogs thousands of shells, corals, sand dollars,

---

 Frommer's Favorite St. Barts Experiences

Making the Scene at Le Select: For more than 50 years this garden cafe has been the most popular gathering spot in Gustavia, and the best place to get a taste of local life. (See "Great Local Restaurants & Bars," below.)

Bronzing on the Beach: St. Barts has several gorgeous beaches, some social, some private. (See "Beaches," below.)

Zipping Around the Island in a Mini-Moke: Few experiences are as exhilarating as zooming along the island's roller-coaster roads in one of these open-air vehicles, half golf cart, half jeep. (See "Getting Around," above.)

sea horses, sea urchins, and fish from around the world. One (now very old) man's obsession, the museum is homemade, though displays are completely endearing and sure to enthrall the child in everyone. Don't miss the collection of sand from beaches around the world: A cocktail umbrella is planted in each specimen. Admission is $3. Doors to this extension of the owner's home are open from 8am to 5pm, Monday through Saturday.

SHOPPING

A duty-free port, St. Barts is a good place to buy liquor, perfume, and other French luxury items. Good buys on apparel, crystal, porcelain, and watches can also be found, especially during April, the biggest sale month. Moisturizer mavens can stock up on the island's own cosmetic line, Ligne St. Barth. Shops are concentrated in Gustavia and St. Jean, where the quality-to-schlock ratio is as high as anywhere in the Caribbean. Most shops and offices close for a long lunch, usually from noon to 2pm.

In Gustavia, **Carat,** Rue de la République, **Fabienne Miot,** Rue de la République, and **Diamond Genesis,** Rue du Général de Gaulle, offer an array of fine jewelry, some handcrafted on the premises. **Dovani,** Rue de la République, and **Privilège,** Rue du Roi Oscar II, are your best bets for perfumes and cosmetics. **St. Barth Style,** Rue Lafayette, near the corner of Rue du Port, stocks fashionable beachwear, while **Mandarine,** Rue de la République, carries chic but casual women's clothing. Higher-style women's fashion is available at **Roberto Cavalli,** Le Carré d'Or, **Stéphane & Bernard,** Rue de la République behind Carat, and **Sorélina,** Rue du Général de Gaulle. Men in search of a new shirt or trousers should try **Images Boutique** or **L'Homme et la Mer,** both on Rue du Général de Gaulle. Men's and women's shoes can be found at **Human Steps,** Rue de la France. **Le Comptoir du Cigare,** Rue du Général de Gaulle, sells cigars from Cuba and the Dominican Republic and connoisseur-quality rums, while **Nilaya,** Rue du Roi Oscar II, stocks unique, handcrafted objets d'art from Asia and elsewhere around the world.

In St. Jean, **Kiwi Saint Tropez** stocks chic beachwear, **Bleu Marine** has French and Italian women's fashions, **Elysees Caraïbes** sells high-style handbags and luggage, and **Boutique Iléna** offers erotic lingerie.

BEACHES

The beaches of St. Barts are first-rate. By official count, the island has 22, each blessed with blindingly white sand. Few are ever crowded, even during the peak season, and all are public, free, and easily accessible by taxi from the cruise pier (make arrangements with your driver to be picked up at a specific time). As St. Barts is a French island, toplessness is common at all beaches. Full nudism is officially prohibited, but bathers at several sites—Saline and Gouverneur, to name a couple (see below)—willfully flout the rules. Defying a common stereotype, most nude bathers on the island actually have attractive bodies.

If you're looking for an active beach strand, with restaurants and watersports, **Grand Cul de Sac** fits the bill. The shallow, protected waters here are warm and relatively calm. Watersports are well represented, with windsurfing especially popular. An even busier and equally social beach, **St. Jean** is actually two beaches divided by a rock promontory. Protected by a coral reef, the calm waters here attract families and water-toy enthusiasts, including windsurfers. When the winds gather greater force, surfer dudes appear. Near the end of the airport's incredibly short runway, St. Jean also provides numerous eating, drinking, shopping, and people-watching opportunities. The scene is considerably more subdued at **Flamands,** a huge stretch of white sand on the northeast coast. Despite a smattering of hotels and restaurants, this expanse is often deserted. Blame it on the waves, which, although frequently intimidating, are seldom dangerous. Also on the north shore, **Marigot** is more popular with locals than visitors, probably because it's so close to the road. It's good for snorkeling, though, and full of parents, children, and sandcastles on Sundays. Another spot favored by St. Barts families, **Lorient** is more than 540m (600 yd.) long. The waters here are generally tranquil, except at the far end, where the waves kick up, making it popular with surfers. If you're more in the mood for a rustic and totally unpretentious stretch of sand, head to the village of **Corossol,** probably the island's quaintest fishing port. Here you can take a dip at the small and relatively unspectacular town beach while getting a taste of what St. Barts was like before it became chic. **Gouverneur,** on the south central coast, is quiet and relatively remote. Its idyllic setting and unspoiled beauty make it No. 1 with locals and discerning visitors who want privacy and serenity. Farther east, in a wild and rustic area that was once the site of salt ponds, **Saline** is reached by a 3-minute hike over a sand dune. Most famous for its adult environment and nude bathers, it also boasts great bodysurfing waves. Closest to port, **Shell Beach** can be reached on foot from Gustavia. Sections of this beach have been artificially covered with thousands of small shells, a treat for kids. St. Barts's most secluded beach, **Colombier,** on the island's northeast tip, is reachable by boat from Gustavia or by foot from a picturesque trail beginning at Petite Anse (allow 30 min. for the walk). It's sometimes referred to as "Rockefeller's Beach" because David Rockefeller once owned the surrounding property. Usually very quiet, it's a popular picnic spot for locals on Sundays and is good for snorkeling.

SPORTS

SAILING, SCUBA DIVING & SNORKELING   Marine Service, Quai du Yacht Club (© **590/27-70-34**), operates from the marina across the harbor from the busier side of Gustavia. Most dive sites served by this five-star PADI operator are a 10- to 20-minute boat ride from the harbor; depths vary from 3 to 30m (10 to 100 ft.). Reef dives are the rule, although one wreck dive for more experienced divers is a possibility. One-tank dives are about $60; two-tank dives are about $80, including beverages and all equipment. The operation also offers half-day snorkeling cruises (about $50, including snorkeling gear and a French snack buffet) and catamaran or sloop charters (starting at $350 for half a day during the low season; $400 during the winter, including cheese, fruit, beverages, and music). Vendors at both St. Jean and Grand Cul de Sac rent snorkel gear and other watersports equipment—jet skis, Sunfish sailboats, and so on.

WINDSURFING   Try St. Barth Wind School (© **590/27-71-22**) near the Tom Beach Hotel at St. Jean or **Windwave Power** (© **590/27-82-57**) at Grand Cul de Sac. Expect to pay about $20 an hour for a full rig.

GREAT LOCAL RESTAURANTS & BARS

Mix lots of rich, discerning diners with the French tradition of culinary expertise, and it's no wonder that so many of St. Barts's restaurants consistently receive high accolades. Craig Claiborne, the fabled *New York Times* food critic, spent every Christmas here for decades, declaring that "no other Caribbean island has such an assortment of fine French foods." It's a pity that some of the best open only for dinner, well after your ship has gone out to sea. Luckily, enough serve lunch to assure you one of the best meals of your cruise.

IN GUSTAVIA   More interested in seeing and being seen than in satisfying your taste buds? Make a beeline to **Le Select,** Rue de la France at Rue du Général de Gaulle (© **590/27-86-87**), the epicenter of Gustavia's social life for more than 50 years. This cafe's tables rest in a tree-shaded garden a block from the harbor. A full bar is available to complement burgers, salads, and other simple fare. Salty locals, celebrities, and chic tourists are among the clientele. The classic, funky ambience inspired Jimmy Buffett's "Cheeseburger in Paradise." At the foot of Gustavia harbor, **La Route des Boucaniers** (© **590/27-73-00**) looks like any seaside restaurant around Chesapeake Bay or on the Jersey shore, but its traditional and nouvelle créole cuisine is anything but run-of-the-mill. Try the octopus gratin served in a potato shell or the braised scallops with passion fruit. **Carl Gustaf Restaurant** (© **590/29-79-47**), at Gustavia's upscale Carl Gustaf Hotel on Rue des Normands, offers a panoramic view of Gustavia harbor, as well as light Antillean and fusion specialties, such as squid and chorizo casserole. It's expensive, with fixed-price lunches from $22 to about $36. **L'Iguane,** Quai de la République (© **590/27-88-46**), offers an international menu that includes sushi and light sandwiches and salads.

AT ST. JEAN   **Eden Rock** (© **590/29-79-99**) has three restaurants at St. Jean beach: one on the rock promontory that bisects the strand, one next to the ocean, and one in the sand. Traditional French cuisine, seafood, and tropical drinks are the trio's strong suits. For great pizza and friendly ambience, try **The Hideaway** (© **590/27-63-62**). Relax on the open-air terrace or get your order to go. If you're more in the mood for a sandwich and want to get back to the sun, head to **KiKi-e Mo** (© **590/27-90-65**), an Italian gourmet shop that whips up divine light fare to go.

AT GRANDE SALINE   A handful of restaurants are within walking distance of Saline beach. **Grain de Sel** (© **590/52-46-05**) looks no-frills, but the seafood and créole specialties are deluxe. Prettier and more upscale, but just as relaxing, **Le Tamarin** (© **590/27-72-12**) specializes in beef, salmon, and tuna carpaccios; fresh grilled lobster; and inventive créole dishes.

AT GRAND CUL DE SAC   Seaside restaurants abound on Grand Cul de Sac beach. **Club Lafayette** (© **590/27-62-51**) has an exclusive and tony, yet congenial, atmosphere. Prices can be astronomical, but try the warm foie gras served with apples or the prodigious lobster salad. More moderately priced menus can be found at **La Gloriette** (© **590/27-75-66**), which offers easygoing ambience, créole specialties, and fresh seafood, and **L'Indigo** (© **590/27-66-60**), at the Hotel Guanahani, where salads and grilled lobster steal the show.

25 St. Croix

Though it's now part of the U.S. Virgin Islands, and though seven different flags have flown over St. Croix in its history, it's the 2½ centuries of Danish influence that are most visible in the island's architecture.

Today, St. Croix, the largest of the USVIs at 212 square km (82 sq. miles), competes with St. Thomas for the Yankee cruise ship dollar. It gets nowhere near the number of visitors that St. Thomas does, but maybe that's a good thing: It's more tranquil and less congested than its smaller sibling. At the east end of the island (which, incidentally, is the easternmost possession of the U.S.), the terrain is rocky and arid. The west end is more lush, with a rain forest of mango and mahogany, tree ferns, and dangling lianas. Rolling hills and upland pastures make up much of the area between the two extremes, and the vivid African tulips are just one of the many tropical flowers that add a splash of color to the landscape, which is dotted with the ruins of sugarcane plantations. The major St. Croix attraction is **Buck Island National Park,** an offshore national treasure of coral reefs. There are some fine beaches here as well, including Sandy Point, Sprat Hall, and Rainbow Beach.

Although large cruise ships moor at **Frederiksted,** most of the action is really in **Christiansted,** located on a coral-bound bay about midway along the north shore, which features more sights and better restaurants and shopping than **Frederiksted.** The town is being handsomely restored, and the entire harborfront area is a national historic site.

St. Croix's population is descended from both Africa and Europe, and some families have been here for 10 generations, with roots dating back to colonial times.

COMING ASHORE   Only cruise ships with fewer than 200 passengers can land directly at the dock at Christiansted. Others moor at newly renovated **Abramson Pier** at Frederiksted, a sleepy town that springs to life only when the ships arrive. There's space for two megaships, and both piers have information centers and telephones. We suggest you spend as little time as possible in Frederiksted and head immediately for Christiansted, some 27km (17 miles) away. It's easy to explore either town on foot (it's the only way, really). You might want to consider one of the shore excursions outlined below to see more of the island, especially its underwater treasures.

Although St. Croix is relatively safe, it's wise to stay on the beaten path and watch your belongings on the beaches (as you should on any island); in late 2001, four incidences of muggings and robberies were reported involving Carnival Cruise Line passengers and crew.

LANGUAGE   **English** is spoken here.

CURRENCY   The **U.S. dollar** is the official currency.

INFORMATION   The **U.S. Virgin Islands Department of Tourism** has offices in Christiansted at Queen Cross Street (© 340/773-0495), and at the Customs House Building, Strand Street in Frederiksted (© 340/772-0357). Open Monday to Friday from 9am to 5pm. To get info before you go, contact the tourism board office in the U.S. (© 800/372-USVI; www.usvi.org/tourism). To get up-to-the-minute info on St. Croix, from taxi and bus rates to maps and info on restaurants and the island's history and culture, pick up a free copy of the pink *St. Croix This Week,* which has a lot more than just ads.

CALLING FROM THE U.S.   When calling St. Croix from the United States, you only need to dial a "1" before the numbers listed throughout this section.

GETTING AROUND

BY TAXI   Taxis are unmetered, and rates are set from point to point. The **St. Croix Taxicab Association** (© 340/778-1088) offers door-to-door service. Taxi tours are a great way to explore the island. For one or two passengers, the cost is about $50 for 2 hours or $70 for 3 hours. It costs $20 to take a taxi from Christiansted to Frederiksted.

BY BUS   Air-conditioned buses run between Christiansted and Frederiksted about every 40 minutes daily between 5:30am and 9pm. The main stop in Christiansted is on Hospital Street, near the National Park office; the main stop in Frederiksted is on Custom House Street, near Fort Frederick and King Street. The fare is $1. For more information, call © **340/778-0898.**

BY SEAPLANE   Regular seaplane shuttles between St. Croix and St. Thomas are available for $150 round-trip; however, special rates are available for nonresidents, running as low as $90 round-trip, provided that you travel from 9:30am to 3:30pm Monday through Friday or any hours on Saturday and Sunday. Book ahead. Flights depart every 15 to 45 minutes in both directions, and flight time is a mere 18 minutes; but figure 30 minutes from dock to dock. For more information, contact **Seaborne Airlines,** 34 Strand St., Christiansted (© **340/773-6442;** www.seaborneairlines.com).

BY RENTAL CAR   We don't recommend renting a car here.

SHORE EXCURSIONS OFFERED BY THE CRUISE LINES

Buck Island National Park Tour/Snorkeling ($50, 4–5 hr.): The most popular tour in St. Croix takes you to a tropical underwater wonderland of blue water, a dazzling rainbow of sea life, and colorful coral reefs. Transportation is provided from the Frederiksted pier to Christiansted, where a powerboat takes you over to Buck Island. An experienced guide provides snorkel lessons.

Island Tour ($31, 4 hr.): This tour is designed to give a taste of the whole island, with visits to the Whim Great House sugar plantation, Christiansted, and other major sites.

St. Croix Bike Tour ($49, 3 hr.): Bike along the coast of St. Croix, passing through the town of Frederiksted before heading out on the Northside Road, past ruins and through forests and rolling grasslands.

Hiking Tour ($40, 2 hr.): Hike through the 90-hectare (225-acre) Butler Bay Preserve—prime bird-watching territory.

Golf at Carambola ($74–$105, self-timed): Your cruise line will probably offer an excursion to Carambola, one of the Caribbean's most famous golf courses. If not, you can do it on your own (see "Sports," below).

EXCURSIONS OFFERED BY LOCAL OPERATORS

Horseback Tour: On this 1½-hour tour, run by **Paul and Jill's Equestrian Stables,** Sprat Hall Plantation, Route 58 (© **340/772-2880;** http://pws.prserv.net/paul-and-jills), you'll pass ruins of abandoned 18th-century plantations and sugar mills, and climb the hills of St. Croix's western end. Tour guides give running

   Frommer's Favorite St. Croix Experiences

Visiting Buck Island Reef National Monument: Within this 800-acre preserve (the only underwater national monument in the United States), you can snorkel over a series of unique marked underwater trails and experience some of the best-preserved coral reefs in the Caribbean. A snorkeling instructor guides the excursion. (See "Shore Excursions Offered by the Cruise Lines," above.)

Biking Along the Coast: On this tour, you'll pass through Frederiksted, past ruins, and through forests and rolling grasslands. (See "Shore Excursions Offered by the Cruise Lines," above.)

St. Croix

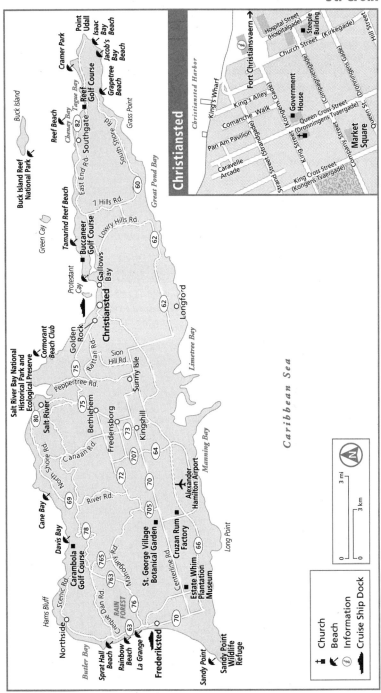

Christiansted

Hospital Street (Hospitalgade)
Steeple Building
Church Street (Kirkegade)
Hill Street
Fort Christiansvaern
King's Wharf
Christiansted Harbor
King's Alley
King's Walk
Comanche Walk
Pan Am Pavilion
Caravelle Arcade
Government House
King Street (Kongens Gade)
Queen Cross Street (Dronningens Tvaergade)
Queen St.
Strand Street (Strandgade)
Market Square
Company Street (Compagniesgade)
Dronningens Gade
King Cross Street (Kongens Tvaergade)

Point Udall
Isaac Bay Beach
Cramer Park
Jacob's Bay Beach
Reef Golf Course
Grapetree Beach
Reef Beach
Chenay Bay
Teague Bay
82
Southgate
Grass Point
Buck Island
Buck Island Reef National Park
East End Rd.
South Shore Rd.
Green Cay
Tamarind Reef Beach
1 Hills Rd.
Buccaneer Golf Course
Lowry Hills Rd.
60
Great Pond Bay
Gallows Bay
62
Protestant Cay
Salt River Bay National Historical Park and Ecological Preserve
Cormorant Beach Club
Christiansted
Longfo'rd
62
Golden Rock
Rattan Rd.
Sion Hill Rd.
Limetree Bay
75
Peppertree Rd.
Sunny Isle
Salt River
80
Bethlehem
75
Fredensborg
73
Kingshill
64
Manning Bay
North Shore Rd.
Canaan Rd.
707
72
70
Alexander Hamilton Airport
69
River Rd.
705
Cane Bay
Davis Bay
78
St. George Village Botanical Garden
Cruzan Rum Factory
66
Long Point
Carambola Golf Course
765
Mahogany Rd.
Centerline Rd.
763
Estate Whim Plantation Museum
Hams Bluff
Scenic Rd.
RAIN FOREST
Cane Dan Rd.
76
Northside
Sprat Hall Beach
Rainbow Beach
63
70
La Grange
Frederiksted
Butler Bay
Sandy Point
Sandy Point Wildlife Refuge

Caribbean Sea

N

3 mi
3 km
0
0

✝ Church
🏖 Beach
ℹ Information
⚓ Cruise Ship Dock

251

commentaries on island fauna and history and on riding techniques. The stables, owned by Paul Wojcie and his wife, Jill Hurd (a daughter of the establishment's original founders), are set on the sprawling grounds of the island's oldest plantation, and are known throughout the Caribbean for the quality of the horses and the exceptionally scenic forest trails. The grounds also boast an exquisite tropical fruit orchard. Both beginner and experienced riders are welcome. Make reservations in advance.

ON YOUR OWN: WITHIN WALKING DISTANCE

IN FREDERIKSTED   Frederiksted is nothing great, but if you decide to hang around, you should begin your tour at russet-colored **Fort Frederik** (© 340/772-2021), next to the cruise ship pier. Some historians claim it was the first fort to sound a foreign salute to the U.S. flag, in 1776. The structure, at the northern end of Frederiksted, has been restored to its 1840 look. You can explore the courtyard and stables, visit the police museum, peruse exhibits of antique cannons and clothing, and see photographs of life on St. Croix in the days of yore. Admission is free. The fort is open Monday to Saturday from 8am to 5pm.

IN CHRISTIANSTED   You can begin your visit at the **visitor bureau** (© 340/773-0495), a yellow building with a cedar roof near the harbor front. It was built as the Old Scalehouse in 1856 to replace a similar, older structure that burned down. In its heyday, all taxable goods leaving and entering the harbor were weighed here. The scales could once accurately weigh barrels of sugar and molasses weighing up to 1,600 pounds.

The **Steeple Building** (© 340/773-1460), or Church of Lord God of Sabaoth, was completed in 1753 as St. Croix's first Lutheran church. It, too, stands near the harbor front, and contains an exhibit on island heritage in general and the church in particular, with photos and artifacts. Get there via Hospital Street. The building was deconsecrated in 1831 and has served at various times as a bakery, a hospital, and a school. It's open daily from 8am to 5pm, and admission is $2, which also includes admission to **Fort Christiansvaern** (© 340/773-1460), the best-preserved colonial fortification in the Virgin Islands. The National Park Service maintains the fort as a historic monument, overlooking the harbor. Its original star-shaped design was at the vanguard of the most advanced military planning of its era. The fort is open Monday to Thursday from 8am to 4:30pm, Friday and Saturday from 9am to 5pm.

ON YOUR OWN: BEYOND THE PORT AREA

Salt River, on the island's northern shore, is the only site that Columbus is known to have landed upon in what is now U.S. territory. To mark the 500th anniversary of the arrival of Columbus, former President George Bush signed a bill creating the 912-acre **Salt River Bay National Historical Park and Ecological Preserve.** The landmass includes the site of the original Carib village explored by Columbus and his men, along with the only Taíno ceremonial ball court (used for ceremonial sporting events) ever discovered in the Lesser Antilles. At the Carib settlement, Columbus's men liberated several Taíno women and children held as slaves. On the way back to their vessels, the Spaniards faced a canoe filled with hostile Caribs, armed with poison arrows. One Spanish soldier was killed, and perhaps six Caribs were either slain or captured. This is the first documented case of hostility between invading Europeans and Native Americans. Sailing away, Columbus named this part of St. Croix "Cape of the Arrows."

The park today is in a natural state. It has the largest mangrove forest in the Virgin Islands, sheltering many endangered animals and plants, plus an underwater canyon attracting scuba divers from around the world. The **St. Croix Environmental Association,** 3 Arawak Building, Gallows Bay (© 340/773-1989; www.seastx.com), conducts tours of the area.

The **Cruzan Rum Factory,** West Airport Road, Route 64 (© 340/692-2280), distills the famous Virgin Islands rum. Guided tours depart from the visitor pavilion; call for reservations and information.

Restored by the St. Croix Landmarks Society, the **Estate Whim Plantation Museum,** Centerline Road, about 3km (2 miles) east of Frederiksted (© 340/772-0598), is composed of only three rooms and is unique among the many old sugar plantations dotting the island, with 3-foot-thick walls made of stone, coral, and molasses. Also on the museum's premises are a woodworking shop, the estate's original kitchen, a museum store, servant's quarters, and tools from the 18th century. The ruins include remains of the plantation's sugar-processing plant, complete with a restored windmill.

The **St. George Village Botanical Garden of St. Croix** (© 340/692-2874) is a much-loved, popular Eden of tropical trees, shrubs, vines, and flowers, located 6.5km (4 miles) east of Frederiksted.

SHOPPING

Americans get a break here, since they can bring home $1,200 worth of merchandise from the U.S. Virgin Islands without paying duty, as opposed to a paltry $400 from most other Caribbean ports. And liquor here is duty-free.

The **King's Alley Complex,** a pink-sided compound created right on the Christiansted waterfront following the hurricanes of 1995, is filled with the densest concentration of shopping options on St. Croix. There are a number of worthwhile specialty shops in Christiansted as well. **Skirt Tails,** Pam Am Pavilion, is one of the most colorful and popular boutiques on the island, specializing in hand-painted batiks for both men and women. The **White House/Black Market,** King's Alley Walk, stocks women's clothing, ranging from dressy to casual and breezy—with all apparel in black and white. **Elegant Illusions Copy Jewelry,** 55 King St., sells credible copies of the baroque and antique jewelry your great-grandmother might have worn, priced from $10 to $1,000. **Larimar,** on The Boardwalk/King's Walk, specializes in its namesake, a pale-blue pectolyte stone prized for its sky-blue color, in various gold settings. **Sonya Ltd.,** 1 Company St., specializes in traditional Caribbean hook bracelets.

Folk Art Traders, 1B Queen Cross St., deals in Caribbean art and folk-art treasures, such as carnival masks, pottery, ceramics, original paintings, and hand-wrought jewelry. **Many Hands,** in the Pan Am Pavilion, Strand Street, sells Virgin Islands handicrafts, spices and teas, handmade jewelry, and more.

There are a wealth of local artists and galleries in Christiansted, all located right in the same area. Check out **Mitchell-Larson Studio,** 58 Company St., for glass art; **Maria Henle Studio,** 55 Company St.; the **Memories of St. Croix** artisan cooperative, diagonally across from the Steeple Building; and **Christensted Gallery,** located at 1 Company St., upstairs.

GAMBLING

St. Croix's first casino opened in early 2000 at the new **Divi Carina Bay Hotel,** 25 Estate Turner Hole, in Christiansted, on the east side of the island (© 340/773-9700; www.divicarina.com). By taxi, it takes approximately 45 minutes and costs about $30 per person to get to the casino from Frederiksted. The casino opens at noon.

BEACHES

Beaches are the biggest attraction on St. Croix. The drawback is that getting to them from Christiansted or Frederiksted isn't always easy. Taxis will take you, but they can be expensive. From Christiansted, you can take a ferry to the **Hotel on the Cay,** a palm-shaded island in the harbor.

NEAR FREDERIKSTED   Most convenient for passengers arriving at Frederiksted is **Sandy Point,** the largest beach in all of the U.S. Virgin Islands. Its waters are shallow and calm, perfect for swimming. You may remember this beach from the last scene of the movie *The Shawshank Redemption.* Sandy Point is also the nesting ground for endangered leatherback and green sea turtles, who lay their eggs every year between early April and early June. Parts of the beach are roped off during this time, but you can watch these fascinating creatures from outside of the protected areas.

On Route 63, a short ride north of Frederiksted, **Rainbow Beach** is inviting, with its white sand and ideal snorkeling conditions. **La Grange** is another good beach in the vicinity, also on Route 63, about 5 minutes north of Frederiksted. You can rent lounge chairs here, and there's a bar nearby.

We highly recommend **Cane Bay** and **Davis Bay.** They're both the type of beaches you'd expect to find on a Caribbean island—palms, white sand, and good swimming and snorkeling. Cane Bay attracts snorkelers and divers with its rolling waves, coral gardens, and drop-off wall. It's near Route 80 on the north shore. Davis Beach, off the South Shore Road (Rte. 60) in the vicinity of the Carambola Beach Resort, draws bodysurfers. There are no changing facilities here.

NEAR CHRISTIANSTED   At the **Cormorant Beach Club,** about 8km (5 miles) west of Christiansted, palm trees shade some 360m (1,200 ft.) of white sands. A living reef lies just off the shore, making snorkeling ideal.

Windsurfers like **Reef Beach,** which opens onto Teague Bay along Route 82, East End Road, a half-hour ride from Christiansted. You can find good beach grub at the popular Duggan's Reef restaurant. **Cramer Park,** at the northeastern end of the island, is a special public park operated by the Department of Agriculture. Lined with sea-grape trees, the beach has a picnic area, a restaurant, and a bar.

SPORTS

GOLF   St. Croix has the best golfing in the U.S. Virgin Islands, hands down. In fact, guests staying on St. John and St. Thomas often fly over to St. Croix for a day, just to play. The 18-hole, par-72 **Carambola Golf Course,** on the northeast side of St. Croix (© **340/778-5638**), was designed by Robert Trent Jones, Sr., who called it "the loveliest course I ever designed." Golfing authorities consider its collection of par-3 holes to be the best in the tropics. Greens fees are $100 (including golf cart). The 18-hole, par-70 **Buccaneer,** 3km (2 miles) east of Christiansted (© **340/773-2100,** ext. 738), is a challenging 5,313m (5,810-yd.) course with panoramic vistas. Players can knock the ball over rolling hills right to the edge of the ocean. Greens fees are $65. The 2,835m (3,100-yd.), nine-hole, par-35 course **Reef Golf Course** is located at Teague Bay on the east end of the island (© **340/773-8844**). Greens fees are $12.

SCUBA DIVING   Divers love St. Croix's sponge life, beautiful black-coral trees, and steep drop-offs near the shoreline. This island is home to the largest living reef in the Caribbean. Its fabled north-shore wall begins in 25 to 30 feet (8 to 9m) of water and drops—sometimes almost straight down—to 13,200 feet (3,960m). There are 22 moored diving sites. Favorites include **Salt River Canyon,** the coral gardens of **Scotch Banks,** and **Eagle Ray,** filled with cruising eagle rays. **Pavilions** is another good dive site, boasting a pristine coral reef. The best site of all, however, is **Buck Island,** an underwater wonderland with a visibility of more than 100 feet (30m) and an underwater nature trail. All minor and major agencies offer scuba and snorkeling tours to Buck Island. **Dive St. Croix,** 59 King's Wharf (© **800/523-DIVE** in the U.S., or 340/773-2628; fax 340/773-7400), operates the 38-foot dive boat *Reliance.* **S.C.O.R.E./V.I. Divers Ltd.,** in the Pan Am Pavilion on Christiansted's waterfront (© **340/773-6045**), is the oldest and one of the best dive operations on the island. *Rodale's Scuba Diving* magazine rated S.C.O.R.E.'s staff as among the top 10 worldwide. This full-service PADI five-star facility offers daily two-tank boat dives, as well as guided snorkeling trips to Green Cay.

GREAT LOCAL RESTAURANTS & BARS
A couple of favorite **local beers** are Carib and Blackbeard's (made on St. Thomas); the favorite **local rum** is Cruzan.

IN CHRISTIANSTED   Annabelle's Tea Room, 51-ABC Company St. (© **340/773-3990**), occupies a quiet courtyard and serves an assortment of sandwiches, salads, and soups. **Harvey's,** 11B Company St. (© **340/773-3433**), features the thoroughly zesty cooking of island matriarch Sarah Harvey. Main dishes are the type of food Sarah was raised on: barbecue chicken, barbecue spareribs (barbecue is big here), boiled fillet of snapper, and lobster when she can get it. **Indies,** 55–56 Company St. (© **340/692-9440**), serves what may be the finest and freshest meals on St. Croix. The swordfish with fresh artichokes, shiitake mushrooms, and thyme is a savory treat, as is the baked wahoo with lobster curry, fresh chutney, and coconut. Helping to promote St. Croix as a food destination, the chic **Restaurant Bacchus,** 52 King St., upstairs, at Queen Cross Street (© **340/692-9922**), is named for the god of wine. There's an impressive wine selection that's won awards of excellence from *Wine Spectator* magazine. Along with a sophisticated menu, they pride themselves on their delicious signature dessert, a bread pudding with bourbon sauce.

Paradise Cafe, Queen Cross St. at 53B Company St., across from Government House (© **340/773-2985**), serves burgers and New York deli-style sandwiches throughout the day—everything from a Reuben to a tuna melt. **Fort Christian Brew Pub,** King's Alley Walk (© **340/713-9820**), has one of the best harbor views in Christiansted and serves beer, plus burgers, sandwiches, and Cajun cuisine. It's the only restaurant/microbrewery in the Virgin Islands. **Tutto Bene,** 2 Company St. (© **340/773-5229**), serves a full range of delectable pastas, plus fish, veggie frittatas, a chicken pesto sandwich, spinach lasagna, and more.

IN FREDERIKSTED   Le St. Tropez, Limetree Court, 67 King St. (© **340/772-3000**), is the most popular bistro in Frederiksted, offering crepes, quiches, soups, and salads for lunch in its sunlit courtyard. **Pier 69,** 69 King St. (© **340/772-0069**), looks like a combination of a 1950s living room and a nautical bar. It's a hangout for Christiansted's counterculture and a top spot for sandwiches and salads.

AROUND THE ISLAND   The popular **Duggan's Reef,** East End Road, Teague Bay (© **340/773-9800**), serves a simple array of salads, crepes, and sandwiches at lunch. **Sunset Grill** (formerly Sprat Hall Beach Restaurant), located on Route 63, 1.5km (1 mile) north of Frederiksted (✆ **340/772-5855**), is an upscale place offering the likes of Parmesan-crusted tuna, buffalo burgers, and chicken quesadillas. Be sure to try their Caribbean seafood pasta—fresh fish, shrimp, and mussels over linguini with a coconut mango broth.

26 St. Kitts

Somewhat off the beaten tourist track, south of St. Martin and north of Guadeloupe, St. Kitts forms the larger half of the combined Federation of St. Kitts and Nevis, which gained self-government from Britain in 1967 and became a totally independent nation in 1983. The two islands are separated by only about 3km (2 miles) of ocean, but the emotional distance is a little wider, with Nevis's citizens often expressing a strong urge for independence from St. Kitts.

St. Kitts—or St. Christopher, a name hardly anyone uses—is by far the more populous of the two islands, with some 35,000 people. It was the first English settlement in the Leeward Islands, and during the plantation age its 176 square km (68 sq. miles) enjoyed one of the richest sugarcane economies in the Caribbean. Of course, the plantation age depended on slave labor for cultivation, and today, though the bulk of the island's revenue still comes from the nationalized sugar industry, the back-breaking and low-paying work of sugar harvesting is shunned by most of St. Kitts's citizens—in their place, Guayanese workers come in for the harvesting season. Cane fields climb the slopes of a volcanic mountain range, and you'll see ruins of old mills and plantation houses as you drive around the island.

St. Kitts is lush and fertile, dotted with rain forests and waterfalls and boasting some lovely beaches along its southeast coastline, but it's also extremely poor and has suffered catastrophically in recent years, being hit with several successive hurricanes in the late 1990s. Despite efforts at wooing tourists, to bring in badly needed cash, the country lags behind in amenities and infrastructure.

The island is crowned by the 1,138m (3,792-ft.) **Mount Liamuiga,** a crater that, thankfully, remains dormant. The island's most impressive landmark is the **Brimstone Hill fortress,** one of the Caribbean's most impressive forts. **Basseterre,** the capital city, is rife with old-time Caribbean architecture, and has a few worthwhile landmarks, but overall the city has little to hold the interest of visitors.

COMING ASHORE In April 1997, the government of St. Kitts and Nevis attempted to replace the older, drab-looking industrial piers of Basseterre by building **Port Zante,** a pier stretching from the center of town into the deep waters offshore, but fate apparently had other plans, and whacked Port Zante hard with successive hurricanes. At press time, the restoration of **Zante** is scheduled for completion in November 2002, after this book is published. Until then, cruise ships will continue to dock at the **Basseterre Deep Water Port,** located at the western side of the Basseterre harbor. Some smaller ships drop passengers off at Basseterre in the morning for tours, then anchor off the beaches at Frigate Bay and South Friar's Bay to pick up passengers after a day of sunbathing and swimming.

LANGUAGE **English** is the language of both islands.

CURRENCY The local currency is the **Eastern Caribbean dollar** (U.S.$1 = EC$2.70; EC$1 = U.S.37¢). Many shops and restaurants quote prices in U.S. dollars. Always determine which currency locals are talking about. We've used U.S.-dollar prices in this section.

INFORMATION You can get local tourist information at the St. Kitts/Nevis Department of Tourism, Pelican Mall, Bay Road, in Basseterre (℗ **800/582-6208** or 869/465-4040), open Monday to Friday from 8am to 4pm. For info before you go, contact the tourism board office in the U.S. (℗ **212/535-1234;** www.stkitts-nevis.com).

CALLING FROM THE U.S. When calling St. Kitts or Nevis from the United States, you just need to dial a "1" before the numbers listed here.

GETTING AROUND

BY TAXI Taxis wait at the docks in Basseterre and in the Circus, a public square near the docks at the intersection of Bank and Fort streets. Since most taxi drivers are also guides, this is the best means of getting around the island. Taxis aren't metered, so you must agree on the price before heading out. Always ask if the rates quoted are in U.S. dollars or Eastern Caribbean dollars.

BY RENTAL CAR We don't recommend renting a car here.

SHORE EXCURSIONS OFFERED BY THE CRUISE LINES

Brimstone Hill Tour ($28, 2½ hr.): Visit this 17th-century citadel, which, at some 240m (800 ft.) above sea level, gives you an inspiring panoramic view of the coastline and the island. Tours typically include a visit to the beautiful Romney Gardens, which lie between Basseterre and the fort. You can check out the lush greenery, say hi to the cows that graze just across the hill, or shop at Cara-belle Boutique.

Rain Forest Adventure Hike ($41, 4 hr.): Departing from Romney Gardens, about 8km (5 miles) from Basseterre, you'll hike along a loop of trail through lush rain forest. With luck, you'll catch sight of some of the island's resident monkey population. This is one of our favorite shore excursions.

Beach Horseback Ride ($38, 1–2 hr.): Cruise ship passengers ride well-trained horses along the Atlantic coastline, where trade winds ensure a cool, breezy trip.

Sail & Snorkel Catamaran Trip ($46, 3–4 hr.): A sailing catamaran takes you to secluded Smitten's Bay for snorkeling among diverse reef fish and coral forma-tions. Complimentary rum punch is served aboard the boat on your return trip.

Nevis Catamaran Trip ($94, 7 hr.): The tour stops at Smitten's Bay for snor-keling before crossing the channel to sister-island Nevis, spending time there on the beach, where a barbecue lunch is served. Food and all drinks are included in the price.

Nevis Botanical Gardens Tour ($75, 3½ hr.): Travel by water taxi to Nevis, vis-iting the Alexander Hamilton Museum before heading for the gardens.

EXCURSIONS OFFERED BY LOCAL AGENCIES

Rain-Forest Tours: For a great rain-forest walk in the thickets around Romney Gardens, contact Addy of **Addy's Rainforest Safaris** (© 869/465-8069). He knows the flora and fauna of St. Kitts like the back of his hand and delivers a sat-isfying, personal rain-forest experience, ending his tour by sharing a plate of his wife's tasty homemade banana bread and some fresh guava and passion fruit juices.

Taxi Tours: You'll find a fleet of taxis waiting in the dock as you disembark from the ship. Taxi drivers will take you on a 3-hour tour of the island for about $60. Lunch can be arranged at one of the local inns. Good inn choices are **Golden Lemon** at Dieppe Bay (© **869/465-7260**) or **Rawlins Plantation,** Mount Pleasant (© **869/465-6221**).

ON YOUR OWN: WITHIN WALKING DISTANCE

The capital city of **Basseterre,** where the docks are located, has typical British colonial architecture and some quaint buildings, a few shops, and a market where locals display fruits and flowers—but even this description might be

---

 Frommer's Favorite St. Kitts Experiences

Visiting Brimstone Hill Fortress: Begun by the British in 1690 and sub-sequently changing hands from British to French and back to British again, this is one of the most impressive forts in the Caribbean, with battlement after battlement leading up to a spectacular view of the sea. (See "Shore Excursions Offered by the Cruise Lines," above and "On Your Own: Beyond the Port Area," below.)

Hiking Mount Liamuiga: The hike up this dormant volcano will take you through a rain forest and along deep ravines up to the rim of the crater at a cool 788m (2,625 ft.). (See "On Your Own: Beyond the Port Area," below.)

giving you the wrong idea about this place. The truth is, it's a very poor town, with few attractions aimed at visitors. Plans call for a revitalization, but we'll have to wait and see.

Rain forest and beaches are the real draw on St. Kitts, so you need only about a half-hour to explore in town. **St. George's Anglican Church,** on Cayon Street (walk straight up Church St. or Fort St. from the dock), is the oldest church in town and is worth a look. **Independence Square,** a stone's throw from the docks along Bank Street, is pretty, with its central fountain and old church, but there's no good reason to linger unless it's to sit in the shade and toss back a bottle of Ting, the refreshing (and very sweet) grapefruit-based local soda.

ON YOUR OWN: BEYOND THE PORT AREA
The **Brimstone Hill Fortress** (© **869/465-6211;** www.brimstonehillfortress. org), 14km (9 miles) west of Basseterre, is the major stop on any tour of St. Kitts. This historic monument, among the largest and best preserved in the Caribbean, is a complex of bastions, barracks, and other structures, ingeniously adapted to the upper slopes of a steep, 240m (800-ft.) hill. The name of the place derives from the odor of sulfur released by nearby undersea vents.

The structure dates from 1690, when the British fortified the hill to help recapture Fort Charles, located below, from the French. In 1782, an invading force of 8,000 French troops bombarded the fortress for a month before its small British garrison, supplemented by local militia, surrendered. When the British took the island back the next year, they proceeded to enlarge the fort into "The Gibraltar of the West Indies." In all, the structure took 104 years to complete.

Today the fortress is the centerpiece of a national park crisscrossed by nature trails and home to a diverse range of plant and animal life, including green vervet monkeys. It's a photographer's paradise, with views of mountains, fields, and the Caribbean Sea—on a clear day you can see six neighboring islands. From below, the fort presents a dramatic picture, poised among diabolical-looking spires and outcroppings of lava rock.

Visitors will enjoy the self-directed tours among the many partially restored structures, including the barrack rooms at Fort George. The gift shop sells prints of rare Caribbean maps and paintings of the Caribbean. Admission is $5 for adults, $2.50 for children. The park is open daily from 9:30am to 5:30pm.

The well-maintained **Romney Gardens** are located amidst the ruins of a sugar estate, just a 15-minute drive from Basseterre, in the town of Old Road. The boiling houses, a chimney, and a stone aqueduct, all enveloped in lush foliage and bright flowering plants, are all that remain of the estate. With pic-turesque views of the sea in the distance, the hillside gardens feature giant ferns, orchids, poinsettias, and "The Tree," a 350-year-old Saman tree. Rain-forest hik-ing excursions depart from here, and most allow time for a short exploration of the gardens and a stop at the Caribelle Batik shop (see "Shopping").

The dormant **Mount Liamuiga volcano,** in the northwest of the island, has long been known as "Mount Misery." It sputtered its last gasp around 1692, and today its summit is a major goal for hikers. A round-trip to the usually cloud-covered peak takes about 4 hours—2½ hours going up, 1½ coming down. Hik-ers usually make the ascent from Belmont Estate near St. Paul on the north end of St. Kitts. The trail winds through a rain forest and travels along deep ravines up to the rim of the crater at a cool 788m (2,625 ft.). Many hikers climb (or crawl) down a steep, slippery trail to a tiny lake in the caldera, some 120m (400 ft.) below the rim.

You can reach the rim without a guide, but it's absolutely necessary to have one to go into the crater. **Greg's Safaris** (© **869/465-4121;** www.skbee.com/safaris) offers guided hikes to the crater for about $60 per person (a minimum of four hikers required), including breakfast, a picnic at the crater's rim, and a cocktail toast at the end. The same outfit also offers half-day rain-forest explorations, also with a picnic, for $40 per person.

SHOPPING

Basseterre is not a shopping town, despite the handout maps you may receive when you arrive, which show a listing of shops that would put St. Thomas's shopping hot spot, Charlotte Amalie, to shame—that is, until you look closer and see entries such as "R. Gumbs Electrical," "TDC/Finco Finance Co.," and "Horsford Furniture Store." Turns out they just listed every business on every street in town, no matter whether it's of interest to visitors or not. Strength in numbers, we suppose.

The closest thing to high-quality shopping is at **Pelican Shopping Mall,** with more than a dozen shops, as well as banking services, a restaurant, and a philatelic bureau where collectors can buy St. Kitts stamps and everyone else can mail letters. Here too, though, don't expect much—and whose idea was it to build a covered mall in the sunny Caribbean, anyway?

At Romney Gardens, you'll find **Caribelle Batik** (© **869/465-6253**), one of the island's most popular boutiques. Inside, artisans demonstrate their Indonesian-style hand-printing amid rack after rack of brightly colored clothes. Brimstone Hill and rain-forest-hike shore excursions typically include a stop here. If you're coming on your own, look for signs indicating a turnoff along the coast road, about 8km (5 miles) north of Basseterre in the town of Old Road.

BEACHES

The narrow peninsula in the southeast contains the island's salt ponds and also boasts the best white-sand beaches (approach via the windy, hilly road for a dramatic and gorgeous view). You'll find the best swimming at **Conaree Beach,** 5km (3 miles) from Basseterre; **Frigate Bay,** with its talcum-powder–fine sand; the twin beaches of **Banana Bay** and **Cockleshell Bay,** at the southeast corner of the island; and **Friar's Bay,** a peninsula beach opening onto both the Atlantic and the Caribbean. All beaches, even those that border hotels, are free and open to the public. However, you must usually pay a fee to use a hotel's beach facilities.

SPORTS

GOLF   The **Royal St. Kitts Golf Course,** Frigate Bay (© **869/465-8339**), is an 18-hole, par-72 championship course with seven beautiful ponds. It's bounded on the south by the Caribbean Sea and on the north by the Atlantic Ocean. Greens fees are $80.

SCUBA DIVING & SNORKELING   One of the best diving spots is **Nagshead,** at the southern tip of St. Kitts. This is an excellent shallow-water dive for certified divers, starting at 3m (10 ft.) and extending to 21m (70 ft.). You'll see a variety of tropical fish, eagle rays, and lobster here. Another good site is **Booby Shoals,** between Cow 'n' Calf Rocks and Booby Island. Booby Shoals has abundant sea life, including nurse sharks, lobster, and stingrays. Dives here are up to 9m (30 ft.) in depth, and are good for both certified and beginning divers.

GREAT LOCAL RESTAURANTS & BARS

The favorite **local beer** is Carib, brewed right on the northern edge of Basseterre. There's a local cane sugar drink called CSR (Cane Spirit Rothschild) that tastes a bit like Brazilian cachaça, but with a slight licorice flavor.

Ballahoo Restaurant ((C) 869/465-4197), located in Basseterre's most picturesque intersection (The Circus, right by the cruise dock), serves some of the best baby-back ribs in town. Seafood platters, such as garlic shrimp, curried conch, or fresh lobster, are served with salad and rice.

27 St. Lucia

With a turbulent history shared by many of its Caribbean neighbors, St. Lucia (pronounced *Loo*-sha), second largest of the Windward Islands at about 622 square km (240 sq. miles), changed hands often during the colonial period, being British seven times and French seven times. Today, though, it's an independent state that's become one of the most popular destinations in the Caribbean, with some of the finest resorts. The heaviest development is concentrated in the northwest, between the capital of Castries and the northern end of the island, where there's a string of white-sand beaches. The interior boasts relatively unspoiled green-mantled mountains and gentle valleys, as well as the volcanic **Mount Soufrière.** Two dramatic peaks (**the Pitons**) rise along the southwest coast.

Castries, the capital, has grown up around an extinct volcanic crater that's now a large harbor surrounded by hills. Because of fires that devastated many of its older structures, the town today has touches of modernity, with glass-and-concrete buildings, although there's still an old-fashioned **Saturday-morning market** on Jeremie Street. The country women dress in traditional cotton headdress to sell their luscious fruits and vegetables, while weather-beaten men sit close by playing warrie (a fast game played with pebbles on a carved board) or fleet games of dominoes using tiles the color of cherries.

COMING ASHORE   Most cruise ships arrive at a fairly new pier at **Pointe Seraphine,** within walking distance of the center of Castries. Unlike piers on other islands, this one boasts St. Lucia's best shopping. You'll find a money exchange, a small visitor information bureau, and a cable and wireless office. Phone cards are sold for use at specially labeled phones.

If Pointe Seraphine is too crowded (not too likely, as six megaships can pull alongside at once), your ship might dock at **Port Castries** (also called Port Careenage) on the other side of the colorful harbor. There's now a shopping terminal here called La Place Careenage, but if you still want to shop in Pointe Seraphine, a water taxi ($1) runs between the two all day. A land taxi will cost you around $4, or you can also walk between the two. Some smaller vessels, such as Star Clippers', Seabourn's, and Clipper's, anchor off Rodney Bay to the north or Soufrière to the south and carry you ashore by tender.

There are telephones right outside the port gate at Port Careenage, the town's cargo dock, and at the pier at Pointe Seraphine.

LANGUAGE   **English** is the official language.

CURRENCY   The official monetary unit is the **Eastern Caribbean dollar** (EC$). The exchange rate is U.S.$1 = EC$2.70; EC$1 = U.S.37¢. Prices quoted in this section are in U.S. dollars, which are accepted by nearly all hotels, restaurants, and shops.

INFORMATION   The **St. Lucia Tourist Board** is at Point Seraphine in Castries ((C) 758/452-4094). It's open Monday to Friday from 9am to 5pm. For info before you go, contact the tourism board office in the U.S. (© **800/456-3984** or 212/867-2950; www.sluonestop.com).

CALLING FROM THE U.S.   When calling St. Lucia from the United States, you just need to dial a "1" before the numbers listed here.

GETTING AROUND

BY TAXI   Most taxi drivers have been trained to serve as guides. Their cars are unmetered, but the government fixes tariffs for all standard trips. Be sure to determine if the driver is quoting a rate in U.S. or EC dollars. You can hire a taxi to go to Soufrière on your own, too. A taxi for four will cost about $120 for a 3- to 4-hour tour, including a beach stop, photo ops, shopping, and sightseeing. Avoid any driver who is not in uniform (which is really just a light-cotton tropical shirt).

BY RENTAL CAR   Driving is on the left, and roads are decent (but not great). We wouldn't recommend renting a car, but if you're set on it, **Avis, Budget,** and **Hertz** all have offices here, as does **Courtesy Rent-A-Car** (© **758/452-8140**).

SHORE EXCURSIONS OFFERED BY THE CRUISE LINES

Because of the difficult terrain, shore excursions are the best means of seeing this beautiful island in a day or less. In addition to the sampling below, most ships typically offer plantation tours, island bus tours, and snorkeling cruises.

Island Tour by Land & Sea ($69–$82, 8 hr.): A picturesque journey from Castries to the Piton peaks, via catamaran, takes you along St. Lucia's verdant coast. Docking at La Soufrière, you'll board a minibus and visit the volcano, the Diamond Baths (see "On Your Own: Beyond the Port Area," below), and sulfur springs. Lunch is included at a restaurant in Soufrière or on the boat.

Mountain Ridge Bike Tour ($75, 3½ hr.): From Castries, travel by bus to the top of Morne Fortune, where your bike ride begins. You'll pedal through hilltop roads with dramatic views of the harbor on one side and a stunning mountain range on the other. The ride goes past banana plantations, and through rural neighborhoods and lush valleys.

Morne Coubaril Plantation Tour ($46, 4 hr.): By minibus, ride along the island's west coast, between the sea and the rain forest, with views of the Pitons peaks. At the Morne Coubaril Estate, tour the working family plantation, and watch how coconuts, coffee, and cocoa are processed.

Pigeon Island Hike & Beach Swim ($44, 4 hr.): A steep walk takes you up to Fort Rodney on Pigeon Island, where St. Lucians last defeated the French. From the summit, you'll have great views of the Pitons, and sometimes you'll even be able to see Martinique. After the walk, there's a pleasant swim in the island's gin-clear waters, as well as complimentary refreshments in the rustic Captain's Cellar pub.

Anse Chastanet Snorkel Trip ($18, 3 hr.): Travel by jeep to St. Lucia's Anse Chastanet National Marine Park, where you'll snorkel among an amazing variety of reef fish.

EXCURSIONS OFFERED BY LOCAL AGENCIES

Horseback Treks: Trim's National Riding Stables, north of Castries, offers picnic trips to the Atlantic side of the island, with a barbecue lunch and drinks included. Departures are at 8:30am, 10am, 2pm, and 4pm. The fee is $70 for a 2-hour ride. Nonriders can also join the excursion; they are transported to the

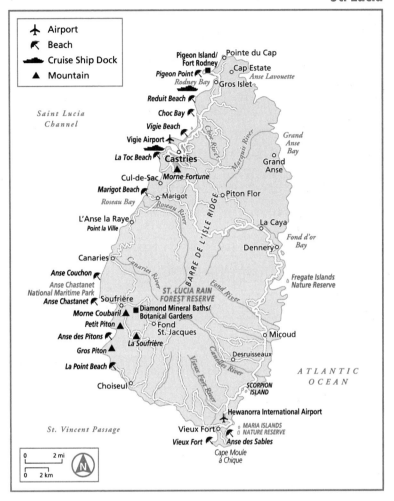

Legend:
- ✈ Airport
- 🏊 Beach
- 🚢 Cruise Ship Dock
- ▲ Mountain

Map labels:
Saint Lucia Channel · Pigeon Island/Fort Rodney · Pointe du Cap · Pigeon Point · Cap Estate · Anse Lavouette · Rodney Bay · Gros Islet · Reduit Beach · Choc Bay · Vigie Beach · Vigie Airport · Grand Anse Bay · La Toc Beach · Castries · Grand Anse · Cul-de-Sac · Morne Fortune · Marigot Beach · Marigot · Piton Flor · Roseau Bay · Roseau River · L'Anse la Raye · Point la Ville · La Caya · Fond d'or Bay · Dennery · Canaries · Canaries River · BARRE DE L'ISLE RIDGE · Fond River · Fregate Islands Nature Reserve · Anse Couchon · Anse Chastanet National Maritime Park · Anse Chastanet · Soufrière · ST. LUCIA RAIN FOREST RESERVE · Diamond Mineral Baths/Botanical Gardens · Morne Coubaril · Petit Piton · Fond St. Jacques · Micoud · Anse des Pitons · Gros Piton · La Soufrière · Desruisseaux · Vieux Fort River · La Point Beach · Choiseul · SCORPION ISLAND · ATLANTIC OCEAN · St. Vincent Passage · Hewanorra International Airport · Vieux Fort · MARIA ISLANDS NATURE RESERVE · Vieux Fort · Anse des Sables · Cape Moule à Chique · Canelles River

Scale: 0 — 2 mi / 0 — 2 km · N

site in a van and pay half price. To make arrangements, contact René Trim at ✆ **758/450-8273,** or trimsridingstables@candw.lc.

ON YOUR OWN: WITHIN WALKING DISTANCE

First, a tip: The last time we were at the duty-free marketplaces right at Castries' dock, a guy was doling out 5-minute massages for $5. If he's still there, this could save you a bundle on those expensive Steiner massages aboard the ship!

The principal streets of Castries are William Peter Boulevard and Bridge Street. Don't miss a walk through town: People are very friendly, and Jeremie Street is chockablock with variety stores of the most authentic local kind, selling everything from spices to housewares. A Roman Catholic cathedral stands on Columbus Square, which has a few restored buildings. Take a gander at the enormous 400-year-old "rain" tree, also called a "no-name" tree, which grows in the square. The nearby **Government House** is a late Victorian structure.

Frommer's Favorite St. Lucia Experiences

Riding a Catamaran Along the Coast: See the lush coast of St. Lucia and the mighty Pitons via catamaran, and then ride a minibus to visit a volcano, the Diamond Baths (warm mineral baths), and sulfur springs. (See "Shore Excursions Offered by the Cruise Lines," above.)

Exploring a Banana Plantation: See how St. Lucia's leading export is grown and harvested. (See "On Your Own: Beyond the Port Area," below.)

Hiking Up to Fort Rodney in Rodney Bay: The beautiful Pigeon Island on Rodney Bay offers the chance to hike up to Fort Rodney, an 18th-century English base that was used as an American signal station during World War II. From the top you can catch sight of Martinique. (See "On Your Own: Beyond the Port Area," below.)

Beyond Government House lies **Morne Fortune,** which means "Hill of Good Luck." Actually, no one's had much luck here, certainly not the French and British soldiers who battled for Fort Charlotte. The fort switched nationalities (from French to English, and vice versa) many times. You can visit the 18th-century barracks, complete with a military cemetery, a small museum, the Old Powder Magazine, and the "Four Apostles Battery"—four grim muzzle-loading cannons. The view of the harbor of Castries is panoramic from this point. You can also see north to Pigeon Island or south to the Pitons. To reach Morne Fortune, head east on Bridge Street. Castries has a very colorful **Central Market,** right near the dock, which is also worth a visit. The airplane-hangar-size emporium sells local food, trinkets, and produce. Buy some banana ketchup or local cinnamon sticks to take home.

ON YOUR OWN: BEYOND THE PORT AREA

Bananas are St. Lucia's leading export, so if you're being taken around the island by a taxi driver, ask him to take you to one of the huge plantations. (Most island tours include a drive through one of the plantations as a matter of course.) We suggest a look at one of the three biggest: the **Cul-de-Sac,** just north of Marigot Bay; **La Caya,** on the east coast in Dennery; or the **Roseau Estate,** south of Marigot Bay.

St. Lucia's first national park, **Pigeon Island National Landmark,** was originally an island but is now joined to the northwest shore of the mainland by a very environmentally unfriendly causeway that has disrupted offshore currents, thereby upsetting the local fishing industry. The 18-hectare (44-acre) island got its name from the red-neck pigeon, or ramier, which once made this island home. It's ideal for picnics and nature walks, and is covered with lemongrass, which spread from original plantings made by British light opera singer Josset, who leased the island for 30 years and grew the grass to provide thatch for her cottage's roof. Every few years the grass, which is full of volatile oils, catches fire and immolates much of the island before it can be put out.

The island's **Interpretation Centre** (© **758/450-0603**) contains artifacts and a multimedia display of local history, covering everything from the Amerindian settlers of A.D. 1000 to 1782's Battle of Saints, when Admiral Rodney's fleet set out from Pigeon Island and defeated the French admiral De Grasse. The center is open from 9am to 5pm daily; admission is $4 for adults, $1 for children 5 to 12. Right below the interpretation center is the cozy **Captain's Cellar pub,** located in what was formerly a soldier's mess. From the tables outside you get wonderful views of the crashing surf on the Atlantic coast, just a few steps away.

From the center, you can walk up the winding and moderately steep path to a lookout from which you can see Martinique. In 1780, Admiral Rodney said of this spot, "This is the post the Governor of Martinique has set his eye on and if possessed by the enemy would deprive us of the best anchorage place in these islands, from which Martinique is always attackable." Remember that when planning your own assault. From the pinnacle you get a wonderful view, and the cannons that ring the space are a nice place to pose for "I was there" pictures.

On Pigeon Island's west coast are two white-sand beaches. There's also a restaurant, **Jambe de Bois** ("Leg of Wood"), named after a peg-legged pirate who once used the island as a hideout.

Pigeon Island National Landmark is open daily from 9am to 5pm. For more information, call the **St. Lucia National Trust** (© **758/452-5005**). The best way to get here is to take a taxi and arrange to be picked up in time to return to your ship (the trip is 30 min., at most, back to the docks). Some small ships anchor here and bring passengers ashore by tender.

La Soufrière, a fishing port and St. Lucia's second largest settlement, is dominated by the dramatic **Pitons,** Petit Piton and Gros Piton, two pointed peaks that rise right from the sea to 738m to 786m, respectively (2,460 and 2,619 ft.). Formed by lava and once actively volcanic, these mountains are now cloaked in green vegetation, with waves crashing around their bases. Their sheer rise from the water makes them such visible landmarks that they've become the very symbol of St. Lucia.

Near the town of Soufrière lies the famous "drive-in" volcano, **La Soufrière,** a rocky lunar landscape of bubbling mud and craters seething with fuming sulfur. You can literally drive into an old crater and walk between the sulfur springs and pools of hissing steam. The fumes are said to have medicinal properties. A local guide is usually waiting nearby; if you do hire a guide, agree—then doubly agree—on what the fee will be.

Nearby are the **Diamond Mineral Baths** (© **758/452-4759**), surrounded by a tropical arboretum. They were constructed in 1784 by order of Louis XVI, whose doctors told him that these waters were similar in mineral content to the waters at Aix-les-Bains. The baths were built to help French soldiers who had been fighting in the West Indies recuperate from wounds and disease. Later destroyed, they were rebuilt after World War II. The water's average temperature is 106°F. You'll also find another fine attraction here: a waterfall that changes colors (from yellow to black to green to gray) several times a day. For about $2.60 you can bathe and benefit from the recuperative effects of the baths yourself.

SHOPPING

Many stores sell duty-free goods, and will deliver tobacco products and liquor to the cruise dock. Keep in mind, you are allowed to purchase only one bottle of liquor here (in St. Thomas, you can buy five). You'll find some good, but not remarkable, buys in bone china, jewelry, perfume, watches, liquor, and crystal. Souvenir items include designer bags and mats, local pottery, and straw hats—again, nothing remarkable. A tip: If your cruise is also calling in St. Thomas, let the local vendors know; it may make them more amenable to bargaining.

Built for cruise ship passengers, **Pointe Seraphine** has the best collection of shops on the island. You must present your cruise pass when making purchases here. Liquor and tobacco will be delivered to the ship.

Gablewoods Mall, on Gros Islet Highway, 3km (2 miles) north of Castries, has three restaurants and one of the densest concentrations of stores on St. Lucia. Since this mall is near some lovely beaches (and near the Sandals St. Lucia resort), it's possible to plan a day that combines shopping and sunbathing.

At **Caribelle Batik,** Howelton House, Old Victoria Road, The Morne (© 758/452-3785), just a 5-minute taxi ride from Castries, you can watch St. Lucian artists creating intricate patterns and colors through the ancient art of batik, which involves application of removable wax before dyes are applied so that the waxed area repels the dye. **Eudovic Art Studio,** Goodlands, Morne Fortune (© 758/452-2747), sells woodcarvings by St. Lucia native Vincent Joseph Eudovic and some of his pupils. Take a taxi from the cruise pier. Southwest of Soufrière, just past the small village of Choiseul, **Choiseul Craft Centre,** La Fargue (© 758/459-3226), is a government-funded retail outlet and training school that perpetuates the tradition of handmade Amerindian pottery and basketware. Some of the best basket weaving on the island is done here, using techniques practiced only in St. Lucia, St. Vincent, and Dominica. Look for place mats, handbags, woodcarvings (including bas-reliefs crafted from screw pine), and pottery. The craft center is open Monday to Friday 8:30am to 4pm and Saturday 10:30am to 2:30pm.

BEACHES

If you don't take a shore excursion, you might want to spend your time on one of St. Lucia's famous beaches, all of which are open to the public, even those at hotel properties (but you must pay to use a hotel's beach equipment). Taxis can take you to any of the island's beaches, but we recommend that you stick to the calmer shores along the western coast, since the rough surf on the windward Atlantic side makes swimming potentially dangerous.

Leading beaches include **Pigeon Island,** off the northern shore, with white sand and picnic facilities; **Vigie Beach,** north of Castries Harbour, with fine sands; **Marigot Beach,** south of Castries Harbour, framed on three sides by steep emerald hills and skirted by palm trees; and **Reduit Beach,** between Choc Bay and Pigeon Point, with fine brown sands. For sheer novelty, you might want to visit the black-volcanic-sand beach at **Soufrière.**

Just north of Soufrière is a beach connoisseur's delight, **Anse Chastanet** (© 758/459-7000), boasting an expanse of white sands at the foothills of lush, green mountains. This is a fantastic spot for snorkeling.

SPORTS

SCUBA DIVING   In Soufrière, **Scuba St. Lucia,** in the Anse Chastanet Hotel (© 758/459-7000; www.scubastlucia.com), is a five-star PADI dive center offering great diving and comprehensive facilities. The hotel is at the southern end of Anse Chastanet's 0.5km (¼-mile) secluded beach. Some of St. Lucia's most spectacular coral reefs—many only 3 to 6m (10 to 20 ft.) below the surface—provide shelter for sea creatures just a short distance offshore.

WATERSPORTS   **St. Lucian Watersports,** on Reduit Beach at the Rex St. Lucian Hotel (© 758/452-8351), is the best place to rent watersports equipment and arrange water-skiing.

GREAT LOCAL RESTAURANTS & BARS

A really, really great **local beer** is Piton—very refreshing on a hot day, like Corona but better. A favorite **local rum** is Bounty.

IN CASTRIES   At the **Green Parrot,** Red Tape Lane, Morne Fortune, about 2.5km (1½ miles) east of the town center (② **758/452-3399**), there's an emphasis on St. Lucian specialties and homegrown produce (the restaurant has trained cruise ship chefs in the use of local products). Try the christophine au gratin (a Caribbean squash with cheese) or the Creole soup made with callaloo (a leafy green) and pumpkin. **Jimmie's,** Vigie Cove Marina (② **758/452-5142**), is known for its fresh-fish menu and tasty Creole cookery.

AT MARIGOT BAY   **Doolittle's,** at the Marigot Beach Club (② **758/451-4974;** www.marigotdiveresort.com/dining.htm), showcases Caribbean and international dishes. To reach the place, you'll have to take a ferryboat across Marigot Bay. The ferry runs from the Moorings Marigot Bay Resort about every 10 minutes throughout the day and evening.

IN THE SOUFRIÈRE AREA   **Chez Camilla Guest House & Restaurant,** 7 Bridge St., 1 block inland from the waterfront (② **758/459-5379**), is the only really good place to eat in the village of Soufrière itself. It serves sandwiches, cold salads, omelets, and burgers at lunch. **Dasheene Restaurant & Bar,** in the Ladera Resort, between Gros and Petit Piton (② **758/459-7323**), serves the most refined and certainly the most creative cuisine in St. Lucia. The chef has a special flair with the seafood pasta and the marinated sirloin steak. Your best bet is the catch of the day, likely to be kingfish or red snapper, grilled to perfection. Other standouts are the dumpling-and-callaloo soup, the fresh pumpkin risotto with red pepper coulis, and the banana-stuffed pork with ginger and coconut sauce. The restaurant is perched atop a 300m (1,000-ft.) ridge and framed by the rising twin peaks of the Pitons. Everything is locally produced, including the furniture.

IN RODNEY BAY   **The Lime,** north of Reduit Beach (② **758/452-0761**), is a casual local place specializing in stuffed crab backs and Creole-seasoned fish steaks. It also serves shrimp, steaks, lamb, pork chops, and rotis (Caribbean burritos). The **Mortar & Pestle,** in the Harmony Marina Suites, Rodney Bay Lagoon (② **758/452-8711**), offers indoor-outdoor dining with a view of the boats moored at the nearby marina. For something truly regional, try the Barbados souse, full of marinated pieces of lean cooked pork, or the frogs' legs from Dominica.

28 St. Martin/Sint Maarten

Who can resist a two-for-one sale? On the island of St. Martin, you get two cultures, two nationalities, and two different experiences for the price of one. Occupying the bend where the Lesser and Greater Antilles meet, about 241km (150 miles) southeast of Puerto Rico, this is the smallest territory in the world that is shared by two sovereign states: France, with 52 square km (20 sq. miles), and the Netherlands, with 44 square km (17 sq. miles). The two nations have shared the island in a spirit of neighborly cooperation and mutual friendship for more than 350 years. Although the border between the two sides is virtually imperceptible—a monument along the road marks the change in administration— each side retains elements of its own heritage. The French side, with some of the best beaches and restaurants in the Caribbean, emphasizes quiet elegance. French fashions and luxury items fill the shops, and the fragrance of croissants mixes with the spicy aromas of West Indian cooking. Although not as chichi as nearby St. Barts, French St. Martin has its share of wealthy, beautiful people. The Dutch side, officially known as Sint Maarten, reflects Holland's anything-goes philosophy: Development is much more widespread, flashy casinos pepper the landscape, and strip malls make the larger towns look as much like Anaheim as Amsterdam. The 100% duty-free shopping has turned both sides of the island into a bargain-hunter's paradise.

St. Martin's first inhabitants, the Stone Age hunter-gatherer Ciboneys, arrived as early as 1800 B.C. A thousand years later, the Arawaks, originally from South America, arrived and dubbed the island "Soualiga," or "land of salt," referring to the salt ponds (which would later figure in St. Martin's colonial economy). The more belligerent Caribs horned in later, absorbing or exterminating the Arawaks. Christopher Columbus was the first European to make the scene. He spotted the island in 1493 and named it in honor of St. Martin of Tours, whose feast day it happened to be. With bigger fish than St. Martin to fry, namely Peru and Mexico, Spain left the island virtually untouched. The first Dutch and French colonists arrived more than 100 year later, in the early 17th century. After some minor stabs at controlling the island, the Spanish decided that St. Martin wasn't worth the headache and abandoned it in 1648. The Dutch and French exchanged some martial rumblings before deciding, in March 1648, to just get along, splitting the island roughly in two (the apocryphal legend that says that the line of demarcation was decided by a race between two runners, a wine-sipping Frenchman and a gin-guzzling Dutchman, is repeated ad nauseam). Coffee, sugar, rum, and salt brought relative prosperity to the island, but not to the slaves brought over from Africa. Tourism supplanted agriculture as the major industry in the last half of the 20th century.

French St. Martin is part of the French overseas region of Guadeloupe and has direct representation in Paris. Sint Maarten is part of the Netherlands Antilles, a component of the Kingdom of the Netherlands based in Curaçao. Today, the Dutch side holds a slight population edge: 41,000 people to the French side's 36,000. Most locals are descendants of African slaves, but residents born in France, Holland, and the U.S. occupy many of the villas and condominiums around the island.

COMING ASHORE   Most cruise ships dock on the Dutch side, at A. C. Wathey Pier, about 1.5km (a mile) southeast of **Philipsburg.** The majority of passengers are then tendered to the smaller Captain Hodge Pier at the center of town, but others choose to walk the distance or take taxis. The Wathey pier has few facilities except for a some credit-card phones, whereas the Hodge Pier offers immediate access to phones, tourist information, and taxis.

Smaller vessels sometimes dock on the French side of the island, at Marina Port la Royale, adjacent to the heart of **Marigot.** The waterfront here features restaurants, shopping arcades, and a tourist office. The pier accommodates only one ship at a time, so passengers on subsequently arriving vessels are tendered ashore.

LANGUAGE   Surprise, surprise: The official language on the **Dutch** side is Dutch, and the official language on the **French** side is French. Most people on both sides also speak **English.** Among locals on the street, patois is often spoken: **Papiamento** on the Dutch side, **Créole** on the French.

CURRENCY   The legal tender in Dutch Sint Maarten is the **Netherlands Antilles guilder,** or NAf (NAf1.9 = U.S.$1; NAf1 = U.S.55¢), and the official currency on the French side is the **euro** (€1.1 = U.S.$1; €1 = U.S.90¢). U.S.

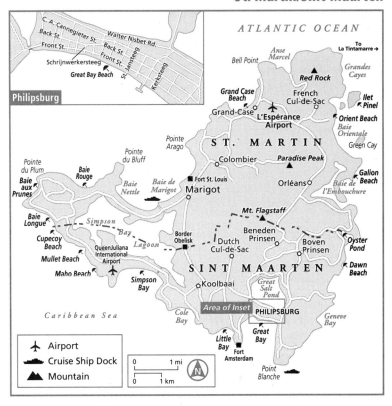

Philipsburg

ATLANTIC OCEAN

Key:
- ✈ Airport
- ⚓ Cruise Ship Dock
- ▲ Mountain

dollars are widely accepted on both sides, though, so there's no need to change money. Most prices are quoted in U.S. dollars, too, so you're spared the work of calculating exchange rates. Credit cards and travelers checks are readily accepted, as well. Prices in this chapter are given in U.S. dollars. ATMs abound in both Philipsburg and Marigot.

INFORMATION   On the Dutch side, the Tourist Information Bureau head-quarters, in the Imperial Building at 23 Walter Nisbeth Road in Philipsburg (*© 599/542-2337*), is open Monday to Friday from 8am to 5pm. There's a smaller but more conveniently located satellite office at the town pier. For information before you go, call the tourist board office in the U.S. (*© 800/786-2278; www.st-maarten.com*).

The Tourist Information office **on the French side** is adjacent to the pier at Port La Royale in Marigot (*© 590/87-57-23*). It's open Monday to Friday from 8:30am to 1pm and 2:30 to 5:30pm. For info before you go, contact the French St. Martin Tourism Board in the U.S. (*© 212/475-8970; www.st-martin.org*).

CALLING FROM THE U.S.   When calling **Dutch Sint Maarten from the United States, simply dial the international access number (011) before the numbers listed here. Calling **French** Saint Martin requires more of an effort: dial 011, then 590 before the numbers listed. Yes, 590 appears in our listed numbers, but those three digits must be dialed twice to make a connection.

GETTING AROUND

BY TAXI   Taxis on both sides of the island are unmetered. Agree on a rate and currency before getting in. Dutch law requires that drivers list government-regulated fares, which assume two passengers (each additional passenger is another $2). Shorter rides, including the route between Marigot and Philipsburg, average around $10; longer trips can climb to $20-plus. Drivers, who greet cruisers in both Philipsburg and Marigot, expect at least a $1 tip for short runs, more for extended 2-hour sightseeing trips around the island. To call a taxi on the Dutch side, dial ℭ **599/542-2359.** On the French side, dial ℭ **590/87-56-54.**

BY MINIVAN   Privately owned and operated minivans are a reasonable way to get around, if you don't mind frequent stops, potential overcrowding, and the local zouk and soca music that's usually playing (a plus or a minus, depending on your tastes). These jitneys run daily from 7am to midnight and serve much of the island. The most popular run, between Philipsburg and Marigot, has almost constant service. Fares range from about $1 to $2. The vans, which have signs to indicate their destination, can be hailed anywhere on the street.

BY RENTAL CAR   Rental cars are a great way to make the most of your day and see both sides of the island. Driving is on the right side, roads are generally in decent shape, and signage is in either international symbols or English. Parking can be a headache in both Philipsburg and Marigot, and road construction and drawbridges sometimes exacerbate congestion. Away from the two main towns, though, zipping along is a breeze. **Avis, Budget,** and **Hertz** all have offices here.

SHORE EXCURSIONS OFFERED BY THE CRUISE LINES

America's Cup Sailing Regatta ($71, 3 hr.): Get a taste of nautical exhilaration by competing in a race aboard Dennis Connor's America's Cup–winning *Stars & Stripes.* This hands-on, extremely popular excursion lets you grind winches, trim sails, and duck under booms—after you've been trained by professionals, of course. Alternatively, sit back and watch others do all the work. In either case, wear your Topsiders (or other soft-soled shoes).

Island Tour ($20, 3 hr.): See both sides of the island from the air-conditioned comfort of your minibus, stopping along the way to marvel at various panoramas. A stopover in Marigot allows time for some on-foot town sightseeing and shopping.

Ilet Pinel Snorkeling Tour ($30, 3 hr.): After a scenic bus ride to the French town of Cul de Sac, along the northeast coast, hop on a tender to the small off-shore island of Ilet Pinel for some of St. Martin's best snorkeling.

Butterfly Farm and Marigot ($28–$38, 3½ hr.): After a scenic drive through both the French and Dutch sides of the island, walk through a surrealistic enclosed garden that features pools, waterfalls, and hundreds of exquisitely beautiful and exotic butterflies from around the world. Amusing guides identify species, describe courtship and mating rituals, and give tips on attracting butterflies to your garden at home. Afterward, absorb the Créole charm and French atmosphere of Marigot.

EXCURSIONS OFFERED BY LOCAL AGENCIES

Horseback Treks: Bayside Riding Club, Coconut Grove, next to the Butterfly Farm (ℭ **590/87-36-64**), offers 2-hour riding expeditions ($55 per person) that conclude on an isolated beach, where horses and riders enjoy a cool post-ride romp in the water (don't forget your bathing suit). Half-hour pony rides with a handler, for the little ones, are $20. Riders of all experience levels are welcome.

Mountain Biking Tours: Frog Legs (© **590/87-05-11**), based in Marigot, offers three tours, which vary in difficulty (5%–30% climb), time (from a little under 2 hr. to more than 4), and price ($40–$45). Some stay along the coast, others move to inland hills.

Scuba Diving: Of the island's 40 dive sites, the 1801 British man-of-war HMS *Proselyte,* which sank to a watery grave on a reef 1.5km (a mile) off the coast, is the most popular. Other favorites include Ilet Pinel, for shallow diving; the Green Key barrier reef; and Flat Island, for its sheltered coves and geologic faults. On the Dutch side, **Pelican Watersports,** Simpson Bay (© **599/544-2640**), employs some the most knowledgeable guides on the island. One of the French side's premier dive operators, **Marine Time,** is in Quartier d'Orléans, not far from Coconut Grove Beach (© **590/87-20-28**). Single-tank dives with all equipment run about $55; two-tank dives are around $95.

ON YOUR OWN: WITHIN WALKING DISTANCE

Shopping, sunbathing, and gambling are the pastimes that interest most cruisers who hit this island, but folks with a taste for culture and history can make a day of it here as well.

ON THE DUTCH SIDE   Directly in front of the Philipsburg town pier, on Wathey Square, the **Courthouse** combines northern European sobriety with Caribbean brightness. Originally built in 1793 of freestone and wood, this venerable old building has suffered numerous hurricanes, but has been restored after each tempest and continues to house government offices. East of the Courthouse, at 7 Front St. (down a little shopping alley), the tiny **Sint Maarten Museum** (© **599/542-4917**) features modest, cluttered exhibits that focus on the island's history and geology. The second-floor gallery is open every day but Sunday. There's no admission fee, but donations are appreciated. The museum is open Monday through Friday, from 10am to 4pm, and Saturday 10am to 2pm. The street-level gift shop stocks handcrafts, postcards, and books. At the far east end of town, the **Vineyard** is another architectural highlight. Imported from Baltimore by the van Romondt family in 1871, this freestone and wood residence features an airy terrace, a grand stone staircase, and walls of windows. The upside-down star that ornaments the pediment looks like something out of Pennsylvania Dutch country.

Historically, **Fort Amsterdam** is the Dutch side's most important colonial site. Since 1631, the fort has looked out over Great Bay from the hill west of Philipsburg. The fort was the Netherlands' first military outpost in the Caribbean. The Spanish captured it 2 years later, making it their most significant bastion east of Puerto Rico. Peter Stuyvesant, who later became governor of New Amsterdam (now New York), lost his leg to a cannonball while trying to reclaim the fort for Holland. The site provides grand views of the bay, but ruins of the walls and a couple of rusty cannons are all that remain of the original fort.

ON THE FRENCH SIDE   **Fort St. Louis** is Marigot's answer to Fort Amsterdam. Built in 1767 to protect the waterfront warehouses that stored the French colony's agricultural riches, the cannons of this bastion frequently fired on hostile British raiders from Anguilla. After restorations and modification in the 19th century, the fort was eventually abandoned. In addition to the fort's

Frommer's Favorite St. Martin Experiences

Sizzling in the Sun: On the French side, colorful open-air restaurants and bars line Orient Beach, a social, very European strand humming with motorized water toys. For privacy, unparalleled beauty, and the freedom to doff it all, head to Cupecoy Beach, at the island's extreme west, just over the border on the Dutch side. (See "Beaches," below.)

Dejeuner Chez Madame Claude's Mini Club: Savor the rich flavors of Créole and French cuisine on the cozy, colorfully painted upstairs terrace of Marigot's oldest restaurant. (See "Great Local Restaurants & Bars," later in this chapter.)

Competing for the America's Cup: Race on and against 12-meter yachts that once competed in the famed America's Cup race. (See "Shore Excursions Offered by the Cruise Lines," above.)

cannons, crumbling walls, and French *tricouleur* flag flapping in the breeze, the short climb up the hill flanking Marigot Bay's north end affords splendid vistas. As a respite from the sun, duck into Marigot's **Museum of Saint Martin** (© 590/29-22-84), next to the Tourism Office and adjacent to the marina. Much more thorough and scholarly than its Philipsburg counterpart, this institution boasts a first-rate collection of Ciboney, Arawak, and Carib artifacts excavated from the island's Amerindian sites, plus a reproduction of a 1,500-year-old burial mound. Another display details the history of the plantation and slavery era, and early-20th-century photographs trace the island's modern development. It's open Monday through Friday 9am to 4pm, Saturday 9am to 1pm. Admission is $5 for adults, $2 for children.

ON YOUR OWN: BEYOND THE PORT AREA

Most tours include a quick stop at the **Border Obelisk** on the main road between Philipsburg and Marigot. Not unlike the Four Corners plaque erected where Arizona, Colorado, New Mexico, and Utah converge, this simple marker commemorates the cooperation treaty of 1648, which formally divided the island between the Netherlands and France. Erected in 1948, 300 years after the treaty signing, it's a testament to more than 350 years of peaceful cohabitation.

Ecocruisers and Tarzan wannabes will probably want to spend much of the day at **Loterie Farm** (© 590/87-86-16), located on the road to Paradise Peak (Pic Paradis), the island's highest hill (1,391 ft.). A sugar factory from 1773 to 1855, today this 64-hectare (160-acre) domain preserves one of the island's last remaining rain forests, an oasis of calm on an island where the drumbeat of development bangs loudly. Five hiking trails meander through verdant foliage bordered by waterfalls and springs. General admission is $5, but the guided tours, which range from $15 to $45 per person and require advance reservations, are recommended.

GAMBLING

Slot machines and game tables can be found in the Dutch side's dozen casinos. Most of the heavy betting takes place after dark, but a handful of casinos open before noon. In the heart of Philipsburg on Front Street, **Coliseum Casino** (© 599/543-2101), **Diamond Casino** (© 599/543-2565), **Paradise Plaza**

Slots World (© 599/543-2721), and **Rouge et Noir** (© 599/542-2952) all open at 11am, early enough to snag cruisers. West of Philipsburg, **Hollywood Casino,** at the Pelican Resort on Simpson Bay (© 599/544-4463), features a panoramic view of the water and offers craps, roulette, blackjack, stud poker, and slots after 1pm. Farther west, at Maho Bay, **Casino Royale** (© 599/545-2590) has roulette, Caribbean stud poker, craps, blackjack, baccarat, minibaccarat, and slots, also after 1pm.

SHOPPING

St. Martin is a true free port—no duties are paid on any item coming in or going out—and neither side of the island has a sales tax.

ON THE DUTCH SIDE   Shops in the much busier Dutch side are concentrated in Philipsburg, along Front Street and the numerous alleys radiating from it. The district is largely nondescript, but you'll find all the usual suspects—the omnipresent jewelry and luxury-item shop **Little Switzerland** and a host of other jewelry/gift/luxury-item shops—as well as some quirky local boutiques. In general, prices in the major stores are nonnegotiable, but at small, family-run shops, you can try your luck with a little polite bargaining. The T-shirt and souvenir epicenter is in the open-air market behind the Courthouse in front of the town pier.

Guavaberry Emporium, 8–10 Front St., sells Guavaberry "island folk liqueur," an aged rum with a distinctive fruity, woody, almost bittersweet flavor; it's available only on St. Martin. Parrot heads in search of all things Jimmy Buffett should cross the street to **Last Mango in Paradise,** 17 Front St., for CDs, T-shirts—you name it, they got it. Walking west, Old Street, off Front Street, features a couple dozen boutiques, including **Colombian Emeralds** and **The Belgian Chocolate Shop.** For cigars, **La Casa del Habano,** 24 Front St., has Cohibas, Montecristos, and the like, while **Lipstick,** 31 Front St., is your best bet for perfumes and cosmetics. Next door, **Dutch Delft Blue,** 29 Front St., stocks the distinctive blue-and-white porcelain.

ON THE FRENCH SIDE   **Marigot** features a much calmer, more charming, and sophisticated ambience, with waterfront cafes where you can rest your weary over-shopped feet. Many shops here close their doors for a 2-hour lunch break starting at noon.

The wide selection of European merchandise is skewed toward an upscale audience, but French crystal, perfume, liqueur, jewelry, and fashion can be up to 50% less expensive than in the States. At Marina Port la Royale, **Havane** offers casual and high-fashion French clothing for men, while **L'Epicerie** stocks caviar, foie gras, and a host of French wines. For chic women's clothing, especially Italian styles, start your search at **La Romana,** 12 Rue de la République. **Oro de Sol Jewelers,** Rue de la République, is one of many purveyors of bracelets, necklaces, and watches, while **Beauty & Scents,** Rue du Général de Gaulle, has your favorite perfumes and cosmetics. For flawless Belgian chocolates, run, don't walk, to **Jeff de Bruges,** 5 Rue de la République. Immediate consumption is de rigueur as the tropical heat will melt your purchases as soon as you walk out the door.

An inviting **open-air craft market** sprawls along the waterfront next to Boulevard de France every day, while on Wednesdays and Saturdays, another open-air market stretches from the base of Fort St. Louis to the wharves below, offering a colorful array of homegrown produce, tropical fruits and spices, and fresh fish. **Gingerbread & Mahogany Gallery,** Marina Port la Royale (in a

---

Fun Fact **You Look Mah-ah-ah-ah-velous**

Despite generous dollops of urbanity, St. Martin can't entirely shake its rural character. In the lush interior village of Colombier, farmers from both sides of the island get together in early July for a beauty contest quite unlike that more famous Atlantic City pageant: The contestants in Colombier are male goats. Led by owners sporting "I ♥ My Ram" T-shirts, the carefully gussied-up competitors parade before a panel of discerning judges, unperturbed by human revelers who dance, drink, and dine in a cloven-footed carnival atmosphere. Winners receive medals, trophies, and cash prizes before returning to the quiet of their pastures; the human crowd parties on till the wee hours of the night.

---

narrow alleyway at the marina), deals in Haitian art by both old masters and talented amateurs.

BEACHES

Beach lovers rejoice: St. Martin has more than 30 beautiful white-sand beaches, some social, some serene. The busier ones boast bars, restaurants, watersports, and hotels, where changing facilities are usually available for a small fee. Toplessness is ubiquitous, and nudism is common on the French side, and increasingly evident on the Dutch side as well.

ON THE DUTCH SIDE   **Great Bay Beach** is your best bet if you want to stay in Philipsburg. This 1.5km (mile-long) stretch is convenient, but because it borders the busy capital, it lacks the tranquility and cleanliness of the more remote beaches. The water is calm, though, and all the amenities of Philipsburg are a step away. Immediately to the west, at the foot of Fort Amsterdam, **Little Bay Beach** looks like a Caribbean postcard, but it can be overrun with visitors, as well. The snorkeling's good at Little Bay Beach.

On the east coast, **Dawn Beach** boasts premier snorkeling (a coral reef is just offshore) and a great view of St. Barts. It's generally peaceful, but the surf is a little strong for small children.

Just west of the airport, on the west side of the island, **Maho Beach** boasts a casino, shade palms, and a popular beachside bar and grill. The biggest attraction, however, seems to be its views of takeoffs and landings (keep your belongings outside the flight path; jumbo jets sometimes blow items into the surf). Farther west, **Mullet Beach** borders the island's golf course. Shaded by palm trees and crowded on weekends, it's popular with swimmers and snorkelers. Onsite vendors rent an array of watersports equipment. Just around the corner to the west (just below the Dutch-French border), but miles away mentally, lies perfectly serene **Cupecoy Beach.** Set against a stunningly beautiful backdrop of mysterious caves and sandstone cliffs that provide morning shade, this beach has no facilities, but a vendor at the parking lot rents beach chairs and shade umbrellas. The clientele is adult, primarily in the buff, quiet, and, not infrequently, gay. The surf can be strong, and aficionados claim that the sun here is more intense than anywhere else on the island.

ON THE FRENCH SIDE   Far and away the island's most visited strand, **Orient Beach,** on the northeast coast, fancies itself "the Saint Tropez of the

Caribbean." Hedonism is the name of the game here: plenty of food, drink, music, and flesh (a naturist resort occupies the beach's southern tip, but nudism isn't confined to any one area). Watersports abound. South of Orient Beach, the waveless waters of Coconut Grove or **Galion Beach** are shallow 30m (100 ft.) out. Protected by a coral reef, this area is No. 1 with kids and popular with windsurfers.

On the island's west coast, just north of the Dutch border, **Baie Longue** is the island's longest beach and another refuge for adults seeking peace and quiet. There are no facilities here, but this wild beach bordering some of the island's grandest mansions is popular with the rich and (sometimes) famous. The water and sand here are silky. Heading north, the kid-friendly beach in the town of **Grand Case** has good swimming and snorkeling. It's most famous, though, for its restaurants. Even the beachside food stands, known as "lolos," serve consistently delicious treats.

SPORTS

GENERAL WATERSPORTS   Most of the large hotels on Orient Beach offer an array of watersports adventures, often from makeshift kiosks on the beach. Two independent operators function from side-by-side positions near the Esmeralda Hotel: **Kon Tiki Watersport** (© 590/87-46-89) and **Bikini Watersports** (© 690/27-07-48). From these operators, jet skis and WaveRunners go for about $40 for 30 minutes, $70 for an hour; parasailing $50 to $80; Wakeboards $25 for 15 minutes, $40 for a half-hour; surfboards $15 per hour; and kayaks $15 per hour.

GOLF   The **Mullet Bay Golf Course** (© 599/545-2850), on the Dutch side, has an 18-hole course designed by Joseph Lee that's considered one of the more challenging in the Caribbean, especially the back nine. Mullet Pond and Simpson Bay lagoon provide both beauty and hazards. Greens fees and cart rental for 18 holes is $110; for 9 holes it's $65; club rental is an additional $25. The course opens at 7am, 7 days a week.

SNORKELING   Tiny coves and calm offshore waters make St. Martin a snorkeler's paradise. Dawn Beach, on the Dutch east coast, is the best snorkeling site on the island (rent equipment from Busby's Beach Bar, which is right on the beach), followed by Maho (Dutch side) and the French side's Baie Rouge and Ilet Pinel, the latter of which can be reached by ferry from Cul de Sac (about $5 per person, round-trip). Most hotels and restaurants at these sites rent equipment for about $10.

WINDSURFING   Because of prevailing winds and calmer, more protected waters, most wind sailors gravitate to the island's easternmost edge, around the French beaches at Coconut Grove and Orient Bay. Two of the best outfits specializing in windsurfing are **Tropical Wave,** Coconut Grove, Le Galion Beach, Baie de l'Embouchure (© 590/87-37-25), and **Club Nathalie Simon,** Orient Beach (© 590/29-41-57). Full rigs are yours for $20 an hour or $60 for the day.

GREAT LOCAL RESTAURANTS & BARS

A favorite **local beer** (on both the Dutch and French sides) is Red White and Blue, while the indigenous **rum liqueur** is the fruity and slightly bitter Guavaberry.

ON THE DUTCH SIDE   As might be expected, food is usually better on the French side, but Dutch St. Maarten has a number of appealing restaurants, too. In Philipsburg, **Da Livio Ristorante,** 159 Front St. (© 599/542-2690), serves delicious seafood, veal, and pasta, including the house specialty, homemade manicotti. Dine alfresco with views of Great Bay, and check out the photos of celebrities who've sated their hunger here. Fully air-conditioned, **Daniella's Courtyard,** 34 Front St. (© **599/542-1333**), features verdant, Mediterranean decor, and tastes from around the world. Try the West Indian crab cakes, the Cajun blackened shrimp, or the Thai chicken salad. Next to the historic court-house, just off Front Street at 6 Hendrikstraat, **Kangaroo Court** (© **599/542-4278**) is Philipsburg's coziest coffeehouse. Stop in for a quick latte and muffin or grab a table in back for a salad, burger, or sandwich. The rich, goocy desserts can satisfy the most insatiable sweet tooth. Indonesian *rijstaffel* is yours for the asking at **Wajang Doll,** 167 Front St. (© **599/542-4278**). Order the 14-dish sampling of Javanese, Balinese, and Sumatran cuisine, or opt for something lighter, such as red snapper with ginger, chili, and lemongrass.

ON THE FRENCH SIDE In Marigot, Madame Claude herself is running the show at **Mini Club** (© **590/87-50-69**), one of the oldest restaurants in town, on the waterfront street Rue des Pêcheurs. Savor the rich flavors of spicy conch stew, Créole-style fresh fish, or other West Indian and French dishes on the cozy, bright-yellow upstairs terrace. **L'Epicerie,** Marina Port la Royale (© **590/87-17-69**), an elegant but welcoming gourmet shop, doubles as a bistro with sit-down meals, delectable cakes, and vintage wines sold by the bottle or glass. Very reasonably priced plats du jour include tastings of Nordic salmon and samplings of Mediterranean cuisines. **La Brasserie de Marigot,** 11 Rue du Général-de-Gaulle (© **590/87-94-43**), is another great choice for good food at modest prices. Dishes include pot-au-feu, duck breast with peaches, and steak tartare. For light salads, sandwiches, and ice-cream concoctions, claim a harbor-side table at **La Vie en Rose,** at the corner of Rue de la République and Boule-vard de France (© **590/87-54-42**).

The pride and joy of St. Martin's Gallic gourmets, the town of Grand Case, on the northeast coast, is famous for its Restaurant Row. Most of the bistros here are open for dinner only, but a handful serve lunch too. **Le Tastevin,** 86 Boule-vard de Grand Case (© **590/87-55-45**), one of the island's premier French eateries, and **Il Nettuno,** 70 Boulevard de Grand Case (© **590/87-77-38**), which, ironically, specializes in Italian cuisine, may be the best of the lunch bunch. For a truly informal introduction to the joy of Créole cuisine, try one of the food stands, or *lolos,* that line the beach. For about $8, you can gorge on fried flying fish, spicy conch stew, or barbecued ribs.

If you're spending the day at Orient Beach, your surfside dining and drinking options include **Kakao** (© **590/87-43-26**) and **Kon Tiki** (© **590/87-43-27**).

29 St. Thomas & St. John

Ever since Columbus discovered the Virgin Islands during his second voyage to the New World in 1493, they have proved to be irresistible to foreign powers seeking territory: The flags of Denmark, Spain, France, England, Holland, and the United States have all flown here at one time or another, beginning with the Danes in 1666. Vacationers discovered **St. Thomas,** the largest of the Virgin Islands (19km/12 miles long, 5km/3 miles wide, and 85 sq. km/33 sq. miles), right after World War II and have been flocking here in increasing numbers ever since to enjoy its world-class dining and elegant resorts. Today, the island is one of the busiest and most developed ports in the Caribbean, often hosting more than six cruise ships a day during the peak winter season. Tourism and U.S.

government programs have raised the standard of living here to one of the highest in the Caribbean. **Charlotte Amalie** (pronounced Ah-*mahl*-yah), named in 1691 in honor of the wife of King Christian V, is the island's capital and has become the Caribbean's major shopping center.

In stark contrast to this busy scene, more than half of nearby **St. John,** the smallest of the U.S. Virgin Islands, is pristinely preserved as the gorgeous Virgin Islands National Park. Ornithologists and zoologists from around the world admire the wildlife here. A rocky coastline, forming crescent-shaped bays and white-sand beaches, rings the whole island. Panoramic views and ruins of 18th-century Danish plantations dot St. John's miles of serpentine hiking trails.

Most cruise ships dock in Charlotte Amalie on St. Thomas, but a few anchor directly off St. John. Many of those that stop only at St. Thomas offer excursions to St. John. If yours doesn't, it's quite easy to get to St. John on your own. **St. Croix,** the third of the U.S. Virgins, is described in its own section, beginning on p. 248.

LANGUAGE   English is spoken on both islands.

CURRENCY   The **U.S. dollar** is the local currency.

INFORMATION   For information before you go, contact the **U.S. Virgin Islands Department of Tourism** (© 800/372-USVI; www.usvitourism.vi).

CALLING FROM THE U.S.   When calling St. Thomas from the United States, you just need to dial a "1" before the numbers listed in this section.

ST. THOMAS

With a population of about 50,000 and a large number of American expatriates and temporary sun-seekers in residence, tiny St. Thomas isn't exactly a tranquil tropical retreat. You won't have any beaches to yourself. Shops, bars, and restaurants (including a lot of fast-food joints) abound here, and most of the locals make their living off the tourist trade. Most native Virgin Islanders are the descendants of slaves brought from Africa. In fact, Charlotte Amalie was one of the major slave-trading centers in the Caribbean.

COMING ASHORE   Most cruise ships anchor at Havensight Mall, at the eastern end of Charlotte Amalie Harbor, 2.5km (1½ miles) from the town center. The mall has a tourist information office, restaurants, a bookstore, a bank, a U.S. postal van, phones that accept long-distance credit cards, and a generous number of duty-free shops. Many people make the long, hot walk to the center of Charlotte Amalie, but it's not a scenic route in any way—you may want to opt for one of the open-air taxis for about $3 per person.

If Havensight Mall is clogged with cruise ships, your ship will dock at the **Crown Point Marina,** to the west of Charlotte Amalie. A taxi is your best bet—the 30-minute walk into Charlotte Amalie feels longer on a hot day, and isn't terribly picturesque. A taxi ride into town from here costs about $4.

INFORMATION   The **U.S. Virgin Islands Department of Tourism** has offices at Tolbod Gade in Charlotte Amalie (© 340/774-8784), open Monday to Friday from 8am to 5pm and Saturday from 8am to noon. Stop by and pick up *St. Thomas This Week,* which includes maps of St. Thomas and St. John. There's also an office at the Havensight Mall.

GETTING AROUND

BY TAXI   Taxis are the chief means of transport here. They're unmetered, but a guide of point-to-point fares around the island is included in most of the tourist magazines. The official fare for sightseeing is about $30 for two passengers for 2 hours; each additional passenger pays another $12. For **radio-dispatch service,** call © 340/774-7457.

BY BUS   Comfortable and often air-conditioned, government-run Vitran buses serve Charlotte Amalie and the countryside as far away as Red Hook, a jumping-off point for St. John. You rarely have to wait more than 30 minutes during the day. A one-way ride costs about 75¢ within Charlotte Amalie, $1 to outer neighborhoods, and $3 for rides as far as Red Hook. For routes, stops, and schedules, call © 340/774-5678.

BY TAXI VAN   Less structured and more erratic are "taxi vans," privately owned vans, minibuses, or open-sided trucks operated by local entrepreneurs. They make unscheduled stops along major traffic arteries and charge the same fares as the Vitran buses. If you look like you want to go somewhere, one will likely stop for you. They may or may not have their final destinations written on a cardboard sign displayed on the windshield.

BY RENTAL CAR   No need to rent a car here.

BY FERRY   Ferries run all day hourly from Charlotte Amalie and Red Hook to St. John. The ride takes approximately 45 minutes and costs $3 from Red Hook and $7 from Charlotte Amalie. © 340/776-6282.

BY SEAPLANE   Regular seaplane shuttles between St. Thomas and St. Croix are available for $150 round-trip; however, special rates are available for nonresidents, running as low as $90 round-trip provided you travel from 9:30am to 3:30pm Monday through Friday (any hours Sat and Sun). Book ahead. Flights depart every 15 to 45 minutes in both directions, and flight time is a mere 18 minutes; but figure 30 minutes from dock to dock. For more information, contact **Seaborne Airlines,** 34 Strand St., Christiansted (© 340/773-6442; www.seaborneairlines.com).

SHORE EXCURSIONS OFFERED BY THE CRUISE LINES
In addition to the excursions below, plenty of organized snorkeling trips, booze cruises, and island tours are offered.

 Frommer's Favorite St. Thomas Experiences

Biking Around the Island: You'll get great views and a great workout too. (See "Shore Excursions Offered by the Cruise Lines," below.) Biking on Water Island is a great experience, too.

Kayaking Among the Island's Mangroves: You'll learn about the local lagoon ecosystem and get some exercise to boot. (See "Shore Excursions Offered by the Cruise Lines," below.)

Visiting the Colorful Village of Frenchtown: Have lunch in a village settled by French-speaking citizenry who were uprooted after the Swedes invaded the island of St. Barts. (See "On Your Own: Beyond the Port Area," below.)

Taking a Nature Walk: The lush St. Peter Greathouse Estate and Gardens has 200 varieties of plants and trees, plus a rain forest, an orchid jungle, and more. (See "On Your Own: Beyond the Port Area," below.)

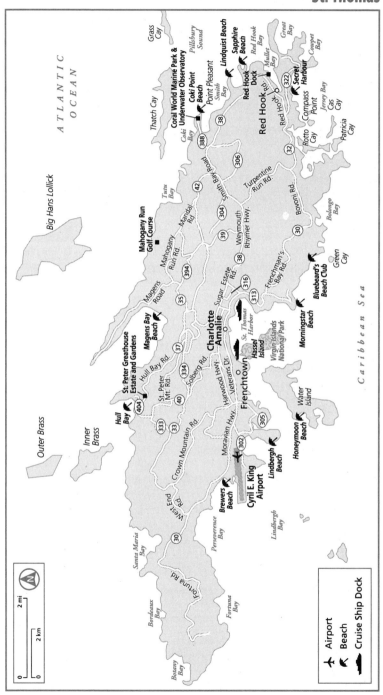

ATLANTIC OCEAN

Grass Cay

Thatch Cay

Pillsbury Sound

Coral World Marine Park & Underwater Observatory
Coki Point
Coki Beach
Point Pleasant
Smith Bay
Lindquist Beach
Sapphire Beach
Red Hook Bay
Great Bay
Coanet Bay
Muller Bay
Red Hook Dock
Secret Harbour
Compass Point
Jersey Bay
Cas Cay
Patricia Cay
Rotto Cay
Red Hook Rd.

38
388
306
32
42
304
39
30

Turpentine Run Rd.

Smith Bay Road

Mahogany Run Golf Course

Tutu Bay

Mandal Rd.

Mahogany Run Rd.

394

35

Magens Road

Magens Bay Beach

St. Peter Greathouse Estate and Gardens

Hull Bay Rd.

37

Solberg Rd.

334

St. Peter Mt. Rd.

40

404

333

33

Crown Mountain Rd.

West End Rd.

Fortuna Rd.

Hull Bay

Sugar Estate Rd.

Charlotte Amalie

Harwood Hwy.
Veterans Dr.
Moravian Hwy.

Frenchtown

Hassel Island

Virgin Islands National Park

St. Thomas Harbor

316
313
38

Weymouth Rhymer Hwy.

Frenchman's Bay Rd.

Bluebeard's Beach Club

Green Cay

Bolongo Bay

Morningstar Beach

Bovoni Rd.

Caribbean Sea

Water Island

305

302

Honeymoon Beach

Lindbergh Beach

Cyril E. King Airport

Brewers Beach

Lindbergh Bay

Perseverence Bay

Santa Maria Bay

Bordeaux Bay

Fortuna Bay

Botany Bay

Big Hans Lollick

Outer Brass

Inner Brass

2 mi
2 km
0
N

Airport
Beach
Cruise Ship Dock

Island Mountain Bike Adventure ($59, 3½ hours): Perfect for great views of the island and some decent exercise, this bike tour starts after a short minivan ride to an elevated part of the island. With a few exceptions, most of the ride is downhill, but you'll definitely work up a sweat. The tour ends at a beach, where there's time for some swimming and relaxing.

Kayaking the Marine Sanctuary ($54, 2½ hr.): Kayak from the mouth of the marine sanctuary at Holmberg's Marina and spend nearly an hour paddling among the mangroves while a naturalist explains the mangrove and lagoon ecosystem. Includes a free half-hour to snorkel or walk along the coral beach at Bovoni Point.

Water Island Bike Trip ($62, 3½ hr.) After a ferry ride to Water Island, a 5-minute bus ride brings you to the island's highest point, from which you get a nice downhill ride. Your guide will point out various historic sites and wildlife en route to Honeymoon Beach, where you can swim and enjoy a drink.

Island Tour by Minibus and Tram ($30, 3 hr.): First drive along the impressive Skyline Drive for panoramic views of St. John and the ship harbor, and then up to the 420m (1,400-ft.) Mountain Top for awesome views of Magens Bay and the British Virgin Islands. From there, 15 minutes on the Paradise Point Tramway brings you to the top of Paradise Point, some 210m (700 ft.) above the sea.

Atlantis Submarine Odyssey ($70–$74, 2 hr.): Descend about 30m (100 ft.) into the ocean in this air-conditioned submarine for views of exotic fish and sea life. (You can also book this tour independently. Call ✆ **800/253-0493**).

Virgin Islands Seaplane Exploration ($68, 1½ hr.): For great views of these islands with their beaches, old sugar plantations, and lush foliage, there's no better vantage point than from above.

EXCURSIONS OFFERED BY LOCAL AGENCIES

St. John Yachting/Snorkeling Excursion: Many yachts and catamarans are available for snorkel and scuba excursions and champagne sails. You can join a full-day or half-day sail aboard the 49-passenger catamaran *Dancing Dolphin* (✆ **340/774-8899;** www.thedancingdolphin.com), visiting local beaches, coves, wrecks, and reefs. The owner, Captain Sharee Winslow, makes special accommodations for handicapped passengers and runs special sails for children as well. Rates are $65 for a half-day cruise, $100 for a full-day cruise, and $45 for a sunset cruise. Captain Sharee also runs special wedding cruises (she's an ordained minister!).

For a more personal experience, the six-passenger *Fantasy* (✆ **340/775-5652;** www.daysailfantasy.com) departs from the American Yacht Harbor at Red Hook (on the west coast of St. Thomas) at 9:30am daily, sailing to St. John and nearby islands for swimming, snorkeling, beachcombing, or trolling. The normal full-day trip departs at 9:30am and returns at 4pm, but shorter sailings can be arranged. The cost is $110 per person, including continental breakfast, open bar, a hot lunch served on board, and snorkel gear.

ON YOUR OWN: WITHIN WALKING DISTANCE

Depending on your level of energy, you can either walk from the port into **Charlotte Amalie** (about 2.5km/1½ miles) or take a taxi. In days of yore, seafarers from all over the globe flocked to this old-world Danish town, including pirates and, during the Civil War, Confederate sailors. The old warehouses that once held pirates' loot still stand and, for the most part, house shops. The main streets (called "Gades" here in honor of their Danish heritage) are a veritable

Charlotte Amalie

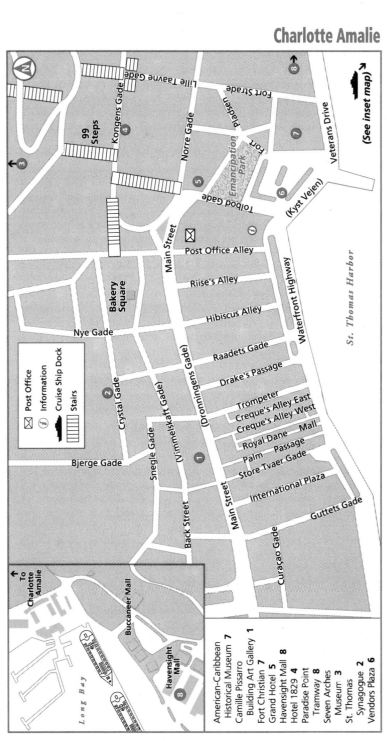

Post Office
Information
Cruise Ship Dock
Stairs

99 Steps

Bakery Square

Nye Gade

Crystal Gade

Snegle Gade

(Vimmelskaft Gade)

Bjerge Gade

Back Street

Main Street

(Dronningens Gade)

Main Street

Post Office Alley

Riise's Alley

Hibiscus Alley

Raadets Gade

Drake's Passage

Trompeter
Creque's Alley East
Creque's Alley West
Royal Dane   Mall
Palm   Passage
Store Tvaer Gade

International Plaza

Guttets Gade

Curaçao Gade

Waterfront Highway

St. Thomas Harbor

(Kyst Vejen)

Veterans Drive

(See inset map)

Kongens Gade

Lille Taavne Gade

Norre Gade

Fort Strade

Emancipation
Park

Fort

Tolbod Gade

Long Bay

To
Charlotte
Amalie

Buccaneer Mall

Havensight
Mall

American-Caribbean
Historical Museum 7
Camille Pissarro
Building Art Gallery 1
Fort Christian 7
Grand Hotel 5
Havensight Mall 8
Hotel 1829 4
Paradise Point
Tramway 8
Seven Arches
Museum 3
St. Thomas
Synagogue 2
Vendors Plaza 6

281

shopping mall, usually packed with visitors. Sandwiched among the shops are a few historic buildings, most of which can be covered on foot in about 2 hours.

Before starting your tour, stop off at the so-called **Grand Hotel,** near Emancipation Park. No longer a hotel, it has a restaurant, a bar, shops, and a visitor center. There are views of the harbor below from the wood-paneled pub/restaurant at **Hotel 1829,** one street farther up Government Hill. It's a great place for a drink or some lunch.

Stray behind the seafront shopping strip (Main St.) of Charlotte Amalie and you'll find pockets of 19th-century houses and the truly charming, cozy, brick-and-stone **St. Thomas Synagogue,** built in 1833 by Sephardic Jews. There's a great view from here as well. It's located high on the steep sloping Crystal Gade.

Dating from 1672, **Fort Christian,** 32 Raadets Gade, rises from the harbor to dominate the center of town. Named after the Danish king Christian V, the structure has been everything from a governor's residence to a jail. Many pirates were hanged in its courtyard. Some of the cells have been turned into the rather minor **American-Caribbean Historical Museum** (© 340/714-5150), displaying Indian artifacts of only the most passing interest. The fort is open Monday to Friday from 8am to 5pm. Admission is free.

Seven Arches Museum, Government Hill (© 340/774-9295), is a 2-century-old Danish house completely restored to its original condition and furnished with antiques. You can walk through the yellow ballast arches and visit the great room with its view of the busy harbor.

The **Paradise Point Tramway** (© 340/774-9809) affords visitors a dramatic view of Charlotte Amalie Harbor at a peak height of 209m (697 ft.). The tramways transport customers from the Havensight area to Paradise Point, where riders disembark to visit shops and a popular restaurant and bar.

ON YOUR OWN: BEYOND THE PORT AREA

Coral World Marine Park & Underwater Observatory, 6450 Coki Point, off Route 38, 20 minutes from downtown Charlotte Amalie (© 340/775-1555; www.coralworldvi.com), is the number-one attraction in St. Thomas. The 1½-hectare (3½-acre) complex features a three-story underwater observation tower 30m (100 ft.) offshore—you'll see sponges, fish, coral, and other underwater life in their natural state through the windows. In the Marine Gardens Aquarium, saltwater tanks display everything from sea horses to sea urchins. An 80,000-gallon reef tank features exotic Caribbean marine life. Another tank is devoted to sea predators, including circling sharks. The entrance is hidden behind a waterfall.

West of Charlotte Amalie, **Frenchtown** was settled by a French-speaking citizenry who were uprooted when the Swedes invaded and took over their home of St. Barts. These settlers were known for wearing cha-chas, or straw hats. Many of the people who live here today are the direct descendants of those long-ago residents. This colorful fishing village contains several interesting restaurants and taverns. To get there, take a taxi down Veterans Drive (Rte. 30) west and turn left at the sign to the Admirals Inn.

The lush **St. Peter Greathouse Estate and Gardens,** at the corner of St. Peter Mountain Road (Rte. 40) and Barrett Hill Road (© 340/774-4999), ornaments 4.5 hectares (11 acres) on the volcanic peaks of the island's northern rim. It's the creation of Howard Lawson DeWolfe, a *Mayflower* descendant who, with his wife, Sylvie, bought the estate in 1987 and set about transforming it into a tropical paradise. It's filled with some 200 varieties of plants and trees, including an umbrella plant from Madagascar. There are also a rain forest, an orchid jungle, waterfalls, and reflecting ponds. From a panoramic deck you can see some 20 of the Virgin Islands. The house itself is worth a visit, its interior filled with local art. Admission is $10 for adults, $5 children.

For a spectacular view of the harbor at Charlotte Amalie, head up to **Drake's Seat** on Route 40. Legend has it that Sir Frances Drake used this place as a lookout to spot enemy fleets. With flamboyant trees in blossom, it makes for a great photo op. There's a small parking area.

SHOPPING

St. Thomas is famous for its shopping opportunities. As in St. Croix and St. John, American shoppers can bring home $1,200 worth of merchandise without paying duty—twice the amount of other Caribbean islands. You'll sometimes find well-known brand names at savings of up to 40% off stateside prices, but you'll often have to plow through a lot of junk to find the bargains. The main goodies are jewelry, watches, cameras, china, and leather.

Many cruise ship passengers shop at the **Havensight Mall,** where the ships dock, but the major shopping goes on along the harbor of Charlotte Amalie. **Main Street** (or Dronningens Gade, its old Danish name) is the main shopping area. Just north of Main Street is merchandise-loaded **Back Street,** or Vimmelskaft. Many shops are also spread along the Waterfront Highway (also called Kyst Vejen). Running between these major streets is a series of side streets, walkways, and alleys, all filled with shops. All the usual Caribbean mega-tourist-shops sell all the usual jewelry, watches, perfume, gift items, and so on, but there are a number of other interesting, and more unique, shops. Just do a little comparison shopping from place to place and be a little cautious of people trying to lure you into their shop and offering you a special rate if you bring in others from your group.

Upstairs at 14 Dronningens Gade, the **Camille Pissarro Building Art Gallery** is in the house where the impressionist painter Pissarro was born on July 10, 1830. In three high-ceilinged and airy rooms, you'll see all the available Pissarro paintings relating to the islands. Many prints and note cards by local artists are available, too, as well as original batiks.

Huddled under oversize parasols, hundreds of street vendors ply their trades in a designated area called **Vendors Plaza,** at the corner of Veterans Drive and Tolbod Gade. It's open Monday to Saturday from 7:30am to 5:30pm, and on Sunday if a cruise ship is expected. Food vendors set up on sidewalks outside.

Need a marital aid? **Lover's Lane,** Raadets Gade 33 (beside Veterans Dr., on the second floor) stocks provocative lingerie, inflatable men and women, vibrators of every conceivable type, and lots of leather and latex—just what you need in the tropical heat.

MAPes MONDc (© 340/776-2886; www.mapesmonde.com) has two locations in St. Thomas—one in Riise Alley and the other at The Grand Hotel—and another at Mongoose Junction on St. John. Its elegant books, reproductions, historic maps, and archival photos of the Caribbean are a nice break from jewelry and tourist knickknacks. They also carry lovely prints, silk screens, and greeting cards featuring indigenous birds and vegetation.

BEACHES

St. Thomas has some good beaches, all of which are easily reached by taxi. Arrange for your driver to return and pick you up at a designated time. All the beaches in the U.S. Virgin Islands are public, but some still charge a fee. Mind your belongings, as St. Thomas has pickpockets and thieves who target visitors.

If you're going to St. John, you may want to do your beaching there (see "Beaches," under St. John, later in this chapter).

THE NORTH SIDE   Located across the mountains, 5km (3 miles) north of the capital, **Magens Bay Beach** was once hailed as one of the world's 10 most beautiful beaches, but its reputation has faded. Though still beautiful, it isn't as well maintained as it should be and is often overcrowded, especially when many cruise ships are in port. It's less than 1.5km (a mile) long and lies between two mountains. Admission is $1 for adults and 25¢ for children under 12. Changing facilities are available along with picnic tables and benches, and you can rent snorkeling gear and lounge chairs. There's no public transportation here, so take a taxi. The gates are open daily from 6am to 6pm (you'll need insect repellent after 4pm).

Located in the northeast near Coral World, **Coki Beach** is good, but it, too, becomes overcrowded when cruise ships are in port. Snorkelers come here often, as do pickpockets—protect your valuables. Lockers can be rented at Coral World, next door. An East End bus runs to Smith Bay and lets you off at the gate to Coral World and Coki.

Also on the north side is **Renaissance Grand Beach Resort,** one of the island's most beautiful beaches. It opens onto Smith Bay, right off Route 38, near Coral World. Many watersports are available here.

THE SOUTH SIDE   On the south side, **Morningstar** lies about 3km (2 miles) east of Charlotte Amalie at Marriott's Frenchman's Reef Beach Resort. You can wear your most daring swimwear here, and you can also rent sailboats, snorkeling equipment, and lounge chairs. The beach can be easily reached via a cliff-front elevator at the Marriott.

The **Bolongo Bay Beach Club** lures those who love a serene spread of sand. You can feed hibiscus blossoms to iguanas and rent snorkeling gear and lounge chairs. They also offer a variety of watersports including parasailing. There's no public transportation, but it's a $5 ride by taxi from Charlotte Amalie. Unlike Magans Bay Beach (see above), where there's only a snack bar, Iggy's Restaurant is right on Bolongo's beach. **Bluebeard's Beach Club** (formerly known as Limetree Beach) offers a secluded setting and is a quick ride from the cruise ship pier.

In 1929, Charles Lindbergh paid a visit to St. Thomas, landing his *Spirit of St. Louis* in a swampy area on the island's southwestern coast. During World War II, the swamp was drained to make way for a military airbase, which today is the island's main international airport. Nearby, on the Fortuna bus route heading west from Charlotte Amalie, **Lindbergh Beach** was named in his honor. It's a sentimental spot for islanders and a nice enough beach, but it's located a little too close to the airport. The Island Beachcomber restaurant is nearby.

Brewer's Beach, one of the island's most popular, lies in the southwest near the University of the Virgin Islands, also along the Fortuna bus route.

THE EAST END   Small and special, **Secret Harbor** sits near a collection of condos. With its white sand and coconut palms, it's a veritable cliché of Caribbean charm. No public transportation stops here, but it's an easy taxi ride east of Charlotte Amalie heading toward Red Hook.

Sapphire Beach is one of the finest on St. Thomas, set against the backdrop of the Doubletree Sapphire Beach Resort & Marina complex, where you can lunch or order drinks. Windsurfers like this beach a lot. You can rent snorkeling gear and lounge chairs here. A large reef lies close to the shore, and there are great views of offshore cays and St. John. To get here, take the East End bus from

Charlotte Amalie, going via Red Hook. Ask to be let off at the entrance to Sapphire Bay; it's a short walk to the water.

SPORTS

GOLF   Designed by Tom and George Fazio, **Mahogany Run** on the north shore, Mahogany Run Road (© **800/253-7103** or 340/777-6006), is one of the most beautiful courses in the West Indies. This 18-hole, par-70 course rises and drops like a roller coaster on its journey to the sea. Cliffs and crashing sea waves are the ultimate hazards at the 13th and 14th holes. The golf course is an $8 taxi ride from the cruise dock. Greens fees are about $100.

SCUBA DIVING & SNORKELING   The waters off the U.S. Virgin Islands are rated as one of the "most beautiful areas in the world" by *Skin Diver* magazine. Thirty spectacular reefs lie just off St. Thomas alone. **Dive In!,** in the Doubletree Sapphire Beach Resort & Marina, Smith Bay Road, Route 36 (© **800/524-2090;** www.diveinusvi.com), offers professional instruction, daily beach and boat dives, custom dive packages, underwater photography and videotapes, and snorkeling trips.

More experienced divers should call the **U.S. Virgin Islands Department of Tourism dive guide** for detailed information on locations and guides (© **340/774-8784;** www.usvitourism.vi).

There are lots of fun things to do at **Coral World** (see "On Your Own: Beyond the Port Area," above). If you're not certified for scuba but want to try something a bit more adventurous than snorkeling, there's **sea trekking** ($59), which allows you to descend about 4.5m (15 ft.) below the water with a helmet and air hose and walk along a trail on the sea floor, with fish swimming all around you. It takes a few minutes to get acclimated to walking under the water and breathing inside the helmet, but it's a ton of fun. **Snuba** ($59) is similar to scuba, except that instead of wearing the air tanks, the tanks stay at the water's surface on little rafts. It requires a bit of orientation before you go down, to a maximum of 6m (20 ft.)—the length of the hose. It's especially fun for couples when only one person is an experienced diver and both would like to experience diving together. An instructor/guide accompanies the group at all times. There are lots of cool underwater photo ops. For more info, visit www.visnuba.com.

GREAT LOCAL RESTAURANTS & BARS

IN CHARLOTTE AMALIE   **Beni Iguana's Sushi Bar,** in the Grand Hotel Court, just behind Emancipation Park in downtown (© **340/777-8744**), is the only Japanese restaurant on St. Thomas. **Greenhouse,** Veterans Drive (© **340/774-7998**), attracts cruise ship passengers with daily specials, including American fare and some Jamaican-inspired dishes. The **Hard Rock Cafe,** 5144 International Plaza (on the second floor of a pink-sided mall), on the Waterfront (© **340/777-5555**), has the best burgers in town, but people mainly come for the good times and the T-shirts. **Virgilio's,** 18 Dronningens Gade, entrance on a narrow alleyway running between Main and Back streets (© **340/776-4920**), is the good northern Italian restaurant that serves excellent lobster ravioli. **Lillian's Caribbean Grill,** 43–46 Norre Gade, in the Grand Galleria Courtyard directly across from Emancipation Park (© **340/774-7900**), serves authentic Caribbean dishes. Conveniently located near the Vendor's Plaza shopping area, it makes for a nice lunch stop.

IN FRENCHTOWN   At **Alexander's,** rue de St. Barthélemy, west of town (© **340/774-4349**), there's a heavy emphasis on seafood—the menu even includes conch schnitzel on occasion. Other dishes include a mouthwatering Wiener schnitzel and homemade paté. **Craig & Sally's,** 22 Honduras (© **340/ 777-9949**), serves dishes that, according to the owner, are not "for the faint of heart, but for the adventurous soul"—roast pork with clams, filet mignon with macadamia-nut sauce, and grilled swordfish with a sauce of fresh herbs and tomatoes.

ON THE NORTH COAST Newly renamed (it used to be Sandra's New Terrace) but with the same Caribbean flair as always, **Glenda's Caribbean Spot,** 66–67 Smith Bay, Route 38, just east of the Coral World turnoff (© **340/ 775-2699**), is one of the island's best-known West Indian restaurants. It oozes local color. The place made news around the world on January 5, 1997, when Bill and Hillary Clinton showed up unexpectedly for lunch. Surrounded by secret-service men, they shared a conch appetizer, then Mrs. Clinton went for the vegetable plate while the president opted for the catch of the day, which he reportedly loved.

ON SAPPHIRE BEACH **Seagrape,** in the Doubletree Sapphire Beach Resort & Marina, Route 6, Smith Bay Rd. (© **340/775-6100**), is counted among the finest dining rooms along the east coast of St. Thomas. The lunch menu includes the grilled catch of the day and freshly made salads.

NEAR THE SUB BASE (east of Frenchtown) **Victor's New Hide Out,** 103 Sub Base, off Route 30 (© **340/776-9379**), has some of the best local dishes on the island, but first you have to find it—this hilltop perch is truly a place to hide out. Take a taxi. Local dishes such as Caribbean lobster, curried chicken, and a variety of fresh fish have sophisticated flair and zest, as opposed to the more down-home cookery found at Glenda's Caribbean Spot (see above).

ST. JOHN

A tiny gem of an island, lush St. John lies about 5km (3 miles) east of St. Thomas across Pillsbury Sound. It's the smallest and least populated of the U.S. Virgins, only about 11km (7 miles) long and 5km (3 miles) wide, with a total land area of some 49 square km (19 sq. miles). The island was slated for big development under Danish control, but a slave rebellion and the decline of the sugarcane plantations ended that idea. Today, St. John leads the Caribbean in eco-tourism or "sustainable tourism"—since 1956, more than half of its land mass, as well as its shoreline waters, have been set aside as the **Virgin Islands National Park.** Miles of winding hiking trails lead to panoramic views and the ruins of 18th-century Danish plantations. Mysterious geometric petroglyphs incised into boulders and cliffs can be seen all over the island (ask a guide to point them out if you can't find them). These figures, of unknown age and origin, have never been deciphered. Since St. John is easy to reach from St. Thomas and the beaches are spectacular, many cruise ship passengers spend their entire day here.

COMING ASHORE Cruise ships cannot dock at either of the piers in St. John. Instead, they moor off the coast at **Cruz Bay,** sending in tenders to the National Park Service Dock, the larger of the two piers. Most cruise ships docking at St. Thomas offer shore excursions to St. John's pristine interior and beaches.

If your ship docks on St. Thomas and you don't take an organized shore excursion to St. John, you can get here from Charlotte Amalie by **ferry.** Ferries leave the Charlotte Amalie waterfront for Cruz Bay at 1- to 2-hour intervals, from 9am until around 5:30pm. The last boat leaves Cruz Bay for Charlotte

Amalie at 3:45pm. The ride takes about 45 minutes and costs $7 each way. Call
© **340/776-6282** for more information. Another ferry leaves from the Red
Hook pier on St. Thomas's eastern tip more or less every half-hour, starting at
6:30am. It's a 30-minute drive from Charlotte Amalie's port to the pier at Red
Hook; the ferry trip takes another 20 minutes each way. The one-way fare is $3
for adults, $1 for children under 11. Schedules can change without notice, so
call in advance (© **340/776-6282**). You can take a Vitran bus from a point near
Market Square (located near the west end of Main St. in Charlotte Amalie)
directly to Red Hook for $1 per person each way, or negotiate a price with a taxi
driver.

GETTING AROUND

BY TAXI   The most popular way to get around is by surrey-style taxi. Typical
fares from Cruz Bay are $3 to Trunk Bay, $3.50 to Cinnamon Bay, or $7 to Maho
Bay. Taxis wait at the pier. In the *very* unlikely event you don't see a taxi at the
pier, you can call St. John Taxi Service at © **340/693-7530.** Almost any taxi at
Cruz Bay can take you on a 2-hour taxi tour of the island. Tours cost from $45
for one or two passengers, or about $12 per person for three or more riders.

BY RENTAL CAR   The extensive Virgin Islands National Park has kept the
island's roads undeveloped and uncluttered, opening onto some of the most
panoramic vistas anywhere. Renting a vehicle is the best way to see these views,
especially if you like to linger at particularly beautiful spots. Open-sided Jeep-
like vehicles are the most fun of the limited rentals here. There's sometimes a
shortage of cars during the busy midwinter season, so try to reserve early.
Remember to drive on the left (even though steering wheels are on the left,
too—go figure). **Avis** and **Hertz** both have offices here. Your car is likely to
come with just enough fuel to get you to one of the island's two gas stations, so
fill 'er up: Due to the distance between stations, it's never a good idea to drive
around St. John with less than half a tank of gas.

SHORE EXCURSIONS OFFERED BY THE CRUISE LINES

Island Tour ($39, 4–5 hr.): Since most ships tie up in St. Thomas, tours of St.
John first require a ferry or tender ride to Cruz Bay in St. John. Then you board
open-air safari buses for a tour that includes a stop at the ruins of a working
plantation (the Annaberg Ruins), as well as a pause at Trunk Bay or one of the
other beaches. The island and sea views from the coastal road are spectacular.

ON YOUR OWN: WITHIN WALKING DISTANCE

Most cruise ship passengers dart through Cruz Bay, a cute little West Indian village with interesting bars, restaurants, boutiques, and pastel-painted houses.
Wharfside Village, near the dock, is a complex of courtyards, alleys, and shady
patios with a mishmash of boutiques, restaurants, fast-food joints, and bars.
Down the road from the dock is **Mongoose Junction** (see "Shopping," below).

Located at the public library, the **Elaine Ione Sprauve Museum** (© **340/
776-6359**) isn't big, but it does have some local artifacts, and will teach you
about some of the history of the island. It's open Monday to Friday from 9am
to 5pm. Admission is free.

ON YOUR OWN: BEYOND THE PORT AREA

In November 1954, the wealthy Rockefeller family began acquiring large tracts
of land on St. John. They then donated more than 5,000 acres to the Department of the Interior for the creation of the **Virgin Islands National Park,**

Frommer's Favorite St. John Experiences

Touring the Island in an Open-air Safari Bus: The views are spectacular from the island's coastal road, and you'll visit the ruins of a plantation and one of St. John's excellent beaches. (See "Shore Excursions Offered by the Cruise Lines," above.)

Beaching Yourself in Trunk Bay: Although it can get somewhat crowded, it's a gorgeous beach and there's some decent snorkeling too. (See "Beaches," below.)

which Congress voted into existence on August 2, 1956. Over the years, the size of the park has grown steadily; it now totals 12,624 acres (50,496 hectares), including over two-thirds of St. John's landmass plus submerged land and water adjacent to the island. Stop off first at the **visitor center** (© 340/776-6201) right on the dock at St. Cruz, where you'll find some exhibits and learn more about what you can see and do in the park. You can explore the park on the more than 32km (20 miles) of biking trails; rent your own car, Jeep, or Mini-Moke; or hike. If you decide to hike, stop at the visitor center first to watch an 18-minute video about the park and to pick up maps and instructions. You can take a taxi for about $5 to the starting point of whatever trail you select. All trails are well marked.

Within the park, try to see the **Annaberg Ruins,** Leinster Bay Road, where the Danes founded thriving plantations and a sugar mill in 1718. You'll find tidal pools, forest, hilltops, wild scenery, and the ruins of several Danish plantations. It's located off North Shore Road, east of Trunk Bay on the north shore. On certain days of the week (dates vary), guided walks of the area are given by park rangers. Check at the visitor center.

SHOPPING
Compared to St. Thomas, St. John is a minor shopping destination, but the boutiques and shops at Cruz Bay are generally more interesting than those on St. Thomas. Most of them are clustered at **Mongoose Junction** (www.usvi.net/shopping/mongoose), in a woodsy area beside the roadway, about a 5-minute walk from the ferry dock. **Bamboula** (© 340/693-8699) has an unusual and appealing collection of gifts from the Caribbean, Haiti, India, Indonesia, and Central Africa. **The Canvas Factory** (© 340/776-6196) produces its own rugged, colorful handmade canvas bags. **Donald Schnell Studio** (© 800/253-7107 or 340/776-6420) deals in handmade pottery, sculpture, and blown glass. The **Fabric Mill** (© 340/776-6194) features silk-screened and batik fabrics from around the world. **R and I Patton Goldsmithing** (© 800/626-3445 or 340/776-6548) has a large selection of locally designed jewelry, made with sterling silver, gold, and precious stones. In case you forgot your Tevas or need a new bathing suit, check out **Big Planet Adventure Outfitters** (© 340/776-6638), which stocks lots of outdoor-gear brands.

At Cruz Bay's Wharfside Village, **Pusser's Company Store** (© 340/775-6379; www.pussers.com) offers a large collection of classically designed, old-world travel and adventure clothing, along with unusual accessories and Pusser's famous (though not terribly good) rum, which was served aboard British Navy

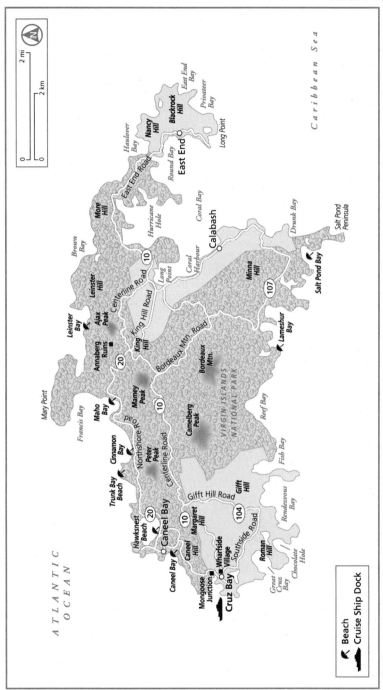

Caribbean Sea

ATLANTIC OCEAN

Beach
Cruise Ship Dock

East End Bay
Privateer Bay
Long Point
Blackrock Hill
Nancy Hill
East End
Round Bay
Haulover Bay
Coral Bay
Drunk Bay
Salt Pond Peninsula
Salt Pond Bay
Calabash
More Hill
Hurricane Hole
Long Point
Coral Harbour
Minna Hill
Lameshur Bay
Brown Bay
East End Road
Centerline Road
King Hill Road
Leinster Hill
Leinster Bay
Ajax Peak
Annaberg Ruins
King Hill
Bordeaux Mtn. Road
Bordeaux Mtn.
VIRGIN ISLANDS NATIONAL PARK
Mary Point
Francis Bay
Maho Bay
Mamey Peak
Camelberg Peak
Reef Bay
Fish Bay
Cinnamon Bay
Northshore Rd.
Peter Peak
Centerline Road
Trunk Bay Beach
Hawksnest Beach
Caneel Bay
Caneel Hill
Margaret Hill
Gifft Hill Road
Gifft Hill
Rendezvous Bay
Roman Hill
Chocolate Hole
Great Cruz Bay
Southside Road
Wharfside Village
Mongoose Junction
Cruz Bay

ships for over 300 years. A good, cheap gift item is packets of Pusser's coasters, on which is written the recipe for that classic Caribbean rum specialty, the Painkiller.

BEACHES

For a true beach lover, missing the great white sweep of **Trunk Bay** would be like touring Europe and skipping Paris. Trouble is, the word is a little more than out. This gorgeous beach is usually overcrowded, and there are sometimes pickpockets lurking about. The beach has lifeguards and rents snorkeling gear to those wanting to explore the underwater trail near the shore. Both taxis and "safari buses" to Trunk Bay meet the ferry as it docks at Cruz Bay.

Caneel Bay, the stamping ground of the rich and famous, has seven perfect beaches on its 68 hectares (170 acres), but only one—Hawksnest Beach—that's open to the public. Since it's the closest beach to Cruz Bay (and is very beautiful, if a bit narrow and windy), it's often overcrowded. Safari buses and taxis from Cruz Bay will take you along North Shore Road.

The campgrounds of **Cinnamon Bay** and **Maho Bay** have their own beaches, where forest rangers sometimes have to remind visitors to put their swimsuits back on. Snorkelers find good reefs here, and it's a great place to spot turtles and schools of parrotfish. Changing rooms and showers are available.

Salt Pond Bay is known to locals but often missed by visitors. The bay here is tranquil, but there are no facilities. The Ram Head Trail begins here and winds for 1.5km (a mile) to a panoramic belvedere overlooking the bay.

SPORTS

HIKING   The network of trails in Virgin Islands National Park is the big thing here. The visitor center at Cruz Bay hands out free trail maps of the park. Since you don't have time to get lost—you don't want the ship to leave without you—it's best to set out with someone who knows his or her way around. Both **Maho Bay Camps** (© 340/776-6226) and **Cinnamon Bay Campground** (© 340/776-6201) conduct nature walks.

KAYAKING & WINDSURFING   The **Cinnamon Bay Watersports Center** on Cinnamon Bay Beach (© 340/776-6330) rents kayaks and 12- or 14-foot Hobie monohull sailboats, and the windsurfing here is some of the best anywhere, for both beginners and experts.

SCUBA DIVING & SNORKELING   Low Key Watersports, Wharfside Village (© 800/835-7718 or 340/693-8999; www.divelowkey.com), offers two-tank, two-location wreck dives on its own custom-built dive boats. They also arrange day-sailing charters, kayaking tours, deep-sea sportfishing, and snorkel tours, and rent watersports gear, including masks, fins, snorkels, and dive skins. **Cruz Bay Watersports,** at Palm Plaza (© 340/776-6234; www.cbw-stjohn. com), is a PADI and NAUI five-star diving center. Snorkel tours are available daily.

GREAT LOCAL RESTAURANTS & BARS

In Wharfside Village, at Cruz Bay, the new, upscale **Cafe Wahoo** (© 340/776-6600) offers a lovely view of Cruz Bay Harbor. For a more casual meal and drinks, try **The Beach Bar,** downstairs (© 340/777-4220), with the same view to go with your burgers and bar food.

The Fish Trap, at Raintree Court, Cruz Bay (© 340/693-9994), is known for its wide selection of fresh fish, but also caters to vegetarians and the burger crowd.

The Italian food at **Paradiso,** Mongoose Junction (© **340/693-8899**), is the best on the island—the chicken picante Willie, a spicy, creamy picante sauce over crispy chicken with linguini and ratatouille, was featured in *Bon Appétit.*

30 Trinidad & Tobago

The southernmost islands in the Caribbean chain, Trinidad and tiny Tobago (which together form a single nation), manage to encompass nearly every facet of Caribbean life. Located less than 16km (10 miles) east of Venezuela's coast, Trinidad is large (the biggest and most heavily populated Caribbean island) and diverse, with an industrial, cosmopolitan capital city, Port of Spain, and an outgoing, vibrant culture that combines African, East Indian, European, Chinese, and Syrian influences. Little-sister Tobago is the more natural of the two, with rain-forested mountains and spectacular secluded beaches.

Trinidad and Tobago won independence from Britain in 1962 and became a republic in 1976, but some British influences, including the residents' love of cricket, remain. Trinidad grew rich from oil, and the islands are still the Western hemisphere's largest oil exporters.

Trinidad's music is another local treasure. The calypso, steel-pan, and soca styles that originated here have influenced musical trends worldwide. Trinidad's rhythmic, soulful music is a main feature of **Carnaval,** the Caribbean-wide bacchanalian celebration held each year on the Monday and Tuesday before Lent. Among all the Carnaval celebrations in the Caribbean, Trinidad's is king.

Trinidad's residents are charming, are friendly, and love to talk. With a literacy rate of 97%, the populace is full of well-informed conversationalists. You'll find Trinis (as residents call themselves) happy to socialize with visitors and discuss just about anything.

LANGUAGE   The official language is **English,** but like many of their Caribbean neighbors, Trinis speak English with a distinct patois. Hindi, Creole, and Spanish are also spoken among various ethnic groups.

CURRENCY   The unit of currency is the Trinidad & Tobago dollar, sometimes designated by the same symbol as the U.S. dollar ($) and sometimes just by "TT." The exchange rate is U.S.$1 = TT$5.55; TT$1 = U.S.18¢. Vacationers can pay in U.S. dollars, but be sure you know what currency prices are being quoted in, and try to get change in U.S. dollars. Local **ATMs** mainly dispense TT notes.

CALLING FROM THE U.S.   When calling Trinidad and Tobago from the United States, you just need to dial "1" before the numbers listed here.

TRINIDAD

Trinidad is one of the most industrialized countries in the Caribbean, and it shows—if you're looking for a sleepy, quiet Caribbean retreat, go to Tobago instead. Trinidad's capital and commercial center, **Port of Spain,** is an energetic, bustling metropolis of 300,000. There are few distinct attractions—Port of Spain isn't necessarily a tourist city—but the central shopping area at the south end of Frederick Street is a colorfully crowded mix of outdoor shopping arcades and air-conditioned minimalls.

Independence Square, in the heart of Port of Spain, is the place to get a taxi, find a bank, and get good, cheap food. There are mosques, shrines, and temples here, and locals gather at Woodford Square to hear public speakers or attend outdoor meetings.

While Port of Spain is interesting and not threatening by day, it's unsafe at night, and strolling around is not recommended if your ship happens to be in port late.

COMING ASHORE   Cruise ships visiting Trinidad dock at Port of Spain's 4-acre cruise terminal, built in the early 1990s to accommodate the island's growing cruise traffic. The complex includes a telephone and communications center, a shopping mall, tourist info, and car-rental agencies. Arriving passengers are usually greeted by steel-pan musicians and colorfully dressed dancers. Outside the terminal, there's a craft market with T-shirts, straw items, and other souvenirs.

INFORMATION   The **Tourism and Industrial Development Corporation of Trinidad and Tobago** (TIDCO) is located at 10–14 Phillips St., at the terminal in Port of Spain (© **868/623-1932** or 888/595-4TNT). It's open Monday to Friday from 8am to 4:30pm. For info before you go, contact the tourism board office in the U.S. (© **212/682-7272;** www.visittnt.com).

GETTING AROUND

BY TAXI   Taxis are available at the cruise terminal. The Port Authority posts cab fares on a board by the main entrance (the cars don't have meters). Always establish a fare before loading into the taxi and shoving off. Private cabs can be relatively expensive.

BY BUS/VAN   Maxi-taxis (minivans operating regular routes within specific zones) have a yellow stripe and are lower priced than taxis. There are also route taxis, shared cabs that travel along a prescribed route and charge about TT$2 to TT$8 (U.S.30¢ to U.S.$1.50) to drop you at any spot along the route.

BY RENTAL CAR   Driving is on the left. Trinidad has a fairly wide network of roads, and roads in town are generally well marked; but traffic is frequently heavy. None of the major rental companies have offices here.

SHORE EXCURSIONS OFFERED BY THE CRUISE LINES

Caroni Bird Sanctuary ($44, 3 hr.): This sanctuary is a pristine network of lush mangroves, quiet canals, and shallow lagoons, and is considered a world-class bird-watching preserve. Following a 30-minute drive from the cruise pier, passengers embark for the tour in flat-bottomed boats, which glide through calm canals and lagoons. Guides will point out unique flora and fauna during the ride. Heron, osprey, and scarlet ibis are among the bird species native to this area.

ON YOUR OWN: WITHIN WALKING DISTANCE

Except for the craft market right outside the terminal, and a small restaurant across the street, there isn't much to see close to the cruise pier.

ON YOUR OWN: BEYOND THE PORT AREA

Among Port of Spain's chief centers of activity, **Independence Square,** a stone's throw from the cruise complex, isn't really a square at all but parallel streets running east and west and connected at one end by a pedestrian mall. The scene here resembles a Middle Eastern bazaar, with a dense thicket of pushcarts, honking cabs, produce hawkers, and inquisitive shoppers moving to the irresistible beat of soca, reggae, and calypso music blaring from nearby stores and sidewalk stands. Some parts of the square have become run-down, and some locals consider the area less than safe. Visitors should keep an eye out for pickpockets and petty thieves.

Woodford Square, laid out by Ralph Woodford, Trinidad's early-19th-century British governor, is among the most attractive areas in town, full of large,

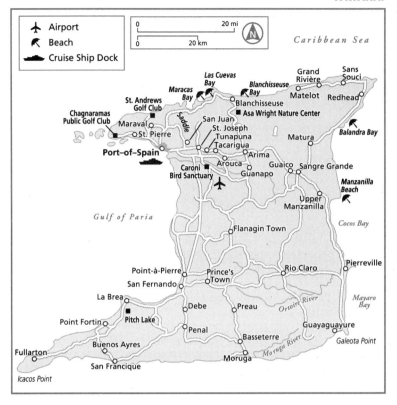

leafy trees surrounding a rich lawn with landscaped walkways. This area has traditionally served as a center for political debates, discussions, and rallies. The **Cathedral of the Holy Trinity,** built in 1818 by Woodford, lies on the square's south side. The church's carved roof is designed as a replica of Westminster Hall in London. Inside the church is a memorial statue of Woodford himself. To reach the square, take Independence Square North and then go left on Abercromby Street, or Wrightson Road to Sackville Street.

On the square's western border is **Red House,** an imposing (and, yes, red) Renaissance-style edifice built in 1906. Today, it houses Trinidad's parliament. The building was badly damaged in 1990 when militants took the prime minister and parliament members hostage. A little farther north of the city center is **Queen's Park Savannah,** originally part of a 80-hectare (200-acre) sugar plantation but now a public park with 32 hectares (80 acres) of open land and walkways, with great shade trees. A depression at the park's northwest section, known as the Hollows, has flower beds, rock gardens, and small ponds. The area has become a popular picnic spot.

There are a number of notable sights along the park's outer, western edge, including the **Magnificent Seven,** a row of seven colonial buildings constructed in the late 19th and early 20th centuries. The buildings include Queen's Royal College, White Hall (the prime minister's office), and Stollmeyer's Castle, which was designed to resemble a Scottish castle—complete with turrets.

Frommer's Favorite Trinidad Experiences

Visiting the Asa Wright Nature Center: This 80-hectare (200-acre) preserve, located in Trinidad's rain forest in the northern hills, features intertwined hiking trails, a bird sanctuary, and a conservation center. (See "On Your Own: Beyond the Port Area," above.)

Trying a Drink with Angostura Bitters: This local specialty contains citrus-tree bark and is made from a secret recipe.

Beyond the northern edge of Queen's Park Savannah lies the **Emperor Valley Zoo** (© 868/622-3530), featuring local animals, including tropical toucans and macaws, porcupine, monkeys, and various snakes. The zoo emphasizes colorful tropical plants, which are in evidence all over the grounds. It's open 9:30am to 5:30pm daily; admission is $1 adults, 25¢ for children.

The 28-hectare (70-acre) **botanical gardens** are east of the zoo. Laid out in 1820, the gardens are landscaped with attractive walkways and great flowering trees, among them the wild poinsettia, whose bright red blossom is the national flower. The **President's House,** built in 1875 as the governor's residence, is adjacent to the gardens.

Near Spring Hill Estate, 48km (30 miles) northeast of Port of Spain beside Blanchisseuse Road, the **Asa Wright Nature Center** (© 868/667-4655; www.asawright.org) is known to bird-watchers throughout the world. Within its 78 hectares (196 acres), set at an elevation of 360m (1,200 ft.) in Trinidad's rain-forested mountains, you can see hummingbirds, toucans, bellbirds, manakins, several varieties of tanagers, and the rare oilbird. Hiking trails line the grounds, and guided tours are available. Call for a schedule.

SHOPPING

Shopping in the Port of Spain area means crafts, fabrics, and fashions made by local artists, a range of spices, and colorful artwork. Most of the shopping opportunities lie in the area around **Independence Square,** particularly near Frederick and Queen streets. Art lovers will find a handful of galleries and studios featuring the work of local and regional artists. **Art Creators,** at Seventh Street and St. Ann's Road in the Aldegonda Park section (© 868/624-4369), is a serious gallery offering year-around exhibits of both newly emerging and established artists. **Aquarela Galleries,** at 1A Dere St., exhibits the work of recognized and up-and-coming Trini artists and also publishes high-end art books. If you're in the mood for distinctive gift and apparel shopping, hire a cab to the **Hotel Normandie,** 10 Nook Ave. in the St. Ann's section (© 868/624-1181), where **Village Market shops** feature clothing and jewelry by some of the country's top designers. The market's **Greer's Textile Designs** carries colorful batiks and pricey jewelry from designer Jillian Bishop. You'll also find **Interiors** here, which sells all manner of unusual gifts.

For craft creations outside of the cruise terminal area, try the **Trinidad and Tobago Blind Welfare Association,** at 118 Duke St. (© 868/624-1613), with accessories and gifts of rattan and other natural materials, all made by blind craftsmen. The **Trinidad and Tobago Handicraft Cooperative,** at King's Wharf (© 868/627-4477), sells small steel pans, hammocks, and other locally produced items. **Art Potters Ltd.,** located at the cruise terminal, is a pottery specialist.

Music is another of Trinidad's signature products, and the latest soca and reggae can be purchased at **Rhyner's Record Shop** at 54 Prince St., Port of Spain (© **868/625-2476**). There's also **Crosby Records** (© **868/622-7622**), located in the St. James area.

BEACHES

Unlike its tiny cousin Tobago, Trinidad was not blessed with many beautiful beaches. The most popular of the beaches is **Maracas Bay,** a scenic, 40-minute drive from Port of Spain. The drive takes vacationers over mountains and through a lush rain forest. As you near the beach, the coastal road descends from a cliff-side. The beach itself is wide and sandy, with a small fishing village on one side and the richly dense mountains in the background. There are a lifeguard, changing rooms and showers, and areas for picnics. There's also a small snack stand selling "shark and bake" sandwiches (a local favorite made with fresh slabs of shark and fried bread).

SPORTS

GOLF   The oldest and best-known golf course on the island is the 18-hole, par-72 **St. Andrews Golf Club** in the suburb of Maraval (© **868/629-2314**). Also known as Moka Golf Course, it was established in the late 19th century. Greens fees are $60.

GREAT LOCAL RESTAURANTS & BARS

A favorite **local beer** is Stag; a favorite **local rum** is Vat 19 Old Oak.

Trinidad is home to some of the most diverse culinary styles in the Caribbean, a result of its African, Chinese, English, French, Indian, Portuguese, Spanish, and Syrian influences. **Rafters,** at 6A Warner St. (© **868/628-9258**), is an old rum house with brick walls and hand-finished ceilings, which offers sandwiches, chili, and chicken in its bar. There's also an elegant dining room for more formal meals. **Plantation House,** at 38 Ariapita Ave. (© **868/628-5551**), is an expensive, quality restaurant housed in a charming colonial house. **Solimar,** at 6 Nook Ave. near the Normandie Hotel (© **868/624-6267**), features a changing menu of international dishes engineered by owner Joe Brown, a peripatetic Englishman who was once a chef for the Hilton hotel chain.

Cricket Wicket, 149 Tragarete Rd. (© **868/628-6766**), is a pub with various bands performing on weekends.

TOBAGO

Tobago is the antithesis of its larger cousin, as peaceful, calm, and easygoing as Trinidad is loud, crowded, and frenetic. The island is filled with magical white-sand beaches, languid palm trees, and clear blue waters, and you'll find lots of spots for diving and snorkeling. There are also magnificent rain forests and hundreds of tiny streams and waterways carved into a steep crest of mountains that rise 600m (2,000 ft.) and snake down the island's center. The bird life and nature trails here are impressive.

COMING ASHORE   Most cruise passengers arrive at a small but orderly cruise terminal in central **Scarborough,** the island's main town. There's usually a fleet of taxis ready to go just outside of the cruise terminal, and detailed cab rates are posted inside the terminal at the main entrance. Larger ships must anchor offshore and transfer passengers to the terminal via tenders.

There are a number of phones inside the terminal, although last time we were here they weren't taking our AT&T phone card and we had to buy a local phone card.

INFORMATION   There is a small information booth at the terminal in Scarborough, open from 9am to 3pm, Monday through Friday. For info before you go, contact the tourism board office in the U.S. (© **212/682-7272;** www.visit tnt.com).

GETTING AROUND
BY TAXI   Taxi is the preferred mode of transportation for visitors here; the island is small enough that any location worth visiting can be reached this way. Distances can be deceiving, though, because some of the roads are in very bad shape and others wind along the coast and twist through the mountains. There is no road that completely circles the island. Taxis are available at the cruise terminal; rates are posted on a board by the main entrance. It pays to agree on a fare before climbing in.

BY RENTAL CAR   There's really no need for a cruise passenger to rent a car on Tobago.

SHORE EXCURSIONS OFFERED BY THE CRUISE LINES
Pigeon Point Beach Trip ($49, 5½ hr., including lunch): By taxi, you'll head toward Tobago's most popular beach, where you'll find a restaurant, a bar, restrooms, and small cabanas lining the beach. You have your pick of watersports, including snorkeling and banana-boat rides (for a fee, of course).

Tobago Island Explorer ($59, 7½ hr., including lunch): Passengers depart the cruise terminal via bus for a trip that starts at Fort King George and the Tobago Museum. After a tour of the museum, the excursion continues along the Windward Coast Road to the Richmond Greathouse for a guided tour. Continuing to the Speyside lookout, a photo stop is made before the tour proceeds to Jemma's Seafood Kitchen for a tasty lunch.

ON YOUR OWN: WITHIN WALKING DISTANCE
The well-restored, British-built **Fort King George,** dating from 1777, overlooks Scarborough's east side. There's no admission charge to enter the grounds. The fort offers a great view of Tobago's Atlantic coast. Other historic buildings here include St. Andrew's church (built in 1819) and the Courthouse (built in 1825). The small **Tobago Museum** (© **868/639-3970**) is located in the Fort's old barracks guardhouse. Scarborough's **botanical gardens** (© **868/639-3421**) are situated between the main highway and the town center, less than 0.5km (a quarter-mile) from the cruise dock, but they are not much more than a glorified public park with a few marked trees.

Other than this, there aren't many attractions within walking distance of the cruise terminal, and even the terminal shops are small and limited.

 Frommer's Favorite Tobago Experiences

Snorkeling at Buccoo Reef: The spot is a must-visit for its exotic fish and impressive underwater coral, which can also be observed by glass-bottom boat. (See "Beaches" and "Sports," below.)

Checking Out Nylon Pool: Named for its crystal-clear water, this small lagoon is located near Buccoo Reef and is filled with tropical fish. It's great for wading and swimming.

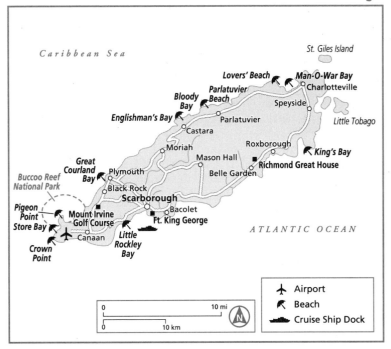

SHOPPING

There simply isn't much here beyond the shops inside the cruise terminal and sporadic craft merchants at the popular beaches at Fort King George. It's best to put aside the shopping excursions for another port and enjoy Tobago's relaxed atmosphere and fine beaches.

BEACHES

Pigeon Point, near the southern tip of Tobago on the Caribbean side, is the best beach on an island filled with great beaches. **Store Bay,** south of Pigeon Point, has white sands and good year-round swimming (there's a lifeguard too). Here you'll find vendors hawking local wares and glass-bottom–boat tours departing to **Buccoo Reef.** Despite their names, **Parlatuvier** and **Bloody Bay,** on Tobago's Caribbean (west) coast, are tranquil, secluded, and beautiful.

SPORTS

GOLF   About 8km (5 miles) from Pigeon Point, the championship, 18-hole, par-72 **Mount Irvine Golf Course,** at the Mount Irvine Hotel (© **868/639-8871**), is among the most scenic courses in the Caribbean, overlooking the sea from gently rolling hills. The clubhouse sits on a promontory and offers great views. Greens fees are $69.

SCUBA DIVING   Tobago is virtually surrounded by shallow-water reefs filled with colorful marine life, easily visible through the clear water. All kinds of diving experiences, from beginner-level dives at Buccoo Reef to drift diving for experienced divers at Grouper Ground, are offered. **Dive Tobago,** at Pigeon Point (© **868/639-0202**), is the island's oldest dive operation, offering resort courses and rentals, and catering to both beginners and experienced divers.

GREAT LOCAL RESTAURANTS & BARS

There are several moderately priced (U.S.$15–U.S.$25 per person) restaurants in Tobago, including The **Old Donkey Cart House,** on Bacolet Street in Scarborough (© **868/639-3551**), which occupies a restored colonial home that once served as Tobago's first guesthouse. Today it's a bistro serving French wines, light snacks, salads, and specialties such as armadillo and opossum (called manicou).

The beach at Store Bay is lined with a row of cheap-food stands offering rotis (chicken or beef wrapped in Indian turnovers and flavored with curry), shark-and-bake, crab with dumplings, and fish lunches. **Chrystal's** (© **868/639-7648**), on the corner of Store Bay and Milford Road, is another local favorite for flying fish, shark-and-bake, and fruit juices.

Index

FROMMER'S® COMPLETE TRAVEL GUIDES

Alaska
Alaska Cruises & Ports of Call
Amsterdam
Argentina & Chile
Arizona
Atlanta
Australia
Austria
Bahamas
Barcelona, Madrid & Seville
Beijing
Belgium, Holland & Luxembourg
Bermuda
Boston
Brazil
British Columbia & the Canadian
  Rockies
Budapest & the Best of Hungary
California
Canada
Cancún, Cozumel & the Yucatán
Cape Cod, Nantucket & Martha's
  Vineyard
Caribbean
Caribbean Cruises & Ports of Call
Caribbean Ports of Call
Carolinas & Georgia
Chicago
China
Colorado
Costa Rica
Denmark
Denver, Boulder & Colorado
  Springs
England
Europe
European Cruises & Ports of Call
Florida

France
Germany
Great Britain
Greece
Greek Islands
Hawaii
Hong Kong
Honolulu, Waikiki & Oahu
Ireland
Israel
Italy
Jamaica
Japan
Las Vegas
London
Los Angeles
Maryland & Delaware
Maui
Mexico
Montana & Wyoming
Montréal & Québec City
Munich & the Bavarian Alps
Nashville & Memphis
Nepal
New England
New Mexico
New Orleans
New York City
New Zealand
Northern Italy
Nova Scotia, New Brunswick &
  Prince Edward Island
Oregon
Paris
Philadelphia & the Amish Country
Portugal
Prague & the Best of the Czech
  Republic

Provence & the Riviera
Puerto Rico
Rome
San Antonio & Austin
San Diego
San Francisco
Santa Fe, Taos & Albuquerque
Scandinavia
Scotland
Seattle & Portland
Shanghai
Singapore & Malaysia
South Africa
South America
South Florida
South Pacific
Southeast Asia
Spain
Sweden
Switzerland
Texas
Thailand
Tokyo
Toronto
Tuscany & Umbria
USA
Utah
Vancouver & Victoria
Vermont, New Hampshire &
  Maine
Vienna & the Danube Valley
Virgin Islands
Virginia
Walt Disney World® & Orlando
Washington, D.C.
Washington State

FROMMER'S® DOLLAR-A-DAY GUIDES

Australia from $50 a Day
California from $70 a Day
Caribbean from $70 a Day
England from $75 a Day
Europe from $70 a Day

Florida from $70 a Day
Hawaii from $80 a Day
Ireland from $60 a Day
Italy from $70 a Day
London from $85 a Day

New York from $90 a Day
Paris from $80 a Day
San Francisco from $70 a Day
Washington, D.C. from $80 a Day

FROMMER'S® PORTABLE GUIDES

Acapulco, Ixtapa & Zihuatanejo
Amsterdam
Aruba
Australia's Great Barrier Reef
Bahamas
Berlin
Big Island of Hawaii
Boston
California Wine Country
Cancún
Charleston & Savannah
Chicago
Disneyland®
Dublin
Florence

Frankfurt
Hong Kong
Houston
Las Vegas
London
Los Angeles
Los Cabos & Baja
Maine Coast
Maui
Miami
New Orleans
New York City
Paris
Phoenix & Scottsdale

Portland
Puerto Rico
Puerto Vallarta, Manzanillo &
  Guadalajara
Rio de Janeiro
San Diego
San Francisco
Seattle
Sydney
Tampa & St. Petersburg
Vancouver
Venice
Virgin Islands
Washington, D.C.

FROMMER'S® NATIONAL PARK GUIDES

Banff & Jasper
Family Vacations in the National
  Parks
Grand Canyon

National Parks of the American
  West
Rocky Mountain

Yellowstone & Grand Teton
Yosemite & Sequoia/ Kings Canyon
Zion & Bryce Canyon

FROMMER'S® MEMORABLE WALKS

Chicago	New York	San Francisco
London	Paris	Washington, D.C.

FROMMER'S® GREAT OUTDOOR GUIDES

Arizona & New Mexico	Northern California	Vermont & New Hampshire
New England	Southern New England	

SUZY GERSHMAN'S BORN TO SHOP GUIDES

Born to Shop: France	Born to Shop: Italy	Born to Shop: New York
Born to Shop: Hong Kong, Shanghai & Beijing	Born to Shop: London	Born to Shop: Paris

FROMMER'S® IRREVERENT GUIDES

Amsterdam	Los Angeles	San Francisco
Boston	Manhattan	Seattle & Portland
Chicago	New Orleans	Vancouver
Las Vegas	Paris	Walt Disney World®
London	Rome	Washington, D.C.

FROMMER'S® BEST-LOVED DRIVING TOURS

Britain	Germany	Northern Italy
California	Ireland	Scotland
Florida	Italy	Spain
France	New England	Tuscany & Umbria

HANGING OUT™ GUIDES

Hanging Out in England	Hanging Out in France	Hanging Out in Italy
Hanging Out in Europe	Hanging Out in Ireland	Hanging Out in Spain

THE UNOFFICIAL GUIDES®

Bed & Breakfasts and Country Inns in:	Southwest & South Central Plains	Mid-Atlantic with Kids
California	U.S.A.	Mini Las Vegas
Great Lakes States	Beyond Disney	Mini-Mickey
Mid-Atlantic	Branson, Missouri	New England and New York with Kids
New England	California with Kids	
Northwest	Chicago	New Orleans
Rockies	Cruises	New York City
Southeast	Disneyland®	Paris
Southwest	Florida with Kids	San Francisco
Best RV & Tent Campgrounds in:	Golf Vacations in the Eastern U.S.	Skiing in the West
California & the West	Great Smoky & Blue Ridge Region	Southeast with Kids
Florida & the Southeast	Inside Disney	Walt Disney World®
Great Lakes States	Hawaii	Walt Disney World® for Grown-ups
Mid-Atlantic	Las Vegas	Walt Disney World® with Kids
Northeast	London	Washington, D.C.
Northwest & Central Plains		World's Best Diving Vacations

SPECIAL-INTEREST TITLES

Frommer's Adventure Guide to Australia & New Zealand
Frommer's Adventure Guide to Central America
Frommer's Adventure Guide to India & Pakistan
Frommer's Adventure Guide to South America
Frommer's Adventure Guide to Southeast Asia
Frommer's Adventure Guide to Southern Africa
Frommer's Britain's Best Bed & Breakfasts and Country Inns
Frommer's Caribbean Hideaways
Frommer's Exploring America by RV
Frommer's Fly Safe, Fly Smart
Frommer's France's Best Bed & Breakfasts and Country Inns
Frommer's Gay & Lesbian Europe

Frommer's Italy's Best Bed & Breakfasts and Country Inns
Frommer's New York City with Kids
Frommer's Ottawa with Kids
Frommer's Road Atlas Britain
Frommer's Road Atlas Europe
Frommer's Road Atlas France
Frommer's Toronto with Kids
Frommer's Vancouver with Kids
Frommer's Washington, D.C., with Kids
Israel Past & Present
The New York Times' Guide to Unforgettable Weekends
Places Rated Almanac
Retirement Places Rated

America Online Keyword: Travel
Booked seat 6A, open return.
Rented red 4-wheel drive.
Reserved cabin, no running water.
Discovered space.